# ACCA

STUDY TEXT

# ADVANCED FINANCIAL MANAGEMENT (AFM)

BPP Learning Media is an **ACCA Approved Content Provider.** This means we work closely with ACCA to ensure this Study Text contains the information you need to pass your exam.

In this Study Text, which has been reviewed by the **ACCA examining team**, we:

- Discuss the best strategies for studying for ACCA exams
- Highlight the most important elements in the syllabus and the key skills you need
- Signpost how each chapter links to the syllabus and the study guide
- Provide lots of exam focus points demonstrating what is expected of you in the exam
- Emphasise key points in regular fast forward summaries
- Test your knowledge of what you've studied in quick quizzes
- Examine your understanding in our practice question bank
- Reference all the important topics in our full index

BPP's **Practice & Revision Kit** also supports the Advanced Financial Management (AFM) syllabus.

**FOR EXAMS IN SEPTEMBER 2018, DECEMBER 2018, MARCH 2019 AND JUNE 2019**

BPP LEARNING MEDIA

First edition 2007
Eleventh edition January 2018

ISBN 9781 5097 1681 4
(Previous ISBN 9781 5097 0846 8)
e-ISBN 9781 5097 1711 8

British Library Cataloguing-in-Publication Data

A catalogue record for this book is available from the
British Library

**Published by**

BPP Learning Media Ltd
BPP House, Aldine Place
142-144 Uxbridge Road
London W12 8AA

www.bpp.com/learningmedia

Printed in the United Kingdom

Your learning materials, published by BPP Learning
Media Ltd, are printed on paper obtained from traceable
sustainable sources.

We are grateful to the Association of Chartered Certified
Accountants for permission to reproduce past examination
questions. The suggested solutions in the practice answer
bank have been prepared by BPP Learning Media Ltd,
unless otherwise stated.

BPP
LEARNING MEDIA

# Contents

# Helping you to pass

## BPP Learning Media – Approved Content Provider

As an ACCA **Approved Content Provider**, BPP Learning Media gives you the **opportunity** to use study materials reviewed by the ACCA examining team. By incorporating the examining team's comments and suggestions regarding the depth and breadth of syllabus coverage, the BPP Learning Media Study Text provides excellent, **ACCA-approved** support for your studies.

These materials are reviewed by the ACCA examining team. The objective of the review is to ensure that the material properly covers the syllabus and study guide outcomes, used by the examining team in setting the exams, in the appropriate breadth and depth. The review does not ensure that every eventuality, combination or application of examinable topics is addressed by the ACCA Approved Content. Nor does the review comprise a detailed technical check of the content as the Approved Content Provider has its own quality assurance processes in place in this respect.

## The PER alert

Before you can qualify as an ACCA member, you have to not only pass all your exams but also fulfil a three year **practical experience requirement** (PER). To help you to recognise areas of the syllabus that you might be able to apply in the workplace to achieve different performance objectives, we have introduced the '**PER alert**' feature. You will find this feature throughout the Study Text to remind you that what you are **learning to pass** your ACCA exams is **equally useful to the fulfilment of the PER requirement**.

Your achievement of the PER should now be recorded in your online *My Experience* record.

## Tackling studying

Studying can be a daunting prospect, particularly when you have lots of other commitments. The **different features** of the Study Text, the **purposes** of which are explained fully on the **Chapter features** page, will help you whilst studying and improve your chances of **exam success**.

## Developing exam awareness

Our Study Texts are completely **focused** on helping you pass your exam.

Our advice on **Studying Advanced Financial Management (AFM)** outlines the **content** of the exam, the **necessary skills** you are expected to be able to demonstrate and any **brought forward knowledge** you are expected to have.

**Exam focus points** are included within the chapters to highlight when and how specific topics were examined, or how they might be examined in the future.

## Testing what you can do

Testing yourself helps you develop the skills you need to pass the exam and also confirms that you can recall what you have learnt.

We include **Questions** – lots of them – both within chapters and in the **Practice Question Bank**, as well as **Quick Quizzes** at the end of each chapter to test your knowledge of the chapter content.

# Chapter features

Each chapter contains a number of helpful features to guide you through each topic.

**Topic list**

| Topic list | Syllabus reference |
|---|---|
|  |  |
|  |  |
|  |  |

Tells you what you will be studying in this chapter and the relevant section numbers, together with ACCA syllabus references.

## Introduction

Puts the chapter content in the context of the syllabus as a whole.

## Study Guide

Links the chapter content with ACCA guidance.

## Exam Guide

Highlights how examinable the chapter content is likely to be and the ways in which it could be examined.

**Knowledge brought forward from earlier studies**

What you are assumed to know from previous studies/exams.

**FAST FORWARD**

Summarises the content of main chapter headings, allowing you to preview and review each section easily.

## Examples

Demonstrate how to apply key knowledge and techniques.

**Key terms**

Definitions of important concepts that can often earn you easy marks in exams.

**Exam focus points**

Tell you when and how specific topics were examined, or how they may be examined in the future.

**Formula to learn**

Formulae that are not given in the exam but which have to be learnt.

This gives you a useful indication of syllabus areas that closely relate to performance objectives in your Practical Experience Requirement (PER).

 Question

Gives you essential practice of techniques covered in the chapter.

 Case Study

Real world examples of theories and techniques.

## Chapter Roundup

A full list of the Fast Forwards included in the chapter, providing an easy source of review.

## Quick Quiz

A quick test of your knowledge of the main topics in the chapter.

## Practice Question Bank

Found at the back of the Study Text with more comprehensive chapter questions. Cross referenced for easy navigation.

# Studying AFM

As the name suggests, AFM examines Advanced Financial Management (AFM) topics and is particularly suited to those who are thinking about a career in treasury or are likely to be involved in strategic financial management decisions.

Members of the AFM examining team have written **several articles** in Student Accountant which are also available on the ACCA website. There are three important new articles, these are *Currency Swaps, Patterns of Behaviour and Investment Appraisal and Real Options*. Make sure you read these articles to gain further insight into what the examining team is looking for.

# 1 What AFM is about

The aim of the syllabus is to develop students' ability to **apply relevant knowledge and skills**, and exercise the **professional judgement** expected of a senior financial adviser, in taking or recommending financial management decisions that are likely to have an impact on the entire organisation.

This is an **advanced level** optional exam which builds on the topics covered in *Financial Management (FM)*. As an advanced exam, it tests much more than just your ability to perform calculations. You must be able to **evaluate** data, **assess** the potential financial and strategic consequences of taking investment decisions and **advise** on alternative courses of action, among other things, in both a **domestic** and **international** context.

The syllabus is divided into **five** main sections.

(a) **The role of the senior financial adviser in the multinational organisation**

More than ever, company management's responsibility towards all stakeholders is under scrutiny. They must be aware of different stakeholder groups' **conflicting needs** and be able to develop suitable financial strategies that fulfil each group's interests as much as possible. The impact of **environmental factors** should also be uppermost in their minds given the increasing importance placed on such factors in the modern business world.

**Ethical issues** cannot be ignored – ethics are expected to be a consistent theme in the examination, and students will be expected to be able to take a **practical approach** to identifying such issues in given scenarios.

**Multinational companies** have their own unique set of challenges, including having operations in international locations. You will be expected to have detailed knowledge and understanding of how to manage international finances and strategic business and financial planning for companies with international operations.

(b) **Advanced investment appraisal**

This section revisits **investment** and **financing** decisions with the emphasis moving from straightforward technical knowledge towards the **strategic issues** associated with making investment decisions, both **domestic** and **international**.

(c) **Acquisitions and mergers**

You will be expected to discuss the logic of a growth strategy based on acquisitions, to **choose** and **apply** an appropriate method of **valuation** and make **strategic decisions** regarding how the merger or acquisition should be **financed**. You will be required to act in an **advisory** as well as technical capacity.

(d) **Corporate reconstruction and reorganisation**

This section looks at how to put together a **restructuring package** and ways in which an organisation might be reorganised (for example, management buyouts and sell-offs). As above, you will be expected to act in both a **technical** and **advisory** capacity in questions on this section.

(e) **Treasury and advanced risk management techniques**

This section covers distinct areas of risk and how to measure and manage them. **Interest rate** and **currency risks** and the derivatives used to hedge against them are considered in detail. You will be required not only to know how the derivatives work but also to **advise** on the best methods of hedging in particular scenarios.

# 2 What skills are required?

## 2.1 Knowledge and application

Even with exams you've previously taken, you'll remember that passing didn't only mean reproducing knowledge. You also had to **apply** what you knew. At Strategic Professional level, the balance is tilted much more towards application. You will need a sound basis of technical knowledge. The exams will detect whether you have the necessary knowledge. However, you won't pass if you just spend your time acquiring knowledge. Developing application skills is vital.

## 2.2 Application skills

What application skills do you need? Many AFM questions will include detail in a scenario about a specific organisation. The following skills are particularly important when you're dealing with question scenarios.

(a) **Identifying the most important features** of the organisation and the organisation's environment. Clues to these will be scattered throughout the scenario. The technical knowledge that you have should help you do this, but you will also need business awareness and imagination. There will be a main theme running through most scenarios that you'll need to identify.

(b) **Using analysis techniques** that will give you more insight into the data that you're given.

(c) **Making informed judgements** that follow from your analysis about what the organisation is doing and should be doing.

(d) **Communicating clearly and concisely** your analysis and recommendations.

# 3 How to improve your chances of passing

## 3.1 Study the whole syllabus

You need to be comfortable with **all areas of the syllabus**. Compulsory Question 1 will always span a number of syllabus areas and other questions may do so as well.

The examining team has also stressed that study and revision should cover the entire syllabus in detail. Students should not question spot or prioritise one area of the syllabus over another. The examining team has identified in its examining team's reports those topics which students who question spotted clearly believed would not be examined, but unfortunately were.

## 3.2 Focus on themes, not lists

There are quite a number of lists in the Texts. This is inevitable because corporate governance guidance quoted as best practice is often in list form. Lists are also sometimes the clearest way of presenting information. However, the examining team has stressed that passing the exam is not a matter of learning and reproducing lists. Good answers will have to **focus on the details in the scenario** and **bring out the underlying themes** that relate to the scenario. The points in them will have more depth than a series of single-line bullet points.

### 3.3 Read around

Wider reading will help you understand the main issues businesses face.

Most importantly you should **read the technical articles on the ACCA website** that are relevant to AFM. Websites such as Reuters.com are also a useful source of information on current trends in the financial environment.

### 3.4 Lots of question practice

You can **develop application skills** by attempting questions in the Practice Question Bank and later on in the BPP Learning Media Practice & Revision Kit.

# 4 Brought forward knowledge

As mentioned previously, this exam builds on knowledge brought forward from *Financial Management (FM)*. If you have not studied FM, you should be aware that the following topics are assumed knowledge and should be considered examinable.

- Management of working capital
- Business finance (including sources of finance and dividend policy)
- The capital structure decision
- Investment appraisal
- Capital rationing
- Cost of capital (including CAPM and WACC)
- Business valuations
- Market efficiency
- Foreign currency and interest rate risk management

# 5 Gaining professional marks

As AFM is a Strategic Professional level exam, **four professional marks** will be awarded in the 50 mark question. The examining team has stated that some marks may be available for presenting your answer in the form of a letter, presentation, memo, report, briefing notes, management reporting, narrative or press statement. You may also be able to obtain marks for the layout, logical flow and presentation of your answer. You should also make sure that you provide the points required by the question.

Whatever the form of communication requested, you will **not** gain professional marks if you fail to follow the basics of good communication. Keep an eye on your **spelling and grammar**. Also think carefully, am I saying things that are **appropriate in a business communication**?

# 6 Answering questions

### 6.1 Analysing question requirements

It's particularly important to **consider the question requirements carefully** to make sure you understand exactly what the question is asking, and whether each question part has to be answered in the **context of the scenario** or is more general. You also need to be sure that you understand all the **tasks** that the question is asking you to perform.

If for example you are asked to:

'Discuss the benefits and disadvantages of a company entering into an overseas joint venture instead of setting up overseas independently', then you would explain:

- The merits of joint venture as a method of entering an overseas market.
- The merits of setting up independently in an overseas market.
- In both cases you would support your argument using the clues in the scenario.

You would **not** discuss whether a company should enter this overseas market (this is an extract from a past exam question, and many candidates made this mistake).

## 6.2 Understanding the question verbs

Important!

> The examining team has highlighted lack of understanding of the requirements of question verbs as the most serious weakness in many candidates' scripts. The examining team will use question verbs very deliberately to signal what is required.

Verbs that are likely to be frequently used in this exam are listed below, together with their intellectual levels and guidance on their meaning.

| Intellectual level | | |
|---|---|---|
| 1 | Calculate | Perform a specific mathematical technique |
| 1 | Describe | Give the key features |
| 1 | Identify | Recognise or select |
| 2 | Apply | Apply relevant concepts to solve problems |
| 2 | Distinguish | Define two different terms, viewpoints or concepts on the basis of the differences between them |
| 2 | Compare and contrast | Explain the similarities and differences between two different terms, viewpoints or concepts |
| 2 | Analyse | Give reasons for the current situation or what has happened |
| 3 | Examine | Critically review in detail |
| 3 | Discuss | Examine by using arguments for and against |
| 3 | Explore | Examine or discuss in a wide-ranging manner |
| 3 | Estimate | Make an appropriate judgement or calculation |
| 3 | Evaluate/critically evaluate | Determine the value of in the light of the arguments for and against (critically evaluate means weighting the answer towards criticisms/arguments against) |
| 3 | Assess | Determine the strengths/weaknesses/importance /significance/ability to contribute |
| 3 | Advise/ Recommend | Use judgement to recommend a course of action(s) in terms the recipient will understand |

At this level of your studies you will normally expect to see Intellectual Level 3 verbs in exam questions.

**Intellectual Level 3 verbs** (advise, report) test your ability to take a complex situation and to use **your judgement and technical knowledge (from a number of DIFFERENT syllabus areas)** to construct appropriate decisions and recommendations.

**In the exam you should actively be looking to synthesise knowledge from different syllabus areas as you construct your answer.**

## 6.3 Content of answers

**Well-judged, clear recommendations** grounded in the scenario will always score well, as markers for this exam have a wide remit to reward good answers. You need to be **selective**. As we've said, lists of points memorised from Texts and reproduced without any thought won't score well.

The examining team identified lack of application skills as a serious weakness in many student answers. What constitutes good application will vary question by question but is likely to include:

- Only including technical knowledge that is **relevant** to the scenario
- Including scenario details that **support the points** you are making
- **Tackling the problems** highlighted in the scenario and the question requirements
- Explaining **why** the factors you're discussing are significant

# The exam and exam formulae

The **time allowed** for the exam is 3 hours 15 minutes.

The paper consists of two sections:

**Section A** consists of one compulsory question worth 50 marks. This question covers topics from across the syllabus but tends to be based on one major area – for example a cross-border merger question (major topic) might bring in ethical issues (smaller topic).

**Section B** consists of two compulsory questions worth 25 marks each.

**Professional marks** are available. The examining team has emphasised that in order to gain all the marks available, students must write in the specified format (such as a report or memo). Reports must have terms of reference, conclusion, appendices and appropriate headings. Make sure you are familiar with how different types of documents are constructed to improve your chances of gaining maximum professional marks.

All topics and syllabus sections will be examinable in either Section A or Section B of the exam, but (from September 2018) every exam will have questions which have a **focus on syllabus Section B** (Advanced Investment Appraisal, covered in Chapter 5–8) **and syllabus Section E** (Treasury and Advanced Risk Management, covered in Chapters 15–17).

# Exam formulae

Set out below are the **formulae you will be given in the exam**. If you are not sure what the symbols mean, or how the formulae are used, you should refer to the appropriate chapter in this Study Text.

*Chapter in Study Text*

*Modigliani and Miller Proposition 2 (with tax)*

$$k_e = k_e^i + (1-T)(k_e^i - k_d)\frac{V_d}{V_e}$$

**7a**

*The capital asset pricing model*

$$E(r_i) = R_f + \beta_i(E(r_m) - R_f)$$

**7a**

*The asset beta formula*

$$\beta_a = \left[\frac{V_e}{(V_e + V_d(1-T))}\beta_e\right] + \left[\frac{V_d(1-T)}{(V_e + V_d(1-T))}\beta_d\right]$$

**7a**

*The growth model*

$$P_0 = \frac{D_0(1+g)}{(r_e - g)}$$

**12**

*Gordon's growth approximation*

$$g = br_e$$

**5**

*The weighted average cost of capital*

$$WACC = \left[\frac{V_e}{V_e + V_d}\right]k_e + \left[\frac{V_d}{V_e + V_d}\right]k_d(1-T)$$

**7a**

*The Fisher formula*

$$(1 + i) = (1 + r)(1 + h)$$

**5**

*Purchasing power parity and interest rate parity*

$$S_1 = S_0 \times \frac{(1+h_c)}{(1+h_b)}$$

$$F_0 = S_0 \times \frac{(1+i_c)}{(1+i_b)}$$

8

*Modified internal rate of return*

$$MIRR = \left[\frac{PV_R}{PV_I}\right]^{\frac{1}{n}} (1+r_e) - 1$$

5

*The Black-Scholes option pricing model*

$$c = P_a N(d_1) - P_e N(d_2) e^{-rt}$$

6

Where $\quad d_1 = \dfrac{\ln(P_a / P_e) + (r + 0.5s^2)t}{s\sqrt{t}}$

6

$$d_2 = d_1 - s\sqrt{t}$$

6

*The put call parity relationship*

$$p = c - P_a + P_e e^{-rt}$$

6

# Analysis of past exams

The table below provides details of when each element of the syllabus has been examined in the ten most recent sittings and the question number and Section (A or B) in which each element was examined (nb until September 2018 there was a choice of 2 questions from 3 in section B of the exam). Further details can be found in the Exam focus points in the relevant chapters.

Since September 2016, ACCA have been issuing two 'hybrid' exams each year, after the December and June exam sessions. These exams are compiled from questions selected from the two preceding sessions eg in December 2017, the hybrid exam questions were compiled from September 2017 and December 2017 exams.

| Covered in Text chapter | | Sep /Dec 17 | Mar /Jun 17 | Sep /Dec 16 | Mar /Jun 16 | Sep /Dec 15 | Jun 15 | Dec 14 | Jun 14 | Dec 13 | Jun 13 |
|---|---|---|---|---|---|---|---|---|---|---|---|
| | **ROLE OF SENIOR FINANCIAL ADVISER** | | | | | | | | | | |
| 1, 2 | Role of senior financial adviser/financial strategy formulation | B | | A, B | A | | B | B | | A | B |
| 3 | Ethical/environmental issues | | | | B | | | | | | A |
| 4a | Trading in a multinational environment | | | | B | B | | | | A | |
| 4b | Planning in a multinational environment | | | | | | | | | | B |
| | **ADVANCED INVESTMENT APPRAISAL** | | | | | | | | | | |
| 5 | Discounted cash flow techniques | B | | B | | | | | | A | |
| 6 | Application of option pricing theory to investment decisions | | | | B | | | B | B | A | |
| 7a, 7b | Impact of financing, adjusted present values/valuation and free cash flows | A | B | A | | B | | | A, B | B | A |
| 8 | International investment/ financing | | B | | A | | A | | | | |
| | **ACQUISITIONS AND MERGERS** | | | | | | | | | | |
| 9, 11, 12 | Strategic/financial/regulatory issues | | A | | B | A | | A | B | | B |
| 10 | Valuation techniques | | | B | B | A | | A | B | B | A, B |
| | **CORPORATE RECONSTRUCTION AND REORGANISATION** | | | | | | | | | | |
| 13 | Financial reconstruction | A | | | | B | B | | | | A |
| 14 | Business reorganisation | B | A | | B | | B | | | B | |

| Covered in Text chapter | | Sep /Dec 17 | Mar /Jun 17 | Sep /Dec 16 | Mar /Jun 16 | Sep /Dec 15 | Jun 15 | Dec 14 | Jun 14 | Dec 13 | Jun 13 |
|---|---|---|---|---|---|---|---|---|---|---|---|
| | **TREASURY AND ADVANCED RISK MANAGEMENT TECHNIQUES** | | | | | | | | | | |
| 15 | Role of the treasury function | B | | A | | | | B | | | |
| 16 | Hedging foreign currency risk | | B | | A | B | | | A | | B |
| 17 | Hedging interest rate risk | B | | B | | B | B | B | A | B | B |

---

**IMPORTANT!**

The table above gives a broad idea of how frequently major topics in the syllabus are examined. It should not be used to question spot and predict for example that Topic X will not be examined because it came up two sittings ago. The examining team's reports indicate that the examining team is well aware some students try to question spot. The examining team avoid predictable patterns and may, for example, examine the same topic two sittings in a row.

# Syllabus and study guide

The complete AFM syllabus and study guide can be found by visiting the exam resource finder on the ACCA website:

www.accaglobal.com/uk/en/student/exam-support-resources.html

P
A
R
T

A

# Role of the senior financial advisor

# The role of the senior financial advisor

| Topic list | Syllabus reference |
|---|---|
| 1 Financial goals and objectives | A1(c) |
| 2 Non-financial objectives | A1(c) |
| 3 Investment decision | A1(c) |
| 4 Financing decision | A1(c) |
| 5 Dividend decision | A1(c) |
| 6 Financial planning and control | A1(c) |
| 7 Risk management | A1(c) |
| 8 Communicating policy to stakeholders | A1(c) |
| 9 Strategies for achieving financial goals | A1(a),(b) |

## Introduction

In this chapter we discuss **the role and responsibility of the senior financial advisor** in the context of setting strategic objectives, financial goals and financial policy development.

This chapter and the next three chapters underpin the rest of the syllabus therefore it is important to read them carefully. This chapter introduces some of the key concepts of financial management, many of these will be familiar to you from the *Financial Management (FM) exam*.

Remember that non-financial objectives are at least as important as financial objectives and will have a significant impact on the three main financial management decisions – investment, financing and dividend.

Bear in mind at all times throughout the syllabus that the company is being run for the benefit of the **shareholders** therefore decisions should reflect their preferences as much as possible.

# Study guide

| | | Intellectual level |
|---|---|---|
| **A1** | **The role and responsibility of senior financial executive/advisor** | |
| (a) | Develop strategies for the achievement of the organisational goals in line with its agreed policy framework. | 3 |
| (b) | Recommend strategies for the management of the financial resources of the organisation such that they are utilised in an efficient, effective and transparent way. | 3 |
| (c) | Advise the board of directors of the organisation in setting the financial goals of the business and in its financial policy development with particular reference to: | 3 |
| | (i) Investment selection and capital resource allocation | |
| | (ii) Minimising the cost of capital | |
| | (iii) Distribution and retention policy | |
| | (iv) Communicating financial policy and corporate goals to internal and external stakeholders | |
| | (v) Financial planning and control | |
| | (vi) The management of risk | |

# 1 Financial goals and objectives

6/11, 6/15

**FAST FORWARD**

In financial management of businesses, the key objective is the **maximisation of shareholders' wealth**.

## 1.1 The principal financial objective of a company

The principal role of the senior financial executive when setting financial goals is the **maximisation of shareholders' wealth**.

A company is financed by ordinary shareholders, preference shareholders, loan stock holders and other long-term and short-term payables. All surplus funds, however, belong to the legal owners of the company, its ordinary (equity) shareholders. Any retained profits are undistributed wealth of these equity shareholders.

**Question**

Financial objectives

It is a common misconception that profit maximisation is the key objective of most publicly owned companies. Give reasons why this objective would be insufficient for investors.

**Answer**

There are several reasons why profit maximisation is not a sufficient objective for investors.

(a) **Risk and uncertainty**. This objective fails to recognise the risk and uncertainty associated with certain projects. Shareholders tend to be very interested in the level of risk and maximising profits may be achieved by raising risk to unacceptable levels.

(b) **Dividend policy**. Shareholders are interested in how much they will receive as dividends. Retained profits can be increased by reducing the dividend payout ratio or by not paying a dividend at all. This is not necessarily in the best interests of the shareholders, who might prefer a certain monetary return on their investment.

(c) **Future profits**. Which profits should management be maximising? Shareholders may not want current profits to be maximised at the expense of future profits.

(d) **Manipulation of profits**. Unlike cash, profits can be easily manipulated – for example, by changing depreciation policy or provision for doubtful debts percentage. It is therefore not difficult to appear to be maximising profits when in reality the company is no better off.

However, you should remember that, while the principal objective is the maximisation of shareholders' wealth, managers should not be pursuing this at any cost. They should not be taking **unacceptable business and financial risks** with shareholders' funds and must act within the law. Managers are aware that any actions that undermine their company's reputation are likely to be **very expensive** in terms of adverse effects on share price and public trust.

### 1.1.1 How do we measure shareholders' wealth?

Key term

**Shareholders' wealth** comes from two sources – dividends received and market value of shares. Shareholders' return on investment = dividend yield + capital gain on shares; this is often referred to as **Total Shareholder Return**.

In order to measure shareholders' wealth, we must be able to measure the value of the company and its shares. How do we do this?

(a) **Statement of financial position valuation**

Assets will be valued on a going concern basis. If retained profits increase year on year then the company is a profitable one. Statement of financial position values are not a measure of market value, although retained profits may give some indication of the level of dividends that could be paid to shareholders.

(b) **Break-up basis**

This basis will only be used when the business is being wound up, there is a threat of liquidation or management has decided to sell off individual assets to raise cash.

(c) **Market value**

Market value is the price at which buyers and sellers will trade shares in a company. Look at your local financial press (for example, the *Financial Times* and *Wall Street Journal*) for a daily summary of market values of individual listed companies' shares. This value is the one that is most relevant to a company's financial objectives.

When shares are in a private company, and are not traded on any stock exchange, there is no easy way to measure their market value. However, the principal objective of such companies should still be the maximisation of ordinary shareholders' wealth.

Shareholders' wealth comes from **two sources – dividends received** and the **market value** of the shares held.

Shareholders' **return on investment** is obtained from **dividends received** and **capital gains** resulting from increases in the market value of the shares. This is often referred to as **Total Shareholder Return**.

### 1.1.2 How is the value of a business increased?

If a company's shares are traded on a stock market, the wealth of shareholders is increased when the share price goes up. The price of a company's shares may increase if the value of future cash flows is expected to rise, this may occur for a number of reasons including the following:

- Potential takeover bid
- News of winning a major contract
- Announcement of attractive strategic initiatives
- Better than expected profit forecasts and published results

- Change in senior staff, such as a new CEO
- Announcement of an increase in the cash being returned to shareholders

**Case Study**

Shares in the Japanese company Nintendo have seen a sharp rise since the release of the augmented reality game Pokemon Go, gaining more than 50%.

Shares closed 16% higher, making an overall increase of 56% since the release (in July 2016) – putting Nintendo's market value at 3.6 trillion yen ($34 billion).

**Pokemon Go** players search locations in the real world to find virtual Pokemon creatures on their smartphone screens.

The game has become a **global phenomenon** since its release.

It topped the app store download chart on both iPhone's App Store and Google Play just days after its initial release in the US, Australia and New Zealand.

Nintendo, which is also behind the iconic Super Mario game, has traditionally relied on sales of its gaming consoles.

However, sales of those have been slowing in recent years as more gamers move online and onto portable devices.

Analysts have long criticised the company for lagging rivals such as Sony and being late in catering to the growing smartphone market.

*(BBC, 2016)*

## 1.2 Earnings per share (EPS) growth

**Formula to learn**

$$\text{Earnings per share (EPS)} = \frac{\text{Profits distributable to ordinary shareholders}}{\text{Number of ordinary shares issued}}$$

EPS is particularly useful for comparing results over a number of years. Investors will be looking for growth in EPS year on year. In addition, companies must demonstrate that they can sustain earnings for dividend payouts and reinvestment in the business for future growth.

**Question**

EPS

As an investor, why might you be wary of using EPS to assess the performance of a company?

**Answer**

EPS is based on past data whereas investors should be more concerned with future earnings. In addition, the measure is very easy to manipulate by changes in accounting policies and by mergers and acquisitions. In reality, the attention given to EPS as a performance measure is probably disproportionate to its true worth.

## 1.3 Other financial targets

In addition to targets for earnings, EPS, and dividend per share, a company might set other financial targets.

| Examples of other financial targets | |
| --- | --- |
| **Restriction on gearing** | Ratio of debt: equity shouldn't exceed 1:1 or finance costs shouldn't be higher than 25% of profit from operations for instance |
| **Profit retentions** | Dividend cover (profit for the year/dividends) should exceed 2.5 for instance |
| **Profit from operations** | Target profit from operations: revenue ratio or minimum return on capital employed |
| **Cash generation** | As well as generating profits, businesses need to generate enough cash to ensure they remain liquid |

These targets are not primary objectives but can help a company to achieve its principal objective without incurring excessive risks. Such targets tend to be measured in the short term (one year) rather than the long term.

# 2 Non-financial objectives

**FAST FORWARD**

Non-financial objectives may limit the achievement of financial objectives. Their existence suggests the assumption that the main purpose of a company is to maximise shareholders' wealth is too simplistic.

Many companies have non-financial objectives that may limit their ability to achieve their financial objectives. They do not negate the financial objectives but emphasise the need for companies to have other targets than the maximisation of shareholders' wealth.

### Question

Non-financial objectives

Suggest a non-financial objective for each of the following companies:

(a)   A major international airline
(b)   A provider of professional education courses
(c)   A large high-street supermarket
(d)   A major pharmaceutical company
(e)   A publicly funded health service

### Answer

Examples include:

(a)   Development of enhanced on-board products (such as extra legroom, more spacious business class seating); improve the customer experience by for example enabling customers to choose their own seats in advance

(b)   Maximise pass rates; provide up to date technology in the classroom; continuous improvement of teaching materials

(c)   Provide services for the communities in which branches operate (for example, Coles supermarket chain in Australia has launched a Community Food program which donates surplus healthy, fresh food to support disadvantaged members of the community); provide excellent staff facilities

(d)   Work with governments to tackle health issues on a global scale; develop new drugs to fight diseases

(e)   Eradicate any hospital-based bugs such as MRSA; reduce waiting times for treatment; improvement in doctor/patient ratio

# 3 Investment decision

> In seeking to attain the financial objectives of the organisation or enterprise, a financial manager has to make three fundamental decisions – investment, financing and dividend. The investment decision involves selecting appropriate investment opportunities that will help to fulfil the company's primary objectives.

The three fundamental decisions that support the objective of maximising shareholders' wealth are:

- Investment decisions
- Financing decisions
- Dividend decisions

Underpinning these decisions is the **management of risk**, including the management of exchange rates and interest rates. At all times the financial managers should remember that they are making decisions with a view to **increasing shareholders' wealth**. It follows that all stakeholders (internal and external) should be kept informed of financial policy and corporate goals through effective communication channels.

As a financial manager you should always bear in mind that these decisions are not made in isolation but are **interconnected**.

This section deals with the first decision identified above – the **investment decision**.

The financial manager will need to **identify** investment opportunities, **evaluate** them and decide on the **optimum allocation of scarce funds** available between investments.

**Investment decisions** may be on the undertaking of new **projects** within the existing business, the **takeover** of, or the **merger** with, another company or the **selling off** of a part of the business. Managers have to take decisions in the light of strategic considerations, such as whether the business wants to **grow internally** (through investment in existing operations) or **externally** (through expansion).

Investment decisions are considered more fully in Chapters 5–10 but some of the key issues are introduced below.

## 3.1 Organic growth

A company which is planning to grow must decide on whether to pursue a policy of 'organic' internal growth or a policy of taking over other established businesses, or a mix of the two.

**Organic growth** requires funding in cash, whereas acquisitions can be made by means of share exchange transactions. A company pursuing a policy of organic growth would need to take account of the following:

(a)  The company must make the **finance available**, possibly out of retained profits. However, the company should then know how much it can afford and, with careful management, should not overextend itself by trying to achieve too much growth too quickly.

(b)  The company can **use its existing staff and systems** to create the growth projects, and this will open up career opportunities for the staff.

(c)  **Overall expansion** can be **planned more efficiently**. For example, if a company wishes to open a new factory or depot, it can site the new development in a place that helps operational efficiency (eg close to other factories to reduce transport costs).

(d)  **Economies of scale** can be achieved from **more efficient use** of central head office functions, such as finance, purchasing, personnel and management services.

## 3.2 Growth by acquisition

Companies may expand or diversify by developing their own internal resources, but they are also likely to consider growth through acquisitions or mergers. In both situations the result is a sudden spurt in company growth, which can clearly cause 'corporate indigestion' typified by problems of communication, blurring of policy decisions and decline in the staff's identity with company and products.

The aim of a merger or acquisition, however, should be to make **profits** in the long term as well as the short term. Acquisitions provide a **means of entering** a market, or building up a market share, more quickly and/or at a lower cost than would be incurred if the company tries to develop its own resources.

## 3.3 Organic growth versus acquisition

**Acquisitions** are probably only desirable if **organic growth alone cannot achieve the targets** for growth that a company has set for itself.

Organic growth takes time. With acquisitions, entire existing operations are assimilated into the company at one fell swoop. Acquisitions can be made without cash, if share exchange transactions are acceptable to both the buyers and sellers of any company which is to be taken over.

However, acquisitions do have their **strategic problems**.

(a)     They might be **too expensive**. Some might be resisted by the directors of the target company. Others might be referred to the Government under the terms of anti-monopoly legislation.

(b)     **Customers** of the target company might **resent** a sudden takeover and consider going to other suppliers for their goods.

(c)     In general, the problems of assimilating new products, customers, suppliers, markets, employees and different systems of operating might create **'indigestion'** and management overload in the acquiring company.

 Case Study

A telecommunications carrier seeks to become a TV network and movie studio owner. A major software company acquires one of the world's largest social networks. A smartphone maker snaps up a manufacturer of internet-connected audio speakers for cars. In 2016, mega deals became ever more transformative.

A drive by some of the world's largest corporations to find new avenues to expand in the face of anaemic economic growth led to major acquisitions in areas adjacent to their core business. This helped make 2016 the third-biggest year on record for mergers and acquisitions, trailing only 2015 and 2007.

"Companies are reinventing themselves, looking at their business in a new way with regards to how can they be a disrupter, and how they can prevent being disrupted – and this opens up deal flow" said Chris Ventresca, global co-head of M&A at JPMorgan Chase & Co.

Among these transformative deals was this year's biggest – U.S. telecommunications company AT&T Inc's $85.4 billion agreement to acquire media company Time Warner Inc, the parent of CNN, TNT, HBO and the Warner Bros movie studio. Other such deals included software behemoth Microsoft Corp's $26.2 billion acquisition of professional social media network LinkedIn Corp, and Samsung Electronics Co Ltd's $8 billion deal to buy car electronics maker Harman International Industries.

*(Reuters, 2016)*

Acquisitions are dealt with in detail in Section C of the Study Text.

## 3.4 Capital resource allocation – capital rationing                     12/12

**Key term**

> **Capital rationing** is a restriction on an organisation's ability to invest capital funds, caused by an internal budget ceiling being imposed on such expenditure by management (**soft capital rationing**), or by external limitations being applied to the company, as when additional borrowed funds cannot be obtained (**hard capital rationing**).                                                                  *(CIMA Official Terminology)*

If an organisation is in a capital rationing situation it will not be able to invest in all available projects (whether involving organic growth or acquisition) because there is not enough capital for all of the investments. Capital is **a limiting factor**. In this situation, which you will have seen earlier in your studies

in the *Financial Management* exam, effective use needs to be made of this limiting factor in order to maximise shareholder wealth.

### 3.4.1 Soft and hard capital rationing

Capital rationing may be necessary in a business due to **internal factors** (soft capital rationing) or **external factors** (hard capital rationing).

**Soft capital rationing** may arise for one of the following reasons:

(a)   Management may be **reluctant to issue additional share capital** because of concern that this may lead to outsiders gaining control of the business.

(b)   Management may be **unwilling to issue additional share capital** if it will lead to a dilution of earnings per share.

(c)   Management may **not want to raise additional debt capital** because they do not wish to be committed to large fixed interest payments.

(d)   **Capital expenditure budgets** may restrict spending.

Note that whenever an organisation adopts a policy that restricts funds available for investment, such a policy may be less than optimal, as the organisation may reject projects with a positive NPV and forgo opportunities that would have enhanced the market value of the organisation.

**Hard capital rationing** may arise for one of the following reasons:

(a)   Raising money through the stock market may not be possible if **share prices are depressed**.

(b)   There may be **restrictions on bank lending** due to government control.

(c)   Lending institutions may consider an organisation to be too **risky** to be granted further loan facilities.

(d)   The **costs** associated with making small issues of capital may be too great.

### 3.4.2 Divisible and non-divisible projects

(a)   **Divisible projects** are those which can be undertaken completely or in fractions. Suppose that project A is divisible and requires the investment of $15,000 to achieve an NPV of $4,000. $7,500 invested in project A will earn an NPV of ½ × $4,000 = $2,000.

(b)   **Indivisible projects** are those which must be undertaken completely or not at all. It is not possible to invest in a fraction of the project.

You may also encounter **mutually exclusive** projects when one, and only one, of two or more choices of project can be undertaken.

### 3.4.3 Single period rationing with divisible projects

With **single period capital rationing**, investment funds are a limiting factor in the current period. The total return will be maximised if management follows the decision rule of maximising the return per unit of the limiting factor. They should therefore **select those projects whose cash inflows have the highest present value per $1 of capital invested**. In other words, rank the projects according to their **profitability index**.

**Formula to learn**

$$\text{Profitability index} = \frac{\text{NPV of project}}{\text{Initial cash outflow}}$$

### 3.4.4 Single period rationing with non-divisible projects

The main problem if projects are non-divisible is that there is likely to be small amounts of unused capital with each combination of projects. The best way to deal with this situation is to use trial and error and test the NPV available for different combinations of projects. This can be a laborious process if there is a large number of projects available.

### 3.4.5 Practical methods of dealing with capital rationing

A company may be able to limit the effects of capital rationing and exploit new opportunities.

(a)   It might **seek joint venture partners** with which to share projects.

(b)   As an alternative to direct investment in a project, the company may be able to consider a **licensing** or **franchising agreement** with another enterprise, under which the licensor/franchisor company would receive royalties.

(c)   It may be possible to **contract** out parts of a project to reduce the initial capital outlay required.

(d)   The company may seek **new** alternative **sources of capital** (subject to any restrictions which apply to it), for example:

| | | | |
|---|---|---|---|
| (i)   | Venture capital | (iv)  | Grant aid |
| (ii)  | Debt finance secured on projects' assets | (v)   | More effective capital management |
| (iii) | Sale and leaseback of property or equipment | (vi)  | Delay a project to a later period |

Having introduced the topic of capital rationing, we will return to it again in Chapter 5 where we will consider how to handle capital rationing that occurs across many periods of time (multi-period capital rationing).

# 4 Financing decision                                                      6/13

FAST FORWARD

**Financing decisions** included both long-term decisions (capital structure) and short-term decisions (working capital management).

The financial manager will need to determine the **source, cost** and effect on **risk** of the possible sources of long-term finance. A balance between **profitability** and **liquidity** (ready availability of funds if required) must be taken into account when deciding on the optimal level of short-term finance. A further issue with financing is that the financial manager will be wanting to **minimise the cost of capital** for an organisation, as this means a lower return is required by the providers of capital.

## 4.1 Sources of funds

The various sources of funds for investment purposes was covered in *Financial Management*. This section is a brief reminder of the sources of funds available. You should consult your previous study notes for details.

### 4.1.1 Short-term sources

(a)   **Overdrafts**

Overdrafts arise when payments from a current account exceed income to the current account – the deficit is financed by an overdraft. Overdrafts are the most important source of short-term finance available to businesses (and individuals!). They can be arranged relatively quickly and offer a degree of flexibility. Interest is only charged when the current account is overdrawn.

(b)   **Short-term loans**

This is a loan of a fixed amount for a specified period of time. The capital is received immediately and is repaid either at a specified time or in instalments. Interest rates and capital repayment structure are often predetermined.

(c)   **Trade credit**

This is one of the main sources of short-term finance for businesses, as they can take advantage of credit periods granted by suppliers. It is particularly useful during periods of high inflation. However, companies must consider the loss of discounts that suppliers may offer for early payment. Any unacceptable delays in payment will have an adverse effect on credit ratings.

(d)    **Leasing**

Leasing is a popular source of finance and is a useful alternative to purchasing an asset.

### 4.1.2 Long-term sources

**Debt**

The choice of debt finance depends on:

- The size of the business (a public issue of bonds is only available to large companies)
- The duration of the loan
- Whether a fixed or floating interest rate is preferred
- The security that can be offered

**Bonds**

Bonds (also called loan notes) are long-term debt capital raised by a company for which interest is paid, usually half-yearly and at a fixed rate. Bonds can be redeemable or irredeemable and come in various forms, including floating rate, zero coupon and convertible.

Bonds have a nominal value (the debt owed by the company) and interest is paid at a stated 'coupon' on this amount. The coupon rate is quoted before tax (ie gross).

One of the issues to be aware of with long-term debt is the ability to pay off debt when the redemption date arrives. The redemption date of current loans is an important piece of information in the statement of financial position, as you can establish how much new finance is likely to be needed by the company and when.

**Equity**

Equity finance is raised through the sale of ordinary shares to investors via a new issue or a rights issue. Holders of equity shares bear the ultimate risk, as they are at the bottom of the creditor hierarchy in the event of liquidation. As a result of this high risk, equity shareholders expect the highest return of long-term finance providers. The cost of equity is always higher than the cost of debt.

Calculating the cost of equity is covered in Chapter 2 and Chapter 7a.

## 4.2 Optimal financing mix

**Key term**

> **Capital structure** refers to the way in which an organisation is financed, by a combination of long-term capital (ordinary shares and reserves, preference shares, loan notes, bank loans, convertible loan stock and so on) and short-term liabilities, such as a bank overdraft and trade creditors. The mix of finance can be measured by **gearing** ratios.

The assets of a business must be financed somehow. When a business is growing, the additional assets must be financed by additional capital.

Although debt is a cheaper source of finance than equity, using debt to finance the business creates financial risk. **Financial risk** can be seen from different points of view.

(a)    **The company as a whole**

If a company builds up debts that it cannot pay when they fall due, it will be forced into liquidation.

(b)    **Lenders**

If a company cannot pay its debts, the company will go into liquidation owing lenders money that they are unlikely to recover in full. Lenders will probably want a **higher interest yield** to compensate them for higher financial risk and gearing.

(c) **Ordinary shareholders**

A company will not make any distributable profits unless it is able to earn enough profit from operations to pay all its interest charges, and then tax. The lower the profits or the higher the interest-bearing debts, the less there will be, if there is anything at all, for shareholders.

Ordinary shareholders will probably want a **bigger expected return** from their shares to compensate them for a **higher financial risk**. The market value of shares will therefore depend on gearing, because of this premium for financial risk that shareholders will want to earn.

### 4.2.1 What determines the optimal financing mix?

**Capital structure theories**

When we consider the capital structure decision, the question arises of whether there is an **optimal mix** of **capital and debt** that a company should try to achieve which will minimise its overall cost of capital. Under one view (the traditional view) there is an optimal capital mix at which the **average cost of capital**, weighted according to the different forms of capital employed, is **minimised**.

However, the alternative view of **Modigliani and Miller** is that the firm's overall **weighted average cost of capital** is **not influenced** by changes in its **capital structure**. Their argument is that the issue of debt causes the cost of equity to rise in such a way that the benefits of debt on returns are exactly offset. Investors themselves adjust their level of personal gearing and thus the level of corporate gearing becomes irrelevant. We shall discuss this debate in detail in Chapter 7a.

**Practical factors**

The appropriate mix of debt and equity will be influenced by a range of practical issues.

(a) **Stage in the company's life cycle**

If a company is just starting up, or is in its early growth phase, a high level of gearing is discouraged. The company will find it difficult to forecast future cash flows with any degree of certainty and any debt that is obtained is likely to have high interest rates attached.

(b) **Stability of earnings**

Shareholders in companies that are in highly volatile industries, for example due to rapid technological change, already face high levels of **business risk**. As interest still has to be paid regardless of earnings levels, unstable earnings are not conducive to high gearing ratios and shareholders are unlikely to want high levels of **financial risk** if business risk is already high.

(c) **Operational gearing (contribution/profit before interest and tax)**

High levels of fixed costs mean that contribution (sales revenue – variable costs) will be high relative to profits after fixed costs – that is, operational gearing will be high. This cost structure means volatile cash flows, therefore high levels of gearing are not recommended.

(d) **Security/collateral for the debt**

If a company is unable to offer sufficient levels of security or collateral then debt will be difficult to obtain. Any debt that is granted will reflect the risk of insufficient collateral in high interest rates.

## 4.3 Other issues

The choice of capital structure will depend not only on company circumstances but also a range of other issues.

### 4.3.1 Loss of control

The directors and shareholders may be unwilling to accept the **conditions** and the **loss of control** that obtaining extra finance will mean. Control may be diminished whether equity or loan funding is sought.

(a) **Issuing shares** to outsiders may **dilute** the **control** of the existing shareholders and directors, and the company will be subject to greater regulatory control if it obtains a stock market listing.

(b) The price of additional debt finance may be **security** restricting disposal of the assets secured and **covenants** that limit the company's rights to **dispose of assets** in general or to pay dividends.

### 4.3.2 Costs

The costs of **arranging new finance sources** may also be significant, particularly if the business is contemplating using a number of different sources over time.

### 4.3.3 Commitments

The interest and repayment schedules that the company is required to meet may be considered **too tight**. The collateral that loan providers require may also be too much, particularly if the directors are themselves required to provide **personal guarantees**.

### 4.3.4 Present sources of finance

Perhaps it's easy to find reasons why new sources of finance may not be desirable, but equally they may be considered more acceptable than drawing on current sources. For example, shareholders may be **unwilling to contribute further funds** in a rights issue; the business may wish to improve its relations with its suppliers, and one condition may be lessening its reliance on trade credit.

### 4.3.5 Foreign currency risk

If the company is receiving income in a foreign currency or has a long-term investment overseas, it can try to limit the **risk of adverse exchange rate movements** by matching. It can take out a long-term loan in the foreign currency and use the foreign currency receipts to repay the loan. Similarly, it can try to **match its foreign assets** (property, plant etc) by a **long-term loan** in the foreign currency. However, if the asset ultimately generates home currency receipts, there will be a long-term currency risk.

In addition, foreign loans may carry a lower **interest rate**, but the principle of **interest rate parity** (covered in Chapter 8) suggests that the **foreign currency** will ultimately strengthen, and therefore loan repayments will become more expensive.

# 5 Dividend decision                                    6/13, Mar/Jun 16, Sep/Dec 16

**FAST FORWARD**

The dividend decision is mainly a reflection of the investment decision and the financing decision.

The senior financial adviser will need to establish an appropriate balance between the amount paid as dividend and the amount of money that is reinvested into a business. The dividend decision is really an interaction between the investment decision and the financing decision, as the amount of money paid out as dividends will affect the level of retained earnings available for investment.

Some of the basic concepts associated with the dividend decision are discussed here, with more detail provided on the dividend decision in Chapter 2.

## 5.1 Dividends and the company's life cycle

A company's dividend policy will vary depending on the stage of the company's life cycle.

A young, growing company with numerous profitable investment opportunities is unlikely to be able to pay dividends, as its cash resources will be used for investment purposes. Shareholders should therefore have low or no expectations of receiving a dividend.

| **Young company** | **Mature company** |
|---|---|
| Zero/low dividend | High stable dividend |
| High growth/investment needs | Lower growth |
| Wants to minimise debt | Able and willing to take on debt |
|  | Possibly share buybacks too |

More mature companies may have built up a sufficient surplus of cash to allow them to pay dividends while still being able to fund dividend payments. Shareholders in such companies may also benefit from share buybacks whereby their shares are repurchased by the company – this is an alternative way of returning surplus cash to shareholders.

## 5.2 Interaction of investment with financing and dividend decisions

Managers will need to consider whether **extra finance** will be required and, if it will be, what the consequences of obtaining it will be. They will have to consider the demands of **providers of finance**, particularly of equity shareholders who require **dividends**. Will equity shareholders be content with projects that maximise their long-term returns, or will they require a minimum return or dividend each year?

When taking financial decisions, managers will have to fulfil the **requirements of the providers of finance**, otherwise finance may not be made available. This may be particularly difficult in the case of equity shareholders, since dividends are paid at the company's discretion; however, if equity shareholders do not receive the dividends they want, they will look to sell their shares, the share price will fall and the company will have more difficulty raising funds from share issues in future.

Although there may be risks in obtaining extra finance, the long-term risks to the business of **failing to invest** may be even greater and managers will have to balance these up.

| Factor | Impact |
|---|---|
| **Loan agreements** | Clauses in loan agreements may restrict payments of dividends. |
| **Tax rules** | Tax rules may prevent small private companies from not distributing earnings, merely to avoid tax payable by the owners on dividends received. |
| **Maintaining control** | If existing stockholders want to retain control they will not want to issue new equity. Hence, they will prefer to raise debt or retain profits giving a lower payout ratio. |

 Case Study

Zero dividend policy

Amazon

Amazon has followed a policy of successfully reinvesting its earnings to create a dominant market position. Because of its high fixed cost base, Amazon has aimed to keep its financial gearing low (it is virtually zero). A consequence of this is that up to 2015 Amazon has never paid a dividend. This does not mean that its shareholders have lost out because, as a consequence of the investments in its value chain, Amazon's share price has risen by over 500% in the 10 years leading up to 2015.

## 5.3 Dividend payout policy

Senior management have to decide on a suitable payout policy that reflects the **expectations** and **preferences** of investors. As mentioned above, dividend payout is linked closely with the life cycle of the company therefore it is unlikely that investors in a growing company will expect dividends in the near future.

The focus of all financial management decisions should be on the **primary objectives** of the company. If shareholders expect dividends to be paid, senior management must balance the dividend payment and retention policies to meet these expectations while ensuring that sufficient funds are available to finance profitable investment opportunities and fulfil the objective of maximising shareholder value.

You will often find that shareholders in a particular company have **similar** expectations and preferences regarding dividends. Those investing in a company that is not paying dividends will not be expecting

dividends (or actually want them) whereas other investors expect dividends and newer shareholders may have purchased shares with this expectation in mind.

**Dividend capacity** (free cash flow to equity) is covered in Chapter 2, and Chapter 4b in a more detailed discussion of dividend policy. It is also covered in Chapter 10 in the context of company valuation.

# 5.4 Share repurchase schemes

Dividends are not the only method of distributing retained earnings to shareholders. In many countries, companies have the right to **buy back shares from shareholders** who are willing to sell them, subject to certain conditions. This is known as a share repurchase or a buyback.

For a **smaller company** with few shareholders, the reason for buying back the company's own shares may be that there is no immediate willing purchaser at a time when a shareholder wishes to sell shares. For a public company, share repurchase could provide a way of withdrawing from the share market and 'going private'.

## 5.4.1 Benefits of a share repurchase scheme

(a)     Finding a **use for surplus cash**, which may be a 'dead asset'

(b)     **Increase in earnings per share** through a reduction in the number of shares in issue. This should lead to a higher share price than would otherwise be the case, and the company should be able to increase dividend payments on the remaining shares in issue

(c)     **Increase in gearing**. Repurchase of a company's own shares allows debt to be substituted for equity, so raising gearing. This will be of interest to a company wanting to increase its gearing without increasing its total long-term funding

(d)     **Readjustment of the company's equity base** to more appropriate levels, for a company whose business is in decline

(e)     Possibly **preventing a takeover** or enabling a quoted company to withdraw from the stock market

## 5.4.2 Drawbacks of a share repurchase scheme

(a)     It can be **hard to arrive at a price** that will be fair both to the vendors and to any shareholders who are not selling shares to the company.

(b)     A repurchase of shares could be seen as an **admission** that the company **cannot make better use of the funds** than the shareholders.

(c)     Some shareholders may suffer from being **taxed on a capital gain** following the purchase of their shares rather than receiving dividend income.

 Case Study

An analysis by Reuters in 2015 shows that spending on buybacks and dividends has surged relative to investment in the business. Among 1,900 US companies that have repurchased their shares since 2010, buybacks and dividends amounted to 113 percent of their capital spending, compared with 60 percent in 2000 and 38 percent in 1990.

And among the approximately 1,000 firms that buy back shares and report R&D spending, the proportion of net income spent on innovation has averaged less than 50 percent since 2009, increasing to 56 percent only in the most recent year as net income fell. It had been over 60 percent during the 1990s.

The phenomenon is the result of several converging forces: pressure from activist shareholders; executive compensation programs that tie pay to per-share earnings and share prices that buybacks can boost; increased global competition; and fear of making long-term bets on products and services that may not pay off.

IBM Corp has spent $125 billion on buybacks since 2005, and $32 billion on dividends, more than its $111 billion in capital spending and R&D during the same period. Pharmaceuticals maker Pfizer Inc spent $139 billion on buybacks and dividends in the past decade, compared to $82 billion on R&D and $18 billion in capital spending. 3M Co, creator of the Post-it Note and Scotch Tape, spent $48 billion on buybacks and dividends, compared to $16 billion on R&D and $14 billion in capital spending.

In theory, buybacks add another way, on top of dividends, of sharing profits with shareholders. Because buybacks increase demand and reduce supply for a company's shares, they tend to increase the share price, at least in the short-term, amplifying the positive effect. By decreasing the number of shares outstanding, they also increase earnings per share, even when total net income is flat.

Companies say buybacks are warranted when demand for their products and services isn't enough to justify spending on R&D, or when they deem their shares to be undervalued, and therefore a better investment than new projects.

But if those buybacks come at the expense of innovation, short-term gains in shareholder wealth could harm long-term competitiveness. "The U.S. is behind on production of everything from flat-panel TVs to semiconductors and solar photovoltaic cells," said Gary Pisano, a professor at Harvard Business School and author of "Producing Prosperity: Why America Needs a Manufacturing Renaissance."

*(Reuters, 2015)*

# 6 Financial planning and control

**Financial planning** covers the monitoring of the company's financial position, the evaluation of its productive capacity needs and the financing requirements of the company.

## 6.1 Strategic cash flow planning

In order to survive, any business must have an adequate net inflow of cash. Businesses should try to plan for positive net cash flows but at the same time it is unwise to hold too much cash.

When a company is cash-rich the senior financial advisor will have to decide whether to do one (or more) of the following:

(a) **Plan to use the cash**, for example for a project investment or a takeover bid for another company

(b) **Pay out the cash** to shareholders as **dividends**, and let the shareholders decide how best to use the cash for themselves

(c) **Repurchase its own shares** (share buyback)

**Strategic fund management** is an extension of cash flow planning, which takes into consideration the ability of a business to overcome unforeseen problems with cash flows. Where cash flow has become a problem, a company may choose to sell off some of its assets. However, it is important to recognise the difference between assets that a company can survive without and those that are essential for the company's continued operation.

Assets can be divided into three categories.

(a) Those that are needed to carry out the core activities of the business (eg plant and machinery)

(b) Those that are not essential for carrying out the main activities of the business and can be sold off at fairly short notice (eg short-term marketable investments)

(c) Those that are not essential for carrying out the main activities of the business and can be sold off to raise cash, but may take some time to sell (eg long-term investments, subsidiary companies)

## 6.2 Financial controls

**Strategic planning and control** is 'the process of deciding on objectives of the organisation, on changes in these objectives, on the resources used to attain these objectives, and on the policies that are to govern the acquisition, use and disposition of these resources'.

**Tactical or management control** is 'the process by which managers assure that resources are obtained and used effectively and efficiently in the accomplishment of the organisation's objectives'.

**Operational control** is 'the process of assuring that specific tasks are carried out effectively and efficiently'.

**Management control** is sometimes called **tactics** or **tactical planning**. Operational control is sometimes called **operational planning**.

| | Investment | Financing | Dividend |
|---|---|---|---|
| **Strategic** | Selection of products and markets<br>Required levels of profitability<br>Purchase of non-current assets fundamental to the business | Target debt/equity mix | Capital growth or high dividend payout |
| **Tactical** | Other non-current asset purchases<br>Efficient use of resources<br>Pricing | Lease versus buy | Scrip or cash dividends |
| **Operational** | Working capital management | Working capital management | N/A |

It is quite common for strategic plans to be in conflict with the shorter-term objectives of management control. Examples are as follows:

(a) It might be in the long-term interests of a company to buy more expensive or technologically advanced machinery to make a product, in the expectation that when market demand for the product eventually declines, customers will buy from producers whose output is of a slightly better quality – ie made on better machinery. In the short run, however, new and expensive machinery will incur higher depreciation charges and therefore **higher unit costs** for the same volume of production.

(b) Similarly, it may be in the long-term interests of a company to invest in R&D, in spite of the costs and loss of profits in the short term.

# 7 Risk management

For investors to be persuaded to take on extra risk, they must be compensated in the form of higher returns.

## 7.1 The risk/return relationship

All businesses face some sort of risk, although the extent of the risk will vary. The risk/return relationship was covered in detail in the *Financial Management* exam therefore you should be familiar with the concept of investors requiring higher returns for taking on more risk.

In a risk-free investment (eg Treasury Bills, Gilts) investors will only be compensated for the fact that they are postponing consumption in favour of investment. As investors take on extra risk, the return they require will not only compensate them for delayed consumption but also include a premium for the additional risk.

The level of risk that a company is willing to expose itself to will depend on the risk appetite of its shareholders. Conservative shareholders are likely to be risk averse, preferring less risk with lower returns, whereas risk takers are prepared to take on more risk in exchange for the chance of higher returns.

The relationship between risk and return is demonstrated in the diagram below.

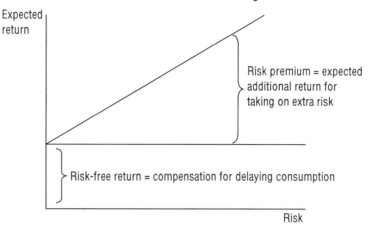

## 7.2 Risk preferences

Shareholders tend to invest in those companies that have a risk profile similar to their own portfolio. Therefore it would be extremely unlikely for a risk-averse investor to buy shares in a company that is perceived to be risky (for example, those involved in R&D and new technology companies).

Financial managers must be aware of the **risk preferences** of their company's shareholders and invest funds accordingly. They should avoid trying to change the risk profile of the company without the approval of the shareholders. This could lead to existing shareholders selling their shares, resulting in a **reduction** in the share price.

Managers should also avoid imposing their own risk preferences on their business decisions. Managers may be risk averse (perhaps worried about their jobs) but if the shareholders are risk takers they will expect business decisions to reflect this. If shareholders are not satisfied they may again sell their shares, with a resultant fall in share price.

## 7.3 Managing risk

Risk can be managed in several different ways.

(a)     **Hedging**. This could include currency risk and interest rate risk (see Section F of this Study Text). Hedging involves taking actions to make an outcome more certain.

(b)     **Diversifying**. This was mentioned earlier in this chapter and is effectively the prevention of 'putting all your eggs in one basket'. A portfolio of different investments, with varying degrees of risk, should help to reduce the overall risk of the business. One way of achieving diversification is via acquisition or merger (see Section D of this Study Text).

(c)     **Risk mitigation**. This involves putting control procedures in place to avoid investments in projects whose risk is above the shareholders' required level.

Risk management is introduced here, but is covered in more detail in Chapters 2 and 17.

# 8 Communicating policy to stakeholders

For financial strategy to be successful it needs to be communicated and supported by the **stakeholder groups**.

- **Internal** – managers, employees
- **Connected** – shareholders, banks, customers, suppliers
- **External** – government, pressure groups, local communities

**Stakeholders** are groups or individuals having a legitimate interest in the activities of an organisation, generally comprising customers, employees, the community, shareholders, suppliers and lenders.

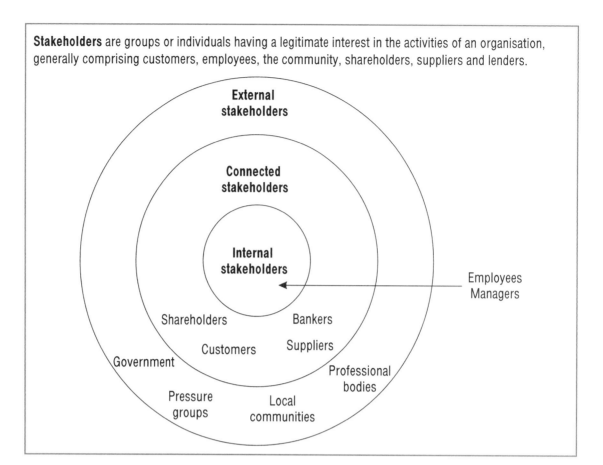

You may be told in a question that a company aims to respect the interests of stakeholders, and determines its policies in the light of that aim. Even if you aren't, you will see at various times in this Text circumstances when stakeholder interests become particularly important, for example in a merger and acquisition situation.

## 8.1 Objectives of stakeholder groups

The various groups of stakeholders in a firm will have different goals which will depend in part on the situation of the organisation.

| Stakeholder goals | |
|---|---|
| **Shareholders** | Providers of risk capital, aim to maximise wealth |
| **Suppliers** | Often other businesses, aim to be paid full amount by date agreed, but want to continue long-term trading relationship, and so may accept later payment |
| **Long-term lenders** | Wish to receive payments of interest and capital on loan by due date for repayment |
| **Employees** | Maximise rewards paid to them in salaries and benefits, also prefer continuity in employment |
| **Government** | Political objectives, such as sustained economic growth and high employment |
| **Management** | Maximising their own rewards |

You might be asked to comment on a situation where the interests of different stakeholders diverge.

## 8.2 Influence of stakeholders

The actions of stakeholder groups in pursuit of their various goals can exert influence on strategy. The **greater** the **power** of the **stakeholder**, the greater their influence will be.

In 2014 the French Government gave itself new powers to block takeovers by foreign companies in a wide range of strategic sectors covering defence, energy, water, transport, telecoms and health. Any such acquisition will need the approval of the economy minister.

Many managers acknowledge that the interests of some stakeholder groups – eg themselves and employees – should be recognised and provided for, even if this means that the interests of shareholders might be adversely affected. Not all stakeholder group interests can be given specific attention in the decisions of management, but those stakeholders for whom management recognises and accepts a responsibility are referred to as **constituents** of the firm.

The influence of stakeholders on an organisation is considered further in Chapter 3.

# 9 Strategies for achieving financial goals 6/11

**FAST FORWARD**

**Strategy** is a course of action to achieve an objective. Strategies to accomplish the objective of maximising shareholder value are set at the corporate, business and operational levels.

## 9.1 Strategy

**Key term**

**Strategy** may be defined as a course of action, including the specification of resources required, to achieve a specific objective.

There are three main levels of strategy.

### 9.1.1 Corporate strategy

This is concerned with broader issues, such as 'what business are we in?'. **Financial aspects** of this level of strategic decision making include the choice of method in entering a market or business. Whether entry should be accomplished through an acquisition or through organic growth is a question with financial implications. It is important to be clear about corporate strategy, as this forms the basis of other strategic decisions.

### 9.1.2 Business strategy or competitive strategy

This covers the question of how strategic business units (SBUs) compete in **individual markets**, and therefore of the resources which should be allocated to them. Business strategy relates to individual SBUs – that is, parts of the organisation where there are distinct external markets for goods or services.

Competitive strategy examines the threat on the performance of the company of such factors as:

(a)　The potential changes in the industry in which the firm operates, through entry of new competitors
(b)　The competition between existing firms in terms of costs, pricing and product quality
(c)　The development of substitute products that may affect the industry as a whole
(d)　The monopolistic power of individual companies in the input markets
(e)　The monopolistic power of companies in the various product markets

Competitive strategy allows a company to forecast revenue and costs much more accurately. Operating profits together with financing and distribution decisions ultimately determine the value of a company.

### 9.1.3 Operational strategy

This is to do with how different functions within the business – including the finance function – contribute to corporate and business strategies. In most businesses, the successful implementation of business

strategies relies to a great extent on decisions that are taken at the operational level. For example, at BPP there are operational strategies in place in terms of updating study materials and the design and presentation of courses.

## 9.2 The management of financial resources

Key term

> The **management of financial resources** is part of the overall financial strategy and consists of the management of the balance sheet items to achieve the desired balance between risk and return.

**Financial strategy** determines the means for the attainment of stated **objectives** or **targets**. An integral part of financial strategy is the **management of financial resources**.

The financial management process provides the framework for co-ordinating and controlling the firm's actions to achieve its financial objectives. It includes strategic financial plans which determine a company's actions and the resulting impact on shareholder value over a period of time and which, in turn, determine the short-term operating plans of the firm.

**Long-term financial strategy** is part of the firm's overall strategy together with a company's marketing strategy, investment strategy and product development strategy. Financial strategy is expressed through a series of annual budget and profit plans.

The long-term financial strategy is supplemented by a **short-term financial strategy** which deals with the management of the financial resources of the company.

The goal of short-term financial management is to manage each of the firm's current assets and liabilities in order to achieve a balance between profitability and risk, which enhances shareholder value. Too much investment in current assets reduces profitability, whereas too little investment in current assets may impair the ability of a company to meet debt payments. Either way, the effect on the value of the firm may be negative.

The efficient management of financial resources of a company is achieved through the construction of annual cash budgets which reflect the firm's planned inflows and outflows of cash. The cash budget presents a useful tool for the estimation of the short-term cash requirements or surpluses of a company.

If a company is predicted to face a deficit, the most efficient method of financing should be considered. This will normally involve the issue of short-term money market instruments. If a company is predicted to have a surplus, then an appropriate investment in short-term money market instruments should be considered.

# Chapter Roundup

- In financial management of businesses, the key objective is the **maximisation of shareholders' wealth**.

- Non-financial objectives may limit the achievement of financial objectives. Their existence suggests the assumption that the main purpose of a company is to maximise shareholders' wealth is too simplistic.

- In seeking to attain the financial objectives of the organisation or enterprise, a financial manager has to make three fundamental decisions – investment, financing and dividend. The investment decision involves selecting appropriate investment opportunities that will help to fulfil the company's primary objectives.

- **Financing decisions** include both long-term decisions (capital structure) and short-term decisions (working capital management).

- The dividend decision is mainly a reflection of the investment decision and the financing decision.

- **Financial planning** covers the monitoring of the company's financial position, the evaluation of its productive capacity needs and the financing requirements of the company.

- **Strategic planning and control** is 'the process of deciding on objectives of the organisation, on changes in these objectives, on the resources used to attain these objectives, and on the policies that are to govern the acquisition, use and disposition of these resources'.

- **Tactical or management control** is 'the process by which managers assure that resources are obtained and used effectively and efficiently in the accomplishment of the organisation's objectives'.

- **Operational control** is 'the process of assuring that specific tasks are carried out effectively and efficiently'.

- **Management control** is sometimes called **tactics** or **tactical planning**. **Operational control** is sometimes called **operational planning**.

- For investors to be persuaded to take on extra risk, they must be compensated in the form of higher returns.

- For financial strategy to be successful, it needs to be communicated and supported by the **stakeholder groups**.

    - **Internal** – managers, employees
    - **Connected** – shareholders, banks, customers, suppliers
    - **External** – government, pressure groups, local communities

- **Strategy** is a course of action to achieve an objective. Strategies to accomplish the objective of maximising shareholder value are set at the corporate, business and operational levels.

# Quick Quiz

1   Why is maximisation of the market value of shares the key objective in the theory of company finance?

2   State **three** ways of measuring the value of a company.

3   What are the **three** main financial management decisions?

4   What are the main forms of growth for a company?

5   What are the **three** groups of stakeholders?

6   What is the objective of risk management policy?

# Answers to Quick Quiz

1   Because it implies maximisation of the market value of shareholder wealth.

2   (1) Going concern basis
    (2) Break-up basis
    (3) Market values

3   (1) Investment decisions
    (2) Financing decisions
    (3) Dividend decisions

4   Organic growth or through acquisitions

5   Internal, connected and external.

6   To choose the combination of risk and return which is consistent with the risk attitude of the company.

## Now try the question below from the Practice Question Bank

| Number | Level | Marks | Time |
|--------|-------|-------|------|
| 1 | Examination | 20 | 39 mins |

# Financial strategy formulation

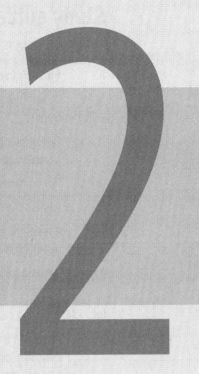

| Topic list | Syllabus reference |
|---|---|
| 1 Assessing corporate performance | A2(a) |
| 2 Other information from companies' accounts | A2(a) |
| 3 Obtaining long-term finance | A2(a) |
| 4 Dividend policy | A2(a) |
| 5 Risk Management | A2(d), (f) |
| 6 Different types of risk | A2(e) |
| 7 Capital investment monitoring | A2(g) |
| 8 Behavioural finance | A2(h) |

## Introduction

This chapter looks in greater detail into four areas of financial strategy, namely the capital structure policy, the dividend distribution policy, the capital investment monitoring process and the risk management process. The Capital Asset Pricing Model underpins a lot of what is covered in the following chapters.

The chapter concludes by introducing behavioural finance and considering its implications for financial strategy.

# Study guide

| | | Intellectual level |
|---|---|---|
| **A2** | **Financial strategy formulation** | |
| (a) | Assess organisational performance using methods such as ratios and trends. | 3 |
| (b) | Recommend the optimum capital mix and structure within a specified business context and capital asset structure. | 3 |
| (c) | Recommend appropriate distribution and retention policy. | 3 |
| (d) | Explain the theoretical and practical rationale for the management of risk. | 3 |
| (e) | Assess the organisation's exposure to business and financial risk including operational, reputational, political, economic, regulatory and fiscal risk. | 3 |
| (f) | Develop a framework for risk management comparing and contrasting risk mitigation, hedging and diversification strategies. | 3 |
| (g) | Establish capital investment monitoring and risk management systems. | 3 |
| (h) | Advise on the impact of behavioural finance on financial strategies/ securities prices and why they may not follow the conventional financial theories (this is also covered in Chapter 10) | 3 |

# Exam guide

You may be asked about the contents of a strategic financial plan. Alternatively, as part of a longer question assessing a specific proposal, you may need to draw on your knowledge of the reasons for mergers and acquisitions, or the differences between vertical integration and diversification. In an investment question, there may be some fairly easy marks in the last part for discussing the benefits of capital investment monitoring.

One of the optional performance objectives in your PER is to advise on the appropriateness and cost of different sources of finance. Another is to identify and raise an appropriate source of finance for a specific business need. This chapter covers some of the common sources of finance and the linked area of dividend policy.

# 1 Assessing corporate performance                     6/12, 6/15

**FAST FORWARD**

Corporate performance can be measured using such means as ratios and trends.

The assessment of your own company's, or someone else's, corporate performance is an important foundation for the formulation of financial strategy. Knowledge of company performance will help management to determine new strategies or amend existing strategies to take account of changing circumstances.

## 1.1 Ratios

You should already be familiar with ratio analysis from *Financial Management (FM)*. However, as a reminder, the main ratios are listed below. **Note that none of these ratios are given in the exam so you will have to learn them.**

**Hierarchy of ratios**

```
                                    Return on equity
                          ┌──────────────────┴──────────────────┐
                  Return on investment        ×        Total assets ÷ equity
           ┌──────────────┴──────────────┐
    Return on sales        ×        Asset turnover
    ┌──────┴──────┐              ┌────────┴────────┐
Net income  ÷   Sales        Sales   ÷   Total assets
 ┌──┴──┐                             ┌────────┴────────┐
Sales — Total costs           Non-current  +  Current
                                assets          assets
```

**Profitability ratios**

**Return on capital employed (ROCE)** $= \dfrac{\text{PBIT}}{\text{Capital employed}}$

**Capital employed** = Shareholders' funds **plus** payables: amounts falling due after more than one year **plus** any long-term provisions for liabilities and charges

= Total assets less current liabilities

When **interpreting** ROCE look for the following:

- How risky is the business?

- How capital intensive is it?

- What ROCE do similar businesses have?

- How does it compare with current market borrowing rates; is it earning enough to be able to cover the costs of extra borrowing?

**Problems**: which items to consider to achieve comparability:

- Revaluation of assets
- Accounting policies, eg goodwill, R&D
- Whether bank overdraft is classified as a short-/long-term liability

**Return on equity** $= \dfrac{\text{Earnings attributable to ordinary shareholders}}{\text{Shareholders' equity}}$

This gives a more **restricted view** of capital than ROCE, but the same principles apply.

**Asset turnover** $= \dfrac{\text{Sales}}{\text{Capital employed}}$

This measures how efficiently the assets have been used. Amend to just non-current assets for capital-intensive businesses.

**Operating profit margin** $= \dfrac{\text{PBIT}}{\text{Sales}}\ \%$ \qquad\qquad Gross profit margin $= \dfrac{\text{Gross profit}}{\text{Sales}}\ \%$

It is useful to compare profit margin to gross profit % to investigate movements which do not match.

**Gross profit margin**

- Sales prices, sales volume and sales mix
- Purchase prices and related costs (discount, carriage etc)
- Production costs, both direct (materials, labour) and indirect (overheads both fixed and variable)
- Inventory levels and valuation, including errors, cut-off and costs of running out of goods

## Operating profit margin

- Sales expenses in relation to sales levels
- Administrative expenses, including salary levels
- Distribution expenses in relation to sales levels

## Liquidity ratios

**Current ratio** $= \dfrac{\text{Current assets}}{\text{Current liabilities}}$

Assume assets realised at book level ∴ theoretical. 2:1 acceptable? 1.5:1? It depends on the industry. Remember that excessively large levels can indicate excessive receivables and inventories, and poor control of working capital.

**Quick ratio (acid test)** $= \dfrac{\text{Current assets} - \text{inventory}}{\text{Current liabilities}}$

Eliminates illiquid and subjectively valued inventory. Care is needed: it could be high if **overtrading** with receivables, but no cash. Is 1:1 OK? Many supermarkets operate on 0.3, as inventories of goods are very liquid and inventory turnover is very fast.

**Receivables collection period (receivables days)** $= \dfrac{\text{Trade receivables}}{\text{Credit sales}} \times 365$

Is it **consistent** with quick/current ratio? If not, investigate.

**Inventory days** $= \dfrac{\text{Inventory}}{\text{Cost of sales}} \times 365$

Note that cost of sales excludes depreciation of any production equipment.

The quicker the turnover the better? But remember:

- Lead times
- Seasonal fluctuations in orders
- Alternative uses of warehouse space
- Bulk buying discounts
- Likelihood of inventory perishing or becoming obsolete

**Payables payment period** $= \dfrac{\text{Trade payables}}{\text{Purchases}} \times 365$

Use **cost of sales (excluding depreciation)** if purchases are not disclosed.

## Cash operating cycle

| | |
|---|---|
| = | Average time raw materials are in inventory |
| − | Period of credit taken from suppliers |
| + | Time taken to produce goods |
| + | Time taken by customers to pay for goods |

## Reasons for changes in liquidity

- Credit control efficiency altered
- Altering payment period of suppliers as a source of funding
- Reducing inventory holdings to maintain liquidity

**Shareholders' investment ratios (stock market ratios)**

**Total shareholder return (TSR)** = $\dfrac{\text{Dividend per share} + \text{capital gain (or loss)}}{\text{Share price at the start of the year}} \times 100$

TSR measures the actual return generated by a company, this can be compared to the expected return (ie the cost of equity) to evaluate whether TSR is acceptable to shareholders.

**Dividend yield** = $\dfrac{\text{Dividend per share}}{\text{Market price per share}}$ %

- **Low yield**: The company retains a large proportion of profits to reinvest
- **High yield**: This is a risky company or slow-growing

Dividend yield is generally less than interest yield. Shareholders will expect price rises, and wish for return (dividends + capital gains) to exceed return investors get from fixed interest securities.

**Earnings per share (EPS)** = $\dfrac{\text{Profits distributable to ordinary shareholders}}{\text{Number of ordinary shares issued}}$

Investors look for growth; earnings levels need to be sustained to pay dividends and invest in the business. In order for comparisons over time to be valid, must be consistent basis of calculation. EPS can be manipulated.

Need to consider possibility of dilution through exercise of warrants or options, or conversion of bonds.

**Dividend cover** = $\dfrac{\text{EPS}}{\text{Dividend per share}}$

This shows **how safe the dividend is**, or the extent of profit retention. Variations are due to maintaining dividend when profits are declining.

The converse of dividend cover is the **dividend payout ratio**.

**Dividend payout ratio** = $\dfrac{\text{Dividend per share}}{\text{EPS}}$

**P/E ratio** = $\dfrac{\text{Market price per share}}{\text{EPS}}$

The **higher the better** here: it reflects the confidence of the market in high earnings growth and/or low risk. A rise in EPS will cause an increase in P/E ratio, but maybe not to same extent.

P/E ratio will be affected by interest rate changes; a rise in rates will mean a fall in the P/E ratio as shares become less attractive. P/E ratio also depends on market expectations and confidence.

**Debt and gearing ratios**

**Financial gearing** = $\dfrac{\text{Prior charge capital}}{\text{Equity capital (including reserves)}}$ (based on statement of financial position values)

**Financial gearing** measures the relationship between shareholders' capital plus reserves, and either prior charge capital or borrowings or both.

**Prior charge capital** is capital which has a right to the receipt of interest or of preferred dividends in precedence to any claim on distributable earnings on the part of the ordinary shareholders.

**Or**

**Financial gearing** = $\dfrac{\text{Market value of prior charge capital}}{\text{Market value of equity} + \text{Market value of prior charge capital}}$ (based on market values)

**Operational gearing** = $\dfrac{\text{Contribution}}{\text{Profit before interest and tax (PBIT)}}$

Contribution is sales minus variable cost of sales.

$$\text{Interest coverage ratio} = \frac{\text{Profit before interest and tax}}{\text{Interest}}$$

**Debt ratio** = Total debts : Total assets

### 1.1.1 Uses of ratio analysis

The key to obtaining meaningful information from ratio analysis is **comparison**; comparing ratios over time within the same business to establish whether the business is **improving** or **declining**, and comparing ratios between similar businesses to see whether the company you are analysing is better or worse than average within its own business sector.

A vital element in effective ratio analysis is understanding the needs of the person for whom the ratio analysis is being undertaken.

(a)   **Investors** will be interested in the **risk and return** relating to their investment, so will be concerned with dividends, market prices, level of debt vs equity etc.

(b)   **Suppliers** and **lenders** are interested in receiving the payments due to them, so will want to know how liquid the business is.

(c)   **Managers** are interested in ratios that indicate how well the business is being run, and also how the business is doing in relation to its **competitors**.

### 1.1.2 Limitations of ratio analysis

Although ratio analysis can be a very useful technique, it is important to realise its limitations.

(a)   **Availability of comparable information**

When making comparisons with other companies in the industry, industry averages may hide **wide variations** in figures. Figures for 'similar' companies may provide a better guide, but then there are problems identifying which companies are similar, and obtaining enough detailed information about them.

(b)   **Use of historical/out of date information**

Comparisons with the previous history of a business may be of limited use if the business has recently undergone, or is about to undergo, **substantial changes**.

(c)   **Ratios are not definitive**

'Ideal levels' vary industry by industry, and even they are not definitive. Companies may be able to exist without any difficulty with ratios that are rather worse than the industry average.

(d)   **Need for careful interpretation**

For example, if comparing two businesses' liquidity ratios, one business may have higher levels. This might appear to be 'good', but further investigation might reveal that the higher ratios are a result of higher inventory and receivable levels which are a result of poor working capital management by the business with the 'better' ratios.

(e)   **Manipulation**

Any ratio including profit may be distorted by **choice of accounting policies**. For smaller companies, working capital ratios may be distorted depending on whether a big customer pays, or a large supplier is paid, before or after the year end.

(f)   **Other information**

**Ratio analysis on its own is not sufficient** for interpreting company accounts, and there are other items of information that should be looked at. These are considered in the next section.

# 2 Other information from companies' accounts

As well as ratios, **other information** can be used to analyse a company's performance and identify possible problem areas. This will include information relating to **non-current assets** and **financial obligations, contingencies** and **events after the reporting period**.

## 2.1 The revaluation of non-current assets

Non-current assets may be stated in the statement of financial position at cost less accumulated depreciation. They may also be revalued from time to time to a current market value to avoid understatement of current value. When this happens:

(a)     The increase in the statement of financial position value of the non-current asset is matched by an increase in the **revaluation reserve**.

(b)     **Depreciation** in subsequent years is based on the revalued amount of the asset, its estimated residual value and its estimated remaining useful life.

## 2.2 Share capital and share issues

The **capital and reserves** section of a company's accounts contains information which appears to be mainly the concern of the various classes of shareholder. However, because the shareholders' interest in the business acts as a **buffer for the creditors** in the event of any financial problems, this section is also of some importance to creditors.

For example, if a company has increased its total share capital and reserves in the year:

(a)     Did it do so by **issuing new shares** resulting in a higher allotted share capital and share premium account?

(b)     Did it do so by **revaluing some non-current assets**, resulting in a higher revaluation reserve?

(c)     Did it make a substantial profit and **retain a good proportion of this profit** in the business resulting in a higher balance in the statement of profit or loss?

A **scrip issue** might also be of some interest. It will result in a **fall** in the **market price** per share. If it has been funded from a company's profit and loss account reserves, a scrip issue would indicate that the company recognised and formalised its long-term capital needs by making some previously distributable reserves non-distributable.

If a company has **issued shares in the form of a dividend**, are there obvious reasons why this should be so? For example, does the company need to retain capital within the business because of poor trading in the previous year, making the directors reluctant to pay out more cash dividend than necessary?

## 2.3 Financial obligations

**Financial obligations** of a company may also be significant, and the timescale over which these become or could become repayable should be considered.

Examples are:

(a)     Levels of **redeemable debt**

(b)     **Earn out arrangements**

(c)     **Potential or contingent liabilities**, such as liabilities under unresolved legal cases or insurance claims

## 2.4 Debentures, loans and other liabilities

Two points of interest about debentures, loans and other liabilities are:

- Whether or not loans are **secured**
- The **redemption dates** of loans

For debentures and loan stock which are **secured**, the details of the security are usually included in the terms of a trust deed. Details of any **fixed or floating charges against assets** must be disclosed in a note to the accounts.

In analysing a set of accounts, particular attention should be paid to some significant features concerning **debenture or loan stock redemption**. These are:

(a)     The **closeness of the redemption date**, which would indicate how much finance the company has to find in the immediate future to repay its loans. It is not unusual, however, to repay one loan by taking out another, and so a company does not necessarily have to find the money to repay a loan from its own resources.

(b)     The **percentage interest rate** on the loans being redeemed, compared with the **current market rate of interest**. This would give some idea, if a company decides to replace loans by taking out new loans, of the likely increase (or reduction) in interest costs that it might face, and how easily it might accommodate any interest cost increase.

## 2.5 Contingencies

**Contingencies** are conditions which exist at the balance sheet date where the outcome will be confirmed only on the occurrence or non-occurrence of one or more uncertain future events.

Contingencies can result in contingent gains or contingent losses. The fact that the condition **exists at the statement of financial position date** distinguishes a contingency from a post balance sheet event.

Some of the **typical types of contingencies** disclosed by companies are as follows:

- Guarantees given by the company
- Uncalled liabilities on shares or loan stock
- Lawsuits or claims pending

Again, knowledge of such contingencies will enhance the quality of the information used in analysis.

## 2.6 Events after the reporting period

> **Events after the reporting period** are those events both favourable and unfavourable which occur between the statement of financial position date and the date on which the financial statements are approved by the board of directors.

The following are examples of events after the reporting period which should normally be disclosed:

- Mergers and acquisitions
- The issue of new shares and debentures
- The purchase and sale of major non-current assets and investments
- Losses of non-current assets or stocks as a result of a catastrophe such as fire or flood
- The opening of new trading activities
- The closure of a significant part of the trading activities
- A decline in the value of property and investments held as non-current assets
- Changes in exchange rates (if there are significant overseas interests)
- Government action, such as nationalisation
- Strikes and other labour disputes

## 3 Obtaining long-term finance                                                    6/12

**FAST FORWARD**

Decisions on how to finance the acquisition of assets are based on an understanding of the advantages and disadvantages of the various sources of finance.

### 3.1 The capital structure decision

The principles behind the capital structure decision have already been outlined in Chapter 1 (and will be expanded in Chapter 7a). Here we focus on the pros and cons of the various **types** of debt and equity finance that are available.

A key part of a financial plan will involve deciding on the type of finance to be used, for example to underpin a proposed investment.

### 3.2 Sources of finance

The main sources of finance for corporations are:

(a)  Retained earnings
(b)  Proceeds from the issue of new ordinary shares to existing or new shareholders
(c)  Proceeds from a flotation of a company
(d)  Preference shares
(e)  Debt

### 3.3 Pros and cons of debt finance

#### 3.3.1 Advantages of debt

(a)  Debt is a **cheaper form of finance** than shares, as debt interest is tax deductible in most tax regimes.
(b)  Debt should be **more attractive** to investors because it will be **secured** against the assets of the company.
(c)  **Debtholders** rank above **shareholders** in the event of a liquidation.
(d)  **Issue costs** are normally **lower** for debt than for shares.
(e)  There is **no immediate change** in the existing structure of control, although this may change over time if the bonds are convertible to shares.
(f)  There is **no immediate dilution** in earnings and dividends per share.
(g)  Lenders do not participate in high profits compared with shares.

#### 3.3.2 Disadvantages of debt

(a)  **Interest** has to be paid on debt no matter what the company's profits in a year are. In particular, the company may find itself locked into long-term debt at unfavourable rates of interest. The company is not legally obliged to pay dividends.

(b)     Money has to be made available for **redemption** or **repayment** of debt. However, redemption values will fall in real terms during a time of inflation.

(c)     Heavy borrowing **increases the financial risks** for ordinary shareholders. A company must be able to pay the interest charges and eventually repay the debt from its cash resources, and at the same time maintain a healthy balance sheet which does not deter would-be lenders. There might be insufficient security for a new loan.

(d)     Shareholders may demand a **higher rate of return** because an increased interest burden increases the risks that dividends will not be paid.

(e)     There might be restrictions on a company's power to borrow. The **company's constitution** may limit borrowing. These borrowing limits cannot be altered except with the approval of the shareholders at a general meeting of the company. **Trust deeds of existing loan stock** may **limit borrowing**. These limits can only be overcome by redeeming the loan stock.

## 3.4 Debt instruments

**FAST FORWARD**

Debt capital takes various forms such as **loan capital, debentures and zero coupon bonds** and the interest on debt is tax deductible.

### 3.4.1 Types of corporate debt

Corporate debt takes many forms which are differentiated in terms of maturity as **redeemable** or **irredeemable**, in terms of the coupon as fixed rate **loan notes, floating rate loan notes**, or **zero coupon bonds**. Finally there are callable bonds which can be redeemed before maturity and **convertible loan stock** which can be converted into equity.

(a)     **Debentures** are **secure loan capital** secured either by a floating charge on all assets of the company, or by a fixed charge on specific assets of the company.

(b)     **Unsecured loan stock** is debt which is not secured on any of the assets of the company and it carries a higher interest.

(c)     **Deep discount bonds** are bonds offered at a large discount on the face value of the debt so that a significant proportion of the return to the investor comes by way of a capital gain on redemption, rather than through interest payment. Deep discount bonds pay a low coupon and have **low servicing costs** but a high cost of redemption at maturity. The only tax advantage is that the gain gets taxed (as **income**) in one lump on maturity or sale, not as amounts of interest each year.

(d)     **Zero coupon bonds** are bonds offering no interest payments, all investor return being gained through capital appreciation. They are issued at a discount to their redemption value, and the investor gains from the difference between the issue price and the redemption value. The advantage for borrowers is that zero coupon bonds can be used to raise cash immediately, and there is no cash repayment until redemption date. The cost of redemption is known at the time of issue, and so the borrower can plan to have funds available to redeem the bonds at maturity. The advantage for lenders is that there is no exposure to interest rate risk and, if held to maturity, they are free of market risk. The investor is of course exposed to credit risk.

(e)     **Convertible unsecured debt** is debt instruments that give the option to the holder to convert them into equity at some time in the future at a predetermined price.

(f)     **Mezzanine debt** is debt with conversion options. It is a subordinated debt because it ranks in terms of seniority of claims below straight debt like debentures and it requires a higher rate of return. Mezzanine debt is the preferred way of financing leveraged buy-outs.

(g)     **Leasing** is used for the financing of certain assets such as buildings, ships and aircraft.

(h)     **Eurobonds** are bonds denominated in currency other than that of the issuer, usually dollar, yen or euro, and trade in the international financial markets.

### 3.4.2 Trust deed

A **loan note (or debenture)** is a written acknowledgement of a debt by a company, usually given under its seal and normally containing provisions as to payment of interest and the terms of repayment of principal. A loan note may be secured on some or all of the assets of the company or its subsidiaries.

A **trust deed** would empower a trustee (such as an insurance company or a bank) to **intervene** on behalf of loan note holders if the conditions of borrowing under which the debentures were issued are not being fulfilled. This might involve:

(a)    **Failure** to **pay interest** on the due dates

(b)    An **attempt** by the company to **sell off important assets** contrary to the terms of the loan

(c)    A company taking out **additional loans** and thereby exceeding previously agreed borrowing limits established either by its constitution or by the terms of the loan note trust deed (a trust deed might place restrictions on the company's ability to borrow more from elsewhere until the loan notes have been redeemed)

### 3.4.3 Issuing corporate bonds

A company that wants to issue corporate bonds will need to appoint an investment bank as the lead manager. The lead manager in turn sets up an underwriting syndicate which purchases the entire issue at an agreed price. The price reflects the coupon of the bond and the credit rating of the bond. The syndicate will then sell the issue to final buyers who are normally clients of the investment banks involved or other investment banks.

### 3.4.4 Cost of debt

The cost of debt capital is the after-tax cost of raising debt in the capital markets. It is the rate of return that investors require for investments with that specific risk. Other factors that influence the cost of debt capital include:

(a)    The general level of interest rate
(b)    The credit rating of the bond which is reflected in the spread over the risk-free rate
(c)    The maturity of the bond
(d)    The type of debt issue; for example callable bonds will be more expensive than non-callable bonds
(e)    The cost of issuing a bond

The mechanics of calculating the cost of debt are covered in Chapter 7a.

## 3.5 Preference shares

Preference shares have priority over ordinary shares in dividend payments and capital repayment.

### 3.5.1 Characteristics of preference shares

**Preference shares** carry priority over ordinary shareholders with regard to dividend payments. They do not carry voting rights. They may be attractive to corporate investors, as (unlike interest receipts) dividends received are generally not subject to tax. However, for the issuing company, dividend payments (unlike interest payments) are generally not tax deductible.

**Preference shares** are shares carrying a fixed rate of dividends, the holders of which, subject to the conditions of issue, have a prior claim to any company profits available for distribution. They are an example of prior charge capital.

Preferred shareholders may also have a prior claim to the repayment of capital in the event of winding up.

### 3.5.2 Types of preference shares

**Cumulative preference shares** are preference shares where any arrears of dividend are carried forward. When eventually the company decides to pay a dividend, the cumulative preference shareholders are entitled to all their arrears before ordinary shareholders are paid a dividend.

**Participating preference shares** are shares that have an additional entitlement to dividend over and above their specified rate. Participating preferred shareholders are entitled to participate along with ordinary shareholders in available profits, normally once the ordinary shareholders have themselves received a specified level of dividend.

**Convertible preference shares** are shares that can be converted into ordinary shares.

### 3.5.3 Advantages and disadvantages of preference shares

From the company's point of view, preference shares have some positive features.

(a) Dividends do **not have** to be **paid** in a year in which **profits are poor**, while this is not the case with interest payments on long-term debt.

(b) Since they do not normally carry voting rights, preferred shares **avoid diluting** the **control** of existing shareholders, while an issue of equity shares would not.

(c) Unless they are redeemable, issuing preference shares will **lower** the company's **gearing**. Redeemable preference shares are normally treated as debt when gearing is calculated.

(d) The issue of preference shares does **not restrict** the company's **borrowing power**, at least in the sense that preferred share capital is not secured against assets of the business.

(e) The non-payment of dividend does **not give** the preferred shareholders the **right** to **appoint a receiver**, a right which is normally given to debenture holders.

From the point of view of the investor, preference shares are less attractive than loan stock because:

(a) They **cannot be secured** on the company's assets.

(b) The **dividend yield** traditionally offered on preferred dividends has been much **too low** to provide an attractive investment compared with the interest yields on loan stock in view of the additional risk involved.

(c) **Dividend payments on preference shares may not be tax deductible** in the way that interest payments on debt are. Furthermore, for preference shares to be attractive to investors, the level of payment needs to be **higher than** for **interest on debt** to compensate for the additional risks.

### 3.5.4 Cost of preference shares

The key feature of preference shares is the **constant interest** that they pay to investors. The cost of preference shares should therefore be calculated in the same way as the cost of corporate bonds.

## 3.6 Retained earnings

**FAST FORWARD**

**Retained earnings** are the **cumulative undistributed earnings** of the company and can be used to finance the **capital expenditure** programme of the company.

For many businesses, the cash needed to finance investments will be available because the earnings the business has made have been retained within the business rather than paid out as dividends. This interaction of investment, financing and dividend policy is the most important issue facing many businesses.

**Advantages of using retentions**

Retentions are a **flexible source** of finance; companies are not tied to specific amounts or specific repayment patterns. Using retentions does **not involve** a **change in the pattern** of **shareholdings**.

#### Disadvantages of using retentions

Shareholders may be **sensitive** to the **loss of dividends** that will result from retention for reinvestment, rather than paying dividends.

### 3.6.1 Cost of retained earnings

Retained profits is not a cost-free method of obtaining funds. There is an **opportunity cost** in that if dividends were paid, the cash received could be invested by shareholders to earn a return. The cost of retained earnings is the rate of return that stockholders require on equity capital that the company has obtained by retaining profits.

The shareholders could have received these earnings as dividends and invested them elsewhere, therefore the company needs to earn at least as good a return as the investors could have received elsewhere for comparable risk. If the company cannot achieve this return it should return the funds to the shareholders and let them invest them elsewhere.

## 3.7 Cost of equity

There are two main alternatives for calculating the cost of equity:

(a)     Theoretical models such as the **Capital Asset Pricing Model (CAPM)** or the **Arbitrage Pricing Theory (APT)**

(b)     **The dividend growth model** (also called the market-implied method) **estimates** using variants of the discounted cash flow approach; however, this model is based on particular assumption on the growth rate of earning of the company

### 3.7.1 CAPM

We have already discussed in Chapter 1 that companies and investors in general will earn a return above the yield of a risk-free asset only if they are prepared to undertake extra risk. The difference between the expected return from a risky investment and the risk-free return is called the **risk premium**. The CAPM and the other valuation models make the assumption that the risk premium is proportional to the risk premium of the market as a whole.

Risk premium on a portfolio = beta of portfolio $\times$ risk premium on the market

The formula for the CAPM is given below.

Exam
formula

$$E(r_i) = r_f + \beta_i(E(r_m) - r_f)$$

CAPM is assumed knowledge from *Financial Management (FM)*; CAPM is revisited in more detail in Chapter 7a.

### 3.7.2 Valuation models – beyond CAPM

The CAPM specifies that the only risk factor that should be taken into account is the market risk premium. Subsequent empirical research has shown that there may be other factors in addition to market risk premium that explain differences in asset returns, such as **interest rates** and **industrial production**.

Unlike the CAPM, which analyses the returns on a share as a function of a single factor – the return on the market portfolio, Arbitrage Pricing Theory (APT) assumes that the return on each security is based on **a number of independent factors**. Four key factors identified by researchers are:

• Inflation
• Industrial production
• Risk premium on bonds (debentures)
• The term structure of interest rates

So now the expected return $E(r_j)$ can be shown as:

$$E(r_j) = r_f + \beta_1(r_1 - r_f) + \beta_2(r_2 - r_f)\ldots$$

where $r_f$ is the risk-free rate of return

$r_1$ is the expected return on a portfolio with unit sensitivity to factor 1 and no sensitivity to any other factor

$r_2$ is the expected return on a portfolio with unit sensitivity to factor 2 and no sensitivity to any other factor

The **APT** generalises the CAPM and suggests the following model for the expected return on a share (or a portfolio):

$$E(r_i) = r_f + (E(r_A) - r_f)\beta_A + (E(r_B) - r_f)\beta_B + .......... + (E(r_m) - r_f)\beta_m + .......$$

Where $(E(r_A) - r_f)$ is the risk premium on factor A

$\beta_{A\ B}$ is the sensitivity of returns on a share to changes in factor A and so on

Another development of the CAPM has been provided by Fama and French (Ryan, 2007, p.167) who identified **two factors** in addition to the **market portfolio** that explain company returns, namely **size** and **distress**.

The **size factor** is measured as the difference in return between a portfolio of the smallest stocks and a portfolio of the largest stocks, whereas the **distress factor** is proxied by the difference in return between a portfolio of the highest book to market value stocks and portfolio of the lowest book to market value stocks.

The Fama and French three factor model is as follows:

$$E(r_j) = r_f + \beta_{i,m} (E(r_m) - r_f) + \beta_{i,S}\ SIZE + \beta_{i,D}\ DIST$$

where $\beta_{i,m}$ is the stock's beta

$\beta_{i,S}$ is beta with respect to size

$\beta_{i,D}$ is the stock's beta with respect to distress

### 3.7.3 Dividend growth (market-implied) method

The dividend growth method is based on a particular assumption about the growth rate of dividends of a company. For example, if we were to assume a constant rate of growth for dividends at the rate of g per annum, the shareholders' required rate of return is $r_e$ per annum, and the next period's dividend payment is $d_1$ then the market value of the share will be:

$$P_0 = \frac{d_0(1+g)}{r_e - g}$$

where $P_0$ = the ex-div market value of the share

$r_e$ = the investors' required rate of return (ie Ke)

$g$ = the expected annual growth rate of the dividends

This formula is given on the formula sheet.

The formula can be rearranged as follows: $k_e - g = \dfrac{d_0(1+g)}{P_0}$

to produce the cost of equity

$$k_e = \frac{d_0(1+g)}{P_0} + g$$

where $d_0$ = the current dividend

$P_0$ = the market value determined by the investor

$g$ = the expected annual growth rate of the dividends

#### Growth rates

The cost of capital we have derived is based on the current market price of shares but also on the growth rate assumptions we have made. If the constant growth assumption in the implied method is not appropriate, then the estimates we have derived will not be accurate.

A company is about to pay a dividend of $1 on its common stock. The shares are currently quoted at $23.00. The dividend is expected to grow at the rate of 10% per annum. Calculate the cost of retained earnings for the company.

Answer

Since we are about to pay the dividend, we will assume that the share is currently cum div. Hence, since we need the ex-div value, we must use the expression:

$$Po_{ex\text{-}div} = Po_{cum\text{-}div} - d_0$$

to calculate the ex-div price as

$$Po_{ex\text{-}div} = \$23.00 - \$1.00 = \$22.00$$

Then using the above formula for the cost of equity, we get

$$k_e = \frac{d_0(1+g)}{P_0} + g$$

$$k_e = \frac{\$1 \times 1.1}{\$22.00} + 0.1$$

$$k_e = \frac{1.10}{\$22.00} + 0.1$$

$$k_e = 0.05 + 0.1 = 0.15 \text{ or } 15\% \text{ per annum}$$

Note that $k_e$ is calculated as dividend yield plus growth rate here.

## 3.8 New share issues by quoted companies

**FAST FORWARD**

New shares can be issued either to existing shareholders or to new shareholders.

A new issue of shares might be made in a variety of different circumstances.

(a) The company might want to **raise more cash**, for example for expansion of its operations.

(b) The company might want to issue new shares partly to raise cash but more importantly to obtain a **stock market listing**. When a UK company is floated, for example on the main stock market, it is a requirement of the stock exchange that at least a minimum proportion of its shares should be made available to the general investing public if the shares are not already widely held.

(c) The company might issue new shares to the shareholders of another company in order to **take it over**.

### 3.8.1 Practicalities for issuing new shares

A lot of the practicalities involved are specific to the type of issue. However, general factors apply to all types.

(a) **Costs.** There will be administrative costs, but how great these are will vary enormously.

(b) **Income to investors.** In the UK and other jurisdictions, companies are not obliged to pay dividends to shareholders in a particular year. However, in the long term shareholders will expect dividends and/or capital appreciation.

(c) **Tax.** Unlike loan finance interest or charges, dividends paid are **not normally tax deductible**.

(d)    **Effect on control.** Unless shares are issued to **existing shareholders** in proportion to their **current holdings**, the balance of voting power will change and there may ultimately be an impact on the **control** of the firm.

### 3.8.2 Timing of new share issues

New equity issues in general will be more common when share prices are high than when share prices are low.

(a)    When **share prices are high**, **investors' confidence** will probably be **high**, and investors will be more willing to put money into companies with the potential for growth.

(b)    By issuing shares at a high price, a company will **reduce** the **number of shares** it must issue to raise the amount of capital it wants. This will reduce the dilution of earnings for existing shareholders.

(c)    Following on from (b), the company's **total dividend commitment** on the new shares, to meet shareholders' expectations, will be **lower**.

(d)    If **share prices are low**, business **confidence** is likely to be **low** too. Companies may not want to raise capital for new investments until expectations begin to improve.

### 3.8.3 A rights issue

A **rights issue** is an offer to existing shareholders for them to buy more shares, usually at lower than the current share price.

A **rights issue** is the raising of new capital by giving existing shareholders the right to subscribe to new shares in proportion to their current holdings. These shares are usually issued at a discount to market price. A shareholder not wishing to take up a rights issue may sell the rights.

A **dilution** is the reduction in the earnings and voting power per share caused by an increase or potential increase in the number of shares in issue.

Existing shareholders have **pre-emption rights** when new shares are issued. So that existing shareholders' rights are not diluted by the issue of new shares, legislation in many countries requires that before any equity shares are allotted for cash, they must first be offered to existing shareholders.

Rights issues are **cheaper** than offers for sale to the general public. This is partly because no **prospectus** is generally required (provided that the issue is for less than 10% of the class of shares concerned), partly because the **administration** is **simpler** and partly because the cost of underwriting will be lower.

Rights issues are **more beneficial** to **existing shareholders** than issues to the general public. New shares are issued at a **discount** to the current market price, to make them attractive to investors. A rights issue secures the discount on the market price for existing shareholders, who may either keep the shares or sell them if they wish.

**Relative voting rights** are **unaffected** if shareholders all take up their rights.

The finance raised may be used to **reduce gearing** in book value terms by increasing share capital and/or to pay off long-term debt which will reduce gearing in market value terms.

A company making a rights issue must set a price which is low enough to **secure the acceptance** of shareholders, who are being asked to provide extra funds, but not so low that EPS are excessively diluted. Other possible problems include getting the issue **underwritten** and an excessive **fall** in the **share price.**

# Example: Rights issue (1)

Seagull can achieve a profit after tax of 20% on the capital employed. At present its capital structure is as follows:

|  | $ |
|---|---|
| 200,000 ordinary shares of $1 each | 200,000 |
| Retained earnings | 100,000 |
|  | 300,000 |

The directors propose to raise an additional $126,000 from a rights issue. The current market price is $1.80.

*Required*

(a)     Calculate the number of shares that must be issued if the rights price is: $1.60; $1.20.

(b)     Calculate the dilution in EPS in each case.

# Solution

The earnings at present are 20% of $300,000 = $60,000. This gives EPS of 30c. The earnings after the rights issue will be 20% of $426,000 = $85,200.

| Rights price $ | No. of new shares ($126,000 ÷ rights price) | EPS ($85,200 ÷ total no. of shares) Cents | Dilution Cents |
|---|---|---|---|
| 1.60 | 78,750 | 30.6 | + 0.6 |
| 1.20 | 105,000 | 27.9 | − 2.1 |

Note that at a high rights price the EPS are increased, not diluted.

A right issue is effectively a call option on the firm's equity and even if issued at the current price – that is, a zero intrinsic value – it may still have time value. The value of the call is effectively a deduction from the existing shareholder value. We will cover call options in more detail in Chapter 6.

## 3.8.4 Scrip dividends

**Scrip dividends**, **scrip issues** and **stock splits** are not methods of raising new equity funds, but they **are** methods of altering the share capital structure of a company or, in the case of scrip dividends and scrip issues, increasing the issued share capital of the company.

**A scrip dividend** is a dividend paid by the issue of additional company shares, rather than by cash.

A scrip dividend effectively converts profit and loss reserves into **issued share capital**. When the directors of a company would prefer to retain funds within the business but consider that they must pay at least a certain amount of dividend, they might offer equity shareholders the choice of a **cash dividend** or a **scrip dividend**. Each shareholder would decide separately which to take.

Recently **enhanced scrip dividends** have been offered by many companies. With enhanced scrip dividends, the value of the shares offered is much greater than the cash alternative, giving investors an incentive to choose the shares.

### Advantages of scrip dividends

They can **preserve** a company's **cash position** if a substantial number of shareholders take up the share option.

Investors may be able to obtain **tax advantages** if dividends are in the form of shares.

Investors looking to **expand their holding** can do so **without incurring** the **transaction costs** of buying more shares.

A small scrip issue will **not dilute the share price significantly.** However, if cash is not offered as an alternative, empirical evidence suggests that the share price will tend to fall.

A share issue will **decrease** the company's **gearing**, and may therefore **enhance** its **borrowing capacity**.

### 3.8.5 Bonus issues

A **bonus/scrip/capitalisation issue** is the capitalisation of the reserves of a company by the issue of additional shares to existing shareholders, in proportion to their holdings. Such shares are normally fully paid-up with no cash called for from the shareholders.

For example, if a company with issued share capital of 100,000 ordinary shares of $1 each made a one for five scrip issue, 20,000 new shares would be issued to existing shareholders, one new share for every five old shares held. Issued share capital would be increased by $20,000, and reserves (probably share premium account, if there is one) reduced by this amount.

By creating more shares in this way, a scrip issue does not raise new funds, but does have the advantage of making shares **cheaper** and therefore (perhaps) **more easily marketable** on the stock exchange. For example, if a company's shares are priced at $6 on the stock exchange, and the company makes a one for two scrip issue, we should expect the share price after the issue to fall to $4 each. Shares at $4 each might be more easily marketable than shares at $6 each.

### 3.8.6 Stock splits

The advantage of a scrip issue is also the reason for a **stock split** which we discussed earlier.

## 3.9 Methods for obtaining a listing

An unquoted company can obtain a listing on the stock market by means of:

- Direct **offer by subscription** to the public
- **Offer for sale**
- **Placing**
- **Introduction**

Of these, an offer for sale or a placing are the most common.

### 3.9.1 Direct offer by subscription to general public

Issues where the issuing firm sells shares directly to the general public tend to be quite rare on many stock exchanges, and the issues that are made tend to be quite large. These issues are sometimes known as **offers by prospectus**. This type of issue is very risky, because of the lack of guarantees that all shares will be taken up.

### 3.9.2 Offer for sale

**Offer for sale** is an invitation to apply for shares in a company based on information contained in a prospectus. It is a means of selling the shares of a company to the public at large. When companies 'go public' for the first time, a **large** issue will probably take the form of an offer for sale. Subsequent issues are likely to be **placings** or **rights issues**, described later.

An offer for sale entails the **acquisition by an issuing house** of a large block of shares of a company, with a view to offering them for sale to the public. An issuing house is usually a merchant bank (or sometimes a firm of stockbrokers). It may acquire the shares either as a direct allotment from the company or by purchase from existing members. In either case, the issuing house publishes an invitation to the public to apply for shares, either at a fixed price or on a tender basis.

The advantage of an offer for sale over a direct offer by the company to the public is that the issuing house **accepts responsibility** to the public, and gives to the issue the support of its own standing.

An issuing house has the job of trying to ensure a successful issue for the company's shares, by advising on an issue price for the shares and trying to interest institutional investors in buying some of the shares.

The offer price must be **advertised a short time in advance**, so it is fixed without certain knowledge of the condition of the market at the time applications are invited. In order to ensure the success of an issue, share prices are often set **lower** than they might otherwise be. An issuing house normally tries to ensure

that a share price rises to a **premium** above its issue price soon after trading begins. A target premium of 20% above the issue price would be fairly typical.

### 3.9.3 Offers for sale by tender

It is often very difficult to decide on the price at which the shares should be offered to the general public. One way of trying to ensure that the issue price reflects the value of the shares as perceived by the market is to make an **offer for sale by tender**. A **minimum price** will be fixed and subscribers will be invited to tender for shares at prices equal to or above the minimum. The shares will be **allotted at the highest price** at which they will **all be taken up**. This is known as the **striking price**.

## Example: Offer for sale by tender

Byte Henderson Inc is a new company that is making its first public issue of shares. It has decided to make the issue by means of an offer for sale by tender. The intention is to issue up to 4,000,000 shares (the full amount of authorised share capital) at a minimum price of 300 cents. The money raised, net of issue costs of $1,000,000, would be invested in projects which would earn benefits with a present value equal to 130% of the net amount invested.

The following tenders have been received: (Each applicant has made only one offer.)

| Price tendered per share $ | Number of shares applied for at this price |
|---|---|
| 6.00 | 50,000 |
| 5.50 | 100,000 |
| 5.00 | 300,000 |
| 4.50 | 450,000 |
| 4.00 | 1,100,000 |
| 3.50 | 1,500,000 |
| 3.00 | 2,500,000 |

(a) How many shares would be issued, and how much in total would be raised, if Byte Henderson Inc chooses:

(i)  To maximise the total amount raised?
(ii) To issue exactly 4,000,000 shares?

(b) Harvey Goldfinger, a private investor, has applied for 12,000 shares at a price of $5.50 and has sent a cheque for $66,000 to the issuing house that is handling the issue. In both cases (a)(i) and (ii), how many shares would be issued to Mr Goldfinger, assuming that any partial acceptance of offers would mean allotting shares to each accepted applicant in proportion to the number of shares applied for? How much will Mr Goldfinger receive back out of the $66,000 he has paid?

(c) Estimate the likely market value of shares in the company after the issue, assuming that the market price fully reflects the investment information given above and that exactly 4,000,000 shares are issued.

## Solution

(a) We begin by looking at the cumulative tenders.

| Price $ | Cumulative number of shares applied for | Amount raised if price is selected, before deducting issue costs $ |
|---|---|---|
| 6.00 | 50,000 | 300,000 |
| 5.50 | 150,000 | 825,000 |
| 5.00 | 450,000 | 2,250,000 |
| 4.50 | 900,000 | 4,050,000 |
| 4.00 | 2,000,000 | 8,000,000 |
| 3.50 | 3,500,000 | 12,250,000 |
| 3.00 | 6,000,000 (4,000,000 max) | 12,000,000 |

(i)     To maximise the total amount raised, the issue price should be $3.50. The total raised before deducting issue costs would be $12,250,000.

(ii)    To issue exactly 4,000,000 shares, the issue price must be $3.00. The total raised would be $12,000,000, before deducting issue costs.

(b)     (i)     Harvey Goldfinger would be allotted 12,000 shares at $3.50 per share. He would receive a refund of 12,000 × $2 = $24,000 out of the $66,000 he has paid.

(ii)    If 4,000,000 shares are issued, applicants would receive two-thirds of the shares they tendered for. Harvey Goldfinger would be allotted 8,000 shares at $3 per share and would receive a refund of $42,000 out of the $66,000 he has paid.

(c)     The net amount raised would be $12,000,000 minus issue costs of $1,000,000 which equals $11,000,000.

The present value of the benefits from investment would be 130% of $11,000,000 which equals $14,300,000. If the market price reflects this information, the price per share would rise to

$$\frac{\$14,300,000}{4,000,000} = \$3.575 \text{ per share.}$$

### 3.9.4 A placing

A **placing** is an arrangement whereby the shares are not all offered to the public but instead the sponsoring market maker arranges for most of the issue to be bought by a **small number of investors**, usually institutional investors such as pension funds and insurance companies.

**The choice between an offer for sale and a placing**

When a company is planning a flotation, is it likely to prefer an offer for sale of its shares, or a placing?

(a)     **Placings** are much **cheaper**. Approaching institutional investors privately is a much cheaper way of obtaining finance, and thus placings are often used for smaller issues.

(b)     Placings are likely to be **quicker**.

(c)     Placings are likely to involve **less disclosure** of **information**.

(d)     However, most of the shares will be placed with a **relatively small number of (institutional) shareholders**, which means that most of the shares are unlikely to be available for trading after the flotation, and that institutional shareholders will have control of the company.

### 3.9.5 A stock exchange introduction

By this method of obtaining a quotation, no shares are made available to the market, neither existing nor newly created; nevertheless, the stock market grants a quotation. This will only happen where shares in a large company are already widely held, so that a market can be seen to exist. A company might want an **introduction** to obtain **greater marketability** for the shares, a known share valuation for inheritance tax purposes and easier access in the future to additional capital.

### 3.9.6 Underwriting

A company about to issue new securities in order to raise finance might decide to have the issue underwritten. **Underwriters** are financial institutions which agree (in exchange for a fixed fee, perhaps 2.25% of the finance to be raised) to buy at the issue price any securities which are **not subscribed** for by the investing public.

Underwriters **remove** the **risk** of a share issue's being undersubscribed, but at a cost to the company issuing the shares. It is not compulsory to have an issue underwritten. Ordinary offers for sale are most likely to be underwritten, although rights issues may be as well.

Because of the costs of underwriting, there has been a trend in recent years for companies whose securities are marketable to adopt the practice known as the **'bought deal'**, whereby an investment bank buys the whole of a new issue at a small discount to the market.

### 3.9.7 Costs of share issue on the stock market

Companies may incur the following costs when issuing shares:

*   Underwriting costs
*   Stock market listing fee (the initial charge) for the new securities
*   Fees of the issuing house, solicitors, auditors and public relations consultant
*   Charges for printing and distributing the prospectus
*   Advertising in national newspapers

### 3.9.8 Costs of equity for new share issue on the stock market

When we are dealing with newly issued equity, the company needs to take into account the flotation cost involved with the new stock. We need to adapt the formula used for retained earnings to allow for the additional cash outflow that the company suffers at time 0, being the **flotation costs**, f. Therefore the cost of equity for the company becomes:

$$k_e = \frac{d_0(1+g)}{P_0(1-f)} + g$$

## Example

Assume that there were flotation costs of 8% and $d_0$ = $1.00, $P_0$ = $22, g = 10%. What is the cost of new shares issued?

## Solution

$$k_e = \frac{\$1.10}{\$22.00(1-0.08)} + 0.1 = 15.4\%$$

Note that the formula for new shares issued could be learned as a general formula for the cost of equity, with retained earnings being a special case where issue costs are zero (f = 0).

# 4 Dividend policy                                    6/13, Sep/Dec 16

FAST FORWARD

Dividend decisions determine the amount of and the way that a company's profits are distributed to its shareholders.

## 4.1 Is dividend policy irrelevant?

Shareholders who hold the shares of a company are entitled to a portion of the income that the company generates and of the assets that it owns. The dividend policy of a company refers to the decision taken by the management of the company with regard to how much of a company's earnings will be distributed to shareholders and how much will be retained within the firm.

In reaching this decision, the management of the company should try, as in all financial management decisions, to maximise the wealth of the company's shareholders. However, there is little agreement as to the impact of dividend policy on shareholder wealth, and the interaction between dividend payments, financing decisions and the value of a company has been the subject of theoretical analysis and empirical investigation.

At one end of the debate, Modigliani and Miller (Watson & Head, 2013, p.320) have maintained that the dividend policy of a corporation is irrelevant because the value of a company is not affected by its financial policy.

Suppose a company pays dividends without changing investment and financing policies. The money that the company will pay as dividends has to come from somewhere else. If the company maintains the amount of debt (does not borrow to pay the dividend), the company needs to issue new shares to finance the dividend. The new shareholders will pay only what the shares are worth, and the old shareholders will receive the money paid by the new shareholders as dividends. After the dividend is paid, the value per share should be equal to the old price minus the dividend paid by the new shareholders. The value of the firm remains the same, but money changed hands from new to old shareholders. Dividend policies are therefore irrelevant.

## 4.2 Ways of paying dividend

Companies have many ways of returning money to the shareholders. The main ones are:

(a) **Cash dividends**. This the most common way of paying dividends by corporations. These dividends are paid in cash, usually quarterly. Companies can declare both regular and 'extra' dividends. Regular dividends usually remain unchanged in the future, but 'extraordinary' or 'special' dividends are unlikely to be repeated.

(b) **Dividends in the form of shares**. These are paid instead of cash dividends by allocating shares of equivalent value to existing shareholders. Shareholders receive new shares in the corporation as a form of a dividend. Like a 'share split', the number of shares increases, but no cash changes hands.

(c) **Share repurchases**. This is an alternative way to distribute cash to shareholders. The firm buys back its own shares. This can be done **on the open market, by tender offer or by buying stock from major shareholders**.

A **major difference** between dividends and share repurchases is their **tax treatment**. **Cash dividends** are **taxed as income** but **share repurchases** are subject to capital gains tax **only if a capital gain has been realised**.

Both cash and stock dividends reduce the value per share.

## 4.3 Dividend capacity                                    6/13, Mar/Jun 16

The **dividend capacity** of a corporation determines how much of a company's income can be paid out as dividend. The dividend capacity of the company is also known as the **free cash flow** to equity (FCFE).

The estimation of dividend capacity of a firm is dealt with in Chapter 4. Here we simply give the definition of the **FCFE**.

FCFE = Net income (EBIT − net interest − tax paid)

| | add | Depreciation |
|---|---|---|
| | less | Total net investment (change in capital investment + change in working capital) |
| | add | Net debt issued (new borrowings less any repayments) |
| | add | Net equity issued (new issues less any equity repurchases) |

The FCFE represents the cash available to the company which could be paid out to shareholders as dividends.

The FCFE is usually not the same as actual dividends in a given year because normally the management of a company deliberately smoothes dividend payments over time. There are also rules which restrict the payment of distributable profits only as dividends.

## 4.4 Theories of dividend policy

The **Modigliani and Miller** argument that dividend policy is irrelevant should have led to a random pattern of dividend payments. In practice, dividend payments tend to be smoothed over time. In this section we review some of the reasons that have been put forward as explanation for the payment of dividends.

### 4.4.1 The residual theory of dividend payments

According to this theory, firms will only pay dividends if all the profitable investment opportunities have been funded. This theory assumes that internal funds are the cheapest source of financing, and the company will resort to external financing only if the available internal funds, current and retained earnings have been exhausted.

### 4.4.2 Target payout ratio

According to the target payout theory, companies pay out as dividends a fixed proportion of their earnings. Firms have long-run target dividend payout ratios.

(a)     Mature companies with stable earnings usually have a higher dividend payout ratio than growth companies.

(b)     Managers focus more on dividend changes than absolute amounts.

(c)     Transitory changes in earnings usually do not affect dividend payouts.

(d)     Only long-term shifts in earnings can be followed by changes in dividends.

(e)     Managers are reluctant to change dividend payout ratios due to the potential signals that such changes may send to the markets (see below).

### 4.4.3 Dividends as signals

Dividends can be used to convey good (or bad) information. A firm that increases its dividend payout ratio may be signalling that it expects future cash flows to increase, as this ratio tends to remain steady over time. Bad firms can also increase dividends to try to convince the markets that they too are expecting increased future cash flows. However, this increase may be unsustainable if the promised increases do not occur and the inevitable reduction in dividend payout ratio will mean heavy penalties from the markets.

### 4.4.4 Agency theory

Dividend payments can be an instrument to monitor managers. When firms pay dividends they often need to subsequently go to the capital markets to fund the projects. When firms go to the financial markets they will be scrutinised by different market participants. For instance, investors will require an analysis of the creditworthiness of the firm. Companies often announce dividend payments in conjunction with trying to raise new capital.

### 4.4.5 Dividends and taxes

A final theory explaining dividend payments is based on the presence of different corporate and personal taxes on one hand and of different income and capital gains taxes on the other. Modigliani and Miller assume that there are no personal taxes. Taxes on dividends (ordinary income) are higher than taxes on capital gains. Thus, under the presence of personal taxes, companies should not pay dividends because investors require a higher return to companies that pay dividends. If payments are to be made to shareholders, the company should opt for other alternatives, such as share repurchases. This is true if taxes on dividend income are higher than taxes on capital gains.

However, different investors have different tax rates. High tax-rate individuals will prefer the firm to invest more, whereas low tax individuals may prefer that the firm does not invest and instead pays dividends. Investors try to select companies with dividend policies that approximate their requirements.

Dividend capacity and dividend policy were also covered in Chapter 1, Section 4 and are considered further in Chapter 4.

**Exam focus point**

> In Sep/Dec 2016 the examining team commented that candidates who achieved high marks demonstrated their ability to apply their knowledge to the companies in the question instead of generalising about the theoretical relevance or irrelevance of dividend policies.

# 5 Risk management

Exposure to risk by corporations should be rewarded and **risk management** is the process through which the company determines the risk/return combination that is consistent with the company's risk appetite. Risk management requires the **identification**, **measurement** and **transfer** of risks. The decision whether to transfer any of the risks to which the company is exposed will depend on the cost of transfer and the risk aversion of the company.

The transfer of risk can take place through the financial or insurance markets, or through product markets. It should be clarified that risk management does not necessarily imply a reduction in risk. If the expected rewards for undertaking risks warrant it, a company may increase its exposure to risk. **Risk mitigation**, on the other hand, is the process through which a company reduces its exposure to risk.

## 5.1 The rationale for risk management                              Sep/Dec 16

**Exam focus point**

The examining team has written an article entitled 'Risk Management – understanding why is as important as understanding how'. Make sure you read this article which is available on the ACCA website.

### 5.1.1 The theoretical rationale

There have been substantial volumes of literature published on the theoretical rationale for risk management. Throughout the literature, the overriding rationale tends to be the **maximisation of shareholder value**.

Companies should be looking to **limit uncertainty** and to **manage speculative risks and opportunities** in order to **maximise positive outcomes and therefore shareholder value**.

Boards should consider the factors that determine **shareholder valuations** of the company, the **risks** associated with these and the ways in which shareholders would like the **risks to be managed**.

Most risks must be managed to some extent, and some should be sought to be eliminated as being outside the scope of the management of a business. For example, a business in a high-tech industry, such as computing, which evolves rapidly within ever-changing markets and technologies, has to accept high risk in its research and development activities; but should it also be speculating on interest and exchange rates within its treasury activities?

Risk management under this view is an integral part of strategy, and involves analysing what the key value drivers are in the organisation's activities, and the risks tied up with those value drivers. In its Risk Management Standard, the Institute of Risk Management linked in key value drivers with major risk categories.

### 5.1.2 The practical rationale

From a practical point of view, companies must be seen to be managing risk to maintain **confidence** in their business operations. Companies that are cavalier with their shareholders' funds may enjoy higher than average returns in the short term but are unlikely to sustain this favourable position for long. While shareholders like to enjoy high returns, most of them will prefer to know that some care is being taken with how their funds are being handled.

### 5.1.3 Management's attitude towards risk management

Managers that have **large equity stakes** (as opposed to equity options) in an organisation are more likely to take positive steps to manage risk. This is due to the fact that such managers will face both systematic and unsystematic risk (whereas external equity shareholders face only systematic risk). However, managers may not increase shareholder value by managing unsystematic risk, as external investors should have already diversified away this risk themselves.

If managers holding large equity stakes can concentrate on risks that they can do something about, it is more likely that they will be able to increase the value of the organisation.

What about managers who hold **share options** rather than actual shares? These managers are more likely to try to increase the risk of an organisation, as they are trying to maximise future profits and share price. Managers may actively seek more risky investments which are not necessarily in the best interests of the organisation in their pursuit of higher profits and share price.

You only need to glance at the business pages of a newspaper on any day to find out why risk management is a key issue in today's business world.

As the effects of the global financial crisis are still being felt, companies face greater pressures to demonstrate the effectiveness of their risk management strategies. Without such strategies in an uncertain and still extremely risky world, confidence in these companies' operations would diminish, leading to fewer investors willing to risk their funds to finance them.

## 5.2 Risk mitigation

**Risk mitigation** is the process of minimising the probability of a risk's occurrence or the impact of the risk should it occur.

**Risk mitigation** is the process through which a corporation reduces its risk exposure. Risk mitigation is therefore closely linked with the process of risk transferring.

The following risk assessment matrix – known as the severity/frequency matrix or the likelihood/consequences matrix – can be used to set **priorities** for **risk mitigation**:

**Severity**

|  |  | Low | High |
|---|---|---|---|
| **Frequency** | Low | Loss of small suppliers | Loss of senior or specialist staff<br><br>Loss of sales to competitor<br><br>Loss of sales due to macroeconomic factors |
|  | High | Loss of lower-level staff | Loss of key customers<br>Failure of computer systems |

A company's risk mitigation strategy can be linked into the matrix above and also the company's **appetite** for risk taking.

**Severity**

|  |  | Low | High |
|---|---|---|---|
| **Frequency** | Low | **Accept**<br>Risks are not significant. Keep under review, but costs of dealing with risks unlikely to be worth the benefits. | **Transfer**<br>Insure risk or implement contingency plans. Reduction of severity of risk will minimise insurance premiums. |
|  | High | **Control or reduce**<br>Take some action, eg enhanced control systems to detect problems or contingency plans to reduce impact. | **Abandon or avoid**<br>Take immediate action, eg changing major suppliers or abandoning activities. |

Consider a company such as **Virgin**. It has many stable and successful brands, and healthy cash flows and profits; little need, you would have thought, to consider risky new ventures.

Yet Virgin operates a subsidiary called **Virgin Galactic** to own and operate privately built spaceships, and to offer 'affordable' sub-orbital **space tourism to everybody** – or everybody willing to pay US$200,000 for the pleasure. The risks are enormous; developing the project will involve investing very large amounts of money, there is no guarantee that the service is wanted by sufficient numbers of people to make it viable, and the risks of catastrophic accidents are self-evident. In 2012 it was reported that almost 500 bookings had already been taken. In October 2014 a test flight ended in disaster when one of the test pilots was killed and the future of the company is now uncertain, although flight testing has recommenced in 2016.

There is little doubt that Virgin's risk appetite derives directly from the **risk appetite** of its chief executive, Richard Branson – a self-confessed adrenaline junkie – who also happens to own most parts of the Virgin Group privately, and so faces little pressure from shareholders.

The most common risk mitigation strategies are **hedging** and **diversification**.

# 5.3 Hedging

Hedging involves the creation of offsetting or counterbalancing flows so that the exposure of a company to risk is either eliminated or reduced. Depending on the instrument that is employed by the company, the hedging strategy can be classified as **financial** or **operational** hedging.

## 5.3.1 Financial hedging

Financial hedging involves the use of financial instruments, mainly derivatives to reduce or eliminate exposure to risks. A company that imports raw materials, for example, may worry about an increase in the price of raw materials due to a depreciation of the home currency, and may want to use forwards, futures or options to hedge such a risk. Financial hedging is considered in detail in Chapters 16 and 17.

## 5.3.2 Operational hedging

Operational hedging is the course of action that **hedges a firm's risk exposure** through operational activities using **non-financial instruments**. The main way of implementing an operational hedging strategy is through **real options**. Real options give the possibility of delaying, abandoning, enhancing or switching activities and are covered in more detail in Chapter 6.

Consider a manufacturing firm, for example, which decides to expand its scale of activity in an overseas subsidiary. The parent company is exposed to both demand and exchange rate risks. The exposure to foreign exchange risk can be hedged using financial instruments eg forward contracts. However, financial tools cannot be used to alter the demand risk exposure. This risk can be managed by postponing the production decision until more accurate information about the demand has been acquired. This kind of operational hedging is achieved by exercising the real option to postpone the extra investment.

# 5.4 Diversification strategies

**Diversification** strategies seek to reduce the volatility of earnings of a company. This can be achieved through **product** or **geographical** diversification.

## 5.4.1 Product diversification

Diversification into new products is considered one of the main strategies of reducing the volatility of earnings and the main motivation of conglomerate mergers which are examined in Chapter 9. Examples of conglomerate mergers include the acquisition of, for example, hotels and holiday resorts by a car manufacturer. The main idea of diversification is that earnings in various industries are subject to different risk factors, which are offset against each other when combined, resulting in aggregate earnings with less volatility.

### 5.4.2 Geographical diversification

Geographical diversification is achieved when the costs and revenues of a firm are aligned in such a way that they are exposed to the same risks. For example, domestic firms selling to overseas markets can ensure that their production costs and sales revenues are exposed to the same exchange rate risk by opening a production facility in the overseas markets.

**Question** — Controls

To demonstrate how controls are an important part of managing risks, we list below a number of the important risks that a business may well face. See if you can suggest some appropriate controls.

| Risks | | Example controls |
|---|---|---|
| Investor | Investors losing confidence in the way the company is run and selling their shares | |
| Investment | Loss-making investments being made | |
| Foreign exchange transaction | Having to pay more on a future transaction because of adverse exchange rate movements | |
| Political | Operations or revenues being disrupted by political activity | |
| Information | Taking the wrong decisions due to inadequate information | |

**Answer**

| Risks | | Example controls |
|---|---|---|
| Investor | Investors losing confidence in the way the company is run and selling their shares | **Corporate governance** arrangements ensuring board exercises proper stewardship over the company and communicates effectively with shareholders |
| Investment | Loss-making investments being made | Use of **different financial measures** to provide extra perspectives on the investment |
| Foreign exchange transaction | Having to pay more on a future transaction because of adverse exchange rate movements | **Purchase an instrument** fixing the exchange rate used in the transaction |
| Political | Operations or revenues being disrupted by political activity | **Monitor** political situation; **negotiate with key stakeholders** (political parties) |
| Information | Taking the wrong decisions due to inadequate information | **Information systems** the organisation chooses providing quality of information needed for decision making |

# 6 Different types of risk

## 6.1 Systematic and unsystematic risk

Knowledge brought forward from earlier studies

**Key terms**

> **Market** or **systematic risk** is risk that cannot be diversified away. **Non-systematic** or **unsystematic risk** applies to a single investment or class of investments, and can be reduced or eliminated by diversification. This is area of brought-forward knowledge is also recapped in the discussion of the CAPM in Chapter 7a.

Whenever an investor invests in some shares, or a company invests in a new project, there will be some risk involved. The actual return on the investment might be better or worse than that hoped for due to company-specific successes or failure. To some extent, risk is unavoidable.

Diversification (ie building a portfolio) reduces company-specific risk. Risks that **can** be diversified away are referred to as **unsystematic risk**.

However, some risk **cannot** be diversified away because an element of share price volatility relates to movements in the stock market as a whole. Some industries are by their very nature more risky than others. This **systematic risk** or **market risk** cannot be diversified away. Systematic risk is measured by a company's beta factor.

## 6.2 Business risk

**Key terms**

> **Business risks** are threats to the net profits arising from decisions an organisation makes in relation to its products or services.

As the name suggests, **business risk** arises from the type of business an organisation is involved in and relates to uncertainty about the future and the organisation's **business prospects**. The cost of capital of any organisation will include a premium for business risk. Business risk will be higher for some firms than for others – for example, you would expect the business risk of a large retail chain such as Walmart to be lower than that of a technological firm such as Microsoft.

Examples of **business risks** include:

*   Threats of long-term **product obsolescence**
*   **Changes in technology** changing the production process

Business risk is a mixture of **systematic** and **unsystematic risk**. The systematic risk comes from such factors as revenue sensitivity and the mix of fixed and variable costs within the total cost structure. Unsystematic risk is determined by such company-specific factors as management ability and labour relations.

### 6.2.1 Degree of operating gearing

One way of measuring business risk is by calculating a company's **operating gearing** or 'operational gearing'.

$$\text{Operating gearing or leverage} = \frac{\text{Contribution}}{\text{Profit before interest and tax (PBIT)}}$$

Contribution is sales minus variable cost of sales.

The significance of operating gearing is as follows:

(a) **If contribution is high but PBIT is low**, fixed costs will be high, and only just covered by contribution. Business risk, as measured by operating gearing (ie the level of fixed costs employed within a business), will be high.

(b) **If contribution is not much bigger than PBIT**, fixed costs will be low, and fairly easily covered. Business risk, as measured by operating gearing, will be low.

## 6.3 Non-business risk and financial risk

**Key term**

> **Non-business risks** are threats to profits that are not influenced by the products or services the organisation supplies.
>
> **Financial risk** is the volatility of earnings due to the financial structure of the business.

Examples of **non-business risks** include:

- Risks arising from the finance structure (**financial risk**)
- Risks from a collapse in trade because of an **adverse event**, an accident or natural disaster

**Financial risk** is the most important type of non-business risk (in the AFM syllabus at least). Financial risk relates to the **structure of finance** the organisation has. In particular, the risks include those relating to the mix of equity and debt capital, the risk of not being able to access funding, and whether the organisation has an insufficient long-term capital base for the amount of trading it is doing (overtrading).

The higher the gearing of an organisation's capital structure, the greater the risk to ordinary shareholders will be. This will be reflected in a higher risk premium and therefore a higher cost of capital.

Organisations must also consider the risks of **fraud and misuse** of financial resources.

**Other shorter-term financial risks include:**

- **Credit risk** – the possibility of payment default by the customer

- **Liquidity risk** – the risk of being unable to finance the credit, arising from cash restrictions or the need for more cash

- **Cash management risk** – risks arising from unpredictable cash flows (eg exchange rate risk and interest risk; these topics are covered in Chapter 16 and Chapter 17 respectively)

## 6.4 Relationship between business and financial risk

In order to increase its share price, a company should aim to achieve higher profits without taking excessive business risk or financial risk.

Most shareholders are willing to accept a certain level of risk in order to earn returns on their investment. Directors and managers are expected to act within these risk parameters in pursuit of the maximisation of shareholders' wealth.

A business with high business risk may be **restricted** in the amount of **financial risk** it can sustain. If business risk is already high, shareholders' may not accept much if any financial risk. The organisation will be unable to add too much debt to its capital structure, as this would increase financial risk and potentially push total risk beyond the shareholders' acceptable level. In this situation a business is also more likely to use currency and interest rate hedging (see Chapters 16 and 17) to control financial risk.

## 6.5 Political risk

Key term

**Political risk** is the risk that political action will affect the position and value of a company.

When a multinational company invests in another country, either by setting up a subsidiary or by entering into a joint venture, it may face a political risk of action by that country's government which may affect the operation of the company. The ultimate political risk is the expropriation of the company's investment by the Government of the host country. Although expropriation or nationalisation is not very common today, a multinational company is still exposed to political risk in the form of various restrictions.

(a) Import quotas could be used to limit the quantities of goods that a subsidiary can buy from its parent company and import for resale in its domestic markets.

(b) Exchange control regulations could be applied that may affect the ability of the subsidiary to remit profits to the parent company.

(c) Government actions could restrict the ability of foreign companies to buy domestic companies, especially those that operate in politically sensitive industries, such as defence contracting, communications and energy supply.

(d) Government legislation may specify minimum shareholding in companies by residents. This would force a multinational to offer some of the equity in a subsidiary to investors in the country where the subsidiary operates.

There are a large number of factors that can be considered to assess political risk, for example government stability, remittance restrictions and product boycotting as a result of deterioration in the relationships between the host country and the country where the parent company is based. Measurement is often by subjective weighting of these factors. Industry-specific factors are also important.

## 6.6 Economic risk

Key term

**Economic risk** arises from changes in economic policy in the host country that affect the macroeconomic environment in which the multinational company operates.

Examples of political risk include the following:

(a) A highly restricted monetary policy may lead to high interest rates and a recession affecting aggregate demand and the demand for the products of the multinational in the host country. On the other hand, inflation in the host country may lead to a devaluation of the currency and it may decrease the value of remittances to the parent company.

(b) Currency inconvertibility for a limited period of time.

(c) The host country may be subjected to economic shocks, eg falling commodity prices which may also affect its exchange rate of fiscal and monetary policy which may in turn affect the state of the economy and the exchange rate.

## 6.7 Fiscal risk

Key term

**Fiscal risk** is the risk that a multinational company is exposed to that the tax arrangements in the host country may change after the investment in the host country is undertaken.

Fiscal risks include:

• The imposition of indirect taxes, such as VAT on the products of the company, raising the price of its products and potentially reducing demand

• The imposition of excise duties on imported goods and services that are used by the subsidiary

• An increase in the corporate tax rate

• The abolition of the accelerated tax depreciation allowances for new investments

• Changes in the tax law regarding admissibility of expenses for tax deductibility

## 6.8 Regulatory risk

> **Regulatory risk** is the risk that arises from the change in the legal and regulatory environment which determines the operation of a company.

For example, a change in employment legislation making the firing of workers more difficult may increase costs of production and affect the profitability of a company. Anti-monopoly laws may also restrict the capacity of a company to expand and it may restrict its profitability. Disclosure requirements or stricter corporate governance may also affect the freedom of a company to operate in the host country. In addition, legal standards of safety or quality (non-tariff barriers) could be imposed on imported goods to prevent multinationals from selling goods through a subsidiary which have been banned as dangerous in other countries.

## 6.9 Operational risk

> **Operational risk** is the risk arising from the execution (operation) of an organisation's business functions.

Operational risk includes such risks as human error, breakdowns in internal procedures and systems or external events.

It is difficult to identify and assess the extent of operational risk – many organisations historically accepted this risk as an inevitable cost of doing business. However, it is becoming more common for organisations to collect and analyse data relating to losses arising from, for example, systems failures or fraud.

Operational risk does not include such strategic risks as losses arising from poor strategic business decisions.

## 6.10 Reputational risk                                              12/12, 6/13

> **Reputational risk** is the risk related to the way in which a business is viewed by others.

Damage to an organisation's reputation can result in lost revenues or significant reductions (permanent or temporary) in shareholder value.

**Reputational risk** can be seen as one of the consequences of operational risk. Damage to an organisation's reputation can arise from **operational failures** and the way in which stakeholders react to such events.

When risks materialise that threaten an organisation's reputation, the organisation should act in a way that minimises the risk and the potential damage. The best course of action will depend on the individual circumstances, including what it is the organisation has done (or is perceived to have done), the likely impact on the organisation's reputation, the effect a damaged reputation may have on the organisation as a whole and the 'damage limitation' options available.

Increasingly, organisations are realising that ignoring the risk and not responding is unlikely to be effective. By not addressing concerns directly, an organisation is likely to be seen as guilty of the accusations and also of not caring. This double whammy is likely to increase significantly the damage to the organisation's reputation. The general public, as well as clients and customers, expect senior management to listen to the concerns of stakeholders and of society – and to respond appropriately.

**Exam focus point**

> Reputational risk was an issue in December 2012 Question 5. It linked in with operational practices, a reduction in quality control, and also ethics, with workers at clothing manufacturers suffering poor working conditions.

In September 2017 Ryanair, the budget Irish airline, suffered significant reputational damage by from having to cancel up to 50 flights a day over a period of about six week (due to mismanagement of pilots holidays). In addition Ryanair is facing fines of approximately £18 million.

## 6.11 Strategies to deal with risks

There are various strategies that multinational companies can adopt to limit the effects of political and other risks.

### Negotiations with host government

The aim of these negotiations is generally to obtain a **concession agreement**. This would cover matters such as the transfer of capital, remittances and products, access to local finance, government intervention and taxation, and transfer pricing. The main problem with concession agreements can be that the initial terms of the agreement may not subsequently prove to be satisfactory. Companies may have different reasons for choosing to set up initially and choosing to stay, while the local Government may be concerned if profits are too high.

### Insurance

In the UK, the Export Credits Guarantee Department provides protection against various threats including nationalisation, currency conversion problems, war and revolution.

### Production strategies

It may be necessary to strike a balance between contracting out to local sources (thus losing control) and producing directly (which increases the investment and therefore the potential loss). Alternatively it may be better to locate key parts of the production process or the distribution channels abroad. Control of patents is another possibility, since these can be enforced internationally.

### Contacts with markets

Multinationals may have contacts with customers which interventionist governments cannot obtain.

### Financial management

If a multinational obtains funds in local investment markets, these may be on terms that are less favourable than on markets abroad, but would mean that local institutions suffered if the local Government intervened. However, governments often do limit the ability of multinationals to obtain funds locally.

Alternatively, guarantees can be obtained from the Government for the investment that can be enforced by the multinational if the Government takes action.

### Management structure

Possible methods include joint ventures or ceding control to local investors and obtaining profits by a management contract.

If governments do intervene, multinationals may have to make use of the advantages they hold or threaten withdrawal. The threat of expropriation may be reduced by negotiation or legal threats.

# 7 Capital investment monitoring                          12/12

**FAST FORWARD**
Capital investment projects require appraisal, and implementation monitoring.

## 7.1 The need for investment monitoring

Capital investment projects require a large proportion of a company's monetary and human resources and their effective implementation is crucial for a company's performance. Implementation is one of the stages of the capital investment process, which consists of the appraisal stage, the budgeting stage, the authorisation stage, the implementation stage and the post-audit report.

The monitoring functions of the implementation stage seek to ensure that:

- The project expenses are within the budgeted limits.
- Any revenues budgeted are achieved.
- The completion time schedule is adhered to.
- The risk factors identified during the appraisal stage remain valid.

## 7.2 Aspects of the monitoring process

Monitoring is a multifaceted function which requires clearly delineated roles and planning as well as recommendations for responding to any violations of the planned targets. Monitoring sets milestones for the assessment of the implementation process and the assessment of the various risks associated with the project implementation. Such risks may stem from industrial action, from changes in raw material prices, from changes in interest and exchange rates or from changes in tastes which may affect the demand for the company's products and therefore its revenues. The monitoring process is therefore closely linked to periodic risk assessment of the project. Below is a list of key activities in the monitoring process, which includes planning, execution and strategic reassessment.

### 7.2.1 Monitoring and risk management planning

(a) Organisation of the monitoring function and roles and responsibilities assigned and communicated to individual members of the monitoring committee

(b) Milestones and risk tracking methods selected

(c) Determination of the critical path in the implementation phase; the critical path is a series of linked activities which make up the entire project

### 7.2.2 Monitoring and risk management execution

(a) Project risk factor database created and risk assessment against the deliverables at each time point to take place

(b) System of revenue and cost evaluation to be used along the critical path to verify compliance with budgets and time scheduling

(c) Project risks assigned impact and probability values eg risks could be classified as

*Probability*

| | |
|---|---|
| Low probability<br>High impact | High probability<br>High impact |
| Low probability<br>Low impact | High probability<br>Low impact |

(d) Risk mitigation actions decided and implemented

### 7.2.3 Project reassessment

Produce final monitoring and risk management report on whether project requires revision of time schedules and financial assumptions and viability reassessed.

## 7.3 Post-completion auditing

Once a project has been completed, an audit should take place to compare the income, costs and timing with the corresponding budgeted items. A valuable aspect of the post-completion audit is the attribution to specific and identifiable factors of any deviations between budgeted items and actual outcomes. Such attribution will be valuable for a company that may undertake similar projects. However, such attribution is not easy and may be costly. It may not be easy to identify the causes of a delay, for example in the execution of a project, as there may be several related and contingent factors. The usefulness of an audit may also be limited especially for projects that are unique.

# 8 Behavioural finance

**FAST FORWARD**

**Behavioural finance** considers the impact of psychological factors on financial decision-making. This challenges the idea that share prices and investor returns are determined by rational economic criteria.

**Exam focus point**

The examining team has written an article entitled 'Patterns of behaviour'. Make sure you read this article, which is available on the ACCA website.

**Behavioural finance** examines the psychological factors that lie behind financial decision making by investors and by financial managers, some of the main factors are listed below.

## 8.1 Psychological factors affecting the decision making of financial managers

### 8.1.1 Motivation

Managers may be motivated by their own objectives, which may sometimes be different from shareholder objectives. For example managers may be motivated by a desire to hit short-term financial targets, this may mean that they are reluctant to invest in projects that do not give good short-term returns. It may also mean that managers attempt to build the size of their business empires to increase their reputation, which may influence decisions on acquiring another business.

### 8.1.2 Analysis

Senior managers have a tendency to overestimate their own abilities. This **'overconfidence'** can lead to acquisitions being chosen based on the belief of senior management that they can turn around a failing company, whatever the evidence to the contrary. This can also explain why many acquisitions are over-valued, this aspect of behavioural finance is covered in Chapter 10.

**Overconfidence** helps to explain why most boards believe that the market undervalues their shares. This can lead to managers taking actions that **may** not be in their shareholders best interests, such as delisting from the stock market or defending against a takeover bid that they believe undervalues their company.

Managers are also reluctant to admit that they are wrong (sometimes referred to as **cognitive dissonance**). This helps to explain why managers persist with investment strategies that are unlikely to succeed. For example, in the face of economic logic managers will often delay decisions to terminate projects because the failure of the project will imply that they have failed as managers.

## 8.2 Psychological factors affecting the decision making of investors

### 8.2.1 Motivation

Investors may be also motivated by their own objectives, which may impair their ability to make rational economic decisions. For example managers may be motivated by a desire to protect their own reputation and so continue to invest in shares that are unlikely to do well in the future, because selling them would imply that they were wrong to invest in them in the first place. This reluctance to admit that they are wrong is sometimes referred to as **cognitive dissonance**. This can also lead to investing companies that are likely to give predictable returns and ignoring companies with higher, but riskier, returns (sometimes called **regret aversion**).

Investors may also want to give the impression that they are actively creating value, and this can lead to irrational movements of funds from one sector to another. Some prefer to invest in well-known companies and ignore smaller companies, this can mean that shares in small companies are undervalued (sometimes called a small capitalisation discount).

Many investors fail to see the bigger picture, and focus too much on short-term fluctuations in share price movements. This is sometimes called **'narrow-framing'**.

### 8.2.2 Analysis

Analysis of financial data may also be affected by behavioural factors. For example, investors may look for available information that can be used to guide decision making even though it is not necessarily relevant information (this is sometimes known as **anchoring**). This might involve analysing a company's **past** returns (when in fact analysing the future is more important) and using this to extrapolate future performance. This type of behaviour can lead to **herding**, where people buy (or sell) shares because share prices are rising (or falling) and can help to explain stock market bubbles (or crashes). Herding is also based on the psychological comfort of following the crowd.

A stock market bubble can emerge because investors buy shares simply because share prices have been rising in the past, this then creates a stronger rise in share prices which in turn creates a stronger demand for shares. Share prices can therefore be driven up to a level that is not justified given the future profit potential due investors following the crowd and continuing to buy shares.

Investors will often focus more on information that is **prominent (available).** Prominent information is often the most **recent information** about a company, and this may help to explain why share prices move significantly shortly after financial results are published.

Investors (and managers) are resistant to changing their opinion and may ignore information that suggests that they are wrong, and focus on information that reinforces their investment decisions (sometimes called **confirmation bias**). So, for example, if a company's profits are better than expected the share price may not react significantly because investors underreact to this news.

## 8.3 CAPM and behavioural finance

**Behavioural finance** conflicts with theories (such as the capital asset pricing model) that suggest that asset prices and investor returns are determined in a rational manner, based on the anticipated risk and future cash flows of a share.

For example, **narrow framing** can mean that if a single share in a large portfolio performs badly in a particular week then logically this should not matter greatly to an investor who is investing in shares over say a twenty year period. However in reality it does seem to matter, so investors are showing a greater aversion to risk than the capital asset pricing model (which argues that diversified investors should only care about systematic risk) suggests they should.

**Exam focus point**

> In the exam, if you are asked to comment on behavioural issues, you should focus on the issues that are likely to be relevant in the scenario presented in the exam – you should not simply repeat all of the points that we have covered here. In the exam you may not be able to identify precisely what is motivating investors or managers but you should be able to identify a range of possible influences.

# Chapter Roundup

- Corporate performance can be measured using such means as ratios and trends.

- As well as ratios, **other information** can be used to analyse a company's performance and identify possible problem areas. This will include information relating **to non-current assets and financial obligations, contingencies** and **events after the reporting period**.

- Decisions on how to finance the acquisition of assets are based on an understanding of the advantages and disadvantages of the various sources of finance.

- Debt capital takes various forms such as **loan capital**, **debentures and zero coupon bonds** and the interest on debt is tax deductible.

- Preference shares have priority over ordinary shares in dividend payments and capital repayment.

- **Retained earnings** are the **cumulative undistributed earnings** of the company and can be used to finance the **capital expenditure** programme of the company.

- New shares can be issued either to existing shareholders or to new shareholders.

- Dividend decisions determine the amount of and the way that a company's profits are distributed to its shareholders.

- **Risk mitigation** is the process of minimising the probability of a risk's occurrence or the impact of the risk should it occur.

- Capital investment projects require appraisal, and implementation monitoring.

- **Behavioural finance** considers the impact of psychological factors on financial decision-making. This challenges the idea that share prices and investor returns are determined by rational economic criteria.

# Quick Quiz

1   What is the significance of high dividend yield?

2   How is dividend capacity, or free cash flow to equity, calculated?

3   Name three advantages and three disadvantages of debt as a source of finance.

4   What is the main difference between operational and financial hedging?

5   Complete the severity/frequency matrix in relation to methods of dealing with risk.

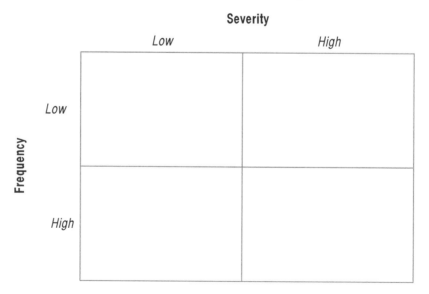

1    Dividend yield is measured by dividing the ordinary dividend per share by the share price. If this is high this normally indicates that dividend payments are high and so the level of reinvestment is low – and is often taken as a signal that the future growth prospects of a company are unattractive.

2    Dividend capacity or **FCFE** =

Net income (EBIT – net interest – tax paid)

| | |
|---|---|
| add | Depreciation |
| less | Total net investment |
| | (change in capital investment + change in working capital) |
| add | Net debt issued (new borrowings less any repayments) |
| add | Net equity issued (new issues less any equity repurchases) |

FCFE represents the cash available to the company which could be paid out to shareholders as dividends.

3    Advantages – any three from:

- Debtholders rank above shareholders in the case of liquidation
- Debt is generally cheaper than equity, as interest is tax deductible in most tax regimes
- Debt is secured against assets ∴ should be more attractive to investors
- Issue costs are normally lower for debt than for equity
- No immediate change in control when debt is issued, but this may change over time if debt is converted into shares
- Lenders do not participate in high profits – payout is restricted to interest and principal
- No immediate dilution in earnings and dividends per share

Disadvantages – any three from:

- There is a legal obligation to pay interest, regardless of the size of annual profit, but there is no such obligation to pay dividends
- The increased burden of interest may cause shareholders to demand a higher return, as the greater burden increases the risk that dividends won't be paid
- The financial risks of ordinary shareholders are increased by heavy borrowing
- There may be restrictions on a company's power to borrow, either from a company's constitution or the trust deeds of existing stock
- Money has to be made available for redemption or repayment of debt

4    Financial hedging involves the use of financial instruments, usually derivatives, whereas operational hedging uses non-financial instruments, usually real options.

5

| | | Severity | |
|---|---|---|---|
| | | Low | High |
| **Frequency** | Low | Accept | Transfer |
| | High | Control | Abandon |

Now try the question below from the Practice Question Bank

| Number | Level | Marks | Time |
|--------|-------|-------|------|
| 2 | Introductory | 15 | 29 mins |

BPP
LEARNING MEDIA

# Ethical and governance issues

| Topic list | Syllabus reference |
|---|---|
| 1 The ethical dimension in business | A3(a) |
| 2 Ethical aspects and functional areas of the firm | A3(b) |
| 3 The elements of an ethical financial policy | A3(c), (d), (e), (f) |
| 4 Stakeholder conflict | A3(e) |
| 5 Strategies for the resolution of stakeholder conflict | A3(g) |
| 6 Triple bottom line (TBL) and integrated reporting | A3(h) |

## Introduction

In this chapter we discuss the ethical dimension to the financial manager's role and how this links to conflicts between stakeholder interests. The chapter considers how financial decisions may impact on sustainability/environmental issues and how reporting may help to give visibility to this.

# Study guide

| | | Intellectual level |
|---|---|---|
| **A3** | **Ethical and governance issues** | |
| (a) | Assess the ethical dimension within business issues and decisions and advise on best practice in the financial management of the organisation. | 3 |
| (b) | Demonstrate an understanding of the interconnectedness of the ethics of good business practice between all of the functional areas of the organisation. | 2 |
| (c) | Recommend, within specified problem domains, appropriate strategies for the resolution of stakeholder conflict and advise on alternative approaches that may be adopted. | 3 |
| (d) | Recommend an ethical framework for the development of an organisation's financial policies and a system for the assessment of their ethical impact on the financial management of the organisation. | 3 |
| (e) | Explore the areas within the ethical framework of the organisation which may be undermined by agency effects and/or stakeholder conflicts and establish strategies for dealing with them. | 3 |
| (f) | Establish an ethical financial policy for the financial management of the organisation which is grounded in good governance, the highest standards of probity and is fully aligned with the ethical principles of the Association. | 3 |
| (g) | Assess the impact on sustainability and environmental issues arising from alternative organisational business and financial decisions. | 3 |
| (h) | Assess and advise on the impact of investment and financing strategies and decisions on the organisation's stakeholders, from an integrated reporting and governance perspective. | 2 |

# Exam guide

The ethical dimension to the financial manager's job is very important and will be a consistent issue in examinations. The concern with ethics is a **practical** one and the examining team will be concerned to see that candidates can identify with reasons where ethical issues might emerge in given scenarios. The student should be able to put forward soundly based arguments to support their views. This should logically lead to a discussion of how such ethical issues may be dealt with.

# 1 The ethical dimension in business                               6/11

**FAST FORWARD**

In the **financial management** of businesses, the key governance objective is the **maximisation of shareholders' wealth**.

**Ethical considerations** are part of the **non-financial objectives** of a company and influence the decisions of management.

**Exam focus point**

Ethics appears regularly as an element of an exam question, for example in the June 2011 exam you were required to discuss issues (including ethical issues) surrounding the commercialisation of a product in an overseas country.

## 1.1 The prime financial objective of a company

The theory of company finance is based on the assumption that the objective of management is to **maximise the market value of the company's shares**. Specifically, the main objective of a company should be to maximise the wealth of its ordinary shareholders.

A company is financed by ordinary shareholders, preference shareholders, loan stock holders and other long-term and short-term payables. All surplus funds, however, belong to the legal owners of the company, its ordinary shareholders. Any retained profits are undistributed wealth of these equity shareholders.

## 1.2 Non-financial objectives                                                6/13

The goal of **maximising shareholder wealth** implies that shareholders are the only stakeholders of a company. In fact, the stakeholders of a company include employees, customers, suppliers and the wider community.

The formulation of the financial policy of the firm takes into account the interests of the shareholders as a stakeholder group and the formulation of non-financial objectives addresses the concerns of other stakeholders. We will discuss later in this chapter the measures that companies adopt in order to address issues related to **sustainability** and **environmental reporting**. Here we provide some other examples of non-financial objectives. Note that these **non-financial objectives** could potentially limit the achievement of **financial objectives**.

| Non-financial objectives | |
| --- | --- |
| **Ethical considerations** | **Actions and strategies** |
| Welfare of employees | Competitive wages and salaries, comfortable and safe working conditions, good training and career development |
| Welfare of management | High salaries, company cars, perks |
| Welfare of society | Concern for environment |
| Provision of service to minimum standard | For example regulations affecting utility (water, electricity providers) |
| Responsibilities to customers | Providing quality products or services, fair dealing |
| Responsibilities to suppliers | Not exploiting power as buyer |
| Leadership in research and development | Failure to innovate may have adverse long-term financial consequences |

Most of these non-financial objectives reflect an **ethical dimension** of business activity.

## 1.3 Ethical dimensions in business                          6/13, Mar/Jun 16

Businesses play an important role in the economic and social life of a nation. They provide **employment and tax revenues** and have been responsible through **research** and **development** for some of the greatest technological breakthroughs which have changed our everyday life. The **downside** of this **dominant role is abuse of power** in the marketplace, **disregard for the environment**, irresponsible use of **depletable resources** and an adverse effect on local culture and customs. Companies like Coca-Cola, Imperial Tobacco and McDonald's have had an impact on developing countries that transcended the economic sphere and have affected dietary habits and ways of life.

Given the power that companies exercise, how do we measure their impact on society? How do we assess their behaviour against some ethical norm as opposed to mere financial norms? The answer to this question is provided by the development of **business ethics** as a branch of **applied morality** that deals specifically with the behaviour of firms and the norms they should follow so that their behaviour is judged as ethical.

It should be stressed that **business ethics** does not invoke a universally acceptable framework of principles that all companies should adhere to, hence the requirement for a corporate governance framework that would ensure a minimum degree of **ethical commitment** by firms became apparent. These movements towards the adoption of **corporate governance norms** have been discussed in Chapter 1.

Ethical considerations are sometimes easy to be incorporated into the policy of a company. For example, during the apartheid years many companies were boycotting South Africa, without any governmental coercion. In this case the ethical aspect was clear and easily identifiable. However, for a multinational company in a developing country not to pay wages to its employees that would render a project uneconomical may not be seen as unethical, as the employees of that country may have remained unemployed without the multinational company's presence.

# 2 Ethical aspects and functional areas of the firm

**Business ethics** should govern the conduct of corporate policy in all functional areas of a company, such as:

- Human resources management
- Marketing
- Market behaviour
- Product development

## 2.1 Human resources management                                    12/12

Employees in a modern corporation are not simply a factor of production which is used in a production process. Employees as human beings have feelings and are entitled to be treated by their employers with respect and dignity. In most advanced countries there are employment laws that determine the **rights** of employees and provide protection against the abuses of their employers.

**Ethical problems** arise when there is a conflict between the financial objectives of the firm and the rights of the employees. These ethical problems arise in relation to minimum wages and discrimination.

### 2.1.1 Minimum wage

Companies are obliged to pay their employees at least the minimum wage. However, when multinational companies operate in countries where there are no minimum wage requirements, then the companies may try to take advantage of the lack of protection and offer low wages. Business ethics would require that companies should not exploit workers and pay lower than the warranted wages.

### 2.1.2 Discrimination

Discrimination on the basis of **race, gender, age, marital status, disability or nationality** is prohibited in most advanced economies, through **equal opportunity legislation**. However, companies may have the power in some instances to circumvent many of the provisions. For example, companies may be able to discriminate against black applicants for certain positions for which they may feel that they are appropriate.

Employers may also wish to discriminate against mothers in certain jobs for which overtime is required. In other circumstances, a company may want to restrict applicants from a certain ethnic background when they deal with people of similar ethnic backgrounds. In all the cases of potential discrimination the company wishing to behave ethically should be aware of the risk of breaking the rules.

## 2.2 Marketing

**Marketing decisions** by the firm are also very important in terms of the impact on firm performance. Marketing is one of the main ways of communicating with its customers and this communication should be **truthful** and sensitive to the **social** and **cultural impact** on society. The marketing strategy should not

target vulnerable groups, create artificial wants or reinforce consumerism. It should also avoid creating stereotypes or creating insecurity and dissatisfaction.

## 2.3 Market behaviour

Companies should not take advantage of their **dominant position** in the market to **exploit suppliers** or **customers**.

Ethical behaviour in this context refers to the exercise of restraint in their pricing policies. Companies which are dominant in the product market and enjoy monopolistic power may charge a price which will result in abnormally high profits. For example, a water company may charge high prices for water in order to increase its profits because the remuneration of managers may be linked to profitability. For example, in many developing countries multinational companies are the only buyers of raw materials and they determine the price they pay to their suppliers.

# 3 The elements of an ethical financial policy

**Ethical policy** can be implemented through measures that ensure that the company takes into account the concerns of its stakeholders.

## 3.1 The ethical framework

An ethical **framework** should be developed as part of a overall company's social responsibility which includes:

(a) Economic responsibility
(b) Legal responsibility
(c) Ethical responsibility
(d) Philanthropic responsibility

The **four responsibilities** have been classified above in terms of **priority** for the firm. **Economic responsibility** is the first and **philanthropic responsibility** the last.

## 3.2 Economic responsibility

The first responsibility of a company is to its shareholders. Shareholders have invested their money in the company and require a return. The company has therefore a responsibility to manage the funds of outside investors in such a way that the required return is generated. The main aspects of the economic responsibility were analysed in Chapter 1 and include the various decisions that the financial manager is responsible for, such as financing, investment, risk management and dividend.

## 3.3 Legal responsibility

Companies operate within a legal framework as defined by company law, the various accounting and environmental standards, labour law etc. It is a duty of the company to comply with all the legal and regulatory provisions, and to ensure that employees are aware of this policy.

As we have already said, ethical responsibilities arise in situations where there is no explicit legal or regulatory provision and the company needs to exercise its judgement as to what is right and fair.

## 3.4 Ethical responsibility

Ethical responsibilities arise not as a result of legal requirements but as a result of a moral imperative for companies to operate in an ethical and fair manner. We have already discussed examples where issues of business ethics arise. How does a company ensure that an ethical approach to the various aspects of a company's activities is adopted? The following approaches are commonly used:

(a) **Mission or value statement**. A corporation has a mission statement in which some social goal is included.

(b) **Codes of ethics** to be followed by the employees, and which specify their attitude and response to ethical dilemmas. The code of ethics should reflect **corporate values** but it should also incorporate **professional codes** of ethics, which individual employees as members of professional bodies need to observe.

(c) **Reporting/advice channels** allow employees to notify unethical behaviour or to seek advice on specific situations.

(d) **Ethics managers**, officers and committees should be appointed to co-ordinate or assume responsibility for the implementation of ethics in the corporation.

(e) **Ethics consultants** should be consulted by corporations on specific issues of business ethics on which the corporation needs advice as to the appropriate course of action or policy formulation.

(f) **Ethics education and training** should be provided for the managers and employees of a corporation to ensure that ethical problems are recognised and dealt with according to the ethics code of the corporation.

(g) **Auditing, accounting and reporting** are necessary aspects of a business ethics programme since the corporation needs to be able to measure and report its economic and social impact to its stakeholders. This is considered in more detail later in this chapter.

## 3.5 Philanthropic responsibility

Philanthropy is the last of the responsibilities of a company and includes all those actions that the company needs to take in order to improve the life of its employees, to contribute to the local community and to make a difference to society as a whole. Philanthropic activities include **charitable donations**, the provision of **recreational facilities** for **employees**, the support to **educational institutions** and the **sponsoring of athletic** and **cultural events**.

## 3.6 Problems with this framework

A problem with the framework is the lack of an **explicit mechanism** for addressing **conflicting corporate responsibilities**, when for example **legal** and **regulatory** compliance may limit the **economic return** that a company can achieve. The resolution of **conflict between stakeholder groups** is considered below.

# 4 Stakeholder conflict

FAST FORWARD

A central source of ethical problems is the conflict between shareholders and other stakeholders.

Ethical issues often arise from a conflict between different stakeholder groups. Questions which include ethical considerations are likely to be of a **practical** nature and are likely to require you to advise the board on the resolution of stakeholder conflict and alternative approaches that may be adopted.

## 4.1 Stakeholders' objectives

Here is a checklist of stakeholders' objectives. It is not comprehensive.

(a) **Employees and managers**

  (i) Job security (over and above legal protection)
  (ii) Good conditions of work (above minimum safety standards)
  (iii) Job satisfaction
  (iv) Career development and relevant training

The fact that the managers of a company are not necessarily the owners of the company leaves open the possibility that **managers may not act in the interests of the owners.** Some examples are given below.

- **Short-termism**

    The longer-term benefits of investment in **research and development** may be ignored in the short-term drive to cut costs and increase profits thus jeopardising the long-term prospects of the company. If bonuses are based on short-term share performance or share options are about to mature, managers may be tempted to make short-term decisions to boost the share price.

    Where managers are unlikely to stay with the business long term, they may prefer to invest in projects that offer high returns initially (and therefore higher rewards), even though these projects ultimately have lower net present values.

    However, shareholders may encourage short-termism by excessive focus on the next profit announcement. This could be due to a lack of reliable information about longer-term cash flows. However, a more significant reason may be that shares are being held for increasingly short periods. Management can argue that they are responding to shareholders' wishes by focusing on the same time horizon.

- **Overpriced acquisitions**

    Takeovers are another manifestation of the non-alignment of the interests of shareholders and managers. In Chapter 10 we explore in more depth the issue of why so many takeovers or mergers fail to increase shareholder value. In brief, the explanation lies in the fact that managers have motives other than shareholder value maximisation.

- **Resistance to takeovers**

    The management of a company may tend to resist takeovers if they feel that their position is threatened, even if in doing so shareholder value is also reduced.

    The relationship between management and shareholders is sometimes referred to as an **agency relationship**, in which managers act as agents for the shareholders.

    The goal of agency theory is to find **governance structures** and **control mechanisms** that minimise the problem caused by the separation of ownership and control. In that sense, agency theory is the cornerstone of the theory of corporate governance. More specifically, agency theory tries to find means for the owners to control the managers in such a way that the managers will operate in the interest of the owners.

(b) **Customers**

(i)     Products of a certain quality at a reasonable price
(ii)    Products that should last a certain number of years
(iii)   A product or service that meets customer needs

(c) **Suppliers**: regular orders in return for reliable delivery and good service

(d) **Providers of loan capital (stock holders)**: reliable payment of interest due and maintenance of the value of any security

(e) **Society as a whole**

(i)     Control pollution
(ii)    Financial assistance to charities, sports and community activities
(iii)   Co-operate with government in identifying and preventing health hazards

Many companies' **pursuit of short-term profits may lead to difficult relationships with their wider stakeholders**.

Relationships with **suppliers** may be disrupted by demands for major improvements in terms and in reduction of prices. **Employees** may be made redundant in a drive to reduce costs and **customers** may be

able to buy fewer product lines and have to face less favourable terms. These policies may aid short-term profits, but in the long term suppliers and employees are able to take full advantage of market conditions and move to other companies, and customers can shop elsewhere or over the internet.

## 4.2 Stakeholder theory

Stakeholder theory proposes **corporate accountability** to a broad range of stakeholders. It is based on companies being so large, and their impact on society being so significant, that they cannot just be responsible to their shareholders. There is a moral case for a business knowing how its decisions affect people both inside and outside the organisation. Stakeholders should also be seen not as just existing, but as **making legitimate demands** on an organisation. The relationship should be seen as a **two-way** relationship.

An organisation might accept the **legitimacy of the expectations of stakeholders other than shareholders** and build those expectations into its stated purposes. This would be because without appropriate relationships with groups such as key suppliers, employers and customers, the organisation would not be able to function.

# 5 Strategies for the resolution of stakeholder conflict

**FAST FORWARD**

Reward systems, corporate governance and reporting can help to resolve conflict between stakeholders.

## 5.1 Reward systems

Agency theory sees employees of businesses, including managers, as individuals, each with their own objectives. Within a department of a business, there are departmental objectives. If achieving these various objectives also leads to the achievement of the objectives of the organisation as a whole, there is said to be **goal congruence**.

**Key term**

> **Goal congruence** is accordance between the objectives of agents acting within an organisation and the objectives of the organisation as a whole.

Goal congruence may be better achieved and the 'agency problem' better dealt with by giving managers some profit-related pay, or by providing incentives which are related to profits or share price. Examples of such remuneration incentives are:

(a) **Profit-related/economic value added pay**

Pay or bonuses related to the size of profits or economic value added.

(b) **Rewarding managers with shares**

This might be done when a private company 'goes public' and managers are invited to subscribe for shares in the company at an attractive offer price. In a **management buy-out** or buy-in (the latter involving purchase of the business by new managers; the former by existing managers), managers become owner-managers.

(c) **Executive share options plans**

In a share option scheme, selected employees are given a number of share options, each of which gives the holder the right after a certain date to subscribe for shares in the company at a fixed price. The value of an option will increase if the company is successful and its share price goes up.

**Exam focus point**

> Discussion of managerial priorities may be part of a longer question in the exam. The integrated approach to the syllabus means that a question on the effect of the introduction of a share option scheme on management motivation may be examined as part of a question on general option theory.

Such measures may be extended to reward management for considering the interests of other key stakeholders such as suppliers, staff or customers. This will require the measurement of a range of **social and environmental measures**. This is covered in Section 6.

## 5.2 Separation of roles

By ensuring that not too much power accrues to a single individual within an organisation, an organisation can reduce the risk of powerful stakeholders pursuing their own agendas. The role of the chairman and the chief executive, for example, should be split.

## 5.3 Corporate governance

Another approach to attempt to monitor managers' behaviour is through the adoption of a **corporate governance** framework of decision making that restricts the power of managers and increases the role of independent non-executive directors in the monitoring of their duties.

This can be achieved for example by establishing 'management audit' procedures, by introducing **additional reporting requirements** (see next section), or by seeking assurances from managers that shareholders' interests will be foremost in their priorities.

# 6 Triple bottom line (TBL) and integrated reporting
**6/11, 12/11**

## 6.1 Sustainability

The extensive use of exhaustible resources and the adoption of production processes which are potentially harmful to the environment have jeopardised the welfare of future generations. There is a growing realisation of this and pressure from the wider stakeholders on companies to take into account the long-term sustainability of their activities.

Although there is no single agreed or precise definition of sustainability, a broad definition is given below based on the common understanding about its underlying principles.

**Key term**

> **Sustainability** refers to the concept of balancing growth with environmental, social and economic concerns.

## 6.2 Environmental concerns

Business activities in general were formerly regarded as problems for the environmental movement, but the two are now increasingly complementary. There has been an increase in the use of the 'green' approach to market products. 'Dolphin friendly' tuna and paper products from 'managed forests' are examples.

## 6.3 The impact of green issues on business practice

**Environmental impacts** on business may be **direct**.

- Changes affecting costs or resource availability
- Impact on demand
- Effect on power balances between competitors in a market

They may also be **indirect**, as legislative change may affect the environment within which businesses operate. Finally, pressure may come from customers or staff as a consequence of concern over environmental problems.

Concern over environmental issues has led to growing pressure for company's to report on the impact of their business activities on the environment. Two approaches have emerged: **triple bottom line (TBL)** reporting and **integrated reporting**. These are covered in the following sections.

## 6.4 The main elements of TBL

Key term

> **Triple bottom line (TBL) reporting** is external reporting that gives consideration to financial outcomes, environmental quality and social equity.

The term **triple bottom line (TBL)** originated among investors seeking investments in enterprises that were socially just, economically profitable and environmentally sound.

The underlying principle is that in order to evaluate a company's true performance and assess the risk to the investor, one must look at a corporation's social, financial and environmental performance.

The triple bottom approach is often conceptualised as a pyramid or a triangle. An example of how this approach has been represented diagrammatically is given below.

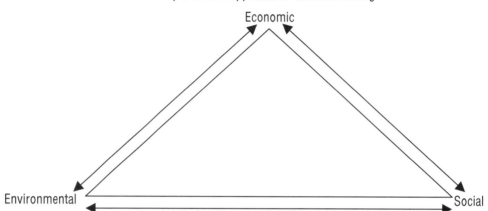

The triple bottom approach to decision making

(*Source*: *'The Triple Bottom Line: A Viable Strategy for Rural Development?'*, *Cornelia Butler Flora*)

Under the triple bottom approach decision making should ensure that each perspective is growing but not at the expense of the other. That is, economic performance should not come at the expense of the environment or society.

The TBL can be defined conceptually as **economic prosperity**, **environmental quality** and **social justice**. TBL reporting is the latest evolution of what is often reported as corporate sustainable development, or corporate social responsibility (sustainable development reporting). **Corporate sustainable development** tends to be very much **forward looking** and **qualitative**. By comparison, **TBL reporting** is a more **quantitative summary** of a company's **economic**, **environmental** and **social performance** over the previous year.

However, more specific methods of measurement are still being defined, making management and reporting difficult. Many companies, thinking it is just a matter of **pollution control**, are missing the bigger picture that meeting the needs of the current generation will destroy the ability of future generations to meet theirs.

### 6.4.1 Reasons for TBL

The concept of **TBL** developed as a response to an increasing demand by community and business groups for reporting the environmental and social impacts as well as the economic impact of a company on the life of a community. Investors, taxpayers, consumers and other stakeholders are demanding that reporting extends beyond economic return or 'output' to cover issues of equity, justice and responsibility. Demands are being made to report on corporate performance in areas such as:

(a)     Assurances of food safety after highly public problems, such as food recalls and food contamination

(b)     Assurances of long-term sustainable production systems and environmental stewardship, eg investments in renewable resources, recycling, waste reduction, and reducing green house gas emissions; demands are on a global basis so that pollution problems are not exported offshore

(c)     Looking after human rights, equity and equality; eg not using child labour, minimum working standards, no human rights violations, work/life balance, social equity for aboriginal communities

(d)     Looking after the welfare of animals, such as no testing on animals (The Body Shop), humane transportation, feeding

(e)     Ethical corporate conduct such as demonstrated due diligence and disclosure of conflicts of interest after the public spectacles of Enron, HIH, One Tel, Nippon Meat Packers and others

(f)     Ethical business investments

The supporters of the TBL approach advocate that a corporation's (whether private or public) ultimate success is measured not just by the financial bottom line but also by the corporation's social and ethical environmental performance.

TBL provides a framework for measuring and reporting **corporate performance** against **economic, social and environmental** benchmarks. Reporting on TBL makes transparent the organisation's decisions that explicitly take into consideration impacts on the environment and people, as well as on financial capital.

## 6.4.2 The advantages of TBL reporting

- **Better risk management and higher ethical standards** through:
    - Identifying stakeholder concerns
    - Employee involvement
    - Good governance
    - Performance monitoring

- **Improved decision making** through:
    - Stakeholder consultation
    - Better information gathering
    - Better reporting processes

- **Attracting and retaining higher calibre employees** through practising sustainability and **ethical values**

The critics of the TBL argue that while the aspirations of the TBL movement are sound, on both practical and conceptual grounds the TBL is an unhelpful addition to the corporate social responsibility debate and it promises more than it can deliver.

Some critics go so far as to argue that the rhetoric behind TBL can 'in fact provide a smokescreen behind which firms can avoid truly effecting social and environmental reporting and performance.'

(*Source: 'Getting to the Bottom of "Triple Bottom Line"', Wayne Norman and Chris MacDonald*)

## 6.4.3 TBL indicators

TBL reporting requires proxies to indicate the economic, environmental and social impact of doing business. Examples of useful proxies are given below.

An indication of **economic impact** can be gained from such items as:

(a)     Gross operating surplus
(b)     Dependence on imports
(c)     Stimulus to the domestic economy by purchasing of locally produced goods and services

An indication of **social impact** can be gained from, for example:

(a)     The organisation's tax contribution
(b)     Employment

An indication of **environmental impact** can be gained from such measures as:

(a)     The ecological footprint
(b)     Emissions to soil, water and air
(c)     Water and energy use

Such indicators can distil complex information into a form that is accessible to stakeholders. Organisations report on indicators that reflect their objectives and are relevant to stakeholders. One difficulty in identifying and using indicators is to ensure consistency within an organisation, over time, and between organisations. This is important for benchmarking and comparisons.

## 6.5 Integrated reporting

In September 2011 the International Integrated Reporting Council (IIRC) launched a discussion document, Towards Integrated Reporting – Communicating Value in the 21st Century. The IIRC subsequently published the International Integrated Reporting Framework in December 2013.

The aim of integrated reporting is to explain how an organisation **creates value over time** and **demonstrate the linkage between strategy, governance and financial performance and the social, environmental and economic contexts** within which it operates. By making these connections, an organisation should be able to take more sustainable decisions, helping to ensure the effective allocation of scarce resources.

Providers of financial capital and other stakeholders should better understand how an organisation is really performing and creating value over time. In particular, they should be able to make a meaningful assessment of the long-term viability of the organisation's business model and its strategy.

Integrated reporting should also achieve the simplification of accounts, with excessive detail being removed and critical information being highlighted.

### 6.5.1 Capitals

Integrated reporting is designed to make visible the **capitals** (resources and relationships used and affected by the organisation) on which the organisation depends, how the organisation uses those capitals and its impact on them.

| Capitals | |
|---|---|
| **Financial** | Funds available for use in production, obtained through financing or generated through operations |
| **Manufactured** | Manufactured physical objects used in production or service provision:<br>Buildings<br>Equipment<br>Infrastructure |
| **Intellectual** | Intangibles providing competitive advantage:<br>Patents, copyrights, software, rights and licences<br>Tacit knowledge, systems, procedures and protocols |
| **Human** | Skills, experience and motivation to innovate<br>Alignment and support for organisation's governance framework and ethical values<br>Ability to understand and implement organisation's strategies<br>Loyalties and motivations for improvements |

| Capitals | |
|---|---|
| Social and relationship | Institutions and relationships within and between communities, groups of stakeholders and other networks, and the ability to share information to enhance wellbeing |
| | Shared norms, common values and behaviours |
| | Key stakeholder relationships, and the associated trust and willingness to engage with stakeholders |
| | Intangibles associated with the brand and reputation |
| | Social licence to operate |
| Natural | Renewable and non-renewable environmental resources and processes |
| | Air, water, land, minerals and forests |
| | Biodiversity and ecosystem health |

### 6.5.2 Principles of reporting

A number of **guiding principles** underpin the content and presentation of an integrated report.

| Guiding principles | |
|---|---|
| **Strategic focus and future orientation** | Insights into strategy and how it relates to ability to create value in the short, medium and long term. Report also on how organisation uses and affects capitals. |
| **Connectivity of information** | Holistic picture of the combination, interrelationships and dependencies between the factors that affect the organisation's ability to create value over time. This includes analysis of resource allocation, how strategy changes when new risks and opportunities are identified and links between the business model and the external environment. |
| **Stakeholder responsiveness** | Insight into organisation's relationships with stakeholders and how organisation takes account of, and responds to, their needs. |
| **Materiality** | Focus on provision of information about matters that substantively affect the organisation's ability to create value over time. |
| **Conciseness** | Inclusion of sufficient context to understand strategy, governance, performance and prospects without the burden of excessive information. |
| **Reliability and completeness** | Inclusion of all material matters, both positive and negative, in a balanced way without material error. |
| **Consistency and comparability** | Presentation of information on a consistent basis over time in a way that, if possible, enables comparison with other organisations. |

### 6.5.3 Content of integrated reports

The **content** follows on from the guiding principles.

(a)   Organisational overview and external environment

(b)   How the governance structure supports value creation

(c)   Business model

(d)   Opportunities and risks that affect ability to create value over the short, medium and long term and how the organisation is dealing with them

(e)   Strategy and resource allocation – where the organisation intends to go and how it intends to get there

(f)   Performance – the extent to which the organisation has achieved its strategic objectives and what the outcomes are in terms of effects on capitals

(g)   Outlook – what challenges and uncertainties the organisation is likely to encounter in pursuing its strategy and the potential implications for its business model and future performance

(h)   Basis of preparation and presentation – how the organisation determines which matters to include in the integrated report and how such matters are quantified or evaluated

The IIRC is operating a pilot programme in integrated reporting in over 25 countries, with over 100 businesses involved, including major global companies.

### 6.5.4 Integrated thinking

The IIRC guidance emphasises the importance of integrated thinking. This essentially involves consideration of relationships between the operating and financial units within the business and the capitals (**including stakeholders**) that the organisation uses or affects.

Integrated thinking considers the issues that influence these relationships, including the connectivity and interdependencies between the factors that influence value creation over time.

### 6.5.5 Relationships with finance providers

As the guidance has evolved it has emphasised the importance of value **creation**, with the aim of producing guidance that will assist investors' decisions. A key selling point of integrated reporting is that it provides a higher quality of information for investors. This should enable them to make more informed decisions and ensure a better allocation of capital across the whole economy, towards sustainable businesses that focus on longer-term value creation within natural limits and the expectations of society.

### 6.5.6 Relationships with other stakeholders

The IIRC guidance also stresses the importance of **responding to key stakeholders' legitimate needs and interests**. In one sense there are limits on this response. The requirement for conciseness in integrated reporting could ultimately mean that not all the information required by all stakeholders will be published in an integrated report.

However, this is not seen as a major issue. The IIRC argues that the information requirements of other stakeholders are not opposed to those investors – all groups are interested in the relationships between value and capitals. In addition, integrated reporting should encourage **better mapping of stakeholder interests** and give organisations more confidence in the information they supply in response to shareholder requests.

Above all, integrated reporting should **promote engagement with stakeholders** that goes beyond provision of information. It should encourage businesses to focus on enhancing the mechanisms for stakeholder feedback, which may identify issues that have not been considered as important previously, but are concerns that should have an impact on strategy.

### 6.5.7 Impact on governance

The IIRC guidance requires a statement from those charged with governance about their responsibility to ensure the integrity of the integrated report and their conclusion about whether the integrated report is presented in accordance with the IIRC framework. The guidance is therefore designed to promote accountability and transparency, but this is not all. The IIRC wishes directors to use integrated reporting to **articulate the case** for the business strategy that they are adopting.

In addition, the information needed for integrated reporting promotes more informed board decision making. A report by KPMG in 2012 found that the focus on material issues that integrated reporting promoted led to better understanding of risks and opportunities and an ability to create strategy more effectively.

The IIRC guidance also stresses the importance of the leadership aspects of governance in promoting integrated reporting. Emphasis by the board of integrated principles should encourage greater awareness of their strategic importance.

## Chapter Roundup

- In the **financial management** of businesses, the key objective is the **maximisation of shareholders' wealth**.

- **Ethical considerations** are part of the **non-financial objectives** of a company and influence the decisions of management.

- **Business ethics** should govern the conduct of corporate policy in all functional areas of a company, such as:

    - Human resources management
    - Marketing
    - Market behaviour
    - Product development

- Companies should not take advantage of their **dominant position** in the market to **exploit suppliers** or **customers**.

- **Ethical policy** can be implemented through measures that ensure that the company takes into account the concerns of its stakeholders.

- A central source of ethical problems is the conflict between shareholders and other stakeholders.

- Reward systems, corporate governance and reporting can help to resolve conflict between stakeholders.

## Quick Quiz

1   On what management objective is the theory of company finance primarily based?

2   List two areas of a company's activity where ethical issues may arise.

3   What are the main elements of an ethical financial policy?

4   What are the main elements through which the ethical responsibility of a company is discharged?

5   Give **two** examples of triple bottom line indicators for each of the following impacts of doing business:

    (a)   Economic
    (b)   Social
    (c)   Environmental

# Answers to Quick Quiz

1   The objective of management is to maximise the market value of the enterprise.

2   Human resources management and marketing

3   Economic responsibility, legal responsibility, ethical responsibility, philanthropic responsibility

4   (a)   Mission or value statement
    (b)   Codes of ethics
    (c)   Reporting/advice channels
    (d)   Ethics managers
    (e)   Ethics consultants
    (f)   Ethics education and training
    (g)   Auditing, accounting and reporting

5   Any two from:

    (a)   Gross operating surplus
          Dependence on imports
          Purchase of locally produced goods
          Services

    (b)   Tax contribution
          Employment
          'Giving back' to the community, eg Tesco's 'Computers for Schools' scheme

    (c)   Water and energy use
          Emissions to air, soil and water
          Ecological footprint

Now try the question below from the Practice Question Bank

| Number | Level | Marks | Time |
|--------|-------|-------|------|
| 5 | Introductory | 20 | 39 mins |

# Trading in a multinational environment

| Topic list | Syllabus reference |
|---|---|
| 1 Corporate strategy in multinational enterprises | A4 |
| 2 Theory and practice of international trade | A4(a) |
| 3 Trade agreements | A4(b) |
| 4 The World Trade Organization (WTO) | A4(c) |
| 5 International monetary institutions | A4(d) |
| 6 International financial markets and global financial stability | A4(e) |
| 7 Developments in world financial markets | A4(f) |
| 8 Developments in international trade and finance | A4(g) |

## Introduction

In this chapter we look at the international environment within which companies need to make financial decisions. We discuss the various aspects of international trade and the benefits and risks for the company. This theme is then developed in Chapter 4b which moves on to look at strategic decision making in a multinational company and the agency issues arising between subsidiaries and the parent company.

# Study guide

| | | Intellectual level |
|---|---|---|
| **A4** | **Management of international trade and finance** | |
| (a) | Advise on the theory and practice of free trade and the management of barriers to trade. | 3 |
| (b) | Demonstrate an up to date understanding of the major trade agreements and common markets and, on the basis of contemporary circumstances, advise on their policy and strategic implications for a given business. | 3 |
| (c) | Discuss how the actions of the World Trade Organisation, the International Monetary Fund, The World Bank and Central Banks can affect a multinational organisation. | 2 |
| (d) | Discuss the role of international financial institutions within the context of a globalised economy, with particular attention to (the Fed, Bank of England, European Central Bank and the Bank of Japan). | 2 |
| (e) | Assess the role of the international financial markets with respect to the management of global debt, the financial development of the emerging economies and the maintenance of global financial stability. | 2 |
| (f) | Discuss the significance to the organisation of latest developments in the world financial markets, such as the causes and impact of the recent financial crisis, growth and impact of dark pool trading systems, the removal of barriers to the free movement of capital and the international regulations on money laundering. | 2 |
| (g) | Demonstrate an awareness of new developments in the macroeconomic environment, assessing their impact upon the organisation, and advising on the appropriate response to those developments both internally and externally. | 2 |

# 1 Corporate strategy in multinational enterprises

**FAST FORWARD**

**Multinational enterprises** undertake **foreign direct investment (FDI)** for reasons including obtaining **cost and revenue advantages**, **tax considerations** and **process specialisation**.

**FDI** can stimulate economic activity in the host country, but it can also lead to a **loss of political and economic sovereignty**.

## 1.1 The nature of multinational enterprises

A company does not become 'multinational' simply by virtue of exporting or importing products: ownership and the control of facilities abroad are involved.

**Key term**

A **multinational enterprise** is one which owns or controls production facilities or subsidiaries or service facilities outside the country in which it is based.

Multinational enterprises range from medium-sized companies having only a few facilities (or 'affiliates') abroad to giant companies having annual revenue larger than the gross national product (GNP) of some smaller countries of the world. Indeed, the largest – such as the US multinationals Ford, General Motors and Exxon Mobil – each have revenue similar to the GNP of a medium-sized national economy.

The **size and significance of multinationals** is increasing. Many companies in 'middle-income' countries such as Singapore are now becoming multinationals, and the annual growth in output of existing multinationals is in the range 10–15%.

The empirical evidence on the growth of multinational companies shows that companies become multinational in a gradual way. First, companies expand their operations into overseas markets by exporting. Then they create overseas sale subsidiaries and enter into licensing agreements. Finally they invest and create production facilities in overseas locations. The key element of the process of expansion is the creation of **competitive advantages**.

## 1.2 Competitive advantages of multinationals

There are many strategic reasons for engaging in foreign investment which include seeking **new markets** for goods, **new sources** of **raw materials**, **production efficiency**, expertise and **political safety**.

The main strategic reasons for engaging in foreign direct investment (FDI) include:

### 1.2.1 Market seeking

'Market seeking' firms engage in FDI either to meet **local demand** or as a way of exporting to markets other than the home market. Examples of this are the manufacturing operations of US and Japanese car producers in Europe. Some FDI is undertaken to provide a sales and market organisation in the overseas economy for the exporter's goods.

### 1.2.2 Raw material seeking

Firms in such industries as oil, mining, plantation and forestry will extract raw materials in the **places where they can be found**, whether for export or for further processing and sale in the host country.

### 1.2.3 Production efficiency seeking

The labour-intensive manufacture of electronic components in Taiwan, Malaysia and Mexico is an example of locating production where one or more **factors of production** are **cheap** relative to their productivity.

### 1.2.4 Knowledge seeking

Knowledge-seeking firms choose to set up operations in countries in which they can **gain access to technology or management expertise**. For example, German, Japanese and Dutch companies have acquired technology by buying US-based electronics companies.

### 1.2.5 Political safety seekers

Firms which are seeking 'political safety' will acquire or set up new operations in those countries which are thought to be **unlikely to expropriate or interfere** with **private enterprise or impose import controls**. More positively, these companies may offer grants and tax concessions.

### 1.2.6 Economies of scale

There are advantages to be gained in production, marketing, finance, research and development, transport and purchasing by virtue of firms being large. **Production economies** can arise from use of large-scale plant or from the possibility of rationalising production by adopting worldwide specialisation. Multinational car manufacturers produce engines in one country, transmissions in another, bodies in another, and assemble cars in yet another country.

### 1.2.7 Managerial and marketing expertise

Managerial expertise may be fostered in the environment of the larger multinational enterprise, and can be developed from previous knowledge of foreign markets. Empirical studies show that multinationals tend to **export to markets** before **establishing production operations** there, thus partly overcoming the possibly superior local knowledge of firms based in the host country.

### 1.2.8 Technology

Empirical studies suggest a link between **research and development (R&D)** work, which enhances technological, scientific and engineering skills and the larger multinationals engaged in FDI. Vernon's **product cycle theory** is based on the idea that multinational firms originate much new technology as a result of R&D activities on new products initially launched in their home markets. Host nations are often interested in FDI for the reason that technology transfer may result from it.

### 1.2.9 Financial economies

Multinationals enjoy considerable cost advantages in relation to finance. They have the advantage of access to the **full range of financial instruments**, such as eurocurrency and eurobonds, which reduces their borrowing costs. Multinationals' financial strength is also achieved through their ability to **reduce risk** by **diversifying their operations** and their sources of borrowing.

## 1.3 Issues in overseas production decisions                    12/10

FAST FORWARD

Commonly used means to establish an **interest abroad** include:

- Joint ventures
- Licensing agreements
- Management contracts
- Branches
- Subsidiaries

Most of the two-way traffic in investment by multinational companies (**FDI**) is between the developed countries of the world. While the present pattern of FDI can be traced back to the initial wave of investment in Europe by the US following the Second World War, more recently Europe, Japan, India and China have become substantial overseas investors.

Developments in international capital markets have provided an environment conducive to FDI.

**Key term**

**Globalisation** describes the process by which the capital markets of each country have become internationally integrated.

The process of integration is facilitated by improved telecommunications and the deregulation of markets in many countries.

There have been significant changes affecting the pattern of multinationals' activities over the last 20 years or so.

### 1.3.1 Destination countries

The focus has shifted from Canada and Latin America in the days when the US was the major source of FDI to other areas, including the countries of South-East Asia which receive significant direct investment from Japanese companies in particular.

### 1.3.2 Centralised control

Centralised control of production activities within multinationals has increased, prompted partly by the need for **strategic management of production planning** and worldwide resource allocation. This process of centralisation has been facilitated by the development of sophisticated worldwide computer and telecommunications links.

### 1.3.3 Type of integration

A firm might develop **horizontally** in different countries, replicating its existing operations on a global basis. **Vertical integration** might have an international dimension through FDI to acquire raw material or component sources overseas (**backwards integration**) or to establish final production and distribution in other countries (**forward integration**). **Diversification** might alternatively provide the impetus to developing international interests.

Different forms of expansion overseas are available to meet various strategic objectives.

(a) Firms may expand by means of **new 'start-up' investments**, for example in manufacturing plants. This does allow flexibility, although it may be slow to achieve, expensive to maintain and slow to yield satisfactory results.

(b) A firm might **take over or merge** with established firms abroad. This provides a means of **purchasing market information**, **market share** and **distribution channels**. If speed of entry into the overseas market is a high priority, then acquisition may be preferred to start-up. However, the better acquisitions may only be available at a **premium**.

(c) **A joint venture with a local overseas partner** might be entered into. A joint venture may be defined as 'the commitment, for more than a very short duration, of funds, facilities and services by two or more legally separate interests to an enterprise for their mutual benefit'. Different forms of joint venture are distinguished below.

### 1.3.4 Joint ventures                                                          12/10

The two distinct types of joint venture are **industrial co-operation (contractual)** and **joint-equity**. A **contractual joint venture** is for a fixed period and the duties and responsibility of the parties are contractually defined. A **joint-equity venture** involves investment, is of no fixed duration and continually evolves. Depending on government regulations, joint ventures may be the **only** means of access to a particular market.

The main advantages of joint ventures are:

(a) Relatively **low-cost access** to new markets

(b) **Easier access** to **local capital markets**, possibly with accompanying tax incentives or grants

(c) **Use of joint venture partner's existing management expertise**, local knowledge, distribution network, technology, brands, patents and marketing or other skills

(d) **Sharing of risks**

(e) **Sharing of costs**, providing economies of scale

The main disadvantages of joint ventures are:

(a) **Managerial freedom** may be **restricted** by the need to take account of the views of all the joint venture partners.

(b) There may be **problems** in **agreeing on partners' percentage ownership**, transfer prices, reinvestment decisions, nationality of key personnel, remuneration and sourcing of raw materials and components.

(c) Finding a **reliable joint venture partner** may take a long time.

(d) Joint ventures are **difficult to value**, particularly where one or more partners have made intangible contributions.

### 1.3.5 Exporting and licensing                                                 6/15

**Exporting** and **licensing** stand as alternatives to FDI. **Exporting** may be direct selling by the firm's own export division into the overseas markets, or it may be indirect through agents, distributors, trading companies and various other such channels. **Licensing** involves conferring rights to make use of the licensor company's production process on producers located in the overseas market.

**Licensing** is an alternative to FDI by which overseas producers are given rights to use the licensor's production process in return for royalty payments.

**Exporting** may be unattractive because of tariffs, quotas or other import restrictions in overseas markets, and local production may be the only feasible option in the case of bulky products, such as cement and flat glass.

The main advantages of licensing are:

(a)     It can allow fairly **rapid penetration of** overseas markets.

(b)     It does **not require substantial financial resources**.

(c)     **Political risks** are **reduced** since the licensee is likely to be a local company.

(d)     **Licensing** may be a **possibility** where direct investment is restricted or prevented by a country.

(e)     For a multinational company, licensing agreements provide a way for **funds** to be **remitted** to the parent company in the form of licence fees.

The main disadvantages of licensing are:

(a)     The arrangement may give the licensee **know-how** and **technology** which it can use in competing with the licensor after the license agreement has expired.

(b)     It may be more **difficult to maintain quality standards**, and lower quality might affect the standing of a brand name in international markets.

(c)     It might be possible for the licensee to **compete** with the licensor by exporting the produce to markets outside the licensee's area.

(d)     Although relatively insubstantial financial resources are required, on the other hand **relatively small cash inflows** will be **generated**.

### 1.3.6 Management contracts

**Management contracts** whereby a firm agrees to sell management skills are sometimes used in combination with licensing. Such contracts can serve as a means of obtaining funds from subsidiaries, and may be a useful way of maintaining cash flows where other remittance restrictions apply. Many multinationals use a **combination** of various methods of servicing international markets, depending on the particular circumstances.

### 1.3.7 Overseas subsidiaries

The basic structure of many multinationals consists of a parent company (a holding company) with subsidiaries in several countries. The subsidiaries may be wholly owned or just partly owned, and some may be owned through other subsidiaries. Whatever the reason for setting up subsidiaries abroad, the aim is to increase the profits of the multinational's parent company. However, there are different approaches to increasing profits that the multinational might take. At one extreme, the parent company might choose **to get as much money as it can** from the subsidiary, and **as quickly as it can**. This would involve the transfer of all or most of the subsidiary's profits to the parent company.

At the other extreme, the parent company might encourage a foreign subsidiary to **develop its business gradually**, to achieve long-term growth in sales and profits. To encourage growth, the subsidiary would be allowed to retain a large proportion of its profits, instead of remitting the profits to the parent company.

### 1.3.8 Branches

Firms that want to establish a definite presence in an overseas country may choose to establish a **branch** rather than a subsidiary. Key elements in this choice are as follows:

### Taxation

In many countries the remitted profits of a subsidiary will be taxed at a higher rate than those of a branch, as profits paid in the form of dividends are likely to be subject to a withholding tax. However, how much impact the withholding tax has is questionable, particularly as a double tax treaty can reduce its import. In many instances a multinational will establish a branch and utilise its initial losses against other profits, and then turn the branch into a subsidiary when it starts making profits.

### Formalities

As a separate entity, a subsidiary may be subject to more legal and accounting formalities than a branch. However, as a separate legal entity, a subsidiary may be able to claim more reliefs and grants than a branch.

### Marketing

A local subsidiary may have a greater profile for sales and marketing purposes than a branch.

# 2 Theory and practice of international trade

> **World output** of **goods** and **services** will increase if countries specialise in the production of goods/services in which they have a **comparative advantage** and **trade** to obtain other goods and services.
>
> Business enterprises are now also becoming increasingly '**internationalised**' by the development of **multinational activities** beyond pure import and export trade.

## 2.1 Theory of international trade

In the modern economy, production is based on a high degree of **specialisation**. Within a country individuals specialise, factories specialise and whole regions specialise. Specialisation increases productivity and raises the standard of living. International trade extends the principle of the division of labour and specialisation to countries. International trade originated on the basis of nations exchanging their products for others which they could not produce for themselves.

International trade arises for a number of reasons:

- Different goods require **different proportions** of **factor inputs** in their production.
- Economic resources are **unevenly distributed** throughout the world.
- The **international mobility** of **resources** is extremely **limited**.

Since it is difficult to move resources between nations, the goods which 'embody' the resources must move. The main reason for trade therefore is that there are differences in the relative efficiency with which different countries can produce different goods and services.

## 2.2 The law of comparative advantage

The significance of the law of comparative advantage is that it provides a justification for the following beliefs:

(a) Countries should **specialise** in what they produce, even when they are less efficient (in absolute terms) in producing every type of good. They should specialise in the goods where they have a **comparative advantage** (they are **relatively** more efficient in producing).

(b) **International trade** should be allowed to take place **without restrictions** on imports or exports – ie there should be **free trade**.

### 2.2.1 Does the law apply in practice?

The law of **comparative advantage** does apply in practice, and countries do specialise in the production of certain goods. However, there are certain limitations or restrictions on how it operates:

(a) **Free trade does not always exist.** Some countries take action to protect domestic industries and discourage imports. This means that a country might produce goods in which it does not have a comparative advantage.

(b) **Transport costs** (assumed to be nil in the examples above) can be **very high** in international trade so that it is cheaper to produce goods in the home country rather than to import them.

## 2.3 The advantages of international trade

The law of comparative advantage is perhaps the major advantage of encouraging international trade. However, there are other advantages to the countries of the world from encouraging international trade. These are as follows:

(a) Some countries have a **surplus** of **raw materials** to their needs, and others have a deficit. A country with a surplus (eg oil) can take advantage of its resources to export them. A country with a deficit of a raw material must either import it, or accept restrictions on its economic prosperity and standard of living.

(b) International trade **increases competition** among suppliers in the world's markets. Greater competition reduces the likelihood of a market for a good in a country being dominated by a monopolist. The greater competition will force firms to be competitive and so will increase the pressures on them to be **efficient**, and also perhaps to produce goods of a high quality.

(c) International trade creates larger markets for a firm's output, and so some firms can benefit from **economies of scale** by engaging in export activities.

(d) There may be **political advantages** to international trade, because the development of **trading links** provides a foundation for **closer political links**. An example of the development of political links based on trade is the **European Union**.

## 2.4 Barriers to entry

> **Barriers to entry** are factors which make it difficult for suppliers to enter a market.

Multinationals may face various entry barriers. All these barriers may be more difficult to overcome if a multinational is investing abroad because of such factors as unfamiliarity with local consumers and government favouring local firms.

Strategies of expansion and diversification imply some logic in carrying on operations. It might be a better decision, although a much harder one, to cease operations or to pull out of a market completely. There are likely to be **exit barriers** making it difficult to pull out of a market.

### 2.4.1 Product differentiation barriers

An **existing major supplier** would be able to exploit its position as supplier of an established product that the consumer/customer can be persuaded to believe is better. A new entrant to the market would have to design a better product, or convince customers of the product's qualities, and this might involve spending substantial sums of money on R&D, advertising and sales promotion.

### 2.4.2 Absolute cost barriers

These exist where an existing supplier has access to **cheaper raw material sources** or know-how that the new entrant would not have. This gives the existing supplier an advantage because its input costs would be cheaper in absolute terms than those of a new entrant.

### 2.4.3 Economy of scale barriers

These exist where the **minimum level of production** needed to achieve the greatest economies of scale is at a high level. New entrants to the market would have to be able to achieve a substantial market share before they could gain full advantage of potential scale economies, and so the existing firms would be able to produce their output more cheaply.

### 2.4.4 Fixed costs

The amount of **fixed costs** that a firm would have to sustain, regardless of its market share, could be a significant entry barrier.

### 2.4.5 Legal barriers

These are barriers where a supplier is fully or partially protected by law. For example, there are some **legal monopolies** (nationalised industries perhaps) and a company's products might be protected by **patent** (for example, computer hardware and software).

# 3 Trade agreements

**FAST FORWARD**

Justifications for **protection** include prevention of the import of cheap goods and dumping, and protection of infant or declining industries.

**Free trade** can lead to greater competition and efficiency, and achieve better economic growth worldwide.

## 3.1 Free trade

Free trade exists where there is no restriction on imports from other countries or exports to other countries. The **European Union** (EU) is a free trade area for trade between its member countries. In practice, however, there are many barriers to free trade because governments wish to protect home industries against foreign competition. **Protectionism** would in effect be intended to hinder the operation of the law of comparative advantage.

## 3.2 Protectionist measures                                                                    12/13

Protectionist measures may be implemented by a government, but **popular demand** for protection commonly exceeds what governments are prepared to allow. In the UK, for example, some protectionist measures have been taken against Japanese imports (eg a voluntary restriction on car imports by Japanese manufacturers) although more severe measures are called for from time to time by popular demand or lobbying interests.

Protection can be applied in several ways, including the following.

### 3.2.1 Tariffs or customs duties

Tariffs or customs duties are taxes on imported goods. The effect of a tariff is to raise the price paid for the imported goods by domestic consumers, while leaving the price paid to foreign producers the same, or even lower. The difference is transferred to the government sector.

For example, if goods imported to the UK are bought for £100 per unit, which is paid to the foreign supplier, and a tariff of £20 is imposed, the full cost to the UK buyer will be £120, with £20 going to the Government.

An *ad valorem* tariff is one which is applied as a percentage of the value of goods imported. A **specific** tariff is a fixed tax per unit of goods.

### 3.2.2 Import quotas

Import quotas are restrictions on the **quantity** of a product that is allowed to be imported into the country. The quota has a similar effect on consumer welfare to that of import tariffs, but the overall effects are more complicated.

- Both domestic and foreign suppliers enjoy a higher price, while consumers buy less.
- Domestic producers supply more.
- There are fewer imports (in volume).
- The Government collects no revenue.

An **embargo** on imports from one particular country is a total ban, ie effectively a zero quota.

### 3.2.3 Hidden export subsidies and import restrictions

An enormous range of government subsidies and assistance for exports and deterrents against imports have been practised, such as:

(a)  **For exports** – export credit guarantees (government-backed insurance against bad debts for overseas sales), financial help (such as government grants to the aircraft or shipbuilding industry) and State assistance via the Foreign Office

(b)  **For imports** – complex import regulations and documentation, or special safety standards demanded from imported goods and so on

### 3.2.4 Government action to devalue the currency

If a government allows its currency to fall in value, imports will become more expensive to buy. This will reduce imports by means of the price mechanism, especially if the demand and supply curves for the products are elastic.

## 3.3 Arguments against protection                                      12/13

Arguments against protection are as follows:

**Reduced international trade**

Because protectionist measures taken by one country will almost inevitably provoke retaliation by others, protection will reduce the volume of international trade. This means that the following benefits of international trade will be reduced:

(a)  **Specialisation**
(b)  **Greater competition**, and so greater efficiency among producers
(c)  The advantages of **economies of scale** among producers who need world markets to achieve their economies and so produce at lower costs

**Retaliation**

Obviously it is to a nation's advantage if it can apply protectionist measures while other nations do not. But because of **retaliation by other countries**, protectionist measures to reverse a balance of trade deficit are unlikely to succeed. Imports might be reduced, but so too would exports.

**Effect on economic growth**

It is generally argued that widespread protection will damage the **prospects for economic growth** among the countries of the world, and protectionist measures ought to be restricted to 'special cases' which might be discussed and negotiated with other countries.

**Political consequences**

Although from a nation's own point of view protection may improve its position, protectionism leads to a **worse outcome for all**. Protection also creates political ill-will among countries of the world and so there are **political disadvantages** in a policy of protection.

## 3.4 Arguments in favour of protection

### Imports of cheap goods

Measures can be taken against imports of cheap goods that compete with higher priced domestically produced goods, and so **preserve output and employment** in domestic industries. In the UK, advocates of protection have argued that UK industries are declining because of competition from overseas, especially the Far East, and the advantages of more employment at a reasonably high wage for UK labour are greater than the disadvantages that protectionist measures would bring.

### Dumping

Measures might be necessary to counter **'dumping'** of surplus production by other countries at an uneconomically low price. Although dumping has short-term benefits for the countries receiving the cheap goods, the longer-term consequences would be a **reduction** in **domestic output** and **employment**, even when domestic industries in the longer term might be more efficient.

### Retaliation

This is why protection tends to spiral once it has begun. Any country that does not take protectionist measures when other countries are doing so is likely to find that it suffers all of the disadvantages and none of the advantages of protection.

### Infant industries

Protectionism can protect a country's **'infant industries'** that have not yet developed to the size where they can compete in international markets. **Less developed countries** in particular might need to protect industries against competition from advanced or developing countries.

### Declining industries

Without protection, the industries might collapse and there would be severe problems of sudden mass unemployment among workers in the industry.

### Reduction in balance of trade deficit

However, because of retaliation by other countries, the success of such measures by one country would depend on the demand by other countries for its exports being inelastic with regard to price and its demand for imports being fairly elastic.

## 3.5 The 'optimal tariff' argument

In each of the above cases, tariffs and other protectionist measures are being advocated instead of alternative policies specifically targeted on the objectives sought.

Another argument in favour of tariffs targets directly the problem of a divergence between social and private marginal costs arising from trade itself. This **optimal tariff argument** provides a clearer demonstration of the possibility of gains in welfare from a tariff.

If a country's imports make up a significant share of the world market for a particular good, an increase in imports is likely to result in the world price of the good rising. The economic agents in the country collectively 'bid up' the price of imports. In a free market, each individual will buy imports up to the point at which the benefit to the individual equals the world price. Because of the price-raising effect referred to above, the cost to the economy as a whole of the last import exceeds the world price, and therefore exceeds its benefit.

In such a case, society can gain by restricting imports up to the point at which the **benefit of the last import equals its cost to society as a whole**. A tariff set to achieve this result is called an 'optimal tariff'.

Tariffs would decrease the welfare of a country in circumstances in which the optimal tariff is zero and there is no longer a need to discourage imports. This is when a country does not 'bid up' the world price of imports, as with a relatively small country in a large world market for a good.

## 3.6 Other measures

As an alternative to protection, a country can try to stimulate its export competitiveness by making efforts to improve the productivity and lower the costs of domestic industries, thus making them more competitive against foreign producers. **Hidden subsidies** and **exchange rate devaluation** are examples of indirect protectionist measures, but other measures, such as **funding industrial training schemes and educational policies**, might in the longer term result in improvements in domestic productivity.

## 3.7 The EU

The **EU** is one of several international economic associations. It dates back to 1957 (the Treaty of Rome) and consists of over 20 countries, including formerly communist Eastern European countries.

The EU incorporates a **common market** combining different aspects.

(a)   A **free trade area exists** when there is no restriction on the movement of goods and services between countries. This has been extended into a **customs union** (see below).

(b)   A **common market** encompasses the idea of a customs union but has a number of additional features. In addition to free trade among member countries there is also **complete mobility** of the **factors of production**. A citizen of a country in the EU has the freedom to work in any other country of the EU. A common market will also aim to achieve stronger links between member countries, for example by harmonising government economic policies and by establishing a closer political confederation.

(c)   The **single European currency**, the **euro**, was adopted by 11 countries of the EU from the inception of the currency at the beginning of 1999.

## 3.8 The customs union

The customs union of the EU **establishes a free trade area between member states**, and also erects **common external tariffs** to charge on imports from non-member countries. The EU thus promotes free trade among member states, while acting as a **protectionist bloc** against the rest of the world. It is accordingly consistent that the EU negotiates in general agreement on tariffs and trade (GATT) talks as a single body.

## 3.9 The European single market

The EU set the end of 1992 as the target date for the removal of all existing physical, technical and fiscal barriers among member states, thus creating a large multinational **European single market**. In practice, these changes have not occurred 'overnight', and many of them are still in progress.

The elimination of these trade barriers will **directly benefit multinational companies**, making it easier for them to engage in business across the European Union without having to deal with differing regulations (and other trade barriers) within each country of the EU.

### 3.9.1 Elimination of trade restrictions

(a)   **Physical barriers** (eg customs inspection) on goods and services have been removed for most products. Companies have had to adjust to a new VAT regime as a consequence.

(b)   **Technical standards** (eg for quality and safety) should be harmonised.

(c)   Governments should not **discriminate** between EU companies in awarding public works contracts.

(d)   **Telecommunications** should be subject to greater competition.

(e)   It should be possible to provide **financial services** in any country.

(f)   There should be **free movement of capital** within the community.

(g)   **Professional qualifications** awarded in one member state should be recognised in the others.

(h)   The EU is taking a **co-ordinated stand** on matters related to consumer protection.

### 3.9.2 Remaining barriers

There are many areas where harmonisation is a long way from being achieved. Here are some examples:

(a) **Company tax rates**, which can affect the viability of investment plans, vary from country to country within the EU.

(b) While there have been moves to harmonisation, there are still differences between **indirect tax** rates imposed by member states.

(c) There are considerable **differences in prosperity** between the wealthiest EU economies (eg Germany) and the poorest (eg Greece). This has meant that grants are sometimes available to depressed regions, which might affect investment decisions; and that different marketing strategies are appropriate for different markets.

(d) **Differences in workforce skills** can have a significant effect on investment decisions. The workforce in Germany is perhaps the most highly trained, but also the most highly paid, and so might be suitable for products of a high added value.

(e) Some countries are better provided with road and rail infrastructure than others. Where accessibility to a market is an important issue, **infrastructure** can mean significant variations in distribution costs.

## 3.10 North American Free Trade Agreement (NAFTA)

Canada, the US and Mexico formed the North American Free Trade Agreement (NAFTA) which came into force in 1994. This free trade area covering a population of 360 million and accounting for economic output of US$6,000 billion annually is almost as large as the European Economic Area (EEA), and is thus the second largest free trade area after the EEA.

Under NAFTA, virtually all tariff and other (non-tariff) barriers to trade and investment between the NAFTA members are to be eliminated over a 15-year period. In the case of trade with non-NAFTA members, each NAFTA member will continue to set its own external tariffs, subject to obligations under GATT. The NAFTA agreement covers most business sectors, with special rules applying to especially sensitive sectors, including agriculture, the automotive industry, financial services and textiles and clothing.

# 4 The World Trade Organization (WTO)      12/13

**FAST FORWARD**

The **World Trade Organization** (WTO) is a global international organisation dealing with the rules of trade between nations.

## 4.1 The World Trade Organization (WTO)

The **World Trade Organization (WTO)** was formed in 1995 to continue to implement the GATT. The WTO has well over 100 members, including the entire EU. Its aims include:

(a) To **reduce existing barriers** to free trade

(b) To **eliminate discrimination** in international trade such as tariffs and subsidies

(c) To **prevent the growth of protection** by getting member countries to consult with others before taking any protectionist measures

(d) To act as a **forum** for assisting free trade, by for example administering agreements, helping countries negotiate and **offering a disputes settlement process**

(e) Establishing **rules and guidelines** to make **world trade more predictable**

### 4.1.1 The most favoured nation principle

**Key term**

**Most favoured nation**: a principle in the GATT international trade agreement binding the parties to grant each other treatment which is as favourable as that offered to any other GATT member in respect of tariffs and other trading conditions.

The WTO encourages free trade by applying the **'most favoured nation'** principle where one country (which is a member of GATT) that offers a reduction in tariffs to another country must offer the same reduction to all other member countries of GATT.

### 4.1.2 Impact on protectionist measures

Although the WTO has helped reduce the level of protection, some problems still remain.

(a) Special circumstances (for example economic crises, the protection of an infant industry, the rules of the EU) have to be **admitted** when protection or special low tariffs between a group of countries are allowed.

(b) A country in the WTO may **prefer not to offer a tariff reduction** to another country because it would have to offer the same reduction to all other GATT members.

(c) In spite of much success in reducing tariffs, the WTO has had **less effect** in dealing with **many non-tariff barriers** to trade that countries may set up. Some such barriers, for example those in the guise of health and safety requirements, can be very difficult to identify.

(d) New agreements are **not always accepted initially** by all members.

Nevertheless, **the WTO exists to help business**, and ultimately businesses should be able to benefit from the **expanded opportunities** a freer global market brings, even if in certain countries some businesses may suffer through losing the benefits of protection.

# 5 International monetary institutions

**FAST FORWARD**

The International Monetary Fund (IMF) and the World Bank are closely related. Both were set up in 1944 as United Nation's agencies to establish a stable global economic framework.

The IMF was set up partly with the role of providing finance for any countries with temporary balance of payments deficits.

The World Bank aims to reduce poverty and to support economic development.

## 5.1 The International Monetary Fund                                    12/12

Most countries of the world have membership of the International Monetary Fund (IMF). The main importance of the IMF to multinational organisation's is that the IMF will step in to provide advice and to **provide financial support** to countries with **temporary balance of payments deficits.**

## 5.2 The IMF and financial support for countries with balance of payment difficulties

If a country has a balance of payments deficit on current account, it must **either borrow capital** or use up official reserves to offset this deficit. Since a country's official reserves will be insufficient to support a balance of payments deficit on current account for very long, it must borrow to offset the deficit.

The IMF **can provide financial support to member countries**. Most IMF loans are repayable in three to five years.

Of course, to lend money, the IMF must also have funds. Funds are made available from subscriptions or 'quotas' of member countries. The IMF uses these subscriptions to lend foreign currencies to countries which apply to the IMF for help.

## 5.3 IMF loan conditions

The preconditions that the IMF places on its loans to debtor countries vary according to the individual situation of each country, but the general position is as follows:

(a) The IMF wants countries which borrow from the IMF to get into a position to start **repaying the loans fairly quickly**. To do this, the countries must take effective action to improve their balance of payments position.

(b) To make this improvement, the IMF generally believes that a country should take action to **reduce the demand for goods and services** in the economy (eg by increasing taxes and cutting government spending). This will reduce imports and help to put a brake on any price rises. The country's industries should then also be able to divert more resources into export markets and hence exports should improve in the longer term.

(c) With 'deflationary' measures along these lines, **standards of living will fall** (at least in the short term) and unemployment may rise. The IMF regards these short-term hardships to be necessary if a country is to succeed in sorting out its balance of payments and international debt problems.

The existence of the IMF **affects multinational companies** by bringing a measure of financial stability by:

(a) Ensuring that national currencies are always convertible into other foreign currencies.

(b) Stabilising the position of countries that are having difficulties repaying international loans.

However it has been suggested that the strict terms attached to IMF loans can lead to economic stagnation as countries struggle to repay these loans. Deflationary policies imposed by the IMF may **damage** the **profitability of multinationals' subsidiaries** by reducing their sales in the local market.

Higher interest rates are likely to be introduced to suppress domestic consumers' demand for imports. However, higher interest rates will tend to dampen domestic investment and could result in increased unemployment and loss of business confidence.

## 5.4 The World Bank                                            Mar/Jun 16

The **World Bank** lends to creditworthy governments of developing nations to finance projects and policies that will stimulate economic development and alleviate poverty.

The World Bank consists of two institutions, the **International Bank for Reconstruction and Development (IBRD)** and the **International Development Association (IDA)**.

The IBRD focuses on middle-income and creditworthy poorer countries, while the IDA focuses exclusively on the world's poorest countries. Both the IBRD and the IDA aim to provide finance for projects concerned with the development of agriculture, electricity, transport (which are likely to have an impact on the poorest people) on attractive terms. IBRD loans must normally be repaid within 15 years, and IDA loans are interest free and have a maturity of up to 40 years.

The existence of the World Bank **affects multinational companies** by bringing a measure of financial stability by **helping to finance infrastructure projects** in developing economies. This allows multinational companies participate directly in infrastructure projects. It also creates a platform for multinational companies to invest in such countries. A pre-condition for such investment is normally that there is a reliable electricity and transport infrastructure and the World Bank helps to provide this.

## 5.5 European Central Bank

The European Central Bank (ECB) was established in 1998 and is based in Frankfurt. It is responsible for administering the monetary policy of the EU Eurozone member states and is thus one of the world's most powerful central banks.

The main objective of the ECB is to maintain price stability within the Eurozone (keep inflation low). Its key tasks are to define and implement monetary policy for the Eurozone member states and to conduct foreign exchange operations.

The main relevance of the ECB to a multinational organisation is that by keeping inflation low, the ECB can help to create long-term financial stability. For example, low inflation should help to protect the value of the euro over the long-term. This is helpful to multinational organisations with assets and profits denominated in Euros.

## 5.6 Bank of England

The Bank of England is the central bank of the UK. In 1997 it became an independent public organisation with independence on setting monetary policy.

The Bank of England performs all the functions of a central bank. The most important of these functions is the maintenance of price stability and support of British economic policies (thus promoting economic growth).

Stable prices and market confidence in sterling are the two main criteria for **monetary stability**. The bank aims to meet inflation targets set by the Government by adjusting interest rates (determined by the Monetary Policy Committee which meets on a monthly basis).

Financial stability is maintained by protecting against threats to the overall financial system. Such threats are detected through the bank's surveillance and market intelligence functions and are dealt with through domestic and international financial operations.

The bank can also operate as a **'lender of last resort'** – that is, it will extend credit when no other institution will. There are several examples of this function during the global financial crisis, for example Northern Rock in 2007. This function is now performed by UK Financial Investments Ltd (set up by the Government) but the Bank of England still remains 'lender of last resort' in the event of any further major shocks to the UK financial system.

## 5.7 US Federal Reserve System

The Federal Reserve System (known as the Fed) is the central banking system of the US. Created in 1913, its responsibilities and powers have evolved significantly over time. Its current main duties include conducting the US monetary policy, maintaining stability of the financial system and supervising and regulating banking institutions.

While the Board of Governors states that the Fed can make decisions without ratification by the President or any other member of government, its authority is derived from US Congress and subject to its oversight.

The Fed also acts as the 'lender of last resort' to those institutions that cannot obtain credit elsewhere and the collapse of which would have serious repercussions for the economy. However, the Fed's role as lender of last resort has been criticised, as it shifts risk and responsibility from the lenders and borrowers to the general public in the form of inflation.

## 5.8 Bank of Japan

The Bank of Japan is Japan's central bank and is based in Tokyo. Following several restructures in the 1940s, the bank's operating environment evolved during the 1970s whereby the closed economy and fixed foreign currency exchange rate was replaced with a large open economy and variable exchange rate.

In 1997, a major revision of the Bank of Japan Act was intended to give the bank greater independence from the Government, although the bank had already been criticised for having excessive independence and lack of accountability before these revisions were introduced. However, the Act has tried to ensure a certain degree of dependence by stating that the bank should always maintain in close contact with the Government to ensure harmony between its currency and monetary policies and those of the Government.

# 6 International financial markets and global financial stability

The globalisation of the financial markets has facilitated the transfer of funds to emerging markets but it has contributed to financial instability.

BPP
LEARNING MEDIA

## 6.1 The rise of global financial markets

One of the main developments of the last few decades has been the globalisation of the financial markets. This globalisation has been buoyed by the expansion of the EU, the rise of China and India as important trading players in the world economy and the creation of the WTO. The globalisation in financial markets is manifested in developments in international equity markets, in international bond markets and in international money markets.

## 6.2 International capital markets and emerging economies development

Private capital flows are important for emerging economies, and the transfer of flows has increased significantly as a result of the development in international capital markets. The capital flows to emerging markets take three forms.

(a)   **Foreign direct investment** by multinational companies.

(b)   **Borrowing from international banks.** Borrowing from international banks is becoming more important. There are several advantages in borrowing from international banks. It is possible to obtain better terms and in currencies which may be more appropriate in terms of the overall risk exposure of the company.

(c)   **Portfolio investment** in emerging markets capital markets. Emerging markets equity has become a distinct area for investment, with many specialist investment managers dedicated to emerging markets.

## 6.3 International capital markets and financial stability

The globalisation of the financial markets has created more liquid, efficient and transparent markets, but it has also created a higher risk of financial contagion, especially in emerging countries. Financial contagion occurs when crisis in one country spills to other countries.

 Case Study

**Risks following Brexit**

The International Monetary Fund cut its forecasts for global economic growth this year (2016) and next as the unexpected UK vote to leave the European Union created a wave of uncertainty amid already-fragile business and consumer confidence.

The economies of the UK and Europe were predicted to be hit the hardest by fallout from the June 23 referendum, which prompted a change of government in Britain. Global growth, already sluggish, was predicted to suffer as a result, putting the onus on policy makers to strengthen banking systems and deliver on plans to carry out much-needed structural reforms.

In particular, policy makers in the UK and the European Union (EU) will play a key role in tempering uncertainty that could further damage growth in Europe and elsewhere, the IMF said. It called on them to engineer a 'smooth and predictable transition to a new set of post-Brexit trading and financial relationships that as much as possible preserves gains from trade between the UK and the EU.'

Brexit's fallout is likely to be felt in Japan, where a stronger yen will limit growth. The IMF cut its 2016 growth forecast by 0.2 percentage point, to 0.3 percent.

Brexit fallout is likely to be muted for China, the world's second-largest economy, because of its limited trade and financial links with the UK.

'However, should growth in the European Union be affected significantly, the adverse effect on China could be material' the IMF said.

*(IMF, 2016)*

Developments in international financial markets have facilitated the growth in trade and the funding of overseas expansion strategies and have opened up more opportunities for investors. The main developments are:

- The global financial crisis
- Dark pool trading systems
- The removal of barriers to the free movement of capital
- International regulations on money laundering

## 7.1 The global credit crisis – the 'credit crunch'

A credit crunch is a crisis caused by banks being too nervous to lend money to customers or to each other. When they do lend, they will charge higher rates of interest to cover their risk.

### 7.1.1 When it all began

One of the first obvious high-profile casualties of the global credit crisis was New Century Financial – the second largest sub-prime lender in the US – which filed for Chapter 11 bankruptcy in early 2007. By August 2007, credit turmoil had hit financial markets around the world.

### Case Study

In September 2007 in the UK, Northern Rock applied to the Bank of England for emergency funding after struggling to raise cash. This led to Northern Rock savers rushing to empty their accounts as shares in the bank plummeted. In February 2008 the UK Chancellor of the Exchequer, Alistair Darling, announced that Northern Rock was to be nationalised.

In August 2008 US investment bank Lehman Brothers also filed for Chapter 11 bankruptcy after suffering significant losses on sub-prime mortgages. Following substantial losses its trading partners lost confidence in the long-term viability of Lehman Brothers and refused to trade with it knowing that there were substantial 'toxic assets' within the bank. The unknown level of 'toxic assets' also prevented anyone purchasing Lehman Brothers as a going concern.

### 7.1.2 What caused the crisis?

Years of lax lending on the part of the financial institutions inflated a huge debt bubble as people borrowed cheap money and ploughed it into property.

Lenders were quite free with their funds – particularly in the US where billions of dollars of 'Ninja' mortgages (no income, no job or assets) were sold to people with weak credit ratings (sub-prime borrowers).

The idea was that if these sub-prime borrowers had trouble with repayments, rising house prices would allow them to remortgage their property.

This was a good idea when US Central Bank interest rates were low – but such a situation could not last. In June 2004, following an interest rate low of 1%, rates in the US started to climb and house prices fell in response. Borrowers began to default on mortgage payments and the seeds of a global financial crisis were sown.

### 7.1.3 How did it turn into a global crisis?

The global crisis stemmed from the way in which **debt was sold onto investors** as mortgage-backed securities.

**Securitisation** is a financing technique where financial assets (such as mortgages) are grouped and the securitised assets can be sold, this transfers the risk of default to the new holder. This allowed banks to issue **further** bonds or use sale proceeds to fund **further** mortgage lending.

The US banking sector packaged sub-prime home loans into mortgage-backed securities known as **collateralised debt obligations** (CDOs). These were sold on to hedge funds and investment banks which saw them as a good way of generating high returns. However, the credit risk rating on these securitised assets often reflected the selling banks AA+ rating and not the real risk of mortgage default.

When borrowers started to default on their loans, the value of these investments plummeted, leading to huge losses by banks on a global scale.

In the UK, many banks had invested large sums of money in sub-prime backed investments and have had to write off billions of pounds in losses.

 Case Study

On 22 April 2008, the day after the Bank of England unveiled a £50 billion bailout scheme to aid banks and ease the mortgage market, Royal Bank of Scotland (RBS) admitted that loan losses hit £1.25 billion in just 6 weeks. In August 2008, RBS reported a pre-tax loss of £691 million (after writing down £5.9 billion on investments hit by the credit crunch) – one of the biggest losses in UK corporate history. At the beginning of 2009, RBS announced that it expected to suffer a loss of up to £28 billion as a result of the credit crunch.

On 3 March 2008, it was reported that HSBC was writing off sub-prime loans at the rate of $51 million per day.

### 7.1.4 Did IFRS exacerbate the problem?

IAS 39 *Financial Instruments: Recognition and Measurement* requires entities to value financial assets and liabilities at **fair value**. Fair value can be defined as:

'The amount for which an asset could be exchanged, or a liability settled, between knowledgeable, willing parties in an arm's length transaction.'

However as the global financial crisis deepened, there were calls to **suspend** fair value accounting. Many viewed fair value as **aggravating** the credit crunch problem. As markets collapsed, banks scrambled desperately to establish values for mortgage-related assets, leading to huge write-downs and in some cases runs on the bank. As banks mark assets down, their **lending capacity** is reduced which affects **liquidity**. This in turn creates further uncertainty, leading to further reductions in market price and so it goes on.

Some argued that not all assets are being disposed of immediately, therefore why should they be valued as such? Market prices of sub-prime debt are low due to the fact that no one is willing to buy, rather than due to the **risk of default**. Fair value prices in the recent economic climate are therefore implying a level of default that is **unrealistic**, which is in turn having an adverse effect on market confidence and activity. No banks will be willing to lend or invest if, by doing so, they have to take an **immediate write-down** as a result of being required to mark the asset to an unrealistic market price.

 Case Study

Prudential disclosed a £459 million nosedive in the fair value of its US insurance assets for the first quarter of 2008. Under the controversial financial instruments standard IAS 39, the value of the assets were hit by more than £794 million in losses and £335 million in gains, resulting in an overall drop of £459 million.

*(Jetuah, 2008)*

However, is this criticism of fair value completely reasonable? After all, the credit crunch was in full swing before most of the large write-downs were announced. Is it not the **threat** of write-downs that is the problem rather than the write-downs themselves? In other words, banks are reacting to the **risk** associated with potential write-downs. They do not know how big the problems are with rivals and are unwilling to risk large amounts of capital to find out.

An article in *Accountancy Age* (Jetuah, 2008) suggested that the **excessive volatility** in the market was caused not by accounting rules but because financial statements do not tell banks whose sub-prime derivatives are better or worse. As mentioned above, banks are unwilling to take the risk of losing large amounts of capital to find out.

### 7.1.5 How businesses were affected

As banks' confidence was at an all-time low, they stopped lending to each other, causing a liquidity problem. Inter-bank lending funds bank operations – without it, banks have insufficient funds to lend to businesses and individuals. By mid-2007 it was obvious there was a severe problem – BNP Paribas had suspended two of its hedge funds blaming 'complete evaporation of liquidity in the asset-backed security market'.

2008 was characterised by multi-billion dollar government bailouts and by the end of the year the US Central Bank had cut interest rates to 0–0.25% in a bid to stem the economic freefall.

With bank lending so low, businesses were unable to obtain funding for investments, resulting in large reductions in output and general business confidence. This lack of confidence had a spiralling effect. As businesses cut back on production and provision of services, workers started to fear for their jobs and thus reduced spending on non-essential items. This led to businesses reducing output further to avoid excessive investment in inventories, workers were made redundant which led to even less consumer spending and so the spiral continued.

## 7.2 The European Sovereign Debt crisis

Although the European debt crisis has no single cause, its roots are in the introduction of the European single currency. This meant that member countries were able to borrow at a cheaper rate than they were previously able to. This was due to the assumption that these countries were following the economic rules of the single currency. This effectively meant that the good credit rating of Germany was improving the credit rating of countries such as Greece, Portugal and Italy.

Some of the European countries used the increased credit offered to increase consumption and build up large balance of payment deficits. The increased borrowing was based on the assumption of certain levels of growth which then did not occur due to the financial crisis of 2007.

The European Sovereign Debt crisis has been increasing in severity since 2010 when Portugal's debt was downgraded and further exacerbated in March 2011 when Greek debt was downgraded to 'junk'. This was followed by Ireland being downgraded in July 2011 and Italy in October 2011. France and Spain were both downgraded in 2012. In a similar manner to the US downgrade of 2011, this could lead to an increase in the cost of government borrowing, which may lead to rising interest rates.

In May 2010 the European Union (EU) created the European Financial Stability Facility (EFSF) which is guaranteed by the Eurozone countries and provides bailout loans to countries that are in severe financial difficulty. In January 2011 the European Financial Stabilisation Mechanism was created to raise funds by using the EU budget as security. The funds raised can be lent to the International Monetary Fund (IMF) or the EFSF.

The EFSF had its credit rating downgraded from AAA to AA+ by Standard & Poor's in January 2012.

## 7.2.1 Austerity measures

Throughout Europe, and indeed globally, countries have been putting austerity measures in place in an attempt to reduce their spiralling debts. The table below summarises certain European countries' financial positions following the debt crisis and some of the austerity measures that were put in place.

| Country | Recent position and austerity measures |
|---|---|
| Greece | Frozen out of international credit markets because of sovereign debt 'junk' status |
| | Pensions, tax thresholds and civil service jobs severely affected |
| | Budget for 2013 involving €9.4bn of spending cuts |
| | Unemployment at 17.7% in 2011 |
| Irish Republic | EU/IMF bailout of €85 billion in December 2010 (length of time to repay loan extended from 7.5 years to 15 years in 2011) |
| | Two banks bailed out in 2011 at a cost of €5.8 billion |
| | Government spending slashed by €4 billion – all public servants' pay cut by at least 5% and social welfare reduced |
| Italy | Debt at 120% of gross domestic product – $2.2 trillion |
| | Austerity measures passed in July 2011 featured savings worth €70 billion, including increases in healthcare fees, cuts to regional subsidies, family tax benefits and pensions of high earners |
| | Original target of balancing budget by 2013 likely to be missed |
| UK | Savings estimated at about £83 billion to be made over 4 years, including cutting 490,000 public sector jobs and increase in retirement age from 65 to 66 by 2020 |
| | In 2008 £37 billion of UK taxpayers' money was used to bail out three major banks (RBS, Lloyds TSB and HBOS), after which the UK Government was forced to borrow a record £44 billion to fund its spending. |
| Spain | Austerity budget for 2011 included tax rise for the rich and 8% spending cuts |
| | €27 billion cut from March 2012 government spending budget |
| | Additional July 2012 austerity budget including €65 billion additional spending cuts and tax increases |
| | Budget deficit of 8.5% in 2011 |
| | Unemployment at 23% in 2012 |

**Exam focus point**

December 2012 part of a question asked students to consider how austerity measures may impact differently on businesses operating in the high-, low- and mid-priced areas of a market sector.

## 7.2.2 Financial contagion

The European Sovereign Debt crisis is a classic example of financial contagion. The initial problems encountered by Greece and Portugal spread throughout Europe as confidence fell in other European economies. Intertrading among European countries meant that, as one country experienced financial difficulties and reduced its imports, those countries providing the imported goods also suffered due to a downturn in trade.

However, it is not just Europe that is suffering. European countries trade worldwide and as their economic growth slows and austerity measures take effect, economies worldwide will be affected. This leads to greater borrowing to fund spending (due to less income from exports and a general slowdown in the economy), leading to increased interest payments on debt and eventually potential downgrade of debt.

## Case Study

**Contagion in Cyprus**

In June 2012 Cyprus applied for bailout assistance for its undercapitalised banking sector. Cyprus was strongly linked and exposed to its neighbour, Greece's, problems. Like Spain, Cyprus also suffered from the deflation of a property bubble. Cyprus's situation was also complicated by having a large offshore banking sector. Negotiations between the Cypriot Government and the European monetary authorities took place during the rest of 2012. At the end of November the Cypriot Government agreed to a bailout, including strong austerity measures such as cuts in public sector salaries, social benefits and pensions and higher taxes and healthcare charges.

When the amount of the package, €10 billion, was agreed in March 2013, a further condition was the imposition of a one-off levy, initially on all deposits but subsequently only on deposits over €100,000. However, this was rejected by the Cypriot Parliament. Instead a deal was reached to close the Cypriot bank in most trouble, the Lakai bank, and impose measures that could result in depositors with over €100,000 at the Bank of Cyprus losing up to 60% of their savings.

While negotiations were going on, banks in Cyprus were shut for two weeks, and restrictions were imposed on individuals and companies when they reopened, including limits on daily withdrawals and restrictions on taking money out of Cyprus and making payments or transfers outside the country, damaging the economy by starving it of the means of payment.

Cyprus was expected to carry out fiscal consolidation of around 4.5%, but its loans were still expected to peak at 140% of GDP, which many considered to be unsustainable. Some commentators suggested that Cyprus's GDP could fall by around 20%.

### 7.2.3 Effect on companies

We mentioned above that exporting companies will suffer as economies slow down. However, it is not just their sales that will suffer. As government debt is downgraded and the cost of debt increases, governments often pass on the cost to companies and consumers in the form of higher interest rates. Therefore companies with debt of their own will find themselves trying to meet increasing interest payments while sales revenue is falling.

To try to combat the problem, companies may increase prices to recoup some of their lost sales revenue. Consumers facing austerity measures in the form of pay cuts or freezes, or more expensive essential services, will be unable to afford these higher prices and reduce their spending. Companies will suffer further reductions in sales revenue and the spiral will continue until either confidence grows again or they go out of business.

Currency fluctuations caused by the crisis can also have a significant effect on company performance. The euro has weakened against the dollar due to the crisis, therefore Eurozone companies purchasing goods from the US face increased prices.

### 7.2.4 Where do we go from here?

**Exam focus point**

The European Sovereign Debt crisis is an important issue. It is important that you keep up to date with developments, not just in Europe but on a global scale. An article on the European Debt Crisis is on the ACCA website.

By the time you read this section there may have been major developments on this topic. It is important that you keep up to date with financial management issues by reading the financial press.

FAST FORWARD

> **Securitisation** is the process of converting **illiquid assets** into **marketable asset-backed securities**. The development of **securitisation** has led to **disintermediation** and a reduction in the role of financial intermediaries, as borrowers can reach lenders directly.
>
> A **tranche** is a slice of a security (typically a bond or other credit-linked security) which is funded by investors who assume different risk levels within the liability structure of that security.

## 7.3.1 Securistisation

Securitisation is the process of converting **illiquid assets** into **marketable securities**. These securities are backed by specific assets and are normally called **asset-backed securities**.

Securitisation started with banks converting their long-term loans such as mortgages into securities and selling them to institutional investors. One of the problems of banks as financial intermediaries is the fundamental mismatch between the maturities of assets and liabilities. Securitisation of loans and sale to investors with more long-term liabilities reduces the mismatch problem and a bank's overall risk profile.

The oldest and most common type of asset securitisation is the **mortgage-backed bond** or **security**, although today one can expect virtually anything that has a cash flow to be a candidate for securitisation.

Cash flows before securitisation

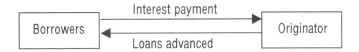

Cash flows after securitisation

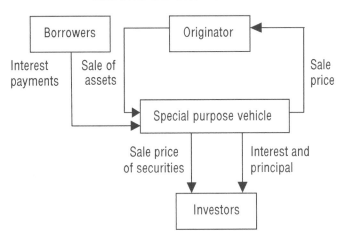

## 7.3.2 How tranching works

The structure of securitisation deals, referred to as **tranching**, is standard. In those transactions, claims on cash flows generated by the collateral are split into several classes of notes, at least three and possibly more than five. Each class is called a **tranche** and has **absolute priority** in the cash flows over the more junior ones.

All the tranches together make up what is known as the deal's **capital structure** or **liability structure**. They are generally paid sequentially, from the most senior to most junior. The more senior tranches generally have higher ratings than the lower-rated tranches. For example, senior tranches may be rated AAA, AA or A. A more junior tranche may be rated BB. Ratings can fluctuate after the debt is issued – even senior tranches could be rated below investment grade (that is, below BBB).

Typical investors of **senior tranches** are insurance companies, pension funds and other risk-averse investors.

**Junior tranches** are **more risky**, as they are not secured by specific assets. These tranches tend to be bought by hedge funds and other investors looking for higher risk-return profiles.

### 7.3.3 Example

A bank is proposing to sell $100 million of mortgage loans by means of a securitization process. The mortgages have a 10 year term and pay a return of 8% per year. The bank will use 90% of the value of the mortgages as collateral.

- 60% of the collateral value will be sold as tranche A – senior debt with a credit rating of A. This will pay interest of 7%.

- 30% of the collateral value will be sold as tranche B – less senior debt with a credit rating of B. This will pay interest of 10%.

- 10% will be sold as subordinated debt with no credit rating.

The estimated cash flows would be:

**Cash inflows**

$8m is expected to be repaid by the mortgage holders ($100m × 8%).

**Cash outflows**

Tranche A is the first to be paid and receive $100m × 0.90 × 0.6 × 0.07 = $3.78m. Tranche B is the next to be paid and receives $100m x 0.90 × 0.3 × 0.1 = $2.7m.

The cash paid to the tranches with security (collateral) ie tranches A and B is $6.48m (3.78 + 2.7).

The difference between the cash received of $8m and the cash paid to tranche's with security ie tranches A and B of $6.48m is $1.52m. This is paid to the holders of the subordinated debt who therefore receive a return of $1.52 on an investment of $9m ($100m × 0.90 × 0.1). This is a return of 1.52 / 9 = 16.9%.

However, in the event of mortgage defaults the cash inflows would fall and this would lead to lower returns for the holders of subordinated debt. Only if cash inflows fell below $6.48m will the holders of tranche B be affected. If the income fell below $3.78m the holders of tranche A would be affected.

### 7.3.4 Benefits of tranching

Tranching is an aspect of securitization. Securitization allows a company to convert assets back into cash and to remove the risk of non-payment associated with those assets.

Tranching involves transferring assets to a special purpose vehicle (SPV) and then selling loan notes/bonds backed by the income stream from these assets. This can allow a company to obtain low cost finance because the finance is directly secured by a reliable income stream.

Tranching can attract investors because it is a good way of **dividing risk**. Anyone who invests in risky loans is taking a chance, but tranching lets you divide the chances up, so that people who want safety can buy the top (senior) tranches, get less of a profit, but know that they're not going to lose out unless things go seriously wrong. People who are willing to take their chances in the lower (junior) tranches know that they're taking a significant risk, but they can potentially make a lot more money.

### 7.3.5 Risks of tranching

(a) Tranches are very **complex**; most investors do not really understand the risks associated with each tranche.

(b) Stripping out low risk assets and transferring them to an SPV may increase the risk faced by the other investors in the company and may lead to an increase in that company's costs of capital.

Securitisation and tranching were both covered in part of an exam question in December 2015, including an analysis of the cash flows to holders of various tranches and a discussion of the benefits and risks of such a scheme.

## 7.4 Credit default swaps

**FAST FORWARD**

A credit default swap is a specific type of counterparty agreement which allows the transfer of third-party credit risk from one party to the other.

### 7.4.1 What are credit default swaps?

Credit default swaps (CDSs) act in a similar way to insurance policies. When two parties enter into a credit default swap, the buyer agrees to pay a fixed **spread** to the seller (see below). In return, the seller agrees to purchase a specified financial instrument from the buyer at the instrument's par value in the event of default. You could liken this transaction to a house insurance policy – in the event of a fire, the buyer of the policy will receive whatever the damaged or destroyed goods are worth in monetary terms.

The **spread** of a CDS is the **annual amount** the protection buyer must pay the protection seller over the length of the contract (like an insurance premium), expressed as a **percentage of the notional amount**. The **more likely** the risk of default, **the larger the spread**. For example, if the CDS spread of the reference entity is 50 basis points (or 0.5%) then an investor buying $10 million worth of protection from a bank must pay the bank $50,000 per year. These payments continue until either the CDS contract expires or the reference entity defaults.

Unlike insurance, however, CDSs are **unregulated**. This means that contracts can be traded – or swapped – from investor to investor without anyone overseeing the trades to ensure the buyer has the resources to cover the losses if the security defaults.

### 7.4.2 The CDS market

By the end of 2007, the CDS market was valued at more than $45 trillion – more than twice the size of the combined GDP of the US, Japan and the EU. An original CDS can go through as many as 15 to 20 trades; therefore, when a default occurs, the so-called 'insured' party or hedged party does not know who is responsible for making up the default or indeed whether the end party has the funds to do so.

When the economy is booming, CDS can be seen as a means of making 'easy' money for banks. Corporate defaults in a booming economy are few, thus swaps are a low-risk way of collecting premiums and earning extra cash.

### 7.4.3 Uses of CDS – speculation

The CDS market expanded into **structured finance** from its original confines of municipal bonds and corporate debt and then into the secondary market where **speculative investors** bought and sold the instruments without having any direct relationship with the underlying investment. Their behaviour was almost like **betting** on whether the investments would succeed or fail.

## Example

A hedge fund believes that a company (Drury Inc) will shortly default on its debt of $10 million. The hedge fund may therefore buy $10 million worth of CDS protection for, say, 2 years, with Drury Inc as the reference entity, at a spread of 500 basis points (5%) per annum.

If Drury Inc does default after, say, one year, then the hedge fund will have paid $500,000 to the bank but will then receive $10 million (assuming zero recovery rate). The bank will incur a $9.5 million loss unless it has managed to offset the position before the default.

If Drury Inc does not default, then the CDS contract will run for two years and the hedge fund will have paid out $1 million to the bank with no return. The bank makes a profit of $1 million; the hedge fund makes a loss of the same amount.

What would happen if the hedge fund decided to liquidate its position after a certain period of time in an attempt to lock in its gains or losses? Say after one year the market considers Drury Inc to be at greater risk of default, and the spread widens from 500 basis points to 1,500. The hedge fund may decide to sell $10 million protection to the bank for one year at this higher rate. Over the two years, the hedge fund will pay the bank $1 million (2 × 5% × $10 million) but will receive $1.5 million (1 × 15% × $10 million) – a net profit of $500,000 (as long as Drury Inc does not default in the second year).

### 7.4.4 Uses of CDS – hedging

CDSs are often used to manage the credit risk (risk of default) which arises from holding debt. For example, the holder of a corporate bond may hedge their exposure by entering into a CDS contract as the buyer of protection. If the bond goes into default, the proceeds from the CDS contract will cancel out the losses on the underlying bond.

## Example

A pension fund owns $10 million of a 5-year bond issued by Drury Inc. In order to manage the risk of losses in the event of a default by Drury Inc, the pension fund buys a CDS from a bank with a notional amount of $10 million. Assume the CDS trades at 300 basis points (3%) which means that the pension fund will pay the bank an annual premium of $300,000.

If Drury Inc does not default on the bond, the pension fund will pay a total premium of 5 × $300,000 = $1.5 million to the bank and will receive the $10 million back at the end of the 5 years. Although it has lost $1.5 million, the pension fund has hedged away the default risk.

If Drury Inc defaults on the bond after, say, 2 years, the pension fund will stop paying the premiums and the bank will refund the $10 million to compensate for the loss. The pension fund's loss is limited to the premiums it had paid to the bank (2 × $300,000 = $600,000) – if it had not hedged the risk, it would have lost the full $10 million.

### 7.4.5 The role of CDS in the global economic crisis

Once an obscure financial instrument for banks and bondholders, CDSs are now at the heart of the recent credit crisis.

American International Group (AIG) – the world's largest insurer – could issue CDSs without putting up any real collateral **as long as it maintained a triple-A credit rating**. There was no real capital cost to selling these swaps; there was no limit. Thanks to **fair value accounting**, AIG could book the profit from, say, a five-year credit default swap as soon as the contract was sold, based on the **expected** default rate. In many cases, the profits it booked never materialised.

On 15 September 2007 the bubble burst when all the major credit-rating agencies downgraded AIG. At issue were the soaring losses in its CDSs. The first big write-off came in the fourth quarter of 2007, when AIG reported an $11 billion charge. It was able to raise capital once, to repair the damage. But the losses kept growing. The moment the downgrade came, AIG was forced to come up with tens of billions of additional collateral immediately. This was on top of the billions it owed to its trading partners. It didn't have the money. The world's largest insurance company was bankrupt.

As soon as AIG went bankrupt, all those institutions which had hedged debt positions using AIG CDSs had to **mark down** the value of their assets, which at once **reduced their ability to lend**. The investment banks had **no ability to borrow**, as the collapse of the CDS market meant that no one was willing to insure their debt. The credit crunch had started in earnest.

**Exam focus point**

Make sure you read the article entitled 'Securitisation and tranching' on the ACCA's website.

> Dark pools are an 'alternative' trading system that allows participants to trade without displaying quotes publicly.

## 7.5.1 What is dark pool trading?

Dark pools are off-exchange facilities that allow trading of large blocks of shares. They allow brokers and fund managers to place and match large orders anonymously to avoid influencing the share price. Traders placing large orders on the transparent exchanges risk signaling that they are large buyers or sellers. Such signals could cause the markets to move against them and put the order at risk.

With dark pool trading, the transactions are only made public after the trades have been completed.

## 7.5.2 What proportion of trading takes place in dark pools?

The proportion of trading that takes place outside the regulated exchanges is difficult to estimate. The Securities and Exchange Commission in the US estimates that dark pools and other alternative platforms accounted for approximately 20% of trade volumes (SEC, 2015). However, in Asia stricter regulation and structural differences in the markets mean that dark pools do not pose such a large threat and account for only 1–3% of trades in the larger, more liquid markets.

## 7.5.3 Problems with dark pool trading

The main problem with dark pool trading is that the regulated exchanges do not know about the transactions taking place until the trades have been completed. As a result, the prices at which these trades are executed remain unknown until after the event.

Such a lack of information on significant trades makes the regulated exchanges less efficient. Although the prices in dark pools are based on those in the regulated exchanges, the dark pool trades do not contribute to the changes in prices, as their liquidity is not displayed. Dark pools also take trade away from the regulated exchanges, resulting in reduced transparency as fewer trades are publicly exposed. Such a practice could reduce liquidity in the regulated exchanges and hinder efficient price-setting.

Transactions in dark pools can almost be viewed as 'over the counter', as prices are not reported and financial risks are not effectively managed. There is the danger that such risks spread in a manner similar to those attached to CDSs and CDOs, which triggered the global financial crisis.

Dark pools and their lack of transparency defeat the purpose of fair and regulated markets with large numbers of participants and threaten the healthy and transparent development of these markets. They could lead to a two-tier system whereby the public would not have fair access to information regarding prices and volumes of shares that is available to dark pool participants.

There are also examples of misconduct by the operators of dark pools. For example, giving preferential access to their own share trading desk or secretly offering high speed traders special order types that gave them an unfair advantage over other subscribers (SEC, 2015).

# 7.6 Free movement of capital

## 7.6.1 Convergence of financial institutions

Traditionally, financial institutions were operating within clearly delineated boundaries. Banks were engaged in **deposit taking** and **loan provision**, **insurance companies** in the **transfer of risks**, **securities firms** and **investment banks** in the provision of **services** related to **capital markets**. The separation of activities was reflected in separate regulatory authorities. In the UK, for example, banks were regulated by the Bank of England, whereas insurance companies were regulated by the Department of Trade and Industry.

Similarly, in the US, the Glass-Steagall Act of 1933 barred banks, brokerages and insurance companies from entering each other's industries, and investment banking and commercial banking were separated.

In the UK, the Financial Services Act 1986 abolished the barriers between the various financial firms, allowing banks to enter the insurance and securities markets and creating a **single regulatory authority**. Similarly, in the US, the Financial Services Modernisation Act of 1999 also did away with restrictions on the integration of banking, insurance and stock trading.

The result of abolishing the barriers to entry in the various segments of the financial services industries has led to the creation of **financial conglomerates** with operations in **banking**, **securities** and **insurance**. The effect of this convergence is:

(a)   The creation of **economies of scale** as operations that were previously performed by different companies are now performed by one company.

(b)   The creation of **economies of scope** since one factor of production can be employed in the production of more than one product.

(c)   The **reduction of volatility of earnings**, since some of the earnings are fee-based and not influenced by the economic cycle.

(d)   The **saving** of **significant search costs for consumers** since they can buy all financial products from one source.

### 7.6.2 Financial reporting

All EU listed companies must use IFRS for their consolidated financial statements. Common accounting standards increase **transparency** and **comparability** for investors. This should lead to a more **efficient capital market**, much more transparency and greater cross-border investment, thereby promoting growth and employment in Europe. Making IFRS work in the EU will also allow greater access of EU companies to global capital markets since it will include removal of the reconciliation requirement to US GAAP for companies which list in the US.

### 7.6.3 Effect on the corporate sector

Globalisation and the single European currency have led to the restructuring of the global and European corporate sector, and the emergence of new companies. The raising of capital through **global equity** and **bond markets** has become commonplace and has made **cross-border mergers** as well as **foreign direct investment** easier. These developments can only favour those companies which may have found it difficult in the past to finance themselves, but which will now be able to raise equity more easily.

The ongoing integration process of the national stock exchanges has also been conducive to this development. Primary issues of European equities has been steadily increasing with whole new markets, such as the Neuer Markt in Frankfurt, becoming prominent internationally. In addition, a number of **Europe-wide equity indices** have been established, thereby contributing to the extension of the trading possibilities and the position-taking opportunities for institutional investors from many European countries. The elimination of exchange rate risks has also allowed many European institutional investors which were previously constrained to investing in the domestic market to invest in any European market, increasing the supply of capital.

Finally, alliances between stock exchanges also foster the integration of stock market infrastructures and trading platforms, creating more competition and making the European markets more resilient and fit for the global economy.

## 7.7 Money laundering legislation

**FAST FORWARD**

The growth of globalisation has created more opportunities for money laundering which governments and international bodies are trying to combat with legislation.

One of the side effects of globalisation and the free movement of capital has been the growth in **money laundering**.

**Money laundering** constitutes any financial transactions whose purpose is to conceal the identity of the parties to the transaction or to make the tracing of the money difficult.

**Money laundering** is used by organised crime and terrorist organisations but it is also used in order to avoid the payment of taxes or to distort accounting information. Money laundering involves therefore a number of agents and entities from criminals and terrorists to companies and corrupt officials or states as well as tax havens.

## 7.7.1 Risks associated with a company's products and services

Some businesses are at a higher risk than others of money laundering. For example, businesses dealing in luxury items of high value can be at risk of the products being resold through the black market or returned to the retailer in exchange for a legitimate cheque from them.

The increasing complexity of financial crime and its increase has prompted national governments and the EU to legislate and regulate the contact of transactions. The Third Money Laundering Directive of the EU was formally adopted on 26 October 2005 and came into force on 15 December 2007. Currently the Fourth Money Laundering Directive is in the process of being implemented across the EU.

At the same time the Financial Services Authority required that professionals who engage in the provision of financial services should warn the authorities when they discover that illegal transactions have taken place.

## 7.7.2 The effects of regulation

Regulations differ across various countries but it is common for companies to be required to assess the risk of money laundering in their business and take necessary action to alleviate this risk.

### Assessing risk – the risk-based approach

The risk-based approach consists of a number of steps:

- Identifying the money laundering risks that are relevant to the business.

- Carrying out a detailed risk assessment on such areas as customer behaviour and delivery channels.

- Designing and implementing controls to manage and reduce any identified risks.

- Monitor the effectiveness of these controls and make improvements where necessary.

- Maintain records of actions taken and reasons for these actions.

The time and cost of carrying out such assessments will depend on the size and complexity of the business but will require considerable effort to ensure compliance with regulations.

### Assessing your customer base

Businesses with certain types of customers are more at risk of money laundering activities and will therefore be required to take more stringent action to protect themselves. Types of customers that pose a risk include the following:

- New customers carrying out large, one-off transactions

- Customers who have been introduced to you by a third party who may not have assessed their risk potential thoroughly

- Customers who aren't local to your business

- Customers whose businesses handle large amounts of cash

Other customers who might pose a risk include those who are unwilling to provide identification and who enter into transactions that do not make commercial sense. Before companies commence business dealings with a customer, they should conduct suitable customer due diligence.

### Customer due diligence

This is an official term for taking steps to check that your customers are who they say they are. In practice, the best and easiest way to do this is to ask for official identification, such as a passport or driving licence, together with utility bills and bank statements. On a personal level, if you are trying to arrange a loan or open a bank account, it is very likely you will be asked to produce such identification.

If customers are acting on behalf of a third party, it is important to identify who the third party is.

### Applying customer due diligence

Businesses should apply customer due diligence whenever they feel it necessary but at least in any of the following circumstances.

(a) When establishing a business relationship. This is likely to be a relationship that will be ongoing, therefore it is important to establish identity and credibility at the start. You may have to establish such information as the source and origin of funds that your customer will be using, copies of recent and current financial statements and details of the customer's business or employment.

(b) When carrying out an 'occasional transaction' worth for example 10,000 euros (this relates to EU legislation) or more – that is, transactions that are not carried out within an ongoing business relationship. You should also look out for 'linked' transactions which are individual transactions of 10,000 euros or more that have been broken down into smaller, separate transactions to avoid due diligence checks.

(c) When you have doubts about identification information that you obtained previously.

(d) When the customer's circumstances change – for example, a change in the ownership of the customer's business and a significant change in the type of business activity of the customer.

### Ongoing monitoring of your business

It is important that you have an effective system of internal controls to protect your business from being used for money laundering. Staff should be suitably trained in the implementation of these internal controls and be alert to any potential issues. A specific member of staff should be nominated as the person to whom any suspicious activities should be reported.

Full documentation of anti money laundering policies and procedures should be kept and updated as appropriate. Staff should be kept fully informed of any changes.

### Maintaining full and up to date records

Businesses are generally required to keep full and up to date records for financial reporting and auditing purposes but these can also be used to demonstrate compliance with money laundering regulations. Such records will include receipts, invoices and customer correspondence. European money laundering regulations require that such information be kept for each customer for five years beginning on either the date a transaction is completed or the date a business relationship ends.

### Ownership

Businesses are often required to hold accurate information on the identity of  individuals who ultimately own or control the company (eg own more than 25% of a company's shares or voting rights). Where beneficial ownership is held through a trust, the trustees (or any individuals who control the activities of the trust) will be recorded as having the relevant interest.

## 7.7.3 The costs of compliance

All the activities listed above do not come cheaply, especially if policies and procedures are being established for the first time. In addition, regulations in the UK state that all accountants in public practice must be supervised and monitored in their compliance and must be registered with a supervisory body.

ACCA is one of the supervisory bodies and is responsible for monitoring its own members. However, such supervision comes at a cost and monitored firms are expected to pay a fee for this service.

# 8 Developments in international trade and finance

> The globalisation and integration of financial markets has contributed to expansion of international trade, but it has also created potentially more uncertainty for multinational companies.

The macroeconomic environment has a catalytic effect on business activities. A **stable macroeconomic environment** with **minimal exchange rate** and **interest rate fluctuations** allows businesses to plan their activities and to predict the key drivers of their value. An economic environment in which there is **uncertainty** about the cost of capital or currency rates is not conducive to long-term planning. In this section we review some developments that have recently taken place and which have an impact on multinational companies.

## 8.1 Trade and world deflation

Trade among nations is a common occurrence and normally benefits both the exporter and the importer. In many countries, international trade accounts for more than 20% of their national incomes. **Foreign trade** can usually be justified on the principle of **comparative advantage**. According to this economic principle, it is economically profitable for a country to specialise in the production of that commodity in which the producer country has the greater comparative advantage and to allow the other country to produce that commodity in which it has the lesser comparative disadvantage. We have already concluded in previous chapters that the risks of foreign trade increase as a company moves from exporting to direct foreign investment and when its activities are directed to less developed countries rather than to developed countries.

The most important application of the principle of **comparative advantage** has been the Chinese economy. China has exploited its comparative advantage stemming from low wages to dominate the production of labour-intensive products which, being produced at a fraction of the production cost in developed countries, has contributed to the worldwide low inflation regime of the last few years. The reduction of the cost has kept prices down and has increased consumer purchasing power worldwide.

## 8.2 Control of monetary policy

One of the most important developments in the macroeconomic environment has been the way monetary policy has been conducted in the advanced economies. Monetary policy has been assigned the task of controlling inflation and is largely outside the control of the national governments.

The **Bank of England** became independent of the Government in 1997 and sets interest rates so as to meet the inflationary target set out by the Government. Similarly, the **European Central Bank** sets the interest rates in the eurozone. The **independence of central banks** from government interference has given credibility to their policies and has stabilised the financial markets. This in turn has affected the expectations about inflation of market participants and has lowered inflation. A **low inflation environment** is conducive to **long-term planning** by business and **stimulates investment**.

## 8.3 Trade zones and international trade

The main obstacles to international trade are capital restrictions and tariffs imposed on imports as well as restrictions on capital mobility. Tariffs are usually imposed to provide revenue or to protect a home industry. The basic arguments for tariffs are:

(a)    To protect infant or key industries
(b)    To equalise costs of production between domestic and foreign producers
(c)    To protect domestic jobs
(d)    To prevent capital being moved to other countries

Other measures that have been used selectively to control imports are **import quotas** which set the maximum absolute amount of a particular commodity that can be imported. **Export subsidies** are also used to encourage exports of certain goods or to prevent discrimination against overseas exporters who sell in a foreign market at a world price lower than the domestic price. **Exchange controls** are also used to control the flow of international trade. Some controls are used to ration a country's scarce foreign exchange. Some countries use different exchange rates for different commodities to encourage or discourage imports.

However, in the last few years there has been an increasing realisation that **tariffs** deny individuals and nations the benefits of **greater productivity** and a higher standard of living and tariffs eliminate or reduce the advantages of specialisation and exchange among nations and prevent the best use of scarce world resources. The presence of tariffs also hinders the expansion of multinational companies and international trade and inhibits their growth and the benefits of consumers.

As a result of the growing movement towards freer trade which culminated with the creation of the World Trade Organization, many countries have come together to create free trade areas. The European Community was a free trade area, before it became the EU. The **North American Free Trade Area** is also a free trade area that was created by the US, Mexico and Canada in 1994. The members of the trade zone have established preferential tariff treatment for certain products traded between these countries, in the form of reduced or zero rate tariffs. By eliminating **trade barriers**, the **trade zone** facilitates **cross-border movement** of **goods and services**, increases **investment opportunities**, promotes fair competition and enforces **intellectual property rights** in the three countries.

## 8.4 Trade financing

A significant development which has boosted international trade is that **trade financing** has become easier to be obtained by companies. Financing sources for international trade transactions include **commercial bank loans** within the host country and loans from **international lending agencies**. Foreign banks can also be used to **discount trade bills** to finance short-term financing. Eurodollar financing is another method for providing foreign financing. A **Eurodollar** is a **dollar deposit** held in a bank outside the US. An active market exists for these deposits. Banks use Eurodollars to make dollar loans to borrowers; the interest rate is usually in excess of the deposit rate. Such loans are usually in very large amounts, are short-term working capital loans, and are unsecured. US firms frequently arrange for lines of credit and revolving credits from Eurodollar banks. No compensating balances are usually required.

The eurobond market is widely used for long-term funds for multinational US companies. A Eurobond is a long-term security issued by an internationally recognised borrower in several countries simultaneously. The bonds are denominated in a single currency. Such bonds are usually fixed income bonds; some bonds are convertible into common stock.

Many countries have organised **development banks** that provide intermediate and long-term loans for private enterprises. Such loans are made to provide **economic development** within a country.

## 8.5 Developments in the non-market environment

We have discussed so far the impact of developments in financial markets and how they may facilitate the funding of investment strategies and the management of risks. These are all the benign effect of globalisation on multinational companies. However, globalisation may also create more uncertainty. This is created in turn by changes in the non-market environments in which multinational companies operate.

The **non-market environments** consist of the **social**, **political** and **legal arrangements** that determine firms' interactions outside of, and in conjunction with, markets. These **non-market environments** are shaped by both **global** and **country-specific factors** and the successful implementation of a multi-domestic strategy involves issue-specific action plans that are tailored to the configuration of institutions and interests in individual countries.

## 8.5.1 Regulation

Many governments have responded to **globalisation** and the loss of control through **tariffs** and other methods by introducing regulation. For example, the wave of **cross-border mergers** and acquisitions of the 1990s, an integral component of globalisation, have created oligopolies in many industries. Major industries (such as automobiles, petroleum exploration, semiconductors, consumer electronics, insurance, banking) now have eight to ten key players that account for 70-80% of the global output. Not surprisingly, then, there is an increased level of **anti-trust scrutiny** especially in the US and the EU, for example the scrutiny of the AB InBev-SABMiller merger. Thus anti-trust actions become non-tariff barriers or cartel-sponsored private barriers become obstacles to trade and investment flows; key issues are whether, when and how to establish an international regime (or modify an extant one) on competition policy. Needless to say, this has an immense bearing on multinational corporations' (MNCs') non-market environments.

Globalisation also creates incentives for governments to intervene in favour of domestic MNCs in terms of 'macroeconomic' and 'macro-structural' policies. It was argued in the 1980s that in industries marked by **imperfect competition**, **high positive externalities** and **supernormal profits** (characteristics of the new oligopolies as well), firms are often locked in a zero-sum game, and governments have incentives to intervene in favour of domestic firms. Boundaries between domestic and international are blurred because domestic interventions can tilt the scale in favour of domestic firms in global markets. Arguably, given the fast pace of product obsolescence, a winner takes all situation is developing in many industries. Consequently, MNCs have incentives to emerge as winners, if not through market processes then through non-market strategies. Thus, globalisation processes create incentives for MNCs to enlist support from their home governments and create an obligation for governments to support them.

## 8.5.2 Pressure groups

Although domestic governments may be willing to support MNCs, a major threat has emerged from **globally networked pressure groups**, which influence the public and put pressure on governments to take measures against MNCs.

### Case Study

Greenpeace, the environmental pressure group, has been responsible for numerous protests against environmentally unfriendly corporate practices. For example, in 2015, Greenpeace and its supporters were partly responsible for Shell agreeing to stop oil exploration in the Arctic region. Greenpeace had been protesting against the company's attempts to explore for fossil fuels off the coast of Alaska, including parking a **double-decker bus-sized polar bear puppet** outside the company's London HQ.

Environmentalists claimed Shell had also suffered huge reputational damage as a result of its activity in the Arctic, with protests in the US and around the world, including activists scaling the Shard in London.

Greenpeace said more than seven million people signed up to the Save The Arctic campaign worldwide, while celebrities such as actors John Hurt, Peter Capaldi and Monty Python star Terry Gilliam have spoken out against drilling in the region.

*(Source: BBC website, October 2015)*

## 8.5.3 Political risks

Because globalisation leads to a high degree of cross-border economic linkages, MNCs become vulnerable to political developments in their home and host countries. Citizen groups in home/host countries can impact MNCs' strategies in yet another country.

In 2015, Santander agreed to stop using an Asian pulp paper company because of its destruction of the Indonesian rainforest.

The message is clear: if MNCs invest in multiple markets, they need to deal with citizen groups in multiple countries. And this would require MNCs to integrate their supranational and multi-domestic non-market strategies.

# Chapter Roundup

- **Multinational enterprises** undertake **foreign direct investment (FDI)** for reasons including obtaining **cost and revenue advantages**, **tax considerations** and **process specialisation**.

- **FDI** can stimulate economic activity in the host country, but it can also lead to **a loss of political and economic sovereignty**.

- There are many strategic reasons for engaging in foreign investment, which include seeking **new markets** for goods, **new sources of raw materials, production efficiency**, expertise and **political safety**.

- Commonly used means to establish an **interest abroad** include:

    - Joint ventures
    - Licensing agreements
    - Management contracts
    - Branches
    - Subsidiaries

- **World output** of **goods** and **services** will increase if countries specialise in the production of goods/services in which they have a **comparative advantage** and **trade** to obtain other goods and services.

- Business enterprises are now also becoming increasingly 'internationalised' by the development of **multinational activities** beyond pure import and export trade.

- Justifications for **protection** include prevention of the import of cheap goods and dumping, and protection of infant or declining industries.

- **Free trade** can lead to greater competition and efficiency, and achieve better economic growth worldwide.

- The **World Trade Organization** (WTO) is a global international organisation dealing with the rules of trade between nations.

- The International Monetary Fund (IMF) and the World Bank are closely related. Both were set up in 1944 as United Nation's agencies to establish a stable global economic framework.

    The IMF was set up partly with the role of providing finance for any countries with temporary balance of payments deficits.

    The World Bank aims to reduce poverty and to support economic development.

- The globalisation of the financial markets has facilitated the transfer of funds to emerging markets but it has contributed to financial instability.

- Developments in international financial markets have facilitated the growth in trade and the funding of overseas expansion strategies and have opened up more opportunities for investors. The main developments are:

    - The global financial crisis
    - Deep pool trading systems
    - The removal of barriers to the free movement of capital
    - International regulations on money laundering

- A credit crunch is a crisis caused by banks being too nervous to lend money to customers or to each other. When they do lend, they will charge higher rates of interest to cover their risk.

- Securitisation is the process of converting illiquid assets into marketable asset-backed securities. The development of securitisation has led to disintermediation and a reduction in the role of financial intermediaries, as borrowers can reach lenders directly. A **tranche** is a slice of a security (typically a bond or other credit-linked security) which is funded by investors who assume different risk levels within the liability structure of that security.

- A credit default swap is a specific type of counterparty agreement which allows the transfer of third-party credit risk from one party to the other.

- Dark pools are an 'alternative' trading system that allows participants to trade without displaying quotes publicly.

- The growth of globalisation has created more opportunities for money laundering which governments and international bodies are trying to combat with legislation.

- The globalisation and integration of financial markets has contributed to expansion of international trade, but it has also created potentially more uncertainty for multinational companies.

# Quick Quiz

1 Define a multinational enterprise.

2 What is meant by the law of comparative advantage?

3 What is meant by:
   (a) A free trade area?
   (b) A customs union?
   (c) A common market?

4 How do deflationary measures help to eliminate a balance of payments deficit?

5 By what methods do governments try to combat money laundering?

# Answers to Quick Quiz

1   A multinational enterprise is one which has a physical presence or property interests in more than one country.

2   The law of comparative advantage or comparative costs states that two countries can gain from trade when each specialises in the industries in which it has the lowest opportunity costs.

3   A free trade area exists when there is no restriction on trade between countries. This is extended into a customs union when common external tariffs are levied on imports from non-member countries. A common market adds free movement of the factors of production, including labour, and may harmonise economic policy.

4   Domestic deflation cuts demand, including demand for imports. Industry is therefore encouraged to switch to export markets.

5   (a)   Legislation that makes it more difficult to happen
    (b)   Asking professionals to report suspect transactions

Now try the questions below from the Practice Question Bank

| Number | Level | Marks | Time |
|--------|-------|-------|------|
| 6 | Introductory | 10 | 20 mins |

# Planning in a multinational environment

## Introduction

In this chapter we continue to look at the international environment within which companies need to make financial decisions. We also look at strategic decision making in a multinational company and the agency issues arising between subsidiaries and the parent company.

# Study guide

| | | Intellectual level |
|---|---|---|
| A5 | **The Strategic business and financial planning for multinational organisations** | |
| (a) | Advise on the development of a financial planning framework for a multinational taking into account: | 3 |
| | (i) Compliance with national governance requirements (for example, the London Stock Exchange admission requirements) | |
| | (ii) The mobility of capital across borders and national limitations on remittances and transfer pricing | |
| | (iii) The pattern of economic and other risk exposures in the different national markets | |
| | (iv) Agency issues in the central co-ordination of overseas operations and the balancing of local financial autonomy with effective central control | |
| A6 | **Dividend policy in multinationals and transfer pricing** | |
| (a) | Determine a corporation's dividend capacity and its policy given: | 3 |
| | (i) The corporation's short- and long-term reinvestment strategy | |
| | (ii) The impact of any other capital reconstruction programmes such as share repurchase agreements and new capital issues on free cash flow to equity | |
| | (iii) The availability and timing of central remittances | |
| | (iv) The corporate tax regime within the host jurisdiction | |
| (b) | Advise, in the context of a specified capital investment programme, on an organisation's current and projected dividend capacity. | 3 |
| (c) | Develop organisational policy on the transfer pricing of goods and services across international borders and be able to determine the most appropriate transfer pricing strategy in a given situation reflecting local regulations and tax regimes. | 3 |

# 1 Framework for financial planning in multinationals

As part of the fulfilment of the performance objective 'evaluate investment and financing decisions' you are expected to be able to identify and apply different finance options to single and combined entities in domestic and multinational business markets. This section looks at the financing options available to multinationals which you can put to good use if you work in such an environment.

**FAST FORWARD**

**Multinational companies** need to develop a **financial planning framework** in order to make sure that the strategic objectives and competitive advantages are realised. Such a financial **planning framework** will include ways of raising **capital** and **risks** related to overseas operations and the **repatriation of profits.**

## 1.1 Financing an overseas subsidiary

Once the decision is taken by a multinational company to start overseas operations in any of the forms that have been discussed in the previous section, there is a need to decide on the source of funds for the proposed expansion. There are some differences in methods of financing the **parent company** itself, and the **foreign subsidiaries**. The parent company itself is more likely than companies which have no foreign interests to raise finance in a foreign currency, or in its home currency from foreign sources.

The **need to finance a foreign subsidiary** raises the following questions:

(a) How much **equity capital** should the parent company put into the subsidiary?

(b) Should the subsidiary be allowed to **retain a large proportion** of its profits, to build up its equity reserves, or not?

(c) Should the parent company hold **100% of the equity** of the subsidiary, or should it try to create a minority shareholding, perhaps by floating the subsidiary on the country's domestic stock exchange?

(d) Should the subsidiary be encouraged to **borrow** as much **long-term debt** as it can, for example by raising large bank loans? If so, should the loans be in the domestic currency of the subsidiary's country, or should it try to raise a foreign currency loan?

(e) Should the subsidiary be listed on the local stock exchange, raising funds from the local equity markets?

(f) Should the subsidiary be encouraged to minimise its working capital investment by relying heavily on trade credit?

The **method of financing** a subsidiary will give some indication of the **nature and length of time** of the investment that the parent company is prepared to make. A sizeable equity investment (or long-term loans from the parent company to the subsidiary) would indicate a long-term investment by the parent company.

## 1.2 Choice of finance for an overseas investment

The choice of the source of funds will depend on:

(a) The **local finance costs**, and any subsidies which may be available

(b) **Taxation systems** of the countries in which the subsidiary is operating; different tax rates can favour borrowing in high tax regimes, and no borrowing elsewhere

(c) Any **restrictions on dividend remittances**

(d) The possibility of **flexibility in repayments** which may arise from the parent/subsidiary relationship

Tax-saving opportunities may be maximised by **structuring the group** and its subsidiaries in such a way as to **take the best advantage** of the different local tax systems.

Because subsidiaries may be operating with a guarantee from the parent company, different gearing structures may be possible. Thus, a subsidiary may be able to operate with a higher level of debt that would be acceptable for the group as a whole.

Parent companies should also consider the following factors;

(a) **Reduced systematic risk.** There may be a small incremental reduction in systematic risk from investing abroad due to the segmentation of capital markets.

(b) **Access to capital.** Obtaining capital from foreign markets may increase liquidity, lower costs and make it easier to maintain optimum gearing.

(c) **Agency costs.** These may be higher due to political risk, market imperfections and complexity, leading to a higher cost of capital.

## 1.3 Dealing with currency risk

To reduce or eliminate the currency risk of an overseas investment, a company might **finance** it with **funds** in the **same currency** as the investment. The advantages of borrowing in the same currency as an investment are as follows:

(a) Assets and liabilities in the same currency can be **matched**, thus avoiding exchange losses on conversion in the group's annual accounts.

(b) **Revenues** in the foreign currency can be used to **repay borrowings** in the same currency, thus eliminating losses due to fluctuating exchange rates.

**Exam focus point** | You must be prepared to answer questions about various methods of financing an overseas subsidiary.

# 2 International debt finance

**FAST FORWARD**

Multinational companies will have access to international debt, such as **eurobonds**.

**PER alert**

As part of the fulfilment of the performance objective 'evaluate potential business/investment opportunities and the required finance options' you are expected to be able to identify and apply different finance options to single and combined entities in domestic and multinational business markets. This section looks at the financing options available to multinationals which you can put to good use if you work in such an environment.

## 2.1 International borrowing

Borrowing markets are becoming increasingly internationalised, particularly for larger companies. Companies are able to borrow long-term funds on the **eurocurrency (money) markets** and on the markets for **eurobonds**. These markets are collectively called 'euromarkets'. Large companies can also borrow on the **syndicated loan market** where a syndicate of banks provides medium- to long-term currency loans.

If a company is receiving income in a foreign currency or has a long-term investment overseas, it can try to **limit the risk** of adverse exchange rate movements by **matching**. It can take out a long-term loan and use the foreign currency receipts to repay the loan.

## 2.2 Eurocurrency markets

**Key terms**

**Eurocurrency** is currency which is held by individuals and institutions outside the country of issue of that currency.

**Eurodollars** are US dollars deposited with, or borrowed from, a bank outside the US.

A UK company might borrow money from a bank or from the investing public, in sterling. However, it might also borrow in a foreign currency, especially if it trades abroad, or if it already has assets or liabilities abroad denominated in a foreign currency. When a company borrows in a foreign currency, the loan is known as a **eurocurrency loan**. (As with euro-equity, it is not only the euro that is involved, and so the 'euro-' prefix is a misnomer.) Banks involved in the eurocurrency market are **not subject to central bank reserve requirements** or regulations in respect of their involvement.

The eurocurrency markets involve the **depositing of funds** with a **bank outside the country** of the currency in which the funds are denominated and **relending these funds for a fairly short term**, typically three months, normally at a floating rate of interest. **Eurocredits** are medium- to long-term international bank loans which may be arranged by individual banks or by **syndicates of banks**. Syndication of loans increases the amounts available to hundreds of millions, while reducing the exposure of individual banks.

## 2.3 Eurobonds

**Key term**

A **eurobond** is a bond sold outside the jurisdiction of the country in whose currency the bond is denominated.
*(OT 2005)*

In recent years, a strong market has built up which allows very large companies to borrow in this way, long term or short term. Again, the market is not subject to national regulations.

Eurobonds are **long-term loans raised by international companies** or other institutions and **sold to investors in several countries** at the same time. Eurobonds are normally repaid after 5 to 15 years, and are for major amounts of capital ie $10m or more.

**Exam focus point**

Don't make the common mistake of thinking that eurobonds are issued in Europe or only denominated in euros.

### 2.3.1 How are eurobonds issued?

**Step 1**  A lead manager is appointed from a major merchant bank; the lead manager liaises with the credit rating agencies and organises a **credit rating** of the eurobond.

**Step 2**  The lead manager organises an **underwriting syndicate** (of other merchant banks) who agree the terms of the bond (eg interest rate, maturity date) and buy the bond.

**Step 3**  The underwriting syndicate then organise the sale of the bond; this normally involves **placing** the bond with **institutional investors**.

### 2.3.2 Advantages of eurobonds

(a)  Eurobonds are '**bearer instruments**', which means that the owner does not have to declare their identity.

(b)  Interest is paid gross and this has meant that eurobonds have been used by investors to avoid tax.

(c)  Eurobonds create a liability in a foreign currency to **match** against a foreign currency asset.

(d)  They are often **cheaper** than a foreign currency bank loan because they can be sold on by the investor, who will therefore accept a lower yield in return for this greater liquidity.

(e)  They are also extremely **flexible**. Most eurobonds are fixed rate but they can be floating rate or linked to the financial success of the company.

(f)  They are typically issued by companies with excellent credit ratings and are normally **unsecured**, which makes it easier for companies to raise debt finance in the future.

(g)  Eurobond issues are not normally advertised because they are **placed** with institutional investors and this reduces issue costs.

### 2.3.3 Disadvantages of eurobonds

Like any form of debt finance, there will be **issue costs** to consider (approximately 2% of funds raised in the case of eurobonds) and there may also be problems if gearing levels are too high.

A borrower contemplating a eurobond issue must consider the **foreign exchange risk** of a long-term foreign currency loan. If the money is to be used to purchase assets which will earn revenue in a currency different to that of the bond issue, the borrower will run the risk of exchange losses if the currency of the loan strengthens against the currency of the revenues out of which the bond (and interest) must be repaid.

# 3 Compliance with listing requirements

**FAST FORWARD**  When a company decides to raise funds from the local equity markets, the company must comply with the requirements of the local exchanges for listing.

## 3.1 Listing requirements for the London Stock Exchange

The listing requirements for the London Stock Exchange are:

### 3.1.1 Track record requirements

The track record requirements are:

(a)  At least 75% of the entity's business must be supported by a revenue earnings record for the three-year period. The UK listing authority has the discretion to allow a shorter period in certain circumstances.

(b)  The company must report significant acquisitions in the three years running up to the flotation.

### 3.1.2 Market capitalisation

Market capitalisation and share in public hands:

(a)   At least £700,000 for shares at the time of listing
(b)   At least 25% of shares should be in public hands

### 3.1.3 Future prospects

The company must show that it has enough working capital for its current needs and for at least the next 12 months.

The company must be able to carry on its business independently and at arm's length from any shareholders with economic interest.

A general description of the future plans and prospects must be given.

If the company gives an optional profit forecast in the document or has already given one publicly, a report will be required from the sponsor and the Reporting Accountant.

### 3.1.4 Audited historical financial information

This must cover the latest three full years and any published later interim period.

If latest audited financial data is more than six months old, interim audited financial information is required.

### 3.1.5 Corporate governance

Although the UK corporate governance rules do not apply to non-UK companies, investors would expect a similar standard, and an explanation for any differences. UK companies are expected to:

(a)   Split the roles of chairman and CEO

(b)   Except for smaller companies (below FTSE 350), at least half of the board, excluding the chairman, should comprise independent non-executive directors; smaller companies should have at least two independent non-executive directors

(c)   Have an independent audit committee, a remuneration committee and a nomination committee

(d)   Provide evidence of a high standard of financial controls and accounting systems

### 3.1.6 Acceptable jurisdiction and accounting standards

The company must be properly incorporated.

International Financial Reporting Standards and equivalent accounting standards are acceptable.

### 3.1.7 Other considerations

Sponsors/underwriters usually recommend that existing shareholders should be barred from selling their shares for a period after initial listing offering of their shares.

The sponsor will need to make sure, through due and careful enquiry, that the applicant has established procedures that enable it to comply with the listing rules and disclosure rules, as well having established procedures which provide a reasonable basis for the applicant to make proper judgements on an ongoing basis as to its financial position and prospects.

# 4 Capital mobility and blocked funds

**FAST FORWARD**

Multinationals can take various measures to combat the risks of political **interference** or **turbulence**, including agreements with governments, insurance, and location elsewhere of key parts of the production process.

Multinationals can **counter exchange controls** by management charges or royalties.

## 4.1 Blocked funds

**Exchange controls** block the flow of foreign exchange into and out of a country, usually to defend the local currency or to protect reserves of foreign currencies. Exchange controls are generally more restrictive in developing and less developed countries, although some still exist in developed countries. Typically, a government might enforce regulations:

(a) **Rationing the supply of foreign exchange**. Anyone wishing to make payments abroad in a foreign currency will be restricted by the limited supply, which stops them from buying as much as they want from abroad.

(b) **Restricting the types of transaction** for which payments abroad are allowed. This could be by suspending or banning the payment of dividends to foreign shareholders, such as parent companies in multinationals, who will then have the problem of **blocked funds**.

## 4.2 Dealing with blocked funds

Ways of overcoming blocked funds include the following:

(a) The parent company could **sell goods or services** to the subsidiary and obtain payment. The amount of this payment will depend on the volume of sales and also on the transfer price for the sales.

(b) A parent company which grants a subsidiary the right to make goods protected by patents can charge a **royalty** on any goods that the subsidiary sells. The size of any royalty can be adjusted to suit the wishes of the parent company's management.

(c) If the parent company makes a **loan** to a subsidiary, it can set the interest rate high or low, thereby affecting the profits of both companies. A high rate of interest on a loan, for example, would improve the parent company's profits to the detriment of the subsidiary's profits.

(d) **Management charges** may be levied by the parent company for costs incurred in the management of international operations.

# 5 Risk exposure

> **FAST FORWARD**
>
> The methods of financing overseas subsidiaries will depend on the **length of investment period** envisaged, as well as the **local finance costs**, **taxation systems** and **restrictions on dividend remittances**.

## 5.1 Political risks for multinationals

**Key term**

> **Political risk** is the risk that political action will affect the position and value of a company.

When a multinational company invests in another country by setting up a subsidiary, it may face a **political risk** of action by that country's government which restricts the multinational's freedom.

If a government tries to prevent the exploitation of its country by multinationals, it may take various measures.

(a) Import **quotas** could be used to limit the quantities of goods that a subsidiary can buy from its parent company and import for resale in its domestic markets.

(b) Import **tariffs** could make imports (such as from parent companies) more expensive and domestically produced goods therefore more competitive.

(c) Legal standards of safety or quality (**non-tariff barriers**) could be imposed on imported goods to prevent multinationals from selling goods through a subsidiary which have been banned as dangerous in other countries.

(d) **Exchange control regulations** could be applied (see below).

(e) A government could **restrict** the ability of foreign companies to buy domestic companies, especially those that operate in politically sensitive industries, such as defence contracting, communications and energy supply.

(f) A government could **nationalise** foreign-owned companies and their assets (with or without compensation to the parent company).

(g) A government could insist on a **minimum shareholding** in companies by residents. This would force a multinational to offer some of the equity in a subsidiary to investors in the country where the subsidiary operates.

## 5.2 Assessment of political risk

In addition to the factors mentioned above, **micro factors** (factors only affecting the company or the industry in which it invests) may be more significant than macro factors, particularly in such companies as hi-tech organisations.

Measurement is often by **subjective weighting** of these factors. Macro analysis may involve use of measures such as those developed by euromoney or the Economist Intelligence Unit. Micro analysis may be more problematic; specially tailored consultancy reports, visits to the country or drawing on the experience of those who know the country may be needed.

## 5.3 Dealing with political risks

There are various strategies that multinational companies can adopt to limit the effects of political risk.

### 5.3.1 Negotiations with host government

The aim of these negotiations is generally to obtain a **concession agreement**. This would cover matters such as the transfer of capital, remittances and products, access to local finance, government intervention and taxation, and transfer pricing.

### 5.3.2 Insurance

In the UK, the Export Credits Guarantee Department provides **protection against various threats**, including nationalisation, currency conversion problems, war and revolution.

### 5.3.3 Production strategies

It may be necessary to strike a balance between **contracting out to local sources** (thus losing control) and **producing directly** (which increases the investment and therefore the potential loss). Alternatively, it may be better to locate key parts of the production process or the distribution channels abroad. Control of patents is another possibility, since these can be enforced internationally.

### 5.3.4 Contacts with markets

Multinationals may have **contacts with customers** which interventionist governments cannot obtain.

### 5.3.5 Financial management

If a multinational obtains funds in local investment markets, these may be on terms that are **less favourable** than on markets abroad, but would mean that local institutions suffered if the local Government intervened. However, governments often do limit the ability of multinationals to obtain funds locally.

Alternatively guarantees can be obtained from the Government for the investment that can be enforced by the multinational if the Government takes action.

### 5.3.6 Management structure

Possible methods include **joint ventures** or **ceding control** to local investors and obtaining profits by a management contract.

If governments do intervene, multinationals may have to make use of the advantages they hold or threaten withdrawal. The threat of expropriation may be reduced by negotiation or legal threats.

# 6 Litigation risks

**FAST FORWARD**

**Litigation risks** can be reduced by keeping abreast of changes, acting as a good corporate citizen and lobbying.

## 6.1 Legal impacts

Companies may face government legislation or action in any jurisdiction that extends over its whole range of activities. Important areas may include:

(a) **Export and import controls** for political, environmental, or health and safety reasons. Such controls may not be overt but instead take the form of bureaucratic procedures designed to discourage international trade or protect home producers.

(b) **Favourable trade status** for particular countries, eg EU membership, former Commonwealth countries.

(c) **Monopolies and mergers legislation**, which may be interpreted not only within a country but also across nations. Thus the acquisition of a company in country A, by company B, which both sell in country C may be seen as a monopolistic restraint of trade.

(d) **Law of ownership**. Especially in developing countries, there may be legislation requiring local majority ownership of a firm or its subsidiary in that country, for example.

(e) **Acceptance of international trademark, copyright and patent conventions**. Not all countries recognise such international conventions.

(f) Determination of minimum **technical standards** that the goods must meet eg noise levels and contents.

(g) **Standardisation measures**, such as packaging sizes.

(h) **Pricing regulations**, including credit (eg some countries require importers to deposit payment in advance and may require the price to be no lower than those of domestic competitors).

(i) **Restrictions on promotional messages**, methods and media.

(j) **Product liability**. Different countries have different rules regarding product liability (ie the manufacturer's/retailer's responsibility for defects in the product sold and/or injury caused). US juries are notoriously generous in this respect.

Bear in mind that organisations may also face legal risks from lack of legislation (or lack of enforcement of legislation) designed to protect them.

## 6.2 Dealing with legal risks

### 6.2.1 Consequences of non-compliance

Businesses that fail to comply with the law run the risk of **legal penalties** and accompanying **bad publicity**. Companies may also be forced into legal action to counter claims of allegedly bad practice that is not actually illegal.

The issues of legal standards and costs have very significant implications for companies that trade internationally. Companies that meet a strict set of standards in one country may face accusations of **hypocrisy** if their practices are laxer elsewhere. Ultimately higher costs of compliance as well as costs of labour may mean that companies **relocate** to countries where costs and regulatory burdens are lower.

### 6.2.2 The legislative process

Policy in many areas only changes slowly over time. However, industries and organisations must be alert for **likely changes in policy**.

Businesses also need to consider the impact of changes in how powers are **devolved** outside central government. In the US, State legislatures have been described as 'the forum for the ideas of the nation'. Directly elected mayors also wield considerable power in major cities.

### 6.2.3 Good citizenship

One aspect of minimising problems from governmental intervention is social and commercial good citizenship, **complying with best practice** and being responsive to **ethical concerns**. Often what is considered good practice at present is likely to acquire some regulatory force in the future. In addition, compliance with voluntary codes, particularly those relating to best practice or relations with consumers, can be **marketed positively**.

### 6.2.4 Other steps

Companies may wish to take all possible steps to avoid the bad publicity resulting from a court action. This includes implementing systems to make sure that the company **keeps abreast** of **changes in the law**, and staff are kept fully informed. Internal procedures may be designed to minimise the risks from legal action, for example **human resource policies** that minimise the chances of the company suffering an adverse judgement in a case brought by a disgruntled ex-employee. Contracts may be drawn up requiring **binding arbitration** in the case of disputes.

Of course, compliance with legislation may involve **extra costs**, including the extra procedures and investment necessary to conform to safety standards, staff training costs and legal costs. However, these costs may also act as a **significant barrier to entry**, benefiting companies that are already in the industry.

# 7 Cultural risks

**FAST FORWARD**

> **Cultural risks** affect the products and services produced and the way organisations are managed and staffed. Businesses should take cultural issues into account when deciding where to sell abroad, and how much to **centralise** activities.

## 7.1 Challenges of different cultures

Where a business trades with, or invests in, a foreign country additional uncertainty is introduced by the existence of different customs, laws and language. Communication between parties can be hindered and potential deals put into jeopardy by ignorance of the expected manner in which such transactions should be conducted.

The following areas may be particularly important:

(a) The **cultures and practices of customers** and consumers in individual markets

(b) The **media and distribution systems** in overseas markets

(c) The **different ways of doing business** (eg it is reputed that Japanese companies are concerned to avoid excessive legalism) in overseas markets

(d) The degree to which **national cultural differences matter** for the product concerned (a great deal for some consumer products, eg washing machines where some countries prefer front-loading machines and others prefer top-loading machines, but less so for products such as gas turbines)

(e) The degree to which a firm can use its own 'national culture' as a selling point

## 7.2 Dealing with cultural risk

### 7.2.1 Deciding which markets to enter

Making the right choices about which markets to enter is a key element in dealing with cultural risk. When deciding what types of country it should enter (in terms of environmental factors, economic development, language used, cultural similarities and so on), the major criteria for this decision should be as follows:

(a) **Market attractiveness**. This concerns such indicators as GNP/head and forecast demand.

(b) **Competitive advantage**. This is principally dependent on prior experience in similar markets, language and cultural understanding.

(c) **Risk**. This involves an analysis of political stability, the possibility of government intervention and similar external influences.

Some products are extremely sensitive to the **environmental differences** which bring about the need for adaptation; others are not at all sensitive to these differences, in which case standardisation is possible.

| Environmentally sensitive | Environmentally insensitive |
|---|---|
| Adaptation necessary | Standardisation possible |
| • Fashion clothes <br> • Convenience foods | • Industrial and agricultural products <br> • World market products, eg jeans |

### 7.2.2 Use of control systems

Local conditions and the scale of operations will influence the organisational structure of companies trading internationally. Conglomerates with widely differing product groups may organise globally by product, with each operating division having its own geographical structure suited to its own needs.

Companies with more integrated operations may prefer their top-level structure to be broken down **geographically**, with product management conducted locally.

Very large and complex companies may be organised as a **heterarchy**, an organic structure with significant local control.

(a) **Some headquarters functions are diffused geographically**. For example, R&D might be in the UK, marketing in the US. Some central functions might be split up: many firms are experimenting with having several centres for R&D.

(b) **Subsidiary managers have a strategic role for the corporation as a whole** (eg through bargaining and coalition forming).

(c) **Co-ordination is achieved through corporate culture and shared values** rather than a formal hierarchy. Employees with long experience might have worked in a number of different product divisions.

(d) **Alliances** can be formed with other company parts and other firms, perhaps in joint ventures or consortia.

### 7.2.3 Management of human resources

The balance between local and expatriate staff must be managed. There are a number of influences:

• The availability of technical skills such as financial management
• The need for control
• The importance of product and company experience
• The need to provide promotion opportunities
• Costs associated with expatriates such as travel and higher salaries
• Cultural factors

For an international company, which has to think globally as well as act locally, there are a number of problems:

- Do you employ mainly **expatriate staff** to control local operations?
- Do you employ **local managers**, with the possible loss of central control?
- Is there such a thing as the **global manager**, equally at home in different cultures?

Expatriate staff are sometimes favoured over local staff.

(a)     Poor **educational opportunities** in the market may require the import of skilled technicians and managers. For example, expatriates have been needed in many Western firms' operations in Russia and Eastern Europe, simply because they understand the importance of profit.

(b)     Some senior managers believe that a business run by expatriates is easier to **control** than one run by local staff.

(c)     Expatriates might be better able than locals to **communicate** with the corporate centre.

(d)     The expatriate may **know more about the firm** overall, which is especially important if they are fronting a sales office.

The use of expatriates in overseas markets has certain disadvantages.

(a)     They **cost** more (eg subsidised housing, school fees).

(b)     **Culture shock**. The expatriate may fail to adjust to the culture (eg by associating only with other expatriates). This is likely to lead to poor management effectiveness, especially if the business requires personal contact.

(c)     A substantial training programme might be needed.

  (i)     **Basic facts** about the country will be given with basic language training, and some briefings about cultural differences.

  (ii)    **Immersion training** involves detailed language and cultural training and simulation of field social and business experiences. This is necessary to obtain an intellectual understanding and practical awareness of the culture.

Employing local managers raises the following issues:

(a)     A **glass ceiling** might exist in some companies. Talented local managers may not make it to board level if most members of the board are drawn from one country.

(b)     In some cases, it may be hard for locals to **assimilate** into the **corporate culture**, and this might lead to communication problems.

(c)     Locals will **have greater knowledge of the country**, but may find it difficult to understand the wider corporate picture.

The following issues may also be important:

(a)     **Recruitment and training**. In countries with low levels of literacy, more effort might need to be spent on basic training.

(b)     **Career management**. Can overseas staff realistically expect promotion to the firm's highest levels if they do well?

(c)     **Appraisal schemes**. These can be a minefield at the best of times, and the possibilities for communications failure are endless. For example, in some cultures, an appraisal is a two-way discussion whereas in others arguing back might be considered a sign of insubordination.

(d)     Problems associated with the **status of women**.

(e)     **Communications**. Human resources management tries to mobilise employees' commitment to the goals of the organisation. In far-flung global firms, the normal panoply of staff newsletters and team briefings may be hard to institute but are vital. Time differences also make communication difficult.

**Agency issues** can be observed in all types and at all levels of organisations, for example between managers at headquarters and managers of subsidiaries. These issues can be addressed by a bundle of corporate governance mechanisms.

## 8.1 Agency problems in multinational companies

We have already studied in Chapter 3 of this Text the **agency problem** between **shareholders** and **managers**. However, these are not the only kinds of dyadic agency relationships. In fact, agency relationships are fairly general and can be observed in all types and levels of organisations. For example, **agency relationships** exist between the CEOs of conglomerates (the principals) and the strategic business unit (SBU) managers that report to these CEOs (agents). The interests of the individual SBU managers may be **incongruent** not only with the interests of the CEOs but also with those of the other SBU managers. Each SBU manager may try to make sure their unit gets access to **critical resources** and achieves the **best performance** at the expense of the performance of other SBUs and the organisation as a whole.

Similarly, **agency relationships** exist between the **managers** at the **headquarters** of **multinational corporations (principals)** and the managers that run the **subsidiaries** of **multinational corporations (agents)**. The **agency relationships** are created between the headquarters and subsidiaries of multinational corporations because the interests of the managers at the headquarters who are responsible for the performance of the whole organisation can be considerably different from the interests of the managers that run the subsidiaries.

The incongruence of interests between the multinationals' headquarters and subsidiaries can arise not only due to concerns that can be seen in any parent-subsidiary relationship but also due to the fact that the multinationals' headquarters and subsidiaries operate in different cultures and have divergent backgrounds.

Finally, similar to what we observe in shareholder-manager relationships, the subsidiary managers in the headquarters-subsidiary relationships are monitored and bonded via bundles of **subsidiary specific corporate governance mechanisms**, so that the **agency costs** are **minimised**. These **subsidiary specific bundles** of **monitoring** and **bonding contracts** represent the **headquarters-subsidiary corporate governance relationships**.

It is also possible that the **corporate governance** mechanisms that make up the bundles that represent corporate governance relationships are institutions that are **internal** to the firm, such as:

- The board of directors
- Large outside shareholders
- Mutual monitoring among managers
- Managerial share ownership
- Managerial compensation packages
- Financial leverage

Other mechanisms involve institutions that are external to the firm, such as:

- Capital market
- Market for corporate control
- External managerial labour market
- Product market

## 8.2 Solutions to the agency problems in multinational companies

### 8.2.1 Board of directors

One way of reducing **agency costs** is to separate the **ratification** and **monitoring** of managerial decisions from their **initiation** and **implementation**. Boards of directors, which consist of top-level executives of firms and non-executive outside members, are institutions that carry out the role of **ratifying** and **monitoring** the managerial decisions with the help of their **non-executive** outside members.

As is the case with all **corporate governance** mechanisms, monitoring by boards of directors is not without costs. Outsiders on the board may lack the expertise about the firm that the managers of the firm have, therefore the outsiders may accept unsound managerial proposals and reject sound ones. The outsiders may also lack the incentives to challenge managerial decisions. **Subsidiary boards** of directors have similar characteristics to the **corporate boards** of directors. However, it must be noted that in subsidiary boards the role of outsiders may be played not only by directors that are not affiliated with the parent company or the subsidiary in any way but also by **directors** that are **employees** of the **parent** but not of the **subsidiary**.

### 8.2.2 Managerial compensation packages

FAST FORWARD

**Managerial compensation packages** can be used to reduce **agency costs** in aligning the interests of top executives with shareholders and the interests of subsidiary managers to those of head office.

**Top executive incentive systems** can reduce **agency costs** and align the interests of the managers to those of the shareholders by making top **executives' pay contingent** on the **value** they **create** for the **shareholders**. **Value** created for the **shareholders** can be measured by various criteria, such as the **growth** in the **firm's market value**, **accounting returns**, **cash flows**, and even **subjective measures**.

Tying managerial compensation to firm value is not without costs. As managers' exposure to firm-specific risk increases, the risk-averse managers may ask to be compensated at higher levels to make up for the risk they are undertaking.

Managerial compensation packages can be used to align the interests of the **subsidiary managers** to those of the headquarters, too. An additional friction that makes using contingent compensation more costly in subsidiaries is that most subsidiaries of multinational corporations are not publicly traded companies. As a result, market value based standards and rewards cannot be used in subsidiary contingent compensation schemes.

### 8.2.3 Bundles of corporate governance mechanisms as the nexus of contracts

As we have emphasised in our review of each **corporate governance mechanism**, none of the mechanisms operate without costs or frictions. As a result, any single mechanism cannot mitigate the agency problem completely. In order to address the agency problem a firm faces, a **multiple of** these **mechanisms** need to work in **unison**. Another important characteristic of corporate governance mechanisms is that they substitute for and complement each other. The frictions related to each mechanism and substitution effects between mechanisms suggest that the mechanisms do not operate independently (ie their effects are not additive); rather, the mechanisms work as **bundles** of **mechanisms** in reducing the **agency costs**.

Finally, we can say that the bundles of corporate governance mechanisms are the **nexus of contracts**, which align the interests of the shareholders and the managers in the public corporation and the interests of the headquarters and the subsidiaries in the multinational corporation. Therefore, the bundles of corporate governance mechanisms represent **shareholder-manager** and **parent-subsidiary corporate governance relationships**.

# 9 Forecasting dividend capacity                       Mar/Jun 16

FAST FORWARD

The dividend capacity of an organisation is measured by its free cash flow to equity.

We have discussed dividend policy already in Chapter 1 and will return to it again in Chapter 10 (in relation to mergers and acquisitions). Here it is considered mainly in the context of a **multinational organization**.

## 9.1 How much can be paid as dividends?

Free cash flow to equity is a measure of what is available for payment to the owners of a firm from this years cash flows, after providing for capital expenditures to maintain existing assets and to create new assets for future growth (it will be covered numerically in Chapter 7b).

In theory, the entire FCFE can be paid as dividends, as this is the amount that is available for this purpose. In practice, however, only a portion of this figure will be given to the shareholders as dividends, as the management team tends to prefer a smooth dividend pattern.

While the dividends can never be less than zero, the FCFE can be **negative**. This can occur even if earnings are positive, if the firm has **substantial working capital and capital expenditure needs**. Negative FCFE is not unusual in **small, high growth firms**, at least in the early years, as reinvestment needs will tend to be substantial. However, as growth rates and capital expenditure **slow down**, FCFE will eventually become **positive**.

# 10 Dividend capacity                                12/10, 6/13

FAST FORWARD

The dividend capacity of a multinational company depends on its after-tax profits, investment plans and foreign dividends.

**Exam focus point**

There was a six-mark section in June 2013 Question 4 asking students to calculate the level of increase in dividends from overseas investments that would raise the investing company's dividend capacity by 10%.

We have introduced the concept of the dividend capacity of an organisation above. Here we extend the treatment to the case of a multinational company and highlight the role of special factors, such as remittances from subsidiaries and the timing of payments.

The potential dividend that can be paid, ie the dividend capacity of the firm, can be estimated as follows:

| | |
|---|---|
| Operating cash flows from domestic operations | **plus** |
| Depreciation | **plus** |
| Dividends from foreign affiliates and subsidiaries | **plus** |
| Net equity issuance (ie new issues net of repurchases) | **plus** |
| Net debt issuance (ie new borrowing net of repayment) | **less** |
| Interest payments on debt, less any interest income | **less** |
| Taxes | **less** |
| Net investment in non-current assets (net of asset sales) | **less** |

Net investment in working capital, inclusive of cash and marketable securities.

Dividend capacity, or FCFE, represents dividends that could be paid to shareholders. This is usually not the same as actual dividends in a given year because normally the management of a company deliberately smoothes dividend payments across time. In the rest of this section we look in greater detail at three of the factors: total net investment, share repurchases and foreign dividends.

**Exam focus point**

You should know how the various parts of the FCFE equation affect dividend capacity.

## 10.1 Effect of investment plans

Total net investment is the single most important factor in determining dividend payouts to the shareholders. According to pecking order hypothesis, funding investments with internal funds is the first choice of management, followed by borrowing or share issues. Consequently, fast-growing companies would be associated with low dividend distributions.

## 10.2 Effect of share repurchases

A company that opts to repurchase its shares transfers funds from the company to the shareholders. The repurchase is financed from the firm's distributable reserves. The effect of a share repurchase is to increase the earnings per share, as the number of issued shares is reduced. The evidence suggests that markets react favourably to announcements of share repurchases. The rationale for the positive reaction is that when there are no investment opportunities then it is preferable for the excess cash to be returned to shareholders rather than to be retained within the company.

Share repurchases as a method of distribution represented a larger amount than dividends in the US. The reason for this is the more favourable tax treatment of share repurchases, which is subject to capital gains tax, whereas dividend payments are subject to income tax which is higher.

## 10.3 Dividends from overseas operations

Corporations paying dividends to common shareholders could, for example, fund these payments by triggering repatriations. Repatriations help parent companies meet their financing needs as larger dividends to external shareholders are associated with larger dividend repatriations inside the firm, and highly levered parent companies with profitable domestic investment opportunities draw more heavily on the resources of their foreign affiliates. In fact, dividend repatriations represent sizeable financial flows for the US companies.

The importance of repatriated dividends is not limited to quoted companies, which it may be argued face pressure from the markets to distribute dividends to shareholders. Even private companies rely heavily on their overseas subsidiaries to finance dividend distributions. The evidence suggests that this is happening even when dividend repatriation is not tax efficient.

# 11 Dividend repatriation policies

**FAST FORWARD**

> The amount of dividends subsidiaries pay to the parent company depend on the parent company's dividend policies, financing needs, taxation and managerial control.

The choice of whether to repatriate earnings from a foreign subsidiary is one of the most important decisions in multinational financial management. As mentioned in the previous section, dividend repatriations represent significant financial flows for parent companies and contribute to dividend payments. The factors that affect dividend repatriation policies can be grouped as follows:

(a) Financing factors
(b) Tax factors
(c) Managerial factors
(d) Timing factors

## 11.1 Financing factors

The factors that shape **repatriation dividend policy** within the multinational firm are the **payment of dividends to external shareholders**, the **level of investment planned by the parent company, after-tax profits** and **financing policies**.

Repatriation policies may reflect financing concerns of parents who draw on subsidiary cash flows to finance domestic expenses. Two examples of such domestic expenses are **dividend payments** to **external shareholders** and **capital expenditures in the home countries**.

## 11.2 Investment financing

Dividend repatriations from foreign affiliates may offer an attractive source of finance for domestic investment expenditures, despite possible associated tax costs, especially when alternative forms of finance are costly. This is true for parent companies with profitable domestic investment opportunities that already maintain large amounts of external debt and do not wish to increase the level of borrowing even

further. Another case is when companies need to expand fast into areas and profitability is not sufficient to finance the expansion.

One of the strong implications of the US tax treatment of foreign income is that US multinational corporations should not simultaneously remit dividends from low-tax foreign locations and transfer equity funds into the same foreign locations. Doing so generates a home-country tax liability that could be easily avoided simply by reducing both dividends and equity transfers.

## 11.3 Dividend policy

Dividend repatriations from foreign affiliates may also offer an attractive source of finance for payments of dividends to common shareholders, especially when the parent company may prefer a smooth dividend payment pattern and domestic profitability is in decline. The dividend payments of a subsidiary may also be affected by the dividend policy of the parent company. For example, if the parent company operates a constant payout ratio policy, then the subsidiary will have to adopt a constant payout ratio policy too.

Empirical evidence shows that dividend payments to parent companies tend to be regular and multinational firms behave as though they select target payouts for their foreign affiliates, gradually adjusting payouts over time in response to changes in earnings.

## 11.4 Tax regime and dividend payments

Tax considerations are thought to be the primary reason for the dividend policies inside the multinational firm. For example, the parent company may reduce its overall tax liability by, for example, receiving larger amounts of dividends from subsidiaries in countries where undistributed earnings are taxed.

For subsidiaries of UK companies, all foreign profits, whether repatriated or not, are liable to UK corporation tax, with a credit for the tax that has already been paid to the host country. Similarly, the US Government does not distinguish between income earned abroad and income earned at home and gives credit to multinational corporations (MNCs) headquartered in the US for the amount of tax paid to foreign governments.

## Example

Assume that the corporate tax rate in the home country is 40% and in the overseas country where a subsidiary is located it is 30%. Assume that both the parent company and the subsidiary have pre-tax profits of $1,000.

Taxes to foreign government = 1,000 × 30% = 300
MNC's profit after foreign tax = 1,000 − 300 = 700
US taxes = 1,000 × 40% = 400
Foreign tax credit = 300
Net tax to IRS = 400 − 300 = 100
Total taxes = 300 + 100 = 400

## 11.5 Managerial control

Another reason that may determine repatriation policies is the inability to fully monitor foreign managers. Regularised dividend payments restrict the financial discretion of foreign managers, thereby reducing associated agency problems. Conflicts of interest are most apt to arise when ownership is divided, as local owners may influence managers to undertake transactions at other than market prices. Control considerations inside the firm may explain the tax-penalised behaviour especially when affiliates are partially owned.

Finally, the desire to control corporate managers around the world carries implications for dividend policies. A multinational firm's central management can use financial flows within the firm to evaluate the financial prospects and needs of far-flung foreign affiliates and to limit the discretion of foreign managers. As this observation suggests, it may be sensible to mandate dividend payments to police and monitor

foreign managers, limit their ability to misallocate funds, and extract returns on investments – much as public shareholders use dividends to monitor and control their firms.

## 11.6 Timing of dividend payments

So far we have concentrated on the size of repatriated dividends. The timing of payments may be equally important. For example, a subsidiary may adjust its dividend payments to a parent company in order to benefit from expected movements in exchange rates. A company would like to collect early (lead) payments from currencies vulnerable to depreciation and to collect late (lag) from currencies which are expected to appreciate.

Also, given that tax liabilities are triggered by repatriation, these tax liabilities can be deferred by reinvesting earnings abroad rather than remitting dividends to parent companies. The incentive to defer repatriation is much stronger for affiliates in low-tax countries, whose dividends trigger significant parent tax obligations, than they are for affiliates in high-tax countries – particularly since taxpayers receive net credits for repatriations from affiliates in countries with tax rates that exceed the parent country tax rate.

# 12 Transfer pricing

**FAST FORWARD**

Transfer prices are set by the MNC not only to recover the cost of services and goods provided but also to achieve objectives such as tax liability minimisation and to offset host country policies.

MNCs supply their affiliates with capital, technology and managerial skills, for which the parent firm receives a stream of dividend and interest payments, royalties and licence fees. At the same time, significant intra-firm transfers of goods and services occur. For example, the subsidiary may provide the parent company with raw materials, whereas the parent company may provide the subsidiary with final goods for distribution to consumers in the host country. For intra-firm trade both the parent company and the subsidiary need to charge prices. These prices for goods, technology or services between wholly or partly owned affiliates of the multinational are called **transfer prices**.

**Key term**

> A **transfer price** may be defined as the price at which goods or services are transferred from one process or department to another or from one member of a group to another.

The extent to which costs and profit are covered by the transfer price is a matter of company policy. A transfer price may be based on any of the following:

- Standard cost
- Marginal cost: at marginal cost or with a gross profit margin added
- Opportunity cost
- Full cost: at full cost, or at a full cost plus price
- Market price
- Market price less a discount
- Negotiated price, which could be based on any of the other bases

A transfer price based on cost might be at **marginal cost** or **full cost**, with no profit or contribution margin, but in a profit centre system it is more likely to be a price based on **marginal cost** or **full cost** plus a margin for contribution or profit. This is to allow profit centres to make a profit on work they do for other profit centres, and so earn a reward for their effort and use of resources on the work.

Transfers based on **market price** might be any of the following:

(a)   The **actual market price** at which the transferred goods or services could be sold on an external market

(b)   The **actual external market price**, minus an amount that reflects the savings in costs (for example selling costs and bad debts) when goods are transferred internally

(c)   The **market price** of **similar goods** which are sold on an external market, although the transferred goods are not exactly the same and do not themselves have an external market

(d)   A **price** sufficient to give an appropriate share of profit to each party

## 12.1 The level of transfer prices

The size of the transfer price will affect the costs of one profit centre and the revenues of another. Since profit centre managers are held accountable for their costs, revenues and profits, they are likely to **dispute** the size of transfer prices with each other, or disagree about whether one profit centre should do work for another or not. Transfer prices affect the behaviour and decisions of profit centre managers.

If managers of individual profit centres are tempted to make decisions that are harmful to other divisions and are not congruent with the goals of the organisation as a whole, the problem is likely to emerge in disputes about the transfer price.

Disagreements about output levels tend to focus on the transfer price. There is presumably a profit-maximising level of output and sales for the organisation as a whole. However, unless each profit centre also **maximises** its **own profit** at the corresponding level of output, there will be **interdivisional disagreements** about output levels and the profit-maximising output will not be achieved.

## 12.2 The advantages of market value transfer prices

Giving profit centre managers the freedom to negotiate prices with other profit centres as though they were independent companies will tend to result in **market-based transfer prices**.

(a)     In most cases where the transfer price is at market price, internal transfers should be expected, because the buying division is likely to benefit from a **better quality of service**, **greater flexibility** and **dependability of supply**.

(b)     Both divisions may benefit from **lower costs** of **administration**, **selling** and **transport**.

A market price as the transfer price would therefore result in decisions which would be in the best interests of the company or group as a whole.

## 12.3 The disadvantages of market value transfer prices

**Market value** as a transfer price does have certain disadvantages.

(a)     The **market price** may be **temporary**, induced by adverse economic conditions or dumping, or it might depend on the volume of output supplied to the external market by the profit centre.

(b)     A **transfer price** at market value might, under some circumstances, act as a **disincentive** to use up any spare capacity in the divisions. A price based on incremental cost, in contrast, might provide an incentive to use up the spare resources in order to provide a marginal contribution to profit.

(c)     Many products do **not have** an **equivalent market price**, so that the price of a similar product might be chosen. In such circumstances, the option to sell or buy on the open market does not exist.

(d)     There might be an **imperfect external market** for the transferred item so that, if the transferring division tried to sell more externally, it would have to reduce its selling price.

(e)     **Internal transfers** are often **cheaper** than **external sales**, with savings in selling costs, bad debt risks and possibly transport costs. It would therefore seem reasonable for the buying division to expect a discount on the external market price, and to negotiate for such a discount.

## 12.4 Example: Transfer prices

A multinational company based in Beeland has subsidiary companies in Ceeland and in the UK. The UK subsidiary manufactures machinery parts which are sold to the Ceeland subsidiary for a unit price of B$420 (420 Beeland dollars), where the parts are assembled. The UK subsidiary shows a profit of B$80 per unit; 200,000 units are sold annually.

The Ceeland subsidiary incurs further costs of B$400 per unit and sells the finished goods on for an equivalent of B$1,050.

All the profits from the foreign subsidiaries are remitted to the parent company as dividends. Double taxation treaties between Beeland, Ceeland and the UK allow companies to set foreign tax liabilities against their domestic tax liability.

The following rates of taxation apply:

|  | UK | Beeland | Ceeland |
| --- | --- | --- | --- |
| Tax on company profits | 25% | 35% | 40% |
| Withholding tax on dividends | – | 12% | 10% |

*Required*

Show the tax effect of increasing the transfer price between the UK and Ceeland subsidiaries by 25%.

## Solution

The current position is as follows:

|  | UK company B$'000 | Ceeland company B$'000 | Total B$'000 |
| --- | --- | --- | --- |
| *Revenues and taxes in the local country* | | | |
| Sales | 84,000 | 210,000 | 294,000 |
| Production expenses | (68,000) | (164,000) | (232,000) |
| Taxable profit | 16,000 | 46,000 | 62,000 |
| Tax (1) | (4,000) | (18,400) | (22,400) |
| Dividends to Beeland | 12,000 | 27,600 | 39,600 |
| Withholding tax (2) | 0 | 2,760 | 2,760 |
| *Revenues and taxes in Beeland* | | | |
| Dividend | 12,000 | 27,600 | 39,600 |
| Add back foreign tax paid | 4,000 | 18,400 | 22,400 |
| Taxable income | 16,000 | 46,000 | 62,000 |
|  | 5,600 | 16,100 | 21,700 |
| Foreign tax credit | (4,000) | (16,100) | (20,100) |
| Tax paid in Beeland (3) | 1,600 | – | 1,600 |
| Total tax (1) + (2) + (3) | 5,600 | 21,160 | 26,760 |

An increase of 25% in the transfer price would have the following effect:

|  | UK company B$'000 | Ceeland company B$'000 | Total B$'000 |
| --- | --- | --- | --- |
| *Revenues and taxes in the local country* | | | |
| Sales | 105,000 | 210,000 | 315,000 |
| Production expenses | (68,000) | (185,000) | (253,000) |
| Taxable profit | 37,000 | 25,000 | 62,000 |
| Tax (1) | (9,250) | (10,000) | (19,250) |
| Dividends to Beeland | 27,750 | 15,000 | 42,750 |
| Withholding tax (2) | 0 | 1,500 | 1,500 |
| *Revenues and taxes in Beeland* | | | |
| Dividend | 27,750 | 15,000 | 42,750 |
| Add back foreign tax paid | 9,250 | 10,000 | 19,250 |
| Taxable income | 37,000 | 25,000 | 62,000 |
| Beeland tax due | 12,950 | 8,750 | 21,700 |
| Foreign tax credit | (9,250) | (8,750) | (18,000) |
| Tax paid in Beeland (3) | 3,700 | – | 3,700 |
| Total tax (1) + (2) + (3) | 12,950 | 11,500 | 24,450 |

The total tax payable by the company is therefore reduced by B$2,310,000 to B$24,450,000.

## 12.5 Motivations for transfer pricing

In deciding on their transfer pricing policies, MNCs take into account many internal and external factors or motivations for transfer pricing. In terms of internal motivations these include the following:

### Performance evaluation

When different affiliates within a multinational are treated as standalone profit centres, transfer prices are needed internally by the multinational to determine profitability of the individual divisions. Transfer prices which deviate too much from the actual prices will make it difficult to properly monitor the performance of an affiliated unit.

### Management incentives

If transfer prices used for internal measures of performance by individual affiliates deviate from the true economic prices, and managers are evaluated and rewarded on the basis of the distorted profitability, then it may result in corporate managers behaving in an irresponsible way.

### Cost allocation

When units within the multinational are run as cost centres, subsidiaries are charged a share of the costs of providing the group service function so that the service provider covers its costs plus a small mark-up. Lower or higher transfer prices may result in a subsidiary bearing less or more of the overheads.

### Financing considerations

Transfer pricing may be used in order to boost the profitability of a subsidiary, with the parent company undercharging the subsidiary. Such a boost in the profitability and its credit rating may be needed by the subsidiary in order to succeed in obtaining funds from the host country.

Transfer pricing can also be used to disguise the profitability of the subsidiary in order to justify high prices for its products in the host country and to be able to resist demands for higher wages.

Several external motivations can affect the multinational's choice of transfer prices. Because multinationals operate in two or more jurisdictions, transfer prices must be assigned for intra-firm trade that crosses national borders.

### Taxes

MNCs use transfer pricing to channel profits out of high tax rate countries into lower ones. A parent company may sell goods at lower than normal prices to its subsidiaries in lower tax rate countries and buy from them at higher than normal prices. The resultant loss in the parent's high-tax country adds significantly to the profits of the subsidiaries. An MNC reports most of its profits in a low-tax country, even though the actual profits are earned in a high-tax country.

### Tariffs

Border taxes, such as tariffs and export taxes, are often levied on crossborder trade. Where the tax is levied on an *ad valorem* basis, the higher the transfer price, the larger the tax paid per unit. Whether an MNC will follow high transfer price strategy or not may depend on its impact on the tax burden. When border taxes are levied on a per-unit basis (ie specific taxes), the transfer price is irrelevant for tax purposes.

### Rule of origin rule

Another external factor is the need to meet the rule of origin that applies to crossborder flows within a free trade area. Since border taxes are eliminated within the area, rules of origin must be used to determine eligibility for duty-free status. Over- or under invoicing inputs is one way to avoid customs duties levied on products that do not meet the rule of origin test.

### Exchange control and quotas

Transfer pricing can be used to avoid currency controls in the host country. For example, a constraint in profit repatriation could be avoided by the parent company charging higher prices for raw materials, or higher fees for services provided to the subsidiary. The parent company will have higher profits and a higher tax liability and the subsidiary will have lower profitability and a lower tax liability.

When the host country restricts the amount of foreign exchange that can be used to import goods, then a lower transfer price allows a greater quantity of goods to be imported.

# 13 Regulation of transfer pricing

**FAST FORWARD**

MNCs have to adhere to pricing guidelines to prevent exploitation of the host country.

## 13.1 The problem of transfer price manipulation

As we have discussed in the previous section, transfer pricing is a normal, legitimate and, in fact, required activity. Firms set prices on intra-firm transactions for a variety of perfectly legal and rational internal reasons and, even where pricing is not required for internal reasons, governments may require it in order to determine how much tax revenues and customs duties are owed by the MNC. **Transfer price manipulation**, on the other hand, exists when MNCs use transfer prices to evade or avoid payment of taxes and tariffs, or other controls that the Government of the host country has put in place.

Governments worry about transfer price manipulation because they are concerned with the loss of revenues through tax avoidance or evasion and they dislike the loss of control. Overall MNC profits after taxes may be raised by either under- or over invoicing the transfer price; such manipulation for tax purposes, however, comes at the expense of distorting other goals of the firm; in particular, evaluating management performance.

### Case Study

**Starbucks became the poster child for corporate tax avoidance in 2012** after details of its meagre tax contribution emerged. It was accused of using artificial corporate structures to shift profits out of the UK into lower tax jurisdictions.

The furore **prompted a deal with HMRC to waive tax deductions and pay £20 million in voluntary corporation tax** over two years, including £11.2 million last year.

(Starbucks said that it sourced UK coffee from its wholesale trading subsidiary in Switzerland. It has been suggested that while this may be sensible to have one team responsible for sourcing all of Starbucks' coffee, it is hard to escape the conclusion that Switzerland would not be a major centre for coffee trading in the first place if it did not charge a lowly 12% tax rate on the trading profits. Starbucks also charges its UK operations for use of its brand name, technology and engineering support).

Starbucks paid nearly as much corporation tax in 2015 as it did in its first 14 years in the UK, after bowing to pressure to scrap its complex tax structures.

The Seattle-based coffee house posted a pre-tax profit of £34.2 million for the year to the end of September 2015, up from £2 million the year before.

It also paid £8.1 million in corporation tax at a rate of 24%, above the UK corporation tax rate of 20% due to a one-off change in accounting practices.

Elements of its European tax structure were ruled unlawful by the European commission in October 2015, with millions of euros of fines expected to follow.

*(Davies, 2015)*

## 13.2 The arm's length standard

**Key term**

> The **arm's length standard** states that intra-firm trade of multinationals should be priced as if they took place between unrelated parties acting at arm's length in competitive markets.

The most common solution that tax authorities have adopted to reduce the probability of the transfer price manipulation is to develop particular transfer pricing regulations as part of the corporate income tax code. These regulations are generally based on the concept of the arm's length standard, which says that all MNC intra-firm activities should be priced as if they took place between unrelated parties acting at arm's length in competitive markets. The 1979 OECD Report defines the arm's length standard as:

'Prices which would have been agreed upon between unrelated parties engaged in the same or similar transactions under the same or similar conditions in the open market' (OECD 1979).

The arm's length standard has two methods.

Method 1: use the price negotiated between two unrelated parties C and D to proxy for the transfer between A and B.

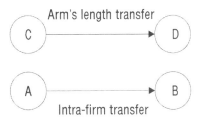

Method 2: use the price at which A sells to unrelated party C to proxy for the transfer price between A and B.

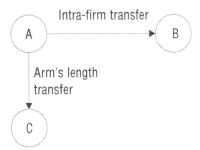

In practice, the method used will depend on the available data. That is the existence of unrelated parties that engage in the same, or nearly the same, transactions under the same or nearly the same circumstances. Does one of the related parties also engage in the same, or nearly the same, transactions with an unrelated party under the same, or nearly the same circumstances? Where there are differences, are they quantifiable? Do the results seem reasonable in the circumstances?

If the answers to these questions are yes, then the arm's length standard will yield a reasonable result. If the answers are no, then alternative methods must be used.

The main methods of establishing 'arm's length' transfer prices of tangible goods include:

- Comparable uncontrolled price (CUP)
- Resale price (RP)
- Cost plus (C+)
- Profit split (PS)

### The CUP method

The CUP method looks for a comparable product to the transaction in question, either in terms of the same product being bought or sold by the MNC in a comparable transaction with an unrelated party, or the same or similar product being traded between two unrelated parties under the same or similar circumstances. The product so identified is called a **product comparable**. All the facts and circumstances that could materially affect the price must be considered.

Tax authorities prefer the CUP method over all other pricing methods for at least two reasons. First, it incorporates more information about the specific transaction than does any other method; ie it is transaction and product specific. Second, CUP takes the interests of both the buyer and seller into account since it looks at the price as determined by the intersection of demand and supply.

### The RP method

Where a product comparable is not available, and the CUP method cannot be used, an alternative method is to focus on one side of the transaction, either the manufacturer or the distributor, and to estimate the transfer price using a functional approach.

Under the RP method, the tax auditor looks for firms at similar trade levels that perform similar distribution functions (ie a **functional comparable**). The **RP** method is best used when the distributor adds relatively little value to the product so that the value of its functions is easier to estimate. The assumption behind the **RP** method is that competition among distributors means that similar margins (returns) on sales are earned for similar functions.

The RP method backs into the transfer price by subtracting a profit margin, derived from margins earned by comparable distributors engaged in comparable functions, from the known retail price to determine the transfer price. As a result, the **RP** method evaluates the transaction only in terms of **the buyer**. The method ensures that the buyer receives an arm's length return consistent with returns earned by similar firms engaged in similar transactions. Since the resale margin is determined in an arm's length manner, but nothing is done to ensure that the manufacturer's profit margin is consistent with margins earned by other manufacturers, the adjustment is one-sided. Under the RP method, having determined the buyer's arm's length margin, all excess profit on the transaction is assigned to the seller. Thus the RP method tends to **overestimate** the transfer price since it gives all unallocated profits on the transaction to the upstream manufacturer. We call this **contract distributor** case, since the manufacturer is contracting out the distribution stage to the lowest bidder.

### The C+ method

The C+ method starts with the costs of production, measured using recognised accounting principles, and then adds an appropriate mark-up over costs. The appropriate mark-up is estimated from those earned by similar manufacturers.

The assumption is that in a competitive market the percentage mark-ups over cost that could be earned by other arm's length manufacturers would be roughly the same. The C+ method works best when the producer is a simple manufacturer without complicated activities so that its costs and returns can be more easily estimated.

In order to use the C+ method, the tax authority or the MNC must know the accounting approach adopted by the unrelated parties, such as what costs are included in the cost base before the mark-up over costs is calculated. Is it actual cost or standard cost?

Are only manufacturing costs included or is the cost base the sum of manufacturing costs plus some portion of operating costs? The larger the cost base, the smaller should be the profit mark-up, or gross margin, over costs.

### The PS method

When there are no suitable product comparables (the CUP method) or functional comparables (the RP and C+ methods), the most common alternative method is the PS method, whereby the profits on a transaction earned by two related parties are split between the parties.

The PS method allocates the consolidated profit from a transaction, or group of transactions, between the related parties. Where there are no comparables that can be used to estimate the transfer price, this method provides an alternative way to calculate or 'back into' the transfer price. The most commonly recommended ratio to split the profits on the transaction between the related parties is return on operating assets (the ratio of operating profits to operating assets).

The PS method ensures that both related parties earn the same ROA.

# Chapter Roundup

- **Multinational companies** need to develop a **financial planning framework** in order to make sure that the strategic objectives and competitive advantages are realised. Such a financial **planning framework** will include ways of raising **capital** and **risks** related to overseas operations and the **repatriation of profits**.

- Multinational companies will have access to international debt, such as **eurobonds**.

- When a company decides to raise funds from the local equity markets, the company must comply with the requirements of the local exchanges for listing.

- Multinationals can take various measures to combat the risks of political **interference** or **turbulence**, including agreements with governments, insurance, and location elsewhere of key parts of the production process.

- Multinationals can **counter exchange controls** by management charges or royalties.

- The methods of financing overseas subsidiaries will depend on the **length of investment period** envisaged, as well as the **local finance costs**, **taxation systems** and **restrictions on dividend remittances**.

- **Litigation risks** can be reduced by keeping abreast of changes, acting as a good corporate citizen and lobbying.

- **Cultural risks** affect the products and services produced and the way organisations are managed and staffed. Businesses should take cultural issues into account when deciding where to sell abroad, and how much to **centralise** activities.

- **Agency issues** can be observed in all types and at all levels of organisations, for example between managers at headquarters and managers of subsidiaries. These issues can be addressed by a bundle of corporate governance mechanisms.

- **Managerial compensation packages** can be used to reduce **agency costs** in aligning the interests of top executives with shareholders and the interests of subsidiary managers to those of head office.

- The dividend capacity of an organisation is measured by its free cash flow to equity.

- The dividend capacity of a multinational company depends on its after-tax profits, investment plans and foreign dividends.

- The amount of dividends subsidiaries pay to the parent company depend on the parent company's dividend policies, financing needs, taxation and managerial control.

- Transfer prices are set by the MNC not only to recover the cost of services and goods provided but also to achieve objectives such as tax liability minimisation and to offset host country policies.

- MNCs have to adhere to pricing guidelines to prevent exploitation of the host country

1   Give three examples of barriers to entry that multinationals might face.

2   Forward integration would involve acquiring final production and distribution facilities in other countries.

True   ☐

False  ☐

3   What principal characteristics is a tax haven most likely to have?

4   Why might a firm looking to establish an overseas presence choose to set up a branch rather than a subsidiary?

5   What are the main differences between a contractual joint venture and a joint-equity venture?

6   What is meant by transfer price manipulation?

7   What are the main methods of establishing 'arm's length' transfer prices?

8   What are the main factors that affect dividend repatriation policies?

# Answers to Quick Quiz

1   Any three of: Product differentiation barriers; Absolute cost barriers; Economy of scale barriers; Fixed costs; Legal barriers

2   True

3   (a)   Tax on foreign investment or sales income earned by resident companies, and withholding tax on dividends paid to parent should be low

    (b)   Stable government and stable currency

    (c)   Adequate financial service support facilities

4   (a)   More favourable tax (not subject to withholding tax)
    (b)   Fewer legal formalities

5   A contractual joint venture is for a fixed period; duties and responsibilities are defined in a contract. A joint-equity venture involves investment, is of no fixed duration and continually evolves.

6   **Transfer price manipulation** is the use of transfer prices to avoid the payment of taxes or tariffs.

7   Comparable uncontrolled price (CUP)

Cost plus (C+)
Resale price (RP)
Profit split (PS)

8   (a)   Financing factors
    (b)   Tax factors
    (c)   Managerial factors
    (d)   Timing factors

Now try the questions below from the Practice Question Bank

| Number | Level | Marks | Time |
| --- | --- | --- | --- |
| 7 | Introductory | 10 | 20 |

# Advanced investment appraisal

# Discounted cash flow techniques

| Topic list | Syllabus reference |
|---|---|
| 1 Net present value (NPV) | B1(a) |
| 2 Monte Carlo simulation and investment appraisal | B1(b) |
| 3 Internal rate of return | B1(c) |
| 4 Comparison of NPV and IRR | B1(c) |
| 5 Modified internal rate of return (MIRR) | B1(c) |

## Introduction

In this chapter we discuss two criteria for investment appraisal, the net present value (NPV) and the internal rate of return (IRR). A number of issues related to the two criteria are explored, such as inflation and taxation effects and Monte Carlo simulation.

# Study guide

| | | Intellectual level |
|---|---|---|
| **B1** | **Discounted cash flow techniques** | |
| (a) | Evaluate the potential value added to an organisation arising from a specified capital investment project or portfolio using the net present value (NPV) model. Project modelling should include explicit treatment of: | 3 |
| | (i) Inflation and specific price variation | |
| | (ii) Taxation including capital allowances and tax exhaustion | |
| | (iii) Single period capital rationing and multi-period capital rationing. Multi-period capital rationing to include the formulation of programming methods and the interpretation of their output | |
| | (iv) Probability analysis and sensitivity analysis when adjusting for risk and uncertainty in investment appraisal | |
| | (v) Risk-adjusted discount rates | |
| | (vi) Project duration as a measure of risk | |
| (b) | Outline the application of Monte Carlo simulation to investment appraisal. Candidates will not be expected to undertake simulations in an examination context but will be expected to demonstrate an understanding of: | 2 |
| | (i) The significance of the simulation output and the assessment of the likelihood of project success | |
| | (ii) The measurement and interpretation of project value at risk | |
| (c) | Establish the potential economic return (using internal rate of return and modified internal rate of return) and advise on a project's return margin. Discuss the relative merits of NPV and IRR. | 3 |

# Exam guide

Discounted cash flow techniques may arise as a means of solving part of a larger problem in the exam. A previous question required candidates to recommend procedures for the appraisal of capital investment projects from the point of view of a senior financial manager, including the provision of advice on a project and its likely impact on the company.

One of the optional performance objectives in your PER is the evaluation of the financial viability of a potential investment. This chapter covers some of the most popular methods of investment appraisal – NPV, IRR and MIRR – which you can regularly put into practice in the real world.

# 1 Net present value (NPV)　　　6/12, 12/12, 6/15, Sep/Dec 16

This section covers material that should be familiar to you from previous studies. However, it is important that you revise this section, as net present value (NPV) is a fundamental investment appraisal technique.

**FAST FORWARD**　　Projects with a positive net present value should be undertaken.

**Key term**　　The **net present value (NPV)** of a project is the sum of the discounted cash flows less the initial investment.

## Question

Project X requires an immediate investment of $150,000 and will generate net cash inflows of $60,000 for the next 3 years. The project's discount rate is 7%. If NPV is used to appraise the project, should Project X be undertaken?

## Answer

| Time | Cash flow | Discount factor | Present value |
|---|---|---|---|
| 0 | −150,000 | 1 | −150,000 |
| 1 | 60,000 | 0.935 | 56,100 |
| 2 | 60,000 | 0.873 | 52,380 |
| 3 | 60,000 | 0.816 | 48,960 |
| | | | 7,440 |

The NPV of this project is $7,440. As NPV is positive, Project X should be undertaken, as it will increase shareholders' wealth.

**Exam focus point**

NPV with taxation and foreign currency complications was examined as part of a 50-mark compulsory question in June 2015. Foreign currency complications are covered in Chapter 8.

## 1.1 NPV and shareholder wealth maximisation

The main advantage of the NPV method is that it evaluates projects in the same way as shareholders would do – that is, it focuses on how individual projects would affect shareholders' wealth. Only those projects with a **positive** NPV are accepted, meaning that only those projects that will **increase** shareholders' wealth will be undertaken.

## 1.2 The effect of inflation

 **FAST FORWARD**

Inflation is present in all economies and must be accounted for when evaluating projects.

**Key terms**

**Real cash flows** have had the effects of inflation removed and should be discounted using the **real discount rate**. **Nominal cash flows** include the effects of inflation and should be discounted using the **nominal discount rate**.

The above example (NPV calculations) assumes that net cash flows do not change from year to year. This is unrealistic, given the existence of inflation. It is important to take proper account of inflation when undertaking investment appraisal, as it could change the NPV of the project and ultimately the decision as to whether the project should be accepted.

NPV calculations can be carried out using either **real** or **nominal** cash flows.

### 1.2.1 Real and nominal interest rates

The **real interest rate** has removed the effects of inflation and represents purchasing power (it is really the nominal interest rate 'deflated' to take out the effects of inflation). When the nominal rate of interest **exceeds** the rate of inflation, the real interest rate will be **positive**. If the nominal rate of interest **is less than** the rate of inflation, the real interest rate will be **negative**.

$(1 + i) = (1 + r)(1 + h)$

Where  i  = nominal (money) rate
        r  = real rate
        h  = inflation rate

This is known as the **Fisher equation**.

Question                                                                      Nominal discount factor

If the real rate of interest is 5% and the expected inflation is 3%, what is the nominal return?

Answer

$(1 + i) = (1 + 0.05)(1 + 0.03) = 1.0815$

The nominal rate is therefore 8.15%.

### 1.2.2 Real rate or nominal rate?

The rule is as follows:

(a)     We use the **nominal** rate if cash flows are expressed in **actual numbers of dollars** that will be
        received or paid at various future dates (remember: 'money at money').

(b)     We use the **real** rate if cash flows are expressed in **constant price terms** (that is, in terms of their
        value at time 0). Remember: 'real at real'.

### 1.2.3 Advantages and misuses of real values and a real rate of return

Although generally companies should discount money values at the nominal cost of capital, there are
some advantages of using real values discounted at a real cost of capital.

(a)     When all costs and benefits rise at the same rate of price inflation, **real values** are the **same as
        current day values**, so that **no further adjustments** need be made to cash flows before
        discounting. In contrast, when nominal values are discounted at the nominal cost of capital, the
        **prices** in **future years** must be **calculated** before discounting can begin.

(b)     The Government might prefer to set a real return as a target for investments, being more suitable
        than a commercial money rate of return.

Question                                                                      Effect of inflation

Rice is considering a project which would cost $5,000 now. The annual benefits, for 4 years, would be a
fixed income of $2,500 a year, plus other savings of $500 a year in year 1, rising by 5% each year because
of inflation. Running costs will be $1,000 in the first year, but would increase at 10% each year because of
inflating labour costs. The general rate of inflation is expected to be 7½% and the company's required
money rate of return is 16%. Is the project worthwhile? (Ignore taxation.)

The cash flows at inflated values are as follows:

| Year | Fixed income | Other savings | Running costs | Net cash flow |
|------|------|------|------|------|
| | $ | $ | $ | $ |
| 1 | 2,500 | 500 | 1,000 | 2,000 |
| 2 | 2,500 | 525 | 1,100 | 1,925 |
| 3 | 2,500 | 551 | 1,210 | 1,841 |
| 4 | 2,500 | 579 | 1,331 | 1,748 |

The NPV of the project is as follows:

| Year | Cash flow | Discount factor | PV |
|------|------|------|------|
| | $ | 16% | $ |
| 0 | (5,000) | 1.000 | (5,000) |
| 1 | 2,000 | 0.862 | 1,724 |
| 2 | 1,925 | 0.743 | 1,430 |
| 3 | 1,841 | 0.641 | 1,180 |
| 4 | 1,748 | 0.552 | 965 |
| | | | + 299 |

The NPV is positive and the project would appear to be worthwhile.

## 1.2.4 Expectations of inflation and the effects of inflation

When managers evaluate a particular project, or when shareholders evaluate their investments, they can only guess at what the rate of inflation is going to be. Their expectations will probably be wrong, at least to some extent, because it is extremely difficult to forecast the rate of inflation accurately. The only way in which uncertainty about inflation can be allowed for in project evaluation is by risk and uncertainty analysis.

Costs and benefits may rise at levels different from the general rate of inflation: inflation may be **general**, affecting prices of all kinds, or **specific** to particular prices. Generalised inflation has the following effects:

(a) Since **non-current assets, inventories** and **other working capital** will **increase in money value**, the same quantities of assets or working capital must be financed by **increasing amounts of capital**.

(b) Inflation means higher costs and higher selling prices. The effect of higher prices on demand is not necessarily easy to predict. A company that raises its prices by 10% because the general rate of inflation is running at 10% might suffer a serious fall in demand.

(c) Inflation, because it affects financing needs, is also likely to affect gearing, and so the cost of capital.

## 1.3 Allowing for taxation

FAST FORWARD

In investment appraisal, tax is often assumed to be payable **one year in arrears**, but you should read the question details carefully.

**Tax-allowable depreciation** details should be checked in any question you attempt.

**Typical assumptions** which may be stated in questions are as follows:

(a) An assumption about the timing of payments will have to be made.

(i) Half the tax is **payable** in the **same year** in which the **profits are earned** and **half in the following year**. This reflects the fact that large companies have to pay tax **quarterly** in some regimes.

(ii) Tax is payable in the **year following** the one in which the taxable profits are made. Thus, if a project increases taxable profits by $10,000 in year 2, there will be a tax payment, assuming tax at (say) 30% of $3,000 in year 3.

(iii) Tax is payable in the **same year** that the **profits arise**.

The question should make clear what assumptions you should use.

(b) Net cash flows from a project should be considered as the taxable profits arising from the project (unless an indication is given to the contrary).

## 1.3.1 Tax-allowable depreciation

Tax-allowable depreciation is used to reduce taxable profits, and the consequent reduction in a tax payment should be treated as a cash saving arising from the acceptance of a project.

For example, suppose tax-allowable depreciation is allowed on the cost of **plant and machinery** at the rate of 25% on a **reducing balance (RB)** basis. Thus if a company purchases plant costing $80,000, the subsequent writing-down allowances would be as follows:

| Year | | Tax-allowable depreciation | RB |
|------|--|---------------------------|-----|
| | | $ | $ |
| 1 | (25% of cost) | 20,000 | 60,000 |
| 2 | (25% of RB) | 15,000 | 45,000 |
| 3 | (25% of RB) | 11,250 | 33,750 |
| 4 | (25% of RB) | 8,438 | 25,312 |

When the plant is eventually sold, the difference between the sale price and the RB amount at the time of sale will be treated as:

(a) A taxable profit if the sale price exceeds the RB
(b) A tax-allowable loss if the RB exceeds the sale price

**Exam focus point**

Examination questions often assume that this loss will be available immediately, though in practice the balance less the sale price may continue to be written off at 25% a year as part of a pool balance.

The cash saving on the tax-allowable depreciation (or the cash payment for the charge) is calculated by multiplying the depreciation (or charge) by the tax rate.

Assumptions about tax-allowable depreciation could be simplified in an exam question. For example, you might be told that tax-allowable depreciation can be claimed at the rate of 25% of cost on a straight-line basis (that is, over four years).

There are two possible assumptions about the time when tax-allowable depreciation starts to be claimed.

(a) It can be assumed that the **first claim** occurs at the **start of the project** (at year 0).
(b) Alternatively, it can be assumed that the **first claim** occurs **later in the first year**.

You should state clearly which assumption you have made. Assumption (b) is more prudent, but assumption (a) is also perfectly feasible. It is very likely, however, that an examination question will indicate which of the two assumptions is required.

## 1.3.2 Example: Taxation

A company is considering whether or not to purchase an item of machinery costing $40,000 in 20X5. It would have a life of four years, after which it would be sold for $5,000. The machinery would create annual cost savings of $14,000.

The machinery would attract tax-allowable depreciation of 25% on the RB basis which could be claimed against taxable profits of the current year, which is soon to end. A balancing allowance or charge would arise on disposal. The tax rate is 30%. Tax is payable half in the current year, half one year in arrears. The after-tax cost of capital is 8%.

Should the machinery be purchased?

## Solution

Tax-allowable depreciation is first claimed against year 0 profits.

Cost: $40,000

| Year | Tax-allowable depreciation $ | RB $ | |
|---|---|---|---|
| (0) 20X5 (25% of cost) | 10,000 | 30,000 | (40,000 – 10,000) |
| (1) 20X6 (25% of RB) | 7,500 | 22,500 | (30,000 – 7,500) |
| (2) 20X7 (25% of RB) | 5,625 | 16,875 | (22,500 – 5,625) |
| (3) 20X8 (25% of RB) | 4,219 | 12,656 | (16,875 – 4,219) |
| (4) 20X9 (25% of RB) | 3,164 | 9,492 | (12,656 – 3,164) |

| | $ |
|---|---|
| Sale proceeds, end of fourth year | 5,000 |
| Less RB, end of fourth year | 9,492 |
| Balancing allowance | 4,492 |

Having calculated the depreciation each year, the tax savings can be computed. The year of the cash flow is one year after the year for which the allowance is claimed.

| Year of claim | Tax-allowable depreciation $ | Tax saved $ | Year of tax payment/saving (50% in each) |
|---|---|---|---|
| 0 | 10,000 | 3,000 | 0/1 |
| 1 | 7,500 | 2,250 | 1/2 |
| 2 | 5,625 | 1,688 | 2/3 |
| 3 | 4,219 | 1,266 | 3/4 |
| 4 | 7,656 | 2,297 | 4/5 |
| | 35,000 * | | |

\* Net cost $(40,000 – 5,000) = $35,000

These tax savings relate to tax-allowable depreciation. We must also calculate the extra tax payments on annual savings of $14,000.

The net cash flows and the NPV are now calculated as follows:

| Year | Equipment $ | Savings $ | Tax on savings $ | Tax saved on tax-allowable depreciation $ | Net cash flow $ | Discount factor 8% | Present value of cash flow $ |
|---|---|---|---|---|---|---|---|
| 0 | (40,000) | | | 1,500 | (38,500) | 1.000 | (38,500) |
| 1 | | 14,000 | (2,100) | 2,625 | 14,525 | 0.926 | 13,450 |
| 2 | | 14,000 | (4,200) | 1,969 | 11,769 | 0.857 | 10,086 |
| 3 | | 14,000 | (4,200) | 1,477 | 11,277 | 0.794 | 8,954 |
| 4 | 5,000 | 14,000 | (4,200) | 1,782 | 16,582 | 0.735 | 12,188 |
| 5 | | | (2,100) | 1,148 | (952) | 0.681 | (648) |
| | | | | | | | 5,530 |

The NPV is positive and so the purchase appears to be worthwhile.

### 1.3.3 An alternative and quicker method of calculating tax payments or savings

An alternative approach to calculating tax payments is to calculate one single tax payment based on a taxable profit figure; it is often helpful to have a measure of taxable profit in situations where there is tax exhaustion (see Section 1.4) or where there is extra tax to pay in another country (overseas NPV is covered in Chapter 8).

In the above example, the tax computations could have been combined, as follows.

| Year | 0 | 1 | 2 | 3 | 4 |
|---|---|---|---|---|---|
| | $ | $ | $ | $ | $ |
| Cost savings | 0 | 14,000 | 14,000 | 14,000 | 14,000 |
| Tax-allowable depreciation | 10,000 | 7,500 | 5,625 | 4,219 | 7,656 |
| Taxable profits | (10,000) | 6,500 | 8,375 | 9,781 | 6,344 |
| Tax at 30% | 3,000 | (1,950) | (2,512) | (2,934) | (1,903) |

The net cash flows would then be as follows:

| Year | Equipment | Savings | Tax | Net cash flow |
|---|---|---|---|---|
| | $ | $ | $ | $ |
| 0 | (40,000) | | 1,500 | (38,500) |
| 1 | | 14,000 | 525 | 14,525 |
| 2 | | 14,000 | (2,231) | 11,769 |
| 3 | | 14,000 | (2,723) | 11,277 |
| 4 | 5,000 | 14,000 | (2,418) | 16,582 |
| 5 | | | (952) | (952) |

The net cash flows are exactly the same as calculated previously.

### 1.3.4 Taxation and discounted cash flow

The effect of taxation on capital budgeting is theoretically quite simple. Organisations must pay tax, and the effect of undertaking a project will be to increase or decrease tax payments each year. These incremental tax cash flows should be included in the cash flows of the project for discounting to arrive at the project's NPV.

When **taxation is ignored** in the discounted cash flow calculations, the discount rate will **reflect the pre-tax rate of return** required on capital investments. When taxation is included in the cash flows, a **post-tax required rate of return** should be used.

If there is inflation and tax in a question, remember that tax flows do not get inflated by an extra year even though they may be paid one year later.

| Question | Effect of taxation |
|---|---|

A project requires an initial investment in machinery of $300,000. Additional cash inflows of $120,000 at current price levels are expected for three years, at the end of which time the machinery will be scrapped. The machinery will attract tax-allowable depreciation of 25% on the RB basis, which can be claimed against taxable profits of the current year, which is soon to end. A balancing charge or allowance will arise on disposal.

The tax rate is 50% and tax is payable 50% in the current year, 50% one year in arrears. The nominal post-tax cost of capital is 11% and the rate of inflation is 10%. Assume that the project is 100% debt financed.

*Required*

Assess whether the project should be undertaken.

| Post-tax: year | Purchase $ | Inflation factor | Cash flow after inflation $ | Tax on cash inflow $ | (W1-3) Tax saved on tax-allowable depreciation $ | Net cash flow $ | Discount factor 11% | Present Value $ |
|---|---|---|---|---|---|---|---|---|
| 0 | (300,000) | 1.000 | (300,000) | | 18,750 | (281,250) | 1.000 | (281,250) |
| 1 | | 1.100 | 132,000 | (33,000) | 32,813 | 131,813 | 0.901 | 118,764 |
| 2 | | 1.210 | 145,200 | (69,300) | 24,609 | 100,509 | 0.812 | 81,613 |
| 3 | | 1.331 | 159,720 | (76,230) | 42,187 | 125,677 | 0.731 | 91,870 |
| 4 | | | | (39,930) | 31,640 | (8,290) | 0.659 | (5,463) |
| | | | | | | | NPV = | 5,534 |

The project should be undertaken at least from the financial viewpoint.

*Workings*

1   *Tax-allowable depreciation (initial cost $300,000)*

| Year | | Tax-allowable depreciation $ | RB $ |
|---|---|---|---|
| 0 | (25% at cost) | 75,000 | 225,000 |
| 1 | (25% of RB) | 56,250 | 168,750 |
| 2 | (25% of RB) | 42,188 | 126,562 |
| 3 | (25% of RB) | 31,641 | 94,921 |

2   *Balancing allowance*

| | $ |
|---|---|
| Sale proceeds, end of third year | – |
| RB, end of third year | 94,921 |
| Balancing allowance | 94,921 |

3   *Tax saved on tax-allowable depreciation*

| Year of claim | Tax-allowable depreciation claimed $ | Tax saved $ | Year of tax saving |
|---|---|---|---|
| 0 | 75,000 | 37,500 | 0/1 |
| 1 | 56,250 | 28,125 | 1/2 |
| 2 | 42,188 | 21,094 | 2/3 |
| 3 | 126,562 | 63,281 | 3/4 |
| | 300,000 | | |

## 1.4 Tax exhaustion

**Capital allowances** in the form of **first-year allowances** or **writing-down allowances** determine the tax liabilities and after-tax earnings.

In most tax systems, capital expenditure is set off against tax liabilities so as to reduce the taxes a company pays and to encourage investment. These **capital allowances** take two forms; **first-year allowances** which are set off against tax liabilities in the year the investment takes place and **writing-down allowances** which are set off against tax liabilities in subsequent years.

The effect of capital allowances can be from the definition of after-tax – earnings

After-tax earnings = earnings before tax – tax liability

Where tax liability = tax rate × (earnings before tax – capital allowances)

There will be circumstances when the capital allowances in a particular year will equal or exceed before-tax earnings. In such a case the company will pay no tax. In most tax systems, unused capital allowances can be carried forward indefinitely, so that the capital allowance that is set off against the tax liability in any one year includes not only the writing down allowance for the particular year but also any unused allowances from previous years.

### Question

Suppose that a company has invested $10 million in a plant. The first year allowance is 40%, whereas the remaining amount is written down over a period of four years. The tax rate is 30%. Earnings before tax over a five-year period are as follows.

| Year 1 | Year 2 | Year 3 | Year 4 | Year 5 |
|---|---|---|---|---|
| $m | $m | $m | $m | $m |
| 3 | 2.5 | 3.5 | 3.8 | 4.2 |

(a)  Calculate the tax liability every year and the after-tax earnings.
(b)  Calculate the impact on earnings if the first-year allowance is 60%.

### Answer

(a)  The first year allowance is 0.4 × $10 = $4m.

Since the capital allowance exceeds the earnings before tax, the tax liability is 0 and the unused capital allowance of $1m will be added to the second-year writing-down allowance of 0.6 × $10m/4 = $1.5m to yield a capital allowance for year 2 of $2.5m. The capital allowance is the same as the before-tax earnings and the tax liability is again zero. However, this time there is no unused capital allowance to be carried forward.

Capital allowance in each year is shown below.

|  | Year 1 | Year 2 | Year 3 | Year 4 | Year 5 |
|---|---|---|---|---|---|
|  | $m | $m | $m | $m | $m |
| Earnings before tax | 3 | 2.5 | 3.5 | 3.8 | 4.2 |
| First-year allowance | 4 |  |  |  |  |
| Unused capital allowance brought forward |  | 1.0 | 0 |  |  |
| Writing-down allowance |  | 1.5 | 1.5 | 1.5 | 1.5 |
| Total allowance | 4 | 2.5 | 1.5 | 1.5 | 1.5 |

The tax liability for every year and the after-tax earnings are shown in the table below.

|  | Year 1 | Year 2 | Year 3 | Year 4 | Year 5 |
|---|---|---|---|---|---|
|  | $m | $m | $m | $m | $m |
| Earnings before tax | 3.0 | 2.5 | 3.5 | 3.8 | 4.2 |
| Total allowance | 4.0 | 2.5 | 1.5 | 1.5 | 1.5 |
| Taxable profit | 0.0 | 0.0 | 2.0 | 2.3 | 2.7 |
| Tax liability (30%) | 0.0 | 0.0 | 0.6 | 0.69 | 0.81 |
| After-tax earnings | 3.0 | 2.5 | 2.9 | 3.11 | 3.39 |

(b)  When the first-year allowance is 60%, the capital allowances are larger in the first three years but lower in the subsequent two years.

|  | Year 1 | Year 2 | Year 3 | Year 4 | Year 5 |
|---|---|---|---|---|---|
|  | $m | $m | $m | $m | $m |
| Earnings before tax | 3 | 2.5 | 3.5 | 3.8 | 4.2 |
| First-year allowance | 6 |  |  |  |  |
| Unused capital allowance brought forward |  | 3.0 | 1.5 | 0.0 | 0 |
| Writing-down allowance |  | 1.0 | 1.0 | 1.0 | 1 |
| Total allowance | 6 | 4.0 | 2.5 | 1.0 | 1 |

The tax liability for every year and the after tax earnings are shown in the table below.

|  | Year 1 $m | Year 2 $m | Year 3 $m | Year 4 $m | Year 5 $m |
|---|---|---|---|---|---|
| Earnings before tax | 3.0 | 2.5 | 3.5 | 3.8 | 4.2 |
| Total allowance | 6.0 | 4.0 | 2.5 | 1.0 | 1.0 |
| Taxable profit | 0.0 | 0.0 | 1.0 | 2.8 | 3.2 |
| Tax liability (30%) | 0 | 0.0 | 0.3 | 0.84 | 0.96 |
| After-tax earnings | 3 | 2.5 | 3.2 | 2.96 | 3.24 |

After-tax earnings are affected by the pattern of writing-down allowances.

## 1.5 Multi-period capital rationing  12/12

**FAST FORWARD**

**Capital rationing** problems exist when there are insufficient funds available to finance all available profitable projects.

**Capital rationing** may occur due to internal factors (**soft** capital rationing) or external factors (**hard** capital rationing).

When capital rationing is present across **multiple periods**, linear programming may be used to solve the problem of **which projects** to undertake.

**Knowledge brought forward from earlier studies**

**Hard and soft capital rationing**

**Soft capital rationing** may arise for such reasons as the following:

(a) Management may be **reluctant** to **issue additional share capital** because of concerns that this may lead to **outsiders** gaining control of the business.

(b) **Capital expenditure budgets** may restrict spending.

(c) Management may wish to **limit investment** to a level that can be financed solely from retained earnings.

**Hard capital rationing** may arise for one of the following reasons:

(a) There may be restrictions on bank lending due to government control.

(b) The costs associated with making small **issues** of capital may be too great.

(c) Lending institutions may consider an organisation to be **too risky** to be granted further loan facilities.

For **single period** capital rationing problems, divisible projects are ranked according to the **profitability index**. This gives the shadow price of capital or **the maximum rate a company should be prepared to pay to obtain short-term funds to release the capital constraint.**

Single period capital rationing was recapped in Chapter 1, Section 3.4; refer to this section if you are unsure of the technique.

### 1.5.1 Introduction

Companies do not have inexhaustible resources therefore it is likely that only limited funds will be available for capital investment in each period. The problem facing financial managers is how best to spend the money in order to meet their objective of maximising shareholders' wealth. This problem can be solved using **linear programming**.

## 1.5.2 An example

The board of Bazza Inc has approved the following investment expenditure over the next three years.

| Year 1 | Year 2 | Year 3 |
|--------|--------|--------|
| $16,000 | $14,000 | $17,000 |

You have identified four investment opportunities which require different amounts of investment each year, details of which are given below.

| Project | Year 1 | Required investment Year 2 | Year 3 | Project NPV |
|---------|--------|--------|--------|-------------|
| Project 1 | 7,000 | 10,000 | 4,000 | 8,000 |
| Project 2 | 9,000 | 0 | 12,000 | 11,000 |
| Project 3 | 0 | 6,000 | 8,000 | 6,000 |
| Project 4 | 5,000 | 6,000 | 7,000 | 4,000 |

Which combination of projects will result in the highest overall NPV while remaining within the annual investment constraints?

The problem can be formulated as a linear programming problem as follows:

Let   Y1 be investment in project 1
      Y2 be investment in project 2
      Y3 be investment in project 3
      Y4 be investment in project 4

**Objective function**

Maximise $Y_1 \times 8,000 + Y_2 \times 11,000 + Y_3 \times 6,000 + Y_4 \times 4,000$

**Subject to the three annual investment constraints:**

$Y_1 \times 7,000 + Y_2 \times 9,000 + Y_3 \times 0 + Y_4 \times 5,000 \leq 16,000$ (Year 1 constraint)
$Y_1 \times 10,000 + Y_2 \times 0 + Y_3 \times 6,000 + Y_4 \times 6,000 \leq 14,000$ (Year 2 constraint)
$Y_1 \times 4,000 + Y_2 \times 12,000 + Y_3 \times 8,000 + Y_4 \times 7,000 \leq 17,000$ (Year 3 constraint)

When the objective function and constraints are fed into a computer program, the results are:

$Y_1 = 1, Y_2 = 1, Y_3 = 0, Y_4 = 0$

This means that project 1 and project 2 will be selected and project 3 and project 4 will not. The NPV of the investment scheme will be equal to $19,000.

Note that the following solution also satisfies the constraints.

$Y_1 = 0, Y_2 = 0, Y_3 = 1, Y_4 = 1$

However, this is not the optimal solution since the combined NPV of projects 3 and 4 is $10,000, which is lower than the value derived above.

**Exam focus point**

> Make sure you understand the different methods for assessing investments if there is single period rationing and for assessing investments if there is rationing for more than one period. The examining team's report for December 2012 highlighted that students used the wrong techniques to deal with the capital rationing situation in a question in that exam.

## 1.6 Risk and uncertainty

Before deciding whether or not to undertake a project, financial managers will want to assess the project's **risk** (which can be predicted), and **uncertainty** (which is unpredictable).

Risk can be built into project appraisal using such tools as **expected values** and different **costs of capital**.

**Uncertainty** can be described using techniques such as simulation, value at risk, payback and project duration.

### 1.6.1 Risk

You should already be familiar with how financial managers incorporate risk into project appraisal. The **cost of capital** of a project gives an indication of its risk – the **higher** the cost of capital, the **greater** the risk.

Investors want higher returns for higher risk investments. The greater the risk attached to future returns, the greater the risk premium required. Investors also prefer cash now to later and require a higher return for longer time periods.

In investment appraisal, a **risk-adjusted discount rate** can be used for particular types or **risk classes** of investment projects to reflect their relative risks. For example, a **high discount rate** can be used so that a cash flow which occurs quite some time in the future will have less effect on the decision. Alternatively, with the launch of a new product, a higher **initial** risk premium may be used with a decrease in the discount rate as the product becomes established.

Risk can also be incorporated into project appraisal using **expected values**, whereby each possible outcome is given a probability. The expected value is obtained by multiplying each present value by its probability and adding the results together. The **lower** the expected value, the **higher** the risk.

**Question**                                                                    Expected values

A project has the following possible outcomes, each of which is assigned a probability of occurrence.

|  | Probability | Present value |
|---|---|---|
|  |  | $ |
| Low demand | 0.3 | 20,000 |
| Medium demand | 0.6 | 30,000 |
| High demand | 0.1 | 50,000 |

What is the expected value of the project?

**Answer**

The expected value is the sum of each present value multiplied by its probability.

Expected value = $(20,000 \times 0.3) + (30,000 \times 0.6) + (50,000 \times 0.1) = \$29,000$

**Question**                                                                    Expected values 2

What would happen to the expected value of the project if the probability of medium demand fell to 0.4 and the probability of low demand increased to 0.5?

**Answer**

Expected value = $(20,000 \times 0.5) + (30,000 \times 0.4) + (50,000 \times 0.1) = \$27,000$

The project is more risky than before, as there is a greater probability of demand being low, which results in a lower expected value.

## 1.6.2 Uncertainty

Uncertainty is more difficult to plan, for obvious reasons. There are several ways in which uncertainty can be dealt with in project appraisal. Three of them – **payback period, sensitivity analysis** and **discounted payback** – will be familiar to you from earlier studies. Make sure you understand how each of them works.

### Example: Sensitivity analysis

Nevers Ure has a cost of capital of 8% and is considering a project with the following 'most-likely' cash flows.

| Year | Purchase of plant $ | Running costs $ | Savings $ |
|---|---|---|---|
| 0 | (7,000) | | |
| 1 | | 2,000 | 6,000 |
| 2 | | 2,500 | 7,000 |

*Required*

Measure the sensitivity (in percentages) of the project to changes in the levels of expected costs and savings.

### Solution

The present values (PVs) of the cash flows are as follows:

| Year | Discount factor 8% | PV of plant cost $ | PV of running costs $ | PV of savings $ | PV of net cash flow $ |
|---|---|---|---|---|---|
| 0 | 1.000 | (7,000) | | | (7,000) |
| 1 | 0.926 | | (1,852) | 5,556 | 3,704 |
| 2 | 0.857 | | (2,143) | 5,999 | 3,856 |
| | | (7,000) | (3,995) | 11,555 | 560 |

The project has a positive NPV and would appear to be worthwhile. The changes in cash flows which would need to occur for the project to break even (NPV = 0) are as follows.

(a)    Plant costs would need to increase by a PV of $560; that is, by:

$$\frac{560}{7,000} \times 100\% = 8\%$$

(b)    Running costs would need to increase by a PV of $560; that is, by:

$$\frac{560}{3,995} \times 100\% = 14\%$$

(c)    Savings would need to fall by a PV of $560; that is, by:

$$\frac{560}{11,555} \times 100\% = 4.8\%$$

### Weaknesses of sensitivity analysis

These are as follows:

(a)    The method requires that **changes** in each key variable are **isolated**. However, management is more interested in the combination of the effects of changes in two or more key variables.

(b)    Looking at factors in isolation is unrealistic since they are often **interdependent**.

(c)    Sensitivity analysis does not examine the **probability** that any particular variation in costs or revenues might occur.

(d)    **Critical factors** may be those over which managers have no control.

(e)    In itself it does not provide a decision rule. Parameters defining **acceptability** must be laid down by managers.

### 1.6.3 Project duration                                            Sep/Dec 16

Project duration is a measure of the **average time over which a project delivers its value**.

It is calculated by weighting each year of the project by the % **of the present value of the cash inflows** received in that year.

**The lower the project duration the lower the risk of the project**.

> ### Question                                              Project duration
>
> Monty Inc is considering a project which requires an initial investment of $100,000. Projected cash flows discounted at Monty's cost of capital of 10% are as follows.
>
> | Year | 0 | 1 | 2 | 3 | 4 | 5 |
> |------|---|---|---|---|---|---|
> | PV | (100,000) | 45,455 | 36,364 | 26,296 | 13,660 | 6,209 |
>
> Calculate the project duration.

### Answer

The first thing we have to do is determine the total cash inflows over the life of the project, which is the sum of the PVs of the cash inflows for years 1 to 5.

Total PV of cash inflows = $127,984

The second step is to calculate each PV as a percentage of $127,984.

| Year | 1 | 2 | 3 | 4 | 5 |
|------|---|---|---|---|---|
| PV | 45,455 | 36,364 | 26,296 | 13,660 | 6,209 |
| Percentage of total PV | 36% | 28% | 21% | 11% | 4% |

Project duration is the sum of the year number multiplied by the relevant percentage:

$$= (1 \times 0.36) + (2 \times 0.28) + (3 \times 0.21) + (4 \times 0.11) + (5 \times 0.04)$$
$$= 2.19$$

This means that this project delivers its value over 2.19 years ie it has the same duration as a project that delivers 100% of its cash inflows in 2.19 years time. This method looks at the cash flows over the whole life of the project (unlike techniques like payback).

## 2 Monte Carlo simulation and investment appraisal

**FAST FORWARD**

> The Monte Carlo method of estimating a project's NPV assumes that the key factors affecting NPV can be modelled as a probability distribution.

### 2.1 Monte Carlo method

This section provides a brief outline of the Monte Carlo method in investment appraisal. The method appeared in 1949 and is widely used in situations involving uncertainty. The method amounts to adopting a particular probability distribution for the uncertain (random) variables that affect the NPV and then using simulations to generate values of the random variables.

The basic idea is to generate through simulation thousands of values for the parameters or variables of interest and use those variables to derive the NPV for each possible simulated outcome.

From the resulting values we can derive the distribution of the NPV.

To illustrate the method, assume that a company has a project with an expected cash flow of $2 million after the first year of operation. Cash flows will increase by 5% annually in perpetuity. The cost of capital is 10% and initial investment is $18 million.

The PV of the project can be calculated using the constant growth model ie:

$$NPV = \frac{2 \times (1+g)}{(0.1-g)} - 18$$

In our simple example, since the only source of uncertainty is the growth rate, we can assume that the growth rate follows a normal distribution with a mean of 5% and a standard deviation of 3%. The probability distribution of the growth rate is shown in the figure below. The Monte Carlo method works as follows. From the normal distribution we sample 1,000 random values of g. This can be done easily in Excel using the random number generator to generate 1,000 random numbers coming from a normal distribution with a mean of 5 and a standard deviation of 3. For each value of g we calculate the NPV from our model.

$$NPV = \frac{2 \times (1+g)}{(0.1-g)} - 18$$

**Probability Distribution of Growth Rates**

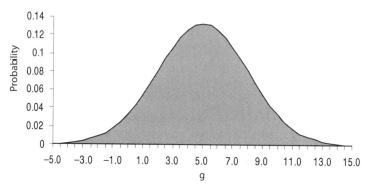

Calculating the NPV for all 1,000 random values of g and plotting the resulting values for the NPV we obtain the following distribution of values for the NPV. While the probability distribution of g is normal, the distribution of the NPV is not normal. The empirical distribution can be constructed from the table below which shows the cumulative frequency distribution of the NPV. Note that you will not be asked to do this in the exam – this is simply to demonstrate how simulations work.

| NPV | Cumulative frequency | NPV | Cumulative frequency |
|---|---|---|---|
| <–5.7 | 1 | <3.6 | 480 |
| <–5.1 | 2 | <4.2 | 563 |
| <–4.5 | 3 | <4.8 | 628 |
| <–3.9 | 4 | <5.4 | 689 |
| <–3.4 | 11 | <6.0 | 756 |
| <–2.8 | 16 | <6.5 | 805 |
| <–2.2 | 29 | <7.1 | 846 |
| <–1.6 | 40 | <7.7 | 875 |
| <–1.0 | 50 | <8.3 | 899 |
| <–0.4 | 76 | <8.9 | 929 |
| <0.0 | 100 | <9.5 | 951 |
| <0.7 | 172 | <10.0 | 971 |
| <1.3 | 217 | <10.6 | 981 |
| <1.9 | 279 | <11.2 | 990 |
| <2.5 | 351 | <11.8 | 996 |
| <3.1 | 417 | <17.0 | 1,000 |

The table provides a complete description of the distribution of the NPV of the model we have employed. For example, the probability of getting a negative NPV is 10% since:

Probability (NPV < 0) = $\dfrac{100}{1,000}$ = 0.1.

Similarly, the probability of getting a NPV of less than 3.6 is equal to:

$\dfrac{480}{1,000}$ or 48%.

The frequency distribution of the NPVs resulting from the simulation is shown in the following diagram. The distribution shows that most of the values for the NPV are around 2 and 6 with a mean value of about 4. Statistical measures, such as the standard deviation, can be calculated to describe the dispersion of prices. The overwhelming conclusion from the analysis is that the NPV of the project under a wide range of assumptions for the growth rate is most likely to be positive.

**Distribution of NPV**

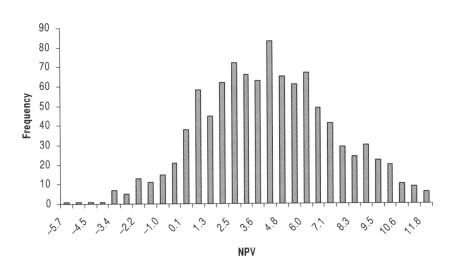

## 2.2 Project value at risk                                           6/12, 12/14

The project value at risk is the potential loss of a project with a given probability.

The empirical distribution of the NPV leads naturally to the concept of the project value at risk.

**Value at risk** (VAR) is the minimum amount by which the value of an investment or portfolio will fall over a given period of time at a given level of probability.

Alternatively, it is defined as the maximum amount that it may lose at a given level of confidence.

For example, we may say that the VAR is $100,000 at 5% probability, or that it is $100,000 at 95% confidence level. The first definition implies that there is a 5% chance that the loss will exceed $100,000, or that we are 95% sure that it will not exceed $100,000. VAR can be defined at any level of probability or confidence, but the most common probability levels are 1, 5 and 10%.

A formal definition of the VAR of a position where the value of the position is denoted by V is the value V* such that values of V less than V* have a chance of only p to appear. The probability level is the area under the curve and it can be calculated as the value of the random variable that determines the desired area under the curve.

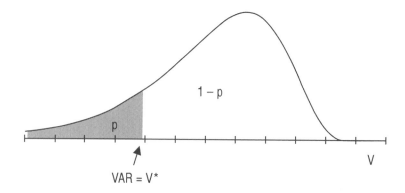

When the random variable follows the normal distribution, the VAR at specific probability levels is easily calculated as a multiple of the standard deviation. For example, the 5% VAR is simply 1.645$\sigma$; the 1% VAR is 2.33$\sigma$.

For example, the annual standard deviation of a position is $200,000. The VAR is 200,000 × 1.645 = $329,000. Only in 5% of the cases will the value fall by a larger amount within a year.

The VAR can be calculated over more than one period by using the standard deviation for the entire period. For example, if we assume that the life of a project is two years and both years have the same variance $\sigma$ = $200,000 and are independent of each other, then the VAR will be:

VAR  =  1.645 × $200,000 × $\sqrt{2}$  = $465,276

That is, there is only a 5% chance that losses will exceed the $465,276 over a 2-year period.

In general the VAR will be given by:

$$VAR = k\sigma\sqrt{N}$$

Where k is determined by the probability level, $\sigma$ is the standard deviation and N is the periods over which we want to calculate the VAR.

Having defined the VAR, we can define the project value at risk (PVAR), as the loss that may occur at a given level of probability over the life of the project.

### 2.2.1 Example

The annual cash flows from a project are expected to follow the normal distribution with a mean of $50,000 and standard deviation of $10,000. The project has a 10 year life. What is the PVAR?

The PVAR for a year is:

PVAR = 1.645 × $10,000 = $16,450

The PVAR that takes into account the entire project life is:

PVAR = 1.645 × $10,000 × $\sqrt{10}$ = $52,019; this is the maximum amount by which the value of the project will fall at a confidence level of 95%.

So far we have used the normal distribution to calculate the VAR. The assumption that project cash flows or values follow the normal distribution may not be plausible. An alternative way is to use the distribution from a Monte Carlo simulation. For example, using the previous table we see that the probability of getting an NPV less or lower than –$1 million is 5%. So the PVAR at 5% probability is –$1 million for the specific example. According to our notation, V* = –1 million. That means that the chance of losing more than $1 million in the above project is only 5%.

The PVAR can be calculated at different probability levels. The PVAR at 1% probability level is –5.7 million. That means that the chance of losses exceeding $5.7 million is only 1%.

# 3 Internal rate of return

A project will only be selected if its internal rate of return **exceeds** the cost of capital or target rate of return.

**Key term**

The **internal rate of return** (IRR) of any investment is the discount rate at which the NPV is equal to zero. Alternatively, the IRR can be thought of as the return that is delivered by a project.

**Knowledge brought forward from earlier studies**

The IRR is used to calculate the exact discount rate at which NPV is equal to zero.

If calculating IRR manually we use the interpolation method as follows.

(a) Calculate an NPV using a discount rate that gives **a whole number** and gives an NPV **close to zero**.

(b) Calculate a second NPV using another discount rate. If the first NPV was **positive**, use a rate that is **higher** than the first rate; if it was **negative**, use a rate that is **lower** than the first rate.

(c) Use the two NPVs to calculate the IRR. The formula to apply is:

$$IRR = a + \left( \left( \frac{NPV_a}{NPV_a - NPV_b} \right)(b-a) \right)\% \quad \text{This formula is not given in the exam.}$$

where
$\quad a$ = the lower of the two rates of return used
$\quad b$ = the higher of the two rates of return used
$\quad NPV_a$ = the NPV obtained using rate a
$\quad NPV_b$ = the NPV obtained using rate b

The project should be accepted if the IRR is **greater** than the **cost of capital** or **target rate of return**.

## 3.1 Example of IRR calculation

A company is considering the purchase of a piece of equipment costing $120,000 that would save $30,000 each year for five years. The equipment could be sold at the end of its useful life for $15,000. The company requires every project to yield a return of 10% or more otherwise they will be rejected. Should this equipment be purchased?

## Solution

Annual depreciation will be $\dfrac{\$(120,000 - 15,000)}{5} = \$21,000$

**Step 1**   Calculate the first NPV, using a rate that is two-thirds of the return on investment.

The return on investment would be:

$$\frac{30,000 - \text{depreciation of } 21,000}{0.5 \times (120,000 + 15,000)} = \frac{9,000}{67,500} = 13.3\%$$

Two-thirds of this is 8.9% and so we can start by trying 9%.

The IRR is the rate for the cost of capital at which the NPV = 0.

| Year | Cash flow $ | PV factor 9% | PV of cash flow $ |
|------|-------------|--------------|-------------------|
| 0 | (120,000) | 1.000 | (120,000) |
| 1–5 | 30,000 | 3.890 | 116,700 |
| 5 | 15,000 | 0.650 | 9,750 |
| | | NPV = | 6,450 |

This is fairly close to zero. It is also **positive**, which means that the actual **rate of return** is **more than 9%**. We can use 9% as one of our two NPVs close to zero.

**Step 2**     Calculate the second NPV, using a rate that is **greater** than the first rate, as the first rate gave a positive answer.

Suppose we try 12%.

| Year | Cash flow $ | PV factor 12% | PV of cash flow $ |
|------|-------------|---------------|-------------------|
| 0 | (120,000) | 1.000 | (120,000) |
| 1–5 | 30,000 | 3.605 | 108,150 |
| 5 | 15,000 | 0.567 | 8,505 |
| | | | NPV = (3,345) |

This is fairly close to zero and **negative**. The real rate of return is therefore greater than 9% (positive NPV of $6,450) but less than 12% (negative NPV of $3,345).

**Step 3**     Use the two NPV values to estimate the IRR.

The interpolation method assumes that the NPV rises in linear fashion between the two NPVs close to 0. The real rate of return is therefore assumed to be on a straight line between NPV = $6,450 at 9% and NPV = –$3,345 at 12%.

Using the formula

$$IRR \approx a + \left( \left( \frac{NPV_a}{NPV_a - NPV_b} \right) (b-a) \right) \%$$

$$IRR \approx 9 + \frac{6,450}{(6,450 + 3,345)} \times (12 - 9)\% = 10.98\%, \text{ say } 11\%$$

If it is company policy to undertake investments which are expected to yield 10% or more, this project would be undertaken.

## 3.2 The multiple IRR problem

> A project being accepted based on IRR may be misleading if the cash flows from the project are not normal.

The example employed to calculate the IRR indicates that the IRR and the NPV produce the same result, ie a positive NPV implies that the IRR is greater than the cost of capital. However, this is true only when the project has normal cash flows, ie a negative initial cash flow followed by a series of positive cash flows. If the cash flows change signs then the IRR may not be unique. This is the multiple **IRR problem**.

**Key term**

> The **multiple IRR** occurs when cash flows change sign and result in more than one value for the IRR.

### 3.2.1 Example

Consider the following example, where the cash flow for the second year is negative. Note that in this case the NPV is equated to zero for two values of IRR, when IRR = 5.1% and when IRR = 39.8%.

| Time | Cash flow | Discount factor | PV |
|------|-----------|-----------------|-----|
| 0 | –245,000 | 1 | –245,000 |
| 1 | 600,000 | 0.909 | 545,455 |
| 2 | –360,000 | 0.826 | –297,521 |
| | | | 2,934 |

If we plot the NPV for this project at various different discount rates, we find the following.

**Multiple IRR problem**

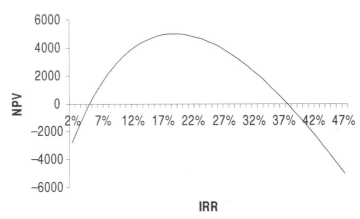

The NPV is initially negative, increases and becomes positive, reaches a maximum value and then declines and becomes negative again. According to the decision rule, we should accept projects for which IRR > k. However, the IRR takes two values.

# 4 Comparison of NPV and IRR

The rule for making investments under the NPV method is that where investments are mutually exclusive, the one with the higher NPV should be preferred. Where investments are independent, all investments should be accepted if they have positive NPVs. The reason for this is that they are generating sufficient cash flows to give an acceptable return to providers of debt and equity finance. This is known as the NPV rule.

The IRR rule states that, where an investment has cash outflows followed by cash inflows, it should be accepted if its IRR exceeds the cost of capital. This is because such investments will have positive NPVs.

## 4.1 Limitations of the IRR technique

Where we are dealing with independent investments, the IRR should usually come to the same decision as the NPV approach. However, it cannot be used to distinguish between mutually exclusive investments. This is because it merely indicates whether or not a project has a positive NPV. It does not tell us the magnitude of the NPV, hence it cannot decide which is the superior project.

## 4.2 Mutually exclusive projects

Question                                                  **Mutually exclusive projects**

We have two projects that both require an initial investment of $10,000. Project A has an IRR of 25% per annum, project B has an IRR of 20% per annum. Which project should we select?

The answer may appear fairly clear-cut, ie that we select the project with the higher IRR. However, we are also told that the company's cost of capital is 10% and are provided with the following data.

| Time | Project A | Project B |
|------|-----------|-----------|
| 0 | (10,000) | (10,000) |
| 1 | 12,000 | 1,000 |
| 2 | 625 | 13,200 |

It is incorrect to decide between these alternatives based on IRRs. If we were to work out the NPVs of these two projects, we could then summarise the findings as follows.

|  | Project A | Project B |
|---|---|---|
| NPV @ 10% | 1,426 | 1,818 |
| IRR | 25% | 20% |

What we can see is that project A has the higher IRR of 25%, but it has a lower NPV at the company's cost of capital. This means that at a 10% cost of capital, project B is preferable, even though it has the lower IRR.

However, when the cost of capital is 20% project A would be preferred since project B would then have a NPV of zero while project A must still have a positive NPV. It can be seen that the decision depends not on the IRR but on the cost of capital being used.

**NPV profile**

Considering this example more fully, if we calculate the NPVs at various costs of capital we find the following:

| Rate % | Project A NPV $ | Project B NPV $ |
|---|---|---|
| 5.0 | 1,995 | 2,925 |
| 7.5 | 1,704 | 2,353 |
| 10.0 | 1,426 | 1,818 |
| 12.5 | 1,160 | 1,319 |
| 15.0 | 907 | 851 |
| 17.5 | 665 | 412 |
| 20.0 | 434 | 0 |
| 22.5 | 212 | (387) |
| 25.0 | 0 | (752) |
| 27.5 | (204) | (1,096) |
| 30.0 | (399) | (1,420) |

Plotting these on a graph we get the following:

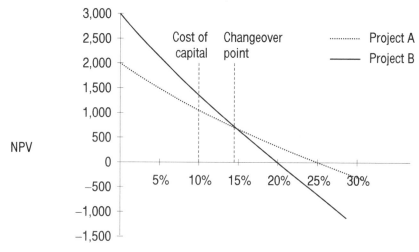

What we can see is that up to a cost of capital of just over 14%, project B has the highest NPV. Above that cost of capital, project A has the greater NPV and would, therefore, be preferable. For both the above projects, the NPV profile is that the NPV falls as the discount rate increases.

## 4.3 Reasons why the NPV profiles differ

The NPV profiles cross over at a discount rate of approximately 14%. There are two reasons why this may occur.

- Differences in the timing of the cash flows for each project
- Differences in the project sizes (or project scales)

In this case, there is no difference in project size, with both projects having an initial investment of $10,000. However, there are differences in the timing of the cash flows, with project B having high cash flows in year 2 and project A having high cash flows in year 1.

The NPV profile for project B shows a far steeper line. This is because it has higher cash inflows in the more distant year. Therefore, it is much more affected by an increasing discount rate. In contrast, project A has higher-value cash flows in the earlier year. This means that it is less affected by the increase in discount rate.

## 4.4 Conflicting rankings using the NPV and IRR methods

Note that, where the discount rate is greater than 15% (the **changeover** or **crossover rate**), selecting an investment based on either the higher NPV or the higher IRR will give the same answer. In this case, for discount rates between 15% and 20%, project A has the higher NPV and it also has the higher IRR.

For discount rates of less than 15%, selecting an investment based on the higher IRR gives an answer which conflicts with the NPV method, since it will select project A, although project B has the higher NPV.

### 4.4.1 Reinvestment rate

The problem with selecting investments based on the **higher IRR** is that it makes an assumption that **cash flows** can be **reinvested** at the **IRR** over the **life of the project**.

In contrast, the **NPV method** assumes that cash flows can be **reinvested** at the **cost of capital** over the life of the project.

If the assumption that the IRR as a reinvestment rate is valid, then the IRR technique will be superior. However, it is unlikely that this will be the case and therefore the NPV method is likely to be superior. The better reinvestment rate assumption will be the cost of capital used for the NPV method.

## 4.5 Other factors

For projects with **non-normal cash flows**, eg flows where the sign changes more than once, there may be more than one IRR. This means that the IRR method cannot be used.

The NPV method gives no indication as to the **sensitivity** of the project to changes in forecast figures or the amount of capital at risk, unlike the IRR method.

# 5 Modified internal rate of return (MIRR)    6/12, 12/14

**FAST FORWARD**

The modified internal rate of return is the IRR that would result if it was **not assumed that project proceeds were reinvested at the IRR**.

The modified internal rate of return (MIRR) overcomes the problem of the **reinvestment assumption** and the fact that **changes in the cost of capital over the life of the project** cannot be incorporated in the IRR method.

**Exam formula**

$$MIRR = \left(\frac{PV_R}{PV_I}\right)^{\frac{1}{n}} \times (1 + r_e) - 1$$

Where  $PV_R$ = the PV of the return phase (the phase of the project with cash inflows)
$PV_I$ = the PV of the investment phase (the phase of the project with cash outflows)
$r_e$  = the cost of capital

> This topic was examined as part of a 30-mark compulsory question in December 2008 – calculations and appreciation of the advantages and disadvantages of the method relative to NPV were required. It was also examined in June 2012 where IRR and MIRR calculations were required.

## 5.1 Example of MIRR calculations

Consider a project requiring an initial investment of $24,500, with cash inflows of $15,000 in years 1 and 2 and cash inflows of $3,000 in years 3 and 4. The cost of capital is 10%.

## Solution

Calculate **PV** of the investment phase and the return phase.

| Year | Cash flow | Discount factor | PV |
|------|-----------|-----------------|-----|
|      | $         | 10%             | $   |
| 0    | (24,500)  | 1.000           | (24,500) |
| 1    | 15,000    | 0.909           | 13,635 |
| 2    | 15,000    | 0.826           | 12,390 |
| 3    | 3,000     | 0.751           | 2,253 |
| 4    | 3,000     | 0.683           | 2,049 |

$PV_R$ = Total PV for years 1–4 = $30,327

$PV_I$ = Cost of investment = $24,500

$$MIRR = \left[\frac{30,327}{24,500}\right]^{\frac{1}{4}} \times (1 + 0.1) - 1 = 16\%$$

The MIRR is calculated on the basis of **investing the inflows** at the **cost of capital**.

**Exam focus point**

> Make sure you read the ACCA article entitled 'Modified internal rate of return'.

## 5.2 Advantages of MIRR

An advantage of MIRR compared to IRR is that MIRR assumes the **reinvestment rate** is the **company's cost of capital**. IRR assumes that the reinvestment rate is the IRR itself, which is usually untrue.

In many cases where there is conflict between the NPV and IRR methods, the MIRR will give the same indication as NPV, which is the **correct theoretical method**. This helps when explaining the appraisal of a project to managers, who often find the concept of rate of return easier to understand than that of NPV.

## 5.3 Disadvantages of MIRR

However, MIRR, like all rate of return methods, suffers from the problem that it may lead an investor to reject a project which has a **lower rate of return** but, because of its size, generates a **larger increase in wealth**.

In the same way, a **high-return** project with a **short life** may be preferred over a **lower-return** project with a longer life.

# Chapter Roundup

- Projects with a positive net present value should be undertaken.

- Inflation is present in all economies and must be accounted for when evaluating projects.

- In investment appraisal, tax is often assumed to be payable **one year in arrears**, but you should read the question details carefully.

- **Tax-allowable depreciation** details should be checked in any question you attempt.

- **Capital allowances** in the form of **first-year allowances** or **writing-down allowances** determine the tax liabilities and after-tax earnings.

- **Capital rationing** problems exist when there are insufficient funds available to finance all available profitable projects.

- **Capital rationing** may occur due to internal factors (**soft** capital rationing) or external factors (**hard** capital rationing).

- When capital rationing is present across **multiple periods**, linear programming may be used to solve the problem of **which projects** to undertake.

- Before deciding whether or not to undertake a project, financial managers will want to assess the project's **risk** (which can be predicted) and **uncertainty** (which is unpredictable).

- Risk can be built into project appraisal using such tools as **expected values** and different **costs of capital**.

- **Uncertainty** can be described using techniques such as simulation, value at risk, payback and project duration.

- The Monte Carlo method of estimating a project's NPV assumes that the key factors affecting NPV can be modelled as a probability distribution.

- The project value at risk is the potential loss of a project with a given probability.

- A project will only be selected if its internal rate of return **exceeds** the cost of capital or target rate of return.

- A project being accepted based on IRR may be misleading if the cash flows from the project are not positive.

- The modified internal rate of return is the IRR that would result if it was **not assumed that project proceeds were reinvested at the IRR**.

# Quick Quiz

1   Why is NPV preferable to IRR as a project selection criterion?

2   When does the multiple value IRR normally occur?

3   What is the appropriate criterion for ranking projects when there is a constraint of funds?

4   What is the main difference between MIRR and IRR?

5   If Project A had a duration of 3.5 years and Project B had a duration of 2.6 years, which project would be preferable and why?

6   What is the advantage of the Monte Carlo calculation of the NPV?

# Answers to Quick Quiz

1     The NPV criterion is consistent with the shareholder wealth maximisation whereas the IRR criterion is not.

2     The multiple value of IRR occurs when there is a negative cash flow.

3     The appropriate criterion is the profitability index.

4     The IRR implies that the profits from a project are reinvested at the IRR whereas the MIRR allows the reinvestment rate to change.

5     Project B is preferable because it delivers its value over a shorter period of time.

6     The Monte Carlo calculation of the NPV derives the NPV under a wide range of assumptions.

Now try the questions below from the Practice Question Bank

| Number | Level | Marks | Time |
|--------|-------|-------|------|
| 8 | Examination | 20 | 39 mins |
| 9 | Examination | 20 | 39 mins |

# Application of option pricing theory in investment decisions

| Topic list | Syllabus reference |
|---|---|
| 1 Overview | B2 |
| 2 Basic concepts | B2(a) |
| 3 Determinants of option values | B2(a) |
| 4 Real options | B2(b) |
| 5 Valuation of real options | B2(c) |

## Introduction

In this chapter we look at how option valuation techniques can be applied to capital budgeting. First we review the basic theory underlying the pricing of financial options and then we examine a number of options embedded in projects, such as the option to delay, the option to abandon, the option to expand and the option to redeploy productive resources.

# Study guide

| | | Intellectual level |
|---|---|---|
| B2 | **Application of option pricing theory in investment decisions** | |
| (a) | Apply the Black-Scholes Option Pricing (BSOP) model to financial product valuation and to asset valuation. | 3 |
| | (i) Determine, using published data, the five principal drivers of option value (value of the underlying, exercise price, time to expiry, volatility and the risk-free rate). | |
| | (ii) Discuss the underlying assumptions, structure, application and limitations of the BSOP model. | |
| (b) | Evaluate embedded real options within a project, classifying them into one of the real option archetypes. | 3 |
| (c) | Assess, calculate and advise on the value of options to delay, expand, redeploy and withdraw using the BSOP model. | 3 |

# 1 Overview

The topic of real options applies the option valuation techniques to capital budgeting exercises in which a project is coupled with a put or call option. For example, the firm may have the option to abandon a project during its life. This amounts to a put option on the remaining cash flows associated with the project. Ignoring the value of these real options (as in standard discounted cash flow techniques) can lead to incorrect investment evaluation decisions.

One of the optional performance objectives in your PER is to review the financial and strategic consequences of undertaking a particular investment decision. This chapter covers the concept of real options which attempts to quantify the strategic characteristics of investments.

# 2 Basic concepts

Options are contracts that give to one party the right to enter into a transaction but not the obligation to do so.

## 2.1 Types of options

### 2.1.1 Definition

An option is a contract that gives one party the option to enter into a transaction either at a specific time in the future or within a specific future period at a price that is agreed when the contract is issued.

### 2.1.2 Exercise price

The exercise or strike price is the price at which the future transaction will take place.

### 2.1.3 Premium

Premium is the price paid by the option buyer to the seller, or writer, for the right to buy or sell the underlying shares.

### 2.1.4 Call and put options

The buyer of a call option acquires the right, but not the obligation, to buy the underlying at a fixed price. The buyer of a put option acquires the right, but not the obligation, to sell the underlying shares at a fixed price.

### 2.1.5 European, American and Bermudan options

A European option can only be exercised at expiration, whereas an American option can be exercised any time prior to expiration. A Bermudan option is an option where early exercise is restricted to certain dates during the life of the option. It derives its name from the fact that its exercise characteristics are somewhere between those of the American and the European style of options and the island of Bermuda lies between America and Europe.

### 2.1.6 Long and short positions                                              6/13

When an investor buys an option the investor is setting up a long position, and when the investor sells an option the investor has a short position.

### 2.1.7 Price quotations

It should be noted that, for simplicity, only one price is quoted for each option in the national newspapers. In practice, there will always be two prices quoted for each option, ie a bid and an offer price. The example below looks at share options.

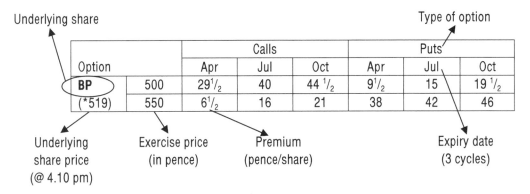

| Option | | Calls | | | Puts | | |
| --- | --- | --- | --- | --- | --- | --- | --- |
| | | Apr | Jul | Oct | Apr | Jul | Oct |
| BP | 500 | $29^1/_2$ | 40 | $44^1/_2$ | $9^1/_2$ | 15 | $19^1/_2$ |
| (*519) | 550 | $6^1/_2$ | 16 | 21 | 38 | 42 | 46 |

## 2.2 Profiles of call options at expiration

**FAST FORWARD**

A long call option position at expiration may lead to unlimited profits, and a short-option position may lead to unlimited losses.

### 2.2.1 Long call

A call option that has been purchased (ie a long call) will be exercised at expiration only if the price of the underlying is higher than the exercise price.

For example, if a call option to buy a BP share at a price of 500p has been purchased, if the BP share price at the expiry date of the option is 600p then the option to buy the share for 500p will be exercised (because the option price is a better price than the market price). If the price of the underlying asset is lower than the exercise price (eg the share price at the expiry date of the option is 400p) then the option will not be exercised.

The value of a call option at expiration is the higher of:

The difference between the value of the underlying security at expiration and the exercise price, if the value of the underlying security > exercise price

Or:

Zero, if value of the underlying security is equal to or less than the exercise price.

Since the buyer of a call option has paid a premium to buy the option, the profit from the purchase of the call option is the value of the option minus the premium paid.

Ie profit = value of call option – premium paid for the purchase of the option

Suppose that you buy the October call option with an exercise price of 550. The premium is 21c. Calculate the potential profit/loss at expiration.

Answer

The profit/loss will be calculated for possible values of the underlying at expiration. Here we examine the profit/loss profile for prices ranging from 500 to 600.

| Value of underlying at expiration | Value of underlying – exercise price | Value of option | Profit/loss |
|---|---|---|---|
| 500 | –50 | 0 | –21 |
| 530 | –20 | 0 | –21 |
| 540 | –10 | 0 | –21 |
| 550 | 0 | 0 | –21 |
| 560 | 10 | 10 | –11 |
| 570 | 20 | 20 | –1 |
| 600 | 50 | 50 | 29 |

The profit or loss at expiration is shown below.

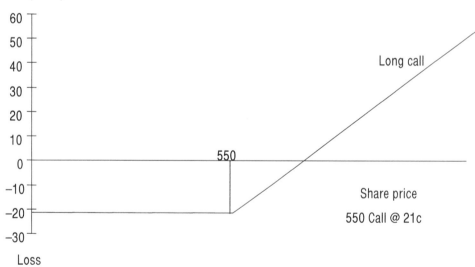

## 2.2.2 Short call

The seller of a call loses money when the option is exercised and gains the premium if the option is not exercised. The value of the call option for a seller is exactly the opposite of the value of the call option for the buyer.

The profit of the short position at expiration is:

Profit = premium received – value of call option

A short call option has a maximum profit, which is the premium, but unlimited losses.

## Question

Suppose that you sell the October call option with an exercise price of 550. The premium is 21c. Calculate the potential profit/loss at expiration for the writer of the option.

## Answer

| Column A<br>Value of underlying at expiration | Column B<br>Value of underlying at expiration – exercise price | Column C<br>Maximum of zero and the difference between the value of the underlying and the exercise price | Negative Column C + premium |
|---|---|---|---|
| 500 | –50 | 0 | 21 |
| 530 | –20 | 0 | 21 |
| 540 | –10 | 0 | 21 |
| 550 | 0 | 0 | 21 |
| 560 | 10 | –10 | 11 |
| 570 | 20 | –20 | –1 |
| 600 | 50 | –50 | –29 |

The profit or loss at expiration is shown below.

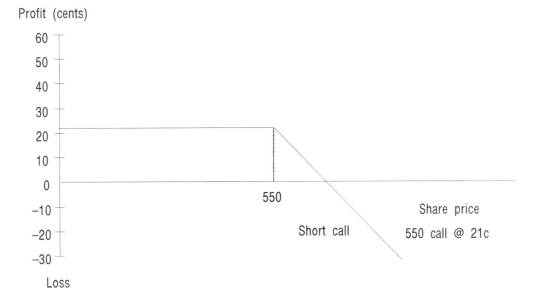

## 2.3 Profiles of put options at expiration

The maximum profit from a long put position and the maximum loss from a short put position occurs when the price of the underlying becomes zero.

### 2.3.1 Long put

A put that has been purchased (ie a long put) will be exercised at expiration only if the price of the underlying asset is lower than the exercise price of the option. The **value** of the option when exercised is the **difference** between the **exercise price** and the **value of the underlying**.

The **profit** from a long position is the **difference** between the **value of the option** at expiration and the **premium paid**.

## Question

Suppose that you buy the October put option with an exercise price of 550. The premium is 46c. Calculate the potential profit/loss at expiration.

## Answer

| Column A<br>Value of underlying<br>at expiration | Column B<br>Exercise price – value<br>of underlying | Column C<br>Maximum of Column B<br>and zero | Column C – premium |
|---|---|---|---|
| 500 | 50 | 50 | 4 |
| 530 | 20 | 20 | –26 |
| 540 | –10 | 10 | –36 |
| 550 | 0 | 0 | –46 |
| 560 | –10 | 0 | –46 |
| 570 | –20 | 0 | –46 |
| 600 | –50 | 0 | –46 |

The profit or loss at expiration is shown below.

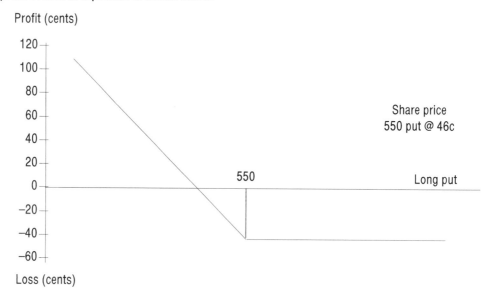

### 2.3.2 Short put

The seller of a put loses money when the option is exercised and gains the premium if the option is not exercised. The value of the put option for a seller is exactly the opposite of the value of the put option for the buyer.

The profit of the short position at expiration is:

Profit = premium received – value of put option

The **maximum profit** for the writer of a put option is the **premium paid** which occurs when the put option is **not exercised** (that is, when the value at expiration = 0). This happens when the value of the underlying at expiration **is greater than** the exercise price.

The profit will be **zero** when the value of the underlying at expiration is **equal to** the sum of the exercise price and the premium paid.

The **highest loss** occurs when the value of the underlying = 0. The maximum loss will be equal to the **exercise price**.

**Question**

Suppose that you sell the October put option with an exercise price of 550. The premium is 46c. Calculate the potential profit/loss at expiration.

**Answer**

| Column A<br>Value of underlying at<br>expiration | Column B<br>Exercise price – value of<br>underlying | Column C<br>Maximum of column B<br>and zero | Column C + premium |
|---|---|---|---|
| 500 | 50 | 50 | –4 |
| 530 | 20 | 20 | 26 |
| 540 | 10 | 10 | 36 |
| 550 | 0 | 0 | 46 |
| 560 | –10 | 0 | 46 |
| 570 | –20 | 0 | 46 |
| 600 | –50 | 0 | 46 |

The profit or loss at expiration is shown below.

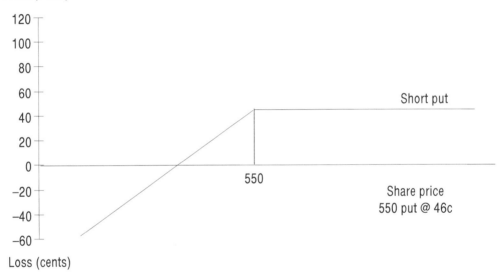

# 3 Determinants of option values

The value of an option is determined by the exercise price, the price of the underlying, the time to expiration, the volatility of the underlying and the interest rate.

## 3.1 Introduction

Options are financial instruments whose value changes all the time. The value of a call or a put option at expiration was derived earlier. In this section we shall identify the factors that affect the price of an option prior to expiration.

### 3.1.1 The exercise price

The higher the exercise price, the lower the probability that a call will be exercised. So call prices will decrease as the exercise prices increase. For the put, the effect runs in the opposite direction. A higher exercise price means that there is higher probability that the put will be exercised. So the put price increases as the exercise price increases.

### 3.1.2 The price of the underlying

As the current stock price goes up, there is a higher probability that the call will be in the money. As a result, the call price will increase. The effect will be in the opposite direction for a put. As the stock price goes up, there is a lower probability that the put will be in the money. So the put price will decrease.

### 3.1.3 The volatility of the underlying

Both the call and put will increase in price as the underlying asset becomes more volatile. The buyer of the option receives full benefit of favourable outcomes but avoids the unfavourable ones (option price value has zero value).

### 3.1.4 The time to expiration

Both calls and puts will benefit from increased time to expiration. The reason is that there is more time for a big move in the stock price. But there are some effects that work in the opposite direction. As the time to expiration increase, the present value (PV) of the exercise price decreases. This will increase the value of the call and decrease the value of the put. Also, as the time to expiration increases, there is a greater amount of time for the stock price to be reduced by a cash dividend. This reduces the call value but increases the put value.

### 3.1.5 The interest rate

The higher the interest rate, the lower the PV of the exercise price. As a result, the value of the call will increase. The opposite is true for puts. The decrease in the PV of the exercise price will adversely affect the price of the put option.

### 3.1.6 The intrinsic and time value

The price of an option has two components; intrinsic value and time value. Intrinsic value is the value of the option if it was exercised now.

*Call options:*   Intrinsic value (at time t) = underlying's current price – call strike price
*Put options:*    Intrinsic value (at time t) = put strike price – underlying's current price

If the intrinsic value is positive, the option is in the money (ITM). If the intrinsic value is zero, the option is at the money (ATM) and if the intrinsic value is negative, the option is out of the money (OTM).

The difference between the market price of an option and its intrinsic value is the time value of the option. Buyers of ATM or OTM options are simply buying time value, which decreases as an option approaches expiration. The more time an option has until expiration, the greater the option's chance of ending up ITM and the larger its time value. On the expiration day the time value of an option is zero and all an option is worth is its intrinsic value. It's either ITM, or it isn't.

## 3.2 The Black-Scholes pricing model    12/10, 6/11, 12/13, Mar/Jun 16

**FAST FORWARD**

The Black-Scholes model predicts the value of an option for given values of its determinants.

The payoffs at expiration for a call option were derived earlier as:
The difference between the value of the underlying at expiration and the exercise price (where value of underlying > exercise price)
Or:
Zero (where value of underlying ≤ exercise price)

The expected value of the payoff will depend on the probability that the option will be on the money, which we do not know. The value of the call option today will be the PV of the expected payoff at expiration. Apart from the probability to be ITM we also need to specify a discount factor, which will reflect the risk of the option. The problem of option valuation concerned financial specialists for a long time until Black, Scholes and Merton resolved the problem.

### 3.2.1 The Black-Scholes formula

The Black-Scholes formula for the value of a **European call option** is given by:

$$c = P_a N(d_1) - P_e N(d_2)e^{-rt}$$

where $P_a$ is the current price of the underlying asset

$P_e$ is the exercise price

r is the continuously compounded risk-free rate

t is the time to expiration measured as a fraction of one year, for example t = 0.5 means that the time to expiration is six months

e is the base of the natural logarithms, $e^{-rt}$ is a form of discount factor

N refers to the use of normal distribution tables – the use of these will be illustrated later

$$d_1 = \frac{\ln\left(\frac{P_a}{P_e}\right) + \left(r + 0.5s^2\right)t}{s\sqrt{t}} \qquad d_2 = d_1 - s\sqrt{t}$$

where s is the standard deviation of the price movement (a measure of volatility)

$\ln\left(\frac{P_a}{P_e}\right)$ is the natural logarithm of the spot price over the exercise price.

### 3.2.2 Value of European put options

The value of a **European put option** can be calculated by using the put call parity relationship which is given to you in the exam formulae sheet.

$$p = c - P_a + P_e e^{-rt}$$

where p is the value of the put option

c is the value of the call option

### 3.2.3 Value of American call options

Although American options can be exercised any time during their lifetime, it is **never optimal** to exercise an option earlier. The value of an American option will therefore be the same as the value of an equivalent European option and the Black-Scholes model can be used to calculate its price.

### 3.2.4 Value of American put options

Unfortunately, no exact analytic formula for the value of an American put option on non dividend paying stock has been produced. Numerical procedures and analytic approximations for calculating American put values are used instead.

---

**Question**                                                                 Black-Scholes calculation

Consider the situation where the stock price 6 months from the expiration of an option is $42, the exercise price of the option is $40, the risk-free interest rate is 10% p.a. and the volatility is 20% p.a. This means $P_a = 42$, $P_e = 40$, r = 0.1, s = 0.2, t = 0.5.

$$d_1 = \frac{\ln(42/40) + (0.1 + \frac{0.2^2}{2})0.5}{0.2\sqrt{0.5}} = 0.7693 = 0.77$$

$$d_2 = 0.7693 - 0.2 \times \sqrt{0.5} = 0.6279 = 0.63$$

and

$$P_e^{-rt} = 40e^{-0.1 \times 0.5} = 40e^{-0.05} = 38.049$$

The values of the standard normal cumulative probability distribution N ($d_1$) and N ($d_2$) can be found from the normal distribution tables which you can find in the Mathematical Tables appendix at the end of this Study Text.

Here $d_1$ = 0.77 so from the normal distribution tables, N ($d_1$) can be found as follows.

**Standard normal distribution table**

|  | 0·00 | 0·01 | 0·02 | 0·03 | 0·04 | 0·05 | 0·06 | 0·07 | 0·08 | 0 |
|---|---|---|---|---|---|---|---|---|---|---|
| 0·0 | 0·0000 | 0·0040 | 0·0080 | 0·0120 | 0·0160 | 0·0199 | 0·0239 | 0·0279 | 0·0319 | 0·0₃ |
| 0·1 | 0·0398 | 0·0438 | 0·0478 | 0·0517 | 0·0557 | 0·0596 | 0·0636 | 0·0675 | 0·0714 | 0·0₇ |
| 0·2 | 0·0793 | 0·0832 | 0·0871 | 0·0910 | 0·0948 | 0·0987 | 0·1026 | 0·1064 | 0·1103 | 0·11 |
| 0·3 | 0·1179 | 0·1217 | 0·1255 | 0·1293 | 0·1331 | 0·1368 | 0·1406 | 0·1443 | 0·1480 | 0·1₅ |
| 0·4 | 0·1554 | 0·1591 | 0·1628 | 0·1664 | 0·1700 | 0·1736 | 0·1772 | 0·1808 | 0·1844 | 0·1₈ |
| 0·5 | 0·1915 | 0·1950 | 0·1985 | 0·2019 | 0·2054 | 0·2088 | 0·2123 | 0·2157 | 0·2190 | 0·2₂ |
| 0·6 | 0·2257 | 0·2291 | 0·2324 | 0·2357 | 0·2389 | 0·2422 | 0·2454 | 0·2486 | 0·2517 | 0·2₅ |
| 0·7 | 0·2580 | 0·2611 | 0·2642 | 0·2673 | 0·2704 | 0·2734 | 0·2764 | 0·2794 | 0·2823 | 0·2₈ |
| 0·8 | 0·2881 | 0·2910 | 0·2939 | 0·2967 | 0·2995 | 0·3023 | 0·3051 | 0·3078 | 0·3106 | 0·31 |
| 0·9 | 0·3159 | 0·3186 | 0·3212 | 0·3238 | 0·3264 | 0·3289 | 0·3315 | 0·3340 | 0·3365 | 0·3₃ |
| 1·0 | 0·3413 | 0·3438 | 0·3461 | 0·3485 | 0·3508 | 0·3531 | 0·3554 | 0·3577 | 0·3599 | 0·3₆ |
| 1·1 | 0·3643 | 0·3665 | 0·3686 | 0·3708 | 0·3729 | 0·3749 | 0·3770 | 0·3790 | 0·3810 | 0·3₈ |
| 1·2 | 0·3849 | 0·3869 | 0·3888 | 0·3907 | 0·3925 | 0·3944 | 0·3962 | 0·3980 | 0·3997 | 0·4₀ |
| 1·3 | 0·4032 | 0·4049 | 0·4066 | 0·4082 | 0·4099 | 0·4115 | 0·4131 | 0·4147 | 0·4162 | 0·41 |
| 1·4 | 0·4192 | 0·4207 | 0·4222 | 0·4236 | 0·4251 | 0·4265 | 0·4279 | 0·4292 | 0·4306 | 0·4₃ |

The text at the bottom of your normal distribution table says:

*'This table can be used to calculate N(d), the cumulative normal distribution functions needed for the Black-Scholes model of option pricing. If $d_i > 0$, add 0.5 to the relevant number above. If $d_i < 0$, subtract the relevant number above from 0.5.'*

So here, because $d_1$ = 0.77, then N ($d_1$) = 0.2794 + 0.5 = 0.7794.

On the same basis, N ($d_2$) = N(0.63) = 0.7357

where the 0.7357 is calculated as 0.2357 from the table + 0.5 (because $d_2$ is a positive number). Hence if the option is a European call, its value is given by:

c = (42 × 0.7794) − (38.049 × 0.7357) = 4.76

If the option is a European put, its value is given by:

$$p = c - P_a + P_e\,e^{-rt}$$

p = 4.76 − 42 + 38.049 = 0.81

The stock price has to rise by $2.76 for the purchaser of the call to break even. Similarly, the stock price has to fall by $2.81 for the purchaser of the put to break even.

### 3.2.5 Assumptions of the Black-Scholes model

Assumptions of the model will be discussed in Section 5.3 of this chapter.

# 4 Real options

6/11, 6/12, 6/14

FAST FORWARD

Real options are alternatives or choices that may be available with a business investment opportunity.

**Exam focus point**

Real options are highly examinable. An optional question in the June 2011 exam focused on the option to delay. The option to follow-on was examined in June 2012.

An option exists when the decision maker has the right, but not the obligation, to take a particular action. They add value as they provide opportunities to take advantage of an uncertain situation as the uncertainty resolves itself over time.

Real options are known as such as they usually relate to **tangible assets**. Options that were discussed earlier in this chapter – and will be discussed further in Chapters 16 and 17 – are financial instruments that relate to such intangibles as exchange rates or interest rates.

A real option embodies flexibility in the development of a project. It gives the company the right but not the obligation to take some course of action that may be desirable if there is an unfortunate turn of events or a new opportunity presents itself. A real option represents either a **form of insurance** or a **means to take advantage** of a favourable situation.

Real options are '**actual options**' – that is, actual choices that a business can make in relation to investment opportunities. For example, a natural resource company may decide to suspend extraction of copper at its mine if the price of copper falls below the extraction cost. Conversely, a company with the right to mine in a particular area may decide to begin operations if the price rises above the cost of extraction. Such options can be extremely important when valuing potential investments but are often overlooked by traditional investment appraisal techniques (eg net present value (NPV)). They can significantly increase the value of an investment by eliminating potentially unfavourable outcomes.

For a real option to exist, there must be uncertainty in terms of future cash flows **and** management must have the flexibility to respond to the uncertainty as it evolves.

In this section we describe the various options embedded in projects and provide examples. In the following section we illustrate how to estimate the value of real options using the Black-Scholes method.

Firstly, however, we look at the shortcomings of the NPV investment appraisal technique.

## 4.1 Limitations of the NPV rule

You should be very familiar with the NPV technique by now (refer to Chapter 5 for examples). However, despite its widespread use in real life, the technique does have several shortcomings.

### 4.1.1 Dealing with uncertainty

Although the cash flows are discounted at an appropriate cost of capital, NPV does not explicitly deal with uncertainty when valuing the project. A risk-adjusted discount rate reduces the PV of the cash flows (the higher the discount rate, the lower the PV) rather than giving the decision maker an indication of the range of cash flows that a project may deliver. The use of a single discount rate means that risk is defined in one measure. This does not allow for the many sources of uncertainty that may surround the project and its cash flows.

### 4.1.2 Flexibility in responding to uncertainty

NPV fails to consider the extent of management's flexibility to respond to uncertainties surrounding the project. Such flexibility can be an extremely valuable part of the project and by failing to account for it, NPV may significantly underestimate the project's value.

Take mining as an example. When a new mining project is being considered, management usually produces a 'life of mine' plan which forms the basis for an NPV evaluation. It includes the information you might expect in an NPV calculation, such as costs of extraction and recovery rates of the mined item, together with the amount, quality and distribution of the item. All of these will affect the estimated cash flows of the project.

However, in practice management will have some degree of flexibility depending on the actual rate at which the item is mined. If external or internal conditions change, they can decide to increase or decrease the rate of mining – or even stop it altogether. When the NPV of the mine is calculated, such flexibilities (or options) are not incorporated. NPV will be based on an assumption that the item will be mined at a predetermined rate. This means that NPV will only provide an accurate estimate of the mine's value if there is no flexibility or no uncertainty (that is, flexibility will have no value as management knows exactly what is going to happen).

In order to correct the shortcomings of the NPV technique, real options can be incorporated into the calculations. The four different types of real options are discussed below.

## 4.2 Option to delay                                                                           6/11

**Exam focus point**

> A 20-mark optional question in the June 2011 exam focused on the valuation of an option to delay. An optional question in the December 2007 exam also focused on an option to delay.

When a firm has exclusive rights to a project or product for a specific period, it can delay taking this project or product until a later date. A traditional investment analysis just answers the question of whether the project is a 'good' one if taken today. Thus, the fact that a project is not selected today either because its NPV is negative, or because its IRR is less than its cost of capital, does not mean that the rights to this project are not valuable.

Consider a situation where a company considers paying an amount C to acquire a licence to mine copper. The company needs to **invest** an extra amount I in order to start operations. The company has three years over which to develop the mine, otherwise it will lose the licence. Suppose that today copper prices are low and the NPV from developing the mine is negative. The company may decide not to start the operation today, but it has the option to start any time over the next three years provided that the NPV is positive. Thus the company has paid a premium C to acquire an American option on the PV of the cash flows from operation, with an exercise price equal to the additional investment (I). The value of the option to delay is therefore:

NPV = PV – I if PV > I
NPV = 0 otherwise

The payoff of the option to delay is shown below and it is the same as the payoff of a **call option**, the only difference being that the underlying is the PV of the project and the exercise price is the additional investment (X = I).

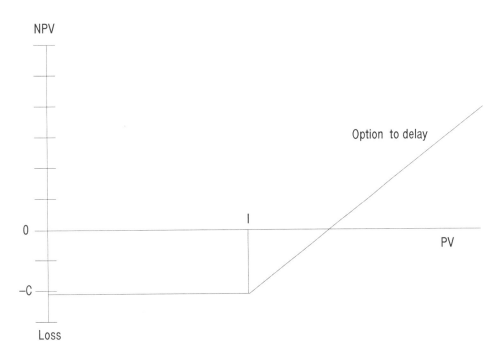

## 4.3 Option to expand

The option to expand exists when firms invest in projects which allow them to make further investments in the future or to enter new markets. The initial project may be found in terms of its NPV as not worth undertaking. However, when the option to expand is taken into account, the NPV may become positive and the project worthwhile. The initial investment may be seen as the premium required to acquire the option to expand.

Expansion will normally require an additional investment, call it **I**. The extra investment will be undertaken only if the PV from the expansion will be higher than the additional investment, ie when PV > **I**. If PV < **I**, the expansion will not take place. Thus the option to expand is again a call option of the PV of the firm with an exercise equal to the value of the additional investment.

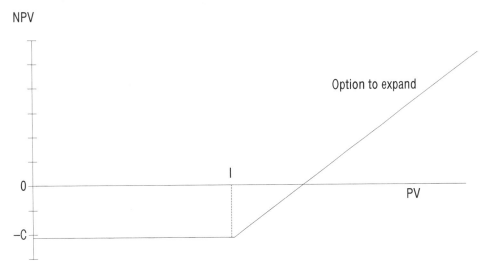

## 4.4 Option to abandon/withdraw                                              12/13

While traditional capital budgeting analysis assumes that a project will operate in each year of its lifetime, the firm may have the option to cease a project during its life. This option is known as an abandonment option. Abandonment options, which are the right to sell the cash flows over the remainder of the project's life for some salvage value, are like American put options. When the PV of the remaining cash flows falls below the liquidation value (L), the asset may be sold. Abandonment is effectively the exercising of a **put option**. These options are particularly important for large capital-intensive projects, such as nuclear plants,

airlines and railroads. They are also important for projects involving new products where their acceptance in the market is uncertain and companies would like to switch to more alternative uses.

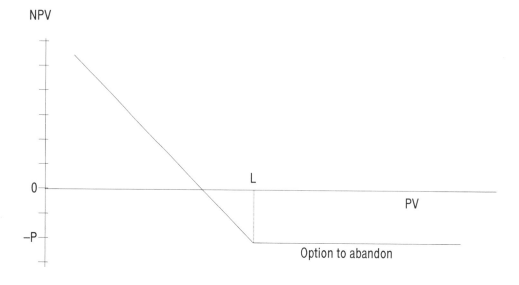

## 4.5 Option to redeploy

The option to redeploy exists when the company can use its productive assets for activities other than the original one. The switch from one activity to another will happen if the PV of cash flows from the new activity will exceed the costs of switching. The option to abandon is a special case of an option to redeploy, and both are valued as **put options** because they involve freeing up assets.

These options are particularly important in agricultural settings. For example, a beef producer will value the option to switch between various feed sources, preferring to use the cheapest acceptable alternative.

These options are also valuable in the utility industry. An electric utility, for example, may have the option to switch between various fuel sources to produce electricity. In particular, consider an electric utility that has the choice of building a coal-fired plant or a plant that burns either coal or gas.

Naïve implementation of discounted cash flow analysis might suggest that the coal-fired plant be constructed since it is considerably cheaper. Whereas the dual plant costs more, it provides greater flexibility. Management has the ability to select which fuel to use and can switch back and forth depending on energy conditions and the relative prices of coal and gas. The value of this operating option should be taken into account.

## 5 Valuation of real options                    12/07, 6/11, 6/14

**FAST FORWARD**

> Real options can be valued using the Black-Scholes model, but certain adjustments need to be made since the underlying is not traded.

**Exam focus point**

In June 2011, students were asked in an optional Section B question to value an option to delay production and marketing of a project. In June 2014 part of a question asked about the use of options and the limitations of the approach used to value options.

## 5.1 Black-Scholes option analysis

Since American call options can be valued using the Black-Scholes model, one could in principle use the Black-Scholes model to estimate the value of the real options we have identified in the previous section. However, there are certain differences between the application of the Black-Scholes model to financial options and real options. The main practical problem is the estimation of volatility. As the underlying asset is not traded, it is very difficult to established the volatility of the value. The main method to overcome this problem is to use simulation methods to estimate the volatility. Since the option to expand is a call option, its value will be given by:

$c = P_a \, N(d_1) - P_e \, N(d_2)e^{-rt}$

In this case

$P_a$ is the value of the project

$P_e$ is the additional investment involved in expansion

$$d_1 = \frac{\ln(P_a/P_e) + \left(r + 0.5s^2\right)t}{s\sqrt{t}}$$

$d_2 = d_1 - s\sqrt{t}$

Similarly the option to abandon is a put option and its value is given by:

$p = c - P_a + P_e e^{-rt}$

**Question**                          Valuation of option to abandon

Assume that Four Seasons International is considering taking a 20-year project which requires an initial investment of $250 million in a real estate partnership to develop time share properties with a Spanish real estate developer, and where the PV of expected cash flows is $339 million. While the NPV of $4 million is small, assume that Four Seasons International has the option to abandon this project any time by selling its share back to the developer in the next 5 years for $150 million. A simulation of the cash flows on this time share investment yields a variance in the PV of the cash flows from being in the partnership of 0.09. The 5-year risk-free rate is 7%.

Calculate the total NPV of the project, including the option to abandon.

**Answer**

The value of the abandonment option can be estimated by determining the value of the put option using the Black-Scholes formula.

Call option = $P_a \, N(d_1) - P_e \, N(d_2)e^{-rt}$

Put option = $c - P_a + P_e e^{-rt}$

Where:

     Value of the underlying asset ($P_a$) = PV of cash flows from project at the point in time when the option is exercised. This is in 5 years' time so 15/20 of the projects' present value will remain: $339m × 15/20 = $254 million
     Strike price ($P_e$) = Salvage value from abandonment = $150 million
     Variance in underlying asset's value = 0.09 (standard deviation (s) = $\sqrt{0.09}$ = 0.3)
     Time to expiration = Life of the project = 5 years
     Risk-free rate of interest (r) = 7%

Value of call option

$$d_1 = \frac{\ln\left(\frac{P_a}{P_e}\right) + \left(r + 0.5s^2\right)t}{s\sqrt{t}}$$

$$d_1 = \frac{\ln\left(\frac{254}{150}\right) + \left(0.07 + 0.50.3^2\right) \times 5}{0.3 \times \sqrt{5}}$$

$$= \frac{0.5267 + 0.115 \times 5}{0.6708}$$

$$= 1.64$$

$$d_2 = d_1 - s\sqrt{t}$$

$$= 1.64 - 0.3 \times \sqrt{5}$$

$$= 0.97$$

Using normal distribution tables:

$N(d_1) = 0.9495$

$N(d_2) = 0.8340$

Value of call option = $254\ (0.9495) - 150\ (0.8340)\ e^{-0.07 \times 5}$

$= 214.17 - 88.16$

$= 153.01$

The value of the put option can be calculated as follows.

Put option $= 153.01 - 254 + \left(150\ e^{-0.07 \times 5}\right)$

$= 153.01 - 254 + 105.70$

$= \$4.71m$

The value of this abandonment option is added to the project's NPV of $89m, which gives a total NPV with abandonment option of $93.71m.

---

## Question

Valuation of option to expand

Pandy Inc is considering a project that currently has an NPV of $(0.5m). However, as part of this project, Pandy Inc will be developing technology that it will be able to use in 5 years' time to break into the Asian market. The expected cost of the investment at year 5 is $20m. The Asian project is currently valued with an NPV of 0 but management believes that NPV could be positive in 5 years' time due to changes in economic conditions.

The standard deviation is 0.25, risk-free rate is 5% and Pandy's cost of capital is 12%.

*Required*

Evaluate the value of the option to expand.

## Answer

The value of the project ($P_a$) is $20m at year 5. We therefore have to discount this back to Year 0 to obtain the PV.

$P_a = \$20m \times 0.567 = \$11.34m$

The other variables are as follows.

$P_e = \$20m$ $\qquad$ $t = 5$ $\qquad$ $s = 0.25$ $\qquad$ $r = 0.05$ $\qquad$ $e^{-rt} = 0.779$

$d_1 = [\ln(11.34/20) + (0.05 + 0.5 \times 0.25^2) \times 5]/(0.25 \times \sqrt{5})$

$\qquad = [-0.5674 + 0.40625]/0.5590$

$\qquad = -0.29$

$d_2 = -0.288 - 0.5590$

$\qquad = -0.85$

$N(d_1) = 0.5 - 0.1141 = 0.3859$

$N(d_2) = 0.5 - 0.3023 = 0.1977$

Option to expand $\quad = (\$11.34m \times 0.3859) - (\$20m \times 0.1977 \times 0.779)$

$\qquad\qquad\qquad\quad = \$4.376m - \$3.080m$

$\qquad\qquad\qquad\quad = \$1.296m$

NPV of the project is now $\$1.296m - \$0.5m = \$0.796m$

We now can see the value of the real options approach. Here a project was originally showing a negative NPV (of $0.5m) and would therefore be rejected. However by valuing a real option associated with the project we can see that the project can be justified and now shows a positive NPV.

## 5.2 What does the real option valuation mean?

The valuation of a real option – and its inclusion in the NPV calculations – takes into account the **uncertainty** of the project. In the Four Seasons question above, for example, the abandonment option increases the attractiveness of the project by increasing its NPV. However, the company **does not actually receive the value of the real option**. What it means is that the project could be abandoned for $150 million in the next five years and the value attached to this choice is $4.72 million. In the ensuing period before the abandonment option can be exercised, Four Seasons can take steps to promote the properties and create a larger potential market. By doing so, Four Seasons can reduce the uncertainty surrounding the project. The time that the company has before it has to make the abandonment decision is reflected in the value of project via the inclusion of real options.

A company may have a project with a negative NPV, which becomes feasible due to the value placed on the real option to expand the project. Again, the company will not receive the value of the real option but the value attached to the option should be used in investment appraisal.

## 5.3 Assumptions of the Black-Scholes model $\qquad\qquad\qquad$ 6/14

The Black-Scholes model makes a number of assumptions which are discussed below.

(a) **Lognormality**. The model assumes that the return on the underlying asset follows a normal distribution which means the return itself follows a lognormal distribution.

(b) **Perfect markets**. This suggests that the direction of the market cannot be consistently predicted and thus the returns on the underlying asset can go up or down at any given moment in time.

(c) **Constant interest rates**. The risk-free rate is used in the Black-Scholes model and this rate is assumed to be constant and known.

(d) **Constant volatility**. The model assumes that the volatility of the project is known and remains constant throughout its life.

(e) **Tradability of asset**. The model assumes that there is a market for the underlying asset and it can therefore be traded.

The two latter assumptions do not necessarily apply to real options. While volatility can be relatively constant in the very short term, it is never constant in the long term. It is not always the case that the underlying asset can be traded therefore this assumption limits the usefulness of the model for valuing real options.

**Exam focus point**

These assumptions can form part of a critique of the Black-Scholes model for option valuation in an exam question. A number of the assumptions are unrealistic and can therefore at best lead to an approximation of the value of options.

An optional question in June 2014 required you to comment on the assumptions made when valuing options.

## 5.4 Implications of real options for capital budgeting

Real options provide a more accurate estimate of a project's value but this greater accuracy comes at a cost. The analysis of real options is a much more complex approach to valuation than NPV and therefore requires a greater investment in time and effort.

However, real options shift the focus away from trying to predict the future 'perfectly' to identifying what can (or should) be done about responding to uncertainty. In addition, this focus on responding in the best possible way to uncertainty promotes a discipline that extends over the entire life of the project (not just when the decision is originally made). Finally, real options give decision makers the ability to identify the **optimal levels of flexibility** by providing estimates of the additional value that increased flexibility can bring.

# Chapter Roundup

- Options are contracts that give to one party the right to enter into a transaction but not the obligation to do so.

- A long call option position at expiration may lead to unlimited profits, and a short option position may lead to unlimited losses.

- The maximum profit from a long put position and the maximum loss from a short put position occurs when the price of the underlying becomes zero.

- The value of an option is determined by an exercise price, the price of the underlying, the time to expiration, the volatility of the underlying and the interest rate.

- The Black-Scholes model predicts the value of an option for given values of its determinants.

- Real options are alternatives or choices that may be available with a business investment opportunity.

- Real options can be valued using the Black-Scholes model, but certain adjustments need to be made since the underlying is not traded.

# Quick Quiz

1   A call option with an exercise price of $60 is bought for $3. On expiry day the underlying is $61. Should the call option be exercised?

2   You have bought a put option, which expires in three months. The day after you bought the put option, the volatility of the underlying asset increased. What would happen to the value of the put option?

3   You have bought an out of the money call option, with an exercise price of $40. The option cost $2 and it expires in 6 months. What would you expect the value of the call option to be in 5 months if the price and volatility of the underlying remain unchanged?

4   What is the impact of increased volatility on the value of an option?

5   Is an option to redeploy valued as a call option or a put option?

# Answers to Quick Quiz

1  The option should be exercised since the price of the underlying is higher than the exercise price. The value of the option at expiration is $61 – $60 = $1.

   The overall result is a loss of $2 since the option was bought for $3.

2  The value of the put option will increase as the volatility increases, because it makes it more likely for the price of the underlying to fall below the exercise price.

3  As an option nears its expiration date its time value goes down. The value of the out of the money option one month before expiration will be lower than the price six months before expiration since there is less time for the price of the underlying to exceed the exercise price.

4  Given that an option will **not** be exercised if it making losses, volatility is beneficial to the option holder. Higher volatility means that there is a greater chance of making gains from an option, so higher volatility increases option value (for both a put and a call option).

5  An option to redeploy (and an option to abandon) involve freeing up assets and are therefore valued as a put option.

Now try the question below from the Practice Question Bank

| Number | Level | Marks | Time |
|--------|-------|-------|------|
| 10 | Examination | 20 | 39 mins |

# Impact of financing on investment decisions and adjusted present values

**7a**

| Topic list | Syllabus reference |
|---|---|
| 1 Sources of finance – appropriateness | B3(a)(b) |
| 2 Cost of capital | B3(c) |
| 3 CAPM and portfolios | B3(d) |
| 4 Project-specific cost of capital | B3(d) |
| 5 Duration | B3(e) |
| 6 Credit risk | B3(f) |
| 7 Credit spreads and cost of debt capital | B3(g) |
| 8 Theories of capital structure – traditional and Modigliani and Miller (MM) | B3(h) |
| 9 Alternative theories of capital structure | B3(i) |
| 10 The adjusted present value (APV) method | B3(j) |
| 11 Effect of alternative financing strategies on financial reporting | B3(i) |

## Introduction

This chapter starts by reviewing a variety of sources of finance (which have been introduced in Chapters 1 and 2), but mainly it examines the impact of sources of finance on the cost of capital and therefore on the investment decision.

This chapter also reviews some of the theories that seek to explain capital structure and the role of capital structure in investment appraisal. We look at the appropriateness of various available sources of finance and then consider the extent of a company's debt exposure to interest rate changes. Exposure to credit risk and credit spreads are followed by a discussion of different theories of capital structure. We will then look at the adjusted present value approach to valuing a firm and conclude the chapter with an assessment of how alternative financing strategies impact on reported financial position.

# Study guide

| B3 | Impact of financing on investment decisions and adjusted present values | Intellectual level |
|---|---|---|
| (a) | Identify and assess the appropriateness of the range of sources of finance available to an organisation including equity, debt, hybrids, lease finance, venture capital, business angel finance, private equity, asset securitisation and sale and Islamic finance. | 3 |
| (b) | Discuss the role of, and developments in, Islamic financing as a growing source of finance for organisations; explaining the rationale for its use, and identifying its benefits and deficiencies. | 2 |
| (c) | Calculate the cost of capital of an organisation, including the cost of equity and cost of debt, based on the range of equity and debt sources of finance. Discuss the appropriateness of using the cost of capital to establish project and organisational value, and discuss its relationship to such value. | 3 |
| (d) | Calculate and evaluate project-specific cost of equity and cost of capital, including their impact on the overall cost of capital of an organisation. Demonstrate detailed knowledge of business and financial risk, the capital asset pricing model and the relationship between equity and asset betas. | 3 |
| (e) | Assess an organisation's debt exposure to interest rate changes using the simple Macaulay duration method and modified duration methods. | 3 |
| (f) | Discuss the benefits and limitations of duration, including the impact of convexity. | 3 |
| (g) | Assess the organisation's exposure to credit risk, including: <br> (i) Explain the role of, and the risk assessment models used by the principal rating agencies <br> (ii) Estimate the likely credit spread over risk free <br> (iii) Estimate the organisation's current cost of debt capital using the appropriate term structure of interest rates and the credit spread | 2 |
| (h) | Assess the impact of financing on investment decisions of: <br> (i) Modigliani and Miller proposition before and after tax <br> (ii) Static trade-off theory <br> (iii) Pecking order propositions <br> (iv) Agency effects | 3 |
| (i) | Apply the adjusted value technique to the appraisal of investment decisions that entail significant alterations in the financial structure of the organisation, including their fiscal and transactions cost implications. | 3 |
| (j) | Assess the impact of a significant capital investment project on the reported financial position and performance of the organisation taking into account alternative financing strategies. | 3 |

1    **The relationship between risk and return**

Risk-averse investors prefer less risk than more. In order to be persuaded to take on more risk, they must be 'compensated' in the form of higher returns.

2    **Diversifiable and non-diversifiable risk**

**Diversifiable risk** (also known as **unsystematic risk**) arises due to **random** and unpredicted factors. It can be diversified away by holding a portfolio of investments.

**Non-diversifiable risk** (also known as **systematic risk**) is caused by factors that **affect all firms** and therefore **cannot** be eliminated by diversification.

3    **The capital asset pricing model (CAPM)**

The following formula is given in the exam.

$E(r_i) = R_f + \beta(E(R_m) - R_f)$

4    **Internal rate of return (IRR)**

The formula for the IRR which is **not** given in the exam is:

$$IRR = a + \left( \left( \frac{NPV_a}{NPV_a - NPV_b} \right)(b - a) \right)\%$$  This formula is not given in the exam.

where      a = the lower of the two rates of return used
           b = the higher of the two rates of return used
        $NPV_a$ = the NPV obtained using rate a
        $NPV_b$ = the NPV obtained using rate b

This formula can be used to calculate the cost of redeemable debt.

5    **Weighted average cost of capital (WACC)**

The formula for the WACC which is given in the exam is:

$$WACC = \left[ \frac{V_e}{V_e + V_d} \right] k_e + \left[ \frac{V_d}{V_e + V_d} \right] k_d (1 - T)$$

This formula can be used to calculate the cost of capital at which potential investment projects should be discounted.

# 1 Sources of finance – appropriateness                     6/12

This section introduces a variety of sources of finance (many of which have been introduced in Chapters 1 and 2, and also feature in *Financial Management (FM))* considering their appropriateness for different organisations and relative cost.

## 1.1 Short-term debt

Short-term debt consists mainly of overdrafts and short-term loans.

The advantage of overdrafts is that they can be arranged relatively quickly and offer the company a degree of flexibility with regard to the amount borrowed. Interest is only paid when the account is overdrawn. However, if the account is overdrawn beyond the authorised amount, penalties can be severe.

Overdrafts are usually most appropriate when a company wants help to finance 'day to day' trading and cash flow requirements. The company is unlikely to be short of cash all the time therefore an informal overdraft agreement that can be called on where necessary would be the best choice of funding.

Short-term loans are more formal than overdrafts in that they are for fixed amounts for a specified period of time. The company knows how much it has to pay back at regular intervals and does not have to worry about the bank withdrawing or reducing an overdraft facility. However, interest has to be paid for the duration of the loan, rather than just when the account is overdrawn.

It may be that a mixture of short-term loans and overdrafts is the most appropriate method of funding. For example, if you are purchasing a shop with inventory, the shop premises might be financed by a loan while the inventory could be funded by an overdraft.

## 1.2 Long-term debt finance

**Exam focus point**

Make sure you read the ACCA article written by the examining team entitled 'Bond valuation and bond yields'. This article deals with how bonds are valued and the relationship between bond value or price, the yield to maturity and the spot yield curve.

Long-term finance is most appropriate for major investments. It tends to be more expensive and less flexible than short-term finance.

Long-term debt comes in various forms – redeemable and irredeemable, fixed and floating rates, convertibles – and the price will vary according to the product and prevailing market conditions. For example, where the coupon rate is fixed at the time of issue, it will be set after considering the credit rating of the company issuing the debt. Although subsequent changes in market and company conditions may cause the market value of the debt to fluctuate, the interest charged (the price of the debt) will remain at the fixed percentage of the nominal value.

Long-term debt tends to be most appropriate for long-term investments. One of the main advantages of long-term debt is that interest is tax deductible, making it cheaper than equity finance.

### 1.2.1 Valuing redeemable bonds                                    Sep/Dec 16 Mar/Jun 17

Calculating the market value of redeemable bonds is necessary for two reasons:

(a)    To allow a business to estimate the funds it will receive from a bond issue
(b)    To calculate the $V_d$ for use in estimating the weighted average cost of capital (see Section 2)

This section introduces the principles of bond valuation, which is then developed further in Section 7 of this chapter.

Bonds are usually **redeemable**. They are issued for a term of 10 years or more, and perhaps 25 to 30 years. At the end of this period, they will 'mature' and become redeemable (at par or possibly at a value above par).

Some redeemable bonds have an earliest and a latest redemption date. For example, 12% Loan Notes 2010/12 are redeemable at any time between the earliest specified date (in 2010) and the latest date (in 2012). The issuing company can choose the date. The decision by a company when to redeem a debt will depend on **how much cash** is available to the company to repay the debt, and on the **nominal rate of interest** on the debt.

Some bonds do not have a redemption date, and are **'irredeemable'** or **'undated'**. Undated bonds might be redeemed by a company that wishes to pay off the debt, but there is no obligation on the company to do so.

Bonds can be valued by estimating the present value of the cash flows associated with the bonds, as follows:

**Formula to learn**

Value of debt = (interest earnings × annuity factor) + (redemption value × discounted cash flow factor)

**200**    **7a: Impact of financing on investment decisions and adjusted present values**  |  Part B Advanced investment appraisal

# Example

Furry has in issue 12% bonds with par value $100,000 and redemption value $110,000, with interest payable quarterly. The redemption yield on the bonds is 8% annually and 2% quarterly. The bonds are redeemable on 30 June 20X4 and it is now 31 December 20X0.

*Required*

Calculate the market value of the bonds.

# Solution

You need to use the redemption yield cost of debt as the discount rate, and remember to use an annuity factor for the interest. We are discounting over 14 periods using the quarterly discount rate (8%/4).

| Period | | Cash flow $ | Discount factor 2% | Present value $ |
|--------|------------|-------------|--------------------|------------------|
| 1–14 | Interest | 3,000 | 12.106 | 36,318 |
| 14 | Redemption | 110,000 | 0.758 | 83,380 |
| | | | | 119,698 |

Market value is $119,698.

## 1.2.2 The term structure of interest rates

Interest rates depend on the **term to maturity** of the asset. For example, government bonds might be short-dated, medium-dated or long-dated depending on when the bonds are to be redeemed and the investor repaid.

The **term structure of interest rates** refers to the way in which the yield on a security varies according to the term of the borrowing, as shown by the **yield curve**.

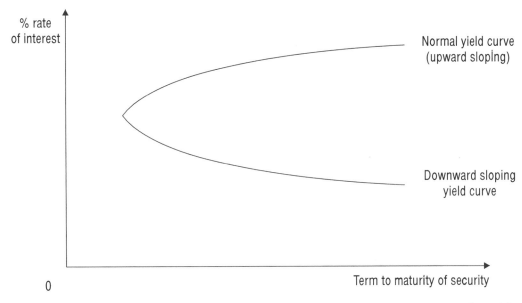

The reasons why, in theory, the yield curve will normally be upward sloping, so that long-term financial assets offer a higher yield than short-term assets, are as follows:

(a) **The investor must be compensated for tying up their money in the asset for a longer period of time**. The only way to overcome this **liquidity preference** of investors is to compensate them for the loss of liquidity; in other words, to offer a higher rate of interest on longer-dated bonds.

(b) **There is a greater risk in lending long term than in lending short term**. To compensate investors for this risk, they might require a higher yield on longer-dated investments.

A yield curve might **slope downwards**, with short-term rates higher than longer-term rates for a number of reasons:

(a) **Expectations**. When interest rates are expected to fall, short-term rates might be higher than long-term rates, and the yield curve would be downward sloping.

(b) **Government policy**. A policy of keeping interest rates relatively high might have the effect of forcing short-term interest rates higher than long-term rates.

(c) The **market segmentation theory**. The slope of the yield curve may reflect demand conditions in different segments of the market. This theory holds that the major investors are confined to a particular segment of the market and will not switch segment even if the forecast of likely future interest rates changes. If demand is high for long-term debt, then the price of long-term bonds will be high which will mean that the return on these bonds will fall.

### 1.2.3 Yield to maturity

The yield to maturity (or **redemption yield**) is the effective yield on a redeemable bond which allows for the time value of money and is effectively the **internal rate of return** of the cash flows.

For example, a 5-year unsecured bond with a coupon of 5% per annum, redeemable at par and issued at a 6% discount to par will have a yield to maturity of 6.47%. This is calculated by assuming a nominal value of $100 and calculating net present values (NPVs) at 5% and 7% discount rates.

| Year | Cash flow $m | Discount factor 5% | Present value $m | Discount factor 7% | Present value $m |
|---|---|---|---|---|---|
| 0 | (94) | 1.000 | (94.00) | 1.000 | (94.00) |
| 1–5 | 5 | 4.329 | 21.64 | 4.100 | 20.50 |
| 5 | 100 | 0.784 | 78.40 | 0.713 | 71.30 |
| NPV | | | 6.04 | | (2.20) |

$$\text{Yield to maturity} = 5\% + \left( \frac{6.04}{(6.04 + 2.20)} \right) \times 2\% = 6.47\%$$

This information is useful if a business is trying to value a new bond issue for a 5 year bond with the same coupon rate.

## 1.3 Equity finance

Equity finance is raised through the sale of ordinary shares to investors, either as a **new issue** or as a **rights issue**.

The issue of equity is at the bottom of the pecking order when it comes to raising funds for investments, not only because of the cost of issue but also because equity finance is more expensive in terms of required returns. Equity shareholders are the ultimate bearers of risk, as they are at the bottom of the creditor hierarchy in a liquidation. This means that there is a significant risk that they will receive nothing at all after all other trade payables' claims have been met.

This high risk means that equity shareholders expect the highest returns of long-term providers of finance. The cost of equity finance is therefore always **higher** than the cost of debt.

As with long-term debt, equity finance will be used for long-term investments. Companies may choose to raise equity rather than debt finance if:

(a) Their gearing ratios are approaching the maximum allowable.
(b) Any further increases in gearing will be perceived as a significant increase in risk by investors.

## 1.4 Venture capital

Venture capital is risk capital which is generally provided in return for an equity stake in the business. It is most suited to private companies with high growth potential. Venture capitalists seek a high return (usually at least 20%), although their principal return is achieved through an **exit strategy**.

Venture capitalists generally like to have a predetermined target exit date (usually 3–7 years). At the outset of their investment, they will have established various exit routes, including the sale of shares to the public or to institutional investors following a flotation of the company's shares.

As well as providing funding for start-up businesses, venture capital is an important source of finance for **management buy-outs** (these are discussed further in Chapter 14).

## 1.5 Business angels

Business angels are wealthy individuals who invest in start-up and growth businesses in return for an equity stake. The investment can involve both time and money depending on the investor. These individuals are prepared to take **high risks** in the hope of **high returns**. As a result, business angel finance can be expensive for the business.

Investments made by business angels can vary but, in the UK, most investments are in the region of £25,000.

Business angels are a very useful tool to fill the gap between venture capital and debt finance, particularly for start-up businesses. One of the main advantages of business angels is that they often follow up their initial investment with later rounds of financing as the business grows. New businesses benefit from their expertise in the difficult early stages of trying to establish themselves.

## 1.6 Lease finance

Some leases, often short-term leases, are rental agreements between a lessor and a lessee, that are structured so that the lessor retains most of the risks of ownership ie the **lessor** is **responsible** for **servicing and maintaining** the leased equipment.

However, some leases are **long-term arrangements** that transfer the risks and rewards of ownership of an asset to the lessee. These are agreements between the lessee and the lessor for most or all of the asset's expected useful life. The **lessee** is responsible for the **upkeep**, **servicing** and **maintenance** of the asset. This can be a cheaper source of finance than a bank loan if the lessor buys a large quantity of assets (eg aircraft) and obtains bulk purchase discounts as a result; some of the savings from such discounts can be shared with the lessee in the form of lower rental payments.

 Case Study

> **Burma's national carrier has signed a nearly $1 billion (£584 million) deal to lease 10 new Boeing 737 jets as it looks to revamp and expand its ageing fleet.**
>
> Myanma Airways will be working with GE Capital Aviation Services (GECAS), the world's largest leasing company, to upgrade its planes and flight routes.
>
> The state-run company flies mainly within Burma, also known as Myanmar.
>
> GECAS – a unit of US conglomerate General Electric - said the aircraft would be delivered by 2020. 'We are pleased at GE to work with Myanma Airways to provide new, state-of-the-art Boeing aircraft,' GECAS president and chief executive Norman Liu **said in a statement**.
>
> *(BBC, 2014)*

## 1.7 Private equity

Private equity consists of equity securities in companies that are not publicly traded on a stock exchange.

In Europe, private equity represents the entire spectrum of the investment sector that includes venture capital and management buy-ins and buy-outs (therefore venture capital is a specific type of private equity). In the US, private equity and venture capital are treated as different types of investment.

In Europe, private equity funds tend to invest in more mature companies with the aim of eliminating inefficiencies and driving growth. Venture capitalists, as we have seen above, are more likely to invest in start-ups and companies in the early stages of development.

Private equity funds might require:

- A 20–30% shareholding
- Special rights to appoint a number of directors
- The company to seek their prior approval for new issues or acquisitions

## 1.8 Asset securitisation

As we have seen in Chapter 4a, asset securitisation involves the aggregation of assets into a pool then issuing new securities backed by these assets and their cash flows. The securities are then sold to investors who share the risk and reward from these assets.

Securitisation is similar to 'spinning off' part of a business, whereby the holding company 'sells' its right to future profits in that part of the business for immediate cash. The new investors receive a premium (usually in the form of interest) for investing in the success or failure of the segment.

Most securitisation pools consist of 'tranches'. Higher tranches carry less risk of default (and therefore lower returns) whereas junior tranches offer higher returns but greater risk.

The main reason for securitising a cash flow is that it allows companies with a credit rating of (for example) BB but with AAA rated cash flows to possibly borrow at AAA rates. This will lead to greatly reduced interest payments, as the difference between BB rates and AAA rates can be hundreds of basis points.

However, securitisation is expensive due to management costs, legal fees and continuing administration fees.

## 1.9 Islamic finance                                            12/13, 12/14, 12/15

Islamic virtues stress the need for ethical behaviour and for honesty and integrity. Businesses should not take unfair advantage, for example charging higher prices because the customer lacks knowledge about what a fair price is. Profit creation should benefit society at large and detrimental business activities, such as alcohol, gambling and armaments, are not acceptable.

Under the tenets of Islamic finance, money should be viewed as a means of exchange and therefore interest cannot be charged on loans. Engaging in speculation is not allowed, which limits the use of derivatives and money markets that are also based on interest.

In Islamic banks or financial institutions money provided as deposits is not loaned but is instead channelled into underlying investment activity, which will earn profits. The depositor receives a share of the profit, after a management charge is deducted by the bank. Sometimes the Islamic financial institution will pool funds and use them for investment purposes, so that there is a three-way relationship between the financial institution's depositors, the financial institution, and the individual corporations that are receiving monies from the bank. However, banks have also developed different types of financial products, which need to comply with Sharia as well as normal financial regulations and law.

Islamic finance has undergone **rapid growth** over recent years up to the point where it is today an industry worth more than $1 trillion. Islamic financing is not only the preserve of Islamic banks but it is also becoming an important revenue stream for some of the world's biggest lenders and many of the major conventional banks, including HSBC and Standard Chartered, have Islamic banking arms also known as 'Islamic Windows'.

Islamic finance products may be suitable for an organisation, either for cultural reasons or because it offers a commercial advantage over conventional financing.

From your *Financial Management* (FM) studies you should remember the following Islamic financial products.

| Islamic finance product | Similar to | Differences |
| --- | --- | --- |
| Murabaha | Trade credit/ loan | The financial institution purchases the asset and sells it to the business or individual. There is a pre-agreed mark-up to be paid, in recognition of the convenience of paying later, for an asset that is transferred immediately. There is no interest charged. |
| Musharaka | Venture capital | Profits are shared according to a pre-agreed contract. There are no dividends paid. Losses are shared according to capital contribution. Both the organisation/investment manager (mudareb) and finance provider (rub-ul-mal) participate in managing and running the venture. Under a diminishing musharaka agreement the mudareb pays greater and greater amounts to the rub-ul-mal, so that eventually the mudareb owns the whole venture or asset. |
| Mudaraba | Equity | Profits are shared according to a pre-agreed contract. There are no dividends paid. Losses are solely attributable to the provider of capital (the rub-ul-mal). The organisation or investment manager (the mudareb) takes sole responsibility for running the business, because they have the expertise in doing so. |
| Ijara | Leasing | The financial institution purchases the asset for the business to use, with lease payments, lease period and payment terms being agreed at the start of the contract. The financial institution is still the owner of the asset and incurs the risk of ownership. This means that the financial institution will be responsible for major maintenance and insurance. |
| Sukuk | Bonds | The sukuk holder shares in the risk and rewards of ownership. The bonds are based on individual assets, groups of assets or securitised Islamic contracts, such as Ijara and Mudaraba. Some have also been based on Murabaha contracts, but there is debate about whether these comply with Sharia rulings, as they can be seen as debt on debt and therefore attracting interest. |
| | | There are two types of sukuk. The first type is asset based (sale and leaseback) where the principal is covered by capital value of the assets but returns to sukuk holders are not directly financed by those assets. Sukuk holders subscribe by paying an issue price to a special purpose vehicle (SPV) company, which in return issues certificates to the sukuk holder indicating the percentage it owns in the SPV. The SPV purchases the asset and obtains legal ownership and then leases the asset back to the seller, which pays rentals to the SPV. The sukuk holders in turn receive rentals from the SPV, redemption is at a pre-agreed value and they have recourse to the lessee if default occurs, so this is like debt. |
| | | The other type is asset backed (securitisation of a leasing portfolio) where the principal is covered by the capital value of assets, and returns and repayments to sukuk holders are directly financed by the assets. Again the sukuk holders subscribe to an SPV, which then purchases a portfolio of assets, which are already generating an income stream. The returns from these assets are paid to the SPV, which then makes distributions to the sukuk holders. The sukuk holders take on risks and rewards and redemption is at market value, possibly zero, so this arrangement is more like equity. |

| Islamic finance product | Similar to | Differences |
|---|---|---|
| Salam | Forward contract | A commodity is sold for future delivery, cash is received from the financial institution in advance and delivery arrangements are determined immediately. The sale by the business will normally be at a discount, so the financial institution can make a profit. The financial institution may sell the contract to another buyer for cash or profit. Salam arrangements are prohibited for gold, silver and other money-type assets. |
| Istisna | Phased payments | These are used for funding large, long-term construction projects. The financial institution funds a project for a client, with the client paying an initial deposit, followed by instalments during the course of construction. At the completion of the project, the property or machinery that has been constructed is delivered to the client. |

Sharia boards oversee and review product offerings made by Islamic financial institutions. They make judgements on their acceptability on an individual basis. The boards also oversee Sharia-compliant training for employees of the financial institution and participate in the preparation and approval of annual reports. Boards are made up of a mixture of Islamic scholars (who may sit on several boards) and finance experts. They have to cope with different interpretations of Sharia law and with precedents that are not binding. Changes in the personnel on the board may shift its opinions on the acceptability of products

## 1.10 Rationale for use of Islamic finance

Islamic finance may be used for either cultural/religious or commercial reasons. Commercial reasons include the fact that Islamic finance may be available when other sources of finance are not. Islamic finance may also appeal to companies due to its more prudent investment and risk philosophy.

Conventional banks aim to profit by taking in money deposits in return for the payment of interest (or **Riba**) and then lending money out in return for the payment of a higher level of interest. Islamic finance does not permit the charging of interest and invests under arrangements which share the profits and losses of the enterprises.

Taken from the perspective of Sharia (Islamic religious law and moral code), the taking of deposits which are subsequently lent out for interest which is paid whether or not the project is profitable is not justifiable. The Islamic bank arranges its business in such a way that the bank's **profitability is closely tied to that of the client**. The bank stands to take profit or make loss in line with the projects it is financing and as such must be more involved in the investment decision making. The bank acts in some ways more like a fund manager than a conventional lending institution. Speculation is not allowed and conventional derivative products are deemed to be un-Islamic.

Exam focus point

Make sure you read the ACCA article written by the examining team entitled 'Aspects of Islamic finance'.

## 1.11 Advantages of Islamic finance

Islamic finance operates on the underlying principle that there should be a link between the economic activity that creates value and the financing of that economic activity. The main advantages of Islamic finance are as follows:

(a)    Following the principles of Islamic finance allows access to a source of worldwide funds. Access to Islamic finance is also not just restricted to Muslim communities, which may make it appealing to companies that are focused on investing ethically.

(b)    Gharar (speculation) is not allowed, reducing the risk of losses.

(c)    Excessive profiteering is also not allowed; only reasonable mark-ups are allowed.

(d)    Banks cannot use excessive leverage and are therefore less likely to collapse.

(e)     The rules encourage all parties to take a longer-term view and focus on creating a successful outcome for the venture, which should contribute to a more stable financial environment.

(f)     The emphasis of Islamic finance is on mutual interest and co-operation, with a partnership based on profit creation through ethical and fair activity benefiting the community as a whole.

## 1.12 Drawbacks of Islamic finance

The use of Islamic finance does not remove all commercial risk. Indeed, there may even be additional risk from the use of Islamic finance. There are the following drawbacks from the use of Islamic finance:

(a)     There is no international consensus on Sharia interpretations, particularly with innovative financial products. Certain financial products may be acceptable in some markets but not in others. For example, some Murabaha contracts have been criticised because their products have been based on prevailing interest rates rather than economic or profit conditions.

(b)     There is no standard Sharia model for the Islamic finance market, meaning that documentation is often tailor-made for the transaction, leading to higher transaction costs than for the conventional finance alternative.

(c)     Due to the need to comply with normal financial laws and Sharia restrictions, Islamic finance institutions are subject to additional compliance work which can also increase the costs of developing new products and transaction costs. Information asymmetry between the borrower and institution will also mean that due diligence work is required.

(d)     Islamic banks cannot minimise their risks in the same way as conventional banks, as hedging is prohibited.

(e)     Some Islamic products may not be compatible with international financial regulation. For example, a diminishing Musharaka contract may not be an acceptable mortgage instrument in law.

(f)     Trading in Sukuk products has been limited. Since the financial crisis, issuance of new Sukuk products has decreased.

(g)     Corporations may not be able to demonstrate that contracts are effectively debt and they therefore may not attract a tax shield, meaning that their cost of capital will increase.

(h)     Because Islamic financial institutions take an active role on some contracts, it may become more complicated for companies to balance the interests of the financial institution with those of other stakeholders.

(i)     The longer focus of arrangements may mean Islamic institutions are slower to react to market changes and may lack short-term flexibility. Approval of new products can take time.

**Exam focus point**

> The different levels of involvement of the finance provider in Mudaraba and Musharaka contracts was an important issue in the December 2013 question on this area.

 Case Study

As Goldman Sachs prepares to borrow via sukuk for the first time, Islamic financing could soon hit the mainstream. Britain has already issued sukuk and other non-Muslim countries look set to follow. One problem: the Islamic academics who interpret Sharia'a law have their focus far above the bottom line.

Goldman understands how this can happen. In 2011 it had to scrap a $2 billion sukuk issue after some Islamic scholars said that its sukuk was not compliant with Sharia'a, which forbids charging interest because it is considered to be usury. Furthermore, the workarounds to meet the rules can be complicated. To comply with Sharia'a a sukuk issuer would instead pay a fixed rent on its own real estate assets to the sukuk holders, rather than typical interest, and at maturity buy back the property – a sale and leaseback structure.

For agnostic capitalists the customer is always right, even if religion must sometimes provide the guidelines. Global sukuk issuance in the first half of 2014 rose 6% to $66 billion, according to the International Islamic Finance Centre, on track to beat its 2012 record of $140bn (up 50% from a decade ago). Global companies are keen to tap the new sources of wealth in the Middle East.

*(Kerr, S. & Braithwaite, T. 2014)*

## 1.13 Hybrids

Hybrids are means of finance that combine debt and equity. Such securities pay a fixed or floating rate of return up to a certain date, after which the holder has such options as converting the securities into the underlying equity.

Examples of hybrids include convertible bonds, debt with attached warrants and preference shares.

Most companies that issue convertible bonds expect them to be converted to equity and view the funds as 'delayed equity'. They are often used either because the company's ordinary share price is considered to be particularly depressed at the time of issue or because the issue of equity shares would result in an immediate and significant drop in earnings per share. The main risk to the company is that there is no guarantee that the security holders will choose to convert to equity. If they do not then the bonds may have to run their full term and need to be redeemed.

| Question | | New business financing |
| --- | --- | --- |

The following two new businesses are trying to raise finance to fund development.

(a)   Nick Payne, a trained sports physiotherapist and personal trainer, is setting up a sports consultancy business where amateur and professional athletes can come for advice on prevention and treatment of injuries. Nick is also considering offering consultancy services on sports kits and training regimes. He is planning to rent small premises until his business becomes established. The location of the business is in a town with excellent sports facilities but with little if any sports consultancy services. He is looking for approximately $30,000 to develop his business, recruit two members of staff and set up a consultancy website. He is hoping that the funds will also help him to go round sports centres and gyms to give presentations on the services his business can offer. Research carried out so far has shown that there are an encouraging number of interested parties in the area. Nick has invested $5,000 of his own money so far on market research and initial advertising but does not have a great deal of previous business knowledge.

(b)   Paula Donnelly is setting up a small hat shop, selling both formal and casual hats. She has considerable experience of making these goods herself and has produced a number of 'one off' hats for private clients. She now wants to expand her expertise into business and has been busy producing inventory for the shop. She has already invested $20,000 of her own money in obtaining and fitting out suitable premises, buying materials, building up inventory and marketing. There are no such shops in the area and research has shown Paula that ladies looking for hats have to travel a considerable distance. She has made contact with two shops in the area that specialise in formal ladieswear for weddings, race meetings, balls etc and the owners have agreed to recommend her shop based on their existing knowledge of the quality of her 'one off' creations.

*Required*

Using the information above, which type(s) of finance do you think will be most suitable for each of the new businesses? Give reasons for your recommendations.

(a) While Nick is a trained physiotherapist and personal trainer, the fact that he has no assets or a 'tangible' product to sell makes his business a more risky investment than Paula's. He does not have a great deal of previous business knowledge which increases the risk, although he has done some market research to determine likely customer base.

Finance for Nick's business is likely to come from sources where risk is not so much of an issue. Business angel finance is a possibility; as such finance providers are prepared to take high risks in the hope of high returns. The amount of investment that Nick is looking for is also typical of what business angels are likely to provide.

Venture capital is another possibility for Nick, as the business is quite unique in an area with a strong sports background. As a personal trainer, Nick is likely to have an understanding of the private health club market and the needs of members. The main problem is that Nick does not have much previous business experience – an attribute that venture capitalists look for in potential investments.

Nick has not invested a great deal of his own money in the business so far and has no assets that could act as collateral for a bank loan. It is likely that any loan that a bank might offer to Nick will come with very high interest rates to reflect the perceived risk therefore this method of financing is not a good option. If he wanted to pursue the possibility of a bank loan he might be advised to apply to the Enterprise Fund Guarantee Scheme or the Small Firms Loan Guarantee Scheme in order to obtain a guarantee for a percentage of the loan amount.

(b) Paula is in a different position to Nick. She has invested a considerable amount of her own money and has built up an asset base already (premises and inventory). Her business has a tangible product (hats) and she has established contacts with complementary businesses to help build up her customer base. Paula has already had some business experience in that she has produced 'one off' designs for private clients that have apparently built up her good reputation (the fashion shops have agreed to recommend her based on these designs).

Paula is in a better position to obtain a bank loan at a reasonable rate. She has assets to support the loan and has already invested a considerable amount of her own cash. Tangible products are usually seen as being less risky than consultancy businesses therefore banks are more likely to grant her a loan.

Business angels and venture capitalists are also available to Paula, although business angels might be less interested due to the lower levels of risk involved. Paula might not be willing to give away a proportion of her business to business angels, in which case a bank loan might be a more favourable option.

## 1.14 Financial position, financial risk and value

The sources of finance available to an organisation depend on several factors, including the **financial position** of the company, the **financial risk** and the **value** of the organisation.

Unless an organisation has a good financial position, several sources of finance may be unavailable. It is difficult to imagine a loss-making organisation which also has net liabilities being able to raise debt or equity finance successfully.

Similarly, a company with a high level of financial gearing may not be able to raise additional debt finance due to the high level of financial risk.

The value of an organisation will also make a difference to the types of finance that are available. An organisation that has a higher value is more likely to attract providers of finance and be able to raise equity or debt finance. Listed companies (which typically are worth more than other organisations) will also have access to international capital markets, in which they will be able to raise funds.

# 2 Cost of capital

You should remember the following material from your studies of *Financial Management (FM)*.

There are two ways of calculating the cost of equity for an organisation – the dividend growth model and the capital asset pricing model (CAPM).

The principles behind the dividend growth model have already been outlined in Chapter 2.

The CAPM has also been introduced in Chapter 2.

## 2.1 The dividend growth model

**Formula to learn**

Cost of ordinary (equity) share capital, having a current ex-div price, $P_0$, having just paid a dividend, $d_0$, with the dividend growing in perpetuity by a constant g% per annum:

$$k_e = \frac{d_0(1+g)}{P_0} + g \text{ or } k_e = \frac{d_1}{P_0} + g$$

**Question** — Cost of equity

A share has a current market value of 96c, and the last dividend was 12c. If the expected annual growth rate of dividends is 4%, calculate the cost of equity capital.

**Answer**

$$
\begin{aligned}
\text{Cost of capital} \quad &= \quad \frac{12(1+0.04)}{96} + 0.04 \\
&= \quad 0.13 + 0.04 \\
&= \quad 0.17 \\
&= \quad 17\%
\end{aligned}
$$

### 2.1.1 Estimating the growth rate

There are two methods for estimating the growth rate that you need to be familiar with.

Firstly, the future growth rate can be predicted from an **analysis of the growth in dividends** over the past few years using the formula

$$1 + g = \sqrt[n]{\frac{\text{newest dividend}}{\text{oldest dividend}}}$$

Alternatively, the growth rate can be estimated using **Gordon's growth approximation**. The **rate of growth in dividends** is sometimes expressed, theoretically, as:

**Exam formula**

$g = br_e$

where  g   is the annual growth rate in dividends

       b   is the proportion of profits that are retained

      $r_e$   is the rate of return to shareholders on new investments

So, if a company retains 65% of its earnings for capital investment projects it has identified and these projects are expected to have an average return of 8%:

$g = br_e = 65\% \times 8 = 5.2\%$

## 2.2 The CAPM formula

The CAPM can be stated as follows.

$E(r_i) = R_f + \beta_i(E(r_m) - R_f)$

where $E(r_i)$ is the cost of equity capital
$R_f$ is the risk-free rate of return
$E(r_m)$ is the return from the market as a whole
$\beta_i$ is the beta factor of the individual security

### Question                                                           Returns

The risk-free rate of return is 7%. The average market return is 11%.

(a)    What will be the return expected from a share whose $\beta$ factor is 0.9?

(b)    What would be the share's expected value if it is expected to earn an annual dividend of 5.3c, with no capital growth?

### Answer

(a)    $7\% + 0.9 (11\% - 7\%) = 10.6\%$

(b)    $\dfrac{5.3c}{10.6\%} = 50c$

### 2.2.1 Problems with applying the CAPM in practice

(a)    The need to **determine** the **average return** $(E(r_m))$. Expected, rather than historical, returns should be used, although historical returns are often used in practice. There are also problems with analysing historical stock market returns because comparing the stock market index between any two periods ignores the fact that some listed companies will have failed (eg have gone into liquidation) over this period and the impact that this would have on investors is ignored.

(b)    The need to **determine** the **risk-free rate**. A risk-free investment might be a government security. However, interest rates vary with the term of the lending.

(c)    **Errors** in the **statistical analysis used** to calculate $\beta$ values. Betas may also **change over** time as companies change their strategies.

(d)    The CAPM does not recognise the extra risk facing investors in **small companies**, or companies with a **high ratio of book value of assets to market value** (ie where the market value is falling towards the book value, which is an indicator of financial distress).

### Question                                                       Beta factor

(a)    What does beta measure, and what do betas of 0.5, 1 and 1.5 mean?
(b)    What factors determine the level of beta which a company may have?

### Answer

(a)    **Beta measures** the systematic risk of a risky investment, such as a share in a company. The total risk of the share can be subdivided into two parts, known as **systematic (or market) risk** and **unsystematic (or unique) risk**. The systematic risk depends on the sensitivity of the return of the share to general economic and market factors, such as periods of boom and recession. The CAPM shows how the return which investors expect from shares should depend only on systematic risk, not on unsystematic risk, which can be eliminated by holding a well-diversified portfolio.

The average risk of stock market investments has a **beta of 1**. Thus shares with betas of 0.5 or 1.5 would have half or 1½ times the average sensitivity to market variations respectively.

This is reflected by higher volatility of share prices for shares with a beta of 1.5 than for those with a beta of 0.5. For example, a 10% increase in general stock market prices would be expected to be reflected as a 5% increase for a share with a beta of 0.5 and a 15% increase for a share with a beta of 1.5, with a similar effect for price reductions.

(b)     The beta of a company will be the **weighted average** of the beta of its shares and the beta of its debt. The beta of debt is very low, but not zero, because corporate debt bears default risk, which in turn is dependent on the volatility of the company's cash flows.

Factors determining the beta of a company's equity shares include:

(i)      **Sensitivity** of the company's **cash flows** to economic factors, as stated above. For example, sales of new cars are more sensitive than sales of basic foods and necessities.

(ii)     The company's **operating gearing**. A high level of fixed costs in the company's cost structure will cause high variations in operating profit compared with variations in sales.

(iii)    The company's **financial gearing**. High borrowing and interest costs will cause high variations in equity earnings compared with variations in operating profit, increasing the equity beta as equity returns become more variable in relation to the market as a whole. This effect will be countered by the low beta of debt when computing the weighted average beta of the whole company.

## 2.3 Cost of debt

### 2.3.1 Irredeemable debt

**Formula to learn**

Cost of irredeemable debt capital, paying interest i in perpetuity, and having a current ex-interest price $P_0$:

$$k_d = \frac{i(1-T)}{P_0}$$

### 2.3.2 Redeemable debt

If the debt is **redeemable** then in the year of redemption the interest payment will be received by the holder as well as the amount payable on redemption.

The cost of redeemable debt to the company will be assessed by comparing the amount of money raised by the sale of the debt to the interest repayments on this debt (post tax) and the amount repaid at the date that the debt is redeemed. This will have to be calculated by trial and error, as an **internal rate of return (IRR)**.

### 2.3.3 Example: cost of debt capital

Owen Allot has in issue 10% bonds of a nominal value of $100. The market price is $90 ex interest. Calculate the cost of this capital if the bond is:

(a)     Irredeemable
(b)     Redeemable at par after 10 years

Taxation is 30%.

## Solution

(a)     **The cost of irredeemable debt capital** is $\frac{i(1-T)}{P_0} = \frac{\$7}{\$90} \times 100\% = 7.8\%$

(b)     **The cost of redeemable debt capital**

| Year | | Cash flow | Discount factor | Present value | Discount factor | Present value |
|---|---|---|---|---|---|---|
| | | $ | 10% | $ | 5% | $ |
| 0 | Market value | (90) | 1.000 | (90.00) | 1.000 | (90.00) |
| 1–10 | Interest (10×(1–t)) | 7 | 6.145 | 43.02 | 7.722 | 54.05 |
| 10 | Capital repayment | 100 | 0.386 | 38.60 | 0.614 | 61.40 |
| | | | | (8.38) | | 25.45 |

The approximate cost of redeemable debt capital is therefore:

$$(5 + \frac{25.45}{(25.45 - -8.38)} \times (10 - 5)) = 8.76\%$$

### 2.3.4 The cost of convertible debt

The cost of capital of convertible to debt is harder to determine. The calculation will depend on whether or not conversion is likely to happen.

(a) If conversion is **not** expected, the conversion value is ignored and the bond is treated as **redeemable debt**, using the IRR method.

(b) If conversion **is** expected, the IRR method for calculating the cost of redeemable debt is used, but the number of years to redemption is replaced by the **number of years to conversion** and the redemption value is replaced by the **conversion value** ie the market value of the shares into which the debt is to be converted.

**Formula to learn**

**Conversion value** = $P_0 (1 + g)^n R$

where
- $P_0$ is the current ex-dividend ordinary share price
- $g$ is the expected annual growth of the ordinary share price
- $n$ is the number of years to conversion
- $R$ is the number of shares received on conversion

### 2.3.5 Example: Cost of convertible debt

A company has issued 8% convertible bonds which are due to be redeemed in 5 years' time. They are currently quoted at $82 per $100 nominal. The bonds can be converted into 25 shares in 5 years' time. The share price is currently $3.50 and is expected to grow at a rate of 3% p.a. Assume a 30% rate of tax.

Calculate the cost of the convertible debt.

## Solution

Conversion value $= P_0(1+g)^n R$

$= 3.50 \times (1+0.03)^5 \times 25$

$= \$101.44$

As the redemption value is $100, investors would **choose to convert** the bonds so the **conversion value** is used in the IRR calculation.

| Year | | Cash flow | Discount factor | Present value | Discount factor | Present value |
|---|---|---|---|---|---|---|
| | | $ | 8% | $ | 12% | $ |
| 0 | Market value | (82.00) | 1.000 | (82.00) | 1.000 | (82.00) |
| 1–5 | Interest (8 ×(1 – 0.3)) | 5.60 | 3.993 | 22.36 | 3.605 | 20.19 |
| 5 | Conversion value | 101.44 | 0.681 | 69.08 | 0.567 | 57.52 |
| | | | | 9.44 | | (4.29) |

Cost of debt = $8\% + \frac{9.44}{9.44 + 4.29} (12\% - 8\%) = 10.75\%$

Note carefully where the market value of debt is used in the examples above. The examining team has commented that students often assume that the book value of debt equals the market value of debt.

## 2.4 The cost of preference shares

For preference shares the future cash flows are the dividend payments in perpetuity so that:

The cost of preference shares can be calculated as $k_{pref} = \dfrac{d}{P_0}$.

## 2.5 General formula for the WACC

A general formula for the WACC $k_0$ is as follows.

$$WACC = \left[\frac{V_e}{V_e + V_d}\right] k_e + \left[\frac{V_d}{V_e + V_d}\right] k_d (1 - T)$$

where  $k_e$   is the cost of equity
       $k_d$   is the cost of debt
       $V_e$   is the market value of equity in the firm
       $V_d$   is the market value of debt in the firm
       $T$    is the rate of company tax

## 2.6 The relationship between company value and cost of capital

The market value of a company depends on its cost of capital. The lower a company's WACC, the higher will be the NPV of its future cash flows and therefore the higher will be its market value.

## 2.7 Using the WACC in investment appraisal

The WACC can be used in investment appraisal if:

(a)   The project being appraised is **small relative** to the company.
(b)   The **existing capital structure** will be maintained (same financial risk).
(c)   The project has the same **business risk** as the company.

## 2.8 Arguments against using the WACC

(a)   New investments undertaken by a company might have different **business risk** characteristics from the company's existing operations. As a consequence, the return required by investors might go up (or down) if the investments are undertaken, because their business risk is perceived to be higher (or lower).

(b)   The finance that is raised to fund a new investment might substantially change the capital structure and the perceived **financial risk** of investing in the company. Depending on whether the project is financed by equity or by debt capital, the perceived financial risk of the entire company might change. This must be taken into account when appraising investments.

(c)   Many companies raise **floating rate** debt capital as well as fixed interest debt capital. With floating rate debt capital, the interest rate is variable, and is altered every three or six months or so in line with changes in current market interest rates. The cost of debt capital will therefore fluctuate as market conditions vary. Floating rate debt is difficult to incorporate into a WACC computation, and the best that can be done is to substitute an 'equivalent' fixed interest debt capital cost in place of the floating rate debt cost.

# 3 CAPM and portfolios

**FAST FORWARD**

The **expected return** of a portfolio of shares can be calculated by calculating the weighted beta of the portfolio and using CAPM.

## 3.1 Beta factors of portfolios

Just as an individual security has a beta factor, so too does a portfolio of securities.

(a) A portfolio consisting of all the **securities** on the **stock market** (in the same proportions as the market as a whole), excluding risk-free securities, will have an expected return equal to the expected return for the market as a whole, and so will have a **beta factor of 1**.

(b) A portfolio consisting entirely of **risk-free securities** will have a beta factor of **0**.

(c) The beta factor of an investor's portfolio is the **weighted average** of the **beta factors** of the securities in the **portfolio**.

### 3.1.1 Example: Beta factors and portfolios

A portfolio consisting of five securities could have its beta factor computed as follows.

| Security | Percentage of portfolio % | Beta factor of security | Weighted beta factor |
|---|---|---|---|
| A Inc | 20 | 0.90 | 0.180 |
| B Inc | 10 | 1.25 | 0.125 |
| C Inc | 15 | 1.10 | 0.165 |
| D Inc | 20 | 1.15 | 0.230 |
| E Inc | 35 | 0.70 | 0.245 |
| | 100 | Portfolio beta = | 0.945 |

If the risk-free rate of return is 12% and the average market return is 20%, the required return from the portfolio using the CAPM equation would be 12% + (20 − 12) × 0.945% = 19.56%.

The calculation could have been made as follows.

| Security | Beta factor | Expected return $E(r_j)$ | Weighting % | Weighted return % |
|---|---|---|---|---|
| A Inc | 0.90 | 19.2 | 20 | 3.84 |
| B Inc | 1.25 | 22.0 | 10 | 2.20 |
| C Inc | 1.10 | 20.8 | 15 | 3.12 |
| D Inc | 1.15 | 21.2 | 20 | 4.24 |
| E Inc | 0.70 | 17.6 | 35 | 6.16 |
| | | | 100 | 19.56 |

## 3.2 CAPM and portfolio management

Practical implications of CAPM theory for an investor are as follows.

(a) They should decide what **beta factor** they would **like to have** for their portfolio. They might prefer a portfolio beta factor of greater than 1, in order to expect above-average returns when market returns exceed the risk-free rate, but they would then expect to lose heavily if market returns fall. On the other hand, they might prefer a portfolio beta factor of 1 or even less.

(b) They should seek to invest in shares with **low beta factors** in a **bear market**, when average market returns are falling. They should then also sell shares with high beta factors.

(c) They should seek to invest in shares with **high beta factors** in a **bull market**, when average market returns are rising.

## 3.3 International CAPM

The possibility of international portfolio diversification increases the opportunities available to investors.

If we assume that the international capital market is a **fully integrated market** like an enlarged domestic market, then we have an international CAPM formula as follows.

$$E(r_i) = r_f + [E(r_w) - r_f]\beta_w$$

where $E(r_w)$ is the expected return from the world market portfolio and $\beta_w$ is a measure of the world systematic risk.

This analysis implies that the risk premium is proportional to the world systematic risk, $\beta_w$, and that investors can benefit from maximum diversification by investing in the world market portfolio consisting of all securities in the world economy. New risk and return combinations may be available.

In practice, such complete diversification will of course not be practicable. However, significant international diversification can be achieved by the following methods:

- Direct investment in companies in different countries
- Investments in multinational enterprises
- Holdings in unit trusts or investment trusts which are diversified internationally

## 3.4 Segmentation and integration

The international picture may be complicated by market segmentation. Segmentation is usually caused by government-imposed restrictions on the movement of capital, leading to restricted capital availability within a country or other geographical segment. Therefore:

- Returns on the same security may differ in different markets.
- Some investments may only be available in certain markets.

In a segmented market the parent company of an international group would use its own country's risk-free rate and market return in CAPM calculations.

In practice, the situation that a multinational company faces will often not be completely integrated nor completely segmented. In this situation a multinational can use CAPM to estimate a local cost of equity and a world cost of equity, and use a cost of equity that is somewhere in between the two.

## 3.5 Limitations of the CAPM for the selection of a portfolio

Under the CAPM, the return required from a security is related to its systematic risk rather than its total risk. If we relax some of the assumptions on which the model is based, then the total risk may be important. In particular, the following points should be considered.

(a) The model assumes that the **costs of insolvency** are **zero** or, in other words, that all **assets** can be **sold** at **going concern prices** and that there are no selling, legal or other costs. In practice, the costs of insolvency cannot be ignored. Furthermore, the risk of insolvency is related to a firm's total risk rather than just its systematic risk.

(b) The model assumes that the **investment market** is **efficient**. If it is not, this will limit the extent to which investors are able to eliminate unsystematic risk from their portfolios.

(c) The model also assumes that **portfolios are well diversified** and so need only be concerned with systematic risk. However, this is not necessarily the case, and undiversified or partly diversified shareholders should also be concerned with unsystematic risk and will seek a total return appropriate to the total risk that they face.

## 4 Project-specific cost of capital      12/12, 6/13, Sep/Dec 16

CAPM can also be used to calculate a **project-specific cost of capital**.

The CAPM produces a required return based on the expected return of the market $E(r_m)$, the risk-free interest rate ($R_f$) and the variability of project returns relative to the market returns ($\beta$). Its main advantage

when used for investment appraisal is that it produces a discount rate which is based on the **systematic** risk of the **individual investment**.

CAPM can therefore be used to calculate a **project-specific cost of capital**.

## 4.1 Beta values and the effect of gearing

The CAPM is consistent with the propositions of Modigliani and Miller. MM argue that as gearing rises, the cost of equity rises to compensate shareholders for the extra financial risk of investing in a geared company. This financial risk is an aspect of systematic risk, and ought to be reflected in the beta factor used to evaluate a specific project.

### 4.1.1 Geared betas and ungeared betas

The connection between MM theory and the CAPM means that it is possible to establish a mathematical relationship between the $\beta$ value of an ungeared company and the $\beta$ value of a similar, but geared, company. The $\beta$ value of a geared company will be higher than the $\beta$ value of a company identical in every respect except that it is all-equity financed. This is because of the extra financial risk. The mathematical relationship between the 'ungeared' (or asset) and 'geared' betas is as follows.

**Exam formulae**

$$\beta_a = \left[ \frac{V_e}{(V_e + V_d(1-T))} \beta_e \right] + \left[ \frac{V_d(1-T)}{(V_e + V_d(1-T))} \beta_d \right]$$

This is the **asset beta formula** on the exam formula sheet.

where  $\beta_a$ is the asset or ungeared beta
$\beta_e$ is the equity or geared beta
$\beta_d$ is the beta factor of debt in the geared company
$V_D$ is the market value of the debt capital in the geared company
$V_E$ is the market value of the equity capital in the geared company
T is the rate of corporate tax

Debt is often assumed to be risk free and its beta ($\beta_d$) is then taken as zero, in which case the formula above reduces to the following form.

$$\beta_a = \beta_e \times \frac{V_e}{V_e + V_d(1-T)} \quad \text{or, without tax,} \quad \beta_a = \beta_e \times \frac{V_e}{V_e + V_d}$$

### 4.1.2 Example: CAPM and geared betas

Two companies are identical in every respect except for their capital structure. Their market values are in equilibrium, as follows.

|  | Geared | Ungeared |
|---|---|---|
|  | $'000 | $'000 |
| Annual profit before interest and tax | 1,000 | 1,000 |
| Less interest (4,000 × 8%) | 320 | 0 |
|  | 680 | 1,000 |
| Less tax at 30% | 204 | 300 |
| Profit after tax = dividends | 476 | 700 |
| Market value of equity | 3,900 | 6,600 |
| Market value of debt | 4,180 | 0 |
| Total market value of company | 8,080 | 6,600 |

The total value of Geared is higher than the total value of Ungeared, which is consistent with MM.

All profits after tax are paid out as dividends, and so there is no dividend growth. The beta value of Ungeared has been calculated as 1.0. The debt capital of Geared can be regarded as risk free.

Calculate:

(a) The cost of equity in Geared
(b) The market return $R_m$
(c) The beta value of Geared

## Solution

(a) Since its market value (MV) is in equilibrium, the cost of equity in Geared can be calculated as:

$$\frac{d}{MV} = \frac{476}{3,900} = 12.20\%$$

(b) The beta value of Ungeared is 1.0, which means that the expected returns from Ungeared are exactly the same as the market returns, and $R_m = 700/6,600 = 10.6\%$.

(c) $\beta_e = \beta_a \times \dfrac{V_e + V_d(1-T)}{V_e}$

$= 1.0 \times \dfrac{3,900 + (4,180 \times 0.70)}{3,900} = 1.75$

The beta of Geared, as we should expect, is higher than the beta of Ungeared.

### 4.1.3 Using the geared and ungeared beta formula to estimate a beta factor

Another way of estimating a beta factor for a company's equity is to use data about the returns of other quoted companies which have similar operating characteristics; that is, to use the beta values of other companies' equity to estimate a beta value for the company under consideration. The beta values estimated for the firm under consideration must be **adjusted to allow for differences in gearing** from the firms whose equity beta values are known. The formula for geared and ungeared beta values can be applied.

If a company plans to invest in a project which involves diversification into a new business, the investment will involve a different level of systematic risk from that applying to the company's existing business. A discount rate should be calculated which is specific to the project, and which takes account of both the project's systematic risk and the company's gearing level. The discount rate can be found using the CAPM.

**Step 1** Get an estimate of the systematic risk characteristics of the project's operating cash flows by obtaining published beta values for companies in the industry into which the company is planning to diversify.

**Step 2** Adjust these beta values to allow for the company's capital gearing level. This adjustment is done in two stages.

(a) Convert the beta values of other companies in the industry to ungeared betas, using the formula:

$$\beta_a = \beta_e \left( \frac{V_e}{V_e + V_d(1-T)} \right)$$

(b) Having obtained an ungeared beta value $\beta_a$, convert it back to a geared beta $\beta_e$, which reflects the company's own gearing ratio, using the formula:

$$\beta_e = \beta_a \left( \frac{V_e + V_d(1-T)}{V_e} \right)$$

**Step 3** Having estimated a project-specific geared beta, use the CAPM to estimate a project-specific cost of equity.

## 4.1.4 Weaknesses in the formula

The problems with using the geared and ungeared beta formula for calculating a firm's equity beta from data about other firms are as follows:

(a)    It is **difficult to identify other firms with identical operating characteristics**. For example there may be **differences in beta values** between firms caused by different cost structures (eg the ratio of fixed costs to variable costs), or size differences between firms.

(b)    **Estimates of beta values** from **share price information are not wholly accurate**. The general problems of the CAPM model were reviewed in the previous section.

| Question | Gearing and ungearing betas |
|---|---|

Backwoods is a major international company with its head office in the UK, wanting to raise £150 million to establish a new production plant in the eastern region of Germany. Backwoods evaluates its investments using NPV, but is not sure what cost of capital to use in the discounting process for this project evaluation.

The company is also proposing to increase its equity finance in the near future for UK expansion, resulting overall in little change in the company's market-weighted capital gearing.

The summarised financial data for the company before the expansion are shown below.

STATEMENT OF PROFIT OR LOSS (EXTRACTS) FOR THE YEAR ENDED 31 DECEMBER 20X1

|  | £m |
|---|---|
| Revenue | 1,984 |
| Gross profit | 432 |
| Profit after tax | 81 |
| Dividends | 37 |
| Retained earnings | 44 |

STATEMENT OF FINANCIAL POSITION (EXTRACTS) AS AT 31 DECEMBER 20X1

|  | £m |
|---|---|
| Non-current assets | 846 |
| Working capital | 350 |
|  | 1,196 |
| Medium-term and long-term loans (see note below) | 210 |
|  | 986 |
| Shareholders' funds |  |
| Issued ordinary shares of £0.50 each nominal value | 225 |
| Reserves | 761 |
|  | 986 |

### Note on borrowings

These include £75m 14% fixed rate bonds due to mature in 5 years' time and redeemable at par. The current market price of these bonds is £120.00 and they have an after-tax cost of debt of 9%. Other medium- and long-term loans are floating rate UK bank loans at LIBOR plus 1%, with an after-tax cost of debt of 7%.

Company rate of tax may be assumed to be at the rate of 30%. The company's ordinary shares are currently trading at 376 pence.

The equity beta of Backwoods is estimated to be 1.18. The systematic risk of debt may be assumed to be zero. The risk-free rate is 7.75% and market return 14.5%.

The estimated equity beta of the main German competitor in the same industry as the new proposed plant in the eastern region of Germany is 1.5, and the competitor's capital gearing is 35% equity and 65% debt by book values, and 60% equity and 40% debt by MVs.

*Required*

Estimate the cost of capital that the company should use as the discount rate for its proposed investment in eastern Germany. State clearly any assumptions that you make.

## Answer

The discount rate that should be used is the WACC, with weightings based on MVs. The cost of capital should take into account the systematic risk of the new investment, and therefore it will not be appropriate to use the company's existing equity beta. Instead, the estimated equity beta of the main German competitor in the same industry as the new proposed plant will be ungeared, and then the capital structure of Backwoods applied to find the WACC to be used for the discount rate.

Since the systematic risk of debt can be assumed to be zero, the German equity beta can be 'ungeared' using the following expression.

$$\beta_a = \beta_e \ \frac{V_e}{V_e + V_d(1-T)}$$

where:  $\beta_a$ = asset beta
$\beta_e$ = equity beta
$V_e$ = proportion of equity in capital structure
$V_d$ = proportion of debt in capital structure
$T$ = tax rate

For the German company:

$$\beta_a = 1.5 \left( \frac{60}{60 + 40(1-0.30)} \right) = 1.023$$

The next step is to calculate the debt and equity of Backwoods based on MVs.

|  |  | £m |
|---|---|---|
| Equity | 450m shares at 376p | 1,692 |
| Debt: bank loans | (210 – 75) | 135 |
| Debt: bonds | (75 million × 1.20) | 90 |
| Total debt |  | 225 |
| Total MV |  | 1,917 |

The beta can now be regeared

$$\beta_e = \frac{1.023(1,692 + 225(1-0.3))}{1,692} = 1.118$$

This can now be substituted into the CAPM to find the cost of equity.

$$E(r_i) = R_f + \beta \ (E(r_m) - R_f)$$

where:  $E(r_i)$ = cost of equity
$R_f$ = risk-free rate of return
$E(r_m)$ = market rate of return
$E(r_i)$ = 7.75% + (14.5% – 7.75%) × 1.118 = 15.30%

The WACC can now be calculated:

$$\left[ 15.3 \times \frac{1,692}{1,917} \right] + \left[ 7 \times \frac{135}{1,917} \right] + \left[ 9 \times \frac{90}{1,917} \right] = 14.4\%$$

**Exam focus point**

> It is worth spending time practising the gearing and ungearing beta calculations and ensuring you are comfortable with them, as the examining team has commented that students often get them wrong.

# 5 Duration

**FAST FORWARD**

> Duration (also known as Macaulay duration) is the weighted average length of time to the receipt of a bond's benefits (coupon and redemption value), the weights being the present value of the benefits involved.

**Exam focus point**

> Macaulay duration was examined as a 17-mark Section B optional question in June 2011. As well as performing calculations, students were required to discuss how useful duration is as a measure of the sensitivity of a bond price to changes in interest rates.

## 5.1 What is duration?

In Chapter 5 we have seen that duration is the average time taken to recover the cash flow from an investment. For investments in bonds, maturity is not only affected by the maturity date of the investment but also by the coupon rate (which determines the interest payments). Duration is useful in allowing bonds of different maturities and coupon rates to be compared.

Duration gives each bond an overall **risk weighting** that allows two bonds to be compared. In simple terms, it is a **composite** measure of the risk expressed in years.

Duration is the **weighted average** length of time to the receipt of a bond's **benefits** (coupon and redemption value), the weights being the **present value** of the benefits involved.

## 5.2 Calculating duration

As already noted, in a different context in Chapter 5, duration is calculated by weighting each year of the project by the % **of the present value of the cash inflows** received in that year.

## Example

Magic Inc has a bond (Bond X) in issue which has a nominal value of $1,000 and is redeemable at par.

Bond X is a 6% bond maturing in 3 years' time and has a gross redemption yield (GRY) of 3.5%. The current price of the bond is $1,070.12.

*Required*

Calculate the duration of the bond.

## Solution

**Bond X**

|  | 1 | 2 | 3 | Total |
|---|---|---|---|---|
| Cash flow | 60 | 60 | 1,060 | |
| Discount factor (3.5%) | 0.966 | 0.934 | 0.902 | |
| Present value | 58 | 56 | 956 | 1,070 |
| % present value in each year | 58/1070 = 5.42% | 56/1070 = 5.23% | 956/1070 = 89.35% | |
| × by year | 5.42/100 × 1= 0.0542 | 5.23/100 × 2= 0.1046 | 89.35/100 × 3= 2.6805 | |

Duration = 0.0542 + 0.1046 + 2.6805 = approximately 2.84 years

## 5.3 Properties of duration

The basic features of sensitivity to interest rate risk will all be mirrored in the duration calculation.

(a) **Longer-dated bonds** will have longer durations.

(b) **Lower-coupon bonds** will have longer durations. The ultimate low-coupon bond is a zero-coupon bond where the duration will be the maturity.

(c) **Lower yields** will give longer durations. In this case, the PV of flows in the future will rise if the yield falls, extending the point of balance, therefore lengthening the duration.

The duration of a bond will shorten as the life span of the bond decays. However, the rate of decay will not be at the same rate. In our example above, a 3-year bond has a duration of 2.84 years. In a year's time the bond will have a remaining life of 2 years and a duration based on the same GRY of 1.94 years. The life span has decayed by a full year, but the duration by only 0.9 years.

## 5.4 Modified duration

**FAST FORWARD**

> **Modified duration** is a measure of the sensitivity of the price of a bond to a change in interest rates.

Rather than looking at the weighted average time it takes to receive the bond's benefits, modified duration measures how sensitive the price of the bond is to a change in the interest rate.

**Formula to learn**

$$\text{Modified duration} = \frac{\text{Macaulay duration}}{1 + \text{GRY}}$$

**Exam focus point**

> In June 2014 modified duration was tested for seven marks in the compulsory section of the exam (Q1).

Using the above example on duration, the modified duration of the bond is:

$2.84/(1 + 0.035) = 2.74$

This can be used to determine the proportionate change in bond price for a given change in yield as follows.

$$\frac{\Delta P}{P} = -\text{Modified duration} \times \Delta Y$$

which can also be expressed as:

**Formula to learn**

$\Delta P = -\text{Modified duration} \times \Delta Y \times P$

Where:

$\Delta P$ = change in bond price          P = current market price of the bond

$\Delta Y$ = change in yield

Remember there is an **inverse relationship** between yield and bond price, therefore the modified duration figure is expressed as a negative number.

If, in the above example, the yield increased by 0.5%, the change in price can be calculated as follows.

$\Delta P = -2.74 \times 0.005 \times \$1,070.12 = \$(14.66)$

Thus for a 0.5% increase in yield, the bond price will fall by $14.66.

### 5.4.1 Properties of modified duration

As the modified duration is derived from the Macaulay duration, it shares the same properties.

(a) **Longer-dated bonds** will have higher modified durations – that is, bonds which are due to be redeemed at a later date are more price-sensitive to changes in interest rates and are therefore more risky.

(b)     **Lower coupon bonds** will have higher modified durations.

(c)     **Lower yields** will give higher modified durations.

The higher the modified duration, then the greater the sensitivity of that bond to a change in the yield.

## 5.5 The benefits and limitations of duration

### 5.5.1 Benefits

The main **benefits** of duration are as follows:

(a)     Duration allows bonds of **different maturities** and **coupon rates** to be directly compared. This makes decision making regarding bond finance easier and more effective.

(b)     If a bond portfolio is constructed based on weighted average duration, it is possible to determine portfolio value changes based on estimated changes in interest rates.

(c)     Managers may be able to modify interest rate risk by changing the duration of the bond portfolio – for example, by adding shorter maturity bonds or those with higher coupons (which will reduce duration), or by adding longer maturity bonds or those with lower coupons (which will increase duration).

### 5.5.2 Limitations

The main limitation of duration is that it **assumes a linear relationship** between interest rates and price – that is, it assumes that for a certain percentage change in interest rates there will be an equal percentage change in price.

However, as interest rates change the bond price is unlikely to change in a linear fashion. Rather, it will have some kind of convex relationship with interest rates (see below).

### Relationship Between Bond Price and Yield

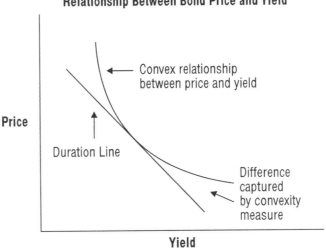

As you can see from the diagram above, the more convex the relationship, the more inaccurate duration is for measuring interest rate sensitivity. Therefore duration should be treated with caution in your predictions of interest rate/price relationships.

Duration can only be applied to measure the approximate change in bond price due to changes in interest rates if the interest rate change does not lead to a change in the shape of the yield curve. This is because it is an average measure based on the GRY (yield to maturity).

However, used in conjunction with each other, convexity and duration can provide a more accurate approximation of the percentage change in price resulting from a percentage change in interest rates. It can also be used to compare bonds with the same duration but different levels of convexity. For example, if Bond X has a higher convexity than Bond Y, its price would fall by a lower percentage in the event of rising interest rates.

# 6 Credit risk

**Key term**

> **Credit risk**, also referred to as **default risk**, is the risk undertaken by the lender that the borrower will default either on **interest payments** or on the **repayment of principal** on the due date, or on both.

## 6.1 Credit risk aspects

Credit risk arises from the inability of a party to fulfil its obligation under the terms of a contract. We have already discussed credit risk in relation to the over the counter derivatives and how exchanges deal with it through the introduction of margins. Creditors to companies, such as corporate bondholders and banks, are also exposed to credit risk. The credit risk of an individual loan or bond is determined by the following two factors.

### The probability of default

This is the probability that the borrower or counterparty will default on its contractual obligations to repay its debt.

### The recovery rate

This is the fraction of the face value of an obligation that can be recovered once the borrower has defaulted. When an company defaults, bondholders do not necessarily lose their entire investment. Part of the investment may be recovered depending on the **recovery rate**.

**Key term**

> The **loss given default** (LGD) is the difference between the **amount of money owed** by the borrower less the **amount of money recovered**.

For example, a bond has a face value of $100 and the recovery rate is 80%. The **LGD** in this case is:

LGD = $100 − $80 = $20

**Key term**

> The **expected loss** (EL) from credit risk shows the amount of money the lender should expect to lose from the investment in a bond or loan with credit risk.

The **EL** is the product of the **LGD** and the **probability of default** (PD).

EL = PD × LGD

If the PD is, say, 10%, the EL from investing in the above bond is:

EL = 0.10 × 20 = $2

## 6.2 Credit risk measurement

We have already discussed how to measure **market risk**, using measures such as the **standard deviation** and the **beta**. The measurement of **credit risk** is slightly more complex. All the approaches concentrate on the estimation of the **default probability** and the **recovery rate**.

The oldest and most common approach is to assess the probability of default using financial and other information on the borrowers and assign a rating that reflects the EL from investing in the particular bond. This assignment of **credit risk ratings** is done by **credit rating companies**, such as Standard & Poor, Moody's Investor Services and Fitch. These ratings are widely accepted as indicators of the credit risk of a bond. The table below shows the credit rating used by Moody's and Standard & Poor.

### Credit risk rating

| Standard & Poor | Moody's | Description of category |
|---|---|---|
| AAA | Aaa | Highest quality, lowest default risk |
| AA | Aa | High quality |
| A | A | Upper medium grade quality |
| BBB | Baa | Medium grade quality |

| | | |
|---|---|---|
| BB | Ba | Lower medium grade quality |
| B | B | Speculative |
| CCC | Caa | Poor quality (high default risk) |
| CC | Ca | Highly speculative |
| C | C | Lowest grade quality |

For Standard & Poor's ratings, those ratings from 'AA' to 'CCC' may be modified by the addition of a plus (+) or minus (−) sign to show relative standing within the major rating categories. For example, a company with BB+ rating is considered to have a better credit rating than a company with a BB rating, although they are in the same major rating category.

With Moody's, numerical modifiers 1, 2 and 3 are added to each ratings category from Aa to Caa, with 1 indicating a higher ranking within the category. For example, a rating of Baa1 is higher than Baa2.

Both credit rating agencies estimate default probabilities from the **empirical performance** of issued **corporate bonds** of each category. The table below shows the probability of default for certain credit categories over different investment horizons. The probability of default within a year for AAA, AA, or A bonds is practically zero whereas for a CCC bond it is 26.38%. However, although the probability of default for a AAA company is **practically zero** over a single year, it becomes 0.98% over a 15-year period (this is consistent with the theory that, the longer the time horizon, the riskier the investment).

**Standard & Poor's cumulative default probabilities (Standard & Poor's, 2015)**

| Initial rating Term | 1 | 5 | 10 | 15 |
|---|---|---|---|---|
| AAA | 0.00% | 0.36 | 0.74 | 0.98 |
| AA | 0.02% | 0.35 | 0.82 | 1.19 |
| A | 0.07% | 0.57 | 1.51 | 2.32 |
| BBB | 0.20% | 1.95 | 4.06 | 5.84 |
| BB | 0.76% | 7.71 | 13.74 | 16.77 |
| B | 3.88% | 18.70 | 25.91 | 29.49 |
| CCC | 26.38% | 46.28 | 450.73 | 53.38 |

## 6.3 Criteria for establishing credit ratings

The criteria for rating international organisations encompasses the following:

| | |
|---|---|
| **Country risk** | No issuer's debt will be rated higher than the country of origin of the issuer (the 'Sovereign Ceiling' concept) |
| **Universal/Country importance** | The company's standing relative to other companies in the country of domicile and globally (measured in terms of sales, profits, relationship with government, importance of the industry to the country, etc) |
| **Industry risk** | The strength of the industry within the country, measured by the impact of economic forces, cyclical nature of the industry, demand factors, etc |
| **Industry position** | Issuer's position in the relevant industry compared with competitors in terms of operating efficiency |
| **Management evaluation** | The company's planning, controls, financing policies and strategies, overall quality of management and succession, merger and acquisition performance and record of achievement in financial results |
| **Accounting quality** | Auditor's qualifications (if any) of the accounts, and accounting policies for inventory, goodwill, depreciation policies and so on |

| Earnings protection | Earnings power including return on capital, pre-tax and net profit margins, sources of future earnings growth |
|---|---|
| Financial gearing | Long-term debt and total debt in relation to capital, gearing, nature of assets, off balance sheet commitments, working capital, management, etc |
| Cash flow adequacy | Relationship of cash flow to gearing and ability to finance all business cash needs. |
| Financial flexibility | Evaluation of financing needs, plans and alternatives under stress (ability to attract capital), banking relationships, debt covenants. |

 Case Study

In January 2017 ratings agency S&P downgraded Rolls-Royce's long-term corporate credit rating, responding to news that the aero-engine maker would pay out 671 million pounds ($835 million) to settle a bribery investigation.

S&P said it now rated Rolls-Royce 'BBB+', down from 'A-'. It added the outlook was stable and it saw profits recovering in 2017.

Shares in Rolls traded down 1.6 percent to 679.8 pence following the ratings cut, underperforming Britain's bluechip index .FTSE which was up 0.2 percent.

As well as announcing the settlement payable over five years with British, U.S. and Brazilian authorities, Rolls said that 2016 profit would beat forecasts.

S&P said its view was that Rolls now had a 'modest' financial risk profile compared with its former classification of 'minimal', adding the company's debt-to-core earnings (EBITDA) ratio would rise to 2.1 times from the 1.4 it had expected. But the agency suggested the downgrade could be short-term.

*(Reuters, 2017)*

In recent years, credit agencies' ratings are coming under greater scrutiny. The US Government launched a lawsuit in 2013 against S&P, alleging that the agency gave excessively high ratings to win business during the boom in mortgage investments. In 2014, the US Securities and Exchange Commission introduced new requirements for credit ratings agencies – to provide for an annual certification by the CEO as to the effectiveness of internal controls and additional certifications to accompany credit ratings attesting that the rating was not influenced by other business activities.

## 6.4 Credit migration

FAST FORWARD

The credit rating of a borrower may change after a bond is issued. This is referred to as credit migration.

There is another aspect of **credit risk** which should be taken into account when investors are investing in **corporate bonds**, beyond the **probability of default**.

A borrower may not default, but due to changing economic conditions or management actions the borrower may become more or less risky than at the time the bond was issued and, as a result, the bond issuer will be assigned a different credit rating by the credit agency. This is called **credit migration**. The significance of credit migration lies in the fact that the assignment of a **lower credit rating** will **decrease the MV** of the corporate bond. This is discussed in the next section in the context of credit spreads.

226    **7a: Impact of financing on investment decisions and adjusted present values** | Part B Advanced investment appraisal

 BPP LEARNING MEDIA

## 6.5 Reducing credit risk – credit enhancement

Credit enhancement is the process of reducing credit risk by requiring collateral, insurance or other agreements to provide the lender with reassurance that it will be compensated if the borrower defaulted.

Credit enhancement is a key part of the securitisation transaction in structured finance and is important for credit rating agencies when raising a securitisation.

### 6.5.1 Internal credit enhancement

There are two main types of internal credit enhancement – excess spread and over-collateralisation.

#### Excess spread

Another name for excess spread is 'excess interest cash flow'. It is the difference between interest received by issuers of asset-based securities (such as mortgages) on the securities sold and the interest paid to the holders of these securities. One example is sub-prime mortgages. Such mortgages are sold at a higher rate of interest than prime mortgages, resulting in higher interest receipts for the mortgage providers.

#### Over-collateralisation

Over-collateralisation is a common form of credit enhancement. In simple terms, it is the **ratio of assets to liabilities**. Over-collateralisation occurs when the value of the assets held to support a security is actually greater than the security itself (the ratio of assets to liabilities is greater than 1). This gives the holder of the assets a 'cushion' in the event of late or non-payment from the security.

How the level of over-collateralisation is determined can be illustrated using an example from Standard & Poor's. A cash flow transaction involves the issue of $80 million of senior debt which is supported (backed) by a collateral pool of assets which has a par value of $100 million (known as an 80/20 liability structure). The level of over-collateralisation is the ratio of assets to liabilities – that is, $100 million/$80 million or 125%.

### 6.5.2 External credit enhancement

External credit enhancement tools include surety bonds, letters of credit and cash collateral accounts.

#### Surety bond

A **surety bond** is a guarantee to pay a loss sustained as a result of a breach of contractual or legal obligations. Strictly speaking, a surety bond is a **contract of guarantee**, not of insurance and involves three persons: the **contractor**, who puts the bond in place, the **employer**, who is contracting with the contractor and requires the surety bond to be provided, and the **guarantor**, who may be an insurer. In the event of the contractor's default, the guarantor compensates the employer for any losses incurred. Often the guarantor provides its guarantees only to securities already of at least investment-grade quality (that is, BBB/Baa or equivalent).

#### Letter of credit

A financial institution (typically a bank) which issues a letter of credit is **obliged** to reimburse any losses incurred up to the required credit-enhancement amount, in return for a fee.

Letters of credit are **often used in international trade** to protect both the importer and exporter. A letter of credit represents a written undertaking given by a bank on behalf of an importer to pay a specified sum of money to the exporter within a certain time. However, in order to be entitled to the payment the exporter must be able to produce necessary documentation that complies with the terms stated in the letter of credit.

In the early 1990s, the long-term debt of some of the banks responsible for issuing letters of credit was **downgraded**, which lessened the appeal of these tools.

## Cash collateral account

A **cash collateral account** is an account that is used to secure and service a loan. Deposits are made into this account but no sums can be withdrawn. When funds are paid in and have cleared, this reduces the loan which is served by this account. As no sums can be withdrawn, it is viewed as a zero-balance account – any money that is paid in goes immediately towards reducing the extent of the loan being served.

As a cash collateral account is an actual deposit of cash, a downgrade of the account provider would not result in a similar downgrade of the security (unlike letters of credit and surety bonds).

# 7 Credit spreads and the cost of debt capital

**FAST FORWARD**

> The cost of debt capital and the market price of corporate bonds depend on the credit risk of the bond.

## 7.1 Credit spreads

**Key term**

> The **credit spread** is the premium required by an investor in a corporate bond to compensate for the **credit risk** of the bond.

The yield to a government bondholder is the compensation to the investor for forgoing consumption today and saving. However, corporate bondholders should require compensation not only for forgoing consumption but also for the credit risk that they are exposed to. As we discussed in the previous section, this is a function of the probability of default, the recovery rate and the probability of migration. Assuming that a government bond such as the one issued by the US or an EU Government is **free** of **credit risk**, the yield on a corporate bond will be:

**Exam focus point**

> Yield on corporate bond = risk free rate + credit spread

Since **credit spreads** reflect the **credit risk** of a bond, they will be inversely related to the credit quality of the bond. **Low credit quality** bonds will be characterised by **large spreads** and **high credit quality** bonds will be characterised by **low spreads**. An example of credit spreads by type of bond and maturity is given below.

**Reuters Corporate Spreads for Industrials (in basis points)**

| Rating | 1 year | 2 year | 3 year | 5 year | 7 year | 10 year | 30 year |
|--------|--------|--------|--------|--------|--------|---------|---------|
| AAA | 5 | 10 | 12 | 18 | 28 | 42 | 65 |
| AA | 11 | 20 | 27 | 37 | 45 | 57 | 82 |
| A | 33 | 47 | 55 | 67 | 76 | 84 | 112 |
| BBB | 47 | 95 | 109 | 127 | 139 | 152 | 191 |
| BB | 240 | 265 | 283 | 304 | 321 | 339 | 377 |
| B | 456 | 482 | 505 | 531 | 555 | 581 | 616 |
| CCC+ | 600 | 626 | 653 | 682 | 712 | 743 | 775 |

*(bondsonline.com, 2014)*

## Example (1)

The current return on a 10-year government bond is 4.2%. Roger Inc, a company rated AA, has 10-year bonds in issue. Using the credit spread table above, calculate the expected yield on Roger Inc's bonds.

## Solution

The credit spread on a 10-year AA bond is 57, which means that 0.57% should be added to the return on the government bond.

Expected yield on Roger Inc's bonds = 4.2% + 0.57% = 4.77%

## Example (2)

A 15-year government bond has a current yield of 5%. Dibble Inc, a B rated company, has equivalent bonds in issue. What is the expected yield on Dibble Inc's bonds?

## Solution

The table does not include credit spreads for 15-year bonds therefore some adjustment is required to the figures we have available.

The credit spread on a 10-year B rated bond is 581 and a 30-year B rated bond is 616. The adjustment can be calculated as follows.

$$581 + \frac{(616 - 581)}{(30 - 10)} \times 5 = 590$$

This means that 5.9% must be added to the yield on government bonds.

The expected yield on Dibble's bonds is therefore 5% + 5.9% = 10.9%

## 7.2 The cost of debt capital

The cost of debt capital for a company is determined by the following.

(a)     Its credit rating
(b)     The maturity of the debt
(c)     The risk-free rate at the appropriate maturity
(d)     The corporate tax rate

**Formula to learn**

> $Cost\ of\ debt\ capital = (1 - tax\ rate)(risk\text{-}free\ rate + credit\ spread)$

**Question**                                                                                   Cost of capital

Jolly Inc, a BBB rated company, has 5-year bonds in issue. The current yield on equivalent government bonds is 3.7% and the current rate of tax is 28%.

*Required*

Using the information in the credit spread table above, calculate:

(a)     The expected yield on Jolly Inc's bonds
(b)     Jolly Inc's post-tax cost of debt associated with these 5-year bonds

**Answer**

(a)     Expected yield on 5-year bonds = 3.7% + 1.27% = 4.97%
(b)     Post-tax cost of debt = (1 − 0.28) × 4.97 = 3.58%

## 7.3 Impact of credit spreads on bond values

**FAST FORWARD**

The deterioration in the credit quality of a bond, referred to as credit migration, will affect the MV of the bond.

We have already mentioned that credit risk is affected by the probability of migration of a certain debt or loan to another credit category. In markets where loans or corporate bonds are traded this migration is reflected in increased spreads. Using only the probability of default and ignoring the probability of migration from one category to another may give a misleading estimate of the risk exposure. Thus a company that has a very low or even zero probability of default but a high probability of being downgraded will have its credit risk significantly underestimated.

To explain how credit migration may impact on bond values, consider a bond which is currently rated as BBB. In a year's time the bond may still be rated BBB, or it may have a higher or lower credit rating. An indication of the probability of being at the same or a different rating in a year's time is reproduced in the table below.

**Value of BBB bond for different credit ratings**

| Year-end rating | Probability of migration |
|---|---|
| AAA | 0.02% |
| AA | 0.33% |
| A | 5.95% |
| BBB | 86.93% |
| BB | 5.30% |
| B | 1.17% |
| CCC | 0.12% |
| Default | 0.18% |

As we have discussed, each credit category implies a different credit spread which in turn implies a different cost of debt capital. The table below is an example of the cost of debt capital for bonds of different credit ratings and different maturities. The cost of debt capital for an AAA bond with a maturity of one year is 3.6%, whereas the cost of capital for a CCC bond with a maturity of four years is 13.52%.

**Yields by credit category (%)**

| Category | Year 1 | Year 2 | Year 3 | Year 4 |
|---|---|---|---|---|
| AAA | 3.60 | 4.17 | 4.73 | 5.12 |
| AA | 3.65 | 4.22 | 4.78 | 5.17 |
| A | 3.72 | 4.32 | 4.93 | 5.32 |
| BBB | 4.10 | 4.67 | 5.25 | 5.63 |
| BB | 5.55 | 6.02 | 6.78 | 7.27 |
| B | 6.05 | 7.02 | 8.03 | 8.52 |
| CCC | 15.05 | 15.02 | 14.03 | 13.52 |

*Source: CreditMetrics Manual*

The value of a bond is the **PV** of the coupons and the redemption value, **discounted** using the appropriate cost of debt capital.

For the BBB bond of our example we need to assume a coupon rate and a face value. Suppose the bond has a face value of $100 and pays an annual coupon of 6%. Using the discount factors from the table above we calculate the value of the bond at the end of a year if it remained rated BBB using:

$$P_{BBB} = \frac{6}{1.041} + \frac{6}{(1.0467)^2} + \frac{6}{(1.0525)^3} + \frac{106}{(1.0563)^4} = 101.53$$

If it is upgraded to A, it will be worth $102.64.

$$P_A = \frac{6}{1.0372} + \frac{6}{(1.0432)^2} + \frac{6}{(1.0493)^3} + \frac{106}{(1.0532)^4} = 102.64$$

If it is downgraded to CCC, it will be worth $77.63.

$$P_{CCC} = \frac{6}{1.1505} + \frac{6}{(1.1502)^2} + \frac{6}{(1.1403)^3} + \frac{106}{(1.1352)^4} = 77.63$$

Calculating the values of the BBB bond for all possible ratings results in the values that are shown in the table below.

**Value of BBB bond for different credit ratings**

| Year-end rating | bond value |
|---|---|
| AAA | $103.35 |
| AA | $103.17 |
| A | $102.64 |
| BBB | $101.53 |
| BB | $96.01 |
| B | $92.09 |
| CCC | $77.63 |

The value of the bond when it defaults will not be zero, as the issuing firm will have some assets. The available empirical evidence from credit rating agencies shows that about 51% of the value of a BBB bond is recovered when the issuing firm defaults.

If bondholders expect to recover in case of bankruptcy, the non-recoverable amount is $49 per $100 of face value. The LGD for a BBB bond will therefore be:

LGD = 0.49 × 100 = $49

The EL for the BBB bond in the example is:

EL = 0.0018 × $49 = $0.0882

The low probability of default reduces the credit risk of a BBB bond despite the fact that it loses nearly 50% of its value in the case of a default.

## 7.4 Predicting credit ratings

Credit rating companies use financial ratios and other information in order to arrive at the credit score of a company. Many researchers have tried to 'guess' the models that are employed by credit rating agencies and have estimated models which link the observed credit rating to financial characteristics of a company. One of these models is the Kaplan-Urwitz model (Ryan, 2007, p.144). This model calculates a numerical value for a company based on certain characteristics which is then used to assign a credit rating to that company.

**Exam focus point**

If a question on the Kaplan-Urwitz model comes up in an exam (which has not happened to date), the formula will be given.

### 7.4.1 Quoted companies

> **Unsubordinated debt** is the debt that has priority claim.

In contrast, subordinated debt has no priority claim, as it is subordinated to other debt.

The Kaplan-Urwitz model for **quoted companies** is as follows.

$$Y = 5.67 + 0.011F + 5.13\pi - 2.36S - 2.85L + 0.007C - 0.87\beta - 2.90\sigma$$

where

Y is the score that the model produces

F is the size of a firm measured in total assets in $ million

$\pi$ is net income/total assets

S is debt status (subordinated debt = 1, otherwise 0)

L is gearing (measured as long-term debt/total assets)

C is interest cover (profit before interest and tax/interest payment)

$\beta$ is beta of the company estimated using CAPM

$\sigma$ is the standard deviation of the residual error from the CAPM model

### 7.4.2 Classification into credit rating categories

The classification of companies into credit rating categories is done in the following way.

| Score (Y) | Rating category |
| --- | --- |
| Y > 6.76 | AAA |
| Y > 5.19 | AA |
| Y > 3.28 | A |
| Y > 1.57 | BBB |
| Y > 0 | BB |

Question                          **Kaplan-Urwitz Model – quoted company**

The following information is available for Trench Inc, a quoted company.

Total assets = $650m

Net income = $250m

Type of debt = unsubordinated

Long-term debt (unsubordinated) = $200m

Profit before interest and tax = $500m

Interest payments = $40m

$\sigma = 0.151$

In addition, the following CAPM model was estimated.

$R_{Trench} = 0.045 + 0.800 \times$ market risk premium

Trench's volatility ($\sigma$) and the standard deviation is volatility of the market are 22% and 20% respectively.

*Required*

What is the predicted credit rating for Trench Inc, using the Kaplan-Urwitz model which is expressed as

$$Y = 5.67 + 0.011F + 5.13\pi - 2.36S - 2.85L + 0.007C - 0.87\beta - 2.90\sigma ?$$

The inputs to the model are as follows (note that we have removed the 'm' from the figures – this is always the case otherwise the results will be distorted).

F = $650

$\pi$ = ($250/$650) = 0.385

S = 0 (unsubordinated debt)

L = ($200/$650) = 0.308

C = ($500/$40) = 12.5 times

$\beta$ = 0.800

$\sigma$ = 0.151

Y =  5.67 + (0.011 × 650) + (5.13 × 0.385) − (2.36 × 0) − (2.85 × 0.308) + (0.007 × 12.5) − (0.87 × 0.800) − (2.90 × 0.151)

Y =  12.87

**The credit rating for Trench Inc = AAA (using the table in Section 7.4.2)**

### 7.4.3 Unquoted companies

The second Kaplan-Urwitz model was estimated using data on unquoted companies.

$$Y = 4.41 + 0.0014F + 6.4\pi - 2.56S - 2.72L + 0.006C - 0.53\sigma$$

You will notice that there is no beta factor in the above equation – this is because we are dealing with unquoted companies.

In this case $\sigma$ is the coefficient of variation of earnings (standard deviation of earnings divided by mean earnings). All the other variables remain the same.

# 8 Theories of capital structure – traditional and Modigliani and Miller (MM)

## 8.1 The traditional view of WACC

The **traditional view** is as follows:

(a)     As the **level of gearing increases**, the **cost of debt** remains **unchanged** up to a certain level of gearing. Beyond this level, the cost of debt will increase as interest cover falls, the amount of assets available for security falls and the risk of bankruptcy increases.

(b)     The **cost of equity** rises as the level of **gearing increases** and **financial risk increases**.

(c)     The **WACC** does **not remain constant**, but rather falls initially as the proportion of debt capital increases, and then begins to increase as the rising cost of equity (and possibly of debt) becomes more significant.

(d)     The **optimum level of gearing** is where the **company's WACC is minimised**.

The traditional view about the cost of capital is illustrated in the following figure. It shows that the WACC will be minimised at a particular level of gearing P.

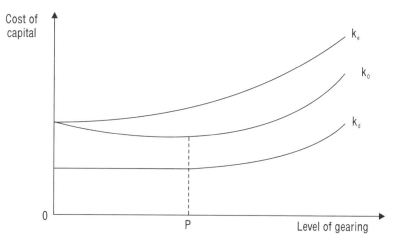

Where $k_e$ is the cost of equity in the geared company

$k_d$ is the cost of debt

$k_0$ is the WACC

The traditional view is that the WACC, when plotted against the level of gearing, is saucer shaped. The optimum capital structure is where the WACC is lowest, at point P.

## 8.2 The net operating income (MM) view of WACC

**FAST FORWARD**

The MM theory predicts that the financial structure has no impact on the cost of capital and therefore the way a project is financed has no impact on the value of the project.

**Exam focus point**

The examining team has stated that you will only need to know the key issues of the MM theory – you will not be asked to enter into any lengthy proofs.

The net operating income approach takes a different view of the effect of gearing on WACC. In their 1958 theory, MM (Watson & Head, 2013, p.299) proposed that the total MV of a company, in the absence of tax, will be determined only by two factors:

- The **total earnings** of the company
- The **level of operating (business) risk** attached to those earnings

The total MV would be computed by discounting the total earnings at a rate that is appropriate to the level of operating risk. This rate would represent the WACC of the company.

Thus MM concluded that **the capital structure of a company would have no effect on its overall value or WACC**.

### 8.2.1 Assumptions of net operating income approach

Modigliani and Miller made various assumptions in arriving at this conclusion, including:

(a)    A **perfect capital market** exists, in which investors have the same information, on which they act rationally, to arrive at the same expectations about future earnings and risks.

(b)    There are no **tax or transaction costs**.

(c)    **Debt is risk free** and freely available at the same cost to investors and companies alike.

MM justified their approach by the use of **arbitrage**.

**Key term**

**Arbitrage** is the simultaneous purchase and sale of a security in different markets, with the aim of making a risk-free profit through the exploitation of any price difference between the markets.

Arbitrage can be used to show that once all opportunities for profit have been exploited, the MVs of two companies with the same earnings in equivalent business risk classes will have moved to an equal value.

If MM's theory holds, it implies:

(a)  The **cost of debt remains unchanged** as the level of gearing increases.
(b)  The **cost of equity rises** in such a way as to keep the **WACC constant**.

This would be represented on a graph as shown below.

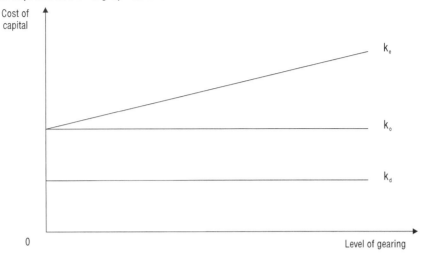

## 8.3 MM theory adjusted for taxation

Having argued that debt has no benefit in the absence of taxation, MM then went on to demonstrate that debt can be beneficial where tax relief applies.

Allowing for **taxation reduces the cost of debt capital** by multiplying it by a factor $(1 - t)$ where t is the rate of tax (assuming the debt to be irredeemable).

MM modified their theory to admit that tax relief on interest payments does makes debt capital cheaper to a company, and therefore **reduces the WACC** where a company has debt in its capital structure. They claimed that the WACC will continue to fall, up to gearing of 100%.

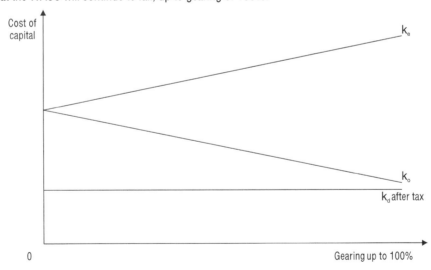

## 8.4 Formula for cost of equity

The principles of the MM theory with tax gave rise to the following formula for cost of equity.

$$k_e = k_e^i + (1-T)(k_e^i - k_d)\frac{V_d}{V_e}$$

Where  $k_e$ is the cost of equity in a geared company

$k_e^i$ is the cost of equity in an ungeared company

$V_d$, $V_e$ are the MVs of debt and equity respectively

$k_d$ is the cost of debt pre-tax

## 8.5 Example of MM cost of equity calculation

Shiny Inc is an ungeared company with a cost of equity of 10%. Shiny is considering introducing debt to its capital structure, as it is tempted by a loan with a rate of 5%, which could be used to repurchase shares. Once the equity is repurchased, the ratio of debt to equity will be 1:4. Assume that corporation tax is 30%.

(a) What will be the revised cost of equity if Shiny takes out the loan?
(b) At what discount rate will Shiny now appraise its projects? Comment on your results.

## Solution

(a) $k_e = 0.10 + (1 - 0.3)(0.10 - 0.05) \times 0.25 = 10.9\%$
(b) $WACC = (0.2 \times 0.7 \times 0.05) + (0.8 \times 0.109) = 9.42\%$

The new WACC figure is lower than that for the ungeared company. This means that future investments will be able to bring greater wealth to the shareholders. More projects will become acceptable to management, given that they are being discounted at a lower discount rate.

## 8.6 Weaknesses in MM theory

MM theory has been criticised as follows:

(a) MM theory assumes that **capital markets are perfect**. For example, a company will always be able to raise finance to fund worthwhile projects. This ignores the danger that higher gearing can lead to **financial distress costs** (see Section 9).

(b) **Transaction costs** will restrict the arbitrage process.

(c) Investors are **assumed to act rationally** which may not be the case in practice.

# 9 Alternative theories of capital structure

## 9.1 Static trade-off theory

**FAST FORWARD**

Static trade-off theory states that firms in a static position will seek to achieve a target level of gearing by adjusting their current gearing levels.

We know that a firm enjoys an increase in tax savings with an increase in debt financing due to the tax deductibility of interest.

However, an increase in debt financing will also result in an increase in the chances of the firm going bankrupt because of its increased commitment in interest payments. It is important to remember that a firm can skip its dividend payments but not its interest payments. Failure, or the risk of failing, to meet those interest payments because of inadequate cash on hand will cause the firm some financial distress, and the ultimate form of financial distress is bankruptcy.

What are some of the financial distress costs faced by a firm? We can classify them into two categories:

(a) Direct financial distress costs
(b) Indirect financial distress costs

### 9.1.1 Direct financial distress costs

The direct financial distress costs faced by a firm are the legal and administrative costs associated with the bankruptcy or reorganisation of the firm. Studies have shown that such costs range from less than 1% to approximately 4–5% of the value of the firm.

### 9.1.2 Indirect financial distress costs

There are different types of cost (mostly implicit) that a firm faces when it is in a financially stressful situation (but not bankruptcy). The following are some of those costs:

(a)    A higher cost of capital (either for debt or equity) due to a firm's high risk of default.

(b)    Lost sales due to customers having concerns that a firm with high gearing may cut back on the quality of goods or services, or may be at risk of failure and so will not be able to provide after sales service or to honour product guarantees.

(c)    Managers and employees will try drastic actions to save the firm that might result in some long-term problems; such actions include closing down plants, downsizing, drastic cost cuts and selling off valuable assets; these actions will ultimately dilute the value of the firm.

(d)    Firms might have trouble keeping highly skilled managers and employees, who may not want to be associated with a firm that is at risk of failing due to high debt levels.

A key drawback of Modigliani and Miller theory is that it ignores the existence of financial distress costs. However, when these are taken into account it can be argued that the **gearing-adjusted** value of the firm should be decreased.

The value of the company in this case will be:

Value of the ungeared firm + present value of tax savings due to interest payments – present value of financial distress costs.

This suggests that a company should gear up to take advantage of any tax benefits available, but only to the extent that the **marginal benefits exceed** the **marginal costs** of **financial distress**. After this point, the market value of the firm will start to fall and its WACC will start to rise. **Myers** (Ryan, 2014, p.207)  argues that the level of gearing that is appropriate for a business depends on its **specific business context.** This is known as the **static trade-off theory** of capital structure.

Myers suggests that mature, asset intensive, industries tend to have high gearing because they are at low risk of default and therefore the present value of financial distress costs are likely to be outweighed by the present value of tax saved from interest payments. On the other companies which high level of intangible assets may well find that the opposite is the case ie the present value of financial distress costs are likely to be higher than the present value of tax saved from interest payments.

## 9.2 Agency theory

The agency theory provides a rationale for an optimal structure based on the existence of agency costs associated with the issue of debt and equity.

### 9.2.1 Agency costs of debt

Agency costs of debt only arise when there is a **risk of default**. If debt is totally free of default risk, debtholders are not concerned about the income, value or the risk of the firm. However, as **gearing increases**, the **probability of default also increases** and with this comes the likelihood of substantial bankruptcy costs.

If the possibility of default exists, **shareholders can gain at the expense of debtholders**. For instance, after issuing debt, a firm may decide to restructure its assets, selling off those with low business risk and acquiring assets that are more risky and thus have a higher possibility of default but also have higher expected returns. If things work out well, then the **shareholders** will get most of the benefit but, if not, then much of the loss will fall on the **bondholders**, who will have already agreed to be anticipated with a lower interest rate than the risk level of the firm presupposes.

### 9.2.2 Agency costs of equity

**Agency costs** also exist in relation to the **new share issues**. The cause of agency costs in this case is the potential conflict between **old shareholders** and **new shareholders**. New shareholders will want to monitor the management of the company to make sure that the original shareholders do not benefit at the expense of new shareholders. These monitoring mechanisms are expensive and the agency costs associated with the issue of new equity is increased with the amount of new equity issued.

The **optimal capital structure** of the firm will be formed at the particular level of debt and equity where the **benefits of the debt** that can be received by the shareholders balance **equal the costs of debt** imposed by the debtholders.

## 9.3 Pecking order theory

**FAST FORWARD**

> Pecking order theory is based on the idea that shareholders have less information about the firm than directors do.
>
> Shareholders and other investors will use directors' actions as signals to indicate what directors believe about the firm, given their superior information.

### 9.3.1 Debt or equity?

When deciding how to finance a project, managers will consider such issues as tax relief on debt and risk of default on debt. However, trying to get the timing right is another consideration.

Managers will prefer to **issue equity** when the **share price is high** (even to the point of being overvalued). They will prefer not to issue equity when the share price is considered to be low (or undervalued). In other words, managers will **issue debt** (increase gearing) when the **share price is low** and issue equity when the share price is high.

As a result, investors will use the issue of debt or equity as a **signal** from managers as to the true worth of the company's shares. Managers typically have better information than investors that can be used to value the shares (**information asymmetry**).

### 9.3.2 Market signals

As mentioned above, investors may use the issue of debt or equity as a signal as to the likely true worth of the company's shares.

If equity is issued, the market will take this as a signal that shares are overvalued. This may result in investors selling their shares (thus making substantial gains) which will lead to a fall in the share price. If this happens, the cost of equity may rise, which will result in a higher marginal cost of finance. To avoid this possibility, managers may decide to issue debt even if shares are seen as being overvalued.

An issue of debt may be interpreted as an undervaluation of the shares. Investors will want to 'get a bargain' and will thus start to buy the shares, leading to an increase in share price.

### 9.3.3 So what is the 'pecking order'?

The preferred 'pecking order' for financing instruments is as follows:

(a)   **Retained earnings**. To avoid any unwanted signals, managers will try to finance as much as possible through internal funds.

(b)   **Debt**. When internal funds have been exhausted and there are still positive NPV opportunities, managers will use debt to finance any further projects until the company's debt capacity has been reached. **Secured debt** (which is less risky) should be **issued first**, followed by unsecured (risky) debt.

(c)   **Equity**. The 'finance of last resort' is the issue of equity.

# 10 The adjusted present value (APV) method   12/10, 6/14

> The **APV** method suggests that it is possible to calculate an **adjusted** cost of capital for use in project appraisal, as well as indicating how the NPV of a project can be increased or decreased by **project financing effects**.
>
> * Evaluate the project as if it was all equity financed
> * Make adjustments to allow for the effects of the financing method

## 10.1 NPV and APV

We have seen that a company's gearing level has implications for both the value of its equity shares and its WACC. The viability of an investment project will depend partly on how the investment is financed and partly on how the method of finance affects gearing.

If an investment uses a unusually high amount of debt finance it can be argued (using Modigliani and Miller theory) that there is a benefit from the financing used (the tax saved from the use of debt finance) as well as from the project itself.

This can be assessed using the **adjusted present value (APV) method**.

**Exam focus point**

> APV was examined in December 2010 as part of an optional question. In this question an investment was planned that would be 100% debt financed. You were expected to realise that this situation required the use of the APV method.

## 10.2 Carrying out an APV calculation

The APV method involves two stages.

**Step 1**   **Evaluate** the **project** first of all as if it was **all equity financed**, and so as if the company were an all equity company to find the 'base case NPV'.

**Step 2**   **Make adjustments** to allow for the effects of the method of financing that has been used.

## 10.3 Example: APV method

A company with gearing of 50% debt and 50% equity (using market values) is considering a project that would cost $100,000. The company's cost of equity is 21.6% and the cost of debt is 12% (pre-tax) and the project's finance would leave the company's WACC unchanged. The cash flows from the project would be $36,000 a year in perpetuity, before interest charges. Tax is at 30%.

Appraise the project using firstly the NPV method and secondly the APV method.

## Solution

We can use the **NPV method** because the company's WACC will be unchanged.

|  | Cost | Weighting | Cost x weighting |
| --- | --- | --- | --- |
|  | % |  | % |
| Equity | 21.6 | 0.5 | 10.8 |
| Debt (70% of 12%) | 8.4 | 0.5 | 4.2 |
| WACC |  |  | 15.0 |

Annual cash flows in perpetuity from the project are as follows.

|  | $ |
| --- | --- |
| Before tax | 36,000 |
| Less tax (30%) | 10,800 |
| After tax | 25,200 |

NPV of project $= -\$100,000 + (25,200 \div 0.15)$
$= -\$100,000 + \$168,000$
$= \$68,000$

Note that the tax relief that will be obtained on debt interest is taken account of **in the WACC, NOT in the project cash flows**.

Since $100,000 of new investment is being created, the value of the company will increase by $100,000 + $68,000 = $168,000, of which 50% must be debt capital.

The company must raise 50% × $168,000 = $84,000 of 12% debt capital, and (the balance) $16,000 of equity. The NPV of the project will raise the value of this equity from $16,000 to $84,000 thus leaving the gearing ratio at 50:50.

The **APV approach** to this example is as follows.

(a)    First, we need to know the cost of equity in an equivalent ungeared company. The MM formula we can use to establish this is as follows.

Cost of ordinary (equity) share capital in a geared firm (with tax):

$$k_e = k_e^i + (1-T)(k_e^i - k_d)\frac{V_d}{V_e}$$

$k_d$ = the **pre-tax** cost of debt. Using the information from the question:

$$21.6\% = k_e^i + (k_e^i - 12\%) \times \left[\frac{50 \times 0.7}{50}\right]$$

$$21.6\% = k_e + 0.70k_e - 8.4\%$$

$$1.70k_e = 30\%$$

$$k_e = 17.647\%$$

(b)    Next, we calculate the **NPV of the project as if it were all equity financed**. The cost of equity would be 17.647%.

$$NPV = \frac{\$25,200}{0.17647} - \$100,000 = \$42,800$$

(c)    Next, we can use an MM formula for the relationship between the value of geared and ungeared companies to establish **the effect of gearing on the value of the project**. $84,000 will be financed by debt.

$V_g$ (APV) = $V_u$ + (value of debt × corporate tax rate)
$= \$42,800 + (\$84,000 \times 0.30)$
$= \$42,800 + \$25,200$
$= \$68,000$

The value of debt × corporate tax rate represents the **PV of the tax shield on debt interest**; that is, the PV of the savings arising from tax relief on debt interest.

This can be proved as follows.

Annual interest charge = 12% of $84,000 = $10,080

Tax saving (30% × $10,080) = $3,024.00

Cost of debt (pre-tax) = 12%

PV of tax savings in perpetuity $= \dfrac{\$3,024}{0.12}$ (by coincidence only this equals the project net of tax cash flows)

$= \$25,200$

Make sure you use the cost of debt to discount the tax relief on interest costs and not the cost of equity.

## 10.4 Example: APV method and limited cash flows

Suppose in the above example the cash flows only lasted for five years, and tax was payable one year in arrears. Calculate the PV of the tax shield.

## Solution

The tax saving will now only last for years 2 to 6. (Remember, interest will be paid in years 1 to 5, but the tax benefits will be felt a year in arrears.)

PV of tax savings = 3,024 × Annuity factor years 2 to 6
$$= 3,024 \times \text{(Annuity factors years 1 to 6 – Annuity factor year 1)}$$
$$= 3,024 \times (4.111 - 0.893)$$
$$= \$9,731$$

The APV and NPV approaches produce the same conclusion.

## 10.5 APV and changes in gearing

However, the APV method can also be adapted to allow for financing which **changes the gearing structure** and the WACC.

In this respect, it is superior to the NPV method. Suppose, for example, that in the previous example the **entire project were to be financed by debt**. The APV of the project would be calculated as follows.

(a)    The NPV of project if all equity financed is:

$$\frac{\$25,200}{0.17647} - \$100,000 = +\$42,800 \text{ (as before)}$$

(b)    The adjustment to allow for the method of financing is the PV of the tax relief on debt interest in perpetuity.

$$DT_c = \$100,000 \times 0.30 = \$30,000$$

(c)    APV = \$42,800 + \$30,000 = +\$72,800

The project would increase the value of equity by \$72,800.

Question | APV

A project costing \$100,000 is to be financed by \$60,000 of irredeemable 12% loan stock and \$40,000 of new equity. The project will yield an after-tax annual cash flow of \$21,000 in perpetuity. If it were all equity financed, an appropriate cost of capital would be 15%. The tax rate is 30%. What is the project's APV?

Answer

|  | $ |
|---|---|
| NPV if all equity financed: \$21,000/0.15 – \$100,000 | 40,000 |
| PV of the tax shield: \$60,000 ×12% ×30%/0.12 | 18,000 |
| APV | 58,000 |

## 10.6 Discounting tax relief at the risk-free rate

Often in exams you will be given the risk-free rate of return. As tax relief is allowed by the Government and is almost certain, there is an argument for saying that **all tax relief** should be discounted at the **risk-free rate**. However, there is the opposing argument that the **risk of the tax relief** is the same as the **risk of the debt** to which it relates, and therefore the tax relief should be discounted at the cost of debt. The risk-free rate would also not be used if the company was unlikely to be in a taxpaying position for some years.

In the exam we suggest that you make clear the reasons for choosing the discount rate that you have chosen to discount the tax relief, and add a comment that an alternative rate might be used.

## 10.7 Other elements in APV calculation

The tax shield may not be the only complication introduced into APV calculations.

### 10.7.1 Issue costs

The costs of issuing the finance needed for the project may also be brought into APV calculations.

### 10.7.2 Example: Issue costs

Edted is about to start a project with an initial investment of $20 million, which will generate cash flow over 4 years. The project will be financed with a $10 million 10-year bank loan and a rights issue. Issue costs are 5% of the amount raised.

Calculate the issue costs that will be used in the APV calculation.

#### Solution

Issue costs will not equal 5% of $10 million ($20 million – $10 million). The $10 million will be the figure left after the issue costs have been paid. Therefore $10 million must be 95%, not 100% of the amount raised, and the

$$\text{Issue costs} = \frac{5}{95} \times \$10 \text{ million} = \$526{,}316$$

In the above example, the issue costs do not need to be discounted, as they are assumed to be paid at time 0. The complication comes if issue costs are allowable for tax purposes.

### 10.7.3 Example: The tax implications of issue costs

Assume in the example above that issue costs are allowable for tax purposes, the tax is assumed to be 30% payable one year in arrears and the risk-free rate of return is assumed to be 8%.

Calculate the tax effect of the issuing costs to be included in the APV calculation.

#### Solution

$$
\begin{aligned}
\text{Tax effect} &= \text{Tax rate} \times \text{Issue costs} \times \text{Discount rate} \\
&= 0.3 \times 526{,}316 \times 0.926 \\
&= \$146{,}211
\end{aligned}
$$

### 10.7.4 Spare debt capacity

Projects may yield other incremental benefits, for example increased borrowing or debt capacity. These benefits should be included in the APV calculations, even if the debt capacity is utilised elsewhere.

### 10.7.5 Example: Spare debt capacity

Continuing with the Edted example, suppose the project increased the borrowing capacity of the company by $6 million, at the risk-free rate of return of 8%. Calculate the effect on the APV calculation.

#### Solution

Remember that we are concerned with the incremental benefit which is the **tax shield effect** of the increased debt finance.

| PV of tax shield effect | = | Increased debt capacity | | Interest rate | | Tax rate | | Discount factor Years 2 to 5 |
|---|---|---|---|---|---|---|---|---|
| | = | $6 million | × | 8% | × | 30% | × | 3.067 |
| | = | $441,648 | | | | | | |

### 10.7.6 Subsidy

You may face a situation where a company can obtain finance at a lower interest rate than its normal cost of borrowing. In this situation you have to include in the APV calculation the tax shield effect of the cheaper finance and the effect of the saving in interest.

### 10.7.7 Example: Subsidy

Gordonbear is about to start a project requiring $6 million of initial investment. The company normally borrows at 12% but a government loan will be available to finance the entire project at 10%. The risk-free rate of interest is 6%.

Tax is payable at 30% one year in arrears. The project is scheduled to last for four years.

Calculate the effect on the APV calculation if Gordonbear finances the project by means of the government loan.

### Solution

(a)    The tax shield is as follows.

We assume that the loan is for the duration of the project (four years) only.

Annual interest  = $6 million × 10%
                  = $600,000

Tax relief        = $600,000 × 0.3
                  = $180,000

This needs to be discounted over years 2 to 5 (remember the one-year time lag). However, we do not use the 10% to discount the loan and the tax effect; instead we assume that the government loan is risk free and the tax effect is also risk free. Hence we use the 6% factor in discounting.

NPV tax relief = $180,000 × Discount factor years 2 to 5
               = $180,000 × 3.269
               = $588,420

(b)    We also need to take into account the benefits of **being able** to pay a **lower interest rate**.

Benefits = $6 million × (12% – 10%) × 6% Discount factor years 1 to 4
         = $6 million × 2% × 3.465
         = $415,800

(c)    Total effect = $588,420 + $415,800 = $1,004,220.

## 10.8 The advantages and disadvantages of the APV method

The main advantages of the APV are as follows.

(a)    APV can be used to **evaluate** all the **effects of financing** a product, including:

    (i)     Tax shield
    (ii)    Changing capital structure
    (iii)   Any other relevant cost

(b)    When using APV you do not have to adjust the WACC using assumptions of perpetual risk-free debt.

The main difficulty with the APV technique is that it is based on Modigliani and Miller theory, we have already identified that there are a number of limitations to this theory.

**Exam focus point**

Always be prepared to discuss the limitations of a technique.

# 11 Effect of alternative financing strategies on financial reporting

Gearing affects the volatility of **earnings per share (EPS)**. The higher the level of gearing, the higher the **volatility of EPS**.

## 11.1 Financial gearing and debt

**Fixed income securities** issued by corporations to fund capital projects include **debt** and **preferred stock**.

**Debt** is **less risky** than **equity** for investors and therefore requires a **lower rate** of **return**. In addition, interest payments attract tax relief, hence the cost of debt will be lower than the cost of equity. The effect of this on the company's WACC is that as a company gears up, its WACC will be reduced due to the higher proportion of the cheaper debt financing in the company's overall financial structure.

The return on debt is not directly linked to the underlying performance of the business. The same predetermined amount is paid whether the profits are high or low and this in turn makes any residual claims that shareholders have on the income of a company more volatile.

## 11.2 Impact of gearing on earnings per share

Financial gearing is an attempt to quantify the **degree of risk** involved in holding equity shares in a company, both in terms of the company's ability to remain in business and in terms of expected ordinary dividends from the company.

The more geared the company is, the **greater the risk** that little (if anything) will be available to distribute by way of dividend to the ordinary shareholders. The more geared the company, the greater the percentage change in **earnings** available for ordinary shareholders for any given percentage change in profit before interest and tax.

This means that there will be greater **volatility in earnings per share**, and presumably therefore greater volatility in dividends paid to those shareholders, where a company is highly geared. That is the risk. You may do extremely well or extremely badly without a particularly large movement in the profit from operations of the company.

Gearing ultimately measures the company's ability to **remain in business**. A highly geared company has a large amount of interest to pay annually. If those borrowings are 'secured' in any way then the holders of the debt are perfectly entitled to force the company to realise assets to pay their interest if funds are not available from other sources. Clearly, the more highly geared a company, the more likely this is to occur if and when profits fall.

# Chapter Roundup

- The **expected return** of a portfolio of shares can be calculated by calculating the weighted beta of the portfolio and using CAPM.

- Duration (also known as Macaulay duration) is the weighted average length of time to the receipt of a bond's benefits (coupon and redemption value), the weights being the present value of the benefits involved.

- **Modified duration** is a measure of the sensitivity of a bond's price to a change in interest rates.

- The credit rating of a borrower may change after a bond is issued. This is referred to as credit migration.

- Credit enhancement is the process of reducing credit risk by requiring collateral, insurance or other agreements to provide the lender with reassurance that it will be compensated if the borrower defaulted.

- Credit enhancement is a key part of the securitisation transaction in structured finance and is important for credit rating agencies when raising a securitisation.

- There are two main types of internal credit enhancement – excess spread and over-collateralisation.

- External credit enhancement tools include surety bonds, letters of credit and cash collateral accounts.

- The cost of debt capital and the market price of corporate bonds depend on the credit risk of the bond.

- The deterioration in the credit quality of a bond, referred to as credit migration, will affect the market value of the bond.

- The MM theory predicts that the financial structure has no impact on the cost of capital and therefore the way a project is financed has no impact on the value of the project.

- Static trade-off theory the level of gearing that is appropriate for a business depends on its **specific business context.**

- Pecking order theory is based on the idea that shareholders have less information about the firm than directors do.

- Shareholders and other investors will use directors' actions as signals to indicate what directors believe about the firm, given their superior information.

- The **APV** method suggests that it is possible to calculate an **adjusted** cost of capital for use in project appraisal, as well as indicating how the net present value of a project can be increased or decreased by project financing effects.

  - Evaluate the project as if it was all equity financed
  - Make adjustments to allow for the effects of the financing method

- Gearing affects the volatility of **earnings per share (EPS)**. The higher the level of gearing, the higher the **volatility of EPS**.

1   Using the beta values for the following companies, calculate the cost of equity if the market risk premium is 5% and the return on a risk-free investment is 4%.

| Company | Beta (as at September 2017) |
|---|---|
| Easyjet (a low cost airline) | 0.58 |
| Volkswagen | 1.57 |

2   You have invested in a bond with a default probability of 10%. In the event of default you hold collateral that amounts to about 70% of the value of the bond. What is your expected loss?

3   What is the relationship between credit rating and the cost of debt capital?

4   What is the most likely rating next year of a BBB bond?

5   What will happen to the value of a corporate bond if its credit rating is downgraded?

# Answers to Quick Quiz

1   **Easyjet**

$r = 0.04 + 0.58 \times 0.05 = 0.069$ or 6.90%

**Volkswagen**

$r = 0.04 + 1.57 \times 0.05 = 0.1185$ or 11.85%

2   The expected loss is equal to $0.10 \times (1 - 0.70) = 0.03$ or 3%.

3   The lower the credit rating, the higher the credit spread and consequently the higher the cost of capital.

4   From the historical migration tables the most likely rating for a BBB bond will be a BBB rating.

5   The value of the bond will fall.

Now try the questions below from the Practice Question Bank

| Number | Level | Marks | Time |
|--------|-------|-------|------|
| 11 | Introductory | 15 | 29 mins |
| 12 | Introductory | 15 | 29 mins |
| 13 | Examination | 10 | 20 mins |

# Valuation and the use of free cash flows

# 7b

| Topic list | Syllabus reference |
|---|---|
| 1 Yield curve and bond price | B4(a) |
| 2 Forecasting a firm's free cash flow | B4(b) |
| 3 Free cash flow to equity | B4(c) |
| 4 Valuations of equity | B4(a) |
| 5 Valuing an organisation using free cash flow | B4(c) |
| 6 Explain use of option pricing models in valuing equity and in assessing default risk | B4(d), (e) |

## Introduction

The purpose of this chapter is to look at different methods of valuing both debt and equity, including the use of free cash flows. It considers how the yield curve can be used to estimate the value of a bond before moving on to look at how an organisation can forecast its free cash flow. Section 4 recaps methods of valuing equity that should be brought forward knowledge from *Financial Management (FM)*, Section 5 looks at valuations using free cash flow and the final section looks at the use of option pricing models and assessment of default risk.

# Study guide

| | | Intellectual level |
|---|---|---|
| **B4** | **Valuation and the use of free cash flows** | |
| (a) | Apply asset-based, income-based and cashflow-based models to value equity. Apply appropriate models, including term structure of interest rates, the yield curve and credit spreads to value corporate debt. | 3 |
| (b) | Forecast an organisation's free cash flow and its free cash flow to equity (pre and post capital reinvestment). | 3 |
| (c) | Advise on the value of a firm using its free cash flow and free cash flow to equity under alternative horizon and growth assumptions. | 3 |
| (d) | Explain the use of the BSOP model to estimate the value of equity of an organisation and discuss the implications of the model for a change in the value of equity. | 2 |
| (e) | Explain the role of the BSOP model in the assessment of default risk, the value of debt and its potential recoverability. | 2 |

## 1 Yield curve and bond price     6/12, Sep/Dec 16, Mar/Jun 17

We have already seen how financial securities can be valued on the basis of their cash flows. The value of a **bond** can be calculated by splitting up the payments associated with one bond into separate bonds and discounting by the relevant rate according to the yield curve.

Question                                   Yield curve

YZ Co wants to issue a five-year redeemable bond with an annual coupon of 4%. The bond is redeemable at par ($100). Tax can be ignored.

The annual spot yield curve for this risk class of bond in the financial press is given as:

1-year 3.3%
2-year 3.8%
3-year 4.2%
4-year 4.8%
5-year 5.5%

*Required*

Using the information above, calculate:

(a) The expected price at which the bond can be issued
(b) The yield to maturity (YTM) of the bond

Answer

(a) The five-year bond can be split into separate bonds as follows.

| Year | 1 | 2 | 3 | 4 | 5 |
|---|---|---|---|---|---|
| Bond 1 | 4 | | | | |
| Bond 2 | | 4 | | | |
| Bond 3 | | | 4 | | |
| Bond 4 | | | | 4 | |
| Bond 5 | | | | | 104 |

Each bond can then be discounted as follows using the yield curve rates

| | | |
|---|---|---|
| Bond 1 | $4 \times 1/1.033$ | $3.87 |
| Bond 2 | $4 \times 1/1.038^2$ | $3.71 |
| Bond 3 | $4 \times 1/1.042^3$ | $3.54 |
| Bond 4 | $4 \times 1/1.048^4$ | $3.32 |
| Bond 5 | $104 \times 1/1.055^5$ | $79.57 |

The total of the discounted cash flows is $94.01 which represents the price at which the bond can be issued.

(b)   An internal rate of return style calculation is needed to calculate the YTM.

Since the current price is below par, the YTM is more than 4%. Therefore we will try 5% and 8%.

| Year | | 5% discount factor | PV | 8% discount factor | PV |
|---|---|---|---|---|---|
| 0 | (94.01) | 1.000 | (94.01) | 1.000 | (94.01) |
| 1–5 | 4 | 4.329 | 17.32 | 3.993 | 15.97 |
| 5 | 100 | 0.784 | 78.40 | 0.681 | 68.10 |
| | | | 1.71 | | (9.94) |

The YTM is therefore

$5 + 1.71 \times (8 - 5)/(1.71 + 9.94) = 5.44\%$

Note that the YTM is lower than the five-year bond yield rate because the bond returns are not all in the fifth year, but in earlier years when the interest rates are lower.

In general the bond price for n time periods can be calculated by the following formula.

$$\text{Price} = \text{coupon} \times \frac{1}{\left(1 + r_1\right)^1} + \text{coupon} \times \frac{1}{\left(1 + r_2\right)^2} + \dots + \text{coupon} \times \frac{1}{\left(1 + r_n\right)^n} + \text{redemption value} \times \frac{1}{\left(1 + r_n\right)^n}$$

Where $r_n$ is the spot rate based on the yield curve.

Note that coupons may be made more frequently than annually and this should be taken into account, as each coupon payment needs to be discounted by an appropriate time period related bond yield rate.

# 2 Forecasting a firm's free cash flow

**FAST FORWARD**

A firm's free cash flow is the actual amount of cash that a company has left from its operations that could be used to pursue opportunities that enhance shareholder value.

In a similar way to bonds, the value of a company's shares (ie equity) can be estimated by discounting the company's future cash flows. The same approach can be used to estimate the value of an organisation as a whole ie value of debt + value of equity.

## 2.1 Definition of free cash flow

**Key term**

The **free cash flow** is the cash flow derived from the operations of a company after subtracting working capital, investment and taxes and represents the funds available for distribution to the capital contributors, ie shareholders **and** debtholders.

The idea of free cash flow is to provide a measure of what is available to the owners of a firm, after providing for capital expenditures to maintain existing assets and to create new assets for future growth and is measured as follows.

Earnings before interest and tax (EBIT)
Less tax on EBIT

Plus non-cash charges (eg depreciation)
Less capital expenditure
Less net working capital increases
Plus net working capital decreases
Plus salvage value received

## Question

Free cash flow calculation

Albion Inc needs to invest $9,000 to increase productive capacity and also to increase its working capital by $1,000. Earnings before taxes are $90,000 and it sets off against tax $6,000 of depreciation. Profits are taxed at 40%. What is the free cash flow?

## Answer

The calculations for the free cash are given below.

| | $ |
|---|---|
| EBIT | 90,000 |
| Less taxes | 36,000 |
| Operating income after taxes | 54,000 |
| Plus depreciation (non-cash item) | 6,000 |
| Less capital expenditures | 9,000 |
| Less changes to working capital | 1,000 |
| Free cash flow | 50,000 |

## 2.2 Forecasting free cash flows

Free cash flows can be forecast in similar ways to such other items as expenses, sales and capital expenditure. We must consider the likely behaviour of each of the elements that make up the free cash flow figure – such as movements in future tax rates, potential spending on capital projects and the associated working capital requirements.

### 2.2.1 Constant growth

One approach to forecasting free cash flows is to assume that they will grow at a constant rate. The calculation of free cash flows is therefore quite straightforward.

$FCF_t = FCF_{t-1}(1 + g)$

Where   $FCF_t$   = the free cash flow at time t
    $FCF_{t-1}$   = the free cash flow in the previous period
        g   = growth rate

If you wish to forecast the total free cash flow over a number of periods where the growth rate is assumed to be constant the following formula can be used.

$FCF = FCF_0(1 + g)^n$

Where   FCF   is the total forecast free cash flow
    $FCF_0$   is the free cash flow at the beginning of the forecast period
        n   is the number of years for which the free cash flow is being forecast

## Question

Forecasting FCF

The current value of the free cash flow is $6 million and it is estimated that the free cash flows will grow at a constant rate of 10% for the next 7 years. What is the total FCF predicted for year 7?

$$FCF_7 = (1 + 0.1)^7 \times \$6 = \$11.7m$$

## 2.2.2 Differing growth rates

When the elements of free cash flow are expected to grow at different rates, each element must be forecast separately using the appropriate rate. Free cash flow can then be estimated using the revised figures for each year.

**Question**                                                                      Future free cash flow

Pokey Inc is trying to forecast its free cash flow for the next three years. Current free cash flow is as follows.

|  | Expected annual increase | |
| --- | --- | --- |
|  | % | $ |
| EBIT | 4 | 500,000 |
| Tax | 30% of EBIT | 150,000 |
| Depreciation | 5 | 85,000 |
| Capital expenditure | 2 | 150,000 |
| Working capital requirements | 3 | 60,000 |

By what percentage will free cash flow have increased between now and the end of year 3?

**Answer**

|  | Year 0 | Year 3 |
| --- | --- | --- |
|  | $ | $ |
| EBIT ($EBIT_0 \times (1 + 0.04)^3$) | 500,000 | 562,432 |
| Tax | (150,000) | (168,730) |
| Depreciation ($Depreciation_0 \times (1 + 0.05)^3$) | 85,000 | 98,398 |
| Capital expenditure ($Cap\ Ex_0 \times (1 + 0.02)^3$) | (150,000) | (159,181) |
| Working capital requirements ($WC_0 \times (1 + 0.03)^3$) | (60,000) | (65,564) |
| Free cash flow | 225,000 | 267,355 |

$$\text{Percentage increase} = \frac{267,355 - 225,000}{225,000} = 18.8\%$$

# 3 Free cash flow to equity

The free cash flow derived in the previous section is the amount of money that is available for distribution to the capital contributors. If the project is financed by equity only, then these funds could be potentially distributed to the shareholders of the company.

However, if the company is financing the project by issuing debt, then the shareholders are entitled to the residual cash flow left over after meeting interest and principal payments. This residual cash flow is called free cash flow to equity (FCFE).

## 3.1 Direct method of calculation

FCFE = Operating profit (EBIT) less interest paid and less tax
Add depreciation
Less total net investment (change in capital investment + change in working capital)
Add net debt issued (new borrowings less any repayments)

**Question**

The following information is available for ABC Co.

Capital expenditure $20 million
Corporate tax rate 35%
Debt repayment $23 million
Depreciation charges $10 million

|  | 20X8 |
| --- | --- |
|  | $m |
| Sales | 650.00 |
| Less cost of goods sold | (438.00) |
| Gross profit | 212.00 |
| Operating expenses | (107.50) |
| EBIT | 104.50 |
| Less interest expense | (8.00) |
| Earnings before tax | 96.50 |
| Less taxes | (33.77) |
| Net income | 62.73 |

What is the FCFE?

**Answer**

The FCFE is calculated as follows.

|  | 20X8 |
| --- | --- |
|  | $m |
| Net income | 62.73 |
| Plus depreciation | 10.00 |
| Less capital expenditures | (20.00) |
| Less debt repayment | (23.00) |
| FCFE | 29.73 |

## 3.2 Indirect method of calculation

Using the indirect method, FCFE is calculated as follows.
Free cash flow (calculated using the formula in Section 2.1 above)
Less interest paid (net of tax)
Add new borrowing (net of any debt repaid)

**Question**                                        Free cash flow to equity – indirect method

Using the information in the question 'Free cash flow to equity' above, calculate the FCFE using the indirect method.

**Answer**

The free cash flow is given by:

| EBIT(1 – Tax rate) | 67.93 |
| --- | --- |
| Plus depreciation expense | 10.00 |
| Less CAPEX | (20.00) |
| Free cash flow | 57.93 |

FCFE = $57.93 – (8 x (1 – 0.35)) + 23 = $29.73

FCFE is also covered in Chapter 2 and 4b as part of a discussion of dividend capacity.

# 4 Valuations of equity

Before we move on to look at valuing equity using free cash flow, we will briefly cover methods of valuing equity which should be familiar to you from *Financial Management (FM)*.

## 4.1 Market capitalisation

**Market capitalisation** is the market value of a company's shares multiplied by the number of issued shares.

## 4.2 The net assets method of share valuation

Using this method of valuation, the value of a share in a particular class is equal to the **net tangible assets** divided by the **number of shares. Intangible assets** (including goodwill) should be excluded, unless they have a market value (for example patents and copyrights, which could be sold).

(a) **Goodwill**, if shown in the accounts, is unlikely to be shown at a true figure for purposes of valuation, and the value of goodwill should be reflected in another method of valuation (for example the earnings basis).

(b) **Development expenditure**, if shown in the accounts, would also have a value which is related to future profits rather than to the worth of the company's physical assets.

### 4.2.1 Advantages and disadvantages of asset-based valuations

**Advantages**

- Valuations can be made relatively simply.
- They provide a base value for the organisation.

**Disadvantages**

- They do not incorporate future earnings potential.
- If based on historical cost, then they are subject to accounting conventions and may not represent market value.
- They exclude the value of intangible assets.

## 4.3 The P/E ratio (earnings) method of valuation

This is a common method of valuing a **controlling interest** in a company, where the owner can decide on **dividend** and **retentions policy**. The P/E ratio relates earnings per share to a share's value.

Since P/E ratio = $\dfrac{\text{Market value}}{\text{EPS}}$,

then market value per share = EPS × P/E ratio

**Exam focus point**

Remember that earnings per share (EPS) = $\dfrac{\text{Profit / loss attributable to ordinary shareholders}}{\text{Weighted average number of ordinary shares}}$

The examining team has commented in the past that students often calculate EPS incorrectly.

The P/E ratio produces an **earnings-based** valuation of shares by deciding a suitable P/E ratio and multiplying this by the EPS for the shares which are being valued.

**Market valuation or capitalisation = P/E ratio × EPS or P/E ratio × Total earnings**

Depending on whether the market value per share, or total market value of the company is being calculated.

The EPS could be a historical EPS or a prospective future EPS. For a given EPS figure, a higher P/E ratio will result in a higher price.

## 4.4 The earnings yield valuation method

Another income-based valuation model is the earnings yield method.

$$\text{Earnings yield (EY)} = \frac{\text{EPS}}{\text{Market price per share}} \times 100\%$$

This method is effectively a variation on the P/E method (the EY being the reciprocal of the P/E ratio), using an appropriate EY effectively as a discount rate to value the earnings:

$$\text{Market value} = \frac{\text{Earnings}}{\text{EY}}$$

### 4.4.1 Advantages and disadvantages of earnings-based valuations

**Advantages**

- They can be used to value a controlling stake in an organisation.
- They are easily understood methods.

**Disadvantages**

- It can be difficult to identify a suitable P/E ratio for an unlisted entity.
- Valuation is based on accounting profits rather than cash flows.
- It can be difficult to establish a realistic sustainable level of earnings.

## 4.5 The dividend growth model

Using the **dividend growth model** we have:

$$P_0 = \frac{D_0(1+g)}{(1+k_e)} + \frac{D_0(1+g)^2}{(1+k_e)^2} + \ldots = \frac{D_0(1+g)}{(k_e - g)} = \frac{D_1}{k_e - g}$$

where
$D_0$ = Current year's dividend
$g$ = Growth rate in earnings and dividends
$D_0(1+g)$ = Expected dividend in one year's time ($D_1$)
$k_e$ = Shareholders' required rate of return
$P_0$ = Market value excluding any dividend currently payable

### 4.5.1 Advantages and disadvantages of dividend-based valuations

**Advantages**

- Based on expected future income
- Useful for valuing a minority stake in an organisation

**Disadvantages**

- Growth rate can be difficult to estimate.
- It can be difficult to estimate a cost of equity for an unlisted company.
- Companies that don't pay and are not expected to pay dividends do not have a zero value.

# 5 Valuing an organisation using free cash flow  6/12, 6/13

In Sections 2 and 3 above we saw that free cash flow could be calculated in two ways, either by calculating it directly or by calculating the FCFE and adding the **cash flows** to **debtholders**. Similarly, we can value an organisation using free cash flows either by using the predicted free cash flows or by adding together all the cash flows payable to the different claimants of the organisation (equity and debtholders).

## 5.1 Valuation using free cash flows

The valuation using free cash flows is very similar to carrying out a net present value calculation. The value of the organisation is simply the **sum of the discounted free cash flows** over the appropriate horizon.

If we assume that free cash flows remain **constant** (that is, with no growth) over the appropriate horizon, then the value of the organisation is the **free cash flow divided by the cost of capital**.

Alternatively, if the free cash flows are growing at a **constant rate** every year, the value can be calculated using the **Gordon Model** (also known as the **Constant Growth Model**).

$$PV_0 = \frac{FCF_0(1+g)}{k-g}$$

Where g is the growth rate
k is the cost of capital

### 5.1.1 Example

Rick Inc currently has free cash flows of $5 million per year and a cost of capital of 12%. Calculate the value of Rick Inc if:

(a)    The free cash flows are expected to remain constant.
(b)    The free cash flows are expected to grow at a constant rate of 4% per annum.

**Solution**

(a)    Value of Rick Inc = $\dfrac{\text{Free cash flow}}{\text{Cost of capital}}$ = $\dfrac{\$5 \text{ million}}{0.12 \text{ million}}$ = $41.67 million

(b)    Use the Gordon Model

Value of Rick Inc = $\dfrac{(\$5 \text{ million} \times 1.04)}{(0.12 - 0.04)}$ = $65 million

## 5.2 Terminal values

**Key term**

> The **terminal value** of a project or a stream of cash flows is the value of all the cash flows occurring from period N + 1 onwards ie beyond the normal prediction horizon of periods 1 to N.

These flows are subject to a greater degree of uncertainty, as they are beyond the horizon 1 to N where normal forecasts are acceptable. As such, simplifying assumptions may need to be made for any flows occurring after period N.

When we refer to a project, the terminal value is equivalent to the **salvage value** remaining at the end of the expected project horizon.

### 5.2.1 Terminal values and company valuation

Terminal values can be used in valuing an organisation. The value of the organisation will be calculated **as the sum of the discounted free cash flows plus the discounted terminal value**.

### 5.2.2 Calculating terminal values

**Assume that free cash flows are constant**

When calculating the terminal value, we can assume that the free cash flows after the 'normal' time horizon (period N) will be constant. Terminal value is determined by dividing the free cash flow at time (N + 1) by the cost of capital (required rate of return).

## Question

Consider the following information on a project.

Cash flow in period N + 1 = $2 million
Required rate of return = 10%

Assuming that the free cash flow will remain at $2 million indefinitely and the initial investment is $18 million, what is the terminal value?

## Answer

The terminal value of the project is:

$$TV_N = \frac{2}{0.1} = \$20 \text{ million}$$

### Assume that cash flows increase at a constant rate

An alternative assumption is to assume that cash flows increase from year to year at a constant rate g, ie:

$$FCF_{N+1} = (1 + g) FCF_N$$

and the terminal value will be:

$$TV_N = \frac{FCF_N (1+g)}{k - g}$$

Provided that $k > g$

## Question

Assume the following values for the expected growth, current cash flows and required return.

$$g = 0.05$$
$$FCF_N = \$2 \text{ million}$$
$$k = 0.10$$

What is the terminal value?

## Answer

The terminal value according to the constant growth model will then be:

$$TV = \frac{2 \times (1 + 0.05)}{0.10 - 0.05} = \$42 \text{ million}$$

## Question

You have completed the following forecast of free cash flows for an eight-year period, capturing the normal business cycle of Marathon Inc.

| Year | FCF |
| --- | --- |
| 20X8 | 1,860.0 |
| 20X9 | 1,887.6 |
| 20Y0 | 1,917.6 |
| 20Y1 | 1,951.2 |

| | 20Y2 | 1,987.2 |
| | 20Y3 | 2,016.0 |
| | 20Y4 | 2,043.6 |
| | 20Y5 | 2,070.0 |

Free cash flows are expected to grow at 3% beyond 20Y5. The cost of capital is assumed to be 12%. What is Marathon's value?

## Answer

| Year | FCF | Discount factor 12% | Present value |
|------|-----|---------------------|---------------|
| 20X8 | 1,860.0 | 0.893 | 1,661 |
| 20X9 | 1,887.6 | 0.797 | 1,504 |
| 20Y0 | 1,917.6 | 0.712 | 1,365 |
| 20Y1 | 1,951.2 | 0.636 | 1,241 |
| 20Y2 | 1,987.2 | 0.567 | 1,127 |
| 20Y3 | 2,016.0 | 0.507 | 1,022 |
| 20Y4 | 2,043.6 | 0.452 | 924 |
| 20Y5 | 2,070.0 | 0.404 | 836 |

Total present value for forecast period = $9,680

$$\text{Terminal value} = \frac{(\$2,070 \times 1.03)}{(0.12 - 0.03)} = \$23,690$$

Discount terminal value back to year 0 = $23,690 × 0.404 = $9,571

Total value of Marathon = $19,431

## 5.3 Organisation valuation using FCFE

The techniques used for the valuation of a company using the FCFE can also be applied for the value of equity. The value of equity is simply the present value of the FCFE, discounted at the cost of equity ($k_e$), plus the terminal value discounted at the cost of equity.

Once the value of equity is calculated, the value of debt needs to be calculated next. The value of the organisation is then simply the value of equity and the value of debt.

# 6 Explain use of option pricing models in valuing equity and in assessing default risk

**FAST FORWARD**

Option pricing models can be used to assess default risk and to value equity.

## 6.1 Options and default probability
6/14

**FAST FORWARD**

The role of **option pricing models** in the assessment of **default risk** is based on the **limited liability property** of **equity investments**.

The **equity** of a company can be seen as a **call option** on the **assets** of the company with an **exercise price** equal to the **outstanding debt**.

**Exam focus point**

The syllabus refers to this syllabus area using the wording 'explain the use of the BSOP (Black Scholes option pricing model)' in estimating default risk and assessing the value of equity. This implies that this area will not be tested numerically.

The role of **option pricing models** in the assessment of **default risk** is based on the **limited liability property** of **equity investments**. Whereas shareholders can participate in an increase in the profits of a company, their losses are limited to the values of their holding.

The probability of asset values falling to a level that would trigger default can be assessed by looking at the past levels of volatility of a firm's asset values and assessing the number of standard deviations that this fall would represent. This would then influence the interest rate that would be charged on the loan.

Consider a firm with assets whose market value is denoted by V. Furthermore, the firm is assumed to have a very simple capital structure where the acquisition of assets is funded by equity whose market value is denoted by E and by debt with market value D. The statement of financial position of this firm is given by:

| Assets | Liabilities |
|---|---|
| V | Equity E |
|  | Debt D |

The **debt** issued by the firm is a **one-year zero coupon bond** with **one year maturity** and **face value F**. The **market value** of **debt** is:

$$D = \frac{F}{1+y}$$

Note that y is not the risk-free return but includes a risk premium over the risk-free rate to reflect the fact that bondholders are exposed to credit risk and they may not receive the promised payment F. This can happen when, on the date the debt matures, the value of the assets $V_1$ are not sufficient to pay the bondholders.

The company will default on its debt if $V_1 < F$ in which case bondholders will receive not F but $V_1$, suffering a loss of $F - V_1$. The lower the value of the assets on maturity, the higher the loss suffered by the bondholders.

Equity is a residual claim on the assets of the company and the value of equity on maturity date will be the difference between the value of the assets and the face value of debt. It will be positive if the value of the assets is higher than the outstanding debt and zero if the value of the assets is lower than the outstanding debt. In summary the value of the equity $E_1$ will be:

$E_1 = V_1 - F$ if $V_1 > F$

$E_1 = 0$ if $V_1 \leq F$

The value of equity on maturity date is shown in Figure 1 below. The value of equity is positive when $V_1 > F$ and zero when $V_1 \leq F$. Because of the limited liability feature of equity, the lowest value it can reach is zero.

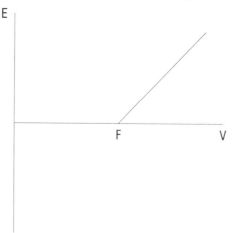

*Figure 1*

As we have already discussed in Chapter 6, this is the payoff of a call option on the assets of a company with an exercise price equal to the face value of debt F.

The value of the firm's equity can therefore be estimated using the **Black-Scholes model** for the valuation of a European call option.

$$C = P_a N(d_1) - P_e N(d_2)e^{-rt}$$

$$d_1 = \frac{\ln\left(\dfrac{P_a}{P_e}\right) + \left(r + 0.5s^2\right)t}{s\sqrt{t}}$$

$$d_2 = d_1 - s\sqrt{t}$$

The value of $N(d_1)$ shows how the value of equity changes when the value of the assets changes. This is the delta of the call option (delta is covered in more detail in Chapter 17). The value of $N(d_2)$ is the probability that a call option will be in the money at expiration. In this case it is the probability that the value of the asset will exceed the outstanding debt, ie $V_1 > F$. The probability of default is therefore given by $1 - N(d_2)$. This is shown as the shaded part in Figure 2 below.

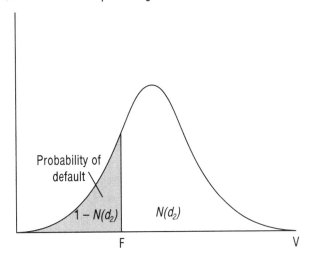

*Figure 2*

## 6.2 Valuing equity

Using the same logic as above, we can use the BSOP model to value a firm's equity.

The value of a firm can be thought of in these terms:

- If the firm fails to generate enough value to repay its loans, then its value = 0; shareholders have the **option** to let the company die at this point.

- If the firm does generate enough value then the extra value belongs to the shareholder

- In this case shareholders can pay off the debt (this is the **exercise price**) and continue in their **ownership** of the company (ie just as the exercise of a **call option** results in the ownership of an asset).

- The Black-Scholes model can be applied because shareholders have a call option on the business. The protection of limited liability creates the same effect as a call option because there is an upside if the firm is successful, but shareholders lose nothing other than their initial investment if it fails.

- So the value of a company can be calculated as the amount that you would pay as a **premium for this call option**.

This is mainly useful for valuing a start-up firm that is high risk and difficult to value using normal valuation techniques.

# Chapter Roundup

- A firm's free cash flow is the actual amount of cash that a company has left from its operations that could be used to pursue opportunities that enhance shareholder value.

- Option pricing models can be used to calculate the expected loss associated with a corporate bond.

- The role of **option pricing models** in the assessment of **default risk** is based on the **limited liability property** of **equity investments**.

- The **equity** of a company can be seen as a **call option** on the **assets** of the company with an **exercise price** equal to the **outstanding debt**.

# Quick Quiz

1  The following information is available for XYZ Co.

Capital expenditure $50 million
Corporate tax rate 25%
Debt repayment $27 million
Depreciation charges $13 million
Shareholders' required return 13%

|  | 20X8 |
|---|---|
|  | $m |
| Sales | 725.00 |
| Less cost of goods sold | (517.00) |
| Gross profit | 208.00 |
| Operating expenses | (91.75) |
| EBIT | 116.25 |
| Less interest expense | (11.00) |
| Earnings before tax | 105.25 |
| Less taxes | (26.31) |
| Net income | 78.94 |

What is the FCFE (using the direct method of calculation)?

2  Using the information above, what is the FCFE using the indirect method of calculation?

3  Using the information above and assuming the free cash flow is expected to grow at a constant rate of 3% per year, what is the valuation of XYZ Co?

4  How can the Black Scholes model be used to find the default probability of a company?

5  How can the Black Scholes model be used to find the value of a company?

# Answers to Quick Quiz

1

|  | 20X8 $m |
|---|---|
| Net income | 78.94 |
| Plus depreciation | 13.00 |
| Less capital expenditures | (50.00) |
| Less debt repayment | (27.00) |
| FCFE | 14.94 |

2

|  |  |
|---|---|
| EBIT(1 – Tax rate) | 87.19 |
| Plus depreciation expense | 13.00 |
| Less CAPEX | (50.00) |
| Free cash flow | 50.19 |

FCFE = $50.19 – (11 × (1 – 0.25)) + 27 = $14.94m

3 Value of XYZ Co = $\dfrac{(\$14.94m \times 1.03)}{(0.13 - 0.03)}$ = $153.9m

4 The value of $N(d_2)$ is the probability that a call option will be in the money at expiration. In this case it is the probability that the value of the asset will exceed the outstanding debt, ie $V_1 > F$. The probability of default is therefore given by $1 - N(d_2)$.

5 The Black-Scholes model can be applied because shareholders have a call option on the business. The protection of limited liability creates the same effect as a call option because there is an upside if the firm is successful, but shareholders lose nothing other than their initial investment if it fails.

So the value of a company can be calculated as the amount that would be paid as a **premium for a call option**.

# International investment and financing decisions

| Topic list | Syllabus reference |
|---|---|
| 1 Overview | B5 |
| 2 Effects of exchange rate assumptions on project values | B5(a) |
| 3 Forecasting cash flows from overseas projects | B5(b) |
| 4 The impact of exchange controls | B5(c) |
| 5 Transaction, translation and economic risks | B5(d), E2(a) |
| 6 Issues in choosing finance for overseas investment | B5(e) |
| 7 Costs and benefits of alternative sources of finance for multinational companies (MNCs) | B5(e) |

## Introduction

In this chapter we look at the international dimension of project appraisal.

Companies that undertake overseas projects are exposed to exchange rate risks as well as other risks, such as exchange control, taxation and political risks.

In this chapter we look at capital budgeting techniques for multinational companies that incorporate these additional complexities in the decision-making process.

# Study guide

# 1 Overview

Many of the projects that companies are appraising may have an international dimension. For example, the assumption can be made that part of the production from a project may be exported. In appraising a tourist development, a company may be making assumptions about the number of tourists from abroad who may be visiting. Imported goods and materials could be a factor in the determination of cash flows. All these examples show that exchange rates will have an influence on the cash flows of the company.

Companies that undertake overseas projects are exposed, in addition to exchange rate risks, to other types of risk, such as exchange control, taxation and political risks. The latter is particularly true in countries with undemocratic regimes that may be subject to changes in a rather disorderly fashion.

Capital budgeting techniques for multinational companies therefore need to incorporate these additional complexities in the decision-making process. These can be based on similar concepts to those used in the purely domestic case which we have examined. Special considerations, examples of which were given above, may apply.

One of the optional performance objectives in your PER is to evaluate projects and to advise on their costs and benefits. This chapter covers how to evaluate international investment decisions.

# 2 Effects of exchange rate assumptions on project values

**FAST FORWARD**

Changes in exchange rates are as important as the underlying profitability in selecting an overseas project.

In a domestic project the net present value (NPV) is the sum of the discounted cash flows plus the terminal value (discounted at the weighted average cost of capital (WACC)) less the initial investment.

When a project in a foreign country is assessed we must take into account some specific considerations such as **local taxes, double taxation agreements, and political risk** that affect the present value of the project. The main consideration in an international project is of course the exchange rate risk; that is, the risk that arises from the fact that the cash flows are denominated in a foreign currency. An appraisal of an

international project requires estimates of the exchange rate. In the rest of this section we discuss some fundamental relationships that help the financial manager form views about exchange rates.

## 2.1 Purchasing power parity                                      Mar/June 16

**Purchasing power parity** theory states that the exchange rate between two currencies is the same in equilibrium when the purchasing power of currency is the same in each country.

Purchasing power parity theory predicts that the exchange value of foreign currency depends on the relative purchasing power of each currency in its own country and that **spot exchange rates will vary over time according to relative price changes**.

Formally, purchasing power parity can be expressed in the following formula.

**Exam formula**

$$S_1 = S_0 \times \frac{(1+h_c)}{(1+h_b)}$$

Where $S_1$ = expected spot rate
$S_0$ = current spot rate
$h_c$ = expected inflation rate in country c
$h_b$ = expected inflation rate in country b

Note that the expected future spot rate will not necessarily coincide with the 'forward exchange rate' currently quoted.

### 2.1.1 Example: Purchasing power parity

The spot exchange rate between UK sterling and the Danish kroner is £1 = 8.00 kroners. Assuming that there is now purchasing parity, an amount of a commodity costing £110 in the UK will cost 880 kroners in Denmark. Over the next year, price inflation in Denmark is expected to be 5% while inflation in the UK is expected to be 8%. What is the 'expected spot exchange rate' at the end of the year?

Using the formula above:

Future (forward) rate, $S_1 = 8 \times \dfrac{1.05}{1.08} = 7.78$

This is the same figure as we get if we compare the inflated prices for the commodity. At the end of the year:

UK price = £110 × 1.08 = £118.80

Denmark price = Kr880 × 1.05 = Kr924

$S_t$ = 924 ÷ 118.80 = 7.78

In the real world, exchange rates move towards purchasing power parity only over the **long term**. However, the theory is sometimes used to predict future exchange rates in **investment appraisal problems** where forecasts of relative inflation rates are available.

 Case Study

An amusing example of purchasing power parity is the Big Mac index (Economist, 2016). Under purchasing power parity, movements in countries' exchange rates should in the long term mean that the prices of an identical basket of goods or services are equalised. The McDonald's Big Mac represents this basket.

The index compares local Big Mac prices with the price of Big Macs in America. This comparison is used to forecast what exchange rates should be, and this is then compared with the actual exchange rates to decide which currencies are over- and undervalued.

## 2.2 Interest rate parity

Under interest rate parity the difference between spot and forward rates reflects differences in interest rates.

**Key term**

Interest rate parity predicts foreign exchange rates based on the hypothesis that the difference between two countries' interest rates should offset the difference between the spot rates and the forward exchange rates over the same period.

Under interest rate parity the difference between spot and forward rates reflects differences in interest rates. If this was not the case then investors holding the currency with the lower interest rate would switch to the other currency, ensuring that they would not lose on returning to the original currency by fixing the exchange rate in advance at the forward rate. If enough investors acted in this way, forces of supply and demand would lead to a change in the forward rate to prevent such risk-free profit making.

The principle of interest rate parity links the foreign exchange markets and the international money markets. The principle can be stated using the following formula which is given in the exam formula sheet.

**Exam formula**

$$F_0 = S_0 \frac{(1+i_c)}{(1+i_b)}$$

where $F_0$ is the forward rate

$S_0$ is the spot rate

$i_c$ is the interest rate in the country overseas

$i_b$ is the interest rate in the base country

This equation links the spot and forward rates to the difference between the interest rates.

## Example

A US company is expecting to receive Zambian kwacha in one year's time. The spot rate is US$1 = ZMK4,819. The company could borrow in kwacha at 7% or in dollars at 9%. There is no forward rate for one year's time.

Estimate the forward rate in one year's time.

## Solution

The base currency is dollars therefore the dollar interest rate will be on the bottom of the fraction.

$$F_0 = 4,819\frac{(1+0.07)}{(1+0.09)} = 4,730.58$$

However, this prediction is subject to considerable inaccuracy, as future events can result in large unexpected currency rate swings that were not predicted by interest rate parity. In general, interest rate parity is regarded as **less accurate** than purchasing power parity for predicting future exchange rates.

### 2.2.1 Use of interest rate parity to compute the effective cost of foreign currency loans

Loans in some currencies are cheaper than in others. However, when the likely strengthening of the exchange rate is taken into consideration, the cost of apparently cheap international loans becomes much more expensive.

## Example

Cato, a Polish company, needs a one-year loan of about 50 million zlotys. It can borrow in zlotys at 10.80% p.a. but is considering taking out a sterling loan which would cost only 6.56% p.a. The current spot exchange rate is zloty/£5.1503. The company decides to borrow £10 million at 6.56% per annum. Converting at the spot rate, this will provide 51.503 million zlotys. Interest will be paid at the end of one year along with the repayment of the loan principal.

Assuming the exchange rate moves in line with interest rate parity, you are required to show the zloty values of the interest paid and the repayment of the loan principal. Compute the effective interest rate paid on the loan.

## Solution

By interest rate parity, the zloty will have weakened in one year to:

$$5.1503 \times \frac{1.1080}{1.0656} = 5.3552$$

| Time | | £'000 | Exchange rate | Zloty '000 |
|------|------|-------|---------------|------------|
| Now | Borrows | 10,000 | 5.1503 | 51,503 |
| In 1 year | 6.56% interest | (656) | | |
| | Repayment | (10,000) | 5.3552 | |
| | | (10,656) | | (57,065) |

The effective interest rate paid is $\frac{57,065}{51,503} - 1 = 10.80\%$, the same as it would have paid in sterling.

This rate would have to be incorporated into the discount rate for any investment projects financed by this loan. As the discount rate would now be higher than originally anticipated, the NPV of the project will be lower (which may result in the project being unviable).

## 2.3 International Fisher effect

**FAST FORWARD**

The International Fisher effect states that currencies with high interest rates are expected to depreciate relative to currencies with low interest rates.

According to the **International Fisher effect**, interest rate differentials between countries provide an unbiased predictor of future changes in spot exchange rates. The currency of countries with relatively high interest rates is expected to depreciate against currencies with lower interest rates, because the higher interest rates are considered necessary to compensate for the anticipated currency depreciation. Given free movement of capital internationally, this idea suggests that the real rate of return in different countries will equalise as a result of adjustments to spot exchange rates.

The International Fisher effect can be expressed as:

**Formula to learn**

$$\frac{1+i_c}{1+i_b} = \frac{1+h_c}{1+h_b}$$

Where 
$i_a$ is the nominal interest rate in country c
$i_b$ is the nominal interest rate in country b
$h_a$ is the inflation rate in country c
$h_b$ is the inflation rate in country b

## Example

The nominal interest rate in the US is 5% and inflation is currently 3%. If inflation in the UK is currently 4.5%, what is its nominal interest rate? Would the dollar be expected to appreciate or depreciate against sterling?

## Solution

The dollar is the base currency.

$$\frac{1+i_c}{1+0.05} = \frac{1+0.045}{1+0.03}$$

$$1 + i_c = (1 + 0.05) \times \frac{1+0.045}{1+0.03}$$

$1 + i_c = 1.065$ therefore $i_c = 6.5\%$

The dollar would be expected to appreciate against sterling, as it has a lower interest rate. According to the International Fisher effect, the currency of a country with a lower interest rate will appreciate against the currency of a country with a higher interest rate.

| Question | Forecasting exchange rates |

Suppose that the nominal interest rate in the UK is 6% and the nominal interest rate in the US is 7%. What is the expected change in the dollar/sterling exchange rate?

| Answer |

Since

$$r_\$ - r_£ = 0.01$$

It means that

$$\frac{e_1 - e_0}{e_0} = 1\%$$

And the implication is that the dollar will depreciate by 1%.

## 2.4 Expectations theory

Expectations theory looks at the relationship between differences in forward and spot rates and the expected changes in spot rates.

The formula for expectations theory is:

$$\frac{\text{Spot}}{\text{Forward}} = \frac{\text{Spot}}{\text{Expected future spot}}$$

## 2.5 Calculating NPV for international projects

> **FAST FORWARD**
>
> The NPV of an international project is normally calculated by converting the overseas cash flows into the domestic currency using a forecast exchange rate.

There are **two alternative approaches** for calculating the NPV from an overseas project.

**First approach**

(a) Forecast **foreign currency** cash flows including inflation
(b) **Forecast exchange rates** and therefore the home currency cash flows
(c) Discount home currency cash flows at the **domestic cost of capital**

**Second approach**

(a) Forecast **foreign currency** cash flows including inflation
(b) Discount at **foreign currency cost of capital** and calculate the foreign currency NPV
(c) Convert into a **home currency NPV** at the spot exchange rate

The second approach is useful because it does not require an exchange rate to be forecast. However, exam questions to date have all been based on using the first approach – this approach is more useful where project's cash flows are in a variety of currencies.

### Question                                                   Overseas investment appraisal

Bromwich Inc, a US company, is considering undertaking a new project in the UK. This will require initial capital expenditure of £1,250 million, with no scrap value envisaged at the end of the five-year lifespan of the project. There will also be an initial working capital requirement of £500 million, which will be recovered at the end of the project. The initial capital will therefore be £1,750 million. Pre-tax net cash inflows of £800 million are expected to be generated each year from the project.

Company tax will be charged in the UK at a rate of 40%, with depreciation on a straight-line basis being an allowable deduction for tax purposes. UK tax is paid at the end of the year following that in which the taxable profits arise.

There is a double taxation agreement between the US and the UK, which means that no US tax will be payable on the project profits.

The current £/$ spot rate is £0.625 = $1. Inflation rates are 3% in the US and 4.5% in the UK. A project of similar risk recently undertaken by Bromwich Inc in the US had a required post-tax rate of return of 10%.

*Required*

Calculate the present value of the project using each of the two alternative approaches.

### Answer

**Method 1 – convert sterling cash flows into $ and discount at $ cost of capital**

Firstly we have to estimate the exchange rate for each of years 1–6. **This can be done using purchasing power parity**.

$$S_1 = S_0 \times \frac{(1+h_c)}{(1+h_b)}$$

| Year | | £/$ expected spot rate |
|---|---|---|
| 0 | | 0.625 |
| 1 | $0.625 \times (1.045/1.03)$ | 0.634 |
| 2 | $0.634 \times (1.045/1.03)$ | 0.643 |
| 3 | $0.643 \times (1.045/1.03)$ | 0.652 |
| 4 | $0.652 \times (1.045/1.03)$ | 0.661 |
| 5 | $0.661 \times (1.045/1.03)$ | 0.671 |
| 6 | $0.671 \times (1.045/1.03)$ | 0.681 |

| | 0 £m | 1 £m | 2 £m | 3 £m | 4 £m | 5 £m | 6 £m |
|---|---|---|---|---|---|---|---|
| Capital | −1,750 | | | | | 500 | |
| Cash inflows | | 800 | 800 | 800 | 800 | 800 | |
| Depreciation | | 250 | 250 | 250 | 250 | 250 | |
| Tax | | | (220) | (220) | (220) | (220) | (220) |
| Net cash flows | (1,750) | 800 | 580 | 580 | 580 | 1080 | (220) |
| Exchange rate $/£ | 0.625 | 0.634 | 0.643 | 0.652 | 0.661 | 0.671 | 0.681 |
| Cash flows in $m | (2,800) | 1,261.83 | 902.02 | 889.57 | 877.46 | 1,609.54 | (323.05) |
| Discount factor | 1 | 0.909 | 0.826 | 0.751 | 0.683 | 0.621 | 0.564 |
| Present value | (2,800) | 1,147.00 | 745.07 | 668.07 | 599.31 | 999.52 | (182.20) |
| NPV in $m | 1,176.77 | | | | | | |

## Method 2 – discount sterling cash flows at adjusted cost of capital

When we use this method we need to find the cost of capital for the project in the host country. If we are to keep the cash flows in sterling they need to be discounted at a rate that takes account of both the US discount rate (10%) and different rates of inflation in the two countries. This is an application of the **International Fisher effect**.

$$\frac{1+i_c}{1+i_b} = \frac{1+h_c}{1+h_b}$$

$$\frac{1+i_c}{1+0.10} = \frac{1+0.045}{1+0.03}$$ where $i_c$ is the UK discount rate

$1 + i_c = 1.116$, therefore $i_c$ is approximately 12%

Sterling cash flows should be discounted at this rate.

| | 0 £m | 1 £m | 2 £m | 3 £m | 4 £m | 5 £m | 6 £m |
|---|---|---|---|---|---|---|---|
| Capital | (1,750) | | | | | 500 | |
| Cash inflows | | 800 | 800 | 800 | 800 | 800 | |
| Depreciation | | 250 | 250 | 250 | 250 | 250 | |
| Tax | | | (220) | (220) | (220) | (220) | (220) |
| Net cash flows | (1,750) | 800 | 580 | 580 | 580 | 1080 | (220) |
| Discount factor | 1 | 0.893 | 0.797 | 0.712 | 0.636 | 0.567 | 0.507 |
| Present value | (1,750.00) | 714.40 | 462.26 | 412.96 | 368.88 | 612.36 | (111.54) |
| NPV in £m | 709.32 | | | | | | |

Translating this present value at the spot rate gives:

$$NPV = \frac{£709.32}{0.625} = \$1,134.91m$$

Note that the two answers are almost identical (with differences being due to rounding). In the first approach the dollar is appreciating due to the relatively low inflation rate in the US (not good news when converting sterling to dollars). In the second approach the UK discount rate is higher due to the relatively high inflation rate in the UK (again, this is bad news, as the NPV of the project will be lower).

## 2.6 The effect of exchange rates on NPV

Now that we have created a framework for the analysis of the effects of exchange rate changes on the NPV from an overseas project we can use the NPV equation to calculate the impact of exchange rate changes on the sterling denominated NPV of a project.

NPV = the sum of the discounted domestic cash flows

Add discounted domestic terminal value
Less initial domestic investment (converted at spot rate)

When there is a devaluation of the domestic currency relative to a foreign currency, then the domestic currency value of the net cash flows increases and thus the NPV increases. The opposite happens when the domestic currency appreciates. In this case the domestic currency value of the cash flows declines and the NPV of the project in sterling declines. The relationship between NPV in sterling and the exchange rate is shown in the diagram below.

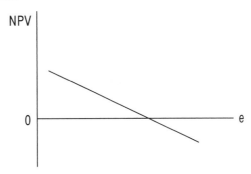

Question                                        Effect of changes in the exchange rate

Calculate the NPV for the UK project of Bromwich Inc under three different scenarios.

(a)     The exchange rate remains constant at £0.625 = $1 for the duration of the project
(b)     The dollar appreciates by 1.5% per year (as per the original question)
(c)     The dollar depreciates by 1.5% per year

Answer

If the dollar depreciates by 1.5% each year the exchange rates are as follows.

| Year | | Exchange rate (£/$) |
|------|------|------|
| 0 | | 0.625 |
| 1 | 0.625/1.015 | 0.616 |
| 2 | 0.616/1.015 | 0.607 |
| 3 | 0.607/1.015 | 0.598 |
| 4 | 0.598/1.015 | 0.589 |
| 5 | 0.589/1.015 | 0.580 |
| 6 | 0.580/1.015 | 0.571 |

The NPV under the three scenarios is given in the table below. Cash flows are discounted at 10%.

|  |  | Cash flows in dollars | | |
| --- | --- | --- | --- | --- |
| Period | Cash flows in £m | Constant exchange rate (£0.625 = $1) | Dollar appreciates 1.5% per year | Dollar depreciates 1.5% per year |
| 0 | (1,750) | (2,800) | (2,800) | (2,800) |
| 1 | 800 | 1,280 | 1,261.83 | 1,298.70 |
| 2 | 580 | 928 | 902.02 | 955.52 |
| 3 | 580 | 928 | 889.57 | 969.90 |
| 4 | 580 | 928 | 877.46 | 984.72 |
| 5 | 580 | 1,728 | 1,609.54 | 1,862.07 |
| 6 | (220) | (352) | (323.05) | (385.29) |
| NPV (discounted at 10%) |  | 1,336 | 1,065.24 | 1,509.78 |

# 3 Forecasting cash flows from overseas projects

## 3.1 Forecasting project cash flows and APV

In Chapter 5 we computed the cash flows that are required for the valuation of a project. The calculation of cash flows for the appraisal of overseas projects may require a number of extra factors to be taken into account.

## 3.2 Effect on exports

When a multinational company sets up a subsidiary in another country to which it already exports, the relevant cash flows for the evaluation of the project should take into account the loss of export earnings in the particular country. The NPV of the project should take explicit account of this potential loss and it should be written as:

Sum of discounted (net cash flows − exports) + discounted terminal value − initial investment

The appropriate discount rate will be WACC.

## 3.3 Taxes

Taxes play an important role in the investment appraisal, as they can affect the viability of a project. The main aspects of taxation in an international context are:

- Corporate taxes in the host country
- Investment allowances in the host country
- Withholding taxes in the host country
- Double taxation relief in the home country
- Foreign tax credits in the home country

The importance of taxation in corporate decision making is demonstrated by the use of **tax havens** by some multinationals as a means of deferring tax on funds prior to their repatriation or reinvestment. A tax haven is likely to have the following characteristics:

(a)    Tax on foreign investment or sales income earned by resident companies, and withholding tax on dividends paid to the parent, should be low.

(b)    There should be a stable government and a stable currency.

(c)    There should be adequate financial services support facilities.

For example, suppose that the tax rate on profits in the Federal West Asian Republic is 20% and the UK corporation tax is 30%, and there is a double taxation agreement between the two countries. A subsidiary

of a UK firm operating in the Federal West Asian Republic earns the equivalent of £1 million in profit, and therefore pays £200,000 in tax on profits. When the profits are remitted to the UK, the UK parent can claim a credit of £200,000 against the full UK tax charge of £300,000, and therefore will only pay £100,000.

## Question

Flagwaver Inc is considering whether to establish a subsidiary in Slovenia at a cost of €20,000,000. The subsidiary will run for four years and the net cash flows from the project are shown below.

|  | Net cash flow |
|  | € |
| Project 1 | 3,600,000 |
| Project 2 | 4,560,000 |
| Project 3 | 8,400,000 |
| Project 4 | 8,480,000 |

There is a withholding tax of 10% on remitted profits and the exchange rate is expected to remain constant at €1.50 = $1. At the end of the four-year period the Slovenian Government will buy the plant for €12,000,000. The latter amount can be repatriated free of withholding taxes.

If the required rate of return is 15%, what is the present value of the project?

## Answer

| € | Remittance $ | Discount factor 15% | Discounted $ |
|---|---|---|---|
| 3,240,000 | 2,160,000 | 0.870 | 1,879,200 |
| 4,104,000 | 2,736,000 | 0.756 | 2,068,416 |
| 7,560,000 | 5,040,000 | 0.658 | 3,316,320 |
| 19,632,000 | 13,088,000 | 0.572 | 7,486,336 |
|  |  |  | 14,750,272 |

The NPV is $14,750,272 − $\dfrac{€20,000,000}{1.50}$ = $1,416,939

## Question

Goody plc is considering whether to establish a subsidiary in the US, at a cost of $2,400,000. This would be represented by non-current assets of $2,000,000 and working capital of $400,000. The subsidiary would produce a product which would achieve annual sales of $1,600,000 and incur cash expenditures of $1,000,000 a year.

The company has a planning horizon of four years, at the end of which it expects the realisable value of the subsidiary's non-current assets to be $800,000.

It is the company's policy to remit the maximum funds possible to the parent company at the end of each year.

Tax is payable at the rate of 35% in the US and is payable one year in arrears. A double taxation treaty exists between the UK and the US and so no UK taxation is expected to arise.

Tax-allowable depreciation is at a rate of 25% on a straight-line basis on all non-current assets. The tax-allowable depreciation can first be claimed one year after the investment ie at $t_1$.

Because of the fluctuations in the exchange rate between the US dollar and sterling, the company would protect itself against the risk by raising a eurodollar loan to finance the investment. The company's cost of capital for the project is 16%.

Calculate the NPV of the project.

The annual writing-down allowance (WDA) is 25% of US$2,000,000 = $500,000. This reduces taxable contribution to $100,000 per year ($600,000 - $500,000). So the tax paid is $100,000 × 0.35 = $35,000.

| Year | Investment $m | Contribution $m | Tax paid $m | Tax on realisable value $m | Net cash flow $m | Discount factor 16% | Present value $m |
|------|------|------|------|------|------|------|------|
| 0 | (2.4) | | | | (2.400) | 1.000 | (2.400) |
| 1 | | 0.6 | | | 0.600 | 0.862 | 0.517 |
| 2 | | 0.6 | (0.035) | | 0.565 | 0.743 | 0.420 |
| 3 | | 0.6 | (0.035) | | 0.565 | 0.641 | 0.362 |
| 4 | 1.2* | 0.6 | (0.035) | | 1.765 | 0.552 | 0.974 |
| 5 | | | (0.035) | (0.280)** | (0.315) | 0.476 | (0.150) |
| | | | | | | | (0.277) |

* Non-current assets realisable value $800,000 plus working capital $400,000

** It is assumed that tax would be payable on the realisable value of the non-current assets, since the tax written-down value of the assets would be zero. Thirty-five per cent of $800,000 is $280,000.

The NPV is negative and so the project would not be viable at a discount rate of 16%.

## 3.4 Subsidies

Many countries offer concessionary loans to multinational companies in order to entice them to invest in the country. The benefit from such concessionary loans should be included in the NPV calculation. The benefit of a concessionary loan is the difference between the repayment when borrowing under market conditions and the repayment under the concessionary loan.

The method of assessing the benefit of a subsidy has already been illustrated in Chapter 7a in the section on adjusted present value (APV).

## 3.5 Exchange restrictions

In calculating the NPV of an overseas project, only the proportion of cash flows that are expected to be repatriated should be included in the calculation of the NPV.

## 3.6 Impact of transaction costs on NPV for international projects

Transaction costs are incurred when companies invest abroad due to currency conversion or other administrative expenses. These should also be taken into account.

## 3.7 A general model using APV

### 3.7.1 A recap of the APV approach

The APV method of investment appraisal was introduced in Chapter 7a in the context of domestic investments. Just to recap, there are three steps.

Step 1    Estimate NPV assuming that the project is financed entirely by equity.

Step 2    Estimate the effects of the actual structure of finance (for example, tax effects of borrowing)

Step 3    Add the values from steps 1 and 2 to obtain the APV.

### 3.7.2 APV in the international context

You should follow the normal procedure of estimating the relevant cash flows and discounting them at an appropriate cost of capital. However, you must also take account of the international dimension of the project, so that the steps become as follows.

**Step 1**     As the initial NPV assumes that the project is financed entirely by equity, the appropriate cost of capital is the cost of equity (allowing for project risk but excluding financial risk).

**Step 2**     Make adjustments for:

- Tax effects of debt and debt issue costs
- Any finance raised in the local markets
- Restrictions on remittances
- Subsidies from overseas governments

**Step 3**     Add the values from the first two steps to obtain the APV.

The steps for calculating the APV of an international project are essentially the same as for domestic projects, although more care has to be taken with the extra adjustments.

# 4 The impact of exchange controls

## 4.1 The nature of exchange controls

**Exchange controls** restrict the flow of foreign exchange into and out of a country, usually to defend the local currency or to protect reserves of foreign currencies. Exchange controls are generally more restrictive in developing and less developed countries, although some still exist in developed countries. These controls take the following forms.

**Rationing the supply of foreign exchange**. Anyone wishing to make payments abroad in a foreign currency will be restricted by the limited supply, which stops them from buying as much as they want from abroad.

**Restricting the types of transaction** for which payments abroad are allowed, for example by suspending or banning the payment of dividends to foreign shareholders, such as parent companies in multinationals, who will then have the problem of **blocked funds**.

## 4.2 Impact of exchange controls on investment decisions

In order to investigate the impact of exchange rate controls we can use the basic equation for the NPV.

**Step 1**     Convert net cash flows to home currency and discount at WACC

**Step 2**     Convert terminal value to home currency and discount at WACC

**Step 3**     Add the values from steps 1 and 2 and deduct the initial investment (converted to home currency)

Assuming that **no repatriation** is possible until period N, when the life of the project will have been completed, then the NPV will be calculated as follows.

**Step 1**     Add all net cash flows together and then add the terminal value

**Step 2**     Convert the value from step 1 to home currency

**Step 3**     Discount the value from step 2 at WACC

**Step 4**     Convert initial investment to home currency

**Step 5**     Deduct the value from step 4 from the value in step 3 to obtain NPV

The above formula assumes that non-repatriated funds are not invested. If in fact we assume that the cash flow is invested each period and earns a return equal to i, then the NPV will be calculated as follows.

**Step 1** Convert terminal value to home currency and discount at WACC

**Step 2** Convert net cash flows to home currency, gross up for interest and add together, before discounting the total using WACC

**Step 3** Convert initial investment to home currency and deduct from the sum of the values in steps 1 and 2

The impact will depend on the interest rate earned and the cost of capital. An example will illustrate how this may be calculated.

## Question                                                                    Exchange controls

Consider again the case of Flagwaver Inc, and its proposed subsidiary in Slovenia in question 'International Investment 1'.

Now assume that no funds can be repatriated for the first 3 years, but all the funds are allowed to be remitted to the home market in year 4. The funds can be invested at a rate of 5% per year.

Is the project still financially viable?

## Answer

| Year | 1st payment | 2nd payment | 3rd payment | 4th payment |
|---|---|---|---|---|
| 1 | €3,600,000 | | | |
| 2 | | €4,560,000 | | |
| 3 | | | €8,400,000 | |
| 4[1] | 4,167,450 | 5,027,400 | 8,820,000 | €8,480,000 |
| Withholding tax | (416,745) | (502,740) | (882,000) | (848,000) |
| Net cash flow | 3,750,705 | 4,524,660 | 7,938,000 | 7,632,000 |
| Exchange rate ($/€) | 1.50 | 1.50 | 1.50 | 1.50 |
| Cash flow ($) | 2,500,470 | 3,016,440 | 5,292,000 | 5,088,000 |

[1] The first payment represents the initial profit of €3,600,000 + 3 years' investment interest of 5% – that is:

$$€3,600,000 \times 1.05^3 = €4,167,150$$

The second payment includes 2 years' investment interest and the third payment 1 year's investment interest.

Total net cash flow receivable in year 4 is $15,896,910. When the salvage value of $8,000,000 (€20,000,000/1.50) is included, total cash receivable is $23,896,910. Discounted at 15% (discount factor at year 4 = 0.572), the present value is $13,669,033.

NPV = $13,669,033 – (€20,000,000/1.5) = $335,700

Note that the exchange controls have reduced the NPV of the project by 76% (original NPV = $1,416,939) but the project is still financially viable.

## 4.3 Strategies for dealing with exchange controls

Multinational companies have used many different strategies to overcome exchange controls, the most common of which are:

(a) **Transfer pricing**, where the parent company sells goods or services to the subsidiary and obtain payment. The amount of this payment will depend on the volume of sales and also on the transfer price for the sales.

(b) **Royalty payments**, when a parent company grants a subsidiary the right to make goods protected by patents. The size of any royalty can be adjusted to suit the wishes of the parent company's management.

(c) **Loans** by the parent company to the subsidiary. If the parent company makes a loan to a subsidiary, it can set the interest rate high or low, thereby affecting the profits of both companies. A high rate of interest on a loan, for example, would improve the parent company's profits to the detriment of the subsidiary's profits.

(d) **Management charges** may be levied by the parent company for costs incurred in the management of international operations.

# 5 Transaction, translation and economic risks

FAST FORWARD ⟫

The main risks faced by companies dealing with foreign currencies are transaction, translation and economic risks.

Exposure to foreign exchange risk can occur in a variety of ways. Most companies and certainly multinational corporations are affected by movements in exchange rates. Generally, exposure to foreign exchange risk can be categorised as **transaction** exposure, **translation** exposure and **economic** exposure.

## 5.1 Transaction exposure

**Key term**

**Transaction risk** is the risk of adverse exchange rate movements occurring in the course of **normal international trading transactions**.

Transaction exposure occurs when a company has a future transaction that will be settled in a foreign currency. Such exposure could arise for example as the result of a US company operating a foreign subsidiary. Operations in foreign countries encounter a variety of transactions; for example, purchases or sales or financial transactions that are denominated in a foreign currency. Under these circumstances it is often necessary for the parent company to convert the home currency in order to provide the necessary currency to meet foreign obligations. This necessity gives rise to a foreign exchange exposure. The cost of foreign obligations could rise as a result of a domestic currency or the domestic value of foreign revenues could depreciate as a result of a stronger home currency. Even when foreign subsidiaries operate independently of the parent company, without relying on the parent company as a source of cash, they will ultimately remit dividends to the parent in the home currency. Once again, this will require a conversion from foreign to home currency.

Transaction risk and its management will be covered in greater detail in Chapter 16 when we look at hedging foreign currency exposure.

## 5.2 Translation exposure

12/12

**Key term**

**Translation risk** is the risk that the organisation will make **exchange losses** when the **accounting results** of its foreign branches or subsidiaries are **translated** into the **home currency**.

Translation exposure occurs in multinational corporations that have foreign subsidiaries with assets and liabilities denominated in foreign currency. Translation exposure occurs because the value of these accounts must eventually be stated in domestic currency for reporting purposes in the company's financial statements. In general, as exchange rates change, the home currency value of the foreign subsidiaries' assets and liabilities will change. Such changes can result in translation losses or gains, which will be recognised in financial statements. The nature and structure of the subsidiaries' assets and liabilities determine the extent of translation exposure to the parent company.

Translation losses can also result from, for example, restating the book value of a foreign subsidiary's assets at the exchange rate on the date of the statement of financial position. Such losses will not have an impact on the firm's cash flow unless the assets are sold.

Translation risk should not need to be hedged if the stock market is efficient and investors understand that no cash flows are involved in any apparent exchange losses. Expenditure to hedge risk in these circumstances would be unnecessary. However, directors may consider that investors will view the losses negatively and take into account the adverse effects on trends and ratios.

Such risk can be reduced if assets and liabilities denominated in particular currencies can be held in balanced accounts.

For example, suppose a UK firm has a European subsidiary that has a European bank deposit of €1 million and payable of €1 million. Also, suppose the exchange rate between the euro and sterling is €1.10 per £. The sterling value of the subsidiary's position in these two accounts is £909,090 in both cases. If sterling was to suddenly appreciate against the euro, say to €1.15/£, the asset and the liability accounts would lose sterling value in the same amount. Both would be revalued in sterling at £869,565. However, there would be no loss to the UK parent, since the sterling loss on the bank deposit is exactly offset by the sterling gain on the payable. In essence, these two accounts hedged each other from translation exposure to exchange rate changes.

 Case Study

The surging value of the U.S. dollar (in 2015) may be posing the biggest threat to U.S. corporate earnings since the 2008 financial crisis, hurting results at most U.S.-based multinationals. The dollar's gain of 22 percent in the past 12 months against a basket of major currencies has landed a double whammy on U.S. companies with big sales abroad. Revenue and earnings from foreign markets are worth less when translated into greenbacks and their costs become relatively less competitive against rivals producing in countries with declining currencies.

The dollar's strength is a particular problem for companies with exposure to Latin America. A massive effective devaluation of Venezuela's bolivar has hurt companies including tissue and diaper maker Kimberly-Clark Corp and Ford Motor Co, which have had to sharply discount the value of their assets in Venezuela. And the weakness of the real and the Mexican peso will only add to issues in those markets.

*(Reuters, 2015)*

## 5.3 Economic exposure                                          12/12

Key term

> **Economic risk** is the risk that exchange rate movements might reduce the international competitiveness of a company. It is the risk that the present value of a company's future cash flows might be reduced by adverse exchange rate movements.

Economic exposure is the degree to which a firm's present value of future cash flows is affected by fluctuations in exchange rates.

Economic exposure differs from transaction exposure in that exchange rate changes may affect the value of the firm even though the firm is not involved in foreign currency transactions. It is more long term in nature.

## Example

### Trends in exchange rates

Suppose a US company sets up a subsidiary in an Eastern European country. The Eastern European country's currency depreciates continuously over a five-year period. The cash flows remitted back to the US are worth less in dollar terms each year, causing a reduction in the investment project.

Another US company buys raw materials which are priced in euros. It converts these materials into finished products which it exports mainly to Singapore. Over a period of several years the US dollar depreciates against the euro but strengthens against the Singapore dollar. The US dollar value of the company's income declines while the US dollar value of its materials increases, resulting in a drop in the value of the company's net cash flows.

The value of a company depends on the **present value** of its **expected future cash flows**. If there are fears that a company is exposed to the type of exchange rate movements described above, this may reduce the

company's value. Protecting against economic exposure is therefore necessary to protect the company's share price.

A company need not even engage in any foreign activities to be subject to economic exposure. For example, if a company trades only in the UK but sterling strengthens significantly against other world currencies, it may find that it loses UK sales to an overseas competitor who can now afford to charge cheaper sterling prices.

### One-off events

As well as trends in exchange rates, one-off events such as a major stock market crash or major economic events such as the UK's referendum vote in favour of exit from the European Union in June 2016 may administer a 'shock' to exchange rate levels.

### Assessing the impact of economic risks

However, none of the above examples are as simple as they seem due to the compensating actions of economic forces. For example, if the exchange rate of an Eastern European country depreciates significantly it is probably because of its high inflation rates.

So if the Eastern European subsidiary of a US company **increases its prices** in line with inflation, its cash flows in the local currency will increase each year. These will be converted at the depreciating exchange rate to produce a fairly constant US dollar value of cash flows. Therefore what is significant for companies is the effect on **real cash flows**, after the effects of inflation have been removed. In order for there to be real operating risk there must be relative price changes between countries.

## 5.3.1 Hedging economic risks

Because economic exposure is long term, it may be difficult to find derivatives that can effectively hedge it. However, various actions can reduce economic exposure, including the following:

(a) **Matching assets and liabilities**

A foreign subsidiary can be financed, as far as possible, with a loan in the currency of the country in which the subsidiary operates. A depreciating currency results in reduced income but also reduced loan service costs. A multinational will try to match assets and liabilities in each country as far as possible. Matching will be discussed further in Chapter 16.

(b) **Diversifying the supplier and customer base**

For example, if the currency of one of the supplier countries strengthens, purchasing can be switched to a cheaper source.

(c) **Diversifying operations worldwide**

On the principle that companies which confine themselves to one country suffer from economic exposure, international diversification is a method of reducing such exposure.

(d) **Change prices**

The amount of scope a company has to change its prices in response to exchange movements will depend on its competitive position. If there are numerous domestic and overseas competitors, an increase in prices may lead to a significant fall in demand.

# 6 Issues in choosing finance for overseas investment

As part of the fulfilment of the performance objective 'evaluate potential business/investment opportunities and the required finance options' you are expected to be able to identify and apply different finance options to single and combined entities in domestic and multinational business markets. This section and Section 7 look at the financing options available to multinationals which you can put to good use if you work in such an environment.

## 6.1 Financing an overseas subsidiary

Once the decision is taken by a multinational company to start overseas operations in any of the forms that have been discussed in the previous section, there is a need to decide on the source of funds for the proposed expansion. There are some differences in methods of financing the **parent company** itself and the **foreign subsidiaries**. The parent company itself is more likely than companies which have no foreign interests to raise finance in a foreign currency, or in its home currency from foreign sources.

The **need to finance a foreign subsidiary** raises the following questions:

(a)     How much **equity capital** should the parent company put into the subsidiary?

(b)     Should the subsidiary be allowed to **retain a large proportion** of its profits to build up its equity reserves, or not?

(c)     Should the parent company hold **100% of the equity** of the subsidiary, or should it try to create a minority shareholding, perhaps by floating the subsidiary on the country's domestic stock exchange?

(d)     Should the subsidiary be encouraged to **borrow** as much **long-term debt** as it can, for example by raising large bank loans? If so, should the loans be in the domestic currency of the subsidiary's country, or should it try to raise a foreign currency loan?

(e)     Should the subsidiary be listed on the local stock exchange, raising funds from the local equity markets?

(f)     Should the subsidiary be encouraged to minimise its working capital investment by relying heavily on trade credit?

The **method of financing** a subsidiary will give some indication of the **nature and length of time** of the investment that the parent company is prepared to make. A sizeable equity investment (or long-term loans from the parent company to the subsidiary) would indicate a long-term investment by the parent company.

## 6.2 Choice of finance for an overseas investment

The choice of the source of funds will depend on:

(a)     The **local finance costs**, and any subsidies which may be available

(b)     **Taxation systems** of the countries in which the subsidiary is operating; different tax rates can favour borrowing in high tax regimes, and no borrowing elsewhere

(c)     Any **restrictions on dividend remittances**

(d)     The possibility of **flexibility in repayments** which may arise from the parent/subsidiary relationship

Tax-saving opportunities may be maximised by **structuring the group** and its subsidiaries in such a way as to **take the best advantage** of the different local tax systems.

Because subsidiaries may be operating with a guarantee from the parent company, different gearing structures may be possible. Thus, a subsidiary may be able to operate with a higher level of debt that would be acceptable for the group as a whole.

Parent companies should also consider the following factors:

(a)     **Reduced systematic risk.** There may be a small incremental reduction in systematic risk from investing abroad due to the segmentation of capital markets.

(b)     **Access to capital.** Obtaining capital from foreign markets may increase liquidity, lower costs and make it easier to maintain optimum gearing.

(c)     **Agency costs.** These may be higher due to political risk, market imperfections and complexity, leading to a higher cost of capital.

| Exam focus point | You must be prepared to answer questions about various methods of financing an overseas subsidiary. |

# 7 Costs and benefits of alternative sources of finance for multinational companies (MNCs)

Multinational companies will have access to international debt facilities, such as eurobonds and syndicated loans.

Multinational companies (MNCs) fund their investments from retained earnings, the issue of new equity or the issue of new debt. Equity and debt funding can be secured by accessing both domestic and overseas capital markets. Thus MNCs have to make decisions not only about their capital structure as measured by the debt/equity ratio and which was discussed extensively in Chapter 7a, but also about the source of funding; that is, whether the funds should be drawn from the domestic or the international markets.

## 7.1 International borrowing

Borrowing markets are becoming increasingly internationalised, particularly for larger companies. Companies are able to borrow long-term funds on the **eurocurrency (money) markets** and on the markets for **eurobonds**. These markets are collectively called '**euromarkets**'. Large companies can also borrow on the **syndicated loan market** where a syndicate of banks provides medium- to long-term currency loans.

If a company is receiving income in a foreign currency or has a long-term investment overseas, it can try to **limit the risk** of adverse exchange rate movements by **matching**. It can take out a long-term loan and use the foreign currency receipts to repay the loan.

## 7.2 Eurocurrency markets

Eurocurrency markets were dealt with in Chapter 4b, Section 2 in the context of international debt finance.

## 7.3 Syndicated loans

**Key term**

> A **syndicated loan** is a loan offered by a group of lenders (a 'syndicate') to a single borrower.

A syndicated loan is a loan put together by a group of lenders (a 'syndicate') for a single borrower. Banks or other institutional lenders may be unwilling (due to excessive risk) or unable to provide the total amount individually but may be willing to work as part of a syndicate to supply the requested funds. Given that many syndicated loans are for very large amounts, the risk of even one single borrower defaulting could be disastrous for an individual lender. Sharing the risk is likely to be more attractive for investors.

Each syndicate member will contribute an agreed percentage of the total funds and receive the same percentage of the repayments.

Originally, syndicated loans were limited to international organisations for acquisitions and other investments of similar importance and amounts. This was mainly due to the following:

(a) **Elimination of foreign exchange risk** – borrowers may be able to reduce exchange rate risk by spreading the supply of funds between a number of different international lenders.

(b) **Speed** – in normal circumstances it may take some time to raise very large amounts of money. The efficiency of the syndicated loans market means that large loans can be put together very quickly.

Syndicated loans are now much more widely available, with small and medium-sized organisations now making use of such provision of funds. These loans can also be made on a 'best efforts' basis – that is, if a sufficient number of investors cannot be found, the amount the borrower receives will be lower than originally anticipated.

## 7.4 The advantages of borrowing internationally

There are three main advantages from borrowing for international capital markets, as opposed to domestic capital markets.

(a) **Availability**. Domestic financial markets, with the exception of the large countries and the Eurozone, lack the depth and liquidity to accommodate either large debt issues or issues with long maturities.

(b) **Lower cost of borrowing**. In Eurobond markets interest rates are normally lower than borrowing rates in national markets.

(c) **Lower issue costs**. The cost of debt issuance is normally lower than the cost of debt issue in domestic markets.

## 7.5 The risks of borrowing internationally

An MNC has three options when financing an overseas project by borrowing. The first is to borrow in the same currency as the inflows from the project. The second option is borrowing in a currency other than the currency of the inflows but with a hedge in place and the third option is borrowing in a currency other than the currency of the inflows but without hedging the currency risk. The last case exposes the company to **exchange rate risk** which can substantially change the profitability of a project.

# Chapter Roundup

- Changes in exchange rates are as important as the underlying profitability in selecting an overseas project.

- **Purchasing power parity** theory states that the exchange rate between two currencies is the same in equilibrium when the purchasing power of currency is the same in each country.

- Under interest rate parity the difference between spot and forward rates reflects differences in interest rates.

- The International Fisher effect states that currencies with high interest rates are expected to depreciate relative to currencies with low interest rates.

- The NPV of an international project is normally calculated by converting the overseas cash flows into the domestic currency using a forecast exchange rate.

- The main risks faced by companies dealing with foreign currencies are transaction, translation and economic risks.

- Multinational companies will have access to international debt facilities, such as eurobonds and syndicated loans.

# Quick Quiz

1 What does the absolute purchasing parity relationship state?

2 Suppose that the annual interest rate is 5% in the US and 6% in the UK, and that the spot exchange rate is £1 = $1.756 and the forward exchange rate, with one-year maturity, is £1 = $1.749. Does interest rate parity hold?

3 Using the data in question 2, how can you profit?

4 What are the two ways NPV can be calculated for an overseas project?

5 What is the impact of exchange controls on the decisions to invest in an international project?

6 What is the difference between transaction and translation exposure?

7 What are the implications of the following on the potential purchasing power of the dollar?

 (a) High $ interest rate
 (b) High $ inflation rate

8 Give four examples of ways in which a company could hedge economic exposure.

9 Give three reasons why a multinational might establish an overseas subsidiary.

10 Give three factors that might influence the choice of finance for an overseas subsidiary.

11 By what methods do governments impose exchange controls?

12 Give four examples of ways companies can overcome exchange controls.

# Answers to Quick Quiz

1    The absolute purchasing parity relationship states that prices in different countries will be the same when expressed in the same currency.

2    Interest rate parity means that

$$\frac{1+i_{US}}{1+i_{UK}} = \frac{\text{Forward rate}}{\text{Spot rate}}$$

However

$$\frac{1+0.05}{1+0.06} < (1.749/1.756)$$

so interest rate parity does not hold.

3    Borrow $1,000,000 at 5% – amount to be repaid $1,050,000

Buy £569,476 spot using $1,000,000

Invest £569,476 in the UK for a year. The value of the investment in a year's time will be £603,645.

Sell £603,645 forward in exchange for $1,055,775 (= £603,645 × $1.749/£)

Resulting profit = $1,055,774 – $1,050,000 = $5,774

4    The first way is to translate the overseas cash flows into domestic currency and use a domestic discount factor.

The second way is to use an appropriate overseas discount factor and calculate the NPV in foreign currency. The NPV can then be converted into domestic currency.

5    Exchange controls will normally lower the NPV from an overseas investment unless they earn a sufficient return from reinvestment in the country of origin until repatriation is allowed.

6    Transaction exposure occurs when a company has a future transaction that will be settled as a foreign currency. Translation exposure occurs when a company has overseas subsidiaries whose assets are denominated in foreign currency. Unlike transaction exposure, translation exposure does not affect the company's cash flows.

7    (a)    A high $ interest rate will lead to a reduction in the purchasing power of the $ (International Fisher effect).

       (b)    A high $ inflation rate means that the purchasing power of the $ will decrease (purchasing power parity).

8    Managing assets and liabilities

Diversifying supplier and customer base

Diversifying operations worldwide

Changing prices in response to exchange rate movements

9    Any three of:

       (a)    Location of markets
       (b)    Need for a sales organisation
       (c)    Opportunity to produce goods more cheaply
       (d)    Need to avoid import controls
       (e)    Need to obtain access for raw materials
       (f)    Availability of grants and tax concessions

10    Any three of:

    (a)    Local finance costs
    (b)    Taxation systems
    (c)    Restrictions on dividend remittances
    (d)    Flexibility in repayments

11    (a)    Rationing the supply of foreign exchange
    (b)    Restricting the types of transaction for which payments abroad are allowed

12    (a)    Selling goods or services to subsidiary
    (b)    Charging a royalty on goods sold by subsidiary
    (c)    Interest rate manipulation
    (d)    Management charges

### Now try the question below from the Practice Question Bank

| Number | Level | Marks | Time |
|---|---|---|---|
| 14 | Introductory | 15 | 29 mins |

P
A
R
T

C

# Acquisitions and mergers

# Acquisitions and mergers versus other growth strategies

| Topic list | Syllabus reference |
|---|---|
| 1 Mergers and acquisitions as a method of corporate expansion | C1(a) |
| 2 Evaluating the corporate and competitive nature of a given acquisition proposal | C1(b) |
| 3 Developing an acquisition strategy | C1(b) |
| 4 Criteria for choosing an appropriate target for acquisition | C1(c) |
| 5 Creating synergies | C1(e) |
| 6 Explaining high failure rate of acquisitions in enhancing shareholder value | C1(d) |
| 7 Reverse takeovers | C1(f) |

## Introduction

In this chapter we discuss the advantages and disadvantages of mergers and acquisitions as forms of expanding the scale of operations of an organisation. We look at the types of mergers and their purpose, illustrating these with real-life examples. We evaluate the merits of a given acquisition proposal and set out the criteria for choosing an appropriate target.

# Study guide

| | | Intellectual level |
|---|---|---|
| **C1** | **Acquisitions and mergers versus other growth strategies** | |
| (a) | Discuss the arguments for and against the use of acquisitions and mergers as a method of corporate expansion. | 2 |
| (b) | Evaluate the corporate and competitive nature of a given acquisition proposal. | 3 |
| (c) | Advise on the criteria for choosing an appropriate target for acquisition. | 3 |
| (d) | Compare the various explanations for the high failure rate of acquisitions in enhancing shareholder value. | 3 |
| (e) | Evaluate, from a given context, the potential for synergy separately classified as:<br><br>(i)    Revenue synergy<br>(ii)   Cost synergy<br>(iii)   Financial synergy | 3 |
| (f) | Evaluate the use of the reverse takeover as a method of acquisition and as a way of obtaining a stock market listing. | 3 |

**PER alert**

One of the performance objectives in your PER is to 'review the financial and strategic consequences of an investment decision'. This chapter evaluates mergers and acquisitions as a method of corporate expansion and also looks at the potential corporate consequences of such activity. This information will be invaluable in practice, as it gives you an idea of the issues that might arise when considering the viability of mergers and acquisitions.

# 1 Mergers and acquisitions as a method of corporate expansion
6/14, Mar/Jun 16

**FAST FORWARD**

Although **growth strategy through acquisition** requires high premiums, it is widely used by corporations as an alternative to **internal organic growth**.

**Exam focus point**

In June 2016 part of an optional question asked for discussion of the pros and cons of a proposed acquisition of a company specialising in online testing by an education company. Many of the clues for this were given in the scenario.

Companies may decide to increase the scale of their operations through a strategy of **internal organic growth** by **investing money** to **purchase** or **create assets** and product lines **internally**.

Alternatively, companies may decide to grow by **buying** other **companies** in the market thus acquiring ready-made tangible and intangible assets and product lines. Which is the right strategy? The decision is one of the most difficult the financial manager has to face.

The right answer is not easy to arrive at. **Organic growth** in areas where the company has been successful and has expertise may present **few risks** but it can be **slow**, **expensive** or sometimes **impossible**. On the other hand, **acquisitions** require **high premiums** that make the **creation** of **value** difficult. Irrespective of the merits of a **growth strategy** by acquisition or not, the fact remains that this is used by corporations extensively.

When companies decide to expand their scale of operations by merging with or acquiring another company, there are many ways that this strategy can be implemented and many possible target companies.

In this section we will look at each type of merger that companies have used for growth and present the arguments for and against each particular case. As a general rule, expansion either by building new plants or by acquisition should not be undertaken unless the expansion results in increased profitability for the company and enhances shareholder wealth.

## 1.1 Advantages of mergers as an expansion strategy

As an **expansion strategy** mergers are thought to provide a quicker way of acquiring productive capacity and **intangible assets** and accessing **overseas markets**.

There are four main advantages that have been put forward in the literature and these are summarised below.

### Speed

The acquisition of another company is a quicker way of implementing a business plan, as the company acquires another organisation that is already in operation. An acquisition also allows a company to reach a certain optimal level of production much quicker than through organic growth. Acquisition as a strategy for expansion is particularly suitable for management with rather short time horizons.

### Lower cost

An acquisition may be a cheaper way of acquiring productive capacity than through organic growth. An acquisition can take place for instance through an exchange of shares which does not have an impact on the financial resources of the firm.

### Acquisition of intangible assets

A firm through an acquisition will acquire not only tangible assets but also intangible assets, such as brand recognition, reputation, customer loyalty and intellectual property, which are more difficult to achieve with organic growth.

### Access to overseas markets

When a company wants to expand its operations in an overseas market, acquiring a local firm may be the only option of breaking into the overseas market.

## 1.2 Disadvantages of mergers as an expansion strategy

An **expansion strategy** through acquisition is associated with exposure to a higher level of **business and financial risk**.

The risks associated with expansion through acquisitions are:

### Exposure to business risk

Acquisitions normally represent large investments by the bidding company and account for a large proportion of its financial resources. If the acquired company does not perform as well as it was envisaged, then the effect on the acquiring firm may be catastrophic.

### Exposure to financial risk

During the acquisition process, the acquiring firm may have less than complete information on the target company, and there may exist aspects that have been kept hidden from outsiders.

### Acquisition premium

When a company acquires another company, it normally pays a premium over its present market value. This premium is normally justified by the management of the bidding company as necessary for the benefits that will accrue from the acquisition. However, too large a premium may render the acquisition unprofitable.

**Managerial competence**

When a firm is acquired, which is large relative to the acquiring firm, the management of the acquiring firm may not have the experience or ability to deal with operations on the new larger scale, even if the acquired company retains its own management.

**Integration problems**

Most acquisitions are beset with problems of integration, as each company has its own culture, history and ways of operation.

# 1.3 Types of mergers

Mergers can be classified as **horizontal, vertical or conglomerate**, depending on the type of company that is acquired.

A merger generally involves two companies pooling their interests and having common ownership of the new company's assets.

An acquisition usually involves a stronger company (the 'bidder') taking over the assets of a smaller company (the 'target') and assuming ownership of these assets.

Mergers and acquisitions can be classified in terms of the company that is acquired or merged with, as **horizontal**, **vertical** or **conglomerate**. Each type of merger represents a **different way** of **expansion** with **different benefits** and **risks**.

**Horizontal mergers**

A **horizontal merger** is one in which one company acquires another company in the **same line of business**. A horizontal merger happens between firms which were formerly competitors and who produce products that are considered **substitutes** by their buyers. The main impact of a horizontal merger is therefore to **reduce competition** in the market in which both firms operate. These firms are also likely to purchase the same or substitute products in the input market. A **horizontal merger** is said to achieve **horizontal integration**.

 Case Study

**US food giant Heinz is to merge with Kraft Foods Group, creating what the companies say will be the THIRD-LARGEST FOOD AND BEVERAGE COMPANY IN THE US.**

**SHARES IN KRAFT** closed up more than 35% on the news at $83.17 in New York.

Heinz shareholders will own 51% of the combined company with Kraft shareholders owning a 49% stake.

The combined firm, Kraft Heinz Company, expects to make annual cost savings of $1.5 billion (£1 billion) by the end of 2017. Its brands will include Kraft, Heinz, and hotdog maker Oscar Mayer, with combined sales worth some $29 billion.

Alex Behring, chairman of Heinz and the managing partner at 3G Capital, said: 'By bringing together these two iconic companies through this transaction, we are creating a strong platform for both US and international growth.'

*(BBC, 2015)*

**Vertical mergers**

Vertical mergers are mergers between firms that operate at different stages of the same production chain, or between firms that produce complementary goods, such as a newspaper acquiring a paper manufacturer. Vertical mergers are either backward when the firm merges with a supplier or forward when the firm merges with a customer.

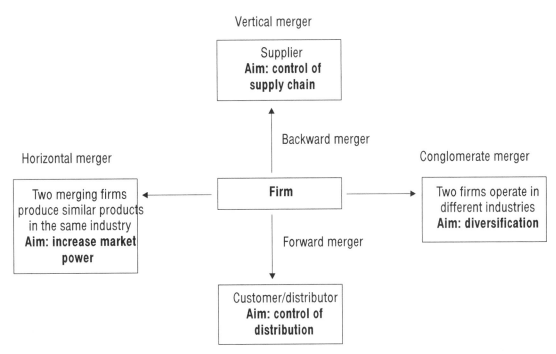

Vertical merger

Supplier
Aim: **control of supply chain**

Backward merger

Horizontal merger

Two merging firms produce similar products in the same industry
Aim: **increase market power**

Firm

Forward merger

Conglomerate merger

Two firms operate in different industries
Aim: **diversification**

Customer/distributor
Aim: **control of distribution**

**Conglomerate mergers**

Conglomerate mergers are mergers which are neither vertical nor horizontal. In a conglomerate merger a company acquires another company in an different, possibly unrelated, line of business.

 Case Study

In 2015 US computer giant Dell agreed a deal to buy data storage company EMC for $67bn (£44bn).

Falling demand for PCs means Dell is looking to expand into more lucrative businesses, and it has identified data storage as a key growth area.

'Our new company will be exceptionally well-positioned for growth in the most strategic areas of next-generation IT,' **said Dell boss Michael Dell.**

Analysts suggested the deal was a brave move by Dell.

'Dell wants to become the old IBM Corp, a one-stop shop for corporate clients,' said Erik Gordon from the University of Michigan's Ross School of Business.

'That model fell apart a couple of decades ago. Reviving it would be a stunning coup for Dell.'

*(BBC, 2015)*

# 2 Evaluating the corporate and competitive nature of a given acquisition proposal

**FAST FORWARD**

Expansion by **organic growth** or by acquisition should only be undertaken if it leads to an **increase** in the **wealth** of the **shareholders**.

We have discussed so far the reasons why a company may opt for growth by acquisition instead of organic growth and the three main types of merger. We should not of course lose sight of the fact that expansion either by organic growth or by acquisitions is only undertaken if it leads to an increase in the wealth of the shareholders. This happens when the merger or acquisition creates **synergies** which either **increase revenues** or **reduce costs**, or when the management of the acquiring company can manage the assets of the

target company better than the incumbent management, thus **creating additional** value for the new owners over and above the current market value of the company. We look at some of the aspects that will have an impact on the competitive position of the firm and its profitability in a given acquisition proposal.

### Market power

The impact on **market power** is one of the most important aspects of an acquisition. By acquiring another firm, in a horizontal merger, the competition in the industry is reduced and the company may be able to charge higher prices for its products. However, competition regulation may prevent this type of acquisition. To the extent that both companies purchase for the same suppliers, the merged company will have greater bargaining power when it deals with its suppliers.

### Barriers to entry

A second aspect of an acquisition proposal and related to the previous one is the possibility of creating **barriers to entry** through **vertical acquisitions** of production inputs.

**FAST FORWARD**

Aspects of a merger that will have an impact on the firm's **competitive position** include **increased market power**, the **creation of barriers to entry, supply chain security** and **economies of scope** and **scale**.

### Supply chain security

A third aspect that has an impact on the competitive position of a firm is the acquisition of a firm which has an important role in the **supply chain**. Companies acquire suppliers to ensure that there is no disruption in the supply of the inputs that will threaten the ability of the company to produce, sell and retain its competitive position. Although the risk of disruption can be eliminated by long-term contracts, acquisition is still considered an important option.

### Economies of scale

The merged company will be bigger in size than the individual companies and it will have a larger scale of operations. The larger scale of operations may give rise to what is called economies of scale from a reduction in the cost per unit resulting from increased production, realised through operational efficiencies. Economies of scale can be accomplished because as production increases, the cost of producing each additional unit falls.

### Economies of scope

Scope economies or changes in product mix are another potential way in which mergers might help improve the performance of the acquiring company. Economies of scope occur when it is more economical to produce two or more products jointly in a single production unit than to produce the products in separate specialising firms. Scope economies can arise from two sources.

(a)     The spreading of fixed costs over an expanded product mix
(b)     Cost complementarities in producing the different products

Economies of scope have been invoked as the main reason driving mergers in the financial sector. The fixed capital of a bank branch for example, or its computer systems, are more fully utilised when they issue not just banking products such as deposits and loans but also insurance products and investment services. These additional services allow the spreading of fixed costs over a larger number of activities, reducing the unit cost of each activity.

## 2.1 Financial synergy: Tax and debt benefits

The final aspect in an acquisition proposal has to do with the existence of financial synergies which take the form of diversification, tax and debt benefit synergies. This will be discussed in detail in **Section 5** of this chapter.

# 3 Developing an acquisition strategy                    12/14

**FAST FORWARD**

The main reasons behind a strategy for acquiring a target firm includes the target being undervalued or to diversify operations in order to reduce risk.

Not all firms considering the acquisition of a target firm have acquisition strategies and, even if they do, they do not always stick to them. We are going to look at a number of different motives for acquisition in this section. A coherent acquisition strategy should be based on one of these motives.

## 3.1 Acquire undervalued firms

This is one of the main reasons for firms becoming targets for acquisition. If a bidder recognises that a firm has been **undervalued** by the market it can take advantage of this discrepancy by purchasing the firm at a 'bargain' price. The difference between the real value of the target firm and the price paid can then be seen as a 'surplus'.

For this strategy to work, the bidder must be able to fulfil three things.

### 3.1.1 Find firms that are undervalued

This might seem to be an obvious point but in practice it is not easy to have such **superior knowledge** ahead of other bidders. The bidder would either have to have access to **better information** than that available to other market players, or have **superior analytical tools** to those used by competitors.

### 3.1.2 Access to necessary funds

It is one thing being able to identify firms that are undervalued – it is quite another **obtaining** the funds to acquire them. Traditionally, **larger firms** tend to have **better access** to capital markets and internal funds than smaller firms. A history of success in **identifying** and **acquiring** undervalued firms will also make funds more accessible and future acquisitions easier.

### 3.1.3 Skills in executing the acquisition

There are **no gains** to be made from driving the share price up in the process of acquiring an undervalued firm. For example, suppose the estimated value of a target firm is $500 million and the current market price is $400 million. In acquiring this firm, the bidder will have to pay a **premium**. If this premium exceeds 25% of the current market price (the difference between estimated value and current market price divided by current market price) then the price paid will actually **exceed** the estimated value. **No value** would thus be created by the bidder.

## 3.2 Diversify to reduce risk

Firm-specific risk (**unsystematic risk**) can be reduced by holding a diversified portfolio. This is another potential acquisition strategy. The managers of bidding firms believe that they may reduce earnings volatility and risk – and increase potential value – by acquiring firms in other industries.

### 3.2.1 Diversifying by acquisition versus diversifying across traded shares

Can diversification be achieved more efficiently at **company** level or at **individual investor** level? Obviously **individual investors** can diversify much more **cheaply** than companies can. All they have to do is buy shares in companies in different industries, whereas companies have to go through long, complicated and expensive processes in order to acquire other companies.

There are **two exceptions** to this:

(a)   Owners of private firms with all or most of their wealth invested in the firm. The owner is exposed to all the risk therefore there is a greater case for diversification.

(b)   Incumbent managers who have large amounts of their wealth invested in the firm. If these managers diversify through acquisition, they will reduce their exposure to total risk. This opens up other arguments as to whether these managers are acting in the best interests of the other shareholders, if the other shareholders do hold well diversified portfolios of other shares.

# 4 Criteria for choosing an appropriate target for acquisition

There are a number of different aspects to successful target identification. One important emerging need is to identify acquisitions in overseas markets. Acquirers must be able to assess the acquisition from the target's point of view, as well as from their own. But understanding the regulatory and competitive environment in another country can be complex and time consuming.

## Case Study

Microsoft uses the enormous resources of its extended enterprise to identify potential acquisitions. The business groups take the lead, looking within their own and related markets for opportunities. Ideas also come from venture capital relationships in both the US and Europe, as well as through the company's alliance and partner community.

Acquirers must also be able to identify and capture new skills in the companies they buy.

## Case Study

Cisco Systems, often known as the 'acquirer of choice' by target companies, is an outstanding example of success in this regard. The maker of internet networking equipment emphasises that it acquires people and ideas, not just technologies. The leadership and talent of the acquired company must be committed to seeing the acquisition and the integration of the company work. It is not the first version of a product that becomes a billion-dollar market, Cisco argues, but the subsequent versions. Cisco needs the acquired company's talent to stay and build those next versions.

The criteria that should be used to assess whether a target is appropriate will depend on the motive for the acquisition. The main criteria that are consistent with the underlying motive are:

### Benefit for acquiring undervalued company

The target firm should trade at a price below the estimated value of the company when acquired. This is true of companies which have assets that are not exploited.

### Diversification

The target firm should be in a business which is different from the acquiring firm's business and the correlation in earnings should be low.

### Operating synergy

The target firm should have the characteristics that create the operating synergy. Thus the target firm should be in the same business in order to create cost savings through economies of scale, or it should be able to create a higher growth rate through increased monopoly power.

### Tax savings

The target company should have large claims to be set off against taxes and not sufficient profits. The acquisition of the target firm should provide a tax benefit to the acquirer.

### Increase the debt capacity

This happens when the target firm is unable to borrow money or is forced to pay high rates. The target firm should have capital structure such that its acquisition will reduce bankruptcy risk and will result in increasing its debt capacity.

### Disposal of cash slack

This is where a cash-rich company seeks a development target. The target company should have great projects but no funds. This happens when for example the target company has some exclusive right to product or use of asset but no funds to start activities.

### Access to cash resources

A company with a number of cash intensive projects or products in its pipeline, or heavy investment in research and development (R&D) might seek a company that has significant cash resources or highly cash generative product lines to support its own needs.

### Control of the company

In this case the objective is to find a target firm which is badly managed and whose stock has underperformed in the market. The management of an existing company is not able to fully utilise the potential of the assets of the company and the bidding company feels that it has greater expertise or better management methods. The bidding company therefore believes that the assets of the target company will generate for them a greater return than for their current owners. The criterion in this case is a market valuation of the company that is lower than for example the value of its assets.

### Access to key technology

Some companies do not invest significantly in R&D but acquire their enabling technologies by acquisition. Pharmaceutical companies who take over smaller biotechs in order to get hold of the technology are a good example of this type of strategy.

## 5 Creating synergies                                    6/13, 12/14

FAST FORWARD

The three main types of synergy to be gained from acquisitions or mergers are **revenue**, **cost** and **financial** synergies.

The existence of synergies has been presented as one of the two main explanations that may increase shareholder value in an acquisition. Indeed, the identification, quantification and announcement of these synergies are an essential part of the process, as shareholders of the companies need to be persuaded to back the merger.

In this section we consider ways, through a series of examples, of identifying revenue, cost and financial synergies when a target company is evaluated for acquisition.

### 5.1 Revenue synergy

**Revenue synergy** exists when the acquisition of the target company will result in **higher revenues** for the acquiring company, **higher return on equity** or a **longer period of growth**. Revenue synergies arise from:

(a)     Increased market power
(b)     Marketing synergies
(c)     Strategic synergies

Revenue synergies are more difficult to quantify relative to **financial** and **cost synergies**. When companies merge, cost synergies are relatively easy to assess pre-deal and to implement post-deal. But revenue synergies are more difficult. It is hard to be sure how customers will react to the new company (in financial services mergers, massive customer defection is quite common), whether customers will actually buy the new, expanded 'total systems capabilities', and how much of the company's declared cost savings they will demand in price concessions (this is common in automotive supplier M&A where the customers have huge purchasing power over the suppliers). Nevertheless, revenue synergies must be identified and delivered. The stock markets will be content with cost synergies for the first year after the deal, but thereafter they will want to see growth. Customer Relationship Management and Product Technology Management are the two core business processes that will enable the delivery of revenue.

## 5.2 Cost synergy

A **cost synergy** results primarily from the existence of **economies of scale**. As the level of operation increases, the marginal cost falls and this will be manifested in greater operating margins for the combined entity. The resulting **costs** from **economies of scale** are normally estimated to be substantial.

## 5.3 Sources of financial synergy

### Diversification

Acquiring another firm as a way of reducing risk cannot create wealth for two publicly traded firms, with diversified stockholders, but it could create wealth for private firms or closely held publicly traded firms. A takeover, motivated only by diversification considerations, has no effect on the combined value of the two firms involved in the takeover. The value of the combined firms will always be the sum of the values of the independent firms. In the case of private firms or closely held firms, where the owners may not be diversified personally, there might be a potential value gain from diversification.

### Cash slack

When a firm with significant excess cash acquires a firm with great projects but insufficient capital, the combination can create value. Managers may reject profitable investment opportunities if they have to raise new capital to finance them. It may therefore make sense for a company with excess cash and no investment opportunities to take over a cash-poor firm with good investment opportunities, or *vice versa*. The additional value of combining these two firms lies in the present value of the projects that would not have been taken if they had stayed apart, but can now be taken because of the availability of cash.

Case Study

Assume that Softscape Inc, a hypothetical company, has a severe capital rationing problem that results in approximately $500 million of investments, with a cumulative net present value of $100 million, being rejected. IBM has far more cash than promising projects, and has accumulated $4 billion in cash that it is trying to invest. It is under pressure to return the cash to the owners. If IBM takes over Softscape Inc, it can be argued that the value of the combined firm will increase by the synergy benefit of $100 million, which is the net present value of the projects possessed by the latter that can now be taken with the excess cash from the former.

### Tax benefits

The tax paid by two firms combined together may be lower than the taxes paid by them as individual firms. If one of the firms has tax deductions that it cannot use because it is losing money, while the other firm has income on which it pays significant taxes, the combining of the two firms can lead to tax benefits that can be shared by the two firms. The value of this synergy is the present value of the tax savings that accrue because of this merger. The assets of the firm being taken over can be written up to reflect new market value, in some forms of mergers leading to higher tax savings from depreciation in future years.

### Debt capacity

By combining two firms, each of which has little or no capacity to carry debt, it is possible to create a firm that may have the capacity to borrow money and create value. Diversification will lead to an increase in debt capacity and an increase in the value of the firm. This has to be weighed against the immediate transfer of wealth that occurs to existing bondholders in both firms from the stockholders. When two firms in different businesses merge, the combined firm will have less variable earnings, and may be able to borrow more (have a higher debt ratio) than the individual firms.

**Exam focus point**

In June 2013 Question 2 students were asked to identify synergies from the information given in the scenario.

# 6 Explaining high failure rate of acquisitions in enhancing shareholder value

A number of theories have been put forward to explain the **high failure rate** of **acquisitions** in **enhancing shareholder value**. These include **agency theory**, **errors in valuing a target firm**, the **pre-emptive theory** and **market irrationality**.

The purpose of this section is to assess the various explanations put forward for the high failure rate of acquisitions in enhancing shareholder value.

One of the most common empirical findings is that in an acquisition the shareholders of the **acquiring company** seldom enjoy any benefits, whereas the shareholders of the **target company** do. What is the reason for the failure to enhance shareholder value? We said earlier that there must be some evidence of synergies or concrete proof of managerial superiority in the acquiring firm to produce an acquisition that would enhance shareholder value. A number of alternative theories explain the phenomenon of failure by postulating that the main motive of the management of a company when they bid for another company is not maximisation of the shareholder value but other motives which have been found to be consistent with empirical evidence.

## 6.1 Agency theory

**Agency theory** suggests that takeovers are primarily motivated by the **self-interest** of the acquirer's management. Reasons that have been advanced to explain the divergence in the interests of the management and the shareholder of a company include:

- Diversification of management's own portfolio
- Use of free cash flow to increase the size of the firm
- Acquiring assets that increase the firm's dependence on management

The common idea of these explanations is that acquisitions is a process that results in value being transferred from the shareholder of the acquiring firm to the managers of the acquiring firm.

The implication of agency theory is that, because the target firm knows that a bid is in the interest of the management rather than the shareholders of the acquiring firm, it sees this bid opportunity to extract some of the value that would have gone to acquiring firm management. How much value the target firm can extract depends on the bargaining power they have.

## 6.2 Errors in valuing a target firm

Managers of the bidding firm may advise their company to bid too much, as they do not know how to value an essentially recursive problem. A risk-changing acquisition cannot be valued without revaluing your own company on the presupposition that the acquisition has gone ahead. The value of an acquisition cannot be measured independently. As a result, the merger fails as the subsequent performance cannot compensate for the high price paid.

## 6.3 Market irrationality

If a **rational manager** observes that their firm's stocks are overvalued in the short run, they have an incentive to exchange the overvalued stocks to real assets before the market corrects the overvaluation. A merger therefore occurs in order to take advantage of market irrationality and it is not related to either synergies or better management. The lack of the latter may in the end lead to a failing merger even though the acquired firm was bought cheaply through the exchange of overvalued shares.

## 6.4 Pre-emptive theory

This theory explains why acquiring firms pursue value-decreasing horizontal mergers even if managers are rational and are trying to maximise shareholders' value. If large cost savings can be achieved through the

merger by several potential acquiring firms, these firms will compete for the opportunity to merge with the target. The winning firm that acquires the target could become a lower cost producer, improve its product market position and gain market share from the rivals. Intuitively, if a firm fears that one of its rivals will gain large cost savings or synergies from taking over some other firm, then it can be rational for the first firm to pre-empt this merger with a takeover attempt of its own.

## 6.5 Window dressing

Another reason for the high failure rate is that companies are acquired not because of the synergies that they may create, but in order to present a better financial picture in the short term.

## 6.6 Poor integration management

In order to integrate two or more organisations effectively there must be effective integration management and recognition that successful integration takes time. Where management is poor or there is an attempt to do too much too soon, potentially successful mergers can actually fail.

**Inflexibility** in the application of integration plans drawn up prior to the event can be damaging. Once the merger has taken place, management must be prepared to adapt plans in the light of changed circumstances or inaccurate prior information.

**Poor man-management** can be detrimental to successful integration. Keeping staff informed in what may be a very unsettling period is important. Lack of communication of goals and future prospects of employees, and failure to recognise and deal with their uncertainties and anxieties can lead to employees being unclear of what is expected of them. Hostilities may develop between the two groups of staff, with an unwillingness to adapt to new procedures and practices.

# 7 Reverse takeovers                                      Mar/Jun 17

A **reverse takeover** involves a large unlisted company being bought by a smaller listed company using a share for share exchange. The larger company will then be the dominant partner in a listed company. This is both a method of acquisition and a way of **obtaining a stock market listing**.

The term '**reverse takeover**' describes a situation where a smaller **quoted** company (Company S) takes over a larger **unquoted** company (Company L) by a **share for share exchange**.

To acquire Company L, a large number of Company S shares will have to be issued to Company L's shareholders. This will mean that **Company L will hold the majority of shares and will therefore have control of the company**.

The company will then often be renamed, and it is normal for the larger company (Company L) to impose its own name on the new entity.

 Case Study

In 2007, Eddie Stobart, a well-known UK road haulage company, used a reverse takeover **to obtain a listing on the London Stock Exchange**.

This deal combined Eddie Stobart's road transport, warehouse and rail freight operations, with Westbury (a property and logistics group).

Eddie Stobart's current owners, William Stobart and Andrew Tinkler were appointed chief executive and chief operating officer of the new company.

Mr Tinkler and Mr Stobart held 28.5% of the new company following the merger.

The merged group was renamed Stobart and took up Westbury's share listing.

## 7.1 Advantages of a reverse takeover

A reverse takeover is a route to a company obtaining a stock market listing. A company may choose to obtain a listing independently (Chapter 2 Sections 3.8 and 3.9 looked at the mechanics of issuing new shares) via an initial public offering (IPO).

Compared to an IPO, a reverse takeover has a number of potential advantages:

### Speed

An IPO typically takes between 1 and 2 years. Over this period a prospectus needs to be prepared, and investor road shows will be required to drum up interest in the listing. The shares will need to be priced and the share issue will need to be administered.

By contrast a reverse takeover can be completed in a matter of months, perhaps even as quickly as one month.

### Cost

An IPO is a lengthy process and will involve guidance an advice from investment banks acting as sponsors. The costs of an IPO can be between 5% and 35% of the amount of finance raised. A reverse takeover will have significantly lower issue costs.

### Availability

In a downturn, it may be difficult to stimulate investor appetite for an IPO. This is not an issue for a reverse takeover.

## 7.2 Disadvantages of a reverse takeover

### Risk

There is the risk that the listed company being used to facilitate a reverse takeover may have some liabilities that are not clear from its financial statements (eg potential future litigation). So it is essential that a full investigation (due diligence) of the listed company is undertaken prior to the reverse takeover.

### Lack of expertise

Running a listed company requires an understanding of the regulatory procedures required to comply with stock market rules. There is the risk that the unlisted company that is engineering the reverse takeover does not have a full understanding of these requirements. To manage this risk it is wise to retain key management from the listed company to act in an advisory capacity.

### Share price decrease

If the shareholders in the listed company sells their shares after the reverse takeover then this could lead to a drop in the share price. This risk can be managed by making the deal conditional on the shareholders guaranteeing that they will not sell their shares for a period of time afterwards (eg six months). This is sometimes called a **lock-up period**.

**Exam focus point**

Make sure you read the ACCA article entitled 'Reverse takeovers'.

# Chapter Roundup

- Although **growth strategy through acquisition** requires high premiums, it is widely used by corporations as an alternative to **internal organic growth**.

- As an **expansion strategy** mergers are thought to provide a quicker way of acquiring productive capacity and **intangible assets** and accessing **overseas markets**.

- An **expansion strategy** through acquisition is associated with exposure to a higher level of **business and financial risk**.

- Mergers can be classified as **horizontal, vertical or conglomerate**, depending on the type of company that is acquired.

- A merger generally involves two companies pooling their interests and having common ownership of the new company's assets.

- An acquisition usually involves a stronger company (the 'bidder') taking over the assets of a smaller company (the 'target') and assuming ownership of these assets.

- Expansion by **organic growth** or by acquisition should only be undertaken if it leads to an **increase** in the **wealth** of the **shareholders**.

- Aspects of a merger that will have an impact on the firm's **competitive position** include **increased market power**, the **creation of barriers to entry, supply chain security** and **economies of scope** and **scale**.

- The main reasons behind a strategy for acquiring a target firm includes the target being undervalued or to diversify operations in order to reduce risk.

- The three main types of synergy to be gained from acquisitions or mergers are **revenue, cost** and **financial** synergies.

- A number of theories have been put forward to explain the **high failure rate** of **acquisitions** in **enhancing shareholder value**. These include **agency theory, errors in valuing a target firm**, the **pre-emptive theory** and **market irrationality**.

- A **reverse takeover** involves a large unlisted company being bought by a smaller listed company using a share for share exchange. The larger company will then be the dominant partner in a listed company. This is both a method of acquisition and a way of **obtaining a stock market listing**.

# Quick Quiz

1   State at least five criteria for choosing an appropriate target.

2   Provide three explanations for the failure of acquisitions to enhance shareholder value.

3   What are the sources of financial synergy?

4   What are the main advantages of mergers as an expansion strategy?

5   What are the main disadvantages of mergers as an expansion strategy?

# Answers to Quick Quiz

1   Undervaluation of target
    Diversification
    Operating synergy
    Tax savings
    Debt capacity
    Use of cash slack
    Control of company

2   Any three of the following:

    Agency theory
    Market irrationality
    Pre-emptive action
    Window dressing

3   Diversification and reduction in volatility
    Cash slack
    Tax benefits
    Debt capacity

4   Speed of growth
    Lower cost
    Acquisition of intangible assets
    Access to overseas markets

5   Exposure to business risk
    Exposure to financial risk
    Acquisition premium
    Managerial incompetence

# References

Arnold, G (2013) *Corporate Financial Management.* 5th edition. Harlow: Pearson.

Now try the questions below from the Practice Question Bank

| Number | Level | Marks | Time |
| --- | --- | --- | --- |
| 15 | Introductory | 8 | 16 mins |
| 16 | Examination | 15 | 29 mins |
| 17 | Examination | 20 | 39 mins |

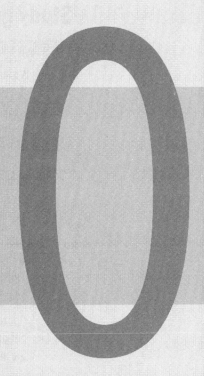

# Valuation of acquisitions and mergers

| Topic list | Syllabus reference |
|---|---|
| 1 The overvaluation problem | C2(a) |
| 2 Principles of business valuation | C2(c) |
| 3 Asset-based models | C2(c) |
| 4 Market-based models | C2(d) |
| 5 Cash-based models | C2(b), (d), (e) |
| 6 Valuation of high growth start-ups | C2(e) |

## Introduction

In this chapter we discuss three main ways of estimating the value of a target company, using asset-based, market-based and cash-based models.

# Study guide

| | | Intellectual level |
|---|---|---|
| **C2** | **Valuation for acquisitions and mergers** | |
| (a) | Discuss the problem of overvaluation. Note that this also covers behavioural finance from syllabus Section A 2(h) | 2 |
| (b) | Estimate the potential near-term and continuing growth levels of a corporation's earnings using both internal and external measures. | 3 |
| (c) | Discuss, assess and advise on the value created from an acquisition or merger of both quoted and unquoted entities using models such as:<br><br>(i)  'Book value-plus' models<br>(ii)  Market based models<br>(iii)  Cash flow models, including free cash flows<br><br>Taking into account the changes in the risk profile and risk exposure of the acquirer and the target entities | 3 |
| (d) | Apply appropriate models, such as: risk adjusted cost of capital, adjusted net present values and changing price-earnings multipliers resulting from the acquisition or merger, to the valuation process where appropriate. | 3 |
| (e) | Demonstrate an understanding of the procedure for valuing high growth start-ups. | 2 |

 One of the optional performance objectives in your PER is to select investment or merger and acquisition opportunities using appropriate appraisal techniques – this is the focus of this chapter.

# 1 The overvaluation problem

**FAST FORWARD**

When a company acquires another company, it will pay a premium above its current market value. Where this premium is excessive, this is known as the overvaluation problem. Behavioural finance helps to why excessive bid premiums are paid.

## 1.1 What gives rise to the overvaluation problem?

We have already discussed the reasons why so many mergers fail to enhance shareholder value in Chapter 9.

Economic theory suggests that mergers only enhance shareholders' value if there are:

(a) **Synergies** which can be exploited

(b) **Significant improvements** in the **management** of the **assets** of the **target** company that could be realised by an acquisition

In Chapter 9 we proposed a number of theories that could explain the **incidence** of **mergers** in the **absence** of the **two conditions** mentioned above.

Most of the theories were based on the existence of **agency problems** and the pursuit by management of takeovers that satisfied **management's goals** rather than those of the shareholders.

A reflection of these managerial motives is the **control premium** that management is prepared to pay in order to acquire the target company.

The larger the agency problem within the **acquiring** company, the larger the premium the **acquiring** company will be willing to pay.

Moreover, if the management/shareholders of the target company are aware that the merger will benefit the **management** of the **acquirer** rather than the **shareholders** of the **acquiring company**, then they will try to extract as much of the benefit as possible resulting in a high bid price.

Empirical studies have shown that during an acquisition there is **normally** a **fall** in the **price** of the **bidder** and an **increase** in the **price** of the **target**.

The consensus of empirical studies is that the target company shareholders enjoy the benefit of the premium as they are paid more than the market value whereas the shareholders of the acquirer do not always benefit and sometimes even lose value as the result of the bidding.

In a sense there is a **transfer of value** from the **acquirer** to the **target**. This is reflected in the **premium** that is paid and is determined by the degree of the **agency problem** prevalent in the acquirer and the ability of the **target's shareholders** to **extract this premium**.

The overvaluation problem may of course arise as a miscalculation of the potential synergies or the overestimation or miscalculation of the ability of the acquiring firm's management to improve performance. One way to reduce the danger of overvaluation is to diligently employ the valuation techniques that are covered in this chapter.

## 1.2 Behavioural finance and overvaluation
Mar/Jun 17

We can also look at psychological factors that may cause acquisitions to be over-valued.

Finance theory assumes that investors behave rationally. **Behavioural finance** (introduced in Chapter 2) studies how **psychological factors** affect financial decision making.

In the context of valuing a takeover target, a number of behavioural factors may come into play, that help to explain the overvaluation problem:

### Overconfidence and confirmation bias

People tend to overestimate their capabilities. If this is happening at Board level it may lead the Board to overestimate their ability to to turn around a firm and to produce higher returns than its previous management.

This overconfidence can partly result from managers paying more attention to evidence that supports the potential logic of an acquisition than they will to evidence that questions this logic. This is sometimes called **confirmation bias**.

### Loss aversion bias

Many takeover bids are contested ie more than one company is involved in bidding for a firm. Especially in this situation there is a likelihood that the bid price will be pushed to excessively high levels.

This can be explained in psychological terms in that there is a stronger desire to possess something because there is a threat of it being taken away from you. This is sometimes called **loss aversion bias**.

### Entrapment

Where a strategy is failing, managers may become unwilling to move away from it because of their personal commitment to it (for example it may have been their idea).

This **entrapment** may mean that they commit even more funds (eg acquisitions) in an increasingly desperate attempt to turn around failing businesses.

Entrapment can help to explain excessive prices being paid to acquire companies that are seen as crucial to helping to turn around a failing strategy.

### Anchoring

In Chapter 2 we saw that decision making may be affected by available information even if this is not necessarily relevant information (**anchoring**). If a Board of directors is asked to value an unlisted company, they may be strongly influenced by that company's asking price ie this becomes a (biased) reference point for the valuation (however irrational the asking price is).

## 1.3 Behavioural finance – other issues

There are many other aspects to behavioural finance, each with some potential relevance to financial strategy.

One illustration of this is **availability bias**

People will often focus more on information that is **prominent (available).** In the context of corporate finance the share price of a train company (for example) may be severely affected by a dramatic train crash (perhaps not even affecting their company directly) regardless of statistics that may suggest that train travel is a relatively safe form of transport.

Prominent information is often the most **recent information** about a company, and this may help to explain why share prices move significantly shortly after financial results are published.

# 2 Principles of business valuation

FAST FORWARD

> Acquisitions may be valued using **asset based, market based or cash based models.**
> Whichever valuation method is used, the **business risk** and **financial risk** associated with the acquisition must be recognised.
>
> Exam questions require a 'reasonable, justified approach', but as in the real world it is recognized that **a business does not have a 'precise' valuation**.

We have already discussed in Chapter 2 that the total risk of the company can be divided into business risk and financial risk.

**Business risk** is the variability in the cash flow or earnings of a company which result from changes in its business environment.

Business risk is a mixture of **systematic** and **unsystematic risk** (covered in Chapter 2). Systematic risk comes from such factors as revenue sensitivity and the mix of fixed and variable costs within the total cost structure. Unsystematic risk is determined by such company-specific factors as management ability and labour relations.

On the assumption that shareholders have a **diversified portfolio** then **systematic risk** (as measured by a beta factor) **is their primary concern. An ungeared (asset) beta** (covered in Chapter 7a) **measures** the **underlying business risk of a company.**

**Financial risk** (covered in Chapter 2) is the additional volatility in cash flow/earnings caused by a company's capital structure.

An acquisition may potentially have an impact on both the financial and the business risk of the acquirer. This impact needs to be incorporated into the analysis of the valuation of an acquisition.

There are **three basic approaches** to valuation.

**Asset-based models**

These models attempt to value the assets that are being acquired as a result of the acquisition.

**Market-based models**

These models use market data to value the acquisition.

**Cash-based models**

These models are based on a discounted value of the future cash flows relating to an acquisition.

These three types of valuation models are covered in the rest of the chapter, and are summarized in the overview below.

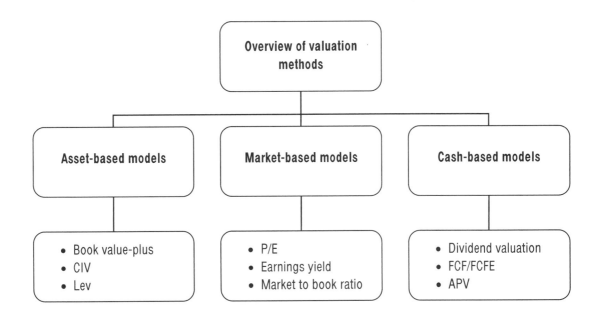

# 3 Asset-based models

**6/13**

Book value or asset-based methods of company valuation are based on the statement of financial position as the starting point in the valuation process.

**Book value** or asset-based methods of **company valuation** use the **statement of financial position** as the starting point in the valuation process.

The statement of financial position records the company's non-current assets (both tangible and intangible), current assets and liabilities to payables, both short and long term. After deducting long-term and short-term payables from the total asset value, we arrive at the company's net asset value (NAV). The book value of net assets is also referred to as 'equity shareholders' funds', as this represents the owners' stake in the company.

**Question**                                                                                  Book value model

The summary STATEMENT OF FINANCIAL POSITION OF CACTUS CO is as follows.

|  | $ | $ | $ |
|---|---|---|---|
| *Non-current assets* | | | |
| Land and buildings | | | 160,000 |
| Plant and machinery | | | 80,000 |
| Motor vehicles | | | 20,000 |
| | | | 260,000 |
| | | | |
| *Current assets* | | | |
| Inventory | | 80,000 | |
| Receivables | | 60,000 | |
| Short-term investments | | 15,000 | |
| Cash | | 5,000 | |
| | | | 160,000 |
| **Total assets** | | | **420,000** |

| | $ | $ | $ |
|---|---|---|---|
| *Equity* | | | |
| Ordinary shares of $1 | | | 80,000 |
| Reserves | | | 120,000 |
| | | | 200,000 |
| 4.9% preference shares of $1 | | | 50,000 |
| | | | 250,000 |
| *Current liabilities* | | | |
| Payables | | 60,000 | |
| Taxation | | 20,000 | |
| Proposed ordinary dividend | | 20,000 | |
| | | | 100,000 |
| *Non-current liabilities* | | | |
| 12% debentures | | 60,000 | |
| Deferred taxation | | 10,000 | 70,000 |
| **Total equity and liabilities** | | | **420,000** |

What is the value of an ordinary share using the net assets basis of valuation?

## Answer

If the figures given for asset values are not questioned, the valuation would be as follows.

| | $ | $ |
|---|---|---|
| Total value of tangible assets | | 420,000 |
| Less    current liabilities | 100,000 | |
| non - current liabilities | 70,000 | |
| preference shares | 50,000 | |
| | | 220,000 |
| NAV of equity | | 200,000 |
| | | |
| Number of ordinary shares | | 80,000 |
| Value per share | | $2.50 |

This technique is sometimes used to estimate a **minimum value for a unquoted company that is in financial difficulties or is difficult to sell**. In this case the owners may be prepared to accept a **minimum bid** that matched the value that they get from a liquidation. In this case it will be more appropriate to use the **realisable value** of the assets (if this is provided in an exam question).

**Alternatively** the book value of the net assets can be used as a **starting point** for negotiating the acquisition price for a small company. However, because this valuation ignores the profit of the company a **premium** is normally negotiated based either on a multiple of the firm's profits or an estimated value of the company's intangible assets (see next section). Where the valuation is based **on book value plus a premium** this is called a '**book value-plus**' model.

In a book value-plus valuation the **replacement value** of the assets may be more useful than the book value, and may be provided in an examination question. The replacement value of the assets of the acquisition target would quantify the cost of setting up the company from scratch without an acquisition ie by acquiring the assets on the open market.

## 3.1 Intangible assets

The book value-plus method discussed earlier excludes most internally generated intangible assets from the computation. This makes this method unsuitable for the valuation of many established businesses, particularly those in the service industry. Here we consider the various types of intangible assets that a business may benefit from and how they might be valued.

In many firms **intangible assets** are of enormous value. A company's knowledge base, its network of contacts with suppliers and customers, and the trust associated with its brand name are often significant sources of value.

The principles of valuation discussed below should be taken as applying to all assets, resources or property that are defined as intangible assets or intellectual capital, which could include, for example:

- Patents, trademarks and copyrights
- Research and development
- Brands
- Customer loyalty
- Distribution channels

We now consider a range of methods for valuing intangibles.

### 3.1.1 Calculated intangible values (CIV)

Calculated intangible values (CIV) calculates an 'excess return' on tangible assets. This figure is then used in determining the proportion of return attributable to intangible assets.

A step by step approach would be as follows:

**Step 1**   Calculate average pre-tax earnings over a time period.

**Step 2**   Calculate average year-end tangible assets over the time period using statement of financial position figures.

**Step 3**   Find the industry's return on assets. Multiply the industry's return on asset percentage by the entity's average tangible asset. Subtract this from the entity's pre-tax earnings to calculate the excess return.

**Step 4**   Adjust the pre-tax excess return for tax to give the after-tax premium attributable to intangible assets.

**Step 5**   Calculate the NPV of the premium by multiplying the after-tax excess return by 1 divided by the entity's cost of capital.

### 3.1.2 Example of CIV method

Jools Inc is trying to value its intangible assets and has decided to use the CIV method. Details for Jools over the last three years are as follows:

|  | 20X6 $m | 20X7 $m | 20X8 $m |
|---|---|---|---|
| Pre-tax earnings | 350.0 | 359.8 | 370.6 |
| Tangible assets | 1,507.5 | 1,528.9 | 1,555.9 |

The current return on assets ratio for the industry as a whole is 21%. Jools' WACC is 8%.

Calculate the fair value of Jools Inc's intangible assets, assuming an average tax rate of 30%.

## Solution

**Average pre-tax earnings** $= \dfrac{350 + 359.8 + 370.6}{3}$ $= \$360.13$ million

**Average tangible assets** $= \dfrac{1,507.5 + 1,528.9 + 1,555.9}{3}$ $= \$1,530.77$ million

**Excess return** $= 360.13 - (0.21 \times 1,530.77) = \$38.67$ million

**After-tax premium** $= 38.67 - (0.3 \times 38.67) = \$27.07$ million

**NPV of premium** $= \$27.07 \times 1/0.08 = \$338.38$ million

### 3.1.3 Problems with the CIV approach

While this seemingly straightforward approach, using readily available information, seems attractive, it does have two problems.

(a) It uses average industry return on assets as a basis for computing excess returns, which may be distorted by extreme values.

(b) CIV assumes that **past profitability** is a sound basis for evaluating the **current value** of intangibles – this will not be true if, for example, a brand has recently been weakened by a corporate scandal or changes in legislation. CIV also assumes that there will be **no growth** in value of the excess profits being created by intangible assets.

### 3.1.4 Lev's knowledge earnings method

> Lev's knowledge earnings method involves separating the earnings that are deemed to come from intangible assets and capitalising these earnings.

This method involves separating the earnings that are deemed to come from intangible assets (these are knowledge earnings) and capitalising them. This is similar to CIV, but this model then proposes a 3 step discounting procedure:

**Step 1**    Discount the first 5 years at the firm's current rate of growth.

**Step 2**    Discount the next 5 years at a declining rate that moves towards the industry average.

**Step 3**    Discount after this at the industry average growth rate.

Lev (Ryan, 2007, p.408) argues that discount rate used should be high to reflect the uncertain nature of intangible assets. This contrasts with CIV which normally uses a weighted average cost of capital.

The main problem with this technique is that it can be very complicated and in the end unrealistic because in practice, most valuations come from intense negotiations between the interested parties rather than complex calculations.

## 4 Market-based models     12/12, 6/13, 12/15, Mar/Jun 16

> Market relative models may be based on the P/E ratio which produces an earnings-based valuation of shares.

A sensible starting point for valuing a listed company is the **market value** of its shares. If the stock market is **efficient** the market price will reflect the market's assessment of the company's future cash flows and risk (both business risk and financial).

It follows that the relationship between a company's share price and its earnings figure ie its **P/E ratio** also indicates the market's assessment of the company's future cash flows and risk (both business risk and financial risk).

**A high P/E ratio (for a company or a sector) may indicate:**

**Optimistic expectations**

**Expectations** that cash flows and earnings will grow rapidly in the years to come, so that a **high price is being paid for future profit prospects**. Many small but successful and fast-growing companies are valued on the stock market on a high P/E ratio.

**Security of earnings**

A well-established low-risk company would be valued on a higher P/E ratio than a similar company whose earnings are subject to greater uncertainty.

**Status**

If a quoted company (the bidder) made a share for share takeover bid for an unquoted company (the target), it would normally expect its own shares to be valued on a higher P/E ratio than the target company's shares. A quoted company ought to be a lower-risk company; but in addition, there is an advantage in having shares which are quoted on a stock market: the shares can be readily sold. **The P/E ratio of an unquoted company's shares will be significantly lower (approximately 30%-50% lower) compared to the P/E ratio of a similar public company with a full stock exchange listing** (the drop in the P/E ratio is not as dramatic when compared to a company whose shares are traded on the Alternative Investment Market (AIM)).

 **Case Study**

Some sample P/E ratios taken from the *Financial Times* on 25 February 2014:

*Industry sector averages (main market)*

| | |
|---|---|
| Chemicals | 23.59 |
| Food producers | 11.30 |
| General retailers | 18.79 |
| Healthcare | 17.10 |
| Telecommunications | 5.85 |

# 4.1 P/E method

A P/E ratio can be applied to valuing a takeover target by taking the latest earnings of the target and multiplying by an appropriate P/E ratio.

**Market-based value = Earnings of target × appropriate P/E ratio**

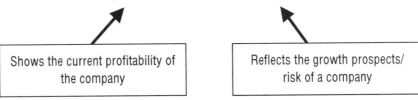

Shows the current profitability of the company

Reflects the growth prospects/ risk of a company

 **Case Study**

Online appliance retailer AO.com achieved a 33% increase in the value of its shares on its first day as a listed company in February 2014. The value of its shares increased from £1.2 billion to £1.6 billion.

However, analysts who focused on its P/E ratio were sceptical of this valuation. They pointed out that in 2013 the company had made £6.8 million profits after tax on revenues of £275 million. This represented a P/E ratio of 175 for a distributor of low margin electrical goods. The company was expanding in the UK and planning to open an operation in Germany, but the valuation appeared to assume that AO would lead

the online market in this sector and its competitors would not fight back. Consistent sustainable profits of around £80 million would represent a more realistic P/E ratio of 20 times' earnings. However, that would be quite a leap from £6.8 million.

There are a number of problems with this method.

### Choice of which P/E ratio to use

The P/E ratio should reflect the risk and growth prospects of the company that is being acquired. However, it is often based on the P/E ratio of another similar company (often called a proxy company) and care has to be taken that the chosen **proxy company has similar business and financial risk (ie capital structure) to the company that is being valued**. This is quite difficult to achieve in practice.

Also, as discussed above, the P/E ratio of a similar company will be **discounted** if the company that is being valued is unlisted. The extent of the discount that should be applied is a matter for negotiation.

### Earnings calculation

The earnings of the target company may need to be adjusted if it includes one-off items that will not to recur, or if it is affected by directors salaries which might be adjusted after a takeover.

Historic earnings will not reflect the potential future synergies that may arise from an acquisition. Earnings may need to be adjusted to reflect such synergies.

Finally, the latest earnings figures might be have been manipulated upwards by the target company if it has been looking to be bought by another company.

### Stock market efficiency

Behavioural finance (see Section 1) suggests that stock market prices (which underpin the P/E ratio) may not be efficient because they are affected by psychological factors. For example P/E ratios at the time of the valuation may be irrationally high or low due to swings in market sentiment.

In practice, using the P/E ratio approach will require you to **make a number of judgements.** In the exam you should make and **state your assumptions clearly**, and **you should not worry about coming up with a precise valuation** because, in reality, **valuations are not a precise science** and are affected by bargaining skills, psychological factors and financial pressures.

## Question — Minimum and maximum bid values

Macleanstein Inc is considering making a bid for 100% of Retina's equity capital. Retina's latest earnings were $25 million.

Retina is an unlisted company in the same industry as Macleanstein Inc, it has been struggling in recent years but Macleanstein Inc's management team believe that they can turn it around so that it shares Macleanstein's growth prospects.

It is expected that $2 million in synergy savings (post tax) will be made as a result of the takeover.

Macleanstein currently has a P/E ratio of 17.

*Required*

Using this information, suggest a sensible range of values within which a bid for Retina could be negotiated.

## Answer

There is no single 'correct answer' here. However, a reasonable approach would be to estimate a maximum and minimum value for Retina and to suggest the negotiation should take place within this range.

### Maximum amount to be paid

Macleanstein must consider the synergies to be made from the acquisition when determining the maximum amount to pay.

Maximum value of Retina     = adjusted earnings × new P/E ratio     = (25 + 2) × 17 = $459m

### Minimum amount that Retina's shareholders should accept

We could argue that Retina is a struggling unlisted company and therefore a P/E ratio of 17 overvalues Retina as an independent unlisted entity. We could therefore reduce the P/E ratio by, say, 50% to 8.5

Approximate minimum value of Retina  = unadjusted earnings x discounted P/E     = 25 × 8.5 = $212.5m

The final amount paid will probably fall between these two extremes.

---

A P/E ratio can also be applied to valuing a takeover target by estimating the **post- acquisition value of the group.**

### Market-based value = Earnings of group × appropriate P/E ratio

The post-acquisition value of the group can then be compared to the pre-acquisition value of the company making the take-over bid; **the difference gives the maximum that the company should pay for the acquisition.**

| Question | Minimum and maximum bid values |

Macleanstein Inc is considering making a bid for 100% of Thomasina Inc's equity capital. Thomasina has a P/E ratio of 14 and earnings of $500 million.

It is expected that $150 million in synergy savings will be made as a result of the takeover and the P/E ratio of the combined company is estimated to be 16.

Macleanstein currently has a P/E ratio of 17 and earnings of $750 million.

*Required*

(a)     What is the maximum amount that Macleanstein should pay for Thomasina?
(b)     What is the minimum bid that Thomasina's shareholders should be prepared to accept?

| Answer |

(a)     **Maximum amount to be paid**

Macleanstein must consider the synergies to be made from the combination when determining the maximum amount to pay.

Value of Thomasina to Macleanstein     = value of combined company – current value of Macleanstein

Value of combined company     = new P/E ratio × combined earnings
= 16 × (500m + 750m + 150m) = $22,400m

Current value of Macleanstein     = 17 × $750m = $12,750m

Value of Thomasina to Macleanstein  = $22,400 – $12,750m = $9,650m

Therefore the maximum amount that Macleanstein should pay for Thomasina is $9,650m.

(b)     **Minimum amount that Thomasina's shareholders should accept**

= current value of Thomasina's equity

= 14 × $500m = $7,000m

The final amount paid will probably fall between these two extremes.

## 4.2 Earnings yield

Earnings yield is calculated as EPS / share price. In other words it is the reciprocal of the P/E ratio ie 1 divided by earnings yield = P/E ratio.

If an exam question provides you with an earnings yield figure divide it into 1 and the you will have a P/E ratio and you can apply the P/E ratio technique that has already been demonstrated.

For example, an earnings yield of 5% is equal to a P/E ratio of 1 / 0.05 = 20

## 4.3 Market to book ratio

The market to book ratio assumes that there is a consistent relationship between market value and net book value.

### Case Study

Some sample price to book value relationships for the US in 2016 are shown below:

*Industry sector averages*

| | |
|---|---|
| Advertising | 6.8 |
| Beverage (alcoholic) | 4.4 |
| Auto Parts | 2.6 |
| Home building | 1.6 |

*(NYU Stern School of Business, 2016)*

These industry average ratios could be used to give an approximate value of a potential acquisition. However these ratios do not take into account the potential acquisition's business or financial risk.

The market –book ratio is based on the 'Q' ratio developed by Nobel prize-winning economist James Tobin (Ryan, 2007, p.369).

# 5 Cash-based models                                              6/11

The final set of valuation models are based on the concept of valuing a company using its forecast cash flows discounted at a rate that reflects that company's business and financial risk.

These models are often seen as the most elegant and theoretically sound methods of business valuation.

## 5.1 Dividend valuation model                          Mar/Jun 16, Sep/Dec 16

The simplest cash flow valuation model is the **dividend valuation model** (this has already been introduced in Chapter 7b). This is based on the theory that an equilibrium price for any share (or bond) on a stock market is the **future expected stream of income** from the security **discounted** at a suitable cost of capital.

**Exam formula**

$$P_0 = \frac{D_0\,(1+g)}{r_e - g}$$

Where   $D_0$ = dividend paid now
        $r_e$ = cost of equity **of the target**
        g  = growth rate in dividends

**Notes**

1   If $D_0$ is given as dividend per share, then $P_0$ will refer to the value of the share.
2   If $D_0$ is given as total dividend, then $P_0$ will refer to the total value of the company.

### 5.1.1 Example: Dividend growth (1)

Hibby Inc has declared a dividend of 35 cents per share. Dividends are expected to grow at 5% in the future in line with previous growth rates. The current cost of equity is 8%.

What is the estimated value of one share in Hibby Inc?

## Solution

$$P_0 = \frac{D_0\,(1+g)}{r_e - g}$$

$P_0 = (35 \times 1.05)/(0.08 - 0.05) = \$12.25$

### 5.1.2 Example: Dividend growth (2)

Janster Inc has declared a dividend of 20 cents per share and has a cost of equity of 15%.

What is the estimated value of one share in Janster Inc in each of the following situations?

(a)   No growth in dividends
(b)   A constant growth in dividends of 6% per annum
(c)   A constant dividend for 4 years and then 7% per annum in perpetuity thereafter

## Solution

(a)   $P_0 = 20/0.15 = \$1.33$ per share

(b)   $P_0 = (20 \times 1.06)/(0.15 - 0.06) = \$2.36$ per share

(c)   (i)   PV of 4 years' dividends with no growth

The dividend is an annuity for the first 4 years, so the present value is calculated by multiplying the dividend by the year 4 annuity factor at 15%.

$\$0.20 \times 2.855 = \textbf{\$0.57}$

(ii)   PV of dividends after year 4

After year 4 the dividend is growing at a constant rate. The dividend valuation model can be used but this model is now valuing the cash flows as at time 4 (looking ahead to the cash flows arising from time 5 onwards) ie

$$P_4 = \frac{D_4\,(1+g)}{r_e - g}$$

Here this becomes $(\$0.20 \times 1.07)/(0.15 - 0.07) = \$2.68$

Because this is a time 4 value it needs to be discounted back to a **present value** at time 0 using a 15% discount factor for **time 4**.

$\$2.68 \times 0.572 = \textbf{\$1.53}$

So the total value of each share = $\$0.57 + \$1.53 = \textbf{\$2.10}$

**Question**                                                                 Dividend valuation model

Target paid a dividend of $250,000 this year. The current return to shareholders of companies in the same industry as Target is 12%, although it is expected that an additional risk premium of 2% will be applicable to Target, being a smaller and unquoted company. Compute the expected valuation of Target if:

(a)   The current level of dividend is expected to continue into the foreseeable future; or
(b)   The dividend is expected to grow at a rate of 4% p.a. into the foreseeable future.

$k_e = 12\% + 2\% = 14\%\ (0.14)$       $d_0 = \$250,000$       g (in (b)) = 4% or 0.04

(a)    $P_0 = \dfrac{d_0}{k_e} = \dfrac{\$250,000}{0.14} = \$1,785,714$

(b)    $P_0 = \dfrac{D_0(1+g)}{K_e - g} = \dfrac{\$250,000(1.04)}{0.14 - 0.04} = \$2,600,000$

### 5.1.3 Estimating dividend growth

There are three ways to estimate the potential **growth rate** of dividends of a company. One is by extrapolating past values, the second is by relying on analysts' forecasts and a third is by looking at the fundamentals of the company.

#### Historical estimate

Historical estimates of the growth rate are estimated by observing the realised growth rates over a specific period.

In Chapter 7a we saw that this can be calculated as:

$$1+g = \sqrt[n]{\dfrac{\text{newest dividend}}{\text{oldest dividend}}}$$

## Example

The historical dividends per share (DPS) for Megatera Inc is shown below.

| Year | DPS (cents) |
| --- | --- |
| 20X6 | 0.53 |
| 20X5 | 0.43 |
| 20X4 | 0.37 |
| 20X3 | 0.26 |
| 20X2 | 0.25 |
| 20X1 | 0.18 |

The rate of growth is given by the formula

$$1+g = \sqrt[n]{\dfrac{\text{newest dividend}}{\text{oldest dividend}}}$$

$$1+g = \left(\dfrac{53}{18}\right)^{1/5} = 1.241 \text{ so } g = 1.241 - 1 = 0.241 \text{ or } 24.1\%$$

Note that although there are 6 years in the table, n = 5 because there are 5 years **between** 20X1 and 20X6.

There are several problems associated with historical estimates.

(a)    First of all a decision needs to be made regarding the length of the estimation period. Too long a period may reflect conditions that are no longer relevant for the future.

(b)    Secondly, even if the same conditions prevail, the average value estimated may not be relevant for the near term especially if growth rates are volatile. An average value may be close to the expected future growth rate over the medium term.

### Analysts forecasts

The second way of estimating the growth in dividends is by using the forecasts of analysts. Analysts regularly produce forecasts on the growth of a company and these estimates can be the base for forming a view of the possible growth prospects for the company.

### Company fundamentals

As we have seen in Chapter 7a, key determinants of the **rate of growth** of a company are the **return on equity** and the **retention rate of earnings** (that is, the proportion of earnings that are not distributed to shareholders as dividends).

---

The **growth** rate = b × $r_e$

Where b = the proportion of profits being retained within the business (sometimes referred to as the retention rate) and $r_e$ = return on investments for shareholders

---

**Question**                                                                Implied retention rate

On 21 December 20X6, Jinky Inc had a dividend yield of 3.8% and a price/earnings (P/E) ratio of 15.3. What is the implied retention rate of Jinky Inc?

**Answer**

$$\text{Dividend yield} = \frac{\text{Dividend per share}}{\text{Market price per share}}$$

$$\text{So dividend yield} \times \text{P/E ratio} = \frac{\text{dividend per share}}{\text{market price per share}} \times \frac{\text{market price per share}}{\text{earnings per share}}$$

Because market price per share cancels out, this leaves $\dfrac{\text{dividend per share}}{\text{earnings per share}}$

This shows the percentage of earnings being paid as a dividend.

In this example this gives 0.038 × 15.3 = 0.5814 ie 58.14% of earnings are being paid as a dividend.

This means that 1 − 0.5814 = 0.4186 or 41.86% of earnings are being reinvested. So the retention rate is 41.86%.

---

There are many disadvantages to the dividend valuation model. As we have seen above, it is **difficult to estimate future dividend growth**. However, having calculated an estimated growth rate **it is not likely that this growth will be constant in future years.**

However, the dividend valuation model can be **adapted to value dividends that are forecast to grow at differing growth rates.** The model needs to be adapted, as shown in the following table.

| Phase 1 (eg next 2 years) | Phase 2 (eg year 3 onwards) |
|---|---|
| Growth is forecast at an unusually high (or low ) rate | Growth returns to a constant rate |
| Use a normal NPV approach to calculate the present value of the dividends in this phase | Use the formula to assess the NPV of the constant growth phase, however the time periods need to be adapted eg $P_0 = \dfrac{d_0(1+g)}{r_e - g}$ is adapted to $P_2 = \dfrac{d_2(1+g)}{r_e - g}$  Then the adjust the value given above by discounting back to a present value (here using a time 2 discount rate). |

## Question

Groady plc wants to acquire an Italian company, Bergerbo SpA,

BERGERBO SPA SUMMARISED STATEMENT OF PROFIT OR LOSS FOR THE YEAR ENDING
31 DECEMBER 20X3

| | €(million) |
|---|---|
| PBIT | 9.8 |
| Interest expense | 2.3 |
| Taxable profit | 7.5 |
| Taxation (25%) | 1.9 |
| Profit after tax | 5.6 |
| Dividend | 5.0 |

There are conflicting views on Bergerbo's future dividend growth potential, some analysts think that the dividend will not grow for the foreseeable future, others estimate that the dividend growth rate will be 3% pa. Bergerbo's beta factor is 0.90; the risk free rate is 3% and the market return is 8.6%.

*Required*

Estimate the value of Bergerbo using the dividend valuation model, assuming 3% growth for the next 3 years and 2% growth after this.

## Answer

$K_e = 3\% + (8.6\% - 3\%)0.90 = 8\%$

**Phase 1**

| Time | 1 | 2 | 3 |
|---|---|---|---|
| Dividend €m | 5.150 | 5.300 | 5.460 |
| d.f. @8% | 0.926 | 0.857 | 0.794 |
| PV | 4.800 | 4.500 | 4.300 |

Total = €13.6m

**Phase 2**

Dividend €m      €5.46m × 1.02 =      €5.57m from time 4 onwards

$$P_0 = \frac{d_0(1+g)}{r_e - g} \quad \text{is adapted to} \quad P_3 = \frac{d_3(1+g)}{r_e - g}$$

$$P_3 = \frac{5.46 \times 1.02}{0.08 - 0.02} = €92.8m$$

Then discounting at a time 3 discount factor of 0.794 = €92.8 × 0.794 = €73.7m

Total = €13.6m + €73.7m = €87.3m

## 5.2 Free cash flow models          6/11, 6/13, 12/13, 12/15, Mar/June 16

The **free cash flow model** is another, more sophisticated, cash flow valuation model. This model attempts to estimate the present value of the actual cash flows being generated by a company.

This means that the **value of synergy** can be built into the model easily in order to determine the value of an individual company that is being acquired or to determine the post-acquisition value of the group.

The free cash flow method was tested in the compulsory question in June 2013 and also in an optional question in December 2013, which required discussion of the results and assumptions.

The free cash flow approach has been explained in detail in Chapter 7b in the context of project appraisal. The procedure for valuing a target company on the basis of its predicted cash flow is the same.

**Formula to learn**

> Free cash flow (FCF) = after-tax operating (pre-interest) cash flows – net investment in assets
>
> Free cash flow to equity (FCFE) = FCF – interest paid (net of tax) + new borrowing (net of any debt repaid)

**Note**. FCFE is sometimes called **dividend capacity** (covered in Chapter 2). Again this reinforces the conceptual link between the dividend valuation model and the approaches being used here. Many of the topics from Section 5.1 of this chapter (eg estimating growth) could also be tested in the valuation techniques that are covered here.

There are **two approaches** to valuing a company using the FCF basis.

| Approach 1 | Approach 2 |
| --- | --- |
| 1  Identify the FCFs of the target company **(before interest)** | 1  Identify the **FCFE** of the target company **(after interest)** |
| 2  Discount FCF at **WACC** to obtain NPV | 2  Discount FCFE at **cost of equity** Ke to obtain NPV |
| 3  NPV of company – **debt**  = **value of the target** | 3  NPV  = **value of the target** |

**Make sure you do not mix the two approaches** – for example, it would be wrong to discount FCFs before interest at the cost of equity.

## Question                                                                 Acquisition

Chunky Trot Inc is planning on making a bid to take over Turkey Lurkey Inc which is in the same industry. Both companies have similar gearing levels of 21.6% (where gearing is debt as a percentage of total finance).

Chunky Trot has estimated that the takeover will increase its annual cash flows over the next few years by the following amounts.

| Year | After-tax (but before interest) cash flows |
| --- | --- |
|  | $m |
| 20X1 | 14.00 |
| 20X2 | 18.50 |
| 20X3 | 20.75 |
| 20X4 onwards | 30.25 |

Turkey Lurkey Inc has 6.5% irredeemable debentures of $37.5 million trading at par.

The risk-free rate is 6.5% and the market rate is 12.5%. Chunky Trot's equity beta is 2.250 and the corporation tax rate is 28%.

*Required*

If Chunky Trot was prepared to bid $100 million for the entire share capital of Turkey Lurkey, would the acquisition increase shareholder wealth? Use both approaches given above to illustrate your answer.

## Answer

$K_e$ (using capital asset pricing model (CAPM)) = 6.5 + 2.25(12.5 − 6.5) = 20%

$K_d = [i/P_0] \times (1 − T) = [6.5/100] \times 0.72 = 4.68\%$

WACC = $(20 \times 0.784) + (4.68 \times 0.216) = 16.69\%$

**Approach 1**

| Year | 20X1 $m | 20X2 $m | 20X3 $m | 20X4 onwards $m |
|---|---|---|---|---|
| Cash flow (after tax, before interest) | 14.00 | 18.50 | 20.75 | 30.25 |
| Perpetuity (1/0.1669) | | | | 5.992 |
| Value at 20X3 | | | | 181.26 |
| Discount factor (16.69%) | 0.857 | 0.734 | 0.629 | 0.629* |
| Present value | 12.00 | 13.58 | 13.05 | 114.01 |

| | |
|---|---|
| Total present value | 152.64 |
| Less debt | (37.50) |
| Value of equity | 115.14 |

As value of equity > the proposed bid, the shareholders' wealth would increase if the target was acquired.

**Approach 2**

Annual interest after tax = (6.5% of $37.5 million) × 0.72 = $1.76 million

| Year | 20X1 $m | 20X2 $m | 20X3 $m | 20X4 $m |
|---|---|---|---|---|
| Cash flow | 14.00 | 18.50 | 20.75 | 30.25 |
| Less interest | (1.76) | (1.76) | (1.76) | (1.76) |
| Cash flow after interest and tax | 12.24 | 16.74 | 18.99 | 28.49 |
| Perpetuity (1/0.2) | | | | 5.000 |
| Value at 20X3 | | | | 142.45 |
| Discount factor (20%) | 0.833 | 0.694 | 0.579 | 0.579* |
| Present value (PV) | 10.200 | 11.62 | 11.00 | 82.48 |

| | |
|---|---|
| Total present value | 115.30 |

*Note that the discount factor used is for 20X3 not 20X4, this is because the perpetuity has created a value as at end 20X3.

Again, as value of equity > the proposed bid, shareholder wealth would increase if the target was acquired.

## 5.2.1 Adjusting for financial risk

Where a company uses high levels of debt to finance an acquisition then this will lead to an increase in financial risk. Acquisitions of this type can be evaluated using **adjusted present value** (APV). The theory behind APV has been explained in Chapter 7a.

Using APV, an acquisition is valued by discounting the FCFs to the firm by the ungeared cost of equity and then adding the PV of the tax shield.

APV = Value of acquired company if all-equity financed + PV of debt tax shields − Initial investment (ie the proposed acquisition price).

If the APV is positive then the acquisition should be undertaken.

### Steps for the calculation of APV

**Step 1**    Calculate the NPV as if ungeared – that is, $K_e^1$.

**Step 2**    Add the PV of the tax saved as a result of the debt used in the project.

**Step 3**    Deduct the debt of the target company to obtain the value of equity and then deduct the proposed cost of the acquisition.

# Example

The management of XERON Inc is considering the acquisition of NERON Inc, an unquoted company. The owners of NERON want $500 million for the business. The analysis of the prospects of NERON by XERON is reflected in the following financial statements.

STATEMENT OF PROFIT OR LOSS

| | Current year 20X7 | | | Years | | | |
| --- | --- | --- | --- | --- | --- | --- | --- |
| | 20X7 | 20X8 | 20X9 | 20Y0 | 20Y1 | 20Y2 | 20Y3 |
| Sales | 620.00 | 682.00 | 750.20 | 825.22 | 907.74 | 998.52 | 998.52 |
| Less cost of goods sold | (410.00) | (441.00) | (475.10) | (512.61) | (553.87) | (599.26) | (599.26) |
| Gross profit | 210.00 | 241.00 | 275.10 | 312.61 | 353.87 | 399.26 | 399.26 |
| Operating expenses | (133.00) | (144.30) | (156.53) | (169.78) | (184.16) | (199.78) | (199.78) |
| EBIT | 77.00 | 96.70 | 118.57 | 142.83 | 169.71 | 199.48 | 199.48 |
| Less interest expense | – | (32.00) | (26.88) | (20.19) | (11.73) | (1.27) | – |
| Earnings before tax | 77.00 | 64.70 | 91.69 | 122.64 | 157.98 | 198.21 | 199.48 |
| Less taxes | (21.56) | (18.12) | (25.67) | (34.34) | (44.23) | (55.50) | (55.85) |
| Net income | 55.44 | 46.58 | 66.02 | 88.30 | 113.75 | 142.71 | 143.63 |

STATEMENT OF FINANCIAL POSITION

| | Current year 20X7 | | | Years | | | |
| --- | --- | --- | --- | --- | --- | --- | --- |
| | 20X7 | 20X8 | 20X9 | 20Y0 | 20Y1 | 20Y2 | 20Y3 |
| Current assets | 100.00 | 100.00 | 100.00 | 100.00 | 100.00 | 242.90 | 404.55 |
| Non-current assets | 400.00 | 378.00 | 354.00 | 328.00 | 300.00 | 270.00 | 238.00 |
| Total assets | 500.00 | 478.00 | 454.00 | 428.00 | 400.00 | 512.90 | 642.55 |
| Debt | 400.00 | 335.95 | 252.35 | 146.63 | 15.94 | – | – |
| Equity | 100.00 | 142.05 | 201.65 | 281.37 | 384.06 | 512.90 | 642.55 |
| Total assets | 500.00 | 478.00 | 454.00 | 428.00 | 400.00 | 512.90 | 642.55 |

## Other information

| | |
| --- | --- |
| Growth rate for sales | 10% |
| Depreciation expense (20X7) | $40m |
| Interest rate on debt (all debt is interest-bearing) | 8% |
| Tax rate | 28% |
| Capital expenditures/year (depreciation charged at 10% per annum) | $20m |
| All available cash flow is applied to repaying debt until repaid in full | |
| Ungeared beta | 1.1 |
| Terminal value reflects level perpetuity equal to year 6 cash flow | |
| Risk-free rate | 6.0% |
| Market risk premium | 7.5% |
| There are no disposals of non-current assets for the duration of the project | |
| XERON proposes to take over NERON in 20X8 | |

**Step 1** Calculation of NPV as if ungeared

---

**Tutorial note.** Don't forget to include the terminal value before calculating the final NPV in this step.

---

|  | 20X8 | 20X9 | 20Y0 | 20Y1 | 20Y2 | 20Y3 |
|---|---|---|---|---|---|---|
| EBIT (1 – Tax rate) | 69.62 | 85.37 | 102.84 | 122.19 | 143.63 | 143.63 |
| Plus: depreciation expense | 42.00 | 44.00 | 46.00 | 48.00 | 50.00 | 52.00 |
| Less CAPEX | (20.00) | (20.00) | (20.00) | (20.00) | (20.00) | (20.00) |
| Firm FCF | 91.62 | 109.37 | 128.84 | 150.19 | 173.63 | 175.63 |
| Discount factor (14%) (W) |  |  |  |  |  |  |
| NPV | 80.35 | 84.11 | 86.97 | 88.91 | 90.11 | 80.09 |

Total NPV before terminal value    510.54

$$\text{Terminal value} = \frac{\$175.63}{0.14} = \$1,254.5m$$

The PV of the terminal value is:

$$\frac{\$1,254.5m}{(1.14)^6} = \$571.53m$$

Total NPV = $510.54m + $571.53m = $1,082.07m

*Working: The discount factor can be calculated using CAPM*

$$E(r_i) = R_f + \beta \ (E(R_m - R_f))$$

$$E(r_i) = 6 + 1.1 \times 7.5$$

$$E(r_i) = 14.25\% \ (\text{say } 14\%)$$

**Step 2** PV of tax saved on debt interest

The tax shield is discounted at the gross cost of debt (8%).

|  | 20X7 $m | 20X8 $m | 20X9 $m | 20Y0 $m | 20Y1 $m | 20Y2 $m | 20Y3 $m |
|---|---|---|---|---|---|---|---|
| Interest tax savings | – | 8.960 | 7.530 | 5.650 | 3.280 | 0.360 | – |
| Discount factor at 8% | – | 0.926 | 0.857 | 0.794 | 0.735 | 0.681 | – |
| PV | – | 8.300 | 6.450 | 4.490 | 2.410 | 0.250 | – |

| | |
|---|---|
| Total PV of tax shield | 21.90 |
| Add PV from step 1 | 1,082.07 |
| Total PV | 1,103.97 |

**Step 3** Deduct current debt and cost of acquisition to obtain equity value

Equity value = $1,103.97m – $500m – $400m = $203.97m

Conclusion – as NERON's equity value exceeds the price paid and the debt, XERON should proceed with the acquisition.

### 5.2.2 Adjusting for business risk

The business risk of the combined entity will be affected by the betas of the target and bidding firms and the beta of the synergy that results from the acquisition.

If the **business risk** is also affected by the acquisition, you will need to follow these steps in order to value an acquisition.

**Step 1**    Calculate the asset beta of both companies.

**Step 2**    Calculate the average asset beta for the group post-acquisition.

**Step 3**    Regear the beta to reflect the group's post-acquisition gearing.

**Step 4**    Calculate the group's new WACC.

**Step 5**    Discount the group's post-acquisition FCFs using the new WACC.

**Step 6**    Calculate the group's revised NPV and subtract debt to calculate the value of the equity.

## Example

Omnivore Inc is considering the acquisition of Sweet Meals Co. The management of Omnivore have estimated that the cash flows of Sweet Meals will grow much faster than theirs over the next ten years, and that considerable savings will be realised by integrating their distribution networks and marketing operations. The estimated cash flows for Omnivore, Sweet Meals and the synergies in the case of a merger are shown below. It is estimated that on acquisition Omnivore will be able to sell one of its storage sites realising an instant income of $5 million.

| Year | Sweet Meals $m | Synergies $m | Omnivore $m | Cash flows of combined entity $m |
|---|---|---|---|---|
| 20X5 | | 5 | | 5.00 |
| 20X6 | 12.00 | 6 | 42 | 60.00 |
| 20X7 | 14.40 | 6 | 45 | 65.40 |
| 20X8 | 17.28 | 6 | 48.01 | 71.29 |
| 20X9 | 20.74 | 6 | 50.97 | 77.71 |
| 20Y0 | 24.88 | 6 | 53.81 | 84.69 |
| 20Y1 | 29.86 | 6 | 56.46 | 92.32 |
| 20Y2 | 35.83 | 6 | 58.79 | 100.62 |
| 20Y3 | 39.41 | 6 | 64.27 | 109.68 |
| 20Y4 | 43.36 | 6 | 70.20 | 119.56 |
| 20Y5 | 45.52 | 6 | 78.79 | 130.31 |
| Terminal value | 682.87 | 50 | 1,663.97 | 2,396.84 |

The following information is available.

| | Omnivore $m | Sweet Meals $m |
|---|---|---|
| Debt | 100 | 20 |
| Equity | 900 | 280 |
| Asset beta | 0.9 | 2.4 |

Omnivore has decided to make a cash offer of $380 million to the shareholders of Sweet Meals for the purchase of 100% of their shares. The cash offer will be funded by additional borrowing.

The tax rate is 30%. Risk-free rate is 5% and the required rate of return for the combined company is 9%. Cost of debt for the combined company is expected to be 7%.

Calculate the change in equity for Omnivore's shareholders that would result from the acquisition.

# Solution

The asset beta of the combined company is:

$$\frac{\text{Total value of Omnivore}}{\text{Total combined value}} \times \text{Beta (Omnivore)} + \frac{\text{Total value of Sweet Meals}}{\text{Total combined value}} \times \text{Beta (Sweet Meals)}$$

$$= \frac{1,000}{1,300} \times 0.9 + \frac{300}{1,300} \times 2.4 = 1.25$$

## Geared beta of combined company

$$\text{Asset beta} \times \left(1 + (1-T) \times \frac{\text{Total debt}}{\text{Total equity}}\right) = 1.25 \times \left(1 + 0.7 \times \frac{500}{1,180}\right) \quad \text{(Total debt includes \$380m for 100\%}$$

of Sweet Meals shares)

$$= 1.62$$

## Cost of equity (using CAPM)

$K_e = 5 + 1.62 \times 4 = 11.48\%$

$$\text{WACC} = \frac{1,180}{1,680} \times 11.48 + \frac{500}{1,680} \times 7 \times 0.7 = 9.52\%$$

Discount cash flows at WACC to find the value of the combined firm

| Year | Combined entity cash flow $m | Discount factor 9.52% | Discounted cash flow $m |
|---|---|---|---|
| 20X5 | 5.00 | 1.000 | 5.00 |
| 20X6 | 60.00 | 0.913 | 54.78 |
| 20X7 | 65.40 | 0.834 | 54.54 |
| 20X8 | 71.29 | 0.761 | 54.25 |
| 20X9 | 77.71 | 0.695 | 54.01 |
| 20Y0 | 84.69 | 0.635 | 53.78 |
| 20Y1 | 92.32 | 0.579 | 53.45 |
| 20Y2 | 100.62 | 0.529 | 53.23 |
| 20Y3 | 109.68 | 0.483 | 52.98 |
| 20Y4 | 119.56 | 0.441 | 52.73 |
| 20Y5 | 130.31 | 0.403 | 52.51 |
| Terminal value | 2,396.84 | 0.403 | 965.93 |

= $1,507.19 million

Value of equity = Value of firm − value of debt
= $1,507.19 − 500
= $1,007.19 million

Omnivore's shareholders' value has increased by ($1,007.19 − 900) million = $107.19 million.

## Question
Nessie Inc

Nessie Inc is considering making a bid for 100% of Patsy Inc, a company in a completely different industry. The bid of $200 million, which is expected to be accepted, will be financed entirely by new debt with a post-tax cost of debt of 7%.

## Pre-acquisition information

### Nessie

Nessie has debt finance totalling $60 million at a pre-tax rate of 7.5%. There are 50 million equity shares with a current market value of $22 each and an equity beta of 1.37.

Post-tax operating cash flows are as follows.

| Year 1 | Year 2 | Year 3 | Year 4 | Year 5 |
| --- | --- | --- | --- | --- |
| $m | $m | $m | $m | $m |
| 60.3 | 63.9 | 67.8 | 71.8 | 76.1 |

### Patsy

Patsy has an equity beta of 2.5 and 65 million shares with a total current market value of $156 million. Current debt – which will also be taken over by Nessie – is $12.5 million.

### Post-acquisition information

Land with a value of $14 million will be sold.

Post-tax operating cash flows of Patsy's current business will be:

| Year 1 | Year 2 | Year 3 | Year 4 | Year 5 |
| --- | --- | --- | --- | --- |
| $m | $m | $m | $m | $m |
| 15.2 | 15.8 | 16.4 | 17.1 | 17.8 |

If the acquisition goes ahead, Nessie will experience an improvement in its credit rating and all **existing** debt will be charged at a rate of 7%.

Cash flows after year 5 will grow at a rate of 1.5% per annum.

### General information

The risk-free rate is 5.2% and the market risk premium is 3%. Corporation tax rate is 28%. Debt beta is 0.

*Required*

Should Nessie go ahead with the acquisition of Patsy? Give reasons for your answer.

### Answer

(1) **Calculate asset betas of both companies**

Assuming a debt beta of 0, asset beta can be calculated using the following formula.

$$\beta_a = \frac{Ve}{(Ve + Vd(1-T))}\beta_e$$

Nessie = (1,100m/[1,100m + (60m × 0.72)]) × 1.37 = 1.32

Patsy = (156m/[156m + (12.5m × 0.72)]) × 2.5 = 2.36

(2) **Combined asset beta**

Combined beta = 1.32 × (1,100/[1,100 + 156]) + 2.36 × (156/[1,100 + 156]) = 1.45

(3) Regear beta to reflect group post-acquisition gearing

> **Tutorial note.** Remember to include the additional debt that is being taken on to fund the acquisition.

Using pre-acquisition debt and equity weightings

Equity beta = 1.45 / (1,256/[1,256 + [(60 + 12.5 + 200) × 0.72]) = 1.68

(4) **Calculate the group's new WACC**

$K_e$ = 5.2 + (1.68 × 3) = 10.24%

WACC = (10.24 × 1,256/[1,256 + 272.5]) + (7 × 272.5/[1,256 + 272.5])

= 8.4144 + 1.2480

= 9.66%

(5)    Discount group's post-acquisition cash flows using this WACC

**Post-acquisition NPV**

| Year | 1 $m | 2 $m | 3 $m | 4 $m | 5 $m | Year 6 onwards $m |
|---|---|---|---|---|---|---|
| Combined cash flow | 75.5 | 79.7 | 84.2 | 88.9 | 93.9 | 95.3 |
| Annuity (1/r–g)) | | | | | | 12.3 |
| Value as at time 5 | | | | | | 1,172.2 |
| at 9.66% | 0.912 | 0.832 | 0.758 | 0.692 | 0.631 | 0.631 |
| PV | 68.900 | 66.3 | 63.8 | 61.5 | 59.3 | 739.7 |

| | |
|---|---|
| Total PV | 1,059.5 |
| Sale of land | 14.0 |
| Nessie's debt | (60.0) |
| Patsy's debt | (12.5) |
| New debt to fund acquisition | (200.0) |
| **Net value** | **801.0** |

The net value of the combined companies is less than Nessie's individual value (50 million shares × $22 = $1,100m) therefore the acquisition of Patsy should not go ahead.

# 6 Valuation of high growth start-ups

## 6.1 Characteristics of high growth start-ups

Due to their unique characteristics high growth start-ups present a number of challenges.

The valuation of **start-ups** presents a number of challenges for the methods that we have considered so far due to their unique characteristics which are summarised below.

(a)    Most start-ups typically have no track record
(b)    Ongoing losses
(c)    Few revenues, untested products
(d)    Unknown market acceptance, unknown product demand
(e)    Unknown competition
(f)    Unknown cost structures, unknown implementation timing
(g)    High development or infrastructure costs
(h)    Inexperienced management

## 6.2 Projecting economic performance

All valuation methods require reasonable projections to be made with regard to the key drivers of the business. The following steps should be undertaken with respect to the valuation of a high growth start-up company.

**Identifying the drivers**

Any market-based approach or discounted cash flow analysis depends on the reasonableness of financial projections. Projections must be analysed in light of the market potential, resources of the business, management team, financial characteristics of the guideline public companies, and other factors.

BPP
LEARNING MEDIA

### Period of projection

One characteristic of high growth start-ups is that in order to survive they need to grow very quickly. Start-ups that do grow quickly usually have operating expenses and investment needs in excess of their revenues in the first years and experience losses until the growth starts to slow down (and the resource needs begin to stabilise). This means that long-term projections, all the way out to the time when the business has sustainable positive operating margins and cash flows, need to be prepared. These projections will depend on the assumptions made about growth. However, rarely is the forecast period less than seven years.

### Forecasting growth

Forecasting growth in earnings can be accommodated in the framework we have already explained for the prediction of earnings. The growth in earnings will be:

$g$ = retention rate $\times$ $r_e$

For most high growth start-ups retention rate = 1 as the company, in order to achieve a high growth rate, needs to invest in research and development, expansion of distribution and manufacturing capacity, human resource development to attract new talent, and development of new markets, products or techniques.

With a $b = 1$, it means that the sole determinant of growth is the return on invested capital. This can be estimated from industry projections from securities analysts or from an evaluation of the company's management, marketing strengths and level of investment.

## 6.3 Valuation methods

Once growth rates have been estimated, the next step is to consider which is the most appropriate of the valuation approaches we have considered so far: net assets, market or discounted cash flows.

### Asset-based method

The asset-based method is not appropriate because the value of capital in terms of tangible assets may not be high. Most of the investment of a start-up is in people, marketing and/or intellectual rights that are treated as expenses rather than as capital.

### Market-based methods

The market approach to valuation also presents special problems for start-ups. This valuation process involves finding other companies, usually sold through private transactions, that are at a similar stage of development and that focus on existing or proposed products similar to those of the company being valued. Complicating factors include comparability problems, differences in fair market value from value paid by strategic acquirers, lack of disclosed information, and the fact that there usually are no earnings with which to calculate price to earnings ratios (in this case price to revenue ratios may be helpful).

### Discounted cash flows

Using the discounted cash flow (DCF) methodology, FCFs are first projected and then discounted to the present using a risk-adjusted cost of capital. For example, one could use the constant growth model which specifies that:

$$V = \frac{FCF}{r - g}$$

Our discussion of the high growth start-up indicates that the growth rates of revenues and costs may vary. Since FCF = Revenue − Costs = R − C, the value of company will be given by:

$$V = \frac{R - C}{r - g}$$

Now assuming that the growth rate of revenues $g_R$ is different than the growth rate of costs $g_C$:

$$V = \frac{R}{r - g_R} - \frac{C}{r - g_C}$$

QuickLeg is an internet legal services provider which next year expects revenue of $100m and costs of $500m. The revenues of the firm are expected to rise by 21% every year but costs will remain at the same level. The required rate of return is assumed to 22%. What is the value of QuickLeg?

Answer

$$V = \frac{\$100m}{0.22 - 0.21} - \frac{\$500m}{0.22 - 0} = \$7,727.27 \text{ million.}$$

The above model seems to capture the phenomenon observed in many start-ups of high losses in the first year of operations with high values of the company. The predicted profits (in $m) for QuickLeg over time (years 1 to 15) are shown in the diagram.

**QuickLeg Profits**

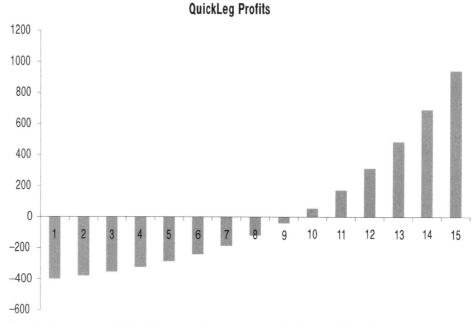

A very important problem with the discounted flow approach is the sensitivity of the valuation model to the underlying assumptions. Changes in the growth rate induced by changes in demand, technology and management of other causes can have a dramatic effect on the value of the start-up. For example, suppose that the growth rate of revenues falls from 21% to 20%. The value of the company now is:

$$V = \frac{\$100}{0.22 - 0.20} - \frac{\$500}{0.22 - 0} = \$2,727.27 \text{ million}$$

That is, the company has lost $5 billion.

Another problem with the DCF is that it cannot reflect managerial flexibilities and the strategic options to expand, delay, abandon, or switch investments at various decision points. The best way of incorporating uncertainty into the DCF analysis for a new company, technology or product is to assign probabilities of success to each of the various possibilities.

## 6.4 Probabilistic valuation methods (expected values)

In a probabilistic cash flow model, we assume a number of scenarios for the drivers of value and derive a value under each scenario. The next step is to assign probabilities to each scenario and arrive at a weighted average value. The procedure to be followed is similar to the Monte Carlo methodology described in Chapter 5.

# Example

Suppose you have calculated three valuations of QuickLeg over a ten-year forecast period. Based on your analysis of value drivers, strategies, competition and other variables, you have assigned the following values to each scenario.

| Scenario | Probability | Value derived from scenario | Expected value |
|---|---|---|---|
| Conservative | 0.2 | 1,000 | 200 |
| Normal | 0.7 | 1,600 | 1,120 |
| High growth | 0.1 | 2,200 | 220 |
| | Overall value | | 1,540 |

Assigning the above values and respective probabilities to each scenario, the expected overall value of QuickLeg is $1,540 million.

# Chapter Roundup

- When a company acquires another company, it will pay a premium above its current market value. Where this premium is excessive, this is known as the overvaluation problem. Behavioural finance helps to why excessive bid premiums are paid.

- Acquisitions may be valued using **asset based, market based or cash based models**. Whichever valuation method is used, the **business risk** and **financial risk** associated with the acquisition must be recognized.

  Exam questions require a 'reasonable, justified approach', but as in the real world it is recognized that **a business does not have a 'precise' valuation**.

- Book value or asset-based methods of company valuation are based on the statement of financial position as the starting point in the valuation process.

- Lev's knowledge earnings method involves separating the earnings that are deemed to come from intangible assets and capitalising these earnings.

- Market relative models may be based on the P/E ratio which produces an earnings-based valuation of shares.

- The business risk of the combined entity will be affected by the betas of the target and bidding firms and the beta of the synergy that results from the acquisition.

- Due to their unique characteristics high growth start-ups present a number of challenges.

1    Give three ways in which the growth rate of a firm's dividendss can be estimated.

2    What is the relationship between earnings growth and retained profits?

3    If the return on equity is 12% and the retention rate is 0.4, what is the estimated growth rate of dividends?

4    What are the three market-based approaches to valuation?

5    What is the most appropriate method for the valuation of an acquisition that changes financial risk?

# Answers to Quick Quiz

1  Historical estimates
   Analysts' forecasts
   Company fundamentals

2  The higher the percentage of earnings retained, the higher the forecast dividend growth

3  Dividend growth = return on equity × retention rate = 0.12 × 0.4 = 0.048 or 4.8%

4  P/E ratio, earnings yield and market to book ratios.

5  The adjusted present value approach (APV).

Now try the questions below from the Practice Question Bank

| Number | Level | Marks | Time |
|--------|-------|-------|------|
| 18 | Introductory | 15 | 29 mins |
| 19 | Examination | 30 | 59 mins |
| 20 | Examination | 50 | 98 mins |
| 21 | Examination | 50 | 98 mins |
| 22 | Introductory | 15 | 29 mins |
| 23 | Examination | 25 | 49 mins |
| 24 | Examination | 20 | 39 mins |

# 11

# Regulatory framework and processes

| Topic list | Syllabus reference |
|------------|--------------------|
| 1 The global regulatory framework | C3(a) |
| 2 Key aspects of takeover regulation | C3(a) |
| 3 Regulation in the UK | C3(b) |
| 4 Defensive tactics in a hostile takeover | C3(b) |

## Introduction

In this chapter we discuss the main factors that have influenced the development of the regulatory framework for mergers and acquisitions globally and compare the two different models of regulation used in the UK and continental Europe respectively. We explain the convergence sought by the implementation of the EU Directive and discuss issues that are likely to arise in a given offer as well as defensive measures available to management in a hostile bid.

# Study guide

| | | Intellectual level |
|---|---|---|
| **C3** | **Regulatory framework and processes** | |
| (a) | Demonstrate an understanding of the principal factors influencing the development of the regulatory framework for mergers and acquisitions globally and, in particular, be able to compare and contrast the shareholder versus the stakeholder models of regulation. | 2 |
| (b) | Identify the main regulatory issues which are likely to arise in the context of a given offer and: | 3 |
| | (i)      Assess whether the offer is likely to be in the shareholders' best interests. | |
| | (ii)      Advise the directors of a target entity on the most appropriate defence if a specific offer is to be treated as hostile. | |

# Exam guide

Questions in this area are likely to involve the application of the regulatory framework to a possibly dubious arrangement, for example arrangements that do not appear to treat shareholders equally.

# 1 The global regulatory framework

## 1.1 Introduction

**FAST FORWARD**

Takeover regulation is an important corporate governance device in protecting the interests of all stakeholders, as the agency problem can have a significant potential impact on mergers and acquisitions.

The **agency problem** (discussed in Part A) and the issues arising from the separation of ownership and control have a significant potential impact on mergers and acquisitions.

Merger booms and a succession of corporate scandals have contributed to the need for adequate regulation from the point of view of both the shareholders and the wider group of stakeholders.

**Takeover regulation** is an important **corporate governance device** that seeks to protect the interests of **minority shareholders** and other types of **stakeholders** and ensure a **well-functioning market** for corporate control.

## 1.2 Potential conflicts of interest

Takeover regulation seeks to regulate the conflicts of interest between the management and shareholders of both the **target** and the **bidder**.

There are **two main agency problems** that emerge in the context of a takeover that regulation seeks to address.

(a) The first is the **protection of minority shareholders**. In addition to existing minority shareholders, transfers of control may turn existing majority shareholders of the target into minority shareholders.

(b) The second is the possibility that the management of the target company may implement **measures** to **prevent the takeover** even if these are **against stakeholder interests**.

## 1.3 Background and brief history of regulation in the UK and continental Europe

### 1.3.1 The City Code on Takeovers and Mergers and UK legislation

The City Code on Takeovers and Mergers is a voluntary set of principles governing takeovers and mergers of UK companies. It is issued and administered by the Takeover Panel, an independent body of representatives from UK financial institutions with key members appointed by the Bank of England.

Takeover regulation in the UK goes back to 1968 when a **voluntary code**, the **City Code on Takeovers** and **Mergers** (known as the City Code), was introduced. Since then the Code, a set of general principles and rules governing takeovers and mergers of UK companies, has been frequently amended.

Mergers and acquisitions in the UK are also regulated by legislation.

In continental Europe, takeover regulation was put in place in the late 1980s based largely on voluntary codes following the UK City Code. However, these were soon replaced by legislation in the mid-1990s.

### 1.3.2 The Takeover Panel

The City Code is issued and administered by the Takeover Panel, an independent body made up of representatives from UK financial institutions and professional associations with key members currently appointed by the Bank of England.

### 1.3.3 Legal status of the City Code

Although the City Code (before the implementation of the EU Directive) was not legally binding, it was in practice mandatory for both UK and non-UK bidders. If a party to a takeover failed to comply with the Code they run the risk that facilities of the London Markets would be withdrawn.

In addition, the Panel could ask the Financial Services Authority under the FSMA to take action if a party's behaviour amounts to market abuse, with sanctions involving unlimited fines.

### 1.3.4 Scope and application of the City Code

The City Code applies to any offer where the target or offeree is a listed or unlisted public company resident in the UK, the Channel Islands or the Isle of Man.

The nature or country of residence of the company or entity making the offer, ie the bidder or offeror, does not affect the application of the City Code.

The main principles of the City Code are detailed in Section 3 below where the principal issues of which a bidder should be aware when making an offer are also discussed.

## 1.4 The two models of regulation

Takeover regulation in the UK is centred around the City Code and is referred to as a 'market-based' model designed to protect a dispersed shareholder base.

Takeover regulation in the UK, centred around the City Code, is based on what is often referred to as a **'market-based model'**[1] designed to protect a wide and dispersed shareholder base. This system which also prevails in the Commonwealth countries and the US is based on case law and the legal rules resulting from it. These seek to a great extent the protection of shareholder rights.

The system prevalent in continental Europe is referred to as the block-holder or stakeholder system and relies on codified civil law designed to protect a broader group of stakeholders.

The second system, prevalent in continental Europe, is referred to as the **stakeholder system** and relies on codified or civil law seeking to protect a broader group of stakeholders, such as creditors, employees and the wider national interest.

The two systems differ in terms of not only their regulatory framework (civil versus common law) but also the underlying structure of ownership and control that they seek to address.

In the UK and the US the system is characterised by wider share ownership than in continental Europe, where companies tend to be owned by majority or near-majority stakes held by a small number of investors.

In the Anglo-American model, the emphasis is on the agency problem and the protection of the widely distributed shareholder base.

The civil law countries rely via **legislation** on the monitoring by large shareholders, **creditors** and **employees**.

### 1.5 Towards European harmonisation – the EU Takeovers Directive

> The Takeovers Directive was introduced by the EU in 2002 and its principles became effective from May 2006 in order to achieve harmonisation and convergence of the market-based and stakeholder systems.

The **Takeovers Directive** lays down for the first time minimum EU rules concerning the regulation of takeovers of companies whose shares are traded on regulated markets. It is one of the measures adopted under the EU Financial Services Action Plan and aims to strengthen the single market in financial services.

The **Takeover Directive** requires that certain of the activities of the **Takeover Panel** are placed within a legal framework bringing an end to the non-statutory approach to regulation in the UK. In terms of approach, the new regulatory model leads to the **convergence** of the **European system** to the **UK-US** one by adopting many of the elements of the **City Code**.

The **European Commission**, seeking to harmonise European takeover regulation, presented a draft Takeover Directive in 2002. This draft introduced the following five main regulatory devices (the rationale of which is explained in Section 2 below):

(a)     Mandatory-bid rule
(b)     The principle of equal treatment of shareholders
(c)     A squeeze-out rule and sell-out rights
(d)     The principle of board neutrality
(e)     A break-through rule

The break-through rule, described below, faced much resistance and the directive allowed individual countries to opt out of it.

## 2 Key aspects of takeover regulation                12/12, 12/15

The following seven regulatory devices feature strongly in European takeover reforms (Goergen, Martynova and Renneboog, 2005).

### The mandatory-bid rule

The aim of this rule is to protect minority shareholders by providing them with the opportunity to exit the company at a fair price once the bidder has accumulated a certain percentage of the shares.

National thresholds vary between countries but the trend has been for these to decrease over the years.

In the UK, this threshold is specified by the City Code for Takeovers and Mergers and is at 30%.

The mandatory-bid rule is based on the grounds that once the bidder obtains control they may exploit their position at the expense of minority shareholders. This is why the mandatory-bid rule normally also specifies the price that is to be paid for the shares.

The bidder is normally required to offer to the remaining shareholders a price not lower than the highest price for the shares already acquired during a specified period prior to the bid.

### The principle of equal treatment

The principle of treating all shareholders equally is fundamental in all western European countries.

In general terms, the principle of equal treatment requires the bidder to offer to minority shareholders the same terms as those offered to earlier shareholders from whom the controlling block was acquired.

### Transparency of ownership and control

The disclosure of information about major shareholdings is an important element of investor protection and a well-functioning corporate market. The transparency enables the regulator to monitor large shareholders, minimise potential agency problems and investigate insider dealing. It also enables both minority shareholders and the market to monitor large shareholders who may be able to exercise undue influence or exact benefits at the expense of other shareholdings.

### The squeeze-out and sell-out rights

Squeeze-out rights give the bidder who has acquired a specific percentage of the equity (usually 90%) the right to force minority shareholders to sell their shares.

The threshold in the UK and in most European countries is 90%, although in Belgium, France, Germany and the Netherlands the threshold is 95% and in Ireland it is the lowest at 80%. The rule enables the bidder to acquire 100% of the equity once the threshold percentage has been reached and eliminates potential problems that could be caused by minority shareholders.

Sell-out rights enable minority shareholders to require the majority shareholder to purchase their shares.

### The one share-one vote principle

Where the one share-one vote principle is upheld, arrangements restricting voting rights are forbidden.

Differentiated voting rights, such as non-voting shares and dual-clan shares with multiple voting rights, enable some shareholders to accumulate control at the expense of other shareholders and could provide a significant barrier to potential takeovers.

### The break-through rule

The effect of the break-through rule, where this is allowed by corporate law, is to enable a bidder with a specified proportion of the company's equity to break through the company's multiple voting rights and exercise control as if one share-one vote existed.

### Board neutrality and anti-takeover measures

Seeking to address the agency issue where management may be tempted to act in their own interests at the expense of the interests of the shareholders, several regulatory devices propose board neutrality. For instance, the board would not be permitted to carry out post-bid aggressive defensive tactics (such as selling the company's main assets, known as crown jewels defence, and entering into special arrangements giving rights to existing shareholders to buy shares at a low price, known as poison pill defence), without the prior authority of the shareholders.

# 3 Regulation in the UK

## 3.1 The City Code: General principles

The City Code is divided into general principles and detailed rules which must be observed by persons involved in a merger or takeover transaction. The key requirements of the City Code include the following:

(a) **All the shareholders of the target company must be treated similarly**

'All holders of the securities of an offeree company of the same class must be afforded equivalent treatment; moreover, if a person **acquires control** of a company, the other holders of securities must be protected.'

In other words, a company making a takeover bid cannot offer one set of purchase terms to some shareholders in the target company, and a different set of terms to other shareholders holding shares of the same class in that company.

An offer must be made for **ALL** other shares if the % shareholding rises above **30%,** at not less than the highest price paid by the bidding company in last year.

(b) **Sufficient time and information to be given for a properly informed decision**

'The holders of the securities of an offeree company must have sufficient time and information to enable them to reach a properly informed decision on the bid; where it advises the holders of securities, the board of the offeree company must give its views on the effects of the implementation of the bid on employment, conditions of employment and the locations of the company's places of business.'

To reinforce this a bid timetable is set – details are provided in the following section but **detailed knowledge of this timetable is not required**.

(c) **The directors of the offeree company must act in the interest of the company as a whole**

'The board of an offeree company must act in the interests of the company as a whole and must not deny the holders of securities the opportunity to decide on the merits of the bid.'

The board may not use poison pills to frustrate a takeover bid without shareholder approval.

## 3.2 Compliance with City Code

The City Code lays down time limits governing the overall period of an offer. The aim of the timetable is to minimise disruption of the normal activities of the target.

Any companies that are identified as potential bidders have a 28 day period within which they must either announce a firm intention to bid or state that they do not intend to make a bid (in which case they cannot make another bid for a 6 month period without the consent of the board of the target company).

An outline timetable is shown in the next section, but this is for interest only and will not be directly examined.

### 3.2.1 Outline timetable for a takeover offer

| Day | Action Required | Note | Rule |
|---|---|---|---|
| −28 | Announcement of intention to bid. | The offer document must be sent to the shareholders within 28 days of the notice of intention to make the offer. | 24.1 |
| 0 | Publication of offer document. | | |
| +14 | Last day for target's written response to offer. | The target company's board should advise its shareholders of its views on the offer. | 25.1 |
| | | The target board's views may already be contained in the offer document if this is an offer which the board recommend. | |
| +21 | Earliest day for offer to close. | The offer cannot close before 21 days have passed from the day on which the offer document was published. | 31.1 |
| +39 | Last day for target to announce material new information including trading results, profit or dividend forecasts and any other relevant information. | | 31.9 |
| +42 | Target shareholders may withdraw their acceptance if offer is not unconditional. | | |
| +46 | Last day for offeror to revise its offer. | Any subsequent revised offer must be kept open for at least 14 days after the revised offer document is posted. Therefore, because the acceptance condition must be met within 60 days, no revised document may be posted after day 46. | 32.1 |
| +60 | Last day for offer to be declared unconditional as to acceptances. | If the acceptance condition (see Section 3.2.2 below) is not satisfied by day 60 then the offer will lapse. | 31.6 |
| +81 | Last day for offer to be made wholly unconditional. | | 31.7 |
| +95 | Last day for paying the offer consideration to the target shareholders who accepted by day 81. | | |

### 3.2.2 The acceptance condition

Whether an offer is successful or not depends on whether the offeror has sufficient acceptances to give it the required degree of control over the target. Therefore the offeror makes the offer subject to the condition that a minimum level of acceptance is achieved. The minimum acceptance condition permitted is 50% of the target's voting rights. Normally, however, a 90% condition will be specified because this is the level that will enable the offeror to force the remaining minority shareholders to sell their shares under the compulsory acquisition per the Companies Acts (CA).

If the specified level of acceptances is not reached within 60 days of posting the offer document, the offer will lapse.

## 3.3 Stake building and the relevant thresholds

Normally, a potential offeror will wish to build a stake prior to making an offer. Any person can acquire a stake of up to 29.9% in a listed or Alternative Investment Market company without being subject to any timing restrictions. Some of the important share stakes and their consequences are outlined below.

| % | Consequence |
|---|---|
| Any | Ability of the company to enquire as to the ultimate ownership |
| 3% | Requirement to disclose interest in the company (the material interests rules). |
| 10% | Shareholders controlling not less than 10% of the voting rights may requisition the company to serve notices to identify another shareholder.<br><br>Notifiable interests rules become operative for institutional investors and non-beneficial stakes. |
| 30% | City Code definition of effective control. Mandatory bid triggered and takeover offer becomes compulsory.<br><br>If the bidder holds between 30% and 50% (normally due to earlier attempts at a takeover) a mandatory offer is triggered with any additional purchase. |
| 50%+ | CA definition of control (since at this level the holder will have the ability to pass ordinary resolutions).<br><br>First point at which a full offer could be declared unconditional with regard to acceptances.<br><br>Minimum acceptance condition. |
| 75% | Major control boundary since at this level the holder will be able to pass special resolutions. |
| 90% | Minorities may be able to force the majority to buy out their stake. Equally, the majority may, subject to the way in which the stake has been acquired, require the minority to sell out their position.<br><br>Compulsory acquisition of remaining 10% is now possible. |

### 3.3.1 Disclosure and Transparency Rules

The **Disclosure and Transparency Rules**, introduced as part of the process of implementation of the **Transparency Directive**, require the notification threshold of a 3% holding, and every 1% thereafter.

The Transparency Directive requires the disclosure of **holdings of shares to which voting rights are attached**.

## 3.4 The Competition and Markets Authority

A UK company might have to consider whether its proposed takeover would be drawn to the attention of the Competition and Markets Authority (formerly called the Competition Commission and the Monopolies and Mergers Commission).

If a transaction is referred to the Competition and Markets Authority and the Authority finds that it results in a substantial lessening of competition in the defined market, it will specify action to remedy or prevent the adverse effects identified, or it may decide that the merger does not take place (or, in the case of a completed merger, is reversed).

Any person aggrieved by a decision of the Competition and Markets Authority in connection with a reference or possible reference may apply to the Competition Appeal Tribunal for a review of that decision.

A number of tests may be used to decide whether there has been a **substantial lessening** of **competition** (SLC). These normally include:

(a) **The revenue test**

No investigation will normally be conducted if the target's revenue is less than £70 million.

(b) **The share of supply test**

An investigation will not normally be conducted unless, following the merger, the combined entity supplies 25%. The 25% share will be assessed by the commission.

(b) **The SLC test**

Even if the thresholds in (a) and (b) above are met, the Competition and Markets Authority will only be involved if there has been an SLC in the market.

## 3.5 The European Union

Mergers fall within the exclusive jurisdiction of the European Union where, following the merger, the following two tests are met:

(a) **Worldwide revenue** of more than **€5 billion per annum**
(b) **European Union** revenue of more than **€250 million per annum**

The European Union will assess the merger in a similar way as the Competition and Markets Authority in the UK by considering the effect on competition in the market.

The merger will be blocked if the merged company results in a market oligopoly or results in such a dominant position in the market that consumer choice and prices will be affected.

# 4 Defensive tactics in a hostile takeover        6/11, 12/15

**FAST FORWARD**

There are a number of defensive measures that can be taken where the management of the takeover target perceives the bid to be hostile. Takeover defences can be categorised into **pre-offer** and **post-offer** defences.

Most takeovers may be referred to as **friendly** and take place when the management of the two firms negotiate an agreement that is **beneficial** to both sides.

However, not all takeovers are negotiated in this way and some are perceived as hostile and resisted by the directors.

There are a number of **defensive** measures that can be taken where the management of the takeover target perceives the bid as **hostile**.

Takeover defences can be categorised into **pre-offer defences** and **post-offer defences**. Both types of defence have developed over the years, mainly in the US during the wave of takeover bids of the 1980s.

The more **aggressive tactics** often **risk shareholders' interests** in favour of those of management. The EU Takeover Directive seeks to override certain of the more aggressive tactics that may be taken by management to frustrate a bid and which may be at the expense of the shareholders.

Both **pre-offer** and **post-offer defences** are set out below, together with an explanation of what can be appropriately used in the UK following the implementation of the Takeover Directive.

(a) **Pre-bid defences** normally include provisions in the company's articles of association whereby **differential share structures** are set up under which **minority shareholders** exercise **disproportionate voting rights**, thus enabling the target to frustrate a takeover bid.

The Takeover Directive restricts the power of such share schemes by preventing their use to block takeovers unless the voting rights relate to shares that are owned by the Government.

(b)    **Post-bid defences** include actions such as selling the major assets of the company (crown jewels) in an attempt to make the target less attractive and setting up schemes where existing shareholders can buy shares at very low prices (poison pill). The Takeover Directive, now incorporated into the **City Code**, requires that the management of the company does not take any such defensive action unless this is authorised by the shareholders.

**Summary of defensive tactics**

| Tactic | Explanation |
|---|---|
| **Golden parachute** | Large compensation payments made to the top management of the target firm if their positions are eliminated due to hostile takeover. This may include cash or bonus payments, stock options or a combination of these. |
| **Poison pill** | This is an attempt to make a company unattractive normally by giving the right to existing shareholders to buy shares at a very low price. Poison pills have many variants. |
| **White knights** | This would involve inviting a firm that would rescue the target from the unwanted bidder. The white knight would act as a friendly counter-bidder. |
| **Crown jewels** | The firm's most valuable assets may be the main reason that the firm became a takeover target in the first place. By selling these or entering into arrangements such as sale and leaseback, the firm is making itself less attractive as a target. |
| **Pacman defence** | This defence is carried out by mounting a counter-bid for the attacker. The Pacman defence is an aggressive rather than defensive tactic and will only work where the original acquirer is a public company with diverse shareholdings. This tactic also appears to suggest that the company's management are in favour of the acquisition but that they disagree about which company should be in control. |
| **Litigation or regulatory defence** | The target company can challenge the acquisition by inviting an investigation by the regulatory authorities or through the courts. The target may be able to sue for a temporary order to stop the bidder from buying any more of its shares. |

# Chapter Roundup

- Takeover regulation is an important corporate governance device in protecting the interests of all stakeholders, as the agency problem can have a significant potential impact on mergers and acquisitions.

- The City Code on Takeovers and Mergers is a voluntary set of principles governing takeovers and mergers of UK companies. It is issued and administered by the Takeover Panel, an independent body of representatives from UK financial institutions, with key members appointed by the Bank of England.

- Takeover regulation in the UK is centred around the City Code and is referred to as a 'market-based' model designed to protect a dispersed shareholder base.

- The system prevalent in continental Europe is referred to as the block-holder or stakeholder system and relies on codified civil law designed to protect a broader group of stakeholders.

- The Takeovers Directive was introduced by the EU in 2002 and its principles became effective from May 2006 in order to achieve harmonisation and convergence of the market-based and stakeholder systems.

- There are a number of defensive measures that can be taken where the management of the takeover target perceives the bid to be hostile. Takeover defences can be categorised into **pre-offer** and **post-offer** defences.

# Quick Quiz

1 What are the two models of takeover regulation?

2 What are the key points of the takeover regulation?

3 Which mergers fall within the jurisdiction of the European Union?

4 What are the main post-bid defensive tactics in a takeover?

5 What are the main pre-bid defensive tactics in a takeover?

1    The market-based model
     The stakeholder system

2    The mandatory-bid rule
     The principle of equal treatment
     Transparency of ownership and control
     The squeeze-out and sell-out rights
     The one share-one vote principle
     The break-through rule
     Board neutrality and anti-takeover measures

3    Mergers where the resulting combined company will have worldwide revenue of more than €5 billion per annum

     Mergers where the resulting combined company will have a European Union revenue in excess of €250 million per annum

4    Golden parachute
     Poison pill
     White knights and white squires
     Crown jewels
     Pacman defence
     Litigation or regulatory defence

5    **Pre-bid defences** normally include provisions in the company's articles of association whereby **differential share structures** are set up under which **minority shareholders** exercise **disproportionate voting rights**, thus enabling the target to frustrate a takeover bid.

Now try the question below from the Practice Question Bank

| Number | Level | Marks | Time |
|--------|-------|-------|------|
| 25 | Introductory | 15 | 29 |

# 12

# Financing mergers and acquisitions

| Topic list | Syllabus reference |
|---|---|
| 1 Methods of financing mergers | C4(a) |
| 2 Assessing a given offer | C4(b) |
| 3 Effect of an offer on financial position and performance | C4(c) |

## Introduction

In this chapter we deal with three issues.

First, we discuss how a bidding firm can finance an acquisition, either by cash or by a share offer or a combination of the two, and discuss the funding of cash offers.

Second, we discuss ways to evaluate a financial offer in terms of the impact on the acquiring company and criteria for acceptance or rejection.

Finally we discuss ways of estimating the possible impact of an offer on the performance and the financial position of the acquiring firm.

# Study guide

| | | Intellectual level |
|---|---|---|
| **C4** | **Financing acquisitions and mergers** | |
| (a) | Compare the various sources of financing available for a proposed cash-based acquisition. | 3 |
| (b) | Evaluate the advantages and disadvantages of a financial offer for a given acquisition proposal using pure or mixed mode financing and recommend the most appropriate offer to be made. | 3 |
| (c) | Assess the impact of a given financial offer on the reported financial position and performance of the acquirer. | 3 |

# Exam guide

Questions in this area are likely to involve some calculations so you will need to bring in your knowledge of company valuation. However, questions will not be purely numerical. Topics you might be asked to discuss include why companies might choose to make an offer in a particular form, takeover tactics, the effect on shareholder wealth, and what happens after the takeover, including post-audits.

You will be expected to demonstrate competence in the analysis of various finance options when fulfilling the performance objective 'evaluate potential investment and financing decisions'. This chapter focuses on the various ways in which mergers could be financed and assesses the costs and benefits of each option – knowledge which you can put into practice if your organisation is involved in merger and acquisition activity.

# 1 Methods of financing mergers          6/11, 12/12, 6/13, 12/13

**FAST FORWARD**

> Payment can be in the form of **cash**, a **share exchange** or **convertible loan stock**. The choice will depend on available cash, desired levels of gearing, shareholders' taxation position and changes in control.

## 1.1 Methods of payment

The terms of a takeover will involve a purchase of the shares of the target company for **cash** or for **'paper'** (shares, or possibly loan stock). A purchase of a target company's shares with shares of the bidding company is referred to as a **share exchange**.

## 1.2 Cash purchases

If the purchase consideration is in **cash**, the shareholders of the target company will simply be bought out. For example, suppose that there are two companies.

| | Big Co | Small Co |
|---|---|---|
| Net assets (book value) | $1,500,000 | $200,000 |
| Number of shares | 100,000 | 10,000 |
| Earnings | $2,000,000 | $40,000 |

Big Co negotiates a takeover of Small Co for $400,000 in cash.

As a result, Big Co will end up with:

(a) Net assets (book value) of

$1,500,000 + $200,000 − $400,000 cash = $1,300,000

(b) 100,000 shares (no change)

(c)     Expected earnings of $2,040,000, minus the loss of interest (net of tax) which would have been obtained from the investment of the $400,000 in cash which was given up to acquire Small Co.

## 1.3 Funding cash offers

A cash offer can be financed from:

(a)     **Cash retained from earnings**. This is a common way when the firm to be acquired is small compared to the acquiring firm, but not very common if the target firm is large relative to the acquiring firm. A company may occasionally divest of some of its own assets to accumulate cash prior to bidding for another company.

(b)     **The proceeds of a debt issue**. That is, the company may raise money by issuing bonds. This is not an approach that is normally taken, because the act of issuing bonds will alert the markets to the intentions of the company to bid for another company and it may lead investors to buy the shares of potential targets, raising their prices.

(c)     **A loan facility from a bank**. This can be done as a short-term funding strategy, until the bid is accepted and then the company is free to make a bond issue.

(d)     **Mezzanine finance**. This may be the only route for companies that do not have access to the bond markets in order to issue bonds.

## 1.4 Purchases by share exchange

One company can acquire another company by **issuing shares** to pay for the acquisition. The new shares might be issued:

(a)     **In exchange** for shares in the target company. Thus, if A Inc acquires B Co, A Inc might issue shares which it gives to B Co's shareholders in exchange for their shares. The B Co shareholders therefore become new shareholders of A Inc. This is a takeover for a 'paper' consideration. Paper offers will often be accompanied by a **cash alternative**.

(b)     **To raise cash** on the stock market, which will then be used to buy the target company's shares. To the target company shareholders, this is a cash bid.

Sometimes, a company might acquire another in a share exchange, but the shares are then **sold immediately** on a stock market to raise cash for the seller.

Whatever the detailed arrangements of a takeover with paper, the end result will be an **increase in the issued share capital of the bidding company**.

## 1.5 Use of convertible loan stock

Alternative forms of paper consideration, including debentures, loan stock and preference shares, are not so commonly used, due to:

- Difficulties in establishing a rate of return that will be attractive to target shareholders
- The effects on the gearing levels of the acquiring company
- The change in the structure of the target shareholders' portfolios
- The securities being potentially less marketable, and possibly lacking voting rights

Issuing **convertible loan stock** will overcome some of these drawbacks, by offering the target shareholders the option of partaking in the future profits of the company if they wish.

**Key term**

> **Convertible loan stock** is a loan which gives the holder the right to convert to other securities, normally ordinary shares, at a predetermined price/rate and time.

## 1.6 The choice between a cash offer and a paper offer

The choice between cash and paper offers (or a combination of both) will depend on how the different methods are viewed by the company and its existing shareholders, and on the attitudes of the shareholders of the target company. Generally speaking, firms which believe that their stock is undervalued will not use stock to make acquisitions. Conversely, firms which believe that their stock is over- or correctly valued will use stock to make acquisitions. Not surprisingly, the premium paid is larger when an acquisition is financed with stock rather than cash. There might be an accounting rationale for using stock as opposed to cash. You are allowed to use pooling instead of purchase. There might also be a tax rationale for using stock. Cash acquisitions create tax liabilities to the selling firm's stockholders.

The use of stock to finance a merger may be a sign of an agency problem – that is, trying to exploit the information advantage the acquirer has over the target firm's shareholders. There is also the possibility that mergers may reflect agency problems between the acquiring firm's managers and its shareholders. There is evidence that mergers increase the private benefits of managers even when they do not benefit a firm's shareholders. A declining stock price may indicate that management is pursuing its own goals rather than solely attempting to maximise shareholder value.

The factors that the directors of the bidding company must consider include the following.

| Company and its existing shareholders | |
|---|---|
| **Dilution of earnings per share (EPS)** | Fall in EPS attributable to existing shareholders may occur if purchase consideration is in equity shares |
| **Cost to the company** | Use of loan stock to back cash offer will attract tax relief on interest and have lower cost than equity. Convertible loan stock can have lower coupon rate than ordinary stock |
| **Gearing** | Highly geared company may not be able to issue further loan stock to obtain cash for cash offer |
| **Control** | Control could change considerably if large number of new shares issued |
| **Authorised share capital increase** | May be required if consideration is in form of shares. This will involve calling a general meeting to pass the necessary resolution |
| **Borrowing limits increase** | General meeting resolution also required if borrowing limits have to change |

| Shareholders in target company | |
|---|---|
| **Taxation** | If consideration is cash, many investors may suffer immediate liability to tax on capital gain |
| **Income** | If consideration is not cash, arrangement must mean existing income is maintained, or be compensated by suitable capital gain or reasonable growth expectations |
| **Future investments** | Shareholders who want to retain stake in target business may prefer shares |
| **Share price** | If consideration is shares, recipients will want to be sure that the shares retain their values |

 Case Study

In 2014 the failed takeover bid made by US pharmaceutical company Pfizer for AstraZeneca was an all-paper bid. This contributed to the failure of the bid because AstraZeneca shareholders would have faced the risk of Pfizer shares (priced in dollars) falling after the acquisition.

## 1.7 Mezzanine finance and takeover bids

When the purchase consideration in a takeover bid is cash, the cash must be obtained somehow by the bidding company, in order to pay for the shares that it buys. Occasionally, the company will have sufficient cash in hand to pay for the target company's shares. More frequently, the cash will have to be raised, possibly from existing shareholders, by means of **a rights issue** or, more probably, by **borrowing from banks** or other financial institutions.

When cash for a takeover is raised by borrowing, the loans would normally be **medium term** and **secured**.

However, there have been many takeover bids, with a cash purchase option for the target company's shareholders, where the bidding company has arranged loans that:

(a)   Are **short to medium term**

(b)   Are **unsecured** (that is, 'junior' debt, low in the priority list for repayment in the event of liquidation of the borrower)

(c)   Because they are unsecured, attract a **much higher rate of interest** than secured debt (typically 4% or 5% above LIBOR)

(d)   Often give the lender the **option to exchange** the loan for shares after the takeover

This type of borrowing is called **mezzanine finance** (because it lies between equity and debt financing) – a form of finance which is also often used in **management buy-outs** (which are discussed later in this chapter).

## 1.8 Earn-out arrangements

The purchase consideration may not all be paid at the time of acquisition. Part of it may be deferred, payable on the target company reaching certain performance targets.

# 2 Assessing a given offer                                      Mar/Jun 16

**FAST FORWARD**

Shareholders of both the companies involved in a merger will be sensitive to the effect of the merger on **share prices** and **EPS**.

## 2.1 The market values of the companies' shares during a takeover bid

**Market share prices** can be very important during a takeover bid. Suppose that Velvet Inc decides to make a takeover bid for the shares of Noggin Inc. Noggin Inc shares are currently quoted on the market at $2 each. Velvet shares are quoted at $4.50 and Velvet offers one of its shares for every two shares in Noggin, thus making an offer at current market values worth $2.25 per share in Noggin. This is only the value of the bid so long as Velvet's shares remain valued at $4.50. If their value falls, the bid will become less attractive.

This is why companies that make takeover bids with a share exchange offer are always concerned that the market value of their shares should not fall during the takeover negotiations, before the target company's shareholders have decided whether to accept the bid.

If the market price of the target company's shares rises above the offer price during the course of a takeover bid, the bid price will seem too low, and the takeover is then likely to fail, with shareholders in the target company refusing to sell their shares to the bidder.

## 2.2 EPS before and after a takeover

If one company acquires another by issuing shares, its EPS will **go up or down** according to the price/earnings (P/E) ratio at which the target company has been bought.

(a)   If the **target company's shares** are **bought** at a **higher P/E** ratio than the bidding company's shares, the bidding company's shareholders will suffer a **fall in EPS**.

(b)   If the target company's shares are valued at a lower **P/E ratio**, the **predator company's shareholders** will benefit from a **rise in EPS**.

## 2.3 Example: Mergers and takeovers (1)

Giant Inc takes over Tiddler Co by offering two shares in Giant for one share in Tiddler. Details about each company are as follows:

|  | Giant Inc | Tiddler Co |
| --- | --- | --- |
| Number of shares | 2,800,000 | 100,000 |
| Market value per share | $4 | – |
| Annual earnings | $560,000 | $50,000 |
| EPS | 20p | 50p |
| P/E ratio | 20 | |

By offering two shares in Giant worth $4 each for one share in Tiddler, the valuation placed on each Tiddler share is $8 and, with Tiddler's EPS of 50c, this implies that Tiddler would be acquired on a P/E ratio of 16. This is lower than the P/E ratio of Giant, which is 20.

If the acquisition produces no synergy, and there is no growth in the earnings of either Giant or its new subsidiary Tiddler, then the EPS of Giant would still be higher than before, because Tiddler was bought on a lower P/E ratio. The combined group's results would be as follows:

|  | Giant group |
| --- | --- |
| Number of shares (2,800,000 + 200,000) | 3,000,000 |
| Annual earnings (560,000 + 50,000) | 610,000 |
| EPS | 20.33c |

If the P/E ratio is still 20, the market value per share would be $4.07 (20.33 × 20), which is 7c more than the pre-takeover price.

## 2.4 Example: Mergers and takeovers (2)

Redwood Inc agrees to acquire the shares of Hawthorn Co in a share exchange arrangement. The agreed P/E ratio for Hawthorn's shares is 15.

|  | Redwood Inc | Hawthorn Co |
| --- | --- | --- |
| Number of shares | 3,000,000 | 100,000 |
| Market price per share | $2 | – |
| Earnings | $600,000 | $120,000 |
| P/E ratio | 10 | |

The EPS of Hawthorn Co is $1.20, and so the agreed price per share will be $1.20 × 15 = $18. In a share exchange agreement, Redwood would have to issue 9 new shares (valued at $2 each) to acquire each share in Hawthorn, and so a total of 900,000 new shares must be issued to complete the takeover.

After the takeover, the enlarged company would have 3,900,000 shares in issue and, assuming no earnings growth, total earnings of $720,000. This would give an EPS of:

$$\frac{\$720,000}{3,900,000} = 18.5c$$

The pre-takeover EPS of Redwood was 20c, and so the EPS would fall. This is because Hawthorn has been bought on a higher P/E ratio (15 compared with Redwood's 10).

The process of buying a company with a lower P/E ratio and looking to boost its P/E ratio of the bidding company P/E ratio is known as **bootstrapping**. Whether the stock market is fooled by this process is debatable. The P/E ratio is likely to fall after the takeover in the absence of synergistic or other gains.

## 2.5 Buying companies on a higher P/E ratio, but with profit growth

Buying companies with a higher P/E ratio will result in a fall in EPS unless there is profit growth to offset this fall. For example, suppose that Starving Inc acquires Bigmeal Inc, by offering two shares in Starving for three shares in Bigmeal. Details of each company are as follows:

| | Starving Inc | Bigmeal Inc |
|---|---|---|
| Number of shares | 5,000,000 | 3,000,000 |
| Value per share | $6 | $4 |
| Annual earnings | | |
| Current | $2,000,000 | $600,000 |
| Next year | $2,200,000 | $950,000 |
| EPS | 40c | 20c |
| P/E ratio | 15 | 20 |

Starving Inc is acquiring Bigmeal Inc on a higher P/E ratio, and it is only the profit growth in the acquired subsidiary that gives the enlarged Starving group its growth in EPS.

| | Starving group |
|---|---|
| Number of shares (5,000,000 + 3,000,000 × 2/3) | 7,000,000 |

Earnings

If no profit growth (2,000,000 + 600,000) = $2,600,000  EPS would have been 37.14c
With profit growth (2,200,000 + 950,000) = $3,150,000  EPS will be 45c

If an acquisition strategy involves buying companies on a higher P/E ratio, it is therefore essential for continuing EPS growth that the acquired companies offer prospects of strong profit growth.

## 2.6 Further points to consider: Net assets per share and the quality of earnings

FAST FORWARD

There are circumstances where a dilution of earnings is acceptable if any of the following benefits arise as a result.

- Earnings growth
- Quality of earnings acquired is superior
- Dilution of earnings compensated by an increase in net asset backing

You might think that **dilution of earnings** must be avoided at all costs. However, there are **three** cases where a dilution of earnings might be accepted on an acquisition if there were other advantages to be gained.

(a)  **Earnings growth** may hide the dilution in EPS as above.

(b)  A company might be willing to accept earnings dilution if the **quality of the acquired company's earnings** is superior to that of the acquiring company.

(c)  A trading company with high earnings, but with few assets, may want to increase its assets base by acquiring a company which is strong in assets but weak in earnings so that assets and earnings get more in line with each other. In this case, **dilution in earnings is compensated for by an increase in net asset backing**.

**Question**
Effect of acquisition

Intangible Inc has an issued capital of 2,000,000 $1 ordinary shares. Net assets (excluding goodwill) are $2,500,000 and annual earnings average $1,500,000. The company is valued by the stock market on a P/E ratio of 8. Tangible Co has an issued capital of 1,000,000 ordinary shares. Net assets (excluding goodwill) are $3,500,000 and annual earnings average $400,000. The shareholders of Tangible Co accept an all-equity offer from Intangible Inc valuing each share in Tangible Co at $4. Calculate Intangible Inc's EPS and assets per share (APS) before and after the acquisition of Tangible Co.

(a)   Before the acquisition of Tangible Co, the position is as follows:

$$EPS = \frac{\$1,500,000}{2,000,000} = 75c$$

$$APS = \frac{\$2,500,000}{2,000,000} = \$1.25$$

(b)   Tangible Co's EPS figure is 40c ($400,000 ÷ 1,000,000), and the company is being bought on a multiple of 10 at $4 per share. As the takeover consideration is being satisfied by shares, Intangible Inc's earnings will be diluted because Intangible Inc is valuing Tangible Co on a higher multiple of earnings than itself. Intangible Inc will have to issue 666,667 (4,000,000/6) shares valued at $6 each (earnings of 75c per share at a multiple of 8) to satisfy the $4,000,000 consideration. The results for Intangible Inc will be as follows.

$$EPS = \frac{\$1,900,000}{2,666,667} = 71.25c \text{ (3.75c lower than the previous 75c)}$$

$$APS = \frac{\$6,000,000}{2,666,667} = \$2.25 \text{ (\$1 higher than the previous \$1.25)}$$

If Intangible Inc is still valued on the stock market on a P/E ratio of 8, the share price should fall by approximately 30c (8 × 3.75c, the fall in EPS) but because the asset backing $\left(\dfrac{\text{Net assets exc goodwill}}{\text{Shares}}\right)$ has been increased substantially the company will probably now be valued on a higher P/E ratio than 8.

The shareholders in Tangible Co would receive 666,667 shares in Intangible Inc in exchange for their current 1,000,000 shares; that is, two shares in Intangible for every three shares currently held.

(a)   **Earnings**

|  | $ |
|---|---|
| Three shares in Tangible earn (3 × 40c) | 1.200 |
| Two shares in Intangible will earn (2 × 71.25c) | 1.425 |
| Increase in earnings, per three shares held in Tangible | 0.225 |

(b)   **Assets**

|  | $ |
|---|---|
| Three shares in Tangible have an asset backing of (3 × $3.5) | 10.50 |
| Two shares in Intangible will have an asset backing of (2 × $2.25) | 4.50 |
| Loss in asset backing, per three shares held in Tangible | 6.00 |

The shareholders in Tangible Co would be trading asset backing for an increase in earnings.

# 3 Effect of an offer on financial position and performance
6/11

FAST FORWARD

Often takeovers fail to achieve their full potential because of lack of attention paid to **post-acquisition integration**. A clear programme should be in place, designed to redefine objectives and strategy, and take appropriate care of the human element.

## 3.1 Effects on earnings

Failures of takeovers often result from **inadequate integration** of the companies after the takeover has taken place. There is a tendency for senior management to devote their energies to the next acquisition rather than to the newly acquired firm. The particular approach adopted will depend on the **culture** of the organisation as well as the **nature** of the company acquired and **how it fits** into the amalgamated organisation (eg horizontally, vertically, or as part of a diversified conglomerate).

One obvious place to start is to assess how the merger will affect earnings. P/E ratios (price to earnings per share) can be used as a rough indicator for assessing the impact on earnings. The higher the P/E ratio of the acquiring firm compared to the target company, the greater the increase in EPS to the acquiring firm. Dilution of EPS occurs when the P/E ratio paid for the target exceeds the P/E ratio of the acquiring company. The size of the target's earnings is also important; the larger the target's earnings relative to the acquirer, the greater the increase to EPS for the combined company. The following examples will illustrate these points.

## Question | Effect of acquisition I

Greer Company has plans to acquire Holt Company by exchanging stock. Greer will issue 1.5 shares of its stock for each share of Holt. Financial information for the two companies is as follows.

|  | Greer | Holt |
| --- | --- | --- |
| Net income | $400,000 | $100,000 |
| Shares outstanding | 200,000 | 25,000 |
| EPS | $2.00 | $4.00 |
| Market price of stock | $40.00 | $48.00 |

Greer expects the P/E ratio for the combined company to be 15. What is the expected share price after the acquisition?

## Answer

Combined earnings = $400,000 + $100,000 = $500,000
Combined shares = 200,000 shares + (25,000 × 1.5) = 237,500
Combined EPS = $500,000/237,500 = $2.11
Expected price of stock = expected P/E ratio × combined EPS = 15 × $2.11 = $31.65

## Question | Effect of acquisition II

Romer Company will acquire all the outstanding stock of Dayton Company through an exchange of stock. Romer is offering $65.00 per share for Dayton. Financial information for the two companies is as follows.

|  | Romer | Dayton |
| --- | --- | --- |
| Net income | $50,000 | $10,000 |
| Shares outstanding | 5,000 | 2,000 |
| EPS | $10.00 | $5.00 |
| Market price of stock | $150.00 |  |
| P/E ratio | 15 |  |

*Required*

(a) Calculate the shares to be issued by Romer
(b) Calculate the combined EPS
(c) Calculate P/E ratio paid: price offered/EPS of target
(d) Compare P/E ratio paid to current P/E ratio
(e) Calculate maximum price before dilution of EPS

(a) Shares to be issued by Romer: $65/$150 × 2,000 shares = 867 shares to be issued.

(b) Combined EPS: ($50,000 + $10,000)/(5,000 + 867) = $10.23

(c) Calculate P/E ratio paid: price offered/EPS of target or $65.00/$5.00 = 13

(d) P/E ratio paid to current P/E ratio: since 13 is less than the current ratio of 15, there should be no dilution of EPS for the combined company.

(e) Maximum price before dilution of EPS: 15 = price/$5.00 or $75.00 per share. $75.00 is the maximum price that Romer should pay before EPS is diluted.

## 3.2 Effects on the statement of financial position

In this example we investigate the effects of a takeover on the financial position of a company by looking at the statement of financial position of the company. ABC Co is planning to bid for DEZ Co. The acquisition will be funded by cash which ABC will borrow.

STATEMENT OF FINANCIAL POSITION OF ABC

| Assets | $m | Liabilities | $m |
|---|---|---|---|
| Non-current assets | 600 | Short-term liabilities | 30 |
| Equity investments | 20 | Long-term liabilities | 100 |
| Receivables | 15 | Equity capital | 15 |
| Cash | 45 | Share premium | 35 |
| | | Earnings | 500 |
| | 680 | | 680 |

STATEMENT OF FINANCIAL POSITION OF DEZ CO

| Assets | $m | Liabilities | $m |
|---|---|---|---|
| Non-current assets | 80 | Short-term liabilities | 10 |
| Equity investments | 5 | Long-term liabilities | 10 |
| Receivables | 25 | Equity capital | 20 |
| Cash | 10 | Share premium | 30 |
| | | Earnings | 50 |
| | 120 | | 120 |

This is a cash offer funded entirely by the issue of debt. The company makes an offer of $120m which is raised by issuing corporate bonds worth $120m.

STATEMENT OF FINANCIAL POSITION OF ABC AFTER THE OFFER

| Assets | $m | Liabilities | $m |
|---|---|---|---|
| Non-current assets | 600 | Short-term liabilities | 30 |
| Equity investments | 20 | Long-term liabilities | 220 |
| Receivables | 15 | Equity capital | 15 |
| Cash | 45 | Share premium | 35 |
| Investment | 120 | Earnings | 500 |
| | 800 | | 800 |

CONSOLIDATED STATEMENT OF FINANCIAL POSITION

| Assets | $m | Liabilities | $m |
|---|---|---|---|
| Non-current assets | 680 | Short-term liabilities | 40 |
| Equity investments | 25 | Long-term liabilities | 230 |
| Receivables | 40 | Equity capital | 15 |
| Cash | 55 | Share premium | 35 |
| Goodwill | 20 | Earnings | 500 |
| | 820 | | 820 |

# Chapter Roundup

- Payment can be in the form of **cash**, a **share exchange** or **convertible loan stock**. The choice will depend on available cash, desired levels of gearing, shareholders' taxation position and changes in control.

- Shareholders of both the companies involved in a merger will be sensitive to the effect of the merger on **share prices** and **EPS**.

- There are circumstances where a dilution of earnings is acceptable if any of the following benefits arise as a result.

  – Earnings growth
  – Quality of earnings acquired is superior
  – Dilution of earnings compensated by an increase in net asset backing

- Often takeovers fail to achieve their full potential because of lack of attention paid to **post-acquisition integration**. A clear programme should be in place, designed to redefine objectives and strategy, and take appropriate care of the human element.

# Quick Quiz

1    What are the main factors a bidding company needs to consider in order to decide between a paper and a cash offer?

2    What are the main factors the shareholders of a target company need to consider in order to decide between a cash and a paper offer?

3    Yellow Company has plans to acquire Brown Company by exchanging stock. Yellow will issue two shares of its stock for each share of Brown. Financial information for the two companies is as follows.

|  | Yellow | Brown |
|---|---|---|
| Net income | 500 | 200 |
| Shares outstanding | 300 | 50 |
| EPS $ | 2.5 | 3.8 |
| Market price of stock | 38 | 50 |

Yellow expects the P/E ratio for the combined company to be 12. Produce an estimate of the value of the shares of the combined company.

# Answers to Quick Quiz

1     Dilution of EPS
      Cost of the company
      Gearing
      Control
      Authorised share capital increase
      Borrowing limits increase

2     Taxation
      Income
      Future investments
      Share price

3     Combined earnings = \$500,000 + \$200,000 = \$700,000
      Combined shares = 300,000 shares + (50,000 × 2) = 400,000
      Combined EPS = \$700,000/400,000 = \$1.75

      Expected price of stock    = expected P/E ratio × combined EPS
                                = 12 × \$1.75 = <u>\$21.00</u>

Now try the question below from the Practice Question Bank

| Number | Level | Marks | Time |
|--------|-------|-------|------|
| 26 | Introductory | 15 | 29 mins |

# Corporate reconstruction and reorganisation

# 13

# Financial reconstruction

| Topic list | Syllabus reference |
|---|---|
| 1 Reconstruction schemes | D1(a) |
| 2 Financial reconstructions | D1(a) |
| 3 Financial reconstruction and firm value | D1(b) |
| 4 Leveraged buy-outs (LBOs) | D1(a), (b) |
| 5 Market response to financial reconstruction | D1(b) |
| 6 Case study in financial reconstruction | D1(b) |

## Introduction

In this chapter we discuss financial restructuring in companies. Financial restructuring and other means of corporate reshaping can take place when companies are in difficulties or seeking to change their focus.

# Study guide

| | | Intellectual level |
|---|---|---|
| **D1** | **Financial reconstruction** | |
| (a) | Assess an organisational situation and determine whether a financial reconstruction is the most appropriate strategy for dealing with the problem as presented. | 3 |
| (b) | Assess the likely response of the capital market and/or individual suppliers of capital to any reconstruction scheme and the impact their response is likely to have upon the value of the organisation. | 3 |

# Exam guide

As with mergers and acquisitions, most questions in this area are likely to be a mixture of calculations (for example, assessing the financing mix for a management buy-out) and narrative (discussing the implications of a scheme of reconstruction on various interested parties). You may be asked to consider a reconstruction scheme and various alternatives (liquidation, selling off part or all of the company).

# 1 Reconstruction schemes

> **FAST FORWARD**
>
> **Reconstruction schemes** are undertaken when companies have got into difficulties or as part of a strategy to enhance the value of the firm for its owners.

## 1.1 Reconstruction schemes to prevent business failure

Not all businesses are profitable. Some incur losses in one or more years, but eventually achieve profitability. Others remain unprofitable, or earn only very small and unsatisfactory profits. Other companies are profitable, but run out of cash.

(a) A poorly performing company which is unprofitable, but has enough cash to keep going, might eventually decide to **go into liquidation**, because it is not worth carrying on in business. Alternatively, it might become the target of a successful takeover bid.

(b) A company which runs out of cash, even if it is profitable, might be forced into liquidation by **unpaid creditors**, who want payment and think that applying to the court to wind up the company is the best way of getting some or all of their money.

However, a company might be on the brink of going into liquidation, but hold out good promise of profits in the future. In such a situation, the company might be able to attract fresh capital and to persuade its creditors to accept some securities in the company as 'payment', and achieve a **capital reconstruction** which allows the company to carry on in business.

## 1.2 Reconstruction schemes for value creation

Reconstruction schemes may also be undertaken by companies which are not in difficulties as part of a strategy to create value for the owners of the company. The management of a company can improve operations and increase the value of the company by:

(a) Reducing costs through the sale of a poorly performing division or subsidiary

(b) Increasing revenue or reducing costs through the acquisition of a company to exploit revenue or cost economies

(c) Improving the financial structure of the company

## 1.3 Types of reconstruction

Depending on the actions that a company needs to take as part of its reconstruction plans, these schemes are usually classified in three categories.

(a) **Financial reconstruction**, which involves changing the capital structure of the firm

(b) **Portfolio reconstruction**, which involves making additions to or disposals from companies' businesses eg through acquisitions and spin-offs

(c) **Organisational restructuring**, which involves changing the organisational structure of the firm

## 1.4 Step by step approach to assessing reconstruction schemes

You can use the following approach to designing reconstructions:

**Step 1** **Estimate** the **position** of each party if **liquidation** is to go ahead. This will represent the minimum acceptable payment for each group.

**Step 2** **Assess additional sources of finance**, for example selling assets, issuing shares, raising loans. The company will most likely need more finance to keep going.

**Step 3** **Calculate** and **assess** the new position after the reconstruction examining how each affected group has fared, and compare with step 1 position.

**Step 4** Check that the company is **financially viable** after the reconstruction.

In addition, you should remember the following points when evaluating the proposed reconstruction:

(a) Anyone providing extra finance for an ailing company must be persuaded that the expected return from the extra finance is attractive. A **profit forecast** and a **cash forecast** or a **funds flow forecast** will be needed to provide reassurance about the company's future, to creditors and to any financial institution that is asked to put new capital into the company. The reconstruction must indicate that the company has a **good chance** of being **financially viable**.

(b) The actual reconstruction might involve the **creation of new share capital** of a **different nominal value** than existing share capital, or the cancellation of existing share capital.

It can also involve the conversion of equity to debt, debt to equity, and debt of one type to debt of another.

(c) For a scheme of reconstruction to be acceptable it needs to **treat all parties fairly** (for example, preference shareholders must not be treated with disproportionate favour in comparison with equity shareholders), and it needs to offer creditors a better deal than if the company went into liquidation. If it did not, the creditors would press for a winding up of the company. A reconstruction might therefore include an arrangement to pay off the company's existing debts in full.

# 2 Financial reconstructions                                   12/10, 12/15

There are many possible reasons why management would wish to restructure a company's finances. A reconstruction scheme might be agreed when a company is in danger of being put into liquidation, owing debts that it cannot repay, and so the creditors of the company agree to accept securities in the company, perhaps including equity shares, in settlement of their debts. On the other hand, a company may be willing to undergo some financial restructuring to better position itself for long-term success.

## 2.1 Leveraged recapitalisations

In leveraged recapitalisation a firm replaces the majority of its equity with a package of debt securities consisting of both senior and subordinated debt. Leveraged capitalisations are employed by firms as defence mechanisms to protect them from takeovers. The high level of debt in the company discourages corporate raiders who will not be able to borrow against the assets of the target firm in order to finance the acquisition.

In order to avoid the possible financial distress arising from the high level of debt, companies that engage in leveraged recapitalisation should be relatively debt free, have stable cash flows and not require substantial ongoing capital expenditure in order to retain their competitive position.

## 2.2 Debt/equity swaps                                                                             6/13

A second way of changing a company's capital is to issue a debt/equity or an equity/debt swap. In the case of an equity/debt swap, all specified shareholders are given the right to exchange their stock for a predetermined amount of debt (ie bonds) in the same company. A debt/equity swap works the opposite way: debt is exchanged for a predetermined amount of equity (or stock). The value of the swap is determined usually at current market rates, but management may offer higher exchange values to entice share- and debtholders to participate in the swap. After the swap takes place, the preceding asset class is cancelled for the newly acquired asset class.

One possible reason that the company may engage in debt/equity swaps is because the company must meet certain contractual obligations, such as maintaining a debt/equity ratio below a certain number. Also, a company may issue equity to avoid making coupon and face value payments because it feels it will be unable to do so in the future. The contractual obligations mentioned can be a result of financing requirements imposed by a lending institution, such as a bank, or may be self-imposed by the company, as detailed in the company's prospectus. A company may self-impose certain valuation requirements to entice investors to purchase its stock. Debt/equity swaps may also be carried out to rebalance a firm's weighted average cost of capital.

| Question | Financing policy |

For illustration, assume there is an investor who owns a total of $2,000 in ABC Inc stock. ABC has offered all shareholders the option to swap their stock for debt at a rate of 1.5. What is the amount worth of debt that the investor will receive?

Answer

The investor would receive, if they elected to take the swap, $3,000 (1.5 × $2,000) worth of debt, gaining $1,000 for switching asset classes. However, the investor would lose all rights as a shareholder, such as voting rights, if they swapped their equity for debt.

## 2.3 Leveraged buy-outs

A leveraged buy-out is a transaction in which a group of private investors uses debt financing to purchase a company or part of a company. In a leveraged buy-out, like a leveraged capitalisation, the company increases its level of leverage but, unlike the case of leveraged capitalisations, the company does not have access to equity markets any more. This is covered in more detail in Section 4 of this chapter.

## 2.4 Dividend policy

A company may change its dividend policy as part of financial restructuring and increase retained earnings and therefore its equity base.

# 3 Financial reconstruction and firm value

The impact of a financial reconstruction scheme on the **value** of the firm can be assessed in terms of its impact on the **growth rate** of the company, its **risk** and its **required rate of return**.

## 3.1 Effect on growth rate

The impact of changes in financial policy on the value of the firm can be assessed through one of the valuation models that we have considered in previous chapters. For example, the growth rate following a financial restructuring can be calculated from the formula $g = b \times re$.

Changes in the level of debt will be reflected in the growth rate through its impact on the debt ratio D/E and therefore its impact on the cost of equity. Similarly, changes in dividend policy can be reflected in the earnings growth rate. Changes in the dividend policy will change the value of b. Decreasing dividends (a higher b) will increase the growth rate, and increasing dividends will decrease the growth rate.

### Question
Financing policy

A firm currently has a debt/equity ratio of 0.12 and a return on equity equal to 16.2%. However, the optimal debt ratio is much lower than the optimal level, since it can raise the debt/equity ratio up to 0.30 without increasing the risk of bankruptcy. The firm plans to borrow and repurchase stock to get to this optimal ratio. The interest rate is expected to increase from 7% to 8%. The tax rate is 25% and the retention rate is 50%. Find the impact of the increase in debt on the growth rate.

### Answer

Before the increase in the debt ratio we have:

$g = b \times re$

$g = 0.5 \times 16.2 = 0.081$ or 8.1%

To see the impact of changing the level of gearing on the cost of equity we will use the Modigliani and Miller theory with tax following formula for cost of equity (introduced in Chapter 7a).

**Exam formula**

$$k_e = k_e^i + (1-T)(k_e^i - k_d)\frac{V_d}{V_e}$$

Where $k_e$ is the cost of equity in a geared company

$k_e^i$ is the cost of equity in an ungeared company

$V_d, V_e$ are the market values of debt and equity respectively

$k_d$ is the cost of debt pre-tax

Currently the $K_e = 16.2$ so the ungeared cost of equity can be calculated using

$$k_e = k_e^i + (1-T)(k_e^i - k_d)\frac{V_d}{V_e}$$

$$16.2 = k_e^i + (1-0.25)(k_e^i - 7)\frac{12}{100}$$

This simplifies to:

$16.2 = k_e^i + 0.09(k_e^i - 7)$

So $16.2 = 1.09 k_e^i - 0.63$

So $16.83 = 1.09 k_e^i$

So $16.83 / 1.09 = k_e^i = 15.44\%$

After the increase in the debt ratio to 0.3 we have:

$$k_e = k_e^i + (1-T)(k_e^i - k_d)\frac{V_d}{V_e}$$

$$k_e = 15.44 + (1-0.25)(15.44-8)\frac{30}{100}$$

So $k_e = 15.44 + 1.67 = 17.11$

$g = b \times re$

$g = 0.5 \times 0.1711 = 0.086$ or 8.6%

The increase in the debt/equity ratio will raise the growth rate from 8.1% to 8.6%.

## Question
Dividend policy

Continuing the previous example, suppose that the firm plans to reduce its dividend payout to 30% instead of increasing the debt ratio. What is the impact on the growth rate?

## Answer

The growth rate before the reduction in the dividend payout ratio is 0.081. The growth rate after the decrease in the payout rate (ie increase in b) is:

$g = b \times re$

$g = 0.7 \times 16.2 = 0.113$ or 11.3%

The increase in the retention rate will raise the growth rate from 8.1% to 11.3%; that is over three percentage points.

## 3.2 Effect on systematic risk

The impact of changes in financial policy on the value of the firm can be assessed through one of the valuation models that we have considered in previous chapters. For example, the risk following a financial restructuring can be calculated from the formula:

**Exam formulae**

$$\beta_a = \left[\frac{V_e}{(V_e + V_d(1-T))}\beta_e\right] + \left[\frac{V_d(1-T)}{(V_e + V_d(1-T))}\beta_d\right]$$

This is the **asset beta formula** on the exam formula sheet, and was introduced in Chapter 7a.

Where $\beta_a$ = is the asset beta
$\beta_e$ = is the geared beta

A higher level of debt will increase the geared beta of the company, and a lower level of debt will reduce it.

## Question
Effect on risk

A firm currently has a debt/equity ratio of 0.12 and an asset beta of 0.9. However, the optimal debt ratio is much lower than the optimal level, since it can raise the debt/equity ratio up to 0.30 without increasing the risk of bankruptcy. The firm plans to borrow and repurchase stock to get to this optimal ratio. The tax rate is 25%. Find the impact of the increase in debt on the geared beta.

The beta of debt can be assumed to be zero.

## Answer

Before the increase in the debt ratio we have:

D/E = 0.12
T = 0.25
$\beta_a$ = 0.9

$$\beta_a = \left[ \frac{V_e}{(V_e + V_d(1-T))} \beta_e \right] + \left[ \frac{V_d(1-T)}{(V_e + V_d(1-T))} \beta_d \right]$$

$$0.9 = \frac{100}{(100 + 12(0.75))} \beta_e$$

$$0.9 = 0.917 \beta_e$$

So $\beta_e = 0.981$

The new beta following the change in the level of debt to a debt to equity ratio of 0.3 will be:

$$\beta_a = \left[ \frac{V_e}{(V_e + V_d(1-T))} \beta_e \right] + \left[ \frac{V_d(1-T)}{(V_e + V_d(1-T))} \beta_d \right]$$

$$0.9 = \frac{100}{(100 + 30(0.75))} \beta_e$$

$$0.9 = 0.816 \beta_e$$

So $\beta_e = 0.9 / 0.816 = 1.10$

# 4 Leveraged buy-outs (LBOs)

**FAST FORWARD**

In an LBO a publicly quoted company is **acquired** by a specially established **private company**. The private company funds the acquisition by substantial borrowing.

## 4.1 Procedures for going private

A public company **'goes private'** when a **small group of individuals**, possibly including existing shareholders and/or managers and with or without support from a financial institution, **buys all the company's shares**. This form of restructuring is relatively common in the US and may involve the shares in the company ceasing to be listed on a stock exchange.

## 4.2 Advantages of LBOs

(a)     The **costs of meeting listing requirements** can be saved.

(b)     The **company is protected** from **volatility** in share prices which financial problems may create.

(c)     The company will be **less vulnerable** to hostile takeover bids.

(d)     Management can **concentrate** on the **long-term needs** of the business rather than the short-term expectations of shareholders.

(e)     Shareholders are likely to be **closer to management** in a private company, reducing costs arising from the separation of ownership and control (the 'agency problem').

### 4.3 Disadvantages of LBOs

The main disadvantage with LBOs is that the company loses its ability to have its shares publicly traded. If a share cannot be **traded** it may **lose some of its value**. However, one reason for seeking private company status is that the company has had difficulties as a quoted company, and the prices of its shares may be low anyway.

# 5 Market response to financial reconstruction

**FAST FORWARD** ▶▶

The **market response** to financial reconstruction has been estimated from **empirical studies** of the **behaviour** of **share prices**.

The empirical evidence shows that the market responds positively to financial restructuring. The available empirical evidence shows that the market reacts positively to firms raising their level of debt up to a certain level, since the constraint that debt imposes on future cash flows makes companies choosier when selecting investment opportunities.

A number of studies have dealt with the performance of **LBOs**. Since the company becomes private as a result of the LBO we cannot assess the impact of the market. However, most studies show that a company does significantly better after the LBO. More specifically, LBOs result in increases in free cash flow, improved operational efficiency and a greater focus on the company's core business. The causes of the improvement following financial restructuring are reportedly benign and cannot be attributed to lay-offs of employees – rather, the increased efficiency of operations coupled with improved control of capital expenditure seem to account for much of the difference.

The empirical evidence also shows that LBOs which involve divisions of companies seem to display larger improvement gains than corporate LBOs. On the other hand, the authors do enter a caveat, as the risk of bankruptcy and financial disaster with LBOs seems to be greater. Moreover, LBOs would appear to underinvest in long-term assets where the risk is greater.

The market reaction to dividend changes has been studied extensively. Most studies show abnormally high returns for dividend increases and abnormally low returns for dividend decreases around the announcement days.

# 6 Case study in financial reconstruction

**FAST FORWARD** ▶▶

A company **goes private** when a small group of individuals buys all the company's shares. Going private may **decrease costs** and make the company **less vulnerable** to hostile takeover bids.

### 6.1 Example: Financial reconstruction schemes

Crosby & Dawson Co is a private company that has for many years been making mechanical timing mechanisms for washing machines. The management was slow to appreciate the impact that new technology would have and the company is now faced with rapidly falling sales.

In July 20X1, the directors decided that the best way to exploit their company's expertise in the future was to diversify into the high precision field of control linkages for aircraft, rockets, satellites and space probes. By January 20X2, some sales had been made to European companies and sufficient progress had been made to arouse considerable interest from the major aircraft manufacturers and from NASA in the US. The cost, however, had been heavy. The company had borrowed $2,500,000 from the Vencap Merchant Bank plc and a further $500,000 from other sources. Its bank overdraft was at its limit of $750,000 and the dividend on its cumulative preference shares, which was due in December, had been unpaid for the fourth year in succession. On 1 February 20X2, the company has just lost another two major customers for its washing machine timers. The financial director presents the following information.

If the company remains in operation, the expected cash flows for the next five periods are as follows:

| | 9 months to 31.12.X2 | Years ending 31 December | | | |
| | | 20X3 | 20X4 | 20X5 | 20X6 |
| --- | --- | --- | --- | --- | --- |
| | $'000 | $'000 | $'000 | $'000 | $'000 |
| Receipts from sales | 8,000 | 12,000 | 15,000 | 20,000 | 30,000 |
| Payments to suppliers | 6,000 | 6,700 | 7,500 | 10,800 | 18,000 |
| Purchase of equipment | 1,000 | 800 | 1,600 | 2,700 | 2,500 |
| Other expenses | 1,800 | 4,100 | 4,200 | 4,600 | 6,400 |
| Interest charges | 800 | 900 | 700 | 400 | 100 |
| | 9,600 | 12,500 | 14,000 | 18,500 | 27,000 |
| Net cash flow | (1,600) | (500) | 1,000 | 1,500 | 3,000 |

The above figures are based on the assumption that the present capital structure is maintained by further borrowings as necessary.

STATEMENTS OF FINANCIAL POSITION

| | 31.12.X0 | 31.12.X1 | 31.3.X2 Projected |
| --- | --- | --- | --- |
| | $'000 | $'000 | $'000 |
| *Assets employed* | | | |
| *Non-current assets* | | | |
| Freehold property | 2,780 | 2,770 | 2,760 |
| Plant and machinery | 3,070 | 1,810 | 1,920 |
| Motor vehicles | 250 | 205 | 200 |
| *Deferred development expenditure* | – | 700 | 790 |
| *Current assets* | | | |
| Inventory | 890 | 970 | 1,015 |
| Receivables | 780 | 795 | 725 |
| | 1,670 | 1,765 | 1,740 |
| *Current liabilities* | | | |
| Trade payables | 1,220 | 1,100 | 1,960 |
| Bank overdraft (unsecured) | 650 | 750 | 750 |
| | 1,870 | 1,850 | 2,710 |
| | (200) | (85) | (970) |
| | 5,900 | 5,400 | 4,700 |
| *Long-term liabilities* | | | |
| 10% debentures 20X8 (secured on freehold property) | (1,000) | (1,000) | (1,000) |
| Other loans (floating charges) | – | (3,000) | (3,000) |
| | 4,900 | 1,400 | 700 |
| | $'000 | $'000 | $'000 |
| Ordinary shares of $1 | 3,500 | 3,500 | 3,500 |
| 8% cumulative preference shares | 1,000 | 1,000 | 1,000 |
| Accumulated reserves/(accumulated deficit) | 400 | (3,100) | (3,800) |
| | 4,900 | 1,400 | 700 |

**Other information**

1    The freehold property was revalued on 31 December 20X0. It is believed that its net disposal value at 31 March 20X2 will be about $3,000,000.

2    A substantial quantity of old plant was sold during the second six months of 20X1 to help pay for the new machinery needed. It is estimated that the break-up value of the plant at 31 March 20X2 will be about $1,400,000.

3    The motor vehicles owned at 31 March 20X2 could be sold for $120,000.

4     Much of the work done on the new control linkages has been patented. It is believed that these patents could be sold for about $800,000, which can be considered as the break-up value of development expenditure incurred to 31 March 20X2.

5     On liquidation, it is expected that the current assets at 31 March 20X2 would realise $1,050,000. Liquidation costs would be approximately $300,000.

A possible reconstruction scheme has been proposed, as follows:

(1)    The **existing ordinary shares** to be **cancelled** and **ordinary shareholders** to be **issued** with **$1,200,000 new $1 ordinary shares** in return for cash.

(2)    The **existing preference shares** to be **cancelled** and the holders to be issued with **$320,000 new $1 ordinary shares** at par.

(3)    The **existing debentures** to be **cancelled** and replaced by **$800,000 15% secured debentures** with a 15-year term and the holders to be issued with $400,000 of new $1 ordinary shares at par.

(4)    The **loan** 'from other sources' to be **repaid**.

(5)    The **Vencap Bank to receive $2,000,000 15% secured debentures** with a **15-year term** in part settlement of the existing loan, to be issued **$680,000 new ordinary shares** in settlement of the balance and to **subscribe cash for $800,000** of new ordinary shares.

(6)    The clearing bank to **transfer the existing overdraft** to a **loan account repayable over five years** and to keep the overdraft limit at $750,000. Both the loan and overdraft to be secured by a floating charge.

Evaluate whether the proposed scheme of reconstruction is likely to be acceptable to all the parties involved. **A full solution follows. Complete the first step yourself as a short question.**

| Question | Liquidation |
|---|---|

Ascertain the likely result of Crosby & Dawson Co (see above) going into liquidation as at 31 March 20X2.

## Answer

| Break-up values of assets at 31 March 20X2 | $'000 |
|---|---|
| Freehold | 3,000 |
| Plant and machinery | 1,400 |
| Motor vehicles | 120 |
| Patents | 800 |
| Current assets | 1,050 |
| | 6,370 |

| Total liabilities at 31 March 20X2 | $'000 |
|---|---|
| Debentures | 1,000 |
| Other loans | 3,000 |
| Bank overdraft | 750 |
| Trade payables | 1,960 |
| | 6,710 |

# Solution to remainder of the example

If the company was forced into liquidation, the debentures and other loans would be met in full but after allowing for the expenses of liquidation ($300,000) the bank and trade creditors would receive a total of $2,070,000 or 76c per dollar. The ordinary and preference shareholders would receive nothing.

If the company remains in operation, the cash position will at first deteriorate but will improve from 20X4 onwards. If the figures can be relied on and the trend of results continues after 20X6, the company will become reasonably profitable.

In the immediate future, after taking into account the additional amounts raised from the existing ordinary shareholders, the company will require finance of $400,000 in 20X2 and $500,000 in 20X3.

Vencap might be persuaded to subscribe **cash for ordinary shares**. It is unlikely that the company's clearing bank would be prepared to accept any shares, but as it would only receive 76c per dollar on a liquidation it may be prepared to transfer part of the overdraft into a (say) five-year loan while maintaining the current overdraft limit. It is unlikely that a suitable arrangement can be reached with the trade payables, as many would be prepared to accept 76c per dollar, rather than agree to a moratorium on the debts or take an equity interest in the company.

Evaluation of the proposed reconstruction scheme:

(1) **Debentureholders**

The debentures currently have **more than adequate asset backing**, and their current nominal yield is 10%. If the reconstruction is to be acceptable to them, they must have either **the same asset backing** or **some compensation** in terms of increased nominal value and higher nominal yield. Under the scheme they will receive securities with a total nominal value of $1,200,000 (an increase of $200,000) and an increase in total yield before any ordinary dividends of $20,000. The new debentures issued to Vencap can be secured on the freehold property (see below).

(2) **Loans from other sources**

It has been suggested that the 'loans from other sources' should be **repaid as**, in general, it is easier to arrange a successful reconstruction that involves fewer parties.

(3) **Vencap**

Vencap's existing loan of $2,500,000 will, under the proposed scheme, be changed into $2,000,000 of 15% debentures secured on the property and $680,000 of ordinary shares. This gives total loans of $2,800,000 secured on property with a net disposal value of $3,000,000. This is **low asset cover** which might increase if property values were to rise. The scheme will offer an improvement in security on the first $2,000,000 to compensate for the risk involved in holding ordinary shares. It has also been suggested that Vencap should be asked to subscribe $800,000 for new ordinary shares. The money is required to repay the 'loans from other sources' and to provide additional working capital. The issue of share capital would give the bank a total of 1,480,000 ordinary shares or 43.5% of the equity. From the company's point of view, issuing new equity is to be preferred to loan stock, as it will improve the gearing position.

(4) **The clearing bank**

In a liquidation now, the clearing bank would **receive approximately $573,000**. In return for the possibility of receiving the full amount owed to it, it is being asked under the scheme to **advance a further $750,000**. By way of compensation, it is receiving the **security of a floating charge**.

(5) **Preference shares**

In a liquidation at the present time, the preference shareholders would receive nothing. The issue of 320,000 $1 ordinary shares should be acceptable, as it is **equivalent to their current arrears of dividend**. If the preference shares were left unaffected by the scheme, the full arrears of dividend would become payable on the company's return to profitability, giving preference shareholders an undue advantage.

(6) **Ordinary shareholders**

In a liquidation, the ordinary shareholders would also receive nothing. Under the scheme, they will **lose control of the company** but, in exchange for their additional investment, will still hold about 35.3% of the equity in a company which will have sufficient funds to finance the expected future capital requirements.

**(7)     Cash flow forecast, on reconstruction**

|                                                   | $'000   |
|---------------------------------------------------|--------:|
| Cash for new shares from equity shareholders      | 1,200   |
| Cash for new shares from Vencap                   | 800     |
|                                                   | 2,000   |
| Repayment of loan from other sources              | (500)   |
| Cash available                                    | 1,500   |

The overdraft of $750,000 is converted into a long-term loan, leaving the company with a further $750,000 of overdraft facility to use.

**(8)     Adequacy of funds**

The statement of financial position below shows the company's position after the implementation of the scheme but before any repayments of short-term debt.

|                                               | $'000    | $'000    |
|-----------------------------------------------|---------:|---------:|
| *Non-current assets*                          |          |          |
| Freehold property                             |          | 2,760    |
| Plant and machinery                           |          | 1,920    |
| Motor vehicles                                |          | 200      |
| Deferred development expenditure              |          | 790      |
|                                               |          | 5,670    |
| *Current assets*                              |          |          |
| Inventory                                     | 1,015    |          |
| Receivables                                   | 725      |          |
| Cash                                          | 1,500    |          |
|                                               | 3,240    |          |
| Less current liabilities: trade payables      | (1,960)  |          |
|                                               |          | 1,280    |
|                                               |          | 6,950    |
| Less long-term liabilities                    |          |          |
| 15% debentures                                |          | (2,800)  |
| Loan from clearing bank                       |          | (750)    |
|                                               |          | 3,400    |
| Ordinary shares of $1                         |          | 3,400    |

It would seem likely that the company will have to make a bigger investment in working capital (ignoring cash) for the following reasons:

(a)     Presumably a substantial proportion of the sales will be exports which generally have a longer collection period than domestic sales.

(b)     It is unlikely that the trade creditors will accept the current payment position (average credit takes over two months) in the long term.

**(9)     Will the reconstructed company be financially viable?**

It is assumed that net current assets excluding cash and any overdraft will, by the end of 20X2, rise from the projected figure of –$220,000 (1,015,000 + 725,000 – 1,960,000) to $500,000 and will then increase in proportion to sales receipts thereafter, as shown below.

|                               | Revised X2                            | X3            | X4              | X5              | X6              |
|-------------------------------|---------------------------------------|---------------|-----------------|-----------------|-----------------|
| Sales change                  |                                       | +50%          | +25%            | +33%            | +50%            |
| Working capital               | 500                                   | 750 +50%      | 940 +25% approx | 1250 +33% approx| 1877 +50% approx|
| Change in working capital     | 720 vs original forecast of –220      | +250          | +190            | +310            | +630            |

It is also assumed that the equipment required in 20X2 and 20X3 will be leased on five-year terms and that the interest charges (including the finance elements in the lease rentals) will be approximately the same as those given in the question.

On these assumptions, the expected cash flows on implementation could be estimated as follows:

|  | 9 months to 31.12.X2 | 20X3 | 20X4 | 20X5 | 20X6 |
|---|---|---|---|---|---|
|  | $'000 | $'000 | $'000 | $'000 | $'000 |
| Receipts from sales | 8,000 | 12,000 | 15,000 | 20,000 | 30,000 |
| Purchase of equipment |  |  | 1,600 | 2,700 | 2,500 |
| Payments to suppliers | 6,000 | 6,700 | 7,500 | 10,800 | 18,000 |
| Other expenses | 1,800 | 4,100 | 4,200 | 4,600 | 6,400 |
| Interest charges | 800 | 900 | 700 | 400 | 100 |
| Lease rentals (excluding finance element) (say) | 200 | 360 | 360 | 360 | 360 |
| Bank loan repayment (say) | 150 | 150 | 150 | 150 | 150 |
| Invt. in working capital | 720 | 250 | 190 | 310 | 630 |
|  | 9,670 | 12,460 | 14,700 | 19,320 | 28,140 |
| Net movement | (1,670) | (460) | 300 | 680 | 1,860 |
| Cash balance b/f | 1,500 | (170) | (630) | (330) | 350 |
| Cash balance c/f | (170) | (630) | (330) | 350 | 2,210 |

These figures suggest that with an agreed overdraft limit of $750,000 the company will have **sufficient funds** to carry it through the next five years, assuming that the figures are reliable and that no dividends are paid until perhaps 20X4 at the earliest.

This scheme of reconstruction might not be acceptable to all parties, if the **future profits of the company** seem **unattractive**. In particular, Vencap and the clearing bank might be reluctant to agree to the scheme. In such an event, an alternative scheme of reconstruction must be designed, perhaps involving another provider of funds (such as another venture capitalist). Otherwise, the company will be forced into liquidation.

**Exam focus point**

In a reconstruction question you may be asked to set out the attributes of a successful reconstruction and discuss alternative strategies.

# Chapter Roundup

- **Reconstruction schemes** are undertaken when companies have got into difficulties or as part of a strategy to enhance the value of the firm for its owners.

- The impact of a financial reconstruction scheme on the **value** of the firm can be assessed in terms of its impact on the **growth rate** of the company, its **risk** and its **required rate of return**.

- In an LBO a publicly quoted company is **acquired** by a specially established **private company**. The private company funds the acquisition by substantial borrowing.

- The **market response** to financial reconstruction has been estimated from **empirical studies** of the **behaviour** of **share prices**.

- A company **goes private** when a small group of individuals buys all the company's shares. Going private may **decrease costs** and make the company **less vulnerable** to hostile takeover bids.

# Quick Quiz

1　Describe the procedures that should be followed when designing a financial reconstruction scheme.

2　Give five advantages of a public company going private.

1   (a)   Calculate what each party's position would be in a liquidation
    (b)   Assess possible sources of finance
    (c)   Assess each party's position as a result of the reconstruction
    (d)   Check that the company is financially viable

2   (a)   Saving of costs of legal formalities
    (b)   Protection from volatility in share prices
    (c)   Less vulnerability to hostile takeover
    (d)   More concentration on long-term needs of business
    (e)   Closer relationships with shareholders

**Now try the question below from the Practice Question Bank**

| Number | Level | Marks | Time |
|--------|-------|-------|------|
| 27 | Examination | 25 | 49 mins |

# 14

# Business reorganisation

| Topic list | Syllabus reference |
|---|---|
| 1 Business reorganisation | D2 |
| 2 Unbundling | D2(a), (b) |
| 3 Management buy-outs (MBOs) and buy-ins (MBIs) | D2(c) |
| 4 Unbundling and firm value | D2(a), (b) |

## Introduction

In this chapter we discuss methods of business reorganisations, concentrating primarily on methods of unbundling companies. Methods discussed include sell-offs, demergers and management buy-ins and buy-outs.

# Study guide

|  |  | Intellectual level |
|---|---|---|
| **D2** | **Business reorganisation** | |
| (a) | Recommend, with reasons, strategies for unbundling parts of a quoted company. | 3 |
| (b) | Evaluate the likely financial and other benefits of unbundling. | 3 |
| (c) | Advise on the financial issues relating to a management buy-out and buy-in. | 3 |

# Exam guide

As with mergers and acquisitions, most questions in this area are likely to be a mixture of calculations (for example, assessing the financing mix for a management buy-out) and narrative analysis (discussing the implications of disposals on various interested parties). You may be asked to advise the board on the various alternatives (demerger, selling off part or all of the company).

# 1 Business reorganisation                                   12/10, Mar/Jun 17

**FAST FORWARD**

> **Business reorganisations** consist of portfolio restructuring and organisational restructuring.

Reorganisations of the operations and structures of business is a constant feature of business life. Companies are restructuring in the pursuit of long-term strategy in order to achieve a higher level of performance or in order to survive when existing structures and activities are problematic. Corporate restructuring is usually the result of extreme changes in corporate governance, such as takeovers and bankruptcy, but it can also be initiated as a response to product market pressures and internal corporate controls. Companies which experience negative earnings due to competition, overexpansion, high costs and excessive debt respond in many ways, such as cutting research and development expenditure, reducing debt levels, reducing employment levels and introducing changes in the internal organisation.

In Chapter 13 we classified business restructuring as financial, portfolio and organisational. The last two types of restructuring are collectively known as business reorganisations. However, all three types of restructuring are linked and it may be necessary for all types to be undertaken for a restructuring to be successful. In this chapter we concentrate primarily on portfolio restructuring.

## 1.1 Portfolio restructuring

**FAST FORWARD**

> **Portfolio restructuring** consists of changes in the mix of assets owned by the firm or the lines of business in which the firm operates in order to increase the performance of the firm.

**Key term**

> **Portfolio restructuring** is the acquisition or disposal of assets or business units by a company in the form of divestments, demergers, spin-offs or management buy-outs.

Portfolio restructuring involves a number of one-off diverse transactions, such as the sale of underperforming assets, spin-offs and acquisitions, which have permanent effects on the financial performance of the company. Thus portfolio restructuring can be seen as part of a strategy to increase the performance of the company which involves not only the buying and selling of a business but also the establishment of performance monitoring and evaluation systems.

## 1.2 Organisational restructuring

> **Organisational restructuring** consists of changes in the organisational structure of the firm, such as divisional changes and hierarchical structures.

Organisational restructuring involves significant changes in the way a company is organised. As part of such a restructuring, a company may redraw divisional boundaries, flatten the hierarchical structure, streamline processes, adopt a different system of corporate governance and reduce employment.

Organisational restructuring on its own does not seem to have a significant effect on the performance of the company. However, when in conjunction with other forms of restructuring, it seems to be a more potent means of increasing performance.

# 2 Unbundling       12/10, 12/15, Mar/Jun 16, Mar/Jun 17

> **Unbundling** is a portfolio restructuring strategy which involves the disposal and sale of assets, facilities, production lines, subsidiaries, divisions or product units.

Unbundling can be voluntary or it can be forced on a company. A company may voluntarily decide to divest part of its business for strategic, financial or organisational reasons. An involuntary unbundling, on the other hand, may take place for regulatory or financial reasons. The main forms of unbundling are:

(a) Divestments
(b) Demergers
(c) Sell-offs
(d) Management buy-outs

## 2.1 Divestments

> **Divestment** is the partial or complete sale or disposal of physical and organisational assets, the shut-down of facilities and the reduction in workforce in order to free funds for investment in other areas of strategic interest.

In a divestment the company ceases the operation of a particular activity in order to concentrate on other activities. The rationale for divestment is normally to reduce costs or to increase return on assets. Divestments differ from the other forms of unbundling because they do not require the formation of a new company.

**Key term**

> A **divestment** is the disposal of a company's assets.

Divestments are undertaken for a variety of reasons. They may take place as a corrective action in order to reverse unsuccessful previous acquisitions, especially when the acquisition has taken place for diversification purposes. Divestments may also take place as a response to a cyclical downturn in the activities of a particular unit or line of business. However, divestments may be proactive in the sense that a company may want to exit lines of business which have become obsolete and redeploy resources to activities with a higher return on invested capital.

Where divestments are part of a strategic response for business realignment, the issue of which assets to divest is as important as the decision of which assets to acquire. A company has to decide what constitutes core activities and where the next growth opportunities exist. The growth opportunities may be realised by concentrating on the core business, organic growth and development of the right product lines, or by acquisitions and investment in the right markets.

This refocus of the company priorities may imply that the company may decide to disengage from certain business activities.

**FAST FORWARD**

> A **demerger, or spin-off,** is the splitting up of corporate bodies into two or more separate bodies, to ensure that share prices reflect the true value of underlying operations.

**Key term**

> A **demerger** is the opposite of a merger. It is the **splitting up of a corporate body into two or more separate and independent bodies**.

For example, the ABC Group plc might demerge by splitting into two independently operating companies AB plc and C plc. Existing shareholders are given a stake in each of the new separate companies.

Demerging, in its strictest sense, stops short of selling out, but is an attempt to ensure that share prices reflect the true value of the underlying operations.

### Case Study

In 2015 BHP Billiton, the Australian mining company, demerged into (new) BHP Billiton and South32. The new BHP Billiton will focus on mining key resources such as iron, copper, potash etc. South32 will focus on areas that had been neglected such as aluminium, nickel, solver etc. Shareholders received one share in each new company in exchange for 1 share in the old company.

### 2.2.1 Advantages of demergers

(a) The main advantage of a demerger is its **greater operational efficiency and the greater opportunity to realise value**. A two-division company with one loss-making division and one profit-making, fast-growing division may be better off splitting the two divisions. The profitable division may acquire a valuation well in excess of its contribution to the merged company.

(b) Even if both divisions are profit making, a demerger may still have benefits. Management can focus on **creating value for both companies individually and implementing a suitable financial structure** for each company. The full value of each company may then become appropriate.

(c) Shareholders will continue to own both companies, which means that the **diversification of their portfolio** will **remain unchanged**.

(d) The **ability** to raise **extra finance**, especially debt finance, to support new investments and expansion may be reduced.

### 2.2.2 Disadvantages of demergers

(a) The **demerger process may be expensive**.

(b) **Economies of scale** may be **lost**, where the demerged parts of the business had operations (and skills) in common to which economies of scale applied.

(c) The **smaller companies** which result from the demerger will have **lower revenue**, profits and status than the group before the demerger.

(d) There may be **higher overhead** costs as a percentage of revenue, resulting from (b).

(e) The **ability** to raise **extra finance**, especially debt finance, to support new investments and expansion may be reduced.

(f) **Vulnerability to takeover** may be **increased**. The impact on a firm's risk may be significant when a substantial part of the company is spun off. The result may be a loss in shareholder value if a relatively low beta element is unbundled.

A **sell-off** is the sale of part of a company to a third party, generally for cash.

**Key term**

> A **sell-off** is a form of **divestment** involving the sale of part of a company to a third party, usually another company. Generally, cash will be received in exchange.

### 2.3.1 Reasons for sell-offs

As part of its strategic planning, a company has decided to **restructure**, concentrating management effort on particular parts of the business. Control problems may be reduced if peripheral activities are sold off.

It wishes to sell off a part of its business which **makes losses**, and so to improve the company's future reported consolidated profit performance. This may be in the form of a management buy-out (MBO) – see below.

In order to **protect the rest of the business from takeover**, it may choose to sell a part of the business which is particularly attractive to a buyer.

The company may be **short of cash, or may have high levels of financial gearing**.

A **subsidiary** with **high risk** in its operating cash flows could be sold, so as to reduce the business risk of the group as a whole. However, as in point (e) in Section 2.2.2 above, the reverse may actually be the case.

A **subsidiary** could be sold at a **profit**. Some companies have specialised in taking over large groups of companies, and then selling off parts of the newly acquired groups, so that the proceeds of sales more than pay for the original takeovers.

### Case Study

Concerns over G4S's high debt levels and poor cash flow could lead the management to signal a cut to the shareholder payout at its half-year results, analysts believe.

The world's largest security business is undertaking a major disposal programme under Ashley Almanza, who took the top job in 2013 with a remit to streamline the business after years of break-neck expansion, and also get it back on track after a series of scandals, most notably its failure to provide sufficient security for the London Olympics in 2012.

G4S said net debt was 3.3 times earnings – close to its banking covenant of 3.5 times – and JP Morgan also cited concerns about this level. The broker noted that post-Brexit uncertainty could make it harder to find buyers for the large divisions G4S is trying to sell, the main route to cutting its debt pile.

Sterling's weakness in the wake of the EU referendum has also increased pressure on the company, which has almost half its £1.78bn of debt in currency other than the pound, making repayments more expensive.

*(Tovey, 2016)*

### 2.3.2 Liquidations

The extreme form of a sell-off is where the entire business is sold off in a **liquidation**. In a voluntary dissolution, the shareholders might decide to close the whole business, sell off all the assets and distribute net funds raised to shareholders.

# 3 Management buy-outs (MBOs) and buy-ins (MBIs)

FAST FORWARD

> An **MBO** is the purchase of all or part of the business by its managers. MBOs can be the best way of maintaining links with a subsidiary, and can ensure the co-operation of management if a disposal is inevitable.
>
> The main complication with **MBOs** is obtaining the consent of all parties involved. Venture capital may be an important source of financial backing.

**Key term**

> An **MBO** is the purchase of all or part of a business from its owners by its managers.

For example, the directors of a subsidiary company in a group might buy the company from the holding company, with the intention of running it as proprietors of a separate business entity.

(a) **To the managers**, the buy-out would be a method of setting up in business for themselves.

(b) **To the group**, the buy-out would be a method of **divestment**, selling off the subsidiary as a going concern.

Where the management team are from outside the existing business, this is referred to as a **management buy-in (MBI)**. In this case the management team will tend to be a group of managers with specialist skills in running a particular type of business. They will often have a strong vision for developing this type of business in the future. They will look to buy underperforming businesses with strong future potential.

Sometimes the management team will be a combination of an MBO (ie existing management) and new managers (with specialist skills that the existing management team do not have eg finance). This is sometimes referred to as a buy-in management buy-out or a **BIMBO**!

## 3.1 The parties to a buy-out

There are usually three parties to an MBO.

(a) A **management team** wanting to make a buy-out. This team ought to have the skills and ability to convince financial backers that it is worth supporting.

(b) **Directors** of a group of companies, who make the divestment decision.

(c) **Financial backers** of the buy-out team, who will usually want an equity stake in the bought-out business, because of the **venture capital risk** they are taking. Often, several financial backers provide the venture capital for a single buy-out.

**The management team making the buy-out** would probably have the aims of setting up in business themselves, being owners rather than mere employees; or avoiding redundancy, when the subsidiary is threatened with closure.

## 3.2 Reasons for an MBO or MBI

**A large organisation's board of directors** may agree to an MBO of a subsidiary for any of a number of different reasons.

(a) The **subsidiary** may be **peripheral** to the group's mainstream activities, and no longer fit in with the group's overall strategy.

(b) The **group may** wish to **sell off a loss-making subsidiary**, and a management team may think that it can restore the subsidiary's fortunes.

(c) The parent company may need to **raise cash quickly**.

(d) The subsidiary may be part of a **group** that has just been **taken over** and the new parent company may wish to sell off parts of the group it has just acquired.

(e) The **best offer price** might come from a **small management group** wanting to arrange a buy-out.

(f)  When a group has taken the decision to sell a subsidiary, it will probably get better co-operation from the management and employees of the subsidiary if the sale is an MBO.

(g)  The sale can be arranged more quickly than a **sale** to an **external party**.

(h)  The selling organisation is more likely to be able to maintain beneficial links with a segment sold to management rather than to an **external party**.

**A private company's shareholders** might agree to sell out to a management team because they need cash, they want to retire, or the business is not profitable enough for them.

To help convince a bank or other institution that it can run the business successfully, the management team should prepare a **business plan** and estimates of sales, costs, profits and cash flows, in reasonable detail.

 Case Study

A businessman who started his career on the factory floor of a manufacturing company before working his way up to become managing director has helped lead a £26 million management buyout of the business.

Richard Lee, managing director of **Jablite**, which also operates under the **Styropack** name, joined with fellow bosses to purchase the business from European owner Synbra.

The company produces expanded polystyrene (EPS), with Jablite delivering products used in the construction industry for insulation, while Styropack makes protective packaging out of the material to be used in industries including food, horticulture and pharmaceuticals.

The deal, which also saw **Mobeus Equity Partners** inject a £5 million equity stake, will create what is believed to be the dominant player in Britain's £160 million EPS industry, with more than a quarter of the market.

The combined companies employ almost 150 staff at five UK locations in Aberdeen, Kent, Lancashire, East Yorkshire and West Sussex. Last year they had total revenues of £44 million and earnings before interest, taxation, depreciation and amortisation of £3.5 million.

The ownership of the business will be split 60:40, with Mobeus holding the smaller portion and the remainder divided between Mr Lee, finance director Ken Hutchins, operations director Wayne Brown and chairman John Colley.

Mr Lee said management first thought about the buyout almost two years ago, having successfully turned around Jablite, which made a £3.5 million loss in 2010, while Styropack was swinging between making losses and profits.

'We wanted to be in control of our own destiny, having made the businesses profitable,' Mr Lee said. 'Synbra is a large operation with its own priorities and we felt we could be more focused.'

The managers are targeting growth mainly though the Jablite business, hoping to take advantage of the housing shortage. 'Both the main [political] parties have said building more homes is a manifesto.'

*(Tovey, 2015)*

## 3.3 The role of the venture capitalist

Knowledge brought forward from earlier studies

---

**Venture capital**

- **Venture capital** is risk capital, normally provided in return for an equity stake.

- Examples of **venture capital organisations** in the UK are 3i, Equity Capital for Industry and the various venture capital subsidiaries of the clearing banks.

- Venture capital **may be provided to fund** business start-ups, business development, MBOs and the purchase of shares from one of the owners of the business.

- Venture capital can also be provided through **venture capital funds**, which is a pool of finance provided by a variety of investors, which will then be applied to MBOs or expansion projects.

- Venture capitalists will normally require an **equity stake** in the company and may wish to have a **representative on the board** to look after its interests.

- A number of clearly defined **exit routes** will be sought by the venture capitalists in order to ensure the easy realisation of their investment when required.

Venture capitalists are far more inclined to fund MBOs, management buy-ins (MBIs) and corporate expansion projects than the more risky and relatively costly early stage investments, such as start-ups. The minimum investment considered in the UK will normally be around £100,000, with average investment of £1 million to £2 million.

While the return required on venture capital for the high-risk, early stage investments may be as high as 80%, where the funding is for a well-established business with sound management, it is more commonly around the 25–30% mark. While this may be achieved by the successful investments, of course there will be many more that fail, and the overall returns on venture capital funds averages out at around 10–15%.

For MBOs and MBIs the venture capitalist will not necessarily provide the majority of the finance – a £50 million buy-out may be funded by, say, £15 million venture capital, £20 million debt finance and £15 million mezzanine debt, discussed earlier.

Venture capital funds may require:

- A significant minority shareholding eg 20–30%
- Special rights to appoint a number of directors
- The company to seek their prior approval for new issues or acquisitions

### 3.3.1 Exit strategies

Venture capitalists generally like to have a predetermined **target exit date**, the point at which they can recoup some or all of their investment in an MBO. At the outset, they will wish to establish various **exit routes**, the possibilities including:

(a) The sale of shares to the public or to institutional investors following a **flotation** of the company's shares on a recognised stock exchange, or on the equivalent of the UK's Alternative Investment Market

(b) The **sale** of the company to another firm

(c) The **repurchase** of the venture capitalist's shares by the company or its owners

(d) The sales of the venture capitalist's shares to an **institution**, such as an investment trust

## 3.4 The appraisal of proposed buy-outs

### 3.4.1 How likely is an MBO to succeed?

Management-owned companies seem to achieve better performance probably because of:

- A **favourable buy-out price** having been achieved
- **Personal motivation and determination**
- **Quicker decision making** and so **more flexibility**
- **Keener decisions** and action on pricing and debt collection
- **Savings in overheads**, eg in contributions to a large head office

However, many MBOs, once they occur, begin with some redundancies to cut running costs.

### 3.4.2 How should an institutional investor evaluate a buy-out?

An institutional investor (such as a venture capitalist) should evaluate a buy-out before deciding whether or not to finance. Aspects of any buy-out that ought to be checked are as follows:

(a)   Does the management team have the **full range of management skills** that are needed (for example, a technical expert and a finance director)? Does it have the right blend of experience? Does it have the commitment?

(b)   **Why** is the **company for sale**? The possible reasons for buy-outs have already been listed. If the reason is that the parent company wants to get rid of a loss-making subsidiary, what evidence is there to suggest that the company can be made profitable after a buy-out?

(c)   What are the **projected profits and cash flows** of the business? The prospective returns must justify the risks involved.

(d)   What is **being bought**? The buy-out team might be buying the shares of the company, or only selected assets of the company. Are the assets that are being acquired sufficient for the task? Will more assets have to be bought? When will the existing assets need replacing? How much extra finance would be needed for these asset purchases? Can the company be operated profitably?

(e)   What is the **price**? Is the price right or is it too high?

(f)   What **financial contribution** can be made by members of the management team themselves?

(g)   What are the **exit routes** and when might they be taken?

## 3.5 The financial arrangements in a typical buy-out

Typically, the **buy-out team** will have a **minority** of the equity in the bought-out company, with the **various financial backers** holding a **majority** of the shares between them. A buy-out might have several financial backers, each providing finance in exchange for some equity.

Investors of venture capital usually want the **managers to be financially committed**. Individual managers could borrow personally from a bank, say, $20,000 to $50,000.

The suppliers of equity finance might insist on investing part of their capital in the form of **redeemable convertible preference shares**. These often have voting rights should the preference dividend fall in arrears, giving increased influence over the company's affairs. They are issued in a redeemable form to give some hope of taking out part of the investment if it does not develop satisfactorily, and in convertible form for the opposite reason: to allow an increased stake in the equity of a successful company.

## 3.6 Problems with buy-outs

A common problem with MBOs is that the managers have little or no experience in **financial management** or **financial accounting**.

Other problems are:

(a)   Tax and legal complications

(b)   Difficulties in deciding on a fair price to be paid

(c)   Convincing employees of the need to change working practices

(d)   Inadequate cash flow to finance the maintenance and replacement of tangible non-current assets

(e)   The maintenance of previous employees' pension rights

(f)   Accepting the board representation requirement that many sources of funds will insist on

(g)   The loss of key employees if the company moves geographically, or wage rates are decreased too far, or employment conditions are unacceptable in other ways

(h)   Maintaining continuity of relationships with suppliers and customers

## 3.7 Buy-ins

**Key term**

> 'Buy-in' is when a team of **outside managers**, as opposed to managers who are already running the business, mount a takeover bid and then run the business themselves.

An MBI might occur when a business venture is running into trouble, and a group of outside managers see an opportunity to take over the business and restore its profitability.

Alternatively, research suggests that buy-ins often occur when the major shareholder of a small family company wishes to retire.

Many features are common to MBOs and MBIs, including **financing**.

Buy-ins work best for companies where the existing managers are being replaced by managers of **much better quality**. However, managers who come in from outside may take **time** to get used to the company, and may encounter **opposition** from employees if they seek to introduce significant changes.

# 4 Unbundling and firm value

**FAST FORWARD**

> The main effect of **unbundling** on the **value** of the **firm** comes through changes in the **return on assets** and the **asset beta**.

## 4.1 Effect on growth rate

The impact of unbundling on the value of the firm can be assessed through one of the valuation models that we have considered in previous chapters. For example, the growth rate following a restructuring can be calculated from the formula $g = b \times re$.

This formula has been introduced in Chapter 7a and Chapter 13.

When firms divest themselves of existing investments, they affect their expected return on assets, as good projects increase the projected return and bad projects reduce the return – and any investment decision taken by firms affects their riskiness and therefore the asset beta $\beta_a$.

**Question**　　　　　　　　　　　　　　　　　　　　　　　　　　　　　Divestment policy

A firm is expected to divest itself of unrelated divisions, which have historically had lower returns. As a result of the divestment, the return on equity is expected to increase from 10% to 15%.

**Answer**

Before the restructuring the growth rate is equal to:

$g = b \times re$

$g = 0.5 \times 0.10 = 0.05$ or 5%

After the restructuring the growth rate is equal to:

$g = 0.5 \times 0.15 = 7.5\%$

The restructuring has increased the growth rate from 5% to 7.5%.

The business risk of an oil company which has diversified into a number of other activities such as leisure and tourism is 1.3. If the oil company divested itself of all other activities and concentrated on its core business, its beta, based on the observed beta of oil companies with similar financial structure, is expected to be 1.4 ($\beta_e = 1.4$). If the tax rate is 0.25 and the debt to equity ratio is 0.30, calculate the business risk following the divestment of business.

Answer

The beta of the company is related to its business beta through the relationship:

**Exam Formulae**

$$\beta_a = \left[ \frac{V_e}{(V_e + V_d(1-T))} \beta_e \right] + \left[ \frac{V_d(1-T)}{(V_e + V_d(1-T))} \beta_d \right]$$

This is the **asset beta formula** on the exam formula sheet, and was introduced in Chapter 7a.

$$\beta_a = \frac{100}{(100 + 30(1-0.25))} 1.4 = 1.14$$

After the restructuring, the business risk of the company is reduced from 1.3 to 1.14, implying a lower cost of equity and consequently a higher value of equity.

# Chapter Roundup

- **Business reorganisations** consist of portfolio restructuring and organisational restructuring.

- **Portfolio restructuring** consists of changes in the mix of assets owned by the firm or the lines of business in which the firm operates in order to increase the performance of the firm.

- **Organisational restructuring** consists of changes in the organisational structure of the firm, such as divisional changes and hierarchical structures.

- **Unbundling** is a portfolio restructuring strategy which involves the disposal and sale of assets, facilities, production lines, subsidiaries, divisions or product units.

- **Divestment** is the partial or complete sale or disposal of physical and organisational assets, the shut-down of facilities and the reduction in workforce in order to free funds for investment in other areas of strategic interest.

- A **demerger, or spin-off** is the splitting up of corporate bodies into two or more separate bodies, to ensure that share prices reflect the true value of underlying operations.

- A **sell-off** is the sale of part of a company to a third party, generally for cash.

- An **MBO** is the purchase of all or part of the business by its managers. MBOs can be the best way of maintaining links with a subsidiary, and can ensure the co-operation of management if a disposal is inevitable.

- The main complication with **MBOs** is obtaining the consent of all parties involved. Venture capital may be an important source of financial backing.

- The main effect of **unbundling** on the **value** of the **firm** comes through changes in the **return on assets** and the **asset beta**.

1    Fill in the blank.

A ........................................ is a splitting up of a corporate body into two independent bodies.

2    Fill in the blank.

A ........................................ involves the sale of part of a company to a third party.

3    Fill in the blank.

In a ........................................ , a new company is created whose shares are owned by the shareholders of the old company.

4    Name three factors that an institutional investor will consider when deciding whether to invest in an MBO.

5    Give four examples of possible exit strategies for a venture capitalist.

6    What is an MBI?

# Answers to Quick Quiz

1    Demerger

2    Sell-off

3    Demerger

4    Any three of:

    (a)    Management skills
    (b)    Reason why company is for sale
    (c)    Projected profits and cash flows of the business
    (d)    What is being bought
    (e)    Price
    (f)    Financial contribution made by the management team
    (g)    Exit routes

5    (a)    Sale of shares to public or institutional investors following a flotation
    (b)    Sale of shares to another company
    (c)    Sale to company itself or its owners
    (d)    Sale to institution management

6    A buy-in is when a team of outside managers mount a takeover bid and run the business.

**Now try the question below from the Practice Question Bank**

| Number | Level | Marks | Time |
|--------|-------|-------|------|
| 28 | Introductory | 12 | 23 mins |

# Treasury and advanced risk management techniques

# The role of the treasury function in multinationals

| Topic list | Syllabus reference |
|---|---|
| 1 The role of financial and money markets | E1(a) |
| 2 Banks and other financial institutions in the money markets | E1(a) |
| 3 Money market instruments | E1(a) |
| 4 The treasury management function | E1(a) |

## Introduction

The purpose of this chapter is to discuss the role of the **treasury function** within a **multinational company**. The treasury function deals primarily with **short-term** decisions but in a way which is consistent with the **long-term** management objective of **maximising shareholder value**.

The chapter starts with a discussion of the role of the **money markets**, and how these provide **short-term finance** for companies. The chapter then discusses the role of banks and **financial institutions** in **financial intermediation** and the various instruments that are traded on this market.

Much of this chapter covers assumed knowledge of material that is covered in *Financial Management (FM)*. However, if you studied FM before 2013, this material will be new to you and must be studied.

The chapter ends with a discussion of **the treasury management function** in a modern organisation.

# Study guide

| | | Intellectual level |
|---|---|---|
| **E1** | **The role of the treasury function in multinationals** | |
| (a) | Discuss the role of the treasury management function within: | 3 |
| | (i)    The short-term management of the organisation's financial resources | |
| | (ii)   The longer-term maximisation of shareholder value | |
| | (iii)  The management of risk exposure | |

The first three sections in this chapter cover material that, from 2013, is part of the *Financial Management (FM)* syllabus and becomes assumed knowledge for this exam. If you have not covered these topics in FM then it is important that you read and understand these sections.

# 1 The role of financial and money markets

## 1.1 Financial markets

**FAST FORWARD**

> Financial markets are the markets where economic units with surplus funds, such as individuals, corporations, the Government and overseas investors, lend funds to other economic units that want to borrow.

Financial markets can be classified in a variety of ways depending on the criterion selected. The most common groupings are primary and secondary markets, over the counter and exchange-based markets and money and capital markets. A brief description follows.

## 1.2 Primary and secondary markets

**FAST FORWARD**

> Markets where a security is first issued are known as primary, and markets where a security is subsequently traded are known as secondary.

**Key term**

> A **primary market** is a financial market in which new issues of a security are sold by the issuer to initial buyers. A **secondary market** is a market in which securities that have already been issued can be bought and sold.

## 1.3 Exchange and over the counter markets

**FAST FORWARD**

> Secondary markets can be organised as exchanges or over the counter (OTC).

**Secondary markets** for financial securities can be organised as **exchanges**, where buyers and sellers of securities buy and sell securities in one location, the exchange. Examples of exchanges include the **London Stock Exchange** and the **New York Stock Exchange** for the trading of shares, the **Chicago Board of Trade** for the trading of commodities, and the **London International Financial Futures and Options Exchange** for the trading of derivatives.

Alternatively, secondary markets can operate as **over the counter (OTC)** markets, where buyers and sellers transact with each other not through an exchange but through individual negotiation. The prices at which securities are bought OTC do not differ from the corresponding transactions in an exchange because participants are in constant contact through computers with other market participants and can therefore transact at the most competitive price.

Securities that are issued in an **OTC market** and can be **resold** are called **negotiable**, and securities that are **not allowed** to be **resold** after they are issued are called **non-negotiable**.

### 1.4 Money and capital markets

**Capital markets** are markets in which the securities that are traded have **long maturities**, ie represent **long-term obligations** for the **issuer**. Securities that trade in capital markets include shares and bonds. **Money markets**, on the other hand, are markets in which the securities that are traded have short maturities, less than a year, and the repayment of funds borrowed is required within a short period of time.

# 2 Banks and other financial institutions in the money markets

**Financial intermediaries** borrow money from the **lender savers** and then in turn make loans to the borrower spenders. The most common financial intermediaries are banks, insurance companies, pension funds, mutual funds and finance companies. The process of **borrowing** and **lending** through **intermediaries** is called **financial intermediation or indirect finance**. As a source of funds for businesses, **indirect finance** is far more common than **direct finance**.

## 2.1 The importance of financial intermediation

Financial intermediation is important for two main reasons, namely the presence of **transaction costs** and the presence of **credit risk**.

#### The presence of transaction costs

Transaction costs (time and money spent carrying out financial transactions) are often prohibitively high for individual borrowers and lenders. Financial intermediaries, by handling a large volume of such transactions, develop an expertise that allows them to make additional transactions much more cheaply than any individual could. Financial intermediaries exploit **economies of scale**. By conducting a very **high volume of business**, they reach a point where the unit cost of transactions becomes smaller and smaller.

#### The presence of credit risk

The second reason for the importance of financial intermediaries is **asymmetric information**. The borrower has much better information about their ability and intention to repay than the lender does. This exposes the lender to **credit risk**. An individual lender will not normally have the ability to ascertain the **credit risk** of another individual. A bank, on the other hand, employs a number of specialists who are in a better position to evaluate the **credit quality** of an individual and it may have access to information on an individual that would be too costly for an individual lender to acquire.

## 2.2 Securitisation

**FAST FORWARD**

> **Securitisation** is the process of converting **illiquid assets** into **marketable asset-backed securities**. The development of **securitisation** has led to **disintermediation** and a reduction in the role of financial intermediaries, as borrowers can reach lenders directly.

Securitisation is the process of converting **illiquid assets** into **marketable securities**. These securities are backed by specific assets and are normally called **asset-backed securities**. This topic has been covered in Chapter 4a.

The development of securitisation has led to **disintermediation** and a reduction in the role of financial intermediaries, as borrowers can reach lenders directly.

**Key term**

> **Disintermediation** describes a decline in the traditional deposit and lending relationship between banks and their customers and an increase in direct relationships between the ultimate suppliers and users of financing.

# 3 Money market instruments

One way in which you can demonstrate competence in the performance objective 'manage cash using active cash management and treasury systems' is to ensure that any financial instruments held to meet liabilities mature on a timely basis. This section introduces various money market instruments and how they can be used to cover liabilities. The various features of each instrument will be useful in practice to determine the best one to use in different situations, not only to cover the risk involved but also to cover the risk for the required period.

**FAST FORWARD**

> **Money markets** are the markets where **short-term instruments** are traded.

**Money markets** are the markets where **short-term instruments** are traded. Money markets are OTC markets and the transactions take place between **institutions** rather than individual investors. The main characteristic of money market instruments, apart from their short maturities (up to 12 months), is that they normally have only one cash flow. Money market instruments can be either **negotiable** or **non-negotiable**. They can also be **coupon bearing** or **discount instruments**.

**Discount instruments** do not pay interest. They are issued and traded at a **discount to the face value**. The discount is equivalent to the interest paid to the investor and is the difference between the purchase price of the instrument and the price at maturity.

Purchase price = face value − discount

The table below shows some of the **money market instruments** in the UK.

| Coupon bearing | Discount | Derivatives |
|---|---|---|
| Money market deposits | Treasury bill (T-bill) | Forwards and futures |
| Certificate of deposit (CD) | Banker's acceptance (BA) | Swaps |
| Repurchase agreement (Repo) | Commercial paper (CP) | Options |

## 3.1 Money market deposits

**Key term**

> **LIBOR** (London Interbank Offered Rate) is the rate of interest at which banks borrow from each other in the London interbank market.

Money market deposits are **very short-term loans** between banks or other institutions, including governments. These deposits can either be **fixed**, where the rate of interest and maturity dates are agreed at the time of the transaction, or call deposits, where the interest is variable and the deposit can be terminated if notice is given. The table below shows examples of market rates for money market instruments.

| | Overnight | 7 days' notice | 1 month | 3 months | 6 months | 1 year |
|---|---|---|---|---|---|---|
| Interbank Sterling | $5\frac{3}{32} - 5$ | $6 - 5\frac{3}{4}$ | $6\frac{1}{16} - \frac{15}{16}$ | $6\frac{3}{16} - 6\frac{1}{16}$ | $6\frac{5}{16} - \frac{3}{16}$ | $6\frac{3}{8} - 6\frac{1}{4}$ |

The table quotes **two rates**. The first figure in each column shows the **interest rate** at which a bank will **lend money**. This is called the **offer price**. The second number is the **rate** at which the bank will pay to **borrow money**. This is called the **bid price**. Note that whereas the convention in London is to quote **Offer/Bid**, in most other markets including the US, what is quoted is **Bid/Offer**.

The rate at which banks borrow from each other in the London market is of particular importance for money market. This is called LIBOR and is the most widely used reference rate for short-term interest rates globally for the settlement of money market derivatives. LIBOR rates are calculated for ten currencies, including the US dollar, pound sterling and the euro. The following table shows examples of LIBOR rates for three currencies for different maturities.

| | € | US$ | £ |
|---|---|---|---|
| Overnight | 3.413 | 5.289 | 5.141 |
| 1 week | 3.592 | 5.305 | 5.150 |
| 1 month | 3.653 | 5.350 | 5.241 |
| 3 months | 3.672 | 5.360 | 5.279 |
| 9 months | 3.851 | 5.313 | 5.420 |
| 12 months | 3.898 | 5.250 | 5.459 |

The LIBOR rates at **different maturities** define the **short-term yield curve** which is shown below.

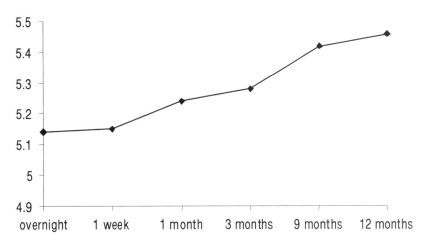

LIBOR yield curve

Note that, while the yield curve is given for specific maturities, the yield curve can be constructed by interpolation.

The LIBOR yield curve can also be used to estimate the **forward yield curve** which gives the interest rate between two future periods. The forward yield curve is used to price many money market derivatives.

## 3.2 Certificates of deposit

> A **certificate of deposit (CD)** is a certificate of receipt for funds deposited at a bank or other financial institution for a specified term and paying interest at a specified rate.

CDs can be either **negotiable** or **non-negotiable**. The holder of a **negotiable CD** has two options: to hold it until maturity, receiving the interest and the principal, or to sell it before maturity at the market price.

## 3.3 Repos

> A **repurchase agreement** is an agreement between two counterparties under which one counterparty agrees to sell an instrument to the other on an agreed date for an agreed price, and simultaneously agrees to buy back the instrument from the counterparty at a later date for an agreed price.

A repurchase agreement is a loan secured by a marketable instrument, usually a treasury bill or a bond. The typical term is 1–180 days and is an attractive instrument because it can accommodate a wide spectrum of maturities. A repo involves two sets of transactions. First, on the start date, the dealer sells the security for cash. On maturity, the dealer will repay the cash with interest and take back the security. The flows in a repo are shown in the following diagram.

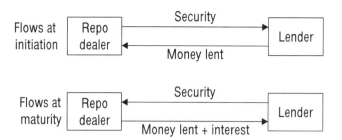

A **reverse repurchase** agreement (reverse repo) is an agreement for the purchase of an instrument with the simultaneous agreement to resell the instrument at an agreed future date and agreed price.

In a **reverse repo**, the dealer purchases the security initially and then sells it on maturity. Because the two parties in a **repo** agreement act as a buyer and a seller of the security, a **repo** to one party is a **reverse repo** to the other.

## 3.4 Treasury bills

Treasury bills (T-bills) are debt instruments issued by the Government, with maturities ranging from one month to one year. The discount rate of a T-bill can be calculated using the following steps.

**Formula to learn**

$$\text{Discount rate} = \frac{\text{Number of days in the year}}{\text{Days to maturity}} \times \frac{\text{Face value} - \text{settlement price}}{\text{Face value}}$$

### Question

T-bill discount

A 91-day T-bill with a face value of $10,000,000 is issued for $9,870,000. What is the discount rate?

### Answer

$$\text{Discount rate} = \frac{365}{91} \times \frac{10,000,000 - 9,870,000}{10,000,000} = 5.2\%$$

## 3.5 Commercial paper

Commercial paper (CP) is **short-term unsecured corporate debt** with maturity up to 270 days. The typical term of this debt is about 30 days. CP can only be issued by large organisations with good credit ratings, normally to fund short-term expenditure. The debt is issued at a discount that reflects the prevailing interest rates.

## 3.6 Banker's acceptance

**Key term**

**Banker's acceptances (BAs)** are negotiable bills issued by companies and guaranteed by a bank.

BAs are issued by firms to finance commercial transactions, such as imports and the purchase of goods. The name derives from the fact that the bank has guaranteed the payment to the holder of the BA; that is, the bank has accepted responsibility for the payment. Banks guaranteed the payment by the company for a fee.

BAs are sold on a **discounted basis** like T-bills and CP. Because BAs are negotiable instruments, they can be bought and sold until they mature. The **rates** on BAs are **low** because, as they are guaranteed by a bank, the credit risk is low.

# 4 The treasury management function

**Treasury management** in a modern enterprise covers a number of areas, including **liquidity management**, **funding management**, **currency management** and **corporate finance**.

One way in which you can demonstrate competence in the performance objective 'manage cash using active cash management and treasury systems' is to manage cash on a centralised basis to both maximise returns and minimise charges. This section introduces the treasury management function and how it can be used to pool cash from various sources which can be placed on deposit.

## 4.1 Treasury management

Large companies rely heavily for both long-term and short-term funds on the financial and currency markets. To manage cash (funds) and currency efficiently, many large companies have set up a separate **treasury department**.

The Association of Corporate Treasurers' **definition of treasury management** is 'the corporate handling of all financial matters, the generation of external and internal funds for business, the management of currencies and cash flows, and the complex strategies, policies and procedures of corporate finance'.

A treasury department, even in a large company, is likely to be quite small, with perhaps a staff of three to six qualified accountants, bankers or corporate treasurers working under a treasurer, who is responsible to the finance director. In some cases, where the company or organisation handles very large amounts of cash or foreign currency dealings, and often has large cash surpluses, the treasury department might be larger.

## 4.2 The role of the treasurer

The diagrams below are based on the Association of Corporate Treasurers' list of experience it requires from its student members before they are eligible for full membership of the Association. Required experience gives a good indication of the roles of treasury departments.

(a)   **Corporate financial objectives**

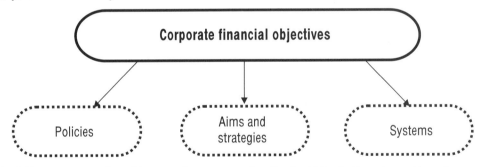

(b)   **Liquidity management**: making sure the company has the liquid funds it needs, and invests any surplus funds, even for very short terms.

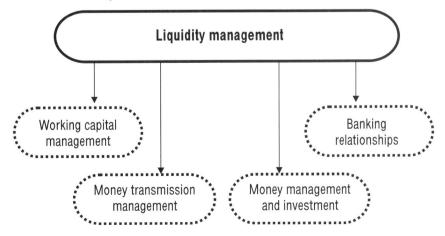

## (c) Funding management

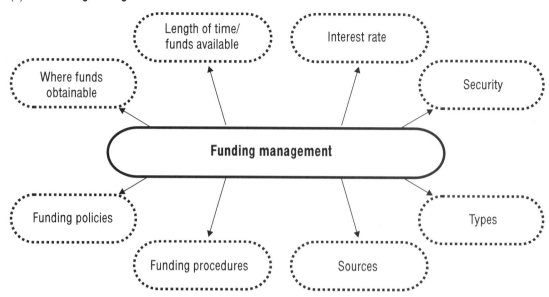

Funding management is concerned with all forms of borrowing, and alternative sources of funds, such as leasing and factoring.

## (d) Currency management

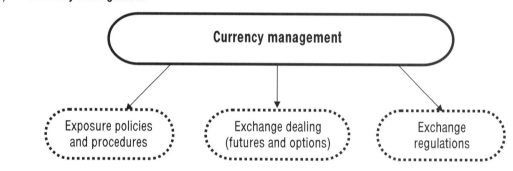

Currency dealings can save or cost a company considerable amounts of money, and the success or shortcomings of the corporate treasurer can have a significant impact on the statement of profit or loss of a company which is heavily involved in foreign trade.

## (e) Corporate finance

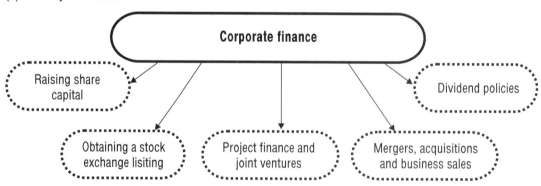

The treasury department has a role in all levels of decision making within the company. It is involved with **strategic** decisions, such as dividend policy and the raising of capital, **tactical** decisions, such as risk management, and **operational** decisions, such as the investment of surplus funds.

## 4.3 Treasury policy

All treasury departments should have a formal statement of treasury policy and detailed guidance on treasury procedures. The aims of a treasury policy are to enable managers to **establish direction**, **specify parameters** and **exercise control**, and also **provide a clear framework and guidelines for decisions**.

The guidance needs to cover the **roles** and **responsibilities** of the **treasury function**, the **risks** requiring management, **authorisation** and **dealing** limits.

Guidance on **risks** should cover:

- Identification and assessment methodology
- Criteria including tolerable and unacceptable levels of risk
- Management guidelines, covering risk elimination, risk control, risk retention and risk transfer
- Reporting guidelines

The areas that might be covered include:

- **Counterparty exposure**, including limits for each counterparty and monitoring of exposures in relation to the limits

- **Currency and interest rate risk**, such as hedging methods, authorised instruments and exposure limits

- **Funding risk**, including limits and targets for different sources of funding

- **Liquidity management**, including permitted banks, netting and inter-group procedures

- **Investment management**, covering sources of funds, authorised counterparties and instruments, and inter-company funding

- **Bank relationships** specifying criteria for the choice of bank

The guidance must also include guidance on **measurement** of **treasury performance**. Measurement must cover both the **management of risk** and the **financial contribution** the department makes.

## 4.4 Advantages of a separate treasury department

Advantages of having a treasury function which is **separate from the financial control function** are as follows:

(a) Centralised liquidity management avoids mixing cash surpluses and overdrafts in different localised bank accounts.

(b) Bulk cash flows allow **lower bank charges** to be negotiated.

(c) Larger volumes of cash can be invested, giving **better short-term investment opportunities**.

(d) Borrowing can be agreed in bulk, probably at **lower interest rates** than for smaller borrowings.

(e) Currency risk management should be improved, through **matching of cash flows in different subsidiaries**. There should be less need to use expensive hedging instruments, such as option contracts.

(f) A specialist department can employ staff with a **greater level of expertise** than would be possible in a local, more broadly based, finance department.

(g) The company will be able to benefit from the use of **specialised cash management software**.

(h) Access to treasury expertise should **improve the quality of strategic planning and decision making**.

## 4.5 Centralised or decentralised cash management?

Centralising the treasury management function allows businesses to **employ experts, deal in bulk cash flows** and therefore **take advantage of lower bank** charges and **avoid a mix of surpluses and deficits**. However, **decentralised** cash management can be **more responsive to local needs**.

A large company may have a number of subsidiaries and divisions. In the case of a multinational, these will be located in different countries. It will be necessary to decide whether the treasury function should be centralised.

With **centralised cash management**, the central treasury department effectively acts as the bank to the group. The central treasury has the job of ensuring that individual operating units have all the funds they need at the right time.

### 4.5.1 Advantages of a specialist centralised treasury department

(a) **Centralised liquidity management** avoids having a mix of cash surpluses and overdrafts in different local bank accounts and facilitates bulk cash flows, so that lower bank charges can be negotiated.

(b) Larger volumes of cash are available to invest, giving better **short-term investment opportunities** (for example, money market deposits, high interest accounts and CDs).

(c) Any borrowing can be arranged **in bulk**, at lower interest rates than for smaller borrowings, and perhaps on the eurocurrency or eurobond markets.

(d) **Foreign currency risk management** is likely to be improved in a group of companies. A central treasury department can match foreign currency income earned by one subsidiary with expenditure in the same currency by another subsidiary. In this way, the risk of losses on adverse exchange rate changes can be avoided without the expense of forward exchange contracts or other 'hedging' (risk-reducing) methods.

(e) A specialist treasury department will employ **experts** with knowledge of dealing in futures, eurocurrency markets, taxation, transfer prices and so on. Localised departments would not have such expertise.

(f) The centralised pool of **funds required for precautionary purposes** will be smaller than the sum of separate precautionary balances which would need to be held under decentralised treasury arrangements.

(g) Through having a separate **profit centre**, attention will be focused on the contribution to group profit performance that can be achieved by good cash, funding, investment and foreign currency management.

(h) Centralisation provides a means of exercising **better control** through use of **standardised procedures** and **risk monitoring**. Standardised practices and performance measures can also create productivity benefits.

### 4.5.2 Possible advantages of decentralised cash management

(a) Sources of finance can be **diversified** and can be **matched with local assets**.

(b) Greater **autonomy** can be given to subsidiaries and divisions because of the closer relationships they will have with the decentralised cash management function.

(c) The decentralised treasury function may be able to be **more responsive** to the needs of individual operating units.

However, since cash balances will not be aggregated at group level, there will be **more limited opportunities to invest** such balances on a short-term basis.

## 4.5.3 Centralised cash management in the multinational firm

If cash management within a **multinational firm** is centralised, each subsidiary holds only the minimum cash balance required for transaction purposes. All excess funds will be remitted to the central treasury department.

Funds held in the central pool of funds can be returned quickly to the local subsidiary by telegraphic transfer or by means of worldwide bank credit facilities. The firm's bank can instruct its branch office in the country in which the subsidiary is located to advance funds to the subsidiary.

**Question**                                                                                     Treasury centralisation

Touten is a US registered multinational company with subsidiaries in 14 countries in Europe, Asia and Africa. The subsidiaries have traditionally been allowed a large amount of autonomy, but Touten is now proposing to centralise most of the group treasury management operations.

*Required*

Acting as a consultant to Touten, prepare a memo suitable for distribution from the group finance director to the senior management of each of the subsidiaries explaining:

(a)     The potential benefits of treasury centralisation

(b)     How the company proposes to minimise any potential problems for the subsidiaries that might arise as a result of treasury centralisation

**Answer**

MEMORANDUM

**To:**    Directors of all foreign subsidiaries
**From:** Group Finance Director
**Date:** 1 July 20X0

### Centralisation of treasury management operations

At its last meeting, the board of directors of Touten made the decision to centralise group treasury management operations. A further memo giving detailed plans will be circulated shortly, but my objective in this memo is to outline the potential benefits of treasury centralisation and how any potential problems arising at subsidiaries can be minimised. Most of you will be familiar with the basic arguments, which we have been discussing informally for some time.

### What it means

Centralisation of treasury management means that most decisions on borrowing, investment of cash surpluses, currency management and financial risk management will be taken by an enhanced central treasury team, based at head office, instead of by subsidiaries directly. In addition, we propose to set most transfer prices for inter-company goods and services centrally.

### The potential benefits

The main benefits are:

(a)     **Cost savings** resulting from reduction of unnecessary banking charges
(b)     **Reduction of the group's total taxation charge**
(c)     **Enhanced control over financial risk**

Reduction in banking charges will result from:

(a)     **Netting off inter-company debts before settlement**. At the moment we are spending too much on foreign exchange commission by settling inter-company debts in a wide range of currencies through the banking system.

(b) **Knowledge of total group currency exposure from transactions**. Amounts receivable in one subsidiary can hedge payables in another, eliminating unnecessary hedging by subsidiaries.

(c) **Knowledge of the group's total cash resources and borrowing requirement**. This will reduce the incidence of one company lending cash while a fellow subsidiary borrows at a higher interest rate and will also eliminate unnecessary interest rate hedging. It will also facilitate higher deposit rates and lower borrowing rates.

Reduction in the group's tax charge will be made possible by a comprehensive centrally set **transfer pricing policy**.

Enhanced control over financial risks will be possible because we will be able to develop a central team of specialists who will have a clear-cut strategy on hedging and risk management. Many of you have requested help in this area.

This team will be able to ensure that decisions are taken in line with **group strategy** and will also be able to provide you with enhanced financial information to assist you with your own decision making.

### Potential problems for subsidiaries and their solution

Our group culture is one of **decentralisation** and **enablement of management at individual subsidiary level**. There is no intention to change this culture. Rather, it is hoped that releasing you from specialist treasury decisions will enable you to devote more time to developing your own business units.

However, the system can only work properly if **information exchange** between head office and subsidiaries is swift and efficient. Enhanced computer systems are to be provided at all centres to assist you with daily reports. It is also important that you keep head office informed of all local conditions that could be beneficial to the treasury function, such as the availability of local subsidised loans, as well as potential local risks, such as the threat of exchange control restrictions.

You will find that movements in your cash balances will be affected by **group policy**, as well as reported profitability. Any adjustments made by head office will be eliminated when preparing the performance reports for your own business units and we will ensure that joint venture partners are not penalised by group policy.

Please contact me with any further comments that you may have on our new treasury policy.

## 4.6 The treasury department as cost centre or profit centre

FAST FORWARD

> The treasury department is usually run as a **cost centre** if its main focus is to keep costs within budgeted spending targets. It may be run as a **profit centre** if there is a high level of foreign exchange transactions, or the business wishes to make speculative profits.

A treasury department might be managed either as a **cost centre** or as a **profit centre**. For a group of companies, this decision may need to be made for treasury departments in separate subsidiaries as well as for the central corporate treasury department.

In a cost centre, managers have an incentive only to **keep the costs** of the department within **budgeted spending targets**. The cost centre approach implies that the treasury is there to perform a service of a certain standard to other departments in the enterprise. The treasury is treated much like any other service department.

However, some companies (for example, BP) are able to make significant profits from their treasury activities. Treating the treasury department as a profit centre recognises the fact that treasury activities such as speculation may earn **revenues** for the company, and may as a result make treasury staff more motivated. It also means that treasury departments have to operate with a greater degree of commercial awareness in, for example, the management of working capital.

## Question

Suppose that your company is considering plans to establish its treasury function as a profit centre. In what ways are the following issues of potential importance to these plans?

(a)    How can we ensure that high quality treasury staff can be recruited?

(b)    How might costly errors and overexposure to risk be prevented?

(c)    Why will the treasury team need extensive market information to be successful?

(d)    Could there be a danger that attitudes to risk in the treasury team will differ from those of the board? If so, how?

(e)    What is the relevance of internal charges?

(f)    What problems could there be in evaluating performance of the treasury team?

## Answer

If a profit centre approach is being considered, the following issues should be addressed.

(a)    **Competence of staff**

Local managers may not have sufficient expertise in the area of treasury management to carry out speculative treasury operations competently. Mistakes in this specialised field may be costly. It may only be appropriate to operate a larger **centralised** treasury as a profit centre, and additional specialist staff demanding high salaries may need to be recruited.

(b)    **Controls**

Adequate controls must be in place to prevent costly errors and overexposure to risks such as foreign exchange risks. It is possible to enter into a very large foreign exchange deal over the telephone.

(c)    **Information**

A treasury team which trades in futures and options or in currencies is competing with other traders employed by major financial institutions who may have better knowledge of the market because of the large number of customers they deal with. In order to compete effectively, the team needs to have detailed and up to date market information.

(d)    **Attitudes to risk**

The more aggressive approach to risk taking which is characteristic of treasury professionals may be difficult to reconcile with the more measured approach to risk which may prevail within the board of directors. The recognition of treasury operations as profit-making activities may not fit well with the main business operations of the company.

(e)    **Internal charges**

If the department is to be a true profit centre, then market prices should be charged for its services to other departments. It may be difficult to put realistic prices on some services, such as arrangement of finance and general financial advice.

(f)    **Performance evaluation**

Even with a profit centre approach, it may be difficult to measure the success of a treasury team for the reason that successful treasury activities sometimes involve **avoiding** the incurring of costs, for example when a currency devalues. For example, a treasury team which hedges a future foreign currency receipt over a period when the domestic currency undergoes devaluation may avoid a substantial loss for the company.

# Chapter Roundup

- Financial markets are the markets where economic units with surplus funds, such as individuals, corporations, the Government and overseas investors, lend funds to other economic units that want to borrow.

- Markets where a security is first issued are known as primary, and markets where a security is subsequently traded are known as secondary.

- Secondary markets can be organised as exchanges or over the counter (OTC).

- **Securitisation** is the process of converting **illiquid assets** into **marketable asset-backed securities**. The development of securitisation has led to disintermediation and a reduction in the role of financial intermediaries, as borrowers can reach lenders directly.

- **Money markets** are the markets where **short-term instruments** are traded.

- **Treasury management** in a modern enterprise covers a number of areas, including **liquidity management**, **funding management**, **currency management** and **corporate finance**.

- Centralising the treasury management function allows businesses to **employ experts**, **deal in bulk cash flows** and therefore **take advantage of lower bank charges** and **avoid a mix of surpluses and deficits**. However, **decentralised** cash management can be **more responsive to local needs**.

- The treasury department is usually run as a **cost centre** if its main focus is to keep costs within budgeted spending targets. It may be run as a **profit centre** if there is a high level of foreign exchange transactions, or the business wishes to make speculative profits.

# Quick Quiz

1   A 91-day T-bill with a face value of $10,000,000 is issued for $9,830,000. What is the discount rate?

2   Fill in the blanks in the statements below, using the words in the box. (Words may be used more than once.)

- Treasury management may be defined as 'the corporate handling of all (1) ................................ matters, the generation of external and internal (2) ................................ for business, the management of (3) ................................ and cash flow, and the complex strategies, policies and procedures of (4) ................................ .

- A treasury department may be managed either as a (5) ................................ centre or a (6) ................................ centre.

- A (7) ................................ treasury department has the role of ensuring that individual operating units have all the funds they need at the right time.

- Futures and options might be employed in (8) ................................ risk management.

- Acquisitions and sales of businesses fall within the area of (9) ................................ .

- Money transmission management is an aspect of (10) ................................ management.

| • Corporate finance | • Centralised | • Profit | • Financial |
|---|---|---|---|
| • Liquidity | • Cost | • Currency/ies | • Funds |

3   Give three possible advantages of decentralisation of the treasury function.

# Answers to Quick Quiz

1  $d = \dfrac{10,000,000 - 9,830,000}{10,000,000} \times \dfrac{365}{91} = 6.82\%$

2  (1) Financial (2) Funds (3) Currencies (4) Corporate finance (5) Cost (6) Profit (7) Centralised
   (8) Currency (9) Corporate finance (10) Liquidity

3  • Diversification of sources of finance and matching with local assets
   • Greater autonomy for subsidiaries and divisions
   • Greater responsiveness to the needs of individual operating units

Now try the question below from the Practice Question Bank

| Number | Level | Marks | Time |
|--------|-------|-------|------|
| 29 | Introductory | 11 | 21 mins |

# The use of financial derivatives to hedge against foreign exchange risk

## Introduction

This chapter focuses on how currency derivatives can be used to manage transaction risk. Any company engaged in international trade will be exposed to such risk where movements in exchange rates can have a significant effect on the value of transactions. There are numerous ways in which a company can hedge against transaction risk – both **internal** and **external** methods are available. It is important to know the characteristics of the various techniques and also the **best strategy** to adopt in particular scenarios.

# Study guide

| | | Intellectual level |
|---|---|---|
| **E1** | **The role of the treasury function in multinationals** | |
| (b) | Discuss the operations of the derivatives market, including: | 3 |
| | (i) The relative advantages and disadvantages of exchange traded versus OTC agreements | |
| | (ii) Key features, such as standard contracts, tick sizes, margin requirements and margin trading | |
| | (iii) The source of basis risk and how it can be minimised | |
| **E2** | **The use of financial derivatives to hedge against FOREX risk** | |
| (a) | Assess the impact on an organisation to exposure in translation, transaction and economic risks and how these can be managed. | 3 |
| (b) | Evaluate, for a given hedging requirement, which of the following is the most appropriate strategy, given the nature of the underlying position and the risk exposure: | 3 |
| | (i) The use of the forward exchange market and the creation of a money market hedge | |
| | (ii) Synthetic foreign exchange agreements (SAFEs) | |
| | (iii) Exchange-traded currency futures contracts | |
| | (iv) Currency swaps | |
| | (v) FOREX swaps | |
| | (vi) Currency options | |
| (c) | Advise on the use of bilateral and multilateral netting and matching as tools for minimising FOREX transactions costs and the management of market barriers to the free movement of capital and other remittances. | 3 |

One of the optional performance objectives in your PER is to advise on managing or using instruments or techniques to manage financial risk. This chapter focuses on a range of techniques for managing exchange rate risk, which is an aspect of financial risk.

# 1 Translation, transaction and economic risks

Translation, transaction and economic risks were covered in Chapter 8, Section 5. It would be a good idea to remind yourself of what each risk is before studying this chapter. The main focus of this chapter is on **transaction risk** – that is, the risk of changes in the exchange rates having an effect on the value of transactions based in a foreign currency (imports or exports).

The effect of exchange rate movements on project values was also covered in Chapter 8. You should review Section 2 of Chapter 8 to remind yourself of how **purchasing power parity**, **interest rate parity** and the **International Fisher effect** can be used to predict exchange rates.

# 2 Exchange rates

**FAST FORWARD**

The **spot rate** is the rate at which currencies can be exchanged now. The **forward rate** is the rate at which currencies will be exchanged on a set future date.

**412** **16: The use of financial derivatives to hedge against foreign exchange risk** | Part E Treasury and advanced risk management techniques

## 2.1 Exchange rates

Exchange rates were covered in detail in *Financial Management (FM)*. However, it is worthwhile revising the basics here, as an understanding of these is essential for the rest of the chapter.

An **exchange rate** is the rate at which a currency can be traded in exchange for another currency.

The **spot exchange rate** is the rate at which currencies can be bought or sold for **immediate delivery**.

The **forward rate** is an exchange rate set for currencies to be exchanged at a future date.

Every traded currency in fact has many exchange rates. There is an exchange rate with every other traded currency on the foreign exchange markets. Foreign exchange dealers make their profit by buying currency for less than they sell it, and so there are really two exchange rates, a selling rate and a buying rate.

## 2.2 Currency quotes

Currencies may be quoted in either direction. For example, the US dollar and euro might be quoted as €/$ = 0.7745 or $/€ = 1.2912. In other words, €0.7745 = $1 and $1.2912 = €1. One rate is simply the reciprocal of the other.

In both cases, the currency on the **right hand side** of the quote is being valued. An exchange rate shows the value of one unit of the currency on the right hand side of the quote; this currency is called the **base currency**.

If a currency is quoted at $1.500:£1, the $ is the **counter currency**, the £ is the **base currency**.

## 2.3 Bid and offer prices

The **bid price** is the rate at which the bank is willing to buy the currency.

The **offer** (or **ask**) **price** is the rate at which the bank is willing to sell the currency.

If an importer has to pay a foreign supplier in a foreign currency, they might ask their bank to sell them the required amount of the currency. For example, suppose that a bank's customer, a UK trading company, has imported goods for which it must now pay $10,000.

(a) In order to pay the bill, the company must obtain (buy) $10,000 from the bank. In other words, the bank will sell $10,000 to the company.

(b) When the bank agrees to sell $10,000 to the company, it will tell the company what the spot rate of exchange will be for the transaction. If the bank's selling rate (known as the **'offer'** or **'ask'** price) is, say, $1.5500 for the currency, the bank will charge the company:

$$\frac{\$10,000}{\$1.5500 \text{ per } £1} = £6,451.61$$

If a UK exporting company receives $10,000 from a customer, the company will want to sell the dollars to obtain sterling (its home currency). The bank will therefore buy the dollars at a quoted **bid price**. If the bank quotes a **bid** price of, say, $1.5595 for the currency the bank will pay the exporter:

$$\frac{\$10,000}{\$1.5595 \text{ per } £1} = £6,412.31$$

Note that the bank buys the dollars for less than it sells them – in other words, it makes a net profit on the transactions. In this case the net profit is £39.30. If you are undecided between which price is the bid price and which is the offer price, remember that the bank's customer will always be offered the **worst rate**. An exporter will pay a high price for the foreign currency and an importer will receive a low price. Just think what happens when you buy currency for a holiday and then sell it back when you come home (ignoring commission).

If you come back to the UK from a holiday in the US with spare dollars, and you are told the spread of $/£ rates is 1.2500–1.2700, will you have to pay the bank $1.25 or $1.27 to obtain £1? Answer: you will have to pay the higher price, $1.27.

**The rule is that banks buy the counter currency (here $s) at a low price and sell the counter currency (here $s) at a high price**.

## Question
Dollar receipts

Calculate how many dollars an exporter would receive or how many dollars an importer would pay, ignoring the bank's commission, in each of the following situations, if they were to exchange currency at the spot rate.

(a)    A US exporter receives a payment from a Danish customer of 150,000 kroner.
(b)    A US importer buys goods from a Japanese supplier and pays 1 million yen.

Spot rates are as follows.

|  | Bank sells (offer) | | Bank buys (bid) |
|---|---|---|---|
| Danish Kr/$ | 9.4340 | – | 9.5380 |
| Japanese Yen/$ | 203.650 | – | 205.781 |

## Answer

(a)    The bank is being asked to buy the Danish kroners and will give the exporter:

$$\frac{150,000}{9.5380} = \$15,726.57 \text{ in exchange}$$

(b)    The bank is being asked to sell the yen to the importer and will charge for the currency:

$$\frac{1,000,000}{203.650} = \$4,910.39$$

## 2.4 Spread

The difference between the bid price and the offer price is known as the **spread**.

One of the easiest ways to find the closing (end of day) exchange rates is to use the financial press (such as the *Financial Times* and *Wall Street Journal*).

The difference between the bid price and the offer price, covering dealers' costs and profit, is called the **spread**. The spread can be quoted in different ways.

£/$0.6500 +/– 0.0005 or £/$0.6495–0.6505

## Question
Exchange rate spreads

Pratt Inc, a US-based company, is engaged in both import and export activities. During a particular month, Pratt sells goods to Posh plc, a UK company, and receives £5 million. In the same month, Pratt imports goods from a UK supplier, which cost £5 million.

If the exchange rates were £/$0.5075 +/– 0.0003, calculate the dollar values of the sterling receipt and payment.

## Answer

(a)    As an exporter, Pratt will pay a high rate to buy dollars (sell pounds sterling) – that is, it will be quoted a rate of 0.5075 + 0.0003 = 0.5078. Pratt will therefore receive £5 million/0.5078 = $9,846,396.

(b) As an importer, Pratt will receive a low rate to sell dollars (buy pounds sterling) – that is, a rate of 0.5075 – 0.0003 = 0.5072. Pratt will therefore pay £5 million/0.5072 = $9,858,044.

# 3 Internal hedging techniques

**FAST FORWARD**

Internal hedging techniques include **leading and lagging, invoicing in home currency, matching and multilateral netting**.

Internal hedging techniques are cheaper than external techniques and should therefore be considered first. There are various internal techniques available which are discussed below.

## 3.1 Leading and lagging

**Key terms**

**Leading** involves **accelerating payments** to avoid potential additional costs due to currency rate movements.

**Lagging** is the practice of **delaying payments** if currency rate movements are expected to make the later payment cheaper.

Companies might try to use lead payments (payments in advance) or lagged payments (delayed payments) in order to take advantage of foreign exchange rate movements.

## Example

Williams Inc – a company based in the US – imports goods from the UK. The company is due to make a payment of £500,000 to a UK supplier in one month's time. The current exchange rate is as follows.

£0.6450 = $1

(a) If the dollar is expected to appreciate against sterling by 2% in the next month and by a further 1% in the second month, what would be Williams Inc's strategy in terms of leading and lagging and by how much would the company benefit from this strategy?

(b) If the dollar was to depreciate against sterling by 2% in the next month and by a further 1% in the second month, how would Williams Inc's strategy probably change and what would the resulting benefit be?

## Solution

(a) **Dollar appreciating against sterling**

If the dollar appreciates against sterling, this means that the dollar value of payments will be smaller in two months' time than if payment was made when due. Williams Inc will therefore adopt a 'lagging' approach to its payment – that is, it will delay payment by an extra month to reduce the dollar cost.

*Payment to UK supplier*

|  | *One month's time* | *Two months' time* |
|---|---|---|
| Exchange rate | £0.6450 × 1.02 = £0.6579 | £0.6579 × 1.01 = £0.6645 |
| $ value of payment | £500,000/0.6579 = $759,994 | £500,000/0.6645 = $752,445 |

By delaying the payment by an extra month, Williams Inc will save $7,549.

(b) **Dollar depreciating against sterling**

The opposite strategy should now be adopted. As the dollar depreciates, there is an incentive for Williams Inc to pay as soon as possible. The dollar value of sterling payments will increase as the dollar depreciates, therefore to save money the company will want to pay on time.

*Payment to UK supplier*

| | One month's time | Two months' time |
|---|---|---|
| Exchange rate | £0.6450 × 0.98 = £0.6321 | £0.6321 × 0.99 = £0.6258 |
| $ value of payment | £500,000/0.6321 = $791,014 | £500,000/0.6258 = $798,977 |

By paying on time Williams Inc will save $7,963.

Companies should be aware of the potential **finance costs** associated with paying early. This is the interest cost on the money used to make the payment, but early settlement discounts may be available. Before deciding on a strategy of making advanced payments, the company should compare how much it saves in terms of currency with the finance costs of making early payment.

By delaying payments there may be a **loss of goodwill** from the supplier which may result in tighter credit terms in the future. While savings may have been made by paying late, the company must compare these savings with potential future costs resulting from, for example, withdrawal of favourable credit terms and early settlement discounts.

## 3.2 Invoicing in home currency

One way of avoiding transaction risk is for an **exporter** to invoice **overseas customers in its own domestic currency**, or for an **importer** to arrange with its overseas supplier **to be invoiced in its home currency**.

(a)  If a Hong Kong exporter is able to quote and invoice an overseas customer in Hong Kong dollars, then the transaction risk is transferred to that customer.

(b)  If a Hong Kong importer is able to arrange with its overseas supplier to be invoiced in Hong Kong dollars, then the transaction risk is transferred to that supplier.

Although either the exporter or the importer avoids transaction risk, the other party to the transaction will bear the full risk. Who ultimately bears the risk may depend on bargaining strength or the exporter's competitive position (it is unlikely to insist on payment in its own currency if it faces strong competition).

An alternative method of achieving the same result is to negotiate contracts expressed in the foreign currency but at a predetermined fixed rate of exchange.

## 3.3 Matching receipts and payments

A company can reduce or eliminate its transaction risk exposure by matching receipts and payments. Wherever possible, a company that expects to make payments and have receipts in the same foreign currency should plan to **offset its payments against its receipts in that currency**. The process of matching is made simpler by having **foreign currency accounts** with a bank.

Offsetting (matching payments against receipts) will be **cheaper** than arranging a forward contract to buy currency and another forward contract to sell the currency, provided that:

- Receipts occur before payments
- The time difference between receipts and payments in the currency is not too long

Any differences between the amounts receivable and the amounts payable in a given currency may be covered by a forward exchange contract (covered later in this chapter) to buy or sell the amount of the difference.

## 3.4 Netting

Netting is a process in which credit balances are netted off against debit balances so that only the reduced net amounts remain due to be paid by actual currency flows.

Exam focus point

Netting was examined as part of a question in June 2013 and also in Sep/Dec 2015.

Unlike matching, netting is not technically a method of managing transaction risk. The objective is simply to save transactions costs by netting off inter-company balances before arranging payment. Many **multinational groups** of companies engage in **intra-group trading**. Where related companies located in different countries trade with each other, there is likely to be inter-company indebtedness denominated in different currencies.

### 3.4.1 Bilateral netting

In the case of bilateral netting, only two companies are involved. The lower balance is netted off against the higher balance and the difference is the amount remaining to be paid.

## Example

Barlow plc and Orange Inc are respectively UK and US subsidiaries of a Swiss-based holding company. On 30 September 20X1 Barlow owed Orange SFr650,000 and Orange owed Barlow SFr450,000. Bilateral netting can reduce the value of the inter-company debts – the two inter-company balances are set against each other, leaving a net debt owed by Barlow to Orange of SFr200,000 (SFr650,000 – SFr450,000).

### 3.4.2 Multilateral netting                                                                    6/13, Sep/Dec 15

Multilateral netting is a more complex procedure in which the debts of more than two group companies are netted off against each other. There are different ways of arranging multilateral netting. The arrangement might be co-ordinated by the company's own central treasury or alternatively by the company's bankers.

The steps to be followed are:

**Step 1**     Construct a table with companies receiving money down the left side and companies making payments across the top.

**Step 2**     Enter all the amounts each company owes to the others and convert to the agreed settlement currency.

**Step 3**     Add across and down the table to determine total receipts and total payments for each company.

Determine the net receivable or payable for each company.

## Example

Maximillian Group is made up of three companies – one in Germany, one in Hong Kong and one in the US. The following inter-company transactions took place during the first quarter of 20X1.

|  | *Paying subsidiary* | | |
| --- | --- | --- | --- |
| *Receiving subsidiary* | *Germany* | *Hong Kong* | *US* |
| Germany | – | €10m | €6m |
| Hong Kong | HK$5m | – | HK$20m |
| US | $12m | $16m | – |

Maximillian has introduced a system of multilateral netting to minimise the number of inter-group payments. The US dollar will be used as the settlement currency. Exchange rates are as follows.

HK$11.2475 = €1          €0.6919 = US$1          HK$7.7821 = US$1

*Required*

Illustrate the effect of multilateral netting on inter-group receipts and payments.

## Solution

Remember the step by step guide above – the US dollar is the settlement currency therefore we convert all the receipts and payments to US dollars using the exchange rates given.

### Paying subsidiary

| Receiving subsidiary | Germany US$m | Hong Kong US$m | US US$m | Total receipts (add across) US$m | Total payments (add down) US$m | Net receipt/ (payt) US$m |
|---|---|---|---|---|---|---|
| Germany | – | 14.4530 | 8.6718 | 23.1248 | (12.6425) | 10.4823 |
| Hong Kong | 0.6425 | – | 2.5700 | 3.2125 | (30.4530) | (27.2405) |
| US | 12.0000 | 16.0000 | – | 28.0000 | (11.2418) | 16.7582 |

This policy of multilateral netting will minimise transactions costs for the group and should prevent the need for foreign currency hedging. Only two transactions are now required – Hong Kong pays US$10.4823m to the US and Hong Kong pays US$16.7582m to the US.

A useful check on the accuracy of your currency conversions can be done by adding up the net receipts/payments column. If your calculations are correct (and the signs attached to receipts and payments are consistent) the column should add up to zero. This is because what is a payment for one company is a receipt for another so they cancel out.

## Question
**Multilateral netting**

Robster, Gazza and Howard are all part of the same group – Robster is based in the US, Gazza in the UK and Howard in Singapore. The following transactions took place between the three companies during the previous quarter of the current year.

### Paying subsidiary

| Receiving subsidiary | Robster | Gazza | Howard |
|---|---|---|---|
| Robster | – | US$50m | US$20m |
| Gazza | £15m | – | £25m |
| Howard | S$33m | S$45m | – |

The settlement currency is £ sterling and the following exchange rates applied at the end of the previous quarter.

$1.5500 = £1     S$2.800 = £1

*Required*

Illustrate the impact of multilateral netting on the group as a whole and the final transactions that are required to settle the net receipts and payments.

## Answer

### Paying subsidiary

| Receiving subsidiary | Robster £m | Gazza £m | Howard £m | Total receipts (add across) £m | Total payments (add down) £m | Net receipt/(payment) £m |
|---|---|---|---|---|---|---|
| Robster | – | 32.26 | 12.9 | 45.16 | (26.79) | 18.37 |
| Gazza | 15.00 | – | 25.0 | 40.00 | (48.33) | (8.33) |
| Howard | 11.79 | 16.07 | – | 27.86 | (37.90) | (10.04) |

The transactions required are reduced to two – Gazza pays Robster £8.33m and Howard pays Robster £10.04m.

## 3.5 Management of barriers

An overseas government may place **restrictions on remittances**. This means that the amount of profit that can be sent back to the parent company is limited. This may be achieved through **exchange controls** or

limits on the amounts that can be remitted. These **barriers** can be avoided/mitigated by the following methods:

(a) Charge overseas subsidiary companies additional head office overhead charges.

(b) Subsidiary companies can lend the equivalent of the dividend to the parent company.

(c) Subsidiary companies can make payments to the parent company in the form of royalties, patents, management fees or other charges.

(d) Increase the transfer prices paid by the subsidiary to the parent company (see Chapter 4b for further discussion of transfer prices).

(e) The overseas subsidiary can lend money to another subsidiary requiring funds in the same country. In return the parent company will receive the loan amount in the home country from the other parent company. This method is sometimes known as **parallel loans**.

Foreign governments may put measures in place to stop the above methods being used.

# 4 Managing transaction risk – forward contracts
## 6/11, 12/12, 6/13, 6/14, Mar/June 16

A **forward contract** is a contract with a bank that covers a **specific amount** of foreign currency for delivery at an **agreed date** at an **exchange rate agreed now**.

## 4.1 What is a forward contract?

**Key term**

A **forward exchange contract** is:

(a) An immediately firm and binding contract, eg between a bank and its customer which must be exercised regardless of the spot rate at the time of exercise

(b) For the purchase or sale of a specified quantity of a stated foreign currency

(c) At a rate of exchange fixed at the time the contract is made

(d) For performance (delivery of the currency and payment for it) at a future time which is agreed when making the contract (this future time will be either a specified date, or any time between two specified dates)

Forward contracts hedge against **transaction exposure** by allowing the importer or exporter to arrange for a bank to sell or buy a quantity of foreign currency at an **agreed future date**, at a **rate of exchange determined** when the **forward contract is made**. The trader will know in advance:

- How much local currency they will receive (if they are selling foreign currency to the bank)
- How much local currency they must pay (if they are buying foreign currency from the bank)

The current spot price is irrelevant to the outcome of a forward contract.

## 4.2 Forward rates and future exchange rate movements

Interest rate parity (IRP) shows that **the forward rate is determined by interest rate differences for the period of the contract.**

 Case Study

In September 2015 the spot rate quoted by HSBC was €1.353 to £1.

The 1 year forward rate quoted by HSBC on the same date was €1.340 to £1.

At this time the 1 year LIBOR rate in the UK was approximately 1% and the Euro LIBOR rate was approximately 0.05%.

**The actual forward rate can be predicted using the formula for IRP:**

$$F_o = S_o \frac{(1+i_c)}{(1+i_b)}$$

Using this formula the forward rate is calculated as

$$F_o = 1.353 \frac{(1+0.0005)}{(1+0.01)} = 1.340 \text{ (this was the } \textbf{actual} \text{ forward rate quoted above)}$$

**The forward rate reflects interest rate differences. It is not a forecast of what the spot rate will be on a given date in the future.** It will be a coincidence if the forward rate turns out to be the same as the spot rate on that future date.

The forward rate can be calculated today without making any estimates of future exchange rates. **Future exchange rates** depend largely on future events and will often turn out to be very different from the forward rate. However, the forward rate is probably an **unbiased predictor of the expected value of the future exchange rate**, based on the information available today

## 4.3 Expectations theory of forward rates

**Expectations theory** of forward rates predicts that the **percentage difference between forward and spot rates now equals the expected change in spot rates over the period**.

For example, given expectations of interest rates and inflation rates, the spot rate three months from now is expected to equal the three-month forward rate quoted now. The forward market is said to be an **unbiased predictor** of exchange rates as, on average, the forward rate is equal to the future spot rate and overestimates it about as often as it underestimates it.

## 4.4 Quotation of forward rates

In Section 2.4 we discussed the spread of spot rates, being the difference between the bid and offer prices. A similar situation applies to the quotation of forward rated – banks will quote a spread based on the forward bid and offer prices. For example, the $/€ 3-month forward rate might be quoted as:

$1.3495–$1.3525 = €1          or          $1.3510 ± 0.0015 = €1

As with the spot rate, a company will always be offered the worst rate by the bank. For example, if the company is selling € (that is, the bank is buying € and paying $) in 3 months' time, the bank will offer $1.3495. If the company is buying € (that is, the bank is buying $ and paying €) in 3 months' time, the bank will require $1.3525 for every € it sells.

## Example

It is now 31 March 20X1. Washington Inc, a US company, has purchased goods from London plc, a UK importer and exporter. Washington is due to pay £5m to London in 3 months' time and wants to hedge the foreign currency payment to reduce transaction risk.

The £/$ spot rates on 31 March 20X1 are £0.6200–£0.6230 = $1. The 3-month forward rates have been quoted as £0.6190–£0.6210 = $1.

Calculate the amount in $ that Washington will have to pay if the company hedges the payment using a forward contract.

## Solution

Washington will want to buy £ (sell $) in 3 months' time – which means that the bank will be selling £ and buying $. Washington will be offered the 'worst' rate – that is, the bank will pay £0.6190 for each $ received from Washington. The $ cost of the payment to London will be:

£5m/0.6190 = $8,077,544

| Question | Forward rates |
| --- | --- |

Using the information in the example above, calculate how much in £ sterling London would have to pay Washington if, in 3 months' time, a payment of $5m is due.

**Answer**

London will be selling £ (buying $) which means that the bank will be selling $. The bank will want to sell $ at a high rate therefore will offer London $1 for every £0.6210 the company pays. The total cost of the payment in 3 months' time will be:

$5m × £0.6210 = £3,105,000

## 4.5 Movement in the spot rate

As discussed above, the forward rate is deemed to be an unbiased predictor of the future spot rate. However, the spot rate at the time the forward contract is to be exercised may be more favourable than the forward rate that was agreed when the contract was entered into. Regardless of what the spot rate is at that time, the forward contract **must be exercised** – the holder does not have the option to let it lapse and perform the transaction at the prevailing spot rate.

## Example

A US importer knows on 1 April that it must pay a foreign seller 26,500 Swiss francs in one month's time, on 1 May. It can arrange a forward exchange contract with its bank on 1 April, whereby the bank undertakes to sell the importer 26,500 Swiss francs on 1 May, at a fixed rate of, say, SFr2.6400 = $1.

The US importer can be certain that, whatever the spot rate is between Swiss francs and US dollars on 1 May, it will have to pay on that date, at this forward rate:

$$\frac{26,500}{2.6400} = \$10,037.88$$

(a) If the spot rate is **lower than 2.6400**, the importer would have successfully protected itself against a weakening of the dollar, and would have avoided paying more dollars to obtain the Swiss francs.

(b) If the spot rate is **higher than 2.6400**, the dollar's value against the Swiss franc would mean that the importer would pay more under the forward exchange contract than it would have had to pay if it had obtained the francs at the spot rate on 1 May. It cannot avoid this extra cost, because a forward contract is binding.

## 4.6 Failure to satisfy a forward contract

A customer might be unable to satisfy a forward contract for any one of a number of reasons.

(a) An **importer** might find that:

   (i)  Its supplier **fails to deliver the goods** as specified, so the importer will not accept the goods delivered and will not agree to pay for them.

   (ii) The **supplier sends fewer goods** than expected, perhaps because of supply shortages, and so the importer has less to pay for.

(iii) The supplier is **late with the delivery**, and so the importer does not have to pay for the goods until later than expected.

(b) An **exporter** might find the same types of situation, but in reverse, so that it do not receive any payment at all, or it receives more or less than originally expected, or it receives the expected amount, but only after some delay.

## 4.7 Close-out of forward contracts

If a customer cannot satisfy a forward exchange contract, the bank will make the customer fulfil the contract.

(a) If the customer has arranged for the bank to buy currency but then cannot deliver the currency for the bank to buy, the bank will:

(i) **Sell currency** to the **customer** at the **spot rate** (when the contract falls due for performance)

(ii) **Buy** the **currency back**, under the terms of the **forward exchange contract**

(b) If the customer has contracted for the bank to sell them currency, the bank will:

(i) Sell the customer the specified amount of currency at the forward exchange rate

(ii) Buy back the unwanted currency at the spot rate

Thus, the bank arranges for the customer to perform their part of the forward exchange contract by either selling or buying the 'missing' currency at the spot rate. These arrangements are known as **closing out** a forward exchange contract.

## 4.8 Synthetic foreign exchange agreements

In order to reduce the volatility of their exchange rates, some governments have banned foreign currency trading. Examples of affected currencies include the Russian ruble, Indian rupee and Philippine peso.

In such markets, **synthetic foreign exchange agreements (SAFEs)** – also known as non-deliverable forwards – are used. These instruments resemble forward contracts but no currency is actually delivered. Instead the two counterparties settle the profit or loss (calculated as the difference between the agreed SAFE rate and the prevailing spot rate) on a notional amount of currency (the SAFE's face value). At no time is there any intention on the part of either party to exchange this notional amount.

SAFEs can be used to create a foreign currency loan in a currency that is of no interest to the lender.

## Example

A borrower might require US dollars but wants to make the loan repayments in a currency that isn't traded. In this case the borrower will receive dollars and repayments will be calculated in dollars. However, actual payment will be in the other preferred currency, calculated using the current exchange rate.

The lender might wish to lend in US dollars and also receive payment in US dollars. Therefore, at the same time as lending the dollars to the borrower, the lender may also enter into a SAFE with a counterparty that matches the cash flows from the foreign currency repayments.

What has happened is that the lender has a synthetic dollar loan, the borrower has a synthetic second currency loan and the counterparty has a SAFE with the lender.

It is important to remember that **settlement of SAFEs will always be in dollars**, as the counterparty will be unable to settle in the alternative currency (as it is not traded).

## Example

A lender enters into a 3-month SAFE with a counterparty to buy $5m worth of Philippine pesos at a rate of PHP44.000 = $1. The spot rate is PHP43.850 = $1.

When the SAFE is due to be settled in 3 months' time, the spot rate is PHP44.050 = $1. This means that the lender will have to pay 5m × (44.050 − 44.000) = PHP250,000 to the counterparty.

As this will be settled in dollars at the prevailing spot rate, the payment to the counterparty will be PHP250,000/44.050 = $5,675.

# 5 Money market hedging

FAST FORWARD

> **Money market hedging** involves borrowing in one currency, converting the money borrowed into another currency and putting the money on deposit until the time at which the transaction is completed, hoping to take advantage of favourable interest rate movements.

**Exam focus point**

> In June 2008, there was an optional question on foreign currency money market hedging. One of the common errors was the incorrect estimation of the appropriate forward rate.

## 5.1 Using the money market

Because of the close relationship between forward exchange rates and the interest rates in the two currencies, it is possible to 'manufacture' a forward rate by using the spot exchange rate and money market lending or borrowing. This technique is known as a **money market hedge** or **synthetic forward**.

## 5.2 Hedging payments

Suppose a British company needs to **pay** a US supplier in US dollars in three months' time. It does not have enough cash to pay now, but will have sufficient in three months' time. Instead of negotiating a forward contract, the company could:

- Borrow the appropriate amount in pounds now
- Convert the pounds to dollars immediately
- Put the dollars on deposit in a US dollar bank account
- When the time comes to pay the company:
    - Pay the supplier out of the dollar bank account
    - Repay the pound loan account

In the exam a tabular approach may be helpful.

| | Importer | |
| --- | --- | --- |
| | **UK £s** | **USA $s** |
| **Now** | 4  withdraw funds from UK account (1 + borrowing rate)* | 3  put money into US account (1 + deposit)* |
| **Three months** | 5  to compare to a forward | 1  pay $ invoice from supplier<br>2  pay off with $ deposit |

\* Remember to take the interest rate quoted and multiply by 3/12 if you have a 3-month loan

What the tabular approach means is that:

(a)    The transaction determines whether you are paying or receiving

(b)    This is the loan repayment which determines

(c)    How much money you have to place on deposit in the US$ account (the size of the loan), which determines

(d)    The payment in £

The effect is exactly the same as using a forward contract, and will usually cost almost exactly the same amount (step 5 above gives you the cost of the money market hedge to compare to the cost of a forward contract). If the results from a money market hedge were very different from a forward hedge, speculators could make money without taking a risk. Therefore market forces ensure that the two hedges produce very similar results.

## Example: Money market hedge (1)

A UK company owes a Danish supplier Kr3,500,000 in three months' time. The spot exchange rate is Kr7.5509–7.5548 = £1. The company can borrow in sterling for 3 months at 8.60% per annum and can deposit kroner for 3 months at 10% per annum.

*Required*

Calculate the cost in sterling with a money market hedge.

## Solution

The interest rates for 3 months are 2.15% to borrow in pounds and 2.5% to deposit in kroner. The company needs to deposit enough kroner now so that the total including interest will be Kr3,500,000 in 3 months' time. This means depositing:

Kr3,500,000/(1 + 0.025) = Kr3,414,634.

These kroner will cost £452,215 (spot rate 7.5509 – remember the company will always receive the worst rate). The company must borrow this amount and, with 3 months' interest of 2.15%, will have to repay:

£452,215 × (1 + 0.0215) = £461,938.

This can be shown in tabular form as follows.

| | Importer | |
| --- | --- | --- |
| | **UK £** | **Danish Kr** |
| **Now** | 4  withdraw funds from UK account Kr3,414,634/7.5509 = £452,215 | 3  put money into Kr account Kr3,500,000/1.025 = Kr3,414,634 |
| | 8.6% × 3/12 = 2.15% (ie 1.0215) | 10% × 3/12 = 2.5% (ie 1.025) |
| **Three months** | 5  to compare to a forward £452,215 × 1.0215 = £461,938 | 1  pay Kr invoice from supplier  3,500,000 2  pay off with Kr deposit  (3,500,000) |

\* Remember to take the interest rate quoted and multiply by 3/12

Cost of hedge = £461,938

Question

A Thai company owes a New Zealand company NZ$3,000,000, payable in 3 months' time. The current exchange rate is Thai Baht 19.0300–19.0500 = NZ$1.

The Thai company elects to use a money market hedge to manage the exchange risk.

The current annual borrowing and investing rates in the two countries are:

| | New Zealand % | Thailand % |
| --- | --- | --- |
| Investing | 2.5 | 4.5 |
| Borrowing | 3.0 | 5.2 |

*Required*

Calculate the cost to the Thai company of using a money market hedge.

| | Importer | | |
|---|---|---|---|
| | **Thai Bt** | | **New Zealand $** |
| **Now** | 4   withdraw funds from Thai account | | 3   put money into NZ account |
| | $2,981,366 × 19.0500 = Bt56,795,022 | | $3,000,000/1.00625 = $2,981,366 |
| | 5.2% × 3/12 = 1.3% (ie 1.013) | | 2.5% × 3/12 = 0.625 (ie 1.00625) |
| **Three months** | 5   to compare to a forward | | 1   pay $ invoice from supplier   3,000,000 |
| | Bt56,795,022 × 1.013 = Bt57,533,357 | | 2   pay off with $ deposit        (3,000,000) |

Cost of hedge = Bt57,533,357

## 5.3 Hedging foreign currency receipts

A similar technique can be used to cover a foreign currency **receipt** from a customer. To manufacture a forward exchange rate, follow the steps below.

- Borrow an appropriate amount in the foreign currency today
- Convert it immediately to home currency
- Place it on deposit in the home currency
- When the supplier's cash is received:
    - Repay the foreign currency loan
    - Take the cash from the home currency deposit account

This can be shown in tabular form as follows (using an example of a UK exporter receiving $ from a US customer).

| | Exporter | | |
|---|---|---|---|
| | **UK £** | | **US $** |
| **Now** | 4   pay $ loan into UK bank account | | 3   take out $ loan |
| | (1 + deposit rate)* | | (1 + borrowing rate)* |
| **Three months** | 5   to compare to a forward | | 1   receive $ from export |
| | | | 2   pay off $ loan with export revenue |

**Exam focus point**

> Variations on these money market hedges are possible in an examination.

## Example: Money market hedge (2)

A US company is owed SFr2,500,000 in 3 months' time by a Swiss company. The spot exchange rate is SFr2.2498–2.2510 = $1. The company can deposit in dollars for 3 months at 8.00% per annum and can borrow Swiss francs for 3 months at 7.00% per annum. What is the receipt in dollars with a money market hedge and what effective forward rate would this represent?

BPP
LEARNING MEDIA

Part E Treasury and advanced risk management techniques  |  **16: The use of financial derivatives to hedge against foreign exchange risk**        **425**

# Solution

| | Exporter | |
|---|---|---|
| | **US $** | **Swiss Fr** |
| **Now** | **4** pay SFr loan into US account<br>SFr2,457,002/2.2510 = $1,091,516 | **3** take out SFr loan<br>SFr2,500,000/1.0175 = SFr2,457,002 |
| | 8% × 3/12 = 2% (ie 1.02) | 7% × 3/12 = 1.75% (ie 1.0175) |
| **Three months** | **5** to compare to a forward<br>$1,091,516 × 1.02 = $1,113,346 | **1** receive SFr from export 2,500,000<br>**2** pay off SFr loan with<br>export revenue (2,500,000) |

The exporter would receive $1,113,346.

The effective forward rate that has been manufactured is

SF2,500,000/$1,113,346 = 2.2455 – that is, SFr2.2455 = $1

This effective forward rate shows the Swiss franc at a premium to the US dollar, as the Swiss franc interest rate is lower than the US dollar rate.

**Question**

Money market hedge 2

An Australian company is due to receive ¥15,000,000 from a Japanese company, payable in 4 months' time. The current exchange rate is ¥62.6000–62.8000 = A$1.

The Australian company elects to use a money market hedge to manage the exchange risk.

The current annual borrowing and investing rates in the two countries are:

| | Australia<br>% | Japan<br>% |
|---|---|---|
| Investing | 4.5 | 2.7 |
| Borrowing | 6.0 | 3.3 |

*Required*

Calculate the amount the Australian company will receive if it uses a money market hedge.

**Answer**

| | Exporter | |
|---|---|---|
| | **Australian $** | **Japanese ¥** |
| **Now** | **4** pay ¥ loan into Australian account<br>¥14,836,795/62.8000 = A$236,255 | **3** take out ¥ loan<br>15,000,000/1.011 = ¥14,836,795 |
| | 4.5% × 4/12 = 1.5% (ie 1.015) | 3.3% × 4/12 = 1.1% (ie 1.011) |
| **Four months** | **5** to compare to a forward<br>A$236,255 × 1.015 = A$239,799 | **1** receive ¥ from export 15,000,000<br>**2** pay off ¥ loan with<br>export revenue (15,000,000) |

The Australian company will receive A$239,799 from the money market hedge.

## 5.4 Forward exchange contracts versus money market hedge

Is one of these methods of hedging likely to be cheaper than the other? The answer is 'perhaps', but not by much. There will be very little difference between borrowing in foreign currency and repaying the loan with currency receivables and borrowing in the domestic currency and selling forward the currency receivables. This is because the premium or discount on the forward exchange rate reflects the interest differential between the two countries.

## 5.5 Arbitrage profits

**Key term**

> **Arbitrage** is the simultaneous purchase and sale of a security in different markets with the aim of making a risk-free profit through the exploitation of any price differences between the two markets.

Arbitrage means exploiting differences:

- Between two markets, selling in one market, buying in another
- Between two products, where similarities between those products suggest they should be traded at the **same price**

Arbitrage differences are **short term**. As others see the differences and exploit them, prices will converge and the opportunities for exploiting differences will disappear as equilibrium is reached.

### 5.5.1 Arbitrage and exchange rates

Interest rate parity suggests that the spot rate in a year forward will reflect differences in interest rates. However, if the difference between the spot rate now and the forward rate being offered now does not reflect differences in the two countries' interest rates, investors can exploit differences. They can:

- Borrow in currency A
- Deposit what they have borrowed in currency B for a period of time
- Take out a forward contract to sell currency B at the end of the period
- At the end of the period, liquidate the investment and convert the currency B proceeds to currency A under the forward contract
- Repay the amount borrowed in currency A and retain the surplus

# 6 Choosing a hedging method

6/11

This is an important section, as you may be asked to compare different hedging methods in the exam and recommend the most appropriate course of action.

**Exam focus point**

> In the June 2011 exam there was a compulsory Section A question that required you to recommend an appropriate hedging strategy for a company due to receive foreign currency income in the future.

## 6.1 Choice of methods

When a company expects to receive or pay a sum of foreign currency in the next few months, it can choose between using the **forward exchange market** and the **money market** to hedge against the foreign exchange risk. The cheaper option available is the one that ought to be chosen. Other methods may also be possible, such as making **lead payments**.

# Example

Trumpton, a UK company, has bought goods from a US supplier, and must pay $4,000,000 for them in three months' time. The company's finance director wishes to hedge against the foreign exchange risk, and the three methods which the company usually considers are:

- Using forward exchange contracts
- Using money market borrowing or lending
- Making lead payments

The following annual interest rates and exchange rates are currently available.

|  | US dollar | | Sterling | |
|---|---|---|---|---|
|  | Deposit rate | Borrowing rate | Deposit rate | Borrowing rate |
|  | % | % | % | % |
| 1 month | 7 | 10.25 | 10.75 | 14.00 |
| 3 months | 7 | 10.75 | 11.00 | 14.25 |

|  | £1 = $ |
|---|---|
| Spot | 1.8625–1.8635 |
| 1 month forward | 1.8565–1.8577 |
| 3 months forward | 1.8445–1.8460 |

Which is the cheapest method for Trumpton? Ignore commission costs.

# Solution

The three choices must be compared on a similar basis, which means working out the cost of each to Trumpton either **now** or **in three months' time**. Here the cost to Trumpton in three months' time will be determined.

### Choice 1: The forward exchange market

Trumpton must buy dollars in order to pay the US supplier. The exchange rate in a forward exchange contract to buy $4,000,000 in three months' time (bank sells) is $1.8445 = £1.

The cost of the $4,000,000 to Trumpton in three months' time will be:

$$\frac{\$4,000,000}{1.8445} = £2,168,609.38$$

This is the cost **in three months**.

### Choice 2: the money markets

Using the money markets involves lending (depositing) in the foreign currency, as Trumpton will eventually pay the currency.

|  | Importer | |
|---|---|---|
|  | **UK £** | **US $** |
| **Now** | 4   withdraw funds from UK account $3,931,304/1.8625 = £2,110,767 | 3   put money into US account $4,000,000/1.0175 = $3,931,204 |
|  | 14.25 × 3/12 = 3.5625% (ie 1.035625) | 7% × 3/12 = 1.75% (ie 1.0175) |
| **Three months** | 5   to compare to a forward £2,110,767 × 1.035625 = £2,185,963 | 1   pay $ invoice from supplier   $4,000,000 <br> 2   pay off with $ deposit     ($4,000,000) |

The cost of the money market hedge is £2,185,963.

## Choice 3: Lead payments

Lead payments should be considered when the currency of payment is expected to strengthen over time, and is quoted forward at a premium on the foreign exchange market.

Here, the cost of a lead payment (paying $4,000,000 now) would be:

$4,000,000 ÷ 1.8625 = £2,147,651.01$

The cost in three months' time is the cost of lost interest:

$£2,147,651 × (1 + 0.11 × 3/12) = £2,206,711$

In this example, the present value of the costs is as follows.

|  | £ |
|---|---|
| Forward exchange contract | 2,168,609 |
| Money markets | 2,185,867 |
| Lead payment | 2,206,711 |

The cheapest method for Trumpton is the forward exchange contract, therefore the company should use this hedging technique to hedge against transaction risk for this transaction.

**Question**            Hedging techniques

Weft is an importer/exporter of textiles and textile machinery. It is based in the UK but trades extensively with countries throughout Europe, particularly in the Eurozone. It has a small subsidiary based in Germany. The company is about to invoice a customer in Germany for 750,000 euros, payable in 3 months' time. Weft's treasurer is considering two methods of hedging the exchange risk. These are:

**Method 1**

Borrow €750,000 for 3 months, convert the loan into sterling and repay the loan out of eventual receipts.

**Method 2**

Enter into a 3-month forward exchange contract with the company's bank to sell €750,000.

The spot rate of exchange is €1.6006 = £1

The 3-month forward rate of exchange is €1.5935 = £1

Annual interest rates for 3 months' borrowing and lending are: euro 3%, sterling 5%.

*Required*

(a) Which of the two methods is the most financially advantageous for Weft?

(b) What are the other factors to consider before deciding whether to hedge the risk using the foreign currency markets?

**Answer**

(a) **Method 1**

Weft borrows €750,000.

| | Exporter | |
|---|---|---|
| | **UK £** | **€** |
| **Now** | 4 pay € loan into UK bank account<br>€744,417/1.6006 = £465,086 | 3 take out € loan<br>€750,000/1.0075 = €744,417 |
| | 5% × 3/12 = 1.25% (ie 1.0125) | 3% × 3/12 = 0.75% (ie 1.0075) |
| **Three months** | 5 to compare to a forward<br>£465,086 × 1.0125 = £470,900 | 1 receive € from export     €750,000<br>2 pay off € loan with<br>    export revenue        (€750,000) |

Using the money market hedge, Weft will receive £470,900.

**Method 2**

The exchange rate is fixed in advance at €1.5935 by the forward contract. Cash received in three months is converted to produce €750,000/1.5935 = £470,662.

**Conclusion**

On the basis of the above calculations, Method 1 gives a slightly higher receipt. However, the difference is quite small, and banker's commission has been excluded from the calculation.

(b) **Factors to consider before deciding whether to hedge foreign exchange risk using the foreign currency markets**

**Defensive strategy**

The company should have a clear strategy concerning how much foreign exchange risk it is prepared to bear. A highly risk-averse or 'defensive' strategy of hedging all transactions can be **expensive** in terms of **commission costs**, but recognises that exchange rates are unpredictable, can be volatile and so can cause severe losses unless the risk is hedged.

**Predictive strategy**

An alternative **'predictive' strategy** recognises that if all transaction exposures are hedged, the chance of making gains from favourable exchange rate movements is lost. It might be possible to predict the future movement in an exchange rate with some confidence. The company could therefore **attempt** to **forecast foreign exchange movements** and only hedge those transactions where **losses from currency exposures** are **predicted**. For example, if inflation is high in a particular country, its currency will probably depreciate, so that there is little to be gained by hedging **future payments** in that currency. However, **future receipts** in a weak currency would be hedged, to provide protection against the anticipated currency loss.

A predictive strategy can be a risky strategy. If exchange rate movements were certain, **speculators** would almost certainly force an **immediate fall** in the exchange rate. However, some corporate treasurers argue that, if predictions are made sensibly, a predictive strategy for hedging should lead to higher profits within acceptable risk limits than a risk-averse strategy of hedging everything. Fewer hedging transactions will also mean lower commission costs payable to the bank. The risk remains, though, that a single large uncovered transaction could cause severe problems if the currency moves in the opposite direction to that predicted.

**Maximum limit**

A sensible strategy for a company could be to set a **maximum limit**, in money terms, for a **foreign currency exposure**. Exposures above this amount should be hedged, but below this limit a predictive approach should be taken or, possibly, all amounts could be left unhedged.

**Offsetting**

Before using any technique to hedge foreign currency transactions, **receipts and payments** in the same currency at the same date should be **offset**. This technique is known as matching. For example, if the company is expecting to receive €750,000 on 31 March and to pay €600,000 at about the same time, only the net receipt of €150,000 needs to be considered as a currency exposure.

Matching can be applied to receipts and payments which do not take place on exactly the same day by simply hedging the period and amount of the difference between the receipt and payment, or even by using a currency bank account. A company that has many receipts and payments in a single currency such as the euro should consider **matching assets with liabilities** in the same currency.

# 7 Currency futures

> **Key term**
>
> A **currency future** is a standardised contract to buy or sell a fixed amount of currency at a fixed rate at a fixed future date.
>
> - **Buying** the futures contract means **receiving** the contract currency.
> - **Selling** the futures contract means **supplying** the contract currency.

## 7.1 Features of currency futures

Futures are **standardised** contracts that are traded on an organised exchange, such as the Chicago Mercantile Exchange and London International Financial Futures and Options Exchange (now part of the ICE group). They fix the exchange rate for a set amount of currency for a specified time period.

When entering into a foreign exchange futures contract, no one is actually buying or selling anything – the participants are **agreeing** to buy or sell currencies on pre-agreed terms at a specified future date if the contract is allowed to reach maturity, which it rarely does. Futures are a **derivative** (their value derives from movements in the spot rate).

Futures are generally **more liquid** and have **less credit risk** than forward contracts, as organised exchanges have clearing houses that guarantee that all traders in the futures market will honour their obligations.

Futures contracts are assumed to mature at the end of either March, June, September or December. One of their limitations is that currencies can only be bought or sold on exchanges for US dollars.

### 7.1.1 Ticks

The price of a currency future moves in 'ticks'. A tick is the **smallest movement in the exchange rate** and is normally four decimal places.

**Tick value = size of futures contract × tick size**

For example, if a futures contract is for £62,500 and the tick size is $0.0001, the tick value is $6.25. (Note that the tick size and tick value are **always quoted in US dollars**.)

What this means is that for every $0.0001 movement in the price, the company will make a profit or loss of $6.25. If the exchange rate moves by $0.004 in the company's favour – which is 40 ticks (0.004/0.0001) – the profit made will be 40 × $6.25 = $250 per contract.

Examples of futures contract specifications – including tick size and tick value – are given below.

| Currency | Contract size | Price quotation | Tick size | Tick value per contract |
|---|---|---|---|---|
| British pound | £62,500 | US$/£1 | $0.0001 | $6.25 |
| Canadian dollar | C$100,000 | US$/C$1 | $0.0001 | $10.00 |
| Euro | €125,000 | US$/€1 | $0.0001 | $12.50 |
| Japanese yen | ¥12,500,000 | US$/¥100 | $0.000001 | $12.50 |
| Swiss franc | SFr125,000 | US$/SFr1 | $0.0001 | $12.50 |
| Australian dollar | A$100,000 | US$/A$1 | $0.0001 | $12.50 |

> **Exam focus point**
>
> You will usually be given the contract size in the exam.

### 7.1.2 Basis risk

**Key term**

> **Basis risk** is the risk that the price of a currency future will vary from the price of the underlying asset (the spot rate).
>
> **Basis** is the **difference** between the **spot rate** and the **futures price**.

Basis risk is the risk that the price of a futures contract will vary from the spot rate as expiry of the contract approaches. It is assumed that the **difference** between the spot rate and futures price (the 'basis') **falls over time** but there is a risk that basis will not decrease in this predictable way (which will create an imperfect hedge). There is no basis risk when a contract is held to maturity.

In order to **manage** basis risk it is important to choose a currency future with the **closest maturity date** to the actual transaction. This reduces the **unexpired basis** when the transaction is closed out.

### Example

A US company trades in Europe and will need to pay €5 million in 5 months' time. It is now 1 March and futures contracts mature at the relevant month end. The current spot rate is \$1.2500/€1. The following futures contracts are available (\$ per €1).

September    1.2456
December     1.2382

If September contracts are used, there will be two months of unexpired basis. If December contracts are used, there will be five months. If basis is assumed to decline at a constant rate, the unexpired basis on 1 August under each contract would be as follows.

|  | September | December |
|---|---|---|
| Futures price | 1.2456 | 1.2382 |
| Spot rate now | 1.2500 | 1.2500 |
| Difference (basis now) | −0.0044 | −0.0118 |
| Months until contract matures | 7 | 10 |
| Unexpired portion of contract on 1 August | 2/7 | 5/10 |
| Unexpired basis | −0.0013 | −0.0059 |

The September contracts have the lower unexpired basis. Given the shorter time horizon there is less risk of significant differences between the predicted futures price and the actual futures prices on 1 August when the contracts are settled.

In this case, however, the September contracts are closed two months before expiry and there is no guarantee that the price of the futures contract will be the same as the predicted price calculated by basis at that date (ie the spot rate less the closing basis of 0.0013). It is **assumed** that the unexpired basis above is −0.0013 on 1 August but it could be either more or less.

This creates a problem in that the futures contract, which in theory gives a fixed interest cost, may vary and therefore the amount of interest is not fixed or predictable. Typically, this risk is much **smaller** than the risk of remaining unhedged and therefore the impact of this risk is smaller and **preferable** to not hedging at all.

**Exam focus point**

> The December 2013 examining team's report commented that most answers to Question 2 calculated basis incorrectly.

## 7.2 Hedge efficiency

Hedgers who need to buy or sell the underlying currency or commodity do not use the margin to trade more than they otherwise would. They can use the futures markets quite safely provided they understand how the system operates. The only risk to hedgers is that the futures market does not always provide a perfect hedge. This can result from two causes.

(a)     The first reason is that amounts must be **rounded to a whole number of contracts**, causing inaccuracies.

(b)     The second reason is **basis risk** – as discussed above. The actions of speculators may increase basis risk.

A measure of **hedge efficiency** compares the profit made on the futures market with the loss made on the cash or commodity market, or *vice versa*.

### 7.2.1 Example: Hedge efficiency

You are given the following details about the results of a hedge by a US company for a payment of SFr650,000 in 30 days' time under two scenarios. In each case compute the hedge efficiency. Assume today's spot rate is $0.5803 = SFr1. Contract size is SFr125,000, and tick size is $12.50.

Number of contracts = 650,000/125,000 = 5.2, round to 5.

|  | Scenario 1 | | Scenario 2 | |
| --- | --- | --- | --- | --- |
| *Futures hedge (5 contracts)* | $/SFr | $ | $/SFr | $ |
| Today: Buy 5 at | 0.5725 | | 0.5725 | |
| In 30 days: Sell 5 at | 0.6030 | | 0.5610 | |
| Gain/(loss) per contract in ticks | 305 | | (115) | |
| Total gain/(loss) on 5 contracts: | | | | |
| 5 × $12.50 × no. of ticks | | 19,063 | | (7,187) |
| | | | | |
| *Cash transaction* | | | | |
| In 30 days: SFr650,000 are | | | | |
| actually bought at | 0.6112 | (397,280) | 0.5680 | (369,200) |
| | | | | |
| Net cost of the Swiss francs | | (378,217) | | (376,387) |

## Solution

The futures hedge gives slightly more or less than the target payment of $377,195 (SFr650,000 × 0.5803) because of hedge inefficiency. To compute the hedge efficiency in each case, compute gain/loss as a percentage. In scenario 1 the gain comes from the futures market. In scenario 2 the gain comes from the cash market.

| *Hedge efficiency* | $ | $ |
| --- | --- | --- |
| Target payment (650,000 × 0.5803) | 377,195 | 377,195 |
| Actual cash payment | 397,280 | 369,200 |
| Gain/(loss) on spot market | (20,085) | 7,995 |
| | | |
| Futures gain/(loss) | 19,063 | (7,187) |
| | | |
| Hedge efficiency | 94.9% | 111.2% |

The hedge efficiency can be further analysed as follows.

In Scenario 1, the futures market gave a gain of 305 ticks on 5 contracts. The spot market price lost 309 ticks on the equivalent of 5.2 contracts.

Hedge efficiency = $\dfrac{305 \times 5}{309 \times 5.2}$ = 94.9%.

In Scenario 2, the spot market gained 123 ticks on 5.2 contracts. The futures price lost 115 ticks on 5 contracts.

Hedge efficiency = $\dfrac{123 \times 5.2}{115 \times 5}$ = 111.2%.

An alternative measure of the hedge efficiency on the futures market might be its success measured against the **results** of **using a forward contract**.

### 7.2.2 Margins and marking to market

There are two types of margin – **initial margin** and **variation margin**.

An **initial margin** is similar to a deposit. When a currency future is set up, the company would be required to deposit some cash (the initial margin) with the futures exchange in a **margin account** – this acts as security against the company defaulting on its trading obligations. This money will remain in the margin account as long as the currency future remains 'open'.

We mentioned above the process of calculating the profit or loss on a contract when there is movement in the exchange rate. This profit or loss is received into or paid from the margin account on a daily basis rather than in one large amount when the contract matures. This procedure is known as **marking to market**.

The futures exchange monitors the margin account on a daily basis. The company will be required to maintain a minimum balance on its margin account; this is called a **'maintenance margin'**. If the company is making significant losses so that the company's balance on their margin account drops beneath the maintenance margin then extra funds will be demanded by the futures exchange. The demand for extra payment is called a **'margin call'** and the extra payment is called a **'variation margin'**. This practice creates uncertainty, as the company will not know in advance the extent (if any) of such margin payments.

### Example

It is now 20 April. Bison Inc, a US company, has used the futures exchange to hedge a receipt in euros by entering into futures contracts **to sell** euros. The euro contracts have a standard size of 125,000 euros.

Bison Inc has, on 20 April, entered into June contracts to sell euros at a rate of $0.6916 per euro. The tick value is 0.0001 × 125,000 = $12.50.

Bison Inc will make losses on this contract if the euro strengthens because it will close out the contract by entering into a contract to buy euros and if the euro is stronger then it is more expensive to buy.

The futures exchange requires a payment of an **initial margin** of $1,250 per contract, which has been paid by Bison Inc.

The exchange also requires a **maintenance margin** of $1,000 per contract.

Over the next two days the futures price moves as follows.

| | |
|---|---|
| 20 April | 0.6916 |
| 21 April | 0.6930 |
| 22 April | 0.6944 |

On 21 April the futures price has risen by 0.6930 – 0.6916 = 14 ticks. This strengthening of the euro creates a loss for Bison Inc of $175 (14 × $12.50) which reduces the balance on its margin account to $1,075 ($1,250 initial margin – $175). This is still above the required maintenance margin of $1,000, so no further payment is required.

On 22 April there has been a further strengthening of the euro of 14 ticks (0.6944 – 0.6930), again incurring a loss of $175. This now means that the balance on Bison's margin account is $900 ($1,075 – $175 = $900). Because Bison's margin account balance is below the **maintenance margin** of $1,000, a

**margin call** will be made by the exchange and Bison will have to make a **variation margin** payment of $100 to top its margin account up to $1,000.

## 7.3 Which type of contract?

As mentioned above, one of the limitations of currency futures is that currencies can only be bought or sold on exchanges for US dollars. The basic rules for choosing the type of contract are given below.

### 7.3.1 Making a payment in a foreign currency (not US$)

If you are going to make a payment in a foreign currency (not US$) on a future date, you will have to **buy** that currency. To hedge, take the following action.

**Step 1**  **Buy** the appropriate **foreign currency futures** contracts **now** (just as you would with a forward contract).

**Step 2**  **Sell** the same number of **foreign currency futures** contracts on the date that you buy the actual currency (closing out).

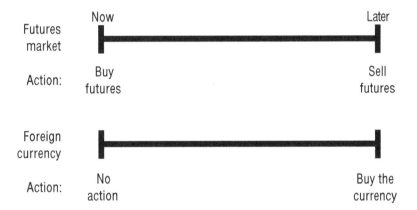

### 7.3.2 Receiving foreign currency on a future date

If you are going to receive money in a foreign currency on a future date, you will need to sell that currency. To hedge this position take the following steps.

**Step 1**  **Sell** the appropriate **foreign currency futures** contracts **now**.

**Step 2**  **Buy** the same number of **foreign currency futures** contracts on the date that you sell the actual currency.

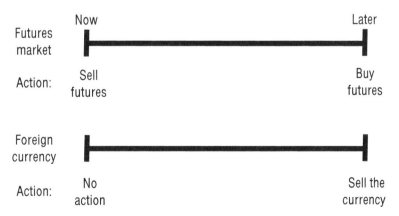

### 7.3.3 Non-American wishing to pay in US$ on a future date

If you are from a country outside the US and are going to make a future payment in US$ you will need to buy US$. To hedge, you cannot buy US$ futures so you will have to sell your own currency's futures.

**Step 1**    Sell your home currency futures contracts now.

**Step 2**    Buy the same number of home currency futures contracts on the date that you buy the US$.

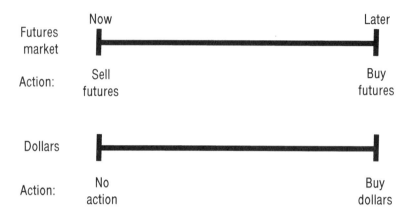

### 7.3.4 Non-American receiving US$ on a future date

If you are from a country outside the US and are going to receive US$ on a future date you will need to sell US$. To hedge you cannot sell US$ futures so you will have to buy your own currency's futures.

**Step 1**    Buy your home currency futures contracts now.

**Step 2**    Sell the same number of home currency futures contracts on the date that you sell the US$.

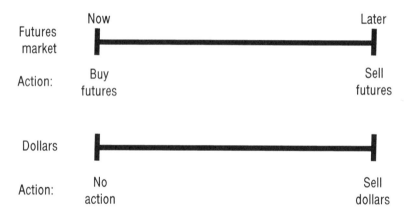

## 7.4 Dealing with a futures question

A number of possible stages are involved.

**Step 1**    **The setup process**

This may involve the following steps.

(a)    **Choose which contract**

You must choose an expiry date after the underlying exposure.

(b)    **Choose type of contract**

A €125,000 contract will be used to buy or sell €. If the company **owes €** it will wish to buy this currency so will **buy € futures**.

However, a UK company receiving $ will wish to sell $ or buy £. As the contract size is quoted in £ (£62,500 to be precise), the company will **buy £ futures**.

(c) **Choose number of contracts**

To find the number of contracts required we divide the amount being hedged by the size of the contract.

We may also have to calculate how much of the currency of the future is required. To find this, we use today's price for the futures contract and then divide by the size of the futures contract.

## Step 2    Estimate the closing futures price

You may be given this in the question, or you may need to estimate this using the concept of basis (covered in Section 7.1.2).

## Step 3    Hedge outcome

(a) **Calculate futures market outcome**

This will be:

Movement in rate × Value of one contract × Number of contracts

(b) **Calculate net outcome**

Spot market payment or receipt translated at closing rate + Futures market profit/(loss)

The currency used for this calculation will be the opposite to the currency of the receipt/payment being hedged. Ultimately, therefore, unless a dollar receipt or payment is being hedged, the value of the futures profit or loss will also have to be converted using the **closing spot rate**.

The gain or loss on the future will accrue during the contract. For exam purposes you will take this gain or loss when the contract is terminated.

# Example

It is 1 April. A US company buys goods worth €745,000 from a German company payable on 1 May. The US company wants to hedge against the euro strengthening against the dollar.

Current spot is $0.9212 = €1 and the June futures rate is 0.9245.

The standard size of a 3-month € futures contract is €125,000.

On 1 May the spot is 0.9351.

*Required*

Evaluate the hedge.

# Solution

## Step 1    Setup

(a) **Which contract?**

We assume that the three-month contract is the best available.

(b) **Type of contract**

We need to buy € or sell $.
As the futures contract is in €, we need to buy futures.

(c)     **Number of contracts**

745,000/125,000 = 5.96, say 6 contracts

**Step 2**     **Closing futures price**

This can be estimated by assuming that the difference between the futures rate and the spot rate (ie basis as covered in Section 7.1) decreases constantly over time. On 1 May there will be two months left of this three-month contract so the basis should have fallen by 1/3, ie 2/3 of the basis on 1 April will remain.

|  | 1 April | 1 May |
|---|---|---|
| Futures price | 0.9245 | |
| Spot rate now | 0.9212 | |
| Basis (future – spot) | 0.0033 | 0.0022 |
| | | (2/3 × 0.0033) |
| Months until June contract matures | 3 | 2 |
| Unexpired portion of contract on 1 May | | 2/3 |

Estimated futures price on 1 May = May spot + 0.0022 = 0.9351 + 0.0022 = 0.9373

**Step 3**     **Hedge outcome**

(a)     **Outcome in futures market**

| Opening futures price | 0.9245 | Buy at low price |
|---|---|---|
| Closing futures price | **0.9373** | Sell at high price |
| Movement | 0.0128 | Profit |

Futures profit/loss = 0.0128 × €125,000 × 6 contracts = $9,600

(b)     **Net outcome**

|  | $ |
|---|---|
| Spot market payment (745,000 × 0.9351) | 696,650 |
| Futures market profit | (9,600) |
| | 687,050 |

In this instance the risk feared was the risk that the payment would go up in $ terms, as you needed more $ to buy each € that you needed to pay the European supplier.

The risk has materialised, as in the end you need to pay $0.9351 to buy each € rather than $0.9212.

Buying the € futures has mitigated this loss because at the end you can sell them for more than you paid, as € have become more valuable.

## 7.4.1 Effective rate

The effective rate obtained on a futures hedge can be analysed by comparing the net outcome to the foreign currency transaction.

In the previous example this would be:

Net outcome                     $687,050

Foreign currency transaction    €745,000

**Effective rate** (687,050/745,000) = $0.9222 to €1.

A **shortcut** that will deliver **approximately** the same answer is:

> **Opening futures price – closing basis = effective futures rate**
>
> Here this gives:
> 0.9245 – 0.0022 (step 2 above) = 0.9223

The slight difference arises because this shortcut does not account for the fact that the futures hedge is for 6 contracts, not 5.96 (step 1). **However, this is a useful shortcut that can be used under exam conditions.**

**Footnote:**

The reason that this quicker method works **(note that this explanation is for interest only and is not directly examinable)** is that the **opening** futures price (used in the quicker method above) can be thought of as the closing spot rate + closing basis – change in the value of the future.

If this is the case then we can restate '**opening futures price** – closing basis' as

'**closing spot + closing basis – change in the value of the future** – closing basis'

This simplifies to:

'closing spot – change in the value of the future'

And this is effectively the approach employed in the longer method shown in the previous example in Section 7.4 (closing spot 0.9351 – 0.0128 movement in future = 0.9223 effective rate).

## 7.5 Useful table to remember

You should remember the following table to help you with exam questions on futures.

| Transaction on future date | | Now | | On future date | |
|---|---|---|---|---|---|
| Receive | Currency | Sell | Currency futures | Buy | Currency futures |
| Pay | Currency | Buy | Currency futures | Sell | Currency futures |

## 7.6 Choosing between forward contracts and futures contracts

**FAST FORWARD**

> Although a foreign exchange **futures** contract is conceptually similar to a **forward** foreign exchange contract, there are important differences between the two instruments.

A futures market hedge attempts to achieve the same result as a forward contract; that is, to fix the exchange rate in advance for a future foreign currency payment or receipt. As we have seen, hedge inefficiencies mean that a futures contract can only fix the exchange rate subject to a margin of error.

Forward contracts are agreed **'over the counter'** between a bank and its customer. Futures contracts are standardised and traded on futures exchanges. This results in the following advantages and disadvantages.

### 7.6.1 Advantages of currency futures

(a)    **Transaction** costs should be **lower** than for forward contracts.

(b)    The **exact date** of **receipt** or **payment** of the currency does **not have to be known**, because the futures contract does not have to be closed out until the actual cash receipt or payment is made. In other words, the futures hedge gives the equivalent of an 'option forward' contract, limited only by the expiry date of the contract.

(c) Because future contracts are traded on exchange regulated markets, **counterparty risk** should be **reduced** and buying and selling contracts should be easy.

## 7.6.2 Disadvantages of currency futures

(a) The **contracts cannot be tailored** to the user's exact requirements.

(b) **Hedge inefficiencies** are **caused** by having to deal in a whole number of contracts and by **basis risk**.

(c) **Only a limited number of currencies** are the subject of futures contracts (although the number of currencies is growing, especially with the rapid development of Asian economies).

(d) The **procedure for converting** between two currencies, neither of which is the US dollar, is twice as complex for futures as for a forward contract.

(e) Using the market will involve various **costs**, including brokers' fees.

In general, the disadvantages of futures mean that the market is much smaller than the currency forward market.

Question                                                                          Currency futures

Allbrit plc, a company based in the UK, imports and exports to the US. On 1 May it signs three agreements, all of which are to be settled on 31 October.

(a) A sale to a US customer of goods for $205,500
(b) A sale to another US customer for £550,000
(c) A purchase from a US supplier for $875,000

On 1 May the spot rate is $1.5500–1.5520 = £1 and the October forward rate is $1.5100–1.5481 = £1. Sterling futures contracts are trading at the following prices.

*Sterling futures (IMM) Contract size £62,500*

| Contract settlement date | Contract price $ per £1 |
| --- | --- |
| Jun | 1.5370 |
| Sep | 1.5180 |
| Dec | 1.4970 |

Tick size is $6.25.

*Required*

(a) Calculate the net amount receivable or payable in pounds if the transactions are covered on the forward market.

(b) Demonstrate how a futures hedge could be set up and calculate the result of the futures hedge if, by 31 October, the spot market price for dollars has moved to 1.5800–1.5820.

Answer

(a) Before covering any transactions with forward or futures contracts, match receipts against payments. The sterling receipt does not need to be hedged. The dollar receipt can be matched against the payment, giving a net payment of $669,500 on 31 October.

Using a forward contract, the sterling cost of the dollar payment will be 669,500/1.5100 = £443,377. The net cash received on 31 October will therefore be £550,000 – 443,377 = £106,623.

(b)   **Step 1**   **Setup**

(a)   **Which contract?**

December contracts

(b)   **Type of contract**

Sell sterling futures in May, we sell the sterling to buy the dollars we need

(c)   **Number of contracts**

Here we need to convert the dollar payment to sterling, as contracts are in sterling.

Using December futures price

$$\frac{669,500}{1.4970} = £447,228$$

No. of contracts = $\dfrac{£447,228}{62,500}$ = 7.16 contracts (round to 7)

**Step 2**   **Closing futures price**

This can be estimated by assuming that the difference between the futures rate and the spot rate decreases constantly over time. On 1 May there are eight months left until the expiry of a December future. By 31 October there are two months left of this contract so the basis should have fallen by 6/8, ie 2/8 of the basis on 1 May will remain.

|  | 1 May | 31 October |
|---|---|---|
| Futures price | 1.4970 | |
| Spot rate now | 1.55 | |
| Basis (future – spot) | –0.0530 | –0.0133 |
| | | (2/8 × –0.0530) |
| Months until December contract matures | 8 | 2 |
| Unexpired portion of contract on 31 Oct | | 2/8 |

Estimated futures price on 31 October = October spot – 0.0133 = 1.58 – 0.0133 = 1.5667

**Step 3**   Result of futures market

(a)   **Futures market outcome**

| | $ | |
|---|---|---|
| Opening futures price | 1.4970 | Sell |
| Closing futures price | 1.5667 | Buy |
| Movement | 0.0697 | Loss |

Futures market loss = 0.0697 × 62,500 × 7 = $30,494

(b) **Net outcome**

| | $ |
|---|---:|
| Spot market payment | (669,500) |
| Futures market loss | (30,494) |
| | (699,994) |
| Translated at closing spot rate | 1.5800 |
| The bank sells low hence we use the rate of 1.5800 | £443,034 |

The effective rate is $669,500/£443,034 = 1.5112

The shortcut to approximately this answer is opening future – closing basis ie 1.4970 – 0.0133 = 1.5103 (closing basis is a negative number in this example)

---

# 8 Currency options    6/11, 12/12, 6/13, 6/14, Mar/June 16

**FAST FORWARD**

**Currency options** protect against adverse exchange rate movements while allowing the investor to take advantage of favourable exchange rate movements. They are particularly useful in situations where the cash flow is not certain to occur (eg when tendering for overseas contracts).

## 8.1 Introduction

**Key term**

A **currency option** is an agreement involving a right, but not an obligation, to buy or sell a certain amount of currency at a stated rate of exchange (the exercise price) at some time in the future.

A forward exchange contract is an agreement to buy or sell a given quantity of foreign exchange, which **must be carried out** because it is a binding contract. However, some exporters might be uncertain about the amount of currency they will earn in several months' time.

An alternative method of obtaining foreign exchange cover, which overcomes much of this problem, is the **currency option**. A currency option **does not have to be exercised**. Instead, when the date for exercising the option arrives, the importer or exporter can either exercise the option or let the option lapse.

The exercise price for the option may be the same as the current spot rate, or it may be more favourable or less favourable to the option holder than the current spot rate.

As with other types of option, buying a currency option involves **paying a premium**, which is the most the buyer of the option can lose. The level of option premiums depends on the following factors:

- The exercise price
- The maturity of the option
- The volatility of exchange and interest rates
- Interest rate differentials, affecting how much banks charge

## 8.2 Basic terminology

This section covers the basic terminology that you will frequently see in questions relating to currency options. Make sure you understand the meaning of each of the terms, as this will help you to interpret questions and make decisions regarding different types of options.

Some of this terminology should be familiar from Chapter 6.

**Key terms**

**Call option** – the right to buy (the contract currency)
**Put option** – the right to sell (the contract currency)

A **call option** gives the **buyer** of the option the **right to buy** the underlying currency at a **fixed rate of exchange** (and the **seller** of the option would be **required to sell** the underlying currency at that rate).

A **put option** gives the **buyer** of the option the **right to sell** the underlying currency at a **fixed rate of exchange** (and the **seller** of the option would be **required to buy** the underlying currency at that rate).

**Key term**

> **Exercise price** – the price at which the future transaction will take place

The exercise price is also known as the **strike price**. It is the price with which the prevailing spot rate should be compared in order to determine whether the option should be exercised or not.

**Key terms**

> **In the money** – where the option strike price is more favourable than the current spot rate
> **At the money** – where the option strike price is equal to the current spot rate
> **Out of the money** – where the option strike price is less favourable than the current spot rate

For example, if a German company holds a call option to purchase £ with a strike price of £0.9174 = €1 and the current spot rate is £0.9200 = €1, the option is '**out of the money**', as the current spot rate is more favourable than the option strike price.

**Key terms**

> A **European option** can only be exercised at the date of expiry.
> An **American option** can be exercised at any date up to and including the date of expiry.

## 8.3 Types of option – over the counter and exchange-traded

Companies can choose whether to buy:

(a) A tailor-made currency option from a bank, suited to the company's specific needs. These are **over the counter** (OTC) or **negotiated** options; or

(b) A standard option, in certain currencies only, from an options exchange. Such options are **traded** or **exchange-traded** options.

### 8.3.1 OTC options                                                                     Mar/Jun 17

OTC options can be purchased directly and are normally **fixed date** (European) options.

## Example

It is now 1 March. Robin Inc anticipates that it may receive €6m from the sale of a European investment in June. It wishes to hedge this potential receipt using options. The current spot rate is €0.7106 = $1. June options with a value of €6m and an exercise price of €0.7200 can be purchased for a premium of $150,000.

*Required*

What will the outcome of the hedge be in each of the following scenarios?

- The spot exchange rate in June is €0.6500.
- The spot exchange rate in June is €0.7500.
- The sale of the investment does not take place.

## Solution

(a) The spot rate is better than the option rate therefore the spot rate is used. This will give a value of $9,230,769 or $9,080,769 after the premium (which is paid up front).

(b) The option rate is better than the spot rate therefore the option will be exercised. This will give a value of $8,333,333 (or $8,183,333 after the premium).

(c) If the sale of the investment is abandoned then the option is no longer necessary. It will be abandoned (as in (a) above). There is no point in exercising the option, as it would cost $8,443,568 to purchase the euros, but Robin Inc would only receive $8,333,333 at the option price (before taking the premium into account). The cost to the company of abandoning the option will be the premium of $150,000.

## 8.3.2 Exchange-traded options

A company wishing to purchase an option to buy or sell sterling might use currency options traded on such US markets as the Philadelphia Stock Exchange. The schedule of prices for $/£ options is set out in tables such as the one shown below.

*Philadelphia SE $/£ options £31,250 (cents per pound)*

| Strike | | Calls | | | Puts | |
| price | Aug | Sep | Oct | Aug | Sep | Oct |
| --- | --- | --- | --- | --- | --- | --- |
| 1.5750 | 2.58 | 3.13 | – | – | 0.67 | – |
| 1.5800 | 2.14 | 2.77 | 3.24 | – | 0.81 | 1.32 |
| 1.5900 | 1.23 | 2.17 | 2.64 | 0.05 | 1.06 | 1.71 |
| 1.6000 | 0.50 | 1.61 | 2.16 | 0.32 | 1.50 | 2.18 |
| 1.6100 | 0.15 | 1.16 | 1.71 | 0.93 | 2.05 | 2.69 |
| 1.6200 | – | 0.81 | 1.33 | 1.79 | 2.65 | 3.30 |

Note the following points.

(a) **What is the contract size?**

The contract size is £31,250.

(b) **What is the meaning of the numbers under each month?**

This is the cost in cents per £ (remember that the market is in the US) – for example, September call at a strike price of $1.6100 will cost $0.0116 × £31,250 = $362.50.

(c) **What is a put US$ per £ option?**

This is the option to sell £ (eg UK importer having to sell £ to obtain $ to pay a US supplier).

(d) **Why is an August call at $1.5800 more expensive than an August call at $1.5900?**

$1.5800 is a better rate than $1.5900 therefore to secure such a rate will be more expensive.

(e) **Why is a call option exercisable in September more expensive than a call option exercisable in August but with the same strike price?**

This is because there is a longer period until the exercise date and it is therefore more likely that exercising the option will be beneficial. The difference also reflects the market's view of the direction in which the exchange rate is likely to move between the two dates.

## 8.3.3 Traded vs OTC options

Both types of options have advantages over the other – the choice of option will depend on particular requirements.

### Advantages of traded options

(a) Traded options are standard sizes and are thus 'tradable' which means they can be sold on to other parties if not required. OTC options are designed for a specific purpose and are therefore unlikely to be suitable for another party.

(b) Traded options are more flexible in that they cover a period of time (American options, whereas OTC options are fixed date (European options).

### Advantages of OTC options

(a) OTC options can be agreed for a longer period than the standard two-year maximum offered by traded options. This gives greater flexibility and protection from currency movements in the longer term should the transaction require it.

(b) OTC options are tailored specifically for a particular transaction, ensuring maximum protection from currency movements. As traded options are of a standard size, the full amount of the transaction may not be hedged, as fractions of options are not available.

Make sure you know these advantages and disadvantages, as they may be useful when making a recommendation regarding hedging strategies.

## 8.4 Choosing the correct type of option

The vast majority of option examples which we consider are concerned with **hedgers** who **purchase** options in order to reduce risk. We are seldom concerned with option writers who sell options.

So, given that we are normally going to **purchase** options, should we **purchase puts or calls**?

(a) A **US company receiving £** in the future and therefore wishing to **sell £** in the future can hedge by **purchasing £ put options** (ie options to sell £).

(b) A **US company paying £** in the future and therefore wishing to **buy £** in the future can hedge by **purchasing £ call options** (ie options to buy £).

(c) A **UK company receiving $** in the future and therefore wishing to **sell $** in the future cannot hedge by purchasing $ put options, as they don't exist. They therefore have to **purchase £ call options**.

(d) A **UK company paying $** in the future and therefore wishing to **buy $** in the future cannot hedge by purchasing $ call options, as they don't exist. They therefore have to **purchase £ put options**.

The following table will be helpful to remember when answering exam questions on currency options.

| Transaction on future date | | Now | | Option on future date | |
|---|---|---|---|---|---|
| Receive | Currency | Buy | Currency put | Sell | Currency |
| Pay | Currency | Buy | Currency call | Buy | Currency |

Note that this table only applies to **traded** options. It would be possible to purchase a dollar put or call option over the counter.

## 8.5 Choosing the price and the number of contracts to be used

A problem arises when a non-US company wishes to buy or sell US dollars using traded options. The amount of US dollars must first be converted into the home currency. For this purpose the best exchange rate to use is the **exercise price**, which means that the number of contracts may vary according to which exercise price is chosen.

## 8.6 Closing out when traded options still have time to run

In practice, most traded options are **closed out**, like futures contracts, because the date when the cash is required does not match the option expiry date.

The position with options is equivalent to the position with **futures**; the expiry date of options must be **on** or **after** the date of the key event. Thus if you were told a company was receiving a payment on 10 September, and you were given a choice of using June, September or December options:

- You could most likely choose September as that expires soonest after 10 September (on 30 September)

- You could choose December

- You would not choose June (as June options expire before 10 September, the date on which you will receive the payment)

## 8.7 Option calculation technique

If an options calculation appears to be complicated, it is best to use a similar method to the method we used for futures to assess the impact of options.

**Set up the hedge**

(a)   Choose contract date
(b)   Decide whether put or call option is required
(c)   Decide which exercise or strike price applies
(d)   How many contracts are required
(e)   Calculate premium (Price in table × 0.01) × Size of contract × Number of contracts

Step 2   **Ascertain closing price**

You should be given this in the question.

Step 3   **Calculate outcome of hedge**

You may have to calculate the outcome under more than one closing spot rate.

(a)   Outcome in options market. This will include:

    (i)   Exercising the option
    (ii)   Cash flows on exercise
    (iii)   Converting amount uncovered/overcovered at spot rate

(b)   Net outcome

# Example

A UK company owes a US supplier $2,000,000 payable in July. The spot rate is $1.5350–1.5370 = £1 and the UK company is concerned that the $ might strengthen.

The details for $/£ £31,250 options (cents per £1) are as follows.

Premium cost per contract

| Strike price | Calls | | | Puts | | |
|---|---|---|---|---|---|---|
| | June | July | August | June | July | August |
| 1.4750 | 6.34 | 6.37 | 6.54 | 0.07 | 0.19 | 0.50 |
| 1.5000 | 3.86 | 4.22 | 4.59 | 0.08 | 0.53 | 1.03 |
| 1.5250 | 1.58 | 2.50 | 2.97 | 0.18 | 1.25 | 1.89 |

Show how traded currency options can be used to hedge the risk at a strike price of 1.525. Calculate the sterling cost of the transaction if the spot rate in July is:

(a)   1.46–1.4620

(b)   1.61–1.6120

# Solution

Step 1   **Set up the hedge**

(a)   Which date contract?  July

(b)   Put or call?  Put, we need to put (sell) pounds in order to generate the dollars we need

(c)   Which strike price?  1.5250

(d)   How many contracts?

$$\frac{2,000,000 \div 1.525}{31,250} = 41.97, \text{ say 42 contracts}$$

(e) Use July put figure for 1.5250 of 1.25. Remember it has to be multiplied by 0.01.

Premium = (1.25 × 0.01) × Contract size × Number of contracts

Premium = 0.0125 × 31,250 × 42

= $16,406 ÷ 1.5350 (to obtain premium in £)

= £10,688

We need to pay the option premium in $ now. Therefore the bank sells low at 1.5350.

## Step 2 Closing spot and futures price

Case (a) $1.46

Case (b) $1.61

## Step 3 Outcome

(a) **Options market outcome**

| | | |
|---|---|---|
| Strike price put | 1.5250 | 1.5250 |
| Closing price | 1.46 | 1.61 |
| Exercise? | Yes | No |
| Outcome of options position (31,250 × 42) | £1,312,500 | – |

**Balance on spot market**

| | $ |
|---|---|
| | $ |
| Exercise option (31,250 × 42 × 1.5250) | 2,001,563 |
| Value of transaction | 2,000,000 |
| Balance | 1,563 |

Translated at spot rate $\dfrac{1,563}{1.46}$ = £1,071

(b) **Net outcome**

| | £ | £ |
|---|---|---|
| Spot market outcome translated at closing spot rate $\dfrac{2,000,000}{1.61}$ | – | (1,242,236) |
| Options position | (1,312,500) | – |
| Difference in hedge at closing rate | 1,071 | |
| The difference is a receipt as the amount owed was overhedged. | | |
| Premium (remember premium has to be added in separately as translated at the opening spot rate) | (10,688) | (10,688) |
| | (1,322,117) | (1,252,924) |

 **Question** Currency options 1

Edted is a UK company that has purchased goods worth $2,000,000 from a US supplier. Edted is due to make payment in three months' time. Edted's treasury department is looking to hedge the risk using an OTC option. A three-month dollar call option has a price of 1.4800.

*Required*

Ignoring premium costs, calculate the cost to Edted if the exchange rate at the time of payment is:

(a) $1.4600 = £1
(b) $1.5000 = £1

As the option is an OTC option, it is possible to have a dollar call option and to cover the exact amount.

(a)    If the exchange rate is 1.4600, the option will be exercised and the cost will be:

$$\frac{2,000,000}{1.4800} = £1,351,351$$

(b)    If the exchange rate is 1.5000, the option will not be exercised, and the cost will be:

$$\frac{2,000,000}{1.5000} = £1,333,333$$

**Question**                                                           Currency options 2

Vinnick, a US company, purchases goods from Santos, a Spanish company, on 15 May on 3 months' credit for €600,000.

Vinnick is unsure in which direction exchange rates will move so has decided to buy options to hedge the contract at a rate of €0.7700 = $1.

The details for €10,000 options at 0.7700 are as follows.

| Calls | | | Puts | | |
|---|---|---|---|---|---|
| July | August | September | July | August | September |
| 2.55 | 3.57 | 4.01 | 1.25 | 2.31 | 2.90 |

The current spot rate is 0.7800.

*Required*

Calculate the dollar cost of the transaction if the spot rate in August is:

(a)    0.7500
(b)    0.8000

**Answer**

**Step 1**    **Set up the hedge**

(a)    Which contract date? August

(b)    Put or call? Call – we need to buy euros

(c)    Which strike price? 0.7700

(d)    How many contracts?

$$\frac{600,000}{10,000} = 60$$

(e)    Use August call figure of 3.57. Remember it has to be multiplied by 0.01.

Premium = (3.57 × 0.01) × contract size × number of contracts

Premium = 0.0357 × 10,000 × 60 = $21,420

**Step 2**  **Closing spot and futures prices**

Case (a)  0.75

Case (b)  0.80

**Step 3**  **Outcome**

(a)  **Options market outcome**

| | | |
|---|---|---|
| Strike price call | 0.77 | 0.77 |
| Closing price | 0.75 | 0.80 |
| Exercise? | Yes | No |
| Outcome of options position | €600,000 | – |

(b)  **Net outcome**

| | $ | $ |
|---|---|---|
| Spot market outcome translated at closing spot rate (600,000/0.80) | – | (750,000) |
| Options position (600,000/0.77) | (779,221) | – |
| Premium | (21,420) | (21,420) |
| | (800,641) | (771,420) |

**Exam focus point**

Under exam conditions it is **quicker** just to illustrate the outcome **if the option is exercised**. This means that you do not have to assess whether the option will be exercised and this saves time. If you do this you should make it clear in your answer that if the option is **not exercised** it will be because the spot rate is better than the option rate. This means that the calculations that show the outcome if the option is exercised are illustrating a **worst-case scenario**.

## 8.8 Graphical illustration of currency options

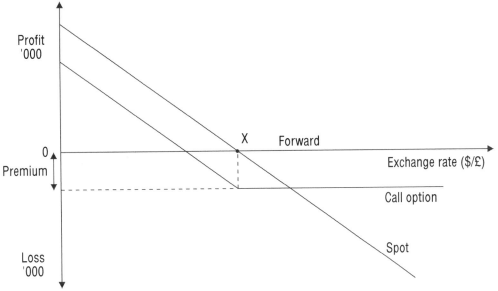

*Currency call option, forward and spot markets: profit/loss profile*

Suppose that a UK-based company expects to receive an amount of export income in dollars in three months' time. This graph illustrates the profit/loss profile of different strategies.

(a) Selling dollars and buying sterling in the **forward market** eliminates all uncertainty. The outcome is represented by a horizontal line.

(b) Relying on the **spot market** results in a net gain or loss compared with the forward market if the spot exchange rate in three months' time turns out to be below or above $X per pound respectively.

(c) If a **call option** is used, it will not be exercised if the exchange rate is less than $X per pound. A currency call option reduces the potential gain compared with the spot market strategy (b) by the amount of the premium on the option, but has the advantage that potential losses are contained, as they will not exceed the value of the premium.

## 8.9 Currency options vs forward and futures contracts

A hedge using a currency future will produce approximately the same result as a currency forward (subject to hedge inefficiencies). When comparing currency options with forward and futures contracts we usually find the following.

(a) If the currency movement is adverse, the option will be exercised. However, the hedge will not normally be as good as that of forward or futures contracts – this is due to the premium cost of the option.

(b) If the currency movement is favourable, the option will not be exercised. The hedge will normally be better than that of forward or futures contracts, as the option allows the holder to profit from the improved exchange rate.

# 9 Currency swaps

6/11, Mar/Jun 17

FAST FORWARD

> **Currency swaps** effectively involve the exchange of debt from one currency to another.
>
> Currency swaps can provide a **hedge** against exchange rate movements for longer periods than the forward market and can be a means of obtaining finance from new countries.

## 9.1 Swap procedures

Key term

> A **swap** is an arrangement whereby two organisations contractually agree to exchange payments on different terms, for example in different currencies, or one at a fixed rate and the other at a floating rate.

In a **currency swap**, the parties agree to swap equivalent amounts of currency for a period. This effectively involves the exchange of debt from one currency to another. Liability on the main debt (the principal) is not transferred and the parties are liable to **counterparty risk**: if the other party defaults on the agreement to pay interest, the original borrower remains liable to the lender. In practice, most currency swaps are conducted between banks and their customers. An agreement may only be necessary if the swap were for longer than, say, one year.

## Example

Consider a US company X with a subsidiary Y in France which owns vineyards. Assume a spot rate of €0.7062 = $1. Suppose the parent company X wishes to raise a loan of €1.6 million for the purpose of buying another French wine company. At the same time, the French subsidiary Y wishes to raise $1 million to pay for new up to date capital equipment imported from the US. The US parent company X could borrow the $1 million and the French subsidiary Y could borrow the €1.6 million, each effectively borrowing on the other's behalf. They would then swap currencies.

## 9.2 Benefits of swaps

(a) **Flexibility**

Swaps are **easy to arrange** and are **flexible** since they can be arranged in any size and are reversible.

(b) **Cost**

**Transaction costs are low**, only amounting to legal fees, since there is no commission or premium to be paid.

(c) **Market avoidance**

The parties can **obtain the currency they require** without subjecting themselves to the **uncertainties** of the foreign exchange markets.

(d) **Access to finance**

The company can gain **access to debt finance in another country** and currency where it is little known, and consequently has a poorer credit rating, than in its home country. It can therefore take advantage of lower interest rates than it could obtain if it arranged the currency loan itself.

(e) **Financial restructuring**

Currency swaps may be used to **restructure the currency base** of the company's liabilities. This may be important where the company is trading overseas and receiving revenues in foreign currencies, but its borrowings are denominated in the currency of its home country. Currency swaps therefore provide a means of reducing exchange rate exposure.

(f) **Conversion of debt type**

At the same time as exchanging currency, the company may also be able to **convert fixed rate debt** to **floating rate or *vice versa***. Thus it may obtain some of the benefits of an interest rate swap in addition to achieving the other purposes of a currency swap.

(g) **Liquidity improvement**

A currency swap could be used to **absorb excess liquidity** in one currency which is not needed immediately, to create funds in another where there is a need.

## 9.3 Disadvantages of swaps

(a) **Risk of default by the other party to the swap (counterparty risk)**

If one party became **unable to meet its swap payment obligations**, this could mean that the other party risked having to make them itself.

(b) **Position or market risk**

A company whose main business lies outside the field of finance should **not increase financial risk** in order to make **speculative gains**.

(c) **Sovereign risk**

There may be a risk of **political disturbances or exchange controls** in the country whose currency is being used for a swap.

(d) **Arrangement fees**

Swaps have arrangement fees payable to third parties. Although these may appear to be cheap, this is because the intermediary accepts **no liability** for the swap. (However, the third party does suffer some spread risk, as it warehouses one side of the swap until it is matched with the other, and then undertakes a temporary hedge on the futures market.)

## Example

**Step 1**  Edted, a UK company, wishes to invest in Germany. It borrows £20 million from its bank and pays interest at 5%. To invest in Germany, the £20 million will be converted into euros at a spot rate of €1.50 = £1. The earnings from the German investment will be in euros, but Edted will have to pay interest on the swap. The company arranges to swap the £20 million for €30 million with Gordonbear, a company in the euro currency zone. Gordonbear is thus the counterparty in this transaction. Interest of 6% is payable on the €30 million. Edted can use the €30 million it receives to invest in Germany.

**Step 2**  Each year when interest is due:

(a)  Edted receives from its German investment cash remittances of €1.8 million (€30 million × 6%)

(b)  Edted passes this €1.8 million to Gordonbear so that Gordonbear can settle its interest liability

(c)  Gordonbear passes to Edted £1 million (£20 million × 5%)

(d)  Edted settles its interest liability of £1 million with its lender

**Step 3**  At the end of the useful life of the investment the original payments are reversed, with Edted paying back the €30 million it originally received and receiving back from Gordonbear the £20 million. Edted uses this £20 million to repay the loan it originally received from its UK lender.

---

**Exam focus point**

> Make sure you read the ACCA article entitled 'Currency swaps'.

## 10 FOREX swaps

**Key term**

> A **FOREX swap** is a spot currency transaction coupled with an agreement that it will be reversed at a pre-specified date by an offsetting forward transaction.

Although the FOREX swap is arranged as a single transaction, it consists of two distinct separate legs. The counterparties agree to exchange two currencies at a particular rate on one date and to reverse payments normally at a different rate on a specified future date. The two legs can therefore be seen as one spot **transaction** and **one forward transaction** going in **opposite directions**.

An FOREX swap is called a **buy/sell** swap when the base currency eg the dollar is bought on the near date and sold on the far date, and is called a **sell/buy** swap when the base currency is sold on the near date and bought on the far date.

A FOREX swap is useful for hedging because it allows companies to shift temporarily into or out of one currency in exchange for a second currency without incurring the exchange rate risk of holding an open position in the currency they temporarily hold. This avoids a change in currency exposure which is the role of the forward contract.

An example of a FOREX swap is where Bank ABC enters into a FOREX swap with Bank 123 to:

- Sell US$1,000,000 worth of Japanese Yen (JPY) today
- Buy US$1,000,000 worth of JPY in one week's time

This FOREX swap (known as a spot to forward date swap) would look something like this.

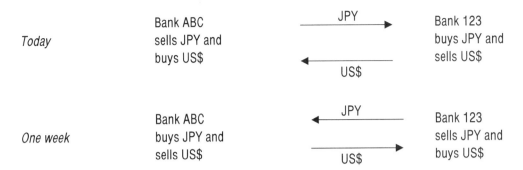

In the above example, the FOREX swap is made up of a spot FOREX transaction and a one-week forward transaction. Other types of FOREX swaps include transactions where both the first and second halves (legs) occur in the future. These are known as forward against forward swaps and are, in effect, two forward transactions operating in parallel.

# 11 Devising a foreign currency hedging strategy

**6/11, 12/12, 6/13**

Given the wide range of financial instruments (both internal and external) available to companies that are exposed to foreign currency risk, how can an appropriate strategy be devised that will achieve the objective of reduced exposure while at the same time keeping costs at an acceptable level and not damaging the company's relationship with its customers and suppliers?

There is no individual best way of devising a suitable hedging strategy – each situation must be approached on its own merits. Unless you are told otherwise, it should be assumed that the company will want to minimise its risk exposure – it is up to you to come up with the most appropriate way of doing so. You should be prepared to justify your choice of strategy.

The following example will give you an idea of how to put together a suitable strategy while justifying your choice of doing so.

## Example – foreign currency hedging strategy

IOU Inc is a large company based in the US that trades mainly within the US and with the UK. It has a significant amount of borrowing in sterling. Debt interest of £725,000 is due to be paid on 31 October and a further £530,000 on 31 December. IOU Inc's policy is to hedge the risks involved in all foreign currency transactions.

Assume it is now 30 September. The company's bank quotes the following rates of exchange, US$ per £:

| Spot | 1 month forward (mid rate) | 3 months forward (mid rate) |
|---|---|---|
| 1.5584–1.5590 | 1.5601 | 1.5655 |

Prices for a $/£ option on a US stock exchange (cents per £, payable on purchase of the option, contract size £31,250) are:

| Strike price ($/£) | Calls | | Puts | |
|---|---|---|---|---|
| | October | December | October | December |
| 1.56 | 2.02 | 3.00 | 1.00 | 2.16 |
| 1.57 | 1.32 | N/A | N/A | N/A |
| 1.58 | 0.84 | 2.12 | 2.18 | 3.14 |

The treasurer is considering two methods of hedging the risk, forward and option contracts. Market expectations, based on current published economic forecasts, are that sterling will appreciate against the US dollar over the next three months. The treasurer thinks the pound might weaken or at least remain stable against the dollar. They suggest that if options are to be used, one-month options should be bought at a strike price of 1.57 and three-month options at a strike price of 1.58.

Ignore transaction costs.

*Required*

(a)     Recommend, with reasons, the most appropriate method for IOU Inc to hedge its foreign exchange risk on the two interest payments due in one and three months' time. Your answer should include appropriate calculations, using the figures in the question, to support your recommendation and a discussion of the factors to consider when choosing between the two hedging mechanisms.

Assume you are a financial manager with the nationally owned postal and telecommunications company in Zorro, a country in Asia. In organisations such as this, periodic settlements are made between local and foreign operators. Net receipts or payments are in US dollars.

(b)     Explain the main types of foreign exchange risk exposure that are likely to affect the organisation and advise the company on policies it could consider to reduce exposure to these risks.

# Solution

(a)     **Spot market position**

The company expects to pay £1,255,000. At today's spot rate this would be converted to $ at $1.5590, giving 1,255,000 × 1.5590 = $1,956,545.

**Forward contracts**

Forward contracts remove the **risk** from **future short-term currency fluctuations** by fixing an exchange rate in advance. If forward contracts are used, the following dollar costs will be incurred.

One month:      £725,000 × 1.5601 = $1,131,073
Three months:   £530,000 × 1.5655 = $829,715
Total payment:  1,131,073 + 829,715 = $1,960,788

A forward contract will mean that the interest payment is of a **predictable amount** and the possibility of exchange losses is **eliminated**. However, IOU will not be able to participate in **exchange gains** if the pound weakens.

**Options**

Options can be used to put a 'ceiling' (or 'cap') on the amount payable while allowing the user to take advantage of **favourable exchange rate movements**.

**Option set-up October payment**

(i)      Contract date – October

(ii)     Option type – Call option; buy £ with $

(iii)    Strike price – Choose $1.57 as recommended by the treasurer

(iv)     Number of contracts

$$\frac{725,000}{31,250} = 23.2 \text{ contracts. Say 23 contracts hedging } 31,250 \times 23$$

= £718,750, leaving £6,250 to be hedged on forward market.

(v)      Premium = 23 × 31,250 × $0.0132 = $9,488

**Outcome**

Option will be exercised if dollar weakens to more than $1.57 in £.

Exercise 23 contracts @ $1.57

|  | $ |
|---|---|
| Option outcome 1.57 × 23 × £31,250 | 1,128,438 |
| Option premium | 9,488 |
| Unhedged amount covered by forward contract £6,250 × 1.5601 | 9,751 |
|  | 1,147,677 |

### Option set-up December payment

(i)     Contract date – December contract

(ii)     Option type – Call option

(iii)     Strike price – Choose $1.58

(iv)     Number of contracts

$$\frac{530,000}{31,250} = 16.96 \text{ contracts, say 17 contracts hedging £31,250} \times 17$$

$$= £531,250, \text{ with difference taken to forward market } (531,250 - 530,000)$$

$$= £1,250)$$

(v)     Premium = $17 \times 31,250 \times \$0.0212 = \$11,263$

### Outcome

Option will be exercised if dollar weakens to more than $1.58 in £.

|  | $ |
|---|---|
| Option outcome 1.58 × 17 × 31,250 | 839,375 |
| Option premium | 11,263 |
| Forward contract receipt £1,250 × 1.5655 | (1,957) |
| Net payment | 848,681 |

### Breakeven rate

The disadvantage of options is that they can be expensive to buy because of the premium. The breakeven rate, the rate below which options will give a more favourable outcome than a forward contract, can be calculated as follows, ignoring the issue of whole contracts.

(Breakeven rate × amount hedged) + premium = forward contract payment

For October breakeven rate = $\dfrac{1,131,073 - 9,488}{725,000} = \$1.5470$

For December breakeven rate = $\dfrac{829,715 - 11,263}{530,000} = \$1.5442$

### Recommendation

Options should only be used if there is thought to be a good chance that the pound will weaken (but protection is still required against its strengthening). If, as the market believes, the pound is likely to strengthen, forward contracts will offer better value.

(b)     **Exchange risks in Zorro**

### Transactions exposure

This is the risk that the exchange rate **moves unfavourably** between the **date of agreement** of a contract price and the **date of cash settlement**.

### Economic exposure

This is the risk of an **adverse change in the present value** of the organisation's future cash flows as a result of longer-term exchange rate movements.

### Netting off

The Zorro postal and telecommunications company will receive **domestic income** in its local currency but will make **settlements** (net receipts or payments) with foreign operators in US dollars. It may appear that most of the **currency risk** is **hedged** because **dollar payments** are balanced against **dollar receipts** before settlement. However, although this is a good way of reducing currency transaction costs, it does not remove currency risk.

### Residual risk

Although the foreign transactions are denominated in dollars, the exchange risk involves all the **currencies of the countries** with which the company deals. For example, if money is owed to Germany and the euro has strengthened against the dollar, then the dollar cost of the transaction has increased. Also, although all of these transactions are short term, their combined effect is to expose the company to **continuous exchange risk** on many currencies. The company needs a strategy to manage this form of **economic exposure**.

### Management of currency risk

One way to manage currency risk in this situation is to attempt to **match assets and liabilities** in each currency as follows:

(i) The company needs to examine each country with which it deals and, having selected those with which it has a material volume of transactions, **determine in each case** whether there is a **net receipt** or **net payment** with that country and the average amount of this net receipt/payment.

(ii) If for a given country there is normally a net receipt, currency risk can be hedged by **borrowing an amount** in that currency equal to the **expected net receipt** for the period for which hedging is required, and **converting this amount** to the home currency.

(iii) For countries where there is **normally a net payment**, a **deposit account** in this currency should be maintained.

### Recommendation

This strategy will go some way towards hedging currency risk in the various countries involved, but will involve **increased currency transaction costs** and possibly **increased interest costs**. It is therefore probably only feasible for major currencies (eg dollar, euro, yen) and for currencies of Asian countries with which there are major transaction volumes.

# Chapter Roundup

- The **spot rate** is the rate at which currencies can be exchanged now. The **forward rate** is the rate at which currencies will be exchanged on a set future date.

- The difference between the bid price and the offer price is known as the **spread**.

- Internal hedging techniques include **leading and lagging, invoicing in home currency, matching** and **multilateral netting**.

- Netting is a process in which credit balances are netted off against debit balances so that only the reduced net amounts remain due to be paid by actual currency flows.

- A **forward contract** is a contract with a bank that covers a **specific amount** of foreign currency for delivery at an **agreed date** at an **exchange rate agreed now**.

- **Money market hedging** involves borrowing in one currency, converting the money borrowed into another currency and putting the money on deposit until the time at which the transaction is completed, hoping to take advantage of favourable interest rate movements.

- Although a foreign exchange **futures** contract is conceptually similar to a **forward** foreign exchange contract, there are important differences between the two instruments.

- **Currency options** protect against adverse exchange rate movements while allowing the investor to take advantage of favourable exchange rate movements. They are particularly useful in situations where the cash flow is not certain to occur (eg when tendering for overseas contracts).

- **Currency swaps** effectively involve the exchange of debt from one currency to another.

- Currency swaps can provide a **hedge** against exchange rate movements for longer periods than the forward market and can be a means of obtaining finance from new countries.

1    A US exporter receives HK$400,000 from a customer. The bank has quoted an offer price of HK$7.7000 and a bid price of HK$7.7425. How many US dollars will the exporter receive from the bank in exchange for HK$400,000?

2    Which factors influence the supply and demand for currencies?

3    Fill in the boxes in the diagram with (A) to (E), to indicate which factors are linked by which theory.

   (A)    Purchasing power parity theory

   (B)    Expectations theory

   (C)    Fisher effect

   (D)    International Fisher effect

   (E)    Interest rate parity

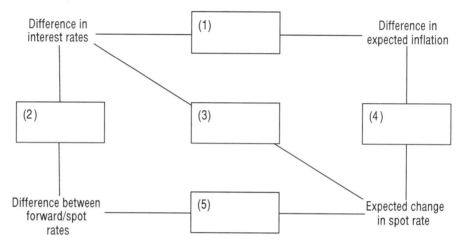

4    Complete the following table using buy or sell.

| Transaction on future date | | Now | | On future date | |
|---|---|---|---|---|---|
| Receive | currency | | currency futures | | currency futures |
| Pay | currency | | currency futures | | currency futures |

5    Complete the following table using buy or sell.

| Transaction on future date | | Now | | | Option on future date | | |
|---|---|---|---|---|---|---|---|
| Receive | currency | | | | | | |
| Pay | currency | | | | | | |

6    What are the key stages in setting up an option hedge?

7    What is the significance of a settlement date in futures?

8    What are the main factors affecting the level of option premiums?

9    Fill in the blank.

   ........................................ risk is the risk of one party on a swap defaulting on the arrangement.

10   Swaps, like other derivatives, can be used as methods of speculation.

   True    ☐

   False    ☐

11    Trebzon Ltd, a UK company, plans to use a money market hedge to hedge its payment of €4,000,000 for Spanish goods in one year. The UK interest rate is 6% and the euro interest rate is 4%. The spot exchange rate is €1.46 = £1. Determine the amount of £ needed if a money market hedge is used.

12    Thalmes Inc is a multinational company that has a bid on a project funded by the Slovenian Government. If the company succeeds in its bid it will have to invest €2,000,000. The decision will be announced three months from now. The management of Thalmes is afraid that dollar devaluation will increase the cost of investment and would like to hedge against the risk of devaluation. Which of the following three strategies (buy forward, buy futures, buy call option) is the most appropriate in your view?

1   The bank is buying the currency therefore the bid price of HK$7.7425 is relevant (remember that the exporter will always pay the higher price). The exporter will receive:

HK$400,000/7.7425 = $51,662.90

2   (a)   Relative rates of inflation    (d)   Market sentiment

    (b)   Relative interest rates    (e)   Speculation

    (c)   Balance of payments position    (f)   Government policy

3   (1)   (C) Fisher effect

    (2)   (E) Interest rate parity

    (3)   (D) International Fisher effect

    (4)   (A) Purchasing power parity

    (5)   (B) Expectations theory

4

| Transaction on future date | | Now | | On future date | |
|---|---|---|---|---|---|
| Receive | currency | Sell | currency futures | Buy | currency futures |
| Pay | currency | Buy | currency futures | Sell | currency futures |

5

| Transaction on future date | | Now | | Option on future date | |
|---|---|---|---|---|---|
| Receive | currency | Buy | currency put | Sell | currency |
| Pay | currency | Buy | currency call | Buy | currency |

6   • Choose contract date
    • Put or call options
    • Strike price
    • No. of contracts
    • Premium

7   A settlement date is the date when trading on a futures contract stops and all accounts are settled.

8   • Exercise price
    • Maturity of option
    • Volatility of exchange/interest rates
    • Interest rate differentials

9   **Counterparty** risk is the risk of one party on a swap defaulting on the arrangement.

10   True

11   Deposit amount to hedge in euro = $\dfrac{4,000,000}{1+0.04} = 3,846,154$

The amount of £ needed is €3,846,154/1.46 = £2,634,352

12   The most appropriate strategy is to buy a call option which will expire in three months. If the bid is successful Thalmes can use the option to purchase the euros needed. Even if the bid is not accepted it will still exercise the option if the euro spot rate exceeds the exercise price and sell the euros in the open market.

| Number | Level | Marks | Time |
|--------|-------|-------|------|
| 30 | Introductory | 15 | 29 mins |
| 31 | Introductory | 25 | 49 mins |
| 32 | Introductory | 15 | 29 mins |
| 33 | Examination | 20 | 39 mins |
| 34 | Examination | 25 | 49 mins |

# 17

# The use of financial derivatives to hedge against interest rate risk

| Topic list | Syllabus reference |
|---|---|
| 1 Interest rate risk | E3 |
| 2 Hedging with forward rate agreements (FRAs) | E3(a)(i) |
| 3 Interest rate futures | E3(a)(ii) |
| 4 Interest rate options | E3(a)(iv) |
| 5 Interest rate swaps | E3(a)(iii) |
| 6 Hedging strategy alternatives – example | E3(a) |
| 7 Issues surrounding the use of derivatives | E1(b) |
| 8 The Greeks – measuring the impact of risk factors | E1(b)(iv) |

## Introduction

This chapter continues our discussion and application of derivatives – this time focusing on **interest rate hedging**. In times of volatile interest rates, companies borrowing large sums of money may wish to hedge against adverse movements in interest rates that could have a significant effect on the level of interest payments. Similarly, companies lending large sums of money may wish to hedge against interest rates falling which will have an adverse effect on interest received.

In this chapter we focus on the different types of interest rate derivatives, their characteristics and how they work. It is important to know how to **apply** these instruments in particular scenarios and also how to **recommend** the best instrument for that scenario. Make sure you are familiar with the advantages and disadvantages of the different instruments for **evaluation** purposes.

We also consider various issues surrounding the use of derivatives in general and finish the chapter with the Greeks.

# Study guide

| | | Intellectual level |
|---|---|---|
| **E1** | **The role of the treasury function in multinationals** | |
| (b) | Discuss the operations of the derivatives market, including: | 3 |
| | (i) The relative advantages and disadvantages of exchange-traded versus OTC agreements | |
| | (ii) Key features, such as standard contracts, tick sizes, margin requirements and margin trading | |
| | (iii) The source of basis risk and how it can be minimised | |
| | (iv) Risks such as delta, gamma, vega, rho and theta, and how these can be managed | |
| **E3** | **The use of financial derivatives to hedge against interest rate risk** | |
| (a) | Evaluate for a given hedging requirement which of the following is the most appropriate given the nature of the underlying position and the risk exposure: | 3 |
| | (i) Forward rate agreements | |
| | (ii) Interest rate futures | |
| | (iii) Interest rate swaps | |
| | (iv) Interest rate options | |

One of the optional performance objectives in your PER is to advise on using instruments or techniques to manage financial risk. This chapter looks at interest rate risk, which is an aspect of financial risk.

# 1 Interest rate risk

**FAST FORWARD**

Factors influencing interest rate risk include:

* Fixed rate versus floating rate debt
* The term of the loan

**Key term**

**Interest rate risk** is the risk to the profitability or value of a company resulting from changes in interest rates.

## 1.1 Managing a debt portfolio

Corporate treasurers will be responsible for managing the company's debt portfolio; that is, in deciding how a company should obtain its short-term funds so as to:

(a) Be able to repay debts as they mature

(b) Minimise any inherent risks, notably invested foreign exchange risk, in the debts the company owes and is owed

There are a number of situations in which a company might be exposed to risk from interest rate movements.

## 1.2 Risks from interest rate movements

(a) **Fixed rate versus floating rate debt**

A company can get caught paying **higher interest rates** by having fixed rather than floating rate debt, or floating rather than fixed rate debt, as market interest rates change.

**Expectations of interest rate movements** will determine whether a company chooses to borrow at a fixed or floating rate. The term structure of interest rates – the rates available on loans of different length – should help businesses determine the market's view on how interest rates are likely to move in the future.

Fixed rate finance may be more expensive; however, the business runs the risk of **adverse upward rate movements** if it chooses floating rate finance.

Other factors include:

(i) **Finance term** (the longer the term the more difficult interest rates are to predict)

(ii) The **differences between fixed and floating rates**, plus arrangement costs or new finance

(iii) The **finance risk tolerance** of the directors

(iv) **Existing debt mix** (greater finance diversification may be desirable to hedge all possibilities)

(v) **Current pressures on liquidity** – if the business is stretched in the short term, it may prefer to take the lower rate available on floating rate debt. In doing so, it is taking the risk that rates may rise and borrowing eventually becomes more expensive. However, the directors are calculating that if this happens, the company will have accumulated sufficient cash to be able to bear the higher rates.

(b) **Currency of debt**

A company can face higher costs if it borrows in a currency for which exchange rates move adversely against the company's domestic currency. The treasurer should seek to **match the currency of the loan** with the **currency of the underlying operations/assets** that generate revenue to pay interest/repay the loans.

(c) **Term of loan**

A company can be exposed by having to **repay a loan earlier** than it can afford to, resulting in a need to reborrow, perhaps at a higher rate of interest.

(d) **Term loan or overdraft facility**

A company might prefer to **pay for borrowings only when it needs the money** as with an overdraft facility: the bank will charge a commitment fee for such a facility. Alternatively, a term loan might be preferred, but this will cost interest even if it is not needed in full for the whole term.

(e) **Rises in interest rates**

A company may plan to take out borrowing at some time in the future, but face the possibility that **interest rates may rise before the term of borrowing commences**. This problem can be addressed by using financial instruments to fix or cap the rate of interest. This is described later in this chapter.

---

**Exam focus point**

In the exam, watch out for information in the scenario about factors affecting the company's attitude to risk, such as company size and risk appetite of directors. This may determine both the composition of the debt portfolio and the methods used to manage its risks.

---

## 1.3 Interest rate risk management

If the organisation faces interest rate risk, it can seek to **hedge the risk**. Alternatively, where the magnitude of the risk is **immaterial** in comparison with the company's overall cash flows or appetite for risks, one option is to **do nothing**. The company then accepts the effects of any movement in interest rates which occur.

The company may also decide to do nothing if **risk management costs are excessive**, both in terms of the costs of using derivatives and the staff resources required to manage risk effectively. **Appropriate products** may not be available and of course the company may consider hedging unnecessary, as it believes that the **chances of an adverse movement** are **remote**.

**Exam focus point**

Bear in mind the possibility that a company may take the decision to do nothing to reduce interest rate risk – it is a situation you should consider when answering exam questions.

The company's **tax situation** may also be a significant determinant of its decision whether or not to hedge risk. If hedging is likely to **reduce variability of earnings**, this may have tax advantages if the company faces a higher rate of tax for higher earnings levels. The directors may also be unwilling to undertake hedging because of the need to **monitor the arrangements**, and the **requirements to fulfil the disclosure requirements** of International Financial Reporting Standards.

## Question

Hedging

Explain what is meant by hedging in the context of interest rate risk.

## Answer

Hedging is a means of reducing risk. Hedging involves coming to an **agreement with another party** who is prepared to take on the risk that you would **otherwise bear**. The other party may be willing to take on that risk because it would otherwise bear an opposing risk which may be 'matched' with your risk; alternatively, the other party may be a speculator who is willing to bear the risk in return for the prospect of making a profit. In the case of interest rates, a company with a variable rate loan clearly faces the risk that the rate of interest will increase in the future as a result of changing market conditions which cannot now be predicted.

Many financial instruments have been introduced in recent years to help corporate treasurers to hedge the risks of interest rate movements. These instruments include forward rate agreements, financial futures, interest rate swaps and options.

## Case Study

**Tate & Lyle** noted in its 2016 annual report that:

> *The Group has an exposure to interest rate risk arising principally from changes in US dollar, sterling and euro interest rates. This risk is managed by fixing or capping portions of debt using interest rate derivatives to achieve a target level of fixed/floating rate net debt, which aims to optimise net finance expense and reduce volatility in reported earnings. The Group's policy is that between 30% and 75% of Group net debt is fixed or capped for more than one year and that no interest rates are fixed for more than 12 years. At 31 March 2016, the longest term of any fixed rate debt held by the Group was until October 2027. The proportion of net debt at 31 March 2016 ... that was fixed or capped for more than one year was 60% (2015 – 31%)%.*

> *(Tate & Lyle annual report, 2016, p.131)*

## 1.4 Interest rate risk management techniques

Methods of reducing interest rate risk include the following:

- **Netting** – aggregating all positions, assets and liabilities, and hedging the net exposure
- **Smoothing** – maintaining a balance between fixed and floating rate borrowing
- **Matching** – matching assets and liabilities to have a common interest rate

- **Pooling** – (see Section 1.4.1 below)
- **Forward rate agreements** (FRAs) (Section 2)
- **Interest rate futures** (Section 3)
- **Interest rate options or interest rate guarantees** (Section 4)
- **Interest rate swaps** (Section 5)

### 1.4.1 Pooling

Pooling means asking the bank to pool the amounts of all its subsidiaries when **considering interest levels and overdraft limits**. It should **reduce the interest payable, stop overdraft limits being breached** and **allow greater control by the treasury department**. It also gives the company the potential to take advantage of **better rates of interest** on **larger cash deposits**.

# 2 Hedging with forward rate agreements (FRAs)    12/13

FRAs hedge risk by **fixing the interest rate** on future borrowing.

**Key term**

An **FRA** is an agreement, typically between a company and a bank, about the interest rate on future borrowing or bank deposits.

## 2.1 How do FRAs work?

An **FRA** does not involve the actual transfer of capital from one party to another. An FRA is an agreement to borrow/lend a notional amount for up to 12 months at an agreed rate of interest (the FRA rate). The 'notional' sum is the amount on which the interest payment is calculated. Only the interest on the notional amount between the rate dealt (that is, the rate when the FRA is traded) and the rate prevailing at the time of settlement (the reference rate) actually changes hands.

If there is a rise in interest rates between the time that the FRA is traded and the date that the FRA comes into effect, the borrower is protected from paying the higher interest rate. If interest rates fall during that time, the borrower must pay the difference between the **traded FRA rate** and the **actual rate** on the notional sum.

If a borrower wishes to hedge against an increase in interest rates to cover a **three-month loan starting in three months' time**, this is known as a **3 v 6 FRA**. A three-month loan starting in one month's time would be a 1 v 4 FRA etc.

### Important dates

| | |
|---|---|
| **Trade date** | The date on which the contract begins (or when the contract is 'dealt'). |
| **Spot date** | The date on which the interest rate of the FRA is determined. |
| **Fixing date** | The date on which the reference rate (which will be compared with the FRA rate on settlement) is determined. The reference rate is the LIBOR on the fixing date. The fixing date is usually two business days before the settlement date. |
| **Settlement date** | The date on which the notional loan is said to begin. This date is used for the calculation of interest on the notional sum. For example, if you entered into a 3 v 6 FRA, this would be 3 months after the spot date. |
| **Maturity date** | The date on which the notional loan expires. For example, in a 3 v 6 FRA, this would be 3 months after the settlement date. |

# Example

It is 30 June. Lynn will need a $10m 6-month fixed rate loan from 1 October. Lynn wants to hedge using an FRA. The relevant FRA rate is 6% on 30 June.

What is the result of the FRA and the effective loan rate if the 6-month FRA benchmark rate has moved to:

(a) 5%?
(b) 6.5%?

# Solution

(a) As there has been a fall in the interest rate Lynn must **pay** the difference between the **traded FRA rate** and the **actual rate** on the notional sum.

This can be analysed in percentage terms as follows:

|  | % |
| --- | --- |
| FRA payment (6%–5%) | (1) |
| Payment on underlying loan 5% | (5) |
| Net payment on loan | (6) |

This can then be shown as a $ cost by multiplying the $10m loan by 6% and multiplying by 6 months (the term of the loan) divided by 12 months (interest rates are quoted in annual terms) ie $10m $\times$ 0.06 $\times$ $^6/_{12}$ = **$300,000**

**Alternatively** this can be shown in $'s as follows:

|  | $ |
| --- | --- |
| FRA payment $10m $\times$ (6% − 5%) $\times$ $^6/_{12}$ | (50,000) |
| Payment on underlying loan 5% $\times$ $10m $\times$ $^6/_{12}$ | (250,000) |
| Net payment on loan | (300,000) |

Effective annual interest rate = $0.3m / $10m $\times$ 12 months / 6 months $\times$ 100 = 6%

(b) As there has been a rise in the interest rate Lynn will **receive** the difference between the **traded rate** and the **actual rate** on the notional sum.

This can be analysed in percentage terms as follows:

|  | % |
| --- | --- |
| FRA receipt (6% − 6.5%) | 0.5 |
| Payment on underlying loan 6.5% | (6.5) |
| Net payment on loan | (6) |

Again, this can then be shown as a $ cost by multiplying the $10m loan by 6% and multiplying by 6 months (the term of the loan) divided by 12 months (interest rates are quoted in annual terms) ie $10m $\times$ 0.06 $\times$ 6/12 = **$300,000**

**Alternatively** this can be shown in $s as follows:

|  | $ |
| --- | --- |
| FRA payment $10m $\times$ (6% − 6.5%) $\times$ $^6/_{12}$ | 25,000 |
| Payment on underlying loan 6.5% $\times$ $10m $\times$ $^6/_{12}$ | (325,000) |
| Net payment on loan | (300,000) |

Effective annual interest rate = $0.3m / $10m $\times$ 12 months / 6 months $\times$ 100 = 6%

BPP
LEARNING MEDIA

## 2.2 Advantages of FRAs

(a) **Protection provided**

An FRA would protect the borrower from **adverse interest rate movements** above the rate negotiated.

(b) **Flexibility**

FRAs are **flexible**; they can in theory be arranged for any amounts and any duration, although they are normally for amounts of over $1m.

(c) **Cost**

FRAs may well be **free** and will in any case **cost little**.

## 2.3 Disadvantages of FRAs

(a) **Rate available**

The rate the bank will set for the FRA will reflect **expectations of future interest rate movements**. If interest rates are expected to rise, the bank may set a **higher rate** than the rate currently available.

(b) **Falling interest rate**

The borrower will **not be able to take advantage** if interest rates fall unexpectedly.

(c) **Term of FRA**

The FRA will **terminate on a fixed date**.

(d) **Binding agreement**

FRAs are **binding agreements** so are less easy to sell to other parties.

### Question

FRAs

Rumple Inc will shortly be making a short-term investment and wants to borrow $4m for 3 months, starting in 3 months' time. However, interest rates are currently volatile and it is worried about adverse movements in these rates before it takes out the loan.

LIBOR (the base rate) is currently 3.5% and Rumple has been offered a 3 v 6 FRA for 3.75%. Rumple can currently borrow at approximately 1% above the base rate.

*Required*

Advise Rumple of the likely outcome of the FRA if the base rate in 3 months' time is:

(a)    4%
(b)    3%

### Answer

(a)    The actual base rate is above the FRA rate, therefore the bank will pay the difference as compensation to Rumple – that is, 0.25%.

Rumple will borrow at the best available rate, which is base rate + 1% – that is, 5% (4 + 1).

Net cost to Rumple = 5% – 0.25% = 4.75%

(b)    As the actual base rate is below the FRA rate, Rumple will pay compensation of 0.75% to the bank.

Rumple will borrow at the best available rate – that is, 4% (3 + 1).

Net cost to Rumple = 4% + 0.75% = 4.75%

This amounts to $0.0475 \times 3/12 \times \$4m = \$47,500$

# 3 Interest rate futures

> **FAST FORWARD**
>
> **Interest rate futures** can be used to hedge against interest rate changes between the current date and the date at which the interest rate on the lending or borrowing is set. Companies who will need to **borrow** money **enter into futures contracts 'to sell'** to hedge against **interest rate rises**. Companies who will have **cash surpluses** will **enter into futures contracts 'to buy'** to hedge against **interest rate falls**.

## 3.1 Futures contracts

We covered currency futures in the previous chapter so you should be familiar with how they work. Interest rate futures are similar to currency futures in that they are used to hedge against movements in the underlying (in this case, interest rates).

Interest rate futures are a similar method of hedging to FRAs, except that the amounts and time periods are standardised. A typical short-term interest rate future would be for a standard amount of £500,000 for a period of 3 months.

### 3.1.1 Contracts to buy and sell

**Key term**

> Companies that will have a cash flow surplus and what to invest/lend it require **contracts to buy**.
> Companies who will borrow require **contracts to sell**.

A company that will have a **cash surplus** over a period of time in the future will be worried about interest rates falling.

This company can arrange a futures contract to 'deposit' and 'receive interest' on a standard amount of money (for example £500,000) at a fixed interest rate for a fixed period (normally 3 months).

This requires a **contract(s) to buy.**

A company that will need to **borrow money** in future due an expected **cash deficit** over a period of time in the future will be worried about interest rates rising.

This company can arrange a futures contract to 'borrow' and 'pay interest' on a standard amount of money (for example £500,000) at a fixed interest rate for a fixed period (normally 3 months).

This requires a **contract(s) to sell.**

## 3.2 Pricing futures contracts

The interest rate (ie the price) on a short-term interest rate futures contract is quoted on an index basis.

- If the interest rate on a short-term futures contract is 8% this will be quoted as a price of 92 (100 − 8).

- If interest rates are 11%, the contract price will be 89 (100 − 11).

## Example

Yew has taken a 3-month $1,000,000 eurodollar loan with interest payable of 8%, the loan is due to be rolled over (ie renewed) on 31 March.

At 1 January, the company treasurer considers that interest rates are likely to rise in the near future. The March futures price is 91 representing a yield of 9%.

Given a standard futures contract size of $1,000,000, the company enters into a **March contract to sell** a eurodollar 3-month contract to hedge against interest on the 3-month loan required at 31 March.

At 31 March the spot interest rate is 11% and a March future is priced at 89.

What is the impact of the futures contract to Yew?

## Solution

| | | | |
|---|---|---|---|
| On 1 January Yew entered into a **contract to sell** at: | 9% | or | 91 |
| On 31 March Yew will enter into a **contract to buy** at: | 11% | or | 89 |
| Yew makes a profit on this futures contract of: | 2% | or | 2 |

The profit of 2 is the percentage profit on a standard loan of $1 million for 3 months. So the **profit on the futures contract is**:

$1,000,000 \times 0.02 \times {}^3/_{12} = \$5,000$

The hedge has effectively reduced the net annual interest cost by 2%.

## 3.3 Use of interest rate futures

The seller of a futures contract does not have to own the underlying instrument. However, the seller may need to deliver it on the contract's delivery date if the buyer requires it. Many, but not all, interest rate contracts are **settled for cash** rather than by delivery of the underlying instrument.

Interest rate futures offer an attractive means of **speculation** for some investors, because there is no requirement that buyers and sellers should actually be lenders and borrowers (respectively) of the nominal amounts of the contracts.

## 3.4 Basis risk

**Basis risk** (which was covered in Chapter 16, Section 7) also occurs for interest rate futures.

If a firm takes a position in the futures contract with a view to closing out the contract before its maturity, there is still likely to be basis. The firm can only **estimate what effect** this will **have on the hedge**. '**Basis risk**' refers to the problem that the **basis may result in an imperfect hedge**. The basis will be **zero** at the **maturity date of the contract**.

The basis risk can be calculated as the difference between the futures price and the current price ('**cash market' price**) of the underlying security.

### 3.4.1 Example: Basis and basis risk

To give an example, if 3-month London Interbank Offered Rate (LIBOR) is 7% and the September price of the 3-month sterling future is 92.70 now (at the end of March, say) then the basis is:

| | | |
|---|---|---|
| Future (100–92.7) | 7.30 | |
| LIBOR | 7.00 | |
| | 0.30 | % |
| | or 30 | basis points |

> **Exam focus point**
>
> In the exam, you might be given other price information and have to calculate the closing futures price from it.

A further cause of basis risk for interest rates is that there are significantly more possible actual interest rates than there are standard contracts. Therefore management may wish to calculate the correlation between the futures price movement and the underlying price movement. This can be used to calculate **hedging ratios** (which were covered in Chapter 16, Section 7) which can be used to determine the overall number of contracts required. **Delta hedging** (covered in Section 8 of this chapter) can also be used to reduce this risk.

## 3.5 Setting up a futures hedge

The basic procedure for setting up an interest rate futures hedge is similar to that for currency futures. The following example illustrates the process.

# Example

Panda has taken a 6-month $10,000,000 loan with interest payable of 8%, the loan being due for rollover on 31 March. At 1 January, the company treasurer considers that interest rates are likely to rise in the near future. The futures price is 91 representing a yield of 9%. Given a standard contract size of $1,000,000, the company enters into a contract to sell a dollar 3-month contract to hedge against interest on the 3-month loan required at 31 March (to sell a contract is to commit the seller to take a deposit). At 31 March the interest rate is 11% and the futures price had fallen to 88.50.

*Required*

Demonstrate how futures can be used to hedge against interest rate movements.

# Solution

The following steps should be taken.

### Setup

(a)  What contract: 3-month contract

(b)  What type: contract to sell (as borrowing and rates expected to rise)

(c)  How many contracts: $\dfrac{\text{Exposure}}{\text{Contract size}} \times \dfrac{\text{Loan period}}{\text{Length of contract}} = \dfrac{10m}{1m} \times {}^{6}/_{3} = 20$ contracts

### Closing price

Closing futures price = 88.50

### Outcome

(a)  **Futures outcome**

| | | | | |
|---|---|---|---|---|
| At opening rate: | 91.00 | or | 9% | sell |
| At closing rate: | 88.50 | or | 11.5% | buy |
| | 2.50 | or | 2.5% | receipt |

Futures outcome:

$$\text{Receipt} \times \text{Size of contract} \times \text{Number of contracts} \times \dfrac{\text{Length of contract}}{\text{One year}}$$

$0.0250 \times 1,000,000 \times 20 \times {}^{3}/_{12} = \$125,000$

(b)  **Net outcome**

| | $ | % |
|---|---|---|
| Payment in spot market $10m × 11% × $^{6}/_{12}$ | (550,000) | (11) |
| Receipt in futures market | 125,000 | 2.5 |
| Net payments | (425,000) | ( 8.5) |

Effective interest rate = $\dfrac{425,000}{10,000,000} \times {}^{12}/_{6} = 8.5\%$

## 3.6 Advantages of interest rate futures

(a) **Cost**

Costs of interest rate futures are reasonably **low**.

(b) **Amount hedged**

A company can **hedge relatively large exposures of cash** with a **relatively small initial employment of cash**.

## 3.7 Disadvantages of interest rate futures

(a) **Inflexibility of terms**

Traded interest rate futures are for **fixed periods** and **cover begins in March, June, September or December**. Contracts are for **fixed**, **large amounts**, so may not entirely match the amount being hedged.

(b) **Basis risk**

The company may be liable to the risk that the **price of the futures contract** may not move in the expected direction.

(c) **Daily settlement**

The company will have to settle **daily profits or losses** on the contract (this concept is covered in Chapter 16 Section 7.2.2).

**Question**                                                                                    Interest rate futures

Rumple Inc (see question 'Forward rate agreements' in Section 2) is now considering using interest rate futures to hedge the $4m loan. It is now 1 March and the Chicago Board of Trade is quoting the following prices on standardised $1m 3-month contracts. Note that these prices are quoted in basis points at (100 – annual yield).

| | |
|---|---|
| March | 96.00 |
| June | 96.10 |
| September | 96.20 |

Contracts are assumed to expire at the end of the quoted months. LIBOR remains at 3.5% and Rumple can still borrow at a rate of approximately LIBOR + 1%.

*Required*

Assuming that Rumple takes out a loan at a fixed rate of LIBOR + 1% at the start of the loan, illustrate the outcome of the futures contract if LIBOR is:

(a)   4%
(b)   3%

**Answer**

The solution to this question shows the outcome of the futures hedge **in percentage terms and then converts into $s at the end.** This is slightly different to the example above and is intended to demonstrate an alternative approach to futures questions. Either approach is acceptable you should use the approach that you prefer.

**Setup**

(a)   What contract? **3 months**

(b)   What type? **Sell** (as Rumple is borrowing and rates are expected to rise)

(c)    How many contracts? $\dfrac{\text{Exposure}}{\text{Contract size}} \times \dfrac{\text{Loan period}}{\text{Length of contract}}$ = ($4m/$1m) × (3/3) = **4 contracts**

(d)    Date? **June** (start of the loan)

### Closing price

The closing price has to be calculated using basis.

| | Now – 1 March | (a) – 1 June | (b) – 1 June |
|---|---|---|---|
| June future | 3.90 | 4.10 | 3.10 |
| LIBOR | 3.50 | 4.00 | 3.00 |
| Basis | 0.40 | 0.10 | 0.10 |

Due to 4 months of time difference between the start of March and the end of June

One month's basis remains (that is, 0.40/4). We know LIBOR therefore price of June future on 1 March is the balancing figure

### Outcome

| | (a) | (b) |
|---|---|---|
| Actual loan rate (LIBOR + 1%) | 5.00 | 4.00 |
| Profit/loss on future | | |
| Opening rate (pay) | 3.90 | 3.90 |
| Closing rate (receive) | 4.10 | 3.10 |
| | 0.20 | 0.80 |
| | PROFIT | LOSS |
| Net rate | 4.80 | 4.80 |
| | Note the fixed outcome | Note the fixed outcome |

In $s this represents 4.8% × $4m × 3/12 = **$48,000**.

Note that the **short-cut** to calculating the effective rate on a currency futures contract (covered in Chapter 16 Section 7.4.1) can also be applied here:

**Opening futures price    – closing basis = effective rate**

3.90              –     0.1     =      3.8

The effective LIBOR rate is 3.8% and Rumple Inc borrows at LIBOR + 1% so the effective borrowing rate is 3.8 + 1 = **4.8%. (The same answer as before but a quicker method.)**

# 4 Interest rate options      12/11, 12/13, 12/14, Sep/Dec 15

Interest rate options allow an organisation to limit its exposure to adverse interest rate movements while also allowing it to take advantage of favourable interest rate movements.

## 4.1 What is an interest rate option?

**Key term**

An **interest rate option** grants the buyer of the option the right, but not the obligation, to deal at an agreed interest rate (strike rate) at a future maturity date. On the date of expiry of the option, the buyer must decide whether or not to exercise the right.

Clearly the buyer of an option to borrow will not wish to exercise it if the market interest rate is now below that specified in the option agreement. Conversely, an option to lend will not be worth exercising if market rates have risen above the rate specified in the option by the time the option has expired.

Tailor-made 'over the counter' interest rate options can be purchased from major banks, with specific values, periods of maturity, denominated currencies and rates of agreed interest. The cost of the option is the 'premium'. Interest rate options offer more flexibility – and are more expensive – than FRAs.

**Exchange traded options** are also available. These have **standardised amounts** and **standard periods**.

## 4.2 Exchange traded options

Exchange traded interest rate options are available as options on interest rate futures which give the holder the right to buy (call option) or sell (put option) one futures contract on or before the expiry of the option at a specified price. The best way to understand the pricing of interest rate options is to look at a schedule of prices. The table below gives an example:.

UK long gilt futures options (LIFFE) £100,000 100ths of 1%

| | Calls | | | Puts | | |
|---|---|---|---|---|---|---|
| Strike price | Nov | Dec | Jan | Nov | Dec | Jan |
| £113.50 | 0.87 | 1.27 | 1.34 | 0.29 | 0.69 | 1.06 |
| £114.00 | 0.58 | 0.99 | 1.10 | 0.50 | 0.91 | 1.32 |
| £114.50 | 0.36 | 0.76 | 0.88 | 0.77 | 1.18 | 1.60 |

This schedule shows that an investor could pay $1.34/100 \times £100,000 = £1,340$ to purchase the right to buy a sterling futures contract in January at a price of £113.50 per £100 stock.

If, say, in December, January futures are priced **below** £113.50 (reflecting an interest rate **rise**), the option will not be exercised. In calculating any gain from the call option, the premium cost must also be taken into account.

If the futures price moves **higher**, as it is likely to if interest rates **fall**, the option will be exercised. The profit for each contract will be current futures prices – 113.50 – 1.34.

## 4.3 Traded put and call options

**Key term**

> A **call option** is the right to **buy** (in this case, to receive interest at the specified rate).
>
> A **put option** is the right to **sell** (that is, the right to pay interest at the specified rate).

To use traded interest rate options for hedging, follow exactly the same principles as for traded currency options.

(a) If a company needs to hedge **borrowing** (where interest will be paid) at a future date it should **purchase put options** to **sell futures**.

(b) Similarly, if a company is lending money (and will therefore be receiving interest) it should **purchase call options** to **buy futures**.

## Example

Panda wishes to borrow £4 million fixed rate in June for 9 months and wishes to protect itself against rates rising above 6.75%. It is 11 May and the spot rate is currently 6%. The data is as follows.

Interest rate guarantees

Short sterling options (LIFFE)

£1,000,000 points of 100%

| Effective interest rate | Calls | | | Puts | | |
|---|---|---|---|---|---|---|
| % | Jun | Sep | Dec | Jun | Sep | Dec |
| 6.75 | 0.16 | 0.03 | 0.03 | 0.14 | 0.92 | 1.62 |
| 6.50 | 0.05 | 0.01 | 0.01 | 0.28 | 1.15 | 1.85 |
| 6.25 | 0.01 | 0.01 | 0.01 | 0.49 | 1.39 | 2.10 |

Panda negotiates the loan with the bank on 12 June (when the £4 million loan rate is fixed for the full 9 months) and closes out the hedge.

What will be the outcome of the hedge and the effective loan rate if prices on 12 June have moved to:

(a) 7.4%?
(b) 5.1%?

## Solution

The following method (similar to currency options) should be used.

### Step 1    Setup

(a) Which contract?      June

(b) What type?      Put (as we are borrowing and therefore paying interest)

(c) Strike price      93.25   $(100 - 6.75)$

(d) How many?      $\dfrac{£4m}{£1m} \times {}^9/_3 = 12$ contracts

(e) Premium      At 93.25 (6.75%) June puts = 0.14p

$$\text{Contracts} \times \text{premium} \times \frac{\text{Size of contract}}{\left( \dfrac{12 \text{ months}}{\text{Length of contract}} \right)} = 12 \times 0.0014 \times \frac{1,000,000}{({}^{12}/_3)} = £4,200$$

### Step 2    Closing prices

(a) 7.4%
(b) 5.1%

### Step 3    Outcome

| Options market outcome | (a) | (b) |
|---|---|---|
| Right to pay interest at | 6.75 | 6.75 |
| Closing rate | 7.40 | 5.10 |
| Exercise? | **Yes** | **No** |
| **Net position** | | |
| | £ | £ |
| Spot (£4m × 9/12 × 5.1%) | | 153,000 |
| Option (£4m × 9/12 × 6.75%) | 202,500 | |
| Option premium | 4,200 | 4,200 |
| Net outcome | 206,700 | 157,200 |
| **Effective interest rate** | *(a)* | *(b)* |
| | (206,700/4,000,000) × (12/9) | (157,200/4,000,000) × (12/9) |
| | = 6.89% | = 5.24% |

## Question

Rumple Inc (see Section 2 question entitled 'Forward rate agreements') is now considering using options to hedge against interest rate movements on its $4 million loan. It is now 1 March and LIBOR remains at 3.5%. Rumple Inc can still borrow at approximately LIBOR + 1%.

Options on 3-month futures ($1,000,000 contract size, premium cost in %) are as follows.

|       | Calls |       |       | Puts  |       |       |
|-------|-------|-------|-------|-------|-------|-------|
|       | Mar   | Jun   | Sep   | Mar   | Jun   | Sep   |
| 96000 | 0.120 | 0.195 | 0.270 | 0.020 | 0.085 | 0.180 |
| 96250 | 0.015 | 0.075 | 0.155 | 0.165 | 0.255 | 0.335 |
| 96500 | 0     | 0.085 | 0.085 | 0.400 | 0.480 | 0.555 |

*Required*

Illustrate an option hedge at 3.75%, assuming that the loan is taken out at LIBOR + 1% and LIBOR is:

(a) 4%
(b) 3%

## Answer

Again this solution takes the approach of leaving everything in % and converting to $ at the end.

**Setup**

(a) **Which contract?** June

(b) **What type?** Put (as we are paying interest on borrowings)

(c) **Strike price** 96.250 (100 – 3.75)

(d) **How many?** $\dfrac{\text{Exposure}}{\text{Contract size}} \times \dfrac{\text{Loan period}}{\text{Length of contract}}$ = ($4m/$1m) × (3/3) = 4 contracts

(e) **Premium** At 96.250 (3.75%) June puts = 0.255%

$\text{Contracts} \times \text{premium} \times \dfrac{\text{Size of contract}}{\left(\dfrac{\text{12 months}}{\text{Length of contract}}\right)}$ = 4 × 0.00255 × [$4m/(12/3)] = $10,200

**Outcome**

| Options market outcome | (a) | (b) |
|---|---|---|
| Right to pay interest at | 5.00% | 4.00% |
| **Profit/loss on option** | | |
| Opening position – put | 3.75% | 3.75% |
| Closing position – future (see calculation in Section 3 question 'Interest rate futures') | 4.10% | 3.10% |
| | 0.35% (profit) | Do not exercise option |
| **Net outcome** | 5.00 + 0.255 − 0.35 | 4.00 + 0.255 |
| | = 4.905% | = 4.255% |
| In $ | 0.04905 × $4m × 3/12 | 0.04255 × $4m × 3/12 |
| | = $49,050 | $42,550 |

## 4.4 Caps, floors and collars

An **interest rate cap** is an option which sets an interest rate ceiling.

An interest rate **floor** is an option which sets a lower limit to interest rates.

Using a **collar** arrangement, the borrower can buy an interest rate cap and at the same time sell an interest rate floor which reduces the cost for the company.

Various cap and collar agreements are possible.

The cost of a collar is lower than for a cap alone. However, the borrowing company forgoes the benefit of movements in interest rates below the floor limit in exchange for this cost reduction.

## Example

Suppose the prevailing interest rate for a company's borrowing is 10%. The company treasurer considers that a rise in rates above 12% will cause serious financial difficulties for the company. How can the treasurer make use of a cap and collar arrangement?

## Solution

The company can buy an interest rate cap from the bank. The bank will reimburse the company for the effects of a rise in rates above 12%. As part of the arrangements with the bank, the company can agree that it will pay at least 9%, say, as a 'floor' rate. The bank will pay the company for agreeing this. In other words, the company has sold the floor to the bank, which partly offsets the costs of the cap. The bank benefits if rates fall below the floor level.

### 4.4.1 Traded caps

Say you are a borrower and have bought a put option (a right to sell the future). The exercise price is 93.00, reflecting an interest rate of 7%.

**Interest rate rises**

- If the interest rate you have to pay **rises to 8%**, the price of the future will fall to 92.00.

- You will buy the future at 92.00 and exercise your option to sell it at 93.00.

- The profit you make on buying and then selling the future can be set against the 8% interest you have to pay, to give an **effective interest rate of 7%**.

**Interest rate falls**

- If the interest rate **falls to 6%**, you **do not exercise the option**.
- Therefore don't worry about buying and selling the future, and just **pay interest at 6%**.

### 4.4.2 Traded floors

In order to set a floor if you are investing/lending, you have to buy a call option – a right to buy a future. Say the exercise price is 95.00, corresponding to an interest rate of 5%.

**Interest rate falls**

- If the interest rate you receive **falls to 4%**, the price of the future will rise to 96.00.

- However, you will exercise your option to buy the future at 95.00 and then you will sell it on at 96.00.

- The profit you make on the future will be added to the 4% interest you receive to give an **effective interest rate of 5%**.

**Interest rate rises**

- If the interest rate **rises to 6%**, you will not exercise the option.
- You will **receive interest at 6%**.

### 4.4.3 Traded collars

With collars, if you're a borrower, you are buying a put and selling a call. Say the exercise price is 96.00, corresponding to an interest rate of 4%.

- Buying a put as above
- Selling a call means that you are selling someone else the right to buy a future from you

**Interest rate falls**

- If the interest rate **falls to 3%**, the price of the future will rise to 97.00.

- You will **pay interest at 3%**.

- However, the holder of the call option will wish to exercise the option to buy the future at 96.00.

- You therefore have to buy the future yourself at 97.00 and sell it to the option holder at 96.00, thus incurring a loss.

- The loss you incur will be added to the 3% interest you have to pay to give an effective net interest rate of 4%.

- If interest rates **fall further**, you will pay a lower interest rate but incur a larger loss on the option, netting out always at an **interest rate of 4%**.

**Interest rate rises**

- If the interest rate rises above 4%, the option holder will not exercise the option.

- You will pay interest at more than 4%, but will be able to offset against this a profit on selling the future, to give an **effective interest rate of 4%**.

## Example

Rumple Inc (continued from the previous example) has decided that interest rate options are too expensive and is therefore considering the use of a collar to hedge interest rate payments on its loan. Illustrate the outcome of a collar with a put option at 3.75% and a call option at 3.5% if LIBOR in 3 months' time is:

(a)   4%
(b)   3%

## Solution

**Setup**

(a)   Which contract?      June
(b)   What type?           Collar (put and call)
(c)   How many?            4 (as before)
(d)   Premium              0.255% − 0.085% = 0.170%

**Outcome**

|  | *(a)* | *(b)* |
|---|---|---|
| Right to pay interest at | 5.00% | 4.00% |
| **Profit/loss on option** | | |
| Put option at 3.75% | 0.35% profit (as before) | |
| Call option at 3.5% | | 0.40% loss |
| | | (Holder of call option receives |
| | | 3.5% − 3.10% future = 0.40%) |
| **Net outcome** | 5.00 + 0.170 − 0.35 | 4.00 + 0.170 + 0.40 |
| | = 4.82% | = 4.57% |
| In $ | 0.0482 × $4m × 3/12 | 0.0457 × $4m × 3/12 |
| | = $48,200 | $45,700 |

BPP
LEARNING MEDIA

## 4.5 Over the counter (OTC) options

Over the counter (OTC) options are tailor-made to the specific requirements of the interested party in terms of size and timing. As these are so specific they will be more expensive than exchange traded options and are much less liquid, as they cannot be sold if not required. As with exchange traded options, caps, floors and collars are available.

## 4.6 Advantages and disadvantages of options

### 4.6.1 Advantages

(a)     **Upside risk** – the company has the choice not to exercise the option and will therefore be able to take advantage of falling interest rates.

(b)     **OTC options** – these are tailored to the specific needs of the company and are therefore more flexible than exchange traded options for a more exact hedge.

(c)     Exchange traded options are useful for **uncertain transactions** – for example you may be unsure if a loan will actually be needed. If it becomes evident that the option is not required it can be sold.

### 4.6.2 Disadvantages

(a)     **Premium** – the premium cost may be **relatively expensive** compared with the costs of other hedging instruments. It will be payable whatever the movement in interest rates and whether or not the option is exercised.

(b)     **Collar** – if the company has a collar, this will limit its ability to take advantage of lower interest rates to the lower limit set by the cap.

(c)     **Maturity** – the maturity of exchange traded options may be **limited to one year**.

(d)     **Traded options** – if the company purchased exchange traded options then the **large fixed amounts** of the available contracts may not match the amount to be hedged. The large amounts of the contracts will also prohibit organisations with smaller amounts to be hedged from using them.

# 5 Interest rate swaps                                6/12, 6/14, 12/14, Sep/Dec 16

**FAST FORWARD**

Interest rate swaps allow companies to take advantage of differences in the conditions connected with fixed and floating rate debt.

**Key term**

An **interest rate swap** is a transaction that exploits different interest rates in different markets for borrowing, to **reduce interest costs** for either **fixed or floating rate loans**.

There are two main types of interest rate swaps – **coupon swaps** and **basis swaps**.

In a **coupon swap**, one party makes payments at a fixed rate of interest in exchange for receiving payments at a floating rate (which changes for each payment). The other party pays the floating rate and receives the fixed rate.

In a **basis swap**, the parties exchange payments on one floating rate basis (for example at three-month LIBOR) for payments on another floating rate basis (for example at six-month LIBOR).

Most interest rate swaps are coupon swaps.

## 5.1 Arranging a swap

An **interest rate swap** is an arrangement whereby two companies, or a company and a bank, swap interest rate commitments with each other. In a sense, each simulates the other's borrowings, with the following effects.

(a) A company which has **debt at a fixed rate of interest** can make a **swap** so that it ends up paying **interest at a variable rate**.

(b) A company which has **debt at a variable rate of interest** (floating rate debt) ends up paying a **fixed rate of interest**.

An example is illustrated below.

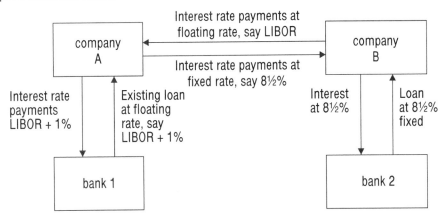

**Interest rate swap**

In this example, company A can use a swap to change from paying interest at a floating rate of LIBOR + 1% to one of paying fixed interest of (8½% + 1%) = 9½%.

A swap may be arranged with a bank, or a counterparty may be found through a bank or other financial intermediary. Fees will be payable if a bank is used. However, a bank may be able to find a **counterparty more easily**, and may have **access to more counterparties** in **more markets** than if the company seeking the swap tried to find the counterparty itself.

Swaps are generally terminated by agreeing a **settlement interest rate**, generally the current market rate.

| Exam focus point | A useful approach to adopt in an exam for a swap organised by a bank is to assume – unless told otherwise – that the variable interest rate payment is at LIBOR. This is what normally happens in reality. |
| --- | --- |

## Example

Goodcredit has been given a high credit rating. It can borrow at a fixed rate of 11%, or at a variable interest rate equal to LIBOR, which also happens to be 11% at the moment. It would like to borrow at a variable rate.

Secondtier is a company with a lower credit rating, which can borrow at a fixed rate of 12½% or at a variable rate of LIBOR plus ½%. It would like to borrow at a fixed rate.

## Solution

|  | Goodcredit | Secondtier | Sum total |
| --- | --- | --- | --- |
| Company wants | Variable | Fixed |  |
| Would pay (no swap) | (LIBOR) | (12.5%) | (LIBOR + 12.5%) |
| Could pay | (11%) | (LIBOR + 0.5%) | (LIBOR + 11.5%) |
| Potential gain |  |  | 1% |
| Split evenly | 0.5% | 0.5% |  |
| Expected outcome | (LIBOR – 0.5%) | (12%) | (LIBOR + 11.5%) |
| **Swap terms** |  |  |  |
| Pay interest on loan that is taken out | (11%) | (LIBOR + 0.5%) | (LIBOR + 11.5%) |
| Swap floating | (LIBOR) | LIBOR |  |
| Swap fixed (Working) | 11.5% | (11.5%) |  |

| | Goodcredit | Secondtier | Sum total |
|---|---|---|---|
| Net paid | (LIBOR – 0.5%) | (12%) | (LIBOR + 11.5%) |
| Would pay | (LIBOR) | (12.5%) | (LIBOR + 12.5%) |
| Gain | 0.5% | 0.5% | 1% |

*Working*

The fixed rate leg of the swap is a balancing figure that enables the potential gain of 1% to be split equally between each party to the swap.

For example, Goodcredit is paying 11% on a fixed rate loan and is also paying LIBOR on the variable leg of the swap. This means that its total payments are LIBOR + 11%, which means that a receipt of 11.5% on the fixed leg of the deal is required in order to create a net payment position of LIBOR – 0.5%.

The results of the swap are that Goodcredit ends up paying variable rate interest, but at a lower cost than it could get from a bank, and Secondtier ends up paying fixed rate interest, also at a lower cost than it could get from investors or a bank.

## 5.2 Reason for gain

If both parties ended up paying interest at a lower rate than was obtainable from the bank, where did this gain come from? To answer this question, set out a table of the rates at which both companies could borrow from the bank.

| | Goodcredit | Secondtier | Difference % |
|---|---|---|---|
| Can borrow at fixed rate | 11% | 12.5% | 1.5 |
| Can borrow at floating rate | LIBOR | LIBOR + 0.5% | 0.5 |
| Difference between differences | | | 1.0 |

Goodcredit has a better credit rating than Secondtier in both types of loan market, but its advantage is comparatively higher in the fixed interest market. The 1% differential between Goodcredit's advantage in the two types of loan may represent a market imperfection or there may be a good reason for it. Whatever the reason, it represents a potential gain which can be made out of a swap arrangement. For a gain to happen:

(a) Each company must borrow in the loan market in which it has **comparative advantage**. Goodcredit has the greatest advantage when it borrows fixed interest. Secondtier has the least disadvantage when it borrows floating rate.

(b) The parties must actually **want** interest of the opposite type to that in which they have comparative advantage. Goodcredit wants floating and Secondtier wants fixed.

Once the target interest rate for each company has been established, there is an infinite number of swap arrangements which will produce the same net result. The example illustrated above is only one of them.

Question | Interest rate swaps

We illustrated above one way in which the swap could work. (Swap fixed 12%, swap floating (LIBOR).) Suggest an alternative arrangement for the swap, based on swapping fixed interest at 11%.

| | Goodcredit | Secondtier |
|---|---|---|
| Pay interest on loan that is taken out | (11%) | (LIBOR + 0.5%) |
| Swap floating | | |
| Swap fixed | | |
| Net interest cost | (LIBOR – 0.5%) | (12%) |

| | Goodcredit | Secondtier |
|---|---|---|
| Pay interest on loan that is taken out | (11%) | (LIBOR + 0.5%) |
| Swap floating (working) | (LIBOR – 0.5%) | LIBOR – 0.5% |
| Swap fixed | 11% | (11%) |
| Net interest cost | (LIBOR – 0.5%) | (12%) |

*Working*

The fixed rate leg of the swap is a balancing figure that enables the potential gain of 1% to be split equally between each party to the swap.

For example, Goodcredit is paying 11% on a fixed rate loan and is also paying LIBOR – 0.5% on the variable leg of the swap. This means that its total payments are LIBOR + 10.5%, which means that a receipt of 11% on the fixed leg of the deal is required in order to create a net position of LIBOR – 0.5%.

## 5.3 Advantages and disadvantages of interest rate swaps

### 5.3.1 Advantages

(a)  **Flexibility and costs**

Swaps are **flexible**, since they can be arranged in any size, and they can be **reversed** if necessary. **Transaction costs are low**, particularly if no intermediary is used, and are potentially much lower than the costs of terminating one loan and taking out another.

(b)  **Credit ratings**

Companies **with different credit ratings** can **borrow in the market** that offers each the best deal and then swap this benefit to reduce the mutual borrowing costs. This is an example of the principle of **comparative advantage**.

(c)  **Capital structure**

Swaps allow **capital restructuring** by changing the nature of interest commitments without renegotiating with lenders.

(d)  **Risk management**

Swaps can be used to **manage interest rate risk** by swapping floating for fixed rate debt if rates are expected to rise. Swaps can also be used to swap a variable rate for a fixed rate investment if interest rates are expected to fall.

(e)  **Convenience**

Swaps are relatively **easy to arrange**.

(f)  **Predictability of cash flows**

If a company's future cash flows are uncertain, it can use a swap to ensure it has **predictable fixed rate commitments**.

### 5.3.2 Disadvantages

(a)  **Additional risk**

The swap is subject to **counterparty risk**, the risk that the other party will default leaving the first company to bear its obligations. This risk can be avoided by using an intermediary.

(b) **Movements in interest rates**

If a company takes on a floating rate commitment, it may be vulnerable to **adverse movements in interest rates**. If it takes on a fixed rate commitment, it won't be able to **take advantage of favourable movements in rates**.

(c) **Lack of liquidity**

The **lack of a secondary market in swaps** makes it **very difficult to liquidate a swap contract**.

**Exam focus point**

Make sure you know the advantages and disadvantages of the different derivatives – it will be useful if you are asked to evaluate them in the context of a particular scenario.

## Question

Interest rate swaps 2

Seeler Muller wishes to borrow 300 million euros for 5 years at a floating rate to finance an investment project in Germany. The cheapest rate at which it can raise such a loan is euro LIBOR + 0.75%.

The company's bankers have suggested that one of their client companies, Overath Maier, would be interested in a swap arrangement. This company needs a fixed interest loan at €300 million. The cheapest rate at which it can arrange the loan is 10.5% per annum. It could, however, borrow in euros at the floating rate of euro LIBOR + 1.5%.

Seeler Muller can issue a fixed interest 5-year bond at 9% per annum interest. The banker would charge a swap arrangement fee of 0.15% per year to both parties. You are required to devise a swap by which both parties can benefit.

## Answer

| | Seeler Muller Floating | Overath Maier Fixed | Sum total |
|---|---|---|---|
| **Company wants** | | | |
| Would pay (no swap) | (LIBOR + 0.75%) | (10.5%) | (LIBOR + 11.25%) |
| Could pay | (9%) | (LIBOR + 1.5%) | (LIBOR + 10.5%) |
| Commission | (0.15%) | (0.15%) | (0.3%) |
| Potential gain (difference between would pay and could pay – commission) | | | 0.45% |
| split evenly | 0.225% | 0.225% | |
| Expected outcome (would pay + potential gain) | (LIBOR + 0.525%) | (10.275%) | (LIBOR + 10.8%) |
| **Swap terms** | | | |
| Pay interest on loan that is taken out | (9%) | (LIBOR + 1.5%) | (LIBOR + 10.5%) |
| Swap floating | (LIBOR) | LIBOR | |
| Swap fixed (W) | 8.625% | (8.625%) | |
| Commission | (0.15%) | (0.15%) | (0.3%) |
| Net paid | (LIBOR + 0.525%) | (10.275%) | (LIBOR + 10.8%) |
| Would pay | (LIBOR + 0.75%) | (10.5%) | (LIBOR + 11.25%) |
| Gain | 0.225% | 0.225% | 0.45% |

Both companies make a net gain of 0.225%. The swap proceeds as follows.

**Step 1** Seeler Muller raises a fixed interest rate 5-year loan for €300m at 9% interest.

**Step 2** Overath Maier raises a floating rate €300m loan at LIBOR + 1.5%.

**Step 3** The companies swap loan principals.

**484** 17: The use of financial derivatives to hedge against interest rate risk | Part E Treasury and advanced risk management techniques

**Step 4**    The fixed rate leg of the swap is a balancing figure that enables the potential gain of 0.45% to be split equally between each party to the swap.

For example, Seeler is paying 9% on a fixed rate loan and is also paying LIBOR on the variable leg of the swap and fees of 0.15%. This means that its total payments are LIBOR + 9.15%, which means that a receipt of 8.625% on the fixed leg of the deal is required in order to create a net position of LIBOR +0.525%.

**Step 5**    At the end of five years the loan principals are swapped back and the companies repay their original loans.

---

### 5.3.3 Valuing interest rate swaps    Sep/Dec 16

An interest rate swap can be valued as the NPV of the net cash flows under the swap. At the start of the swap the swap contract is designed to give an NPV of zero based on the current FRA rates, however the value of the swap will change as interest rates fluctuate.

## Example

Annual spot rates (derived from the yield curve) available to Celine Co for the next three years are as follows:

| One year | Two years | Three years |
|----------|-----------|-------------|
| 3.50% | 4.60% | 5.40% |

This means that if Celine Co wants to borrow for two years (for example) it will able to borrow at 4.60% per year for the two-year period.

FRA rates can be calculated from this data, as follows:

An FRA for one year would be 3.5% (as above).

An FRA starting in one year and ending a year later would be calculated by comparing the borrowing costs for two years to the borrowing costs for one year, ie:

$$\frac{1.046^2}{1.035} - 1 = 0.0571 \text{ ie } 5.71\%$$

If Celine Co wanted to have a FRA starting in two years and ending a year later this would be calculated by comparing the borrowing costs for three years to the borrowing costs for two years, ie:

$$\frac{1.054^3}{1.046^2} - 1 = 0.0702 \text{ ie } 7.02\%$$

Celine Co has $100 million of variable rate borrowings repayable in three years' time and is concerned about interest rates rising.

A variable – fixed swap deal is being negotiated with a bank. This will be based on paying the bank a fixed rate over the three year period in exchange for a variable rate less 0.50%.

Required

Estimate the fixed rate that will be paid as part of the swap.

## Solution

The swap will be designed so that the bank makes a reasonable return; the bank will expect to at least make an NPV of 0 from the deal.

The bank's expected payments (receipts to the company) at a variable rate are estimated, using the FRA rates as:

|  | One year | Two years | Three years |
|---|---|---|---|
| FRA | 3.50% | 5.71% | 7.02% |
| FRA – 0.5% | 3.00% | 5.21% | 6.52% |
| In $m | $3.0m | $5.21m | $6.52m |
|  | (0.03 × $100m) | (0.0521 × $100m) | (0.0652 × $100m) |

The bank's expected receipts (payments by the company) at a fixed rate = R

The bank's net cash flows will be:

|  | One year | Two years | Three years |
|---|---|---|---|
| In $m | R – $3.0m | R – $5.21m | R – $6.52m |

These are discounted at the spot yield rates of 3.5% for one year, 4.6% for two years and 5.4% for three years:

| Time | 1 | 2 | 3 | Total NPV |
|---|---|---|---|---|
| Net cash flows | R – 3.0 | R – 5.21 | R – 6.52 | |
| df 3.5% | 0.966 | | | |
| df 4.6% | | 0.914 | | |
| df 5.4% | | | 0.854 | |
| Total | 0.966R – 2.898 | 0.914R – 4.762 | 0.854R – 5.568 | 2.734R – 13.228 |

For the NPV to be zero then 2.734R = 13.228 so R = 13.228 / 2.734 = $4.838m per year.

As a percentage this is $4.838m / $100m = 4.838%.

**Exam focus point**

An article written by the examining team titled 'Determining interest rate forwards and their application to swap valuation' is available on ACCA's website.

## 5.4 Interest rate swaptions

**Key terms**

**Swaptions** are options on swaps, giving the holder the right but not the obligation to enter into a swap with the seller.

A **payer swaption** gives the holder the right to enter into a swap as the fixed rate payer (and the floating rate receiver).

A **receiver swaption** gives the holder the right to enter the swap as the fixed rate receiver (and the floating rate payer).

A **Bermudan** swaption allows the owner to enter the swap on multiple specified dates.

A **European** swaption allows the owner to enter the swap only on the maturity date.

An **American** swaption allows the owner to enter the swap on any day that falls within a range of two dates.

Swaptions generate a worst-case scenario for buyers and sellers. For example, an organisation that is going to issue floating rate debt can buy a payer swaption that offers the option to convert to being a fixed rate payer should interest rates increase.

## Example

Suppose a party purchases a 1 × 5 payer swaption at a rate of 5%. A year later if the 4-year swap is 6% the buyer will exercise the swaption and pay 5% fixed rate for LIBOR on a 4-year swap. If instead the 4-year swap rate is 4%, the buyer will not exercise the swaption.

# 6 Hedging strategy alternatives – example          12/13

**FAST FORWARD** ≫ It is important to be able to compare and contrast the different hedging instruments in a particular scenario and make recommendations on the best available strategy.

## 6.1 Hedging instruments

Different hedging instruments often offer alternative ways of managing risk in a specific situation. In this section, we consider the different ways in which a company can hedge interest rate risk.

## Example

It is 31 December. Octavo needs to borrow £6 million in 3 months' time for a period of 6 months. For the type of loan finance which Octavo would use, the rate of interest is currently 13% per year and the corporate treasurer is unwilling to pay a higher rate.

The treasurer is concerned about possible future fluctuations in interest rates, and is considering the following possibilities.

(a)    FRAs
(b)    Interest rate futures
(c)    Interest rate guarantees or short-term interest rate caps

*Required*

Explain briefly how each of these three alternatives might be useful to Octavo.

## Solution

### FRAs

Entering into an FRA with a bank will allow the treasurer of Octavo to **effectively lock in an interest rate** for the six months of the loan. This agreement is independent of the loan itself, on which the prevailing rate will be paid. If the FRA were negotiated to be at a rate of 13%, and the actual interest rate paid on the loan were higher than this, the bank will pay the difference between the rate paid and 13% to Octavo. Conversely, if the interest paid by Octavo turned out to be lower than 13%, they would have to pay the difference to the bank. Thus the cost to Octavo will be 13% regardless of movements in actual interest rates.

### Interest rate futures

Interest rate futures have the same effect as FRAs, in effectively **locking in an interest rate**, but they are standardised in terms of size, duration (see Chapter 7a, Section 5) and terms. They can be **traded on an exchange** (such as LIFFE in London), and they will generally be **closed out before the maturity date**, yielding a profit or loss that is offset against the loss or profit on the money transaction that is being hedged. So, for example, as Octavo is concerned about rises in interest rates, the treasurer can sell future contracts now; if that rate does rise, their value will fall, and they can then be bought at a lower price, yielding a profit which will compensate for the increase in Octavo's loan interest cost. If interest rates fall, the lower interest cost of the loan will be offset by a loss on their futures contracts.

There may not be an **exact match** between the **loan and the future contract** (100% hedge), due to the standardised nature of the contracts, and margin payments may be required while the futures are still held. Basis risk can also cause hedge inefficiency. Basis risk has been covered in Chapter 16, Section 7 and in Section 3 of this chapter.

### Interest rate options

Short-term interest rate options give Octavo the opportunity to **benefit from favourable interest rate movements** as well as protecting it from the effects of adverse movements. They give the holder the **right** but not the **obligation** to deal at an agreed interest rate at a future maturity date. This means that if interest rates rise, the treasurer would exercise the option, and 'lock in' to the predetermined borrowing rate. If, however, interest rates fall, then the option would simply lapse, and Octavo would feel the benefit of lower interest rates.

The main disadvantage of options is that a premium will be payable to the seller of the option, whether or not it is exercised. This will therefore add to the interest cost. The treasurer of Octavo will need to consider whether this cost, which can be quite expensive, is justified by the potential benefits to be gained from favourable interest rate movements.

**Exam focus point**

> When considering interest rate or currency hedging, don't discuss every possible technique that you can recall. Marks will only be awarded for techniques that are appropriate to the circumstances described in the question.

# 7 Issues surrounding the use of derivatives

## 7.1 Rationale for the use of derivatives

**FAST FORWARD**

Two general arguments have been put forward for the growth in derivatives.

- The first is that derivatives complete the market.
- The second argument is that they make markets more efficient.

### 7.1.1 Market completeness

Derivatives allow investors to achieve payoffs that would be impossible without using them. Although in theory continuous trading can create the payoffs of derivatives, rendering derivatives redundant, in practice this is not possible because investors face **trading costs** that make closely replicating the payoff of even as simple a derivative as a call option **prohibitively expensive**.

In the case of call options the payoff of the call option on shares, for instance, can be replicated by holding treasury bills and shares. When the price of the shares rises, the portfolio is adjusted in favour of shares so that it behaves more or less like the underlying. When the price of shares falls, the portfolio is adjusted in favour of treasury bills, creating a minimum value in the portfolio which is the value of the treasury bill position.

Replication also requires the investor to trade every time the price changes. In the absence of continuous trading, the replication is only approximate.

Finally, the correct replicating strategy is often difficult to work out because there is uncertainty as to which is the true statistical process that drives asset prices. For example, if price changes are characterised by trends, then a policy of replication will be successful since a rebalancing of the portfolio in favour of equities following a change in share prices will be followed by further rises in share prices. If, on the other hand, prices change in a random way, then rebalancing the portfolio in favour of equities, as a result of an increase in share prices, will not be effective if the prices subsequently fall.

### 7.1.2 Market efficiency

Derivatives make markets more efficient by providing investors with **information** that **cash markets** alone **cannot generate**. For example, swaps can generate **yield curves** even in the absence of corresponding cash markets. The option markets can produce valuable estimates of the implied volatilities in the various markets.

## 7.2 The role of hedging for the firm                                                    6/14

Derivative instruments are used either for **speculation** or for **hedging**. Derivatives are used for speculation when they are used on their own and not in conjunction with the underlying instrument. For example, a long position in a futures contract is a bet that the price of the underlying will move in a certain direction

by a certain date. Similarly, the writer of a call option bets that the price will not move above a certain range over a period of time. In both cases the derivatives position can result in losses if the price does not move in the anticipated direction. When derivatives are used for **hedging** they are always used in combination with the **underlying**. The principle of **hedging** is that any profits or losses in the **cash position** will be offset by losses or profits in the **derivatives position**. We have seen this in the examples involving derivatives in this chapter and the previous chapter.

The empirical evidence on the use of derivatives by corporations shows that firms primarily use derivatives for **hedging** rather than **speculation**.

One unresolved issue is why companies need to hedge their risks since investors can themselves diversify away all risks by including the shares of the company in a portfolio. Here we review the arguments that have been put forward to explain the use of hedging. The main arguments are:

(a) Hedging reduces the risk imposed on the firm's managers, employees, suppliers and customers.

(b) Hedging can control the conflict of interest between bondholders and shareholders, thus reducing the agency costs of debt.

(c) The use of derivatives increases the value of a firm. As we have already discussed in Chapter 7a, Modigliani and Miller showed that firm value and financial policy decisions are unrelated in the absence of market imperfections. Models have been developed that show that hedging can increase the value of a firm if capital market imperfections exist. Thus the following additional justifications have been provided:

   (i) Hedging **lowers the probability** of the firm encountering **financial distress** which in turn lowers the expected costs of financial distress and the cost of capital.

   (ii) Hedging encourages investment by the firm. According to **agency theory** between shareholders and bondholders, the issuance of bonds which have higher priority than equity creates incentives for the firm's equity holders to underinvest. Hedging reduces the incentive to underinvest since it reduces uncertainty and the risk of loss. Because firms with more valuable growth opportunities and higher leverage are more likely to be affected by the underinvestment problem, these firms are also more likely to hedge.

## 7.3 Risks from the use of derivatives

The main risks from the use of derivatives are the role of mispricing (**valuation** or **model risk**), **liquidity risk** and **reporting risk**.

### 7.3.1 Valuation (model) risk

The most common risk for OTC derivative users is the **risk of mispricing** the derivatives position. Since OTC derivatives do not trade in **liquid markets** where they can always be bought or sold at the market price, valuation models need to be used. However, these models are based on assumptions which may not be valid.

For example, the Black-Scholes option valuation model assumes that markets have no frictions, that the stock price is lognormally distributed, that interest rates are fixed, that the volatility of return is constant and that trading is possible all the time.

However, it is well known that these assumptions are at variance with reality. Interest rates are not constant and neither is the volatility. Demand and supply may have an impact on prices and there are certainly frictions in the market.

There are many examples of firms losing money due to valuation errors. For example, the National Australian Bank reported currency option losses in excess of 360 million Australian dollars (approximately 280 million in US dollars) that were attributed to rogue traders and risk management failures and involved incorrect valuations and misreporting. It is much harder to value more complicated derivatives.

### 7.3.2 Liquidity risk

Exchange-traded derivative products are highly liquid and a transaction can take place at the market price. The market value of a derivatives contract is thus realised when it is sold. In the case of OTC derivatives

and especially where complex contracts are involved it is not always possible for these contracts to be sold, and their model-calculated value to be realised. The reasons for this are:

(a) Uncertainty about the **valuation model** and the **risks** of the **position**

(b) In the case of complex contracts, there may be only a small number of counterparties who both want that particular set of risk characteristics and are confident that they understand what they are receiving

### 7.3.3 Reporting risk

OTC complex derivative positions especially with long maturities can be manipulated so that the true value and the true risks of the positions are not revealed. For example, Enron had a huge portfolio of derivatives, including many contracts with extremely long maturities, whose risks were not revealed before it collapsed.

# 8 The Greeks – measuring the impact of risk factors 12/10

FAST FORWARD ▶▶

Changes in the value of an option can be measured in terms of its **Greeks**; that is, in terms of its **risk factors**.

We discussed the basic concepts of options in Chapter 6 and have looked at how they are used to hedge currency risk and interest rate risk in Chapters 16 and 17 respectively. In this section we look at how changes in risk factors can affect the value of an option by using 'the Greeks'.

## 8.1 Risk factors in options positions

The factors that affect the value of a call or put option are:

- The value of the underlying
- The exercise price
- The risk-free interest rate
- The volatility
- The time to expiration

Since these factors are the ones that may adversely affect the value of an option, they are also known as **risk factors**.

The Black-Scholes model we used in Chapter 6 gives a mathematical expression of the relationship between the **value of an option** and the **factors** that **affect** its **value**. This is reproduced below.

The Black-Scholes model states that the value (c) of a call option is given by the following formula.

**Exam formula**

$$c = P_a N(d_1) - P_e N(d_2)e^{-rt}$$

$$\text{Where} \quad d_1 = \frac{\ln\left(\dfrac{P_a}{P_e}\right) + (r + 0.5s^2)t}{s\sqrt{T}}$$

$$d_2 = d_1 - s\sqrt{T}$$

The model has three main elements.

(a) The share price, $P_a$

(b) The delta value, $N(d_1)$, which measures how option prices vary with share prices (discussed below)

(c) $(P_e\ N(d_2)e^{-rt})$, which represents the borrowing element that must be combined with the share investment to produce an option equivalent

**Exam focus point**

Remember that the volatility is represented by the standard deviation, **not** the variance. The variance is the standard deviation squared.

Within the model:

(a) The difference between the share price and the option exercise price ($P_a - P_e$) is the intrinsic value of the option

(b) $e^{-rt}$ is a discount factor, reflecting the fact that the option will be exercised in the future

(c) The model is very dependent on $\sigma$, the factor representing the share price volatility. This is likely to be calculated on the basis of historical movements, and different conditions may apply in the future

## 8.2 Measuring the impact of risk factors: The Greeks

FAST FORWARD

The 'Greeks' are an important element in option theory.

- **Delta** – change in call option price/change in value of share
- **Gamma** – change in delta value/change in value of share
- **Theta** – change in option price over time
- **Rho** – change in option price as interest rates change
- **Vega** – change in option price as volatility of the underlying asset changes

Various elements of the Black-Scholes model can be analysed separately. Collectively they are known as the Greeks.

**Exam focus point**

Calculation of deltas in delta hedging is examinable. You will not be required to calculate the other Greeks but you must know what they are and what they are used for.

## 8.3 Delta                                                                 12/10, 12/13

If we accept the Black-Scholes model, the value of $N(d_1)$ can be used to indicate the amount of the underlying shares (or other instrument) which the writer of an option should hold in order to hedge (eliminate the risk of) the option position.

The appropriate 'hedge ratio' $N(d_1)$ is referred to as the **delta value**: hence the term delta hedge. The delta value is valid if the price changes are **small**.

**Key term**

**Delta** = Change in call option price ÷ Change in the price of the shares $\left( \dfrac{\Delta C}{\Delta S} = \text{delta} \right)$

Delta is used to measure the slope of the option value line at any particular time/price point.

For example, if we know that a change in share price of 3 cents results in a change in the option price of 1 cent, then:

Delta = 1c ÷ 3c = 1/3

For long call options (and/or short put options), delta has a value between 0 and 1.

For long put options (and/or short call options), delta has a value between 0 and –1.

## 8.4 Delta hedging                                                          12/13

The significance of the delta value is illustrated by the process of delta hedging.

Delta hedging allows us to determine the number of shares that we must buy to create the equivalent portfolio to an option, and hedge it.

We have seen that:

Buying call options = Buying share portfolio + Borrowing at risk-free rate

As the opposite of borrowing is investing, therefore:

Buying call options + Investing at risk-free rate = Buying share portfolio

As the opposite of buying call options is selling call options, therefore:

Investing at risk-free rate = Buying share portfolio + Selling call options

Therefore we can eliminate investment risk by buying shares and selling call options, as an adverse movement in the share price will be offset by a favourable movement in the option price. Delta hedging tells us in what proportion shares should be purchased and call options sold.

Delta hedges are only valid for small movements in the share price. The delta value is likely to change during the period of the option, and so the option writer may need to change their holdings to maintain a delta hedge position.

## Example: Delta hedge

What is the number of call options that you would have to sell in order to hedge a holding of 200,000 shares, if the delta value ($N(d_1)$) of options is 0.8?

Assume that option contracts are for the purchase or sale of units of 1,000 shares.

## Solution

The delta hedge can be calculated by the following formula.

$$\text{Number of contracts} = \frac{\text{Number of shares}}{\text{Delta of option} \times \text{size of contract}}$$

$$= \frac{200,000}{0.8 \times 1,000}$$

$$= 250$$

If in this example the price of shares increased by $1, the value of the call options would increase by $800 per contract (80 cents per share). However, since we were selling these contracts the increase in the value of our holding of shares, 200,000 × $1, would be matched by the decrease in our holding of option contracts, 250 × $800.

## 8.5 Other points about delta values

The table below shows approximate values of delta for different types of options and the position of the exercise price relative to the share price.

| | In the money | At the money | Out of the money |
|---|---|---|---|
| Long call/short put | Approaching 1 | Approx 0.5 | Approaching 0 |
| Long put/short call | Approaching –1 | Approx –0.5 | Approaching 0 |

At expiry the value of delta will be as follows.

| | In the money | Out of the money |
|---|---|---|
| Long call/short put | 1 | 0 |
| Long put/short call | –1 | 0 |

The factors influencing delta when the option is either in the money or out of the money can be appreciated by looking at the variables in the $N(d_1)$ formula given earlier. These factors are:

- The exercise price of the option relative to the share price (ie its intrinsic value)
- The time to expiration
- The risk-free rate of return
- The volatility of returns on the share

## 8.6 Uses of delta factors

Delta factors are often used when deciding which options to **sell** or **buy**, with investors considering the delta value of each option and the **trend** – are delta values of options currently held getting stronger or weaker? Not all the Greeks relate to all the derivatives – delta relates to them all.

## 8.7 Gamma                                                                                                   6/13

**Key term**

> **Gamma** = Change in delta value ÷ Change in the price of the underlying share

Gamma is important, as it measures the extent to which delta changes when the share price changes. We know from above that delta changes as the option moves in or out of the money but we don't know by how much. This is where gamma is useful.

The **higher** the **gamma value**, the more difficult it is for the option writer to **maintain** a **delta hedge** because the delta value increases more for a given change in share price. Gamma is effectively a measure of **how easy risk management** will be.

Gamma values will be highest for a share which is **close to expiry** and is **'at the money'**. For example, suppose that an option has an exercise price of 340 cents and is due to expire in a few minutes' time.

(a)     If the share price is 338 cents, there is a very low chance of the option being exercised. The delta hedge ratio will be approximately zero. In other words, no hedge is necessary.

(b)     If the share price rises suddenly to 342 cents, it becomes highly probable that the option will be exercised and the delta hedge ratio will approximate to 1, suggesting the need to hedge through holding the underlying shares.

The table below summarises the types of positions of gamma and delta that might arise for different types of options.

| Type | Delta value | Gamma value |
|---|---|---|
| Long call option | Positive delta | Positive gamma |
| Short call option | Negative delta | Negative gamma |
| Long put option | Negative delta | Positive gamma |
| Short put option | Positive delta | Negative gamma |
| Long call option | Positive delta | Positive gamma |
| Short call option | Negative delta | Negative gamma |

Note that gamma is the same for calls and puts. If you are long a put or call, gamma will be a positive number. If you are short a put or call, then gamma will be negative.

## 8.8 Theta

**Key term**

> **Theta** is the change in an option's price (specifically its time premium) over time.

Remember that an option's price has two components, its **intrinsic value** and its **time premium**. When it expires, an option has no time premium.

Thus the time premium of an option diminishes over time towards zero and theta measures **how much value is lost over time**, and therefore how much the option holder will lose through retaining their options. Theta is usually expressed as an amount lost per day. If a dollar option has a theta of –0.05, it will theoretically lose 5 cents a day, assuming there are no other changes in conditions.

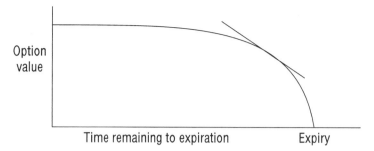

At the money options have the **greatest time premium** and thus the **greatest theta**. Their time decay is not linear; their theta increases as the date of expiration approaches. By contrast, the more in the money or out of the money the option is, the more its theta decays in a straight line.

Generally, options that have a **negative theta** have a **positive gamma** (and *vice versa*). A **positive gamma** means a **position benefits from movement**. **Negative theta** means that the **position loses money** if the **underlying asset** does **not move**.

## 8.9 Rho                                                      Mar/Jun 16

Key term

> **Rho** measures the sensitivity of option prices to interest rate changes.

An option's rho is the amount of change in value for a 1% change in the risk-free interest rate. Rho is positive for calls and negative for puts, ie:

| Prices | Interest rate rises | Interest rate falls |
|---|---|---|
| Calls | Increase | Decrease |
| Puts | Decrease | Increase |

If a dollar call option that has one year until expiration has a rho of 0.2, a 1% increase in interest rates will result in a 20 cent increase in the price of the option. However, the impact on the price of an option that has 6 months left until expiry would only be a 10 cent increase.

Generally, the **interest rate** is the **least significant influence** on change in price and, in addition, interest rates tend to change slowly and in small amounts.

Long-term options have larger rhos than short-term options. The more time there is until expiration, the greater the effect of a change in interest rates.

## 8.10 Vega                                                      6/14

Key term

> **Vega** measures the sensitivity of an option's value to a change in the implied volatility of the underlying asset.

Vega is the **change in value of an option that results from a 1% point change in the volatility of the underlying asset**. If a dollar option has a vega of 0.2, its price will increase by 20 cents for a 1% point increase in its volatility. Vega is the same for both calls and puts.

We have seen earlier that the Black-Scholes model is very dependent on accurately estimating the volatility of the option price. Vega is a measure of the consequences of an incorrect estimation.

**Long-term options** have **larger vegas** than **short-term options**. The longer the time period until the option expires, the more uncertainty there is about the expiry price. Therefore a given change in volatility will have more impact on an option with longer until expiration than one with less time until expiration.

Volatility means the market's current assessment of volatility. It is influenced by the balance between option **demand** and **supply** (the greater the balance, the less the volatility), as well as matters such as takeover rumours. Once announcements of definite plans have been made, volatility will generally decrease.

With company options with the same month of expiry, **vega** is generally greatest **for at the money options**. Vega is small if an option is deeply in the money or out of the money.

| Summary of Greeks | | |
|---|---|---|
| | **Change in** | **With** |
| Delta | Option value | Underlying asset value |
| Gamma | Delta | Underlying asset value |
| Theta | Time premium | Time |
| Rho | Option value | Interest rates |

**Exam focus point**

Questions on the Black Scholes model may be computational or discussion based and have appeared in both Section A and Section B exam questions.

## 8.11 Greeks and risk measurement

The values of the Greek parameters can give an approximate estimate of the value of a position if one or more of the factors that determine the value of an option change. The change in the value of the option can be approximated using the formula:

Change in option value = Delta × (Change in underlying) + ½ × Gamma × (Change in underlying)$^2$ + Vega × (Change in volatility) + Theta × (Change in time) + Rho × (Change in interest rate)

$$\Delta C = \text{Delta} \times \Delta S + \tfrac{1}{2}\,\text{Gamma} \times (\Delta S)^2 + \text{Vega} \times \Delta \sigma + \text{Theta} \times \Delta t + \text{Rho} \times \Delta r$$

The gamma term is added to explain the fact that delta itself changes when the price of the underlying changes.

**Question**           **Using the Greeks**

Suppose that the Greeks of a call option are as follows.

Delta = 0.5
Gamma = 0.03

What will be the impact on the value of the call option if the value of the underlying increases by 5 units?

**Answer**

The value of the option will change by

$\Delta C = 0.5 \times 5 + \tfrac{1}{2}\,0.03 \times (5)^2 = 2.5 + 0.375 = 2.875$

Note that the changes in the option price could have been calculated directly using the Black-Scholes option pricing model. However, using the Greeks is convenient for two reasons.

- First, this method provides a quick way to calculate the Greeks of a portfolio of options.
- The second reason is that the methods allow a simple estimation of the value at risk of an option position to be calculated.

# Chapter Roundup

- Factors influencing interest rate risk include:
    - Fixed rate versus floating rate debt
    - The term of the loan

- FRAs hedge risk by **fixing the interest rate** on future borrowing.

- **Interest rate futures** can be used to hedge against interest rate changes between the current date and the date at which the interest rate on the lending or borrowing is set. Borrowers enter into **contracts to sell** to hedge against **interest rate rises**. Companies with a cash flow surplus enter into **contracts to buy** to hedge against **interest rate falls**.

- Interest rate options allow an organisation to limit its exposure to adverse interest rate movements while also allowing it to take advantage of favourable interest rate movements.

- Interest rate swaps allow companies to take advantage of differences in the conditions connected with fixed and floating rate debt.

- It is important to be able to compare and contrast the different hedging instruments in a particular scenario and make recommendations on the best available strategy.

- Two general arguments have been put forward for the growth in derivatives.
    - The first is that derivatives complete the market.
    - The second argument is that they make markets more efficient.

- The main risks from the use of derivatives are the role of mispricing (**valuation** or **model risk**), **liquidity risk** and **reporting risk**.

- Changes in the value of an option can be measured in terms of its **Greeks**; that is, in terms of its **risk factors**.

- The 'Greeks' are an important element in option theory.
    - **Delta** – change in call option price/change in value of share
    - **Gamma** – change in delta value/change in value of share
    - **Theta** – change in option price over time
    - **Rho** – change in option price as interest rates change
    - **Vega** – change in option price as volatility changes

**496**    **17: The use of financial derivatives to hedge against interest rate risk** | Part E Treasury and advanced risk management techniques

BPP
LEARNING MEDIA

1    Identify three aspects of a debt in which a company may be exposed to risk from interest rate movements.

2    What are 'FRAs'?

3    Fill in the blanks.

     If a company wishes to hedge borrowing at a future date, it should purchase

     . ........................................ options; if it wishes to hedge lending, it should purchase
     ........................................ options.

4    Fill in the blanks.

     With a **collar**, the borrower buys ...................... and at the same time sells ...................... .

5    What aspect of the valuation of an option does the standard deviation measure?

     A      Asset price

     B      Exercise price

     C      Volatility of asset value

     D      Time to expiration

6    What happens if one party to a interest rate swap defaults on the arrangements to pay interest?

7    Give **three** uses of an interest rate swap.

8    Under the terms of a swap arrangement, Louie has paid interest at 10%, Dewie at LIBOR + 1%.

     The parties have swapped floating rate interest at LIBOR + 1%. What amount of fixed rate interest do they need to swap for Louie to end up paying net interest of LIBOR − 0.5%?

# Answers to Quick Quiz

1 Any **three** of:

- Fixed rate versus floating rate debt
- Debt in different currencies
- Different terms of loan
- Term loan or overdraft facility

2 Forward interest rate agreements

3 If a company wishes to hedge borrowing at a future date, it should purchase **put** options; if it wishes to hedge lending, it should purchase **call** options.

4 With a **collar** the borrower buys **an interest rate cap** and at the same time sells **an interest rate floor**.

5 C Volatility of asset value

6 The original party is liable to the lender.

7 Any **three** of:

(a) Switching from paying one type of interest to another
(b) Raising less expensive loans
(c) Securing better deposit rates
(d) Acting as a cost-effective method of managing interest rate risk
(e) Avoiding charges for early termination of loans
(f) Accessing a type of finance that could not be accessed directly

8 Fixed interest swapped – Louie interest paid – Floating rate interest swapped = – (LIBOR – 0.5%)
Fixed interest swapped – 10% – (LIBOR + 1%) = – (LIBOR – 0.5%)
Fixed interest swapped = 10% + (LIBOR + 1%) – (LIBOR – 0.5%) = 11.5%

Now try the questions below from the Practice Question Bank

| Number | Level | Marks | Time |
|--------|-------|-------|------|
| 35 | Introductory | 15 | 29 mins |
| 36 | Introductory | 15 | 29 mins |
| 37 | Examination | 12 | 23 mins |
| 38 | Introductory | 15 | 29 mins |

# Appendix: Mathematical tables

**Present Value Table**

Present value of 1 ie $(1 + r)^{-n}$

Where  $r$ = discount rate
  $n$ = number of periods until payment

*Discount rate (r)*

| Periods (n) | 1% | 2% | 3% | 4% | 5% | 6% | 7% | 8% | 9% | 10% | |
|---|---|---|---|---|---|---|---|---|---|---|---|
| 1 | 0·990 | 0·980 | 0·971 | 0·962 | 0·952 | 0·943 | 0·935 | 0·926 | 0·917 | 0·909 | 1 |
| 2 | 0·980 | 0·961 | 0·943 | 0·925 | 0·907 | 0·890 | 0·873 | 0·857 | 0·842 | 0·826 | 2 |
| 3 | 0·971 | 0·942 | 0·915 | 0·889 | 0·864 | 0·840 | 0·816 | 0·794 | 0·772 | 0·751 | 3 |
| 4 | 0·961 | 0·924 | 0·888 | 0·855 | 0·823 | 0·792 | 0·763 | 0·735 | 0·708 | 0·683 | 4 |
| 5 | 0·951 | 0·906 | 0·863 | 0·822 | 0·784 | 0·747 | 0·713 | 0·681 | 0·650 | 0·621 | 5 |
| 6 | 0·942 | 0·888 | 0·837 | 0·790 | 0·746 | 0·705 | 0·666 | 0·630 | 0·596 | 0·564 | 6 |
| 7 | 0·933 | 0·871 | 0·813 | 0·760 | 0·711 | 0·665 | 0·623 | 0·583 | 0·547 | 0·513 | 7 |
| 8 | 0·923 | 0·853 | 0·789 | 0·731 | 0·677 | 0·627 | 0·582 | 0·540 | 0·502 | 0·467 | 8 |
| 9 | 0·914 | 0·837 | 0·766 | 0·703 | 0·645 | 0·592 | 0·544 | 0·500 | 0·460 | 0·424 | 9 |
| 10 | 0·905 | 0·820 | 0·744 | 0·676 | 0·614 | 0·558 | 0·508 | 0·463 | 0·422 | 0·386 | 10 |
| 11 | 0·896 | 0·804 | 0·722 | 0·650 | 0·585 | 0·527 | 0·475 | 0·429 | 0·388 | 0·350 | 11 |
| 12 | 0·887 | 0·788 | 0·701 | 0·625 | 0·557 | 0·497 | 0·444 | 0·397 | 0·356 | 0·319 | 12 |
| 13 | 0·879 | 0·773 | 0·681 | 0·601 | 0·530 | 0·469 | 0·415 | 0·368 | 0·326 | 0·290 | 13 |
| 14 | 0·870 | 0·758 | 0·661 | 0·577 | 0·505 | 0·442 | 0·388 | 0·340 | 0·299 | 0·263 | 14 |
| 15 | 0·861 | 0·743 | 0·642 | 0·555 | 0·481 | 0·417 | 0·362 | 0·315 | 0·275 | 0·239 | 15 |

| (n) | 11% | 12% | 13% | 14% | 15% | 16% | 17% | 18% | 19% | 20% | |
|---|---|---|---|---|---|---|---|---|---|---|---|
| 1 | 0·901 | 0·893 | 0·885 | 0·877 | 0·870 | 0·862 | 0·855 | 0·847 | 0·840 | 0·833 | 1 |
| 2 | 0·812 | 0·797 | 0·783 | 0·769 | 0·756 | 0·743 | 0·731 | 0·718 | 0·706 | 0·694 | 2 |
| 3 | 0·731 | 0·712 | 0·693 | 0·675 | 0·658 | 0·641 | 0·624 | 0·609 | 0·593 | 0·579 | 3 |
| 4 | 0·659 | 0·636 | 0·613 | 0·592 | 0·572 | 0·552 | 0·534 | 0·516 | 0·499 | 0·482 | 4 |
| 5 | 0·593 | 0·567 | 0·543 | 0·519 | 0·497 | 0·476 | 0·456 | 0·437 | 0·419 | 0·402 | 5 |
| 6 | 0·535 | 0·507 | 0·480 | 0·456 | 0·432 | 0·410 | 0·390 | 0·370 | 0·352 | 0·335 | 6 |
| 7 | 0·482 | 0·452 | 0·425 | 0·400 | 0·376 | 0·354 | 0·333 | 0·314 | 0·296 | 0·279 | 7 |
| 8 | 0·434 | 0·404 | 0·376 | 0·351 | 0·327 | 0·305 | 0·285 | 0·266 | 0·249 | 0·233 | 8 |
| 9 | 0·391 | 0·361 | 0·333 | 0·308 | 0·284 | 0·263 | 0·243 | 0·225 | 0·209 | 0·194 | 9 |
| 10 | 0·352 | 0·322 | 0·295 | 0·270 | 0·247 | 0·227 | 0·208 | 0·191 | 0·176 | 0·162 | 10 |
| 11 | 0·317 | 0·287 | 0·261 | 0·237 | 0·215 | 0·195 | 0·178 | 0·162 | 0·148 | 0·135 | 11 |
| 12 | 0·286 | 0·257 | 0·231 | 0·208 | 0·187 | 0·168 | 0·152 | 0·137 | 0·124 | 0·112 | 12 |
| 13 | 0·258 | 0·229 | 0·204 | 0·182 | 0·163 | 0·145 | 0·130 | 0·116 | 0·104 | 0·093 | 13 |
| 14 | 0·232 | 0·205 | 0·181 | 0·160 | 0·141 | 0·125 | 0·111 | 0·099 | 0·088 | 0·078 | 14 |
| 15 | 0·209 | 0·183 | 0·160 | 0·140 | 0·123 | 0·108 | 0·095 | 0·084 | 0·074 | 0·065 | 15 |

## Annuity Table

Present value of an annuity of 1 ie $\dfrac{1-(1+r)^{-n}}{r}$

Where
$r$ = discount rate
$n$ = number of periods

*Discount rate (r)*

| Periods (n) | 1% | 2% | 3% | 4% | 5% | 6% | 7% | 8% | 9% | 10% | |
|---|---|---|---|---|---|---|---|---|---|---|---|
| 1 | 0·990 | 0·980 | 0·971 | 0·962 | 0·952 | 0·943 | 0·935 | 0·926 | 0·917 | 0·909 | 1 |
| 2 | 1·970 | 1·942 | 1·913 | 1·886 | 1·859 | 1·833 | 1·808 | 1·783 | 1·759 | 1·736 | 2 |
| 3 | 2·941 | 2·884 | 2·829 | 2·775 | 2·723 | 2·673 | 2·624 | 2·577 | 2·531 | 2·487 | 3 |
| 4 | 3·902 | 3·808 | 3·717 | 3·630 | 3·546 | 3·465 | 3·387 | 3·312 | 3·240 | 3·170 | 4 |
| 5 | 4·853 | 4·713 | 4·580 | 4·452 | 4·329 | 4·212 | 4·100 | 3·993 | 3·890 | 3·791 | 5 |
| 6 | 5·795 | 5·601 | 5·417 | 5·242 | 5·076 | 4·917 | 4·767 | 4·623 | 4·486 | 4·355 | 6 |
| 7 | 6·728 | 6·472 | 6·230 | 6·002 | 5·786 | 5·582 | 5·389 | 5·206 | 5·033 | 4·868 | 7 |
| 8 | 7·652 | 7·325 | 7·020 | 6·733 | 6·463 | 6·210 | 5·971 | 5·747 | 5·535 | 5·335 | 8 |
| 9 | 8·566 | 8·162 | 7·786 | 7·435 | 7·108 | 6·802 | 6·515 | 6·247 | 5·995 | 5·759 | 9 |
| 10 | 9·471 | 8·983 | 8·530 | 8·111 | 7·722 | 7·360 | 7·024 | 6·710 | 6·418 | 6·145 | 10 |
| 11 | 10·37 | 9·787 | 9·253 | 8·760 | 8·306 | 7·887 | 7·499 | 7·139 | 6·805 | 6·495 | 11 |
| 12 | 11·26 | 10·58 | 9·954 | 9·385 | 8·863 | 8·384 | 7·943 | 7·536 | 7·161 | 6·814 | 12 |
| 13 | 12·13 | 11·35 | 10·63 | 9·986 | 9·394 | 8·853 | 8·358 | 7·904 | 7·487 | 7·103 | 13 |
| 14 | 13·00 | 12·11 | 11·30 | 10·56 | 9·899 | 9·295 | 8·745 | 8·244 | 7·786 | 7·367 | 14 |
| 15 | 13·87 | 12·85 | 11·94 | 11·12 | 10·38 | 9·712 | 9·108 | 8·559 | 8·061 | 7·606 | 15 |

| (n) | 11% | 12% | 13% | 14% | 15% | 16% | 17% | 18% | 19% | 20% | |
|---|---|---|---|---|---|---|---|---|---|---|---|
| 1 | 0·901 | 0·893 | 0·885 | 0·877 | 0·870 | 0·862 | 0·855 | 0·847 | 0·840 | 0·833 | 1 |
| 2 | 1·713 | 1·690 | 1·668 | 1·647 | 1·626 | 1·605 | 1·585 | 1·566 | 1·547 | 1·528 | 2 |
| 3 | 2·444 | 2·402 | 2·361 | 2·322 | 2·283 | 2·246 | 2·210 | 2·174 | 2·140 | 2·106 | 3 |
| 4 | 3·102 | 3·037 | 2·974 | 2·914 | 2·855 | 2·798 | 2·743 | 2·690 | 2·639 | 2·589 | 4 |
| 5 | 3·696 | 3·605 | 3·517 | 3·433 | 3·352 | 3·274 | 3·199 | 3·127 | 3·058 | 2·991 | 5 |
| 6 | 4·231 | 4·111 | 3·998 | 3·889 | 3·784 | 3·685 | 3·589 | 3·498 | 3·410 | 3·326 | 6 |
| 7 | 4·712 | 4·564 | 4·423 | 4·288 | 4·160 | 4·039 | 3·922 | 3·812 | 3·706 | 3·605 | 7 |
| 8 | 5·146 | 4·968 | 4·799 | 4·639 | 4·487 | 4·344 | 4·207 | 4·078 | 3·954 | 3·837 | 8 |
| 9 | 5·537 | 5·328 | 5·132 | 4·946 | 4·772 | 4·607 | 4·451 | 4·303 | 4·163 | 4·031 | 9 |
| 10 | 5·889 | 5·650 | 5·426 | 5·216 | 5·019 | 4·833 | 4·659 | 4·494 | 4·339 | 4·192 | 10 |
| 11 | 6·207 | 5·938 | 5·687 | 5·453 | 5·234 | 5·029 | 4·836 | 4·656 | 4·486 | 4·327 | 11 |
| 12 | 6·492 | 6·194 | 5·918 | 5·660 | 5·421 | 5·197 | 4·988 | 4·793 | 4·611 | 4·439 | 12 |
| 13 | 6·750 | 6·424 | 6·122 | 5·842 | 5·583 | 5·342 | 5·118 | 4·910 | 4·715 | 4·533 | 13 |
| 14 | 6·982 | 6·628 | 6·302 | 6·002 | 5·724 | 5·468 | 5·229 | 5·008 | 4·802 | 4·611 | 14 |
| 15 | 7·191 | 6·811 | 6·462 | 6·142 | 5·847 | 5·575 | 5·324 | 5·092 | 4·876 | 4·675 | 15 |

## Standard Normal Distribution Table

|      | 0·00   | 0·01   | 0·02   | 0·03   | 0·04   | 0·05   | 0·06   | 0·07   | 0·08   | 0·09   |
|------|--------|--------|--------|--------|--------|--------|--------|--------|--------|--------|
| 0·0  | 0·0000 | 0·0040 | 0·0080 | 0·0120 | 0·0160 | 0·0199 | 0·0239 | 0·0279 | 0·0319 | 0·0359 |
| 0·1  | 0·0398 | 0·0438 | 0·0478 | 0·0517 | 0·0557 | 0·0596 | 0·0636 | 0·0675 | 0·0714 | 0·0753 |
| 0·2  | 0·0793 | 0·0832 | 0·0871 | 0·0910 | 0·0948 | 0·0987 | 0·1026 | 0·1064 | 0·1103 | 0·1141 |
| 0·3  | 0·1179 | 0·1217 | 0·1255 | 0·1293 | 0·1331 | 0·1368 | 0·1406 | 0·1443 | 0·1480 | 0·1517 |
| 0·4  | 0·1554 | 0·1591 | 0·1628 | 0·1664 | 0·1700 | 0·1736 | 0·1772 | 0·1808 | 0·1844 | 0·1879 |
| 0·5  | 0·1915 | 0·1950 | 0·1985 | 0·2019 | 0·2054 | 0·2088 | 0·2123 | 0·2157 | 0·2190 | 0·2224 |
| 0·6  | 0·2257 | 0·2291 | 0·2324 | 0·2357 | 0·2389 | 0·2422 | 0·2454 | 0·2486 | 0·2517 | 0·2549 |
| 0·7  | 0·2580 | 0·2611 | 0·2642 | 0·2673 | 0·2703 | 0·2734 | 0·2764 | 0·2794 | 0·2823 | 0·2852 |
| 0·8  | 0·2881 | 0·2910 | 0·2939 | 0·2967 | 0·2995 | 0·3023 | 0·3051 | 0·3078 | 0·3106 | 0·3133 |
| 0·9  | 0·3159 | 0·3186 | 0·3212 | 0·3238 | 0·3264 | 0·3289 | 0·3315 | 0·3340 | 0·3365 | 0·3389 |
| 1·0  | 0·3413 | 0·3438 | 0·3461 | 0·3485 | 0·3508 | 0·3531 | 0·3554 | 0·3577 | 0·3599 | 0·3621 |
| 1·1  | 0·3643 | 0·3665 | 0·3686 | 0·3708 | 0·3729 | 0·3749 | 0·3770 | 0·3790 | 0·3810 | 0·3830 |
| 1·2  | 0·3849 | 0·3869 | 0·3888 | 0·3907 | 0·3925 | 0·3944 | 0·3962 | 0·3980 | 0·3997 | 0·4015 |
| 1·3  | 0·4032 | 0·4049 | 0·4066 | 0·4082 | 0·4099 | 0·4115 | 0·4131 | 0·4147 | 0·4162 | 0·4177 |
| 1·4  | 0·4192 | 0·4207 | 0·4222 | 0·4236 | 0·4251 | 0·4265 | 0·4279 | 0·4292 | 0·4306 | 0·4319 |
| 1·5  | 0·4332 | 0·4345 | 0·4357 | 0·4370 | 0·4382 | 0·4394 | 0·4406 | 0·4418 | 0·4429 | 0·4441 |
| 1·6  | 0·4452 | 0·4463 | 0·4474 | 0·4484 | 0·4495 | 0·4505 | 0·4515 | 0·4525 | 0·4535 | 0·4545 |
| 1·7  | 0·4554 | 0·4564 | 0·4573 | 0·4582 | 0·4591 | 0·4599 | 0·4608 | 0·4616 | 0·4625 | 0·4633 |
| 1·8  | 0·4641 | 0·4649 | 0·4656 | 0·4664 | 0·4671 | 0·4678 | 0·4686 | 0·4693 | 0·4699 | 0·4706 |
| 1·9  | 0·4713 | 0·4719 | 0·4726 | 0·4732 | 0·4738 | 0·4744 | 0·4750 | 0·4756 | 0·4761 | 0·4767 |
| 2·0  | 0·4772 | 0·4778 | 0·4783 | 0·4788 | 0·4793 | 0·4798 | 0·4803 | 0·4808 | 0·4812 | 0·4817 |
| 2·1  | 0·4821 | 0·4826 | 0·4830 | 0·4834 | 0·4838 | 0·4842 | 0·4846 | 0·4850 | 0·4854 | 0·4857 |
| 2·2  | 0·4861 | 0·4864 | 0·4868 | 0·4871 | 0·4875 | 0·4878 | 0·4881 | 0·4884 | 0·4887 | 0·4890 |
| 2·3  | 0·4893 | 0·4896 | 0·4898 | 0·4901 | 0·4904 | 0·4906 | 0·4909 | 0·4911 | 0·4913 | 0·4916 |
| 2·4  | 0·4918 | 0·4920 | 0·4922 | 0·4925 | 0·4927 | 0·4929 | 0·4931 | 0·4932 | 0·4934 | 0·4936 |
| 2·5  | 0·4938 | 0·4940 | 0·4941 | 0·4943 | 0·4945 | 0·4946 | 0·4948 | 0·4949 | 0·4951 | 0·4952 |
| 2·6  | 0·4953 | 0·4955 | 0·4956 | 0·4957 | 0·4959 | 0·4960 | 0·4961 | 0·4962 | 0·4963 | 0·4964 |
| 2·7  | 0·4965 | 0·4966 | 0·4967 | 0·4968 | 0·4969 | 0·4970 | 0·4971 | 0·4972 | 0·4973 | 0·4974 |
| 2·8  | 0·4974 | 0·4975 | 0·4976 | 0·4977 | 0·4977 | 0·4978 | 0·4979 | 0·4979 | 0·4980 | 0·4981 |
| 2·9  | 0·4981 | 0·4982 | 0·4982 | 0·4983 | 0·4984 | 0·4984 | 0·4985 | 0·4985 | 0·4986 | 0·4986 |
| 3·0  | 0·4987 | 0·4987 | 0·4987 | 0·4988 | 0·4988 | 0·4989 | 0·4989 | 0·4989 | 0·4990 | 0·4990 |

This table can be used to calculate $N(d_i)$, the cumulative normal distribution functions needed for the Black-Scholes model of option pricing. If $d_i > 0$, add 0·5 to the relevant number above. If $d_i < 0$, subtract the relevant number above from 0·5.

# Practice question and answer bank

# 1 Goals

Assume you are Finance Director of a large multinational company, listed on a number of international stock markets. The company is reviewing its corporate plan. At present, the company focuses on maximising shareholder wealth as its major goal. The Managing Director thinks this single goal is inappropriate and asks his co-directors for their views on giving greater emphasis to the following.

(a)     Cash flow generation

(b)     Profitability as measured by profits after tax and return on investment

(c)     Risk-adjusted returns to shareholders

(d)     Performance improvement in a number of areas, such as concern for the environment, employees' remuneration and quality of working conditions and customer satisfaction

*Required*

Provide the Managing Director with a report for presentation at the next board meeting which:

(a)     Evaluates the argument that maximisation of shareholder wealth should be the only true objective of a company

(b)     Discusses the advantages and disadvantages of the MD's suggestions about alternative goals

**(20 marks)**

# 2 XYZ

The table below shows earnings and dividends for XYZ Inc over the past five years.

| Year | Net earnings per share $ | Net dividend per share $ |
|------|------|------|
| 20W9 | 1.40 | 0.84 |
| 20X0 | 1.35 | 0.88 |
| 20X1 | 1.35 | 0.90 |
| 20X2 | 1.30 | 0.95 |
| 20X3 | 1.25 | 1.00 |

There are 10,000,000 shares issued and the majority of these shares are owned by private investors. There is no debt in the capital structure.

It is clear from the table that the company has experienced difficult trading conditions over the past few years. In the current year, net earnings are likely to be $10 million, which will be just sufficient to pay a maintained dividend of $1 per share.

Members of the board are considering a number of strategies for the company, some of which will have an impact on the company's future dividend policy.

The company's shareholders require a return of 15% on their investment.

Four options are being considered, as follows.

(1)     Pay out all earnings as dividends
(2)     Pay a reduced dividend of 50% of earnings and retain the remaining 50% for future investment
(3)     Pay a reduced dividend of 25% of earnings and retain the remaining 75% for future investment
(4)     Retain all earnings for an aggressive expansion programme and pay no dividend at all

The directors cannot agree on any of the four options discussed so far. Some of them prefer option (1) because they believe to do anything else would have an adverse impact on the share price. Others favour either option (2) or option (3) because the company has identified some good investment opportunities and they believe one of these options would be in the best long-term interests of shareholders. An adventurous minority favours option (4) and thinks this will allow the company to take over a small competitor.

*Required*

(a) Discuss the company's dividend policy between 20W9 and 20X3 and its possible consequences for earnings. **(4 marks)**

(b) Advise the directors of the share price for XYZ Inc which might be expected immediately following the announcement of their decision if they pursued each of the four options, using an appropriate valuation model. You should also show what percentage of total return is provided by dividend and capital gain in each case. You should ignore taxation for this part of the question. Make (and indicate) any realistic assumptions you think necessary to answer this question. **(6 marks)**

(c) Discuss the reliability you can place on the figures you have just produced and on the usefulness of this information to the company's directors. **(5 marks)**

**(Total = 15 marks)**

# 3 Remuneration                                             23 mins

A company is considering improving the methods of remuneration for its senior employees. As a member of the executive board, you are asked to give your opinions on the following suggestions.

(a) A high basic salary with usual 'perks' such as company car and pension scheme but no performance-related bonuses

(b) A lower basic salary with usual 'perks' plus a bonus related to their division's profit before tax

(c) A lower basic salary with usual 'perks' plus a share option scheme which allows senior employees to buy a given number of shares in the company at a fixed price at the end of each financial year

*Required*

Discuss the arguments for and against each of the three options from the point of view of both the company and its employees. Detailed comments on the taxation implications are not required.

**(12 marks)**

# 4 Stakeholders                                            29 mins

(a) Many decisions in financial management are taken in a framework of conflicting stakeholder viewpoints. Identify the stakeholders and some of the financial management issues involved in the situation of a company seeking a stock market listing. **(5 marks)**

(b) XYZ plc is a medium-sized company operating in the chemical industry. It is a profitable business, currently producing at below maximum capacity. It has one large factory located on the outskirts of a small industrial town. It is the region's main employer. The company is evaluating a project which has substantial environmental implications.

*Required*

Discuss the inclusion of environmental costs and benefits into the investment appraisal procedure and explain how this might be done. **(10 marks)**

**(Total = 15 marks)**

# 5 Ethical dimension                                       39 mins

(a) What are the main responsibilities faced by companies when developing an ethical framework, and in what ways can these responsibilities be addressed? **(10 marks)**

(b) Discuss how ethical considerations impact on each of the main functional areas of a firm.

**(10 marks)**

**(Total = 20 marks)**

# 6 Developments

20 mins

International trade has expanded substantially in the last few decades; however, this has led to greater uncertainty for multinational companies.

*Required*

Discuss ways in which increased globalisation may adversely affect multinational organisations.

**(10 marks)**

# 7 Transfer prices

20 mins

A multinational company based in Beeland has subsidiary companies in Ceeland and in the UK.

The UK subsidiary manufactures machinery parts which are sold to the Ceeland subsidiary for a unit price of B$420 (420 Beeland dollars), where the parts are assembled. The UK subsidiary shows a profit of B$80 per unit; 200,000 units are sold annually.

The Ceeland subsidiary incurs further costs of B$400 per unit and sells the finished goods on for an equivalent of B$1,050.

All the profits from the foreign subsidiaries are remitted to the parent company as dividends.

Double taxation treaties between Beeland, Ceeland and the UK allow companies to set foreign tax liabilities against their domestic tax liability.

The following rates of taxation apply.

|  | UK | Beeland | Ceeland |
|---|---|---|---|
| Tax on company profits | 25% | 35% | 40% |
| Withholding tax on dividends | – | 12% | 10% |

*Required*

(a)  Show the tax effect of increasing the transfer price between the UK and Ceeland subsidiaries by 25%.

**(6 marks)**

(b)  Outline the various problems which might be encountered by a company which adjusts a transfer price substantially.

**(4 marks)**

**(Total = 10 marks)**

# 8 Solden

39 mins

Solden plc is a UK company which is considering setting up a manufacturing operation to make ski-boot warmers in a country called Ober. The currency of Ober is the Gurgle and these are currently G16 to the pound sterling. If the operation were to be set up the plant would be purchased in Ober costing G600,000 now and some equipment would be sent from the UK immediately. This equipment is fully written off in the UK but has a market value of £12,500 or G200,000. All plant and equipment is written off on a straight-line basis by Solden plc over 5 years.

The ski-boot warmers will sell for an initial price of G160 but this price will increase in line with inflation in Ober which is expected to continue at its current rate of 10% p.a. It is also expected that 4,000 ski-boot warmers will be sold in the first year increasing at a rate of 5% each year. The costs of making ski-boot warmers consist of local variable costs of G80 per unit and selling and administration costs of G40,000 p.a., both of which will increase in line with inflation in Ober. The warmers also require some specialist parts sent over from the UK each year. These will be transferred at the beginning of the first year of production at a cost of G40,000 (£2,500) which includes a 25% mark-up on cost. The transfer price and cost of these items are expected to increase by 5% p.a., and they will be billed to the Ober operation at the beginning of the year and paid for at the end of the year. The working capital for this project will be required at the beginning of each year and will be equal to 10% of the expected sales value for the year.

Solden plc estimates that it will lose some of its own exports worth £5,000 now and increasing by 5% p.a. due to the setting up of the operation in Ober. However, Solden plc will be receiving a licence fee from the Ober operation equal to 10% of sales each year.

Corporation tax in Ober is only 20% and operating costs, licence fees and depreciation at 25% on a straight-line basis are all tax-allowable expenses. Corporation tax in the UK is at 33%. There is a one-year tax delay in both countries.

Solden plc wishes to assess this project from the point of view of both investors in Ober (required return 15%) and investors in the UK (required return 10%). The assessment will take place using Solden's usual five-year time 'horizon' and valuing the Ober operation at three times its net cash inflow during the fifth year. If the operation were to be sold at this value, tax would be payable at 30% on the proceeds.

It is expected that the Gurgle will depreciate against the pound by 4% p.a. from year 2, the first depreciation affecting year 2 cash flows. Assume that all prices have just altered, and that all cash flows occur at the end of the year unless specified otherwise.

*Required*

(a) Calculate (to the nearest 100 Gurgles) whether the operation would be worthwhile for investors based in Ober. **(12 marks)**

(b) If all cash surpluses can be remitted to the UK, calculate whether Solden plc should set up the operation. Assume no further UK tax is payable on income taxed on Ober. **(8 marks)**

**(Total = 20 marks)**

# 9 Mover

**39 mins**

(a) You have been asked to provide preliminary advice on whether or not your company's pension fund should make an investment in the shares of Mover Inc, a large construction company which is leading a consortium that is proposing to build a rail tunnel between Gibraltar and Morocco. The tunnel is scheduled to open in 20X4.

PROJECTED CASH FLOWS OF THE TUNNEL PROJECT

|  | $m |
|---|---|
| 20X0 | −450 |
| 20X1 | −500 |
| 20X2 | −550 |
| 20X3 | −650 |
| 20X4 | −200 |
| 20X5 | 200 |
| 20X6 | 300 |
| 20X7 | 320 |
| 20X8 | 340 |
| 20X9 | 360 |
| 20Y0 | 400 |
| Each year after 20Y0 | 400 |

All projections exclude inflation.

The current domestic nominal risk-free rate is 6% while the real rate is approximately 4%. The market risk premium for the project has been estimated at 7%.

*Required*

Undertake an analysis of the proposed tunnel project and advise on whether or not the pension fund should invest in shares of Mover Inc. Relevant calculations must be shown.

State clearly all assumptions that you make. In this question **only** reasoned assumptions regarding a discount rate are encouraged. **(15 marks)**

(b) Explain how inflation affects the rate of return required on an investment project, and the distinction between a real and a nominal (or 'money terms') approach to the evaluation of an investment project under inflation. **(5 marks)**

**(Total = 20 marks)**

# 10 PS Ltd

**39 mins**

(a) A European call option on shares has 3 months to expiry. The exercise price of the option is £2.50, and the current price of the share is £3. The standard deviation of the share is 20% and the risk-free rate is 5%.

*Required*

Calculate the value of the call option per share using the Black-Scholes formula. **(10 marks)**

(b) Explain:

(i) The five input variables involved in the Black-Scholes pricing model

(ii) How the five input variables can be adapted to value real options as opposed to traded share options **(10 marks)**

**(Total = 20 marks)**

# 11 Nile Inc

**29 mins**

Nile Inc is considering an investment of capital to be raised from the issue of new ordinary shares and debentures in a mix which will hold its gearing ratio approximately constant. It wishes to estimate its weighted average cost of capital.

The company has an issued share capital of 1 million ordinary shares of $1 each; it has also issued $800,000 of 8% debentures. The market price of ordinary shares is $4.76 per share and debentures are priced at $77 per cent. Dividends and interest are payable annually. An ordinary dividend has just been paid; the next instalment of interest is payable in the near future. Debentures are redeemable at par in 15 years' time.

A summary of the most recent statement of financial position runs as follows.

| | $'000 | | $'000 | $'000 |
|---|---|---|---|---|
| Ordinary share capital | 1,000 | Non-current assets | | 1,276 |
| Reserves | 1,553 | Current assets | 4,166 | |
| Deferred taxation | 164 | Less current | | |
| Debentures | 800 | liabilities | 1,925 | |
| | | | | 2,241 |
| | 3,517 | | | 3,517 |

Dividends and earnings have been as follows.

| | Dividends (excluding tax credit) $'000 | Earnings before tax $'000 | Earnings after tax $'000 |
|---|---|---|---|
| 20X4 | 200 | 575 | 350 |
| 20X5 | 230 | 723 | 452 |
| 20X6 | 230 | 682 | 410 |
| 20X7 | 260 | 853 | 536 |
| 20X8 | 300 | 906 | 606 |

Assume that there have been no changes in the system or rates of taxation during the last five years, that the rate of corporation tax is 35% and that the standard rate of income tax is 30%. Assume that 'now' is 20X8.

*Required*

(a) Calculate Nile Inc's weighted average cost of capital. **(12 marks)**

(b) Discuss briefly any difficulties and uncertainties in your estimation. **(3 marks)**

**(Total = 15 marks)**

# 12 Crystal Inc

**29 mins**

The following figures have been extracted from the most recent accounts of Crystal Inc.

STATEMENT OF FINANCIAL POSITION AS AT 30 JUNE 20X9

|  | $'000 | $'000 |
|---|---|---|
| Non-current assets |  | 10,115 |
| Investments |  | 821 |
| Current assets | 3,658 |  |
| Less current liabilities | 1,735 |  |
|  |  | 1,923 |
|  |  | 12,859 |
| Ordinary share capital |  |  |
| Authorised: 4,000,000 shares of $1 |  |  |
| Issued: 3,000,000 shares of $1 |  | 3,000 |
| Reserves |  | 6,542 |
| Shareholders' funds |  | 9,542 |
| 7% debentures |  | 1,300 |
| Deferred taxation |  | 583 |
| Corporation tax |  | 1,434 |
|  |  | 12,859 |

SUMMARY OF PROFITS AND DIVIDENDS

| Year ended 30 June | 20X5 | 20X6 | 20X7 | 20X8 | 20X9 |
|---|---|---|---|---|---|
|  | $'000 | $'000 | $'000 | $'000 | $'000 |
| Profit after interest and before tax | 1,737 | 2,090 | 1,940 | 1,866 | 2,179 |
| Less tax | 573 | 690 | 640 | 616 | 719 |
| Profit after interest and tax | 1,164 | 1,400 | 1,300 | 1,250 | 1,460 |
| Less dividends | 620 | 680 | 740 | 740 | 810 |
| Added to reserves | 544 | 720 | 560 | 510 | 650 |

The current (1 July 20X9) market value of Crystal Inc's ordinary shares is $3.27 per share cum div. An annual dividend of $810,000 is due for payment shortly. The debentures are redeemable at par in 10 years' time. Their current market value is $77.10 per cent. Annual interest has just been paid on the debentures. There have been no issues or redemptions of ordinary shares or debentures during the past five years.

The current rate of corporation tax is 30%, and the current basic rate of income tax is 25%. Assume that there have been no changes in the system or rates of taxation during the last 5 years.

*Required*

(a) Estimate the cost of capital which Crystal Inc should use as a discount rate when appraising new investment opportunities. **(10 marks)**

(b) Discuss any difficulties and uncertainties in your estimates. **(5 marks)**

**(Total = 15 marks)**

# 13 Espondera Inc

Espondera Inc is a small unquoted company that needs to raise funds in order to invest in a new project. The company wants to issue ten-year bonds and its finance director is trying to work out the cost of debt in order to assess the profitability of the company.

The following information is available for the company.

| | |
|---|---|
| Total assets | $120m |
| Net income | $6m |
| Type of proposed debt | Subordinated |
| Long-term debt | $14m |
| Income before interest and taxes | $8m |
| Interest payments | $1.0m |

The earnings of the company for the last five years are as follows.

| Year | Earnings |
|---|---|
| 20X6 | $5m |
| 20X5 | $4.2m |
| 20X4 | $3.2m |
| 20X3 | $3.8m |
| 20X2 | $2.2m |

The finance director has decided to use the Kaplan-Urwitz model for unquoted companies to assess the cost of debt.

The Kaplan-Urwitz model for unquoted companies is given by:

$$Y = 4.41 + 0.001SIZE + 6.40PROFITABILITY - 2.56DEBT - 2.72LEVERAGE + 0.006INTEREST - 0.53COV$$

The classification of companies into credit rating categories is done in the following way.

| Score (Y) | Rating category |
|---|---|
| Y > 6.76 | AAA |
| Y > 5.19 | AA |
| Y > 3.28 | A |
| Y > 1.57 | BBB |
| Y > 0 | BB |

The following table gives the yield to maturity for ten-year corporate bonds by credit category.

| Rating | Cost of debt (yield to maturity) |
|---|---|
| AAA | 6.8% |
| AA | 7.3% |
| A | 7.8% |
| BBB | 8.4% |
| BB | 9.4% |
| B | 10.5% |

Calculate the cost of debt for Espondera Inc.

**(10 marks)**

# 14 Canada

**29 mins**

PG plc is considering investing in a new project in Canada which will have a life of 4 years. The initial investment is C$150,000, including working capital. The net after-tax cash flows which the project will generate are C$60,000 per annum for years 1, 2 and 3 and C$45,000 in year 4. The terminal value of the project is estimated at C$50,000, net of tax.

The current spot rate of Canadian dollars against the pound sterling is 1.7000. Economic forecasters expect the pound to strengthen against the Canadian dollar by 5% per annum over the next 4 years.

The company evaluates UK projects of similar risk at 14%.

*Required*

(a) Calculate the NPV of the Canadian project using the following two methods.

    (i) Convert the currency cash flows into sterling and discount the sterling cash flows at a sterling discount rate.

    (ii) Discount the cash flows in Canadian dollars using an adjusted discount rate which incorporates the 12-month forecast spot rate and explain briefly the theories and/or assumptions which underlie the use of the adjusted discount rate approach. **(10 marks)**

(b) The company had originally planned to finance the project with internal funds generated in the UK. However, the finance director has suggested that there would be advantages in raising debt finance in Canada.

    Discuss the advantages and disadvantages of matching investment and borrowing overseas as compared with UK-sourced debt or equity.

    Wherever possible, relate your answer to the details in this question for PG plc. **(5 marks)**

**(Total = 15 marks)**

# 15 Organic growth

**16 mins**

Discuss the advantages to a company of establishing an overseas operating subsidiary by either:

(a) Organic growth; or

(b) Acquisition. **(8 marks)**

# 16 Canon Burger

**29 mins**

Canon Burger has been expanding its operation rapidly by acquiring a number of restaurants. Canon has been funding its acquisitions by bank borrowing and it has a high level of gearing. Canon Burger has been specialising in fast food outlets and although the market is supported by a booming young population, the older generation prefer more traditional outlets. Canon is considering the acquisition of Templar Restaurant, a continental type of establishment with a steady clientele and good reputation. The owners of Templar have been rather conservative and have not exploited the brand value of the restaurant to expand, as they approach retirement. The owners of Templar are prepared to accept a cash offer of $200,000. Canon Burger has a cost of capital of 16% due to its high gearing. Templar Restaurant, on the other hand, is free of debt. As a result of the acquisition, Canon Burger expects the debt/equity ratio of the combined equity to decrease and the cost of capital to fall to 12%. The acquisition of Templar Restaurant is expected to increase Canon's cash flow by $25,000 per year forever.

(a) Assess the synergies that the acquisition of Templar Restaurants should create. **(5 marks)**

(b) Recommend whether Canon Burger should proceed with the acquisition. **(5 marks)**

(c) If the acquisition was funded by borrowing so that there is no impact on the level of gearing of the combined entity and the cost of capital was not reduced, recommend whether Canon should still proceed with the acquisition. **(5 marks)**

**(Total = 15 marks)**

# 17 Takeovers

**39 mins**

Despite substantial evidence, drawn from different countries and different time periods, that suggests the wealth of shareholders in a bidding company is unlikely to be increased as a result of taking over another company, takeovers remain an important part of the business landscape.

*Required*

(a) Explain, in economic terms, what a company, which is committed to increasing shareholder wealth, should look for when seeking to acquire another company. **(3 marks)**

(b) Describe four ways in which a takeover may lead to an increase in wealth for the bidding company's shareholders. **(8 marks)**

(c) Discuss four reasons why a takeover may fail to deliver an expected increase in wealth for the bidding company's shareholders. **(9 marks)**

**(Total = 20 marks)**

# 18 Univo Inc

**29 mins**

Summarised financial data for Univo Inc is shown below.

STATEMENTS OF PROFIT OR LOSS

|  | 20W9 $'000 | 20X0 $'000 | 20X1[1] $'000 |
|---|---|---|---|
| Revenue | 76,270 | 89,410 | 102,300 |
| Taxable income | 10,140 | 12,260 | 14,190 |
| Taxation | 3,346 | 4,046 | 4,683 |
|  | 6,794 | 8,214 | 9,507 |
| Dividend | 2,516 | 2,654 | 2,800 |
| Retained earnings | 4,278 | 5,560 | 6,707 |

STATEMENT OF FINANCIAL POSITION

|  | 20X1[1] $'000 |
|---|---|
| Non-current assets | 54,200 |
| Current assets | 39,500 |
| Current liabilities | (26,200) |
|  | 67,500 |
|  |  |
| Ordinary shares (50 cents par value) | 20,000 |
| Reserves | 32,500 |
| 10% debentures 20X6 ($100 par value) | 15,000 |
|  | 67,500 |

[1] 20X1 figures are unaudited estimates.

As a result of recent capital investment, stock market analysts expect post-tax earnings and dividends to increase by 15% for two years and then to revert to the company's existing growth rates.

Univo's beta of debt is 0.20 and beta of equity is 1.02. The risk-free rate is 4% and the market return 9%.

The current market price of Univo's shares is 267 cents cum 20X1 dividend.

*Required*

(a)   Using the dividend growth model, estimate what a fundamental analyst might consider to be the intrinsic (or realistic) value of the company's shares. Comment on the significance of your estimate for the fundamental analyst.

Assume, for this part of the question only, that the cost of equity is not expected to change. The cost of equity may be estimated by using the CAPM.   **(10 marks)**

(b)   If interest rates were to increase by 2% and expected dividend growth to remain unchanged, estimate what effect this would be likely to have on the intrinsic value of the company's shares.

**(5 marks)**

**(Total = 15 marks)**

# 19 Black Raven Co

**59 mins**

Black Raven Co is a prosperous private company, whose owners are also the directors. The directors have decided to sell their business, and have begun a search for organisations interested in its purchase. They have asked for your assessment of the price per ordinary share a purchaser might be expected to offer. Relevant information is as follows.

MOST RECENT STATEMENT OF FINANCIAL POSITION

|  | $'000 | $'000 | $'000 |
|---|---|---|---|
| Non-current assets (net book value) |  |  |  |
| Land and buildings |  |  | 800 |
| Plant and equipment |  |  | 450 |
| Motor vehicles |  |  | 55 |
| Patents |  |  | 2 |
|  |  |  | 1,307 |
| Current assets |  |  |  |
| Inventory |  | 250 |  |
| Receivables |  | 125 |  |
| Cash |  | 8 |  |
|  |  | 383 |  |
| Current liabilities |  |  |  |
| Payables | 180 |  |  |
| Taxation | 50 |  |  |
|  |  | 230 |  |
|  |  |  | 153 |
|  |  |  | 1,460 |
| Long-term liability |  |  |  |
| Loan secured on property |  |  | 400 |
|  |  |  | 1,060 |
| Share capital (300,000 ordinary shares of $1) |  |  | 300 |
| Reserves |  |  | 760 |
|  |  |  | 1,060 |

The profits after tax and interest but before dividends over the last five years have been as follows.

| Year | $ |
|---|---|
| 1 | 90,000 |
| 2 | 80,000 |
| 3 | 105,000 |
| 4 | 90,000 |
| 5 (most recent) | 100,000 |

The company's 5-year plan forecasts an after-tax profit of $100,000 for the next 12 months, with an increase of 4% a year over each of the next 4 years. The annual dividend has been $45,000 (gross) for the last 6 years.

As part of their preparations to sell the company, the directors of Black Raven Co have had the non-current assets revalued by an independent expert, with the following results.

| | $ |
|---|---|
| Land and buildings | 1,075,000 |
| Plant and equipment | 480,000 |
| Motor vehicles | 45,000 |

The gross dividend yields and P/E ratios of three quoted companies in the same industry as Black Raven Co over the last three years have been as follows.

| | Albatross Inc | | Bullfinch Inc | | Crow Inc | |
|---|---|---|---|---|---|---|
| | Div. yield % | P/E ratio | Div. yield % | P/E ratio | Div. yield % | P/E ratio |
| Recent year | 12 | 8.5 | 11.0 | 9.0 | 13.0 | 10.0 |
| Previous year | 12 | 8.0 | 10.6 | 8.5 | 12.6 | 9.5 |
| Three years ago | 12 | 8.5 | 9.3 | 8.0 | 12.4 | 9.0 |
| Average | 12 | 8.33 | 10.3 | 8.5 | 12.7 | 9.5 |

Large companies in the industry apply an after-tax cost of capital of about 18% to acquisition proposals when the investment is not backed by tangible assets, as opposed to a rate of only 14% on the net tangible assets.

Your assessment of the net cash flows which would accrue to a purchasing company, allowing for taxation and the capital expenditure required after the acquisition to achieve the company's target five-year plan, is as follows.

| | $ |
|---|---|
| Year 1 | 120,000 |
| Year 2 | 120,000 |
| Year 3 | 140,000 |
| Year 4 | 70,000 |
| Year 5 | 120,000 |

*Required*

Use the information provided to suggest alternative valuations which prospective purchasers might make.

**(30 marks)**

# 20 Margate

**98 mins**

Margate Group plc is a large, long-established company whose primary interests are in transport and distribution within the UK. It is considering a bid to acquire Hastings plc, a company also in the transport and distribution industry. Hastings plc, however, has a strong operations base in Europe as well as in the UK. Both companies are listed on a recognised stock exchange. They both have a wide share ownership, including many institutional investors.

Hastings plc has recently fought off a bid from a company based in the US and has made a public statement that it will defend itself against any future bids. The company has recently won a fiercely contested five-year contract to undertake transport and distribution services for a major supermarket group. Margate Group plc also tendered for this contract. Press comment suggests this contract will allow Hastings plc's earnings to grow at 10% a year for at least the next five years. However, some industry experts believe Hastings plc tendered a price that was so low that the contract could result in very little profit, or even losses.

If the acquisition were to succeed, it would create the largest company of its kind in the UK. A concern is that this would attract the interest of the competition authorities. However, as both companies have recently restructured their operations, redundancies are likely to be few and concentrated mainly in central administration.

## Financial statements

Key financial information for the two companies for the latest financial year is given below. All figures are in £ million unless otherwise stated.

STATEMENTS OF PROFIT OR LOSS FOR THE YEAR TO 31 AUGUST 20X1

|  | Margate Group plc £m | Hastings plc £m |
|---|---|---|
| Revenue | 2,763 | 1,850 |
| Operating costs | 1,950 | 1,380 |
| Operating profit | 813 | 470 |
| Net interest | 125 | 85 |
| Profit before tax | 688 | 385 |
| Tax | 185 | 85 |
| Earnings | 503 | 300 |
| Dividends declared | 201 | 135 |
| Retained profit for the year | 302 | 165 |
| | | |
| Earnings per share (pence) | 47.90 | 35.29 |
| EPS for year to 31 August 20X0 (pence) | 34.85 | 29.50 |

STATEMENTS OF FINANCIAL POSITION AT 31 AUGUST 20X1

|  | Margate Group plc £m | Hastings plc £m |
|---|---|---|
| Non-current assets (net book value) | 3,250 | 2,580 |
| *Current assets* | | |
| Inventory | 125 | 175 |
| Receivables | 550 | 425 |
| | 450 | 45 |
| *Payables: due within 1 year* | | |
| Bank overdraft | 0 | 420 |
| Trade payables | 755 | 365 |
| *Payables: due after 1 year* | | |
| Debentures | 1,450 | 950 |
| Tax | 150 | 40 |
| Net assets | 2,020 | 1,450 |
| | | |
| *Capital and reserves* | | |
| Share capital (£1 each) | 1,050 | 850 |
| Share premium | 220 | 150 |
| Retained earnings | 750 | 450 |
| Total shareholders' funds | 2,020 | 1,450 |

**Note**. Margate Group plc's debenture is 8%, repayable 20X5. Hastings plc's is 9%, repayable 20X4.

### Share price information (prices in pence)

|  | Margate Group plc | Hastings plc |
|---|---|---|
| Share price movements: High for last financial year | 705 | 590 |
| Low for last financial year | 470 | 440 |
| Share price today (20 November 20X1) | 671 | 565 |
| P/E ratios today | 14 | 16 |
| Equity betas | 1.1 | 1.2 |

### Other information

- The average P/E for the industry is currently estimated as 13.

- The return on the market is currently estimated as 12%, the risk-free rate as 6%. These rates are expected to remain constant for the next 12 months and are post-tax.

- The average debt ratio for the industry (long-term debt as proportion of total long-term funding) is 30% based on book values.

- Economic forecasts provided by Margate Group plc's financial advisers expect inflation and interest rates to remain at their current levels for the foreseeable future. Inflation is currently 2% a year.

**Terms of the proposed bid**

Margate Group plc's directors are planning to offer a share exchange to Hastings plc's shareholders.

*Required*

(a) Calculate and discuss briefly three key ratios for both companies that are relevant to the evaluation of the proposed acquisition. **(9 marks)**

(b) Calculate a range of possible values that Margate Group plc could place on Hastings plc, using both P/E basis and the dividend growth model.

Accompany your calculations by brief comments or explanations. Where necessary, explain any assumptions you have made. **(9 marks)**

(c) Assume you are the Financial Manager with Margate Group plc. Write a report to the directors of the group that evaluates the proposed acquisition.

You should use the figures you have calculated in answer to parts (a) and (b) to support your recommendations/advice where relevant. If you have not been able to do the calculations for parts (a) and (b), you should make, and state, appropriate assumptions.

Your report should include the following topics.

(i) Recommendation to the directors of a bid price and offer terms, assuming a share for share exchange.

(ii) Advice on a strategy for making the offer to Hastings plc to minimise the likelihood of outright rejection by the Hastings plc board, and a discussion of the other risks involved in making the bid.

(iii) Discussion of the strategic and financial advantages that might arise from the acquisition by Margate Group plc of Hastings plc.

Support your discussion with calculations of the post-acquisition value of the combined group and how the estimated gains are likely to be split between the shareholders of Margate Group plc and Hastings plc. **(28 marks)**

Professional marks will be awarded for the structure and presentation of the report. **(4 marks)**

**(Total = 50 marks)**

# 21 Canadian Inc                                                       98 mins

Canadian Inc is a regional electricity generating company with several coal, oil and gas powered generating stations. The opportunity to bid for the coal mine supplying one of its local stations has arisen, and you have been asked to assess the project. If Canadian does not bid for the pit, then it is likely to close, in which case coal for the station would have to be obtained from overseas.

Canadian's bid is likely to be successful if priced at $6 million. Regional development fund finance is available at a subsidised interest rate of 4% for the full cost of the purchase, as against Canadian's marginal cost of debt if financed commercially. If Canadian invests a further $6 million in updated machinery, the pit is likely to generate $10 million of coal per annum for the next 5 years at current domestic coal prices. Operating costs will total $3 million per annum, plus depreciation. Thereafter it will have to close, at a net cost after asset sales of $17 million at current price, which includes redundancy, cleanup and associated costs, at present prices.

You have ascertained the following information about the coal industry.

|  | Coal industry (average) |
|---|---|
| Gearing (debt/equity): | |
| Book values | 1 to 0.5 |
| Market values | 1:1 |
| Equity beta | 0.7 |
| Debt beta | 0.2 |

Capital allowances would be available at 25% on a reducing balance basis for all new machinery. The purchase price of the mine can be depreciated for tax at 25% per annum straight line. All other costs are tax allowable in full.

Other than the regional development fund loan (repayable after 5 years), the project would be financed by retained earnings. The project is likely to add another $3 million of borrowing capacity to Canadian, in addition to the $6 million regional development fund loan. Corporation tax is expected to remain at 30% during the life of the project. The company as a whole expects to be in a tax-payable position for all years except the third year of the project.

Assume that all prices rise with the RPI, currently by 3% p.a., except coal prices, which in view of reduced demand are set to remain static. You may assume that original investment cash flows arise at the start of the first year, and that all other cash flows arise at the end of the year in which the costs are incurred, except for tax, which lags one year. Treasury bills currently yield 8%, and the return required of the market portfolio is currently 16%.

You have discovered the following information concerning Canadian.

|  | Canadian Inc |
|---|---|
| Gearing (debt/equity): | |
|  | 1 to 1 |
|  | 1:2 |
| Equity beta | 1.0 |
| Debt beta | 0.25 |
| P/E ratio | 14 |
| Dividend yield | 6% |
| Share price | 220c |
| Number of ordinary shares | 8m |

*Required*

Write a memorandum for the finance director advising on whether the mine should be acquired. You should divide your memorandum into the following sections.

| (a) | Overall summary and conclusion | **(8 marks)** |
|---|---|---|
| (b) | Detailed numerical workings | **(25 marks)** |
| (c) | Assumptions behind the report | **(10 marks)** |
| (d) | Areas for further research | **(3 marks)** |

Professional marks will be awarded for the structure and presentation of the memorandum.     **(4 marks)**

**(Total = 50 marks)**

# 22 Peden and Tulen

29 mins

The total values (equity plus debt) of two companies, Peden and Tulen, are expected to fluctuate according to the state of the economy.

|  | | Economic state | |
|---|---|---|---|
|  | Recession | Slow growth | Rapid growth |
| Probability | 0.15 | 0.65 | 0.20 |
| Total values |  |  |  |
| Peden (£m) | 42 | 55 | 75 |
| Tulen (£m) | 63 | 80 | 120 |

Peden currently has $45 million of debt, and Tulen $10 million of debt.

*Required*

(a)     If the two companies were to merge, and assuming that no operational synergy occurs as a result of the merger, calculate the expected value of debt and equity of the merged company. Explain the reasons for any difference that exists from the expected values of debt and equity if they do not merge.   **(11 marks)**

(b)     Discuss the importance of financial post-audits following a merger or takeover.          **(4 marks)**

(Total = 15 marks)

# 23 Gasco

49 mins

Gasco, a public limited company with a market value of around £7 billion, is a major supplier of gas to both business and domestic customers. The company also provides maintenance contracts for both gas and central heating customers using the well-known brand name Gas For All. Customers can call emergency lines for assistance with any gas-related incident, such as a suspected leak. Gasco employs its own highly trained workforce to deal with all such situations quickly and effectively. The company also operates a major new credit card, which has been extensively marketed and which gives users concessions, such as reductions in their gas bills.

Gasco has recently bid £1.1 billion for CarCare, a long-established mutual organisation (ie it is owned by its members) that is the country's leading motoring organisation. CarCare is financed primarily by an annual subscription to its 4.4 million members. In addition, the organisation obtains income from a range of other activities, such as a high profile car insurance brokerage, a travel agency and assistance with all types of travel arrangements. Its main service to members is the provision of a roadside breakdown service, which is now an extremely competitive market with many other companies involved. Although many of its competitors use local garages to deal with breakdowns, CarCare uses its own road patrols.

CarCare members have to approve the takeover, which once completed would provide them each with a windfall of around £300 each.

Gasco intends to preserve the CarCare name which is extremely well known to consumers.

*Required*

(a)     Discuss the possible reasons why Gasco is seeking to buy CarCare.          **(9 marks)**

(b)     Discuss how the various stakeholders of CarCare might react to the takeover.          **(8 marks)**

(c)     Discuss the potential problems that Gasco may face in running CarCare now that the takeover has been achieved.          **(8 marks)**

(Total = 25 marks)

# 24 Olivine

**39 mins**

Olivine is a holiday tour operator that is committed to a policy of expansion. The company has enjoyed record growth in recent years and is now seeking to acquire other companies in order to maintain its growth momentum. It has recently taken an interest in Halite, a charter airline business, as the board of directors of Olivine believes that there is a good strategic fit between the two companies. Both companies have the same level of risk. Abbreviated financial statements relating to each company are set out below.

ABBREVIATED STATEMENT OF PROFIT OR LOSS
FOR THE YEAR ENDED 30 NOVEMBER 20X3

|  | Olivine | Halite |
|---|---|---|
|  | $m | $m |
| Sales | 182·6 | 75·2 |
| Operating profit | 43·6 | 21·4 |
| Interest charges | 12·3 | 10·2 |
| Net profit before taxation | 31·3 | 11·2 |
| Company tax | 6·3 | 1·6 |
| Net profit after taxation | 25·0 | 9·6 |
| Dividends | 6·0 | 4·0 |
| Accumulated profits for the year | 19·0 | 5·6 |

SUMMARISED STATEMENTS OF FINANCIAL POSITION
AS AT 30 NOVEMBER 20X3

|  | Olivine | Halite |
|---|---|---|
|  | $m | $m |
| Non-current assets | 135.4 | 127.2 |
| Net current assets | 65.2 | 3.2 |
|  | 200.6 | 130.4 |
| Payables due after more than one year | 120.5 | 104.8 |
|  | 80.1 | 25.6 |
| *Capital and reserves* |  |  |
| $0·50 ordinary shares | 20.0 | 8.0 |
| Retained profit | 60.1 | 17.6 |
|  | 80.1 | 25.6 |
| Price/earnings ratio before the bid | 20 | 15 |

The board of directors of Olivine is considering making an offer to the shareholders of Halite of five shares in Olivine for every four shares held. It is believed that a rationalisation of administrative functions arising from the merger would reap after-tax benefits of $2.4 million.

*Required*

(a) Calculate:

    (i)    The total value of the proposed offer

    (ii)    The earnings per share of Olivine following the successful acquisition of Halite

    (iii)    The share price of Olivine following acquisition, assuming that the benefits of the acquisition are achieved and that the price/earnings ratio declines by 5% **(10 marks)**

(b) Calculate the effect of the proposed takeover on the wealth of the shareholders of each company.

**(5 marks)**

(c) Discuss your results in (a) and (b) above and state what recommendations, if any, you would make to the directors of Olivine. **(5 marks)**

**(Total = 20 marks)**

## 25 Takeover regulation
**29 mins**

(a) Discuss the key aspects of takeover regulation in the UK and continental Europe in the context of European harmonisation.

(b) As hostile takeovers increase, discuss some of the defensive measures that could be taken by a target in Europe and compare these briefly with what would be permissible in the US regulatory environment.
**(15 marks)**

## 26 Atlas International
**29 mins**

Atlas International Inc is considering a bid for Olympic Global Inc. The following information is given for both companies.

|                          | Atlas | Olympic |
|--------------------------|-------|---------|
|                          | $     | $       |
| Forecast dividend per share | 4     | 0.90    |
| Share price              | 70    | 22      |
| Number of shares         | 1,000,000 | 500,000 |

The consensus view is that Olympic will grow at a rate of 5%. The management of Atlas believe that without additional investment they can raise the growth rate to 7%.

(a) Calculate the gain from the acquisition.
**(5 marks)**

(b) Calculate the cost of acquisition if Atlas pays $30 per share in cash for each share of Global and recommend whether the acquisition should go ahead.
**(5 marks)**

(c) Calculate the cost of acquisition if Atlas offers one of its own shares for every two shares of Global and recommend whether the acquisition should go ahead.
**(5 marks)**

**(Total = 15 marks)**

## 27 Brive Inc
**49 mins**

The latest statement of financial position for Brive Inc is summarised below.

|                                              | $'000 | $'000 | $'000 |
|----------------------------------------------|-------|-------|-------|
| Non-current assets at net book value         |       |       | 5,700 |
| Current assets                               |       |       |       |
| Inventory and work in progress               |       | 3,500 |       |
| Receivables                                  |       | 1,800 |       |
|                                              |       | 5,300 |       |
| Less current liabilities                     |       |       |       |
| Unsecured payables                           | 4,000 |       |       |
| Bank overdraft (unsecured)                   | 1,600 |       |       |
|                                              |       | 5,600 |       |
| Working capital                              |       |       | (300) |
| Total assets less current liabilities        |       |       | 5,400 |
| Liabilities falling due after more than one year |    |       |       |
| 10% secured debentures                       |       |       | 3,000 |
| Net assets                                   |       |       | 2,400 |
|                                              |       |       | $'000 |
| Capital and reserves                         |       |       |       |
| Called up share capital                      |       |       | 4,000 |
| Reserves                                     |       |       | (1,600) |
|                                              |       |       | 2,400 |

Brive Inc's called-up capital consists of 4,000,000 $1 ordinary shares issued and fully paid. The non-current assets comprise freehold property with a book value of $3,000,000 and plant and machinery with a book value of $2,700,000. The debentures are secured on the freehold property.

In recent years the company has suffered a series of trading losses which have brought it to the brink of liquidation. The directors estimate that in a forced sale the assets will realise the following amounts.

|  | $ |
|---|---|
| Freehold premises | 2,000,000 |
| Plant and machinery | 1,000,000 |
| Inventory | 1,700,000 |
| Receivables | 1,700,000 |

The costs of liquidation are estimated at $770,000. However, trading conditions are now improving and the directors estimate that if new investment in plant and machinery costing $2,500,000 were undertaken the company should be able to generate annual profits before interest of $1,750,000. In order to take advantage of this they have put forward the following proposed reconstruction scheme.

(a)   Freehold premises should be written down by $1,000,000, plant and machinery by $1,100,000, inventory and work in progress by $800,000 and receivables by $100,000.

(b)   The ordinary shares should be written down by $3,000,000 and the debit balance on the statement of profit or loss written off.

(c)   The secured debentureholders would exchange their debentures for $1,500,000 ordinary shares and $1,300,000 14% unsecured loan stock repayable in 5 years' time.

(d)   The bank overdraft should be written off and the bank should receive $1,200,000 of 14% unsecured loan stock repayable in 5 years' time in compensation.

(e)   The unsecured payables should be written down by 25%.

(f)   A rights issue of 1 for 1 at par is to be made on the share capital after the above adjustments have been made.

(g)   $2,500,000 will be invested in new plant and machinery.

*Required*

(a)   Prepare the statement of financial position of the company after the completion of the reconstruction.                                                                                    **(6 marks)**

(b)   Prepare a report, including appropriate calculations, discussing the advantages and disadvantages of the proposed reconstruction from the point of view of:

(i)     The ordinary shareholders
(ii)    The secured debentureholders
(iii)   The bank
(iv)    The unsecured payables

**Note.** Ignore taxation.                                                                                    **(19 marks)**

**(Total = 25 marks)**

# 28 Reorganisation

**23 mins**

(a) Discuss the potential problems with management buy-outs. **(5 marks)**

(b) Company X's hotel division is experiencing considerable financial difficulties. The management is prepared to undertake a buy-out, and Company X is willing to sell for $15 million. After an analysis of the division's performance, the management concluded that the division required a capital injection of $10 million.

Possible funding sources for the buy-out and the additional capital injection are as follows.

From management:

Equity shares of 25c each                                    $12 million

From venture capitalist:

Equity shares of 25c each                                    $5.5 million
Debt: 9.5% fixed rate loan                                   $7.5 million

The fixed rate loan principal is repayable in 10 years' time.

Forecasts of earnings before interest and tax for the next 5 years following the buy-out are as follows.

|       | Year 1 $'000 | Year 2 $'000 | Year 3 $'000 | Year 4 $'000 | Year 5 $'000 |
|-------|--------------|--------------|--------------|--------------|--------------|
| EBIT  | 2,200        | 3,100        | 3,900        | 4,200        | 4,500        |

Corporation tax is charged at 30%. Dividends are expected to be no more than 12% of profits for the first 5 years.

Management has forecast that the value of equity capital is likely to increase by approximately 15% per annum for the next 5 years.

*Required*

On the basis of the above forecasts, determine whether management's estimate that the value of equity will increase by 15% per annum is a viable one. **(7 marks)**

**(Total = 12 marks)**

# 29 Treasury management

**21 mins**

Many large international organisations have a central treasury department which might be a separate profit centre within the group. The responsibilities of this department will include the management of business risk and market risk for the group as a whole.

*Required*

(a) Describe the functions of a central treasury department.

(b) Describe the information that the treasury department needs, from inside and outside the organisation, to perform its function.

**(11 marks)**

# 30 Expo Inc
**29 mins**

Expo Inc is an importer/exporter of textiles and textile machinery which trades extensively with countries throughout Europe. It has a small subsidiary based in Switzerland. The company is about to invoice a customer in Switzerland 750,000 Swiss francs, payable in three months' time. Expo Inc's treasurer is considering two methods of hedging the exchange risk. These are:

Method 1: borrow SFr750,000 for 3 months, convert the loan into dollars and repay the loan out of eventual receipts.

Method 2: enter into a 3-month forward exchange contract with the company's bank to sell SFr750,000.

The spot rate of exchange is SFr2.3834 to $1. The 3-month forward rate of exchange is SFr2.3688 to $1. Annual interest rates for 3 months' borrowing are: Switzerland 3%, US 6%.

*Required*

(a) Advise the treasurer on:

    (i)     Which of the two methods is the most financially advantageous for Expo Inc

    (ii)     The factors to consider before deciding whether to hedge the risk using the foreign currency markets

    Include relevant calculations in your advice.     **(10 marks)**

(b) Assume that Expo Inc is trading in and with developing countries rather than Europe and has a subsidiary in a country with no developed capital or currency markets. Expo Inc is now about to invoice a customer in that country in the local currency. Advise Expo Inc's treasurer about ways in which the risk can be managed in these circumstances. No calculations are required for this part of the question.     **(5 marks)**

**(Total = 15 marks)**

# 31 Fidden plc
**49 mins**

(a) Discuss briefly four techniques a company might use to hedge against the foreign exchange risk involved in foreign trade.     **(8 marks)**

(b) Fidden plc is a medium-sized UK company with export and import trade with the US. The following transactions are due within the next six months. Transactions are in the currency specified.

Purchases of components, cash payment due in three months: £116,000.
Sale of finished goods, cash receipt due in three months: $197,000.
Purchase of finished goods for resale, cash payment due in six months: $447,000.
Sale of finished goods, cash receipt due in six months: $154,000.

Exchange rates (London market)

| | $/£ |
|---|---|
| Spot | 1.7106–1.7140 |
| Three months forward | 1.7024–1.7063 |
| Six months forward | 1.6967–1.7006 |

Interest rates

| Three months or six months | Borrowing | Lending |
|---|---|---|
| Sterling | 12.5% | 9.5% |
| Dollars | 9% | 6% |

| Exercise price ($) | Calls | | | Puts | | |
|---|---|---|---|---|---|---|
| | Mar | Jun | Sep | Mar | Jun | Sep |
| 1.60 | – | 15.20 | – | – | – | 2.75 |
| 1.70 | 5.65 | 7.75 | – | – | 3.45 | 6.40 |
| 1.80 | 1.70 | 3.60 | 7.90 | – | 9.32 | 15.35 |

Assume that it is now December with three months to the expiry of March contracts and that the option price is not payable until the end of the option period, or when the option is exercised.

*Required*

(i) Calculate the net sterling receipts and payments that Fidden might expect for both its three- and six-month transactions if the company hedges foreign exchange risk on:

    (1) The forward foreign exchange market

    (2) The money market        **(7 marks)**

(ii) If the actual spot rate in six months' time turned out to be exactly the present six-month forward rate, calculate whether Fidden would have done better to have hedged through foreign currency options rather than the forward market or the money market. **(7 marks)**

(iii) Explain briefly what you consider to be the main advantage of foreign currency options.
**(3 marks)**

**(Total = 25 marks)**

# 32 Exchange rate forecasts      29 mins

(a) Your managing director has received forecasts of euro exchange rates in two years' time from three leading banks.

$/euro two-year forecasts

| | |
|---|---|
| Lottobank | 1.452 |
| Kadbank | 1.514 |
| Gross bank | 1.782 |

The current spot mid-rate is $1.667/euro.

A non-executive director of your company has suggested that in order to forecast future exchange rates, the interest rate differential between countries should be used. She states that 'as short-term interest rates are currently 3.5% in the US, and 6% in the Euro bloc, the exchange rate in two years' time will be $1.747/euro'.

*Required*

(i) Prepare a brief report discussing the likely validity of the non-executive director's estimate.
**(4 marks)**

(ii) Explain briefly whether or not forecasts of future exchange rates using current interest rate differentials are likely to be accurate. **(3 marks)**

(b) You have also been asked to give advice to your managing director about a tender by the company's Italian subsidiary for an order in Kuwait. The tender conditions state that payment will be made in Kuwait dinars 18 months from now. The subsidiary is unsure as to what price to tender. The marginal cost of producing the goods at that time is estimated to be €340,000 and a 25% mark-up is normal for the company.

Exchange rates
Euro/dinar
Spot            0.256–0.260

No forward rate exists for 18 months' time.

|  |  | Italy | Kuwait |
|---|---|---|---|
|  |  | % | % |
| Annual inflation rates |  | 3 | 9 |
| Annual interest rates available to the Italian subsidiary: | Borrowing | 6 | 11 |
|  | Lending | 2.5 | 8 |

*Required*

Discuss how the Italian subsidiary might protect itself against foreign exchange rate changes, and recommend what tender price should be used. **(8 marks)**

All relevant calculations must be shown. **(Total = 15 marks)**

# 33 US options                                                          39 mins

(a) Your UK-based company has won an export order worth $1.8 million from the US. Payment is due to be made to you in dollars in 6 months' time. It is now 15 November. You wish to protect the exchange rate risk with currency options, but do not wish to pay an option premium of more than £10,000.

Your bank has suggested using a particular currency option which has no premium. The option would allow a worst case exchange rate at which the option could be exercised of $1.65/£. If the contract moved in your favour then the bank would share (participate in) the profits, and would take 50% of any gains relative to the current spot exchange rate.

You also have access to currency options on the Philadelphia Stock Exchange.

Current option prices are:

Sterling contacts, £31,250 contract size. Premium is US cents per £.

| | | Calls | | | Puts | |
|---|---|---|---|---|---|---|
| Exercise price | Dec | Mar | Jun | Dec | Mar | Jun |
| 1.55 | 6.8 | 7.9 | 10.1 | 0.2 | 0.5 | 0.9 |
| 1.60 | 2.1 | 3.8 | 5.3 | 1.9 | 3.1 | 4.0 |
| 1.65 | 0.6 | 0.9 | 1.1 | 5.1 | 7.2 | 9.6 |
| 1.70 | 0.1 | 0.2 | 0.4 | 10.1 | 12.3 | 14.1 |

The current spot rate is $1.6055–1.6100/£. Any option premium would be payable immediately.

*Required*

Evaluate whether a participating option or traded option is likely to offer a better foreign exchange hedge. **(15 marks)**

(b) Your company is trading in and with developing countries and has a subsidiary in a country with no developed capital or currency markets. Your company is now about to invoice a customer in that country in the local currency. Advise your treasurer about ways in which the risk can be managed in these circumstances. **(5 marks)**

**(Total = 20 marks)**

# 34 Curropt plc

49 mins

It is now 1 March and the treasury department of Curropt plc, a quoted UK company, faces a problem. At the end of June the treasury department may need to advance to Curropt's US subsidiary the amount of $15,000,000. This depends on whether the subsidiary is successful in winning a franchise. The department's view is that the US dollar will strengthen over the next few months, and it believes that a currency hedge would be sensible. The following data is relevant.

Exchange rates US$/£
1 March spot 1.4461–1.4492; 4 months forward 1.4310–1.4351.
Futures market contract prices
Sterling £62,500 contracts:
March contract 1.4440; June contract 1.4302.
Currency options: Sterling £31,250 contracts (cents per £)

| | Calls | Puts |
|---|---|---|
| | June | June |
| Exercise price | | |
| $1.400/£ | 3.40 | 0.38 |
| $1.425/£ | 1.20 | 0.68 |
| $1.450/£ | 0.40 | 2.38 |

*Required*

(a)   Explain whether the treasury department is justified in its belief that the US dollar is likely to strengthen against the pound.                                                                                    **(3 marks)**

(b)   Explain the relative merits of forward currency contracts, currency futures contracts and currency options as instruments for hedging in the given situation.                                             **(6 marks)**

(c)   Assuming the franchise is won, illustrate the results of using forward, future and option currency hedges if the US$/£ spot exchange rate at the end of June is:

   (i)     1.3500
   (ii)    1.4500
   (iii)   1.5500                                                                                                                  **(16 marks)**

(Total = 25 marks)

# 35 Carrick plc

29 mins

(a)   Explain the term risk management in respect of interest rates and discuss how interest risk might be managed.                                                                                                              **(7 marks)**

(b)   It is currently 1 January 20X7. Carrick plc receives interest of 6% per annum on short-term deposits on the London money markets amounting to £6 million. The company wishes to explore the use of a collar to protect, for a period of seven months, the interest yield it currently earns. The following prices are available, with the premium cost being quoted in annual percentage terms.

LIFFE interest rate options on three-month money market futures (contract size: £500,000).

| | Calls | | Puts | |
|---|---|---|---|---|
| Strike price | Jun | Sep | Jun | Sep |
| 92.50 | 0.71 | 1.40 | 0.02 | 0.06 |
| 93.00 | 0.36 | 1.08 | 0.10 | 0.14 |
| 93.50 | 0.12 | 0.74 | 0.20 | 0.35 |
| 94.00 | 0.01 | 0.40 | 0.57 | 0.80 |
| 94.50 | – | 0.06 | 0.97 | 1.12 |

Evaluate the use of a collar by Carrick plc for the purpose proposed above. Include calculations of the cost involved and indicate appropriate exercise price(s) for the collar. Ignore taxation, commission and margin requirements. **(8 marks)**

**(Total = 15 marks)**

# 36 Burger Queen                                    29 mins

The three-month dollar interest rate futures are quoted as follows on 30 July.

| | |
|---|---|
| September | 92.90 |
| December | 92.70 |
| March | 92.50 |

Each futures contract has a notional value of $500,000. Burger Queen will need to borrow $10 million floating at the end of December for three months and is concerned that interest rates may rise.

(a) Recommend a hedging strategy that Burger Queen could use to reduce interest rate risk.

**(5 marks)**

(b) Calculate the effective rate of interest that Burger Queen will have to pay if it hedged its exposure and interest rates have risen to 9% in December. **(5 marks)**

(c) Calculate the effective rate of interest after taking into account the derivative transaction if three-month spot rates are 6% in December. **(5 marks)**

**(Total = 15 marks)**

# 37 Theta Inc                                       23 mins

(a) Theta Inc wants to borrow $10 million for five years with interest payable at six-monthly intervals. It can borrow from a bank at a floating rate of LIBOR plus 1% but wants to obtain a fixed rate for the full five-year period. A swap bank has indicated that it will be willing to receive a fixed rate of 8.5% in exchange for payments of six-month LIBOR.

*Required*

Calculate the fixed interest six-monthly payment with the swap in place. **(4 marks)**

(b) Show the interest payments by Theta if:

(i) LIBOR is 10%. **(4 marks)**
(ii) LIBOR is 7.5%. **(4 marks)**

**(Total = 12 marks)**

# 38 Kilber Inc                                      29 mins

Kilber Inc is a mining company with exclusive rights to the mining of Kilbe. Kilbe is a new metal that is used in the construction industry. The demand for Kilbe is highly dependent on the state of the housing market and the price is highly volatile. Kilber would like to hedge its exposure but there are no traded derivatives for Kilbe. The treasurer of Kilber has approached a number of banks but has found the OTC market is expensive, as Kilber is considered to be too risky, and is therefore reluctant to use forward contracts for hedging. One of the bankers they have sought advice from suggested that they should use futures contracts on copper. She explained that the price of Kilbe is highly correlated with the price of copper and therefore copper futures contracts are good substitutes.

*Required*

(a) Explain why the company should care about hedging its risks and comment on the risks that Kilber Inc may face if it adopts the recommendation and uses copper futures contracts as a hedging instrument. **(6 marks)**

(b) Discuss some of the advantages and disadvantages of OTC derivatives. **(3 marks)**

(c) The management of Kilber is currently reviewing its funding strategies. All its borrowing is at variable rate and there are strong indications that interest rates will increase. Advise management on how to reduce the impact of higher rates on its interest payments. **(6 marks)**

**(Total = 15 marks)**

# 1 Goals

The conclusion sums up how the possible objectives can be fitted into the overall strategy of the organisation.

(a) and (b)                                                    REPORT

To:          Managing Director
From:        Finance Director
Date:        17 November 20X5
Subject:     Definition of corporate objectives

### Introduction

(1)    This report has been drafted for use as a discussion document at the forthcoming board meeting. It deals with the validity of continuing to operate with the single major goal of **shareholder wealth maximisation**. The remaining sections of the report contain an analysis of the advantages and disadvantages of some of the alternative objectives that have been put forward in recent discussions.

### Maximisation of shareholder wealth

(2)    The concept that the **primary financial objective** of the firm is to **maximise** the **wealth** of shareholders underpins much of modern financial theory. However, there has been some recent debate as to whether this should or can be the only true objective, particularly in the context of the multinational company.

(3)    The **stakeholder view** of corporate objectives is that **many groups** of people have a stake in what the company does. Each of these groups, which include suppliers, workers, managers, customers and governments as well as shareholders, has its own objectives, and this means that a compromise is required. For example, in the case of the multinational firm with a facility in a politically unstable developing economy, the directors may at times need to place the **interests of local government and economy** ahead of those of its shareholder, in part at least to ensure its own continued stability there.

(4)    While the relevance of the wealth maximisation goal is under discussion, it might also be useful to consider the way in which this type of objective is defined, since this will impact on both parallel and subsidiary objectives. A widely adopted approach is to seek to **maximise the present value of the projected cash flows**. In this way, the objective is both made measurable and can be translated into a yardstick for financial decision making. It cannot be defined as a single attainable target but rather as a criterion for the continuing allocation of the company's resources.

### Cash flow generation

(5) The validity of **cash flow generation** as a major corporate objective depends on the timescale over which performance is measured. If the business maximises the net present value of the cash flows generated in the medium to long term, then this objective is effectively the same as that discussed above. However, if the aim is to **maximise all cash flows**, then decisions are likely to be disproportionately focused on **short-term performance**, and this can work against the long-term health of the business. Defining objectives in terms of long-term cash flow generation makes the shareholder wealth maximisation goal more clearly definable and measurable.

### Profitability

(6) Many companies use **return on investment** targets to **assess performance** and **control the business**. This is useful for the comparison of widely differing divisions within a diverse multinational company, and can provide something approaching a 'level playing field' when setting targets for the different parts of the business. It is important that the **measurement techniques** to be used in respect of both profits and the asset base are **very clearly defined**, and that there is a clear and consistent approach to accounting for inflation. As with the cash flow generation targets discussed above, the selection of the time frame is also important in ensuring that the selected objectives do work for the long-term health of the business.

### Risk-adjusted returns

(7) It is assumed that the use of **risk-adjusted returns** relates to the criteria used for investment appraisal, rather than to the performance of the group as a whole. As such, risk-adjusted returns cannot be used in defining the top level major corporate goals; however, they can be one way in which **corporate goals** are made **congruent** with operating decisions. At the same time, they do provide a **useful input** to the goal setting process in that they focus attention on the company's policy with regard to making risky investments. Once the overall corporate approach to risk has been decided, this can be made effective in operating decisions, for example by **specifying the amount** by which the **cost of capital** is to be **augmented** to allow for risk in various types of investment decisions.

### Performance improvement in non-financial areas

(8) As discussed in the first section of this report, recent work on corporate objectives suggests that firms should take specific account of those areas which impact only indirectly, if at all, on **financial performance**. The firm has responsibilities towards many groups in addition to the shareholders, including:

    (i) **Employees:** to provide good working conditions and remuneration, the opportunity for personal development, outplacement help in the event of redundancy and so on

    (ii) **Customers:** to provide a product of good and consistent quality, good service and communication, and open and fair commercial practice

    (iii) **The public:** to ensure responsible disposal of waste products

(9) There are many **other interest groups** that should also be included in the discussion process. Non-financial objectives may often work indirectly to the financial benefit of the firm in the long term, but in the short term they do often appear to compromise the primary financial objectives.

### Conclusions

(10) It is very difficult to find a comprehensive and appropriate alternative primary financial objective to that of **shareholder wealth maximisation**. However, achievement of this goal can be pursued, at least in part, through the setting of specific **subsidiary targets** in terms of items such as return on investment and risk-adjusted returns. The definition of non-financial objectives should also be addressed in the context of the overall review of the corporate plan.

Signed: Finance Director

# 2 XYZ

(a)     **Ratios**

During this period, **earnings per share** have declined by 10.7% while at the same time **dividend per share** has increased by 19.0%. The **payout ratio** has increased from 60% in 20W9 to 80% in 20X3, and thus the proportion of earnings retained has fallen to 20%. If it is assumed that the capital structure has not changed over the period, then it can be seen that both **actual earnings** and the **return on capital employed** have declined over the period.

**Retention policy**

One possible implication of this policy is that **insufficient earnings** have been **retained** to finance the investment required to at least maintain the rate of return on capital employed. If this means that the company is falling behind its competitors, then this could have a serious **impact** on the **long-term profitability** of the business.

(b)     **Rate of return**

For the purposes of calculation it is assumed that any new investment will earn a rate of return equivalent to that **required by the shareholders** (ie 15%), and that this will also be the level of return that is earned on existing investments for the foreseeable future. It is further assumed that investors are indifferent as to whether they receive their returns in the form of dividend or as capital appreciation.

**Option 1**

The amount of dividend per share is $1 with no growth forecast. The rate of return required by shareholders is 15%. The theoretical share price can be estimated using the dividend valuation model.

$K_e = d_1/p_0$

Where   $K_e$  = Cost of equity

$d_1$  = Dividend per share
$p_0$  = Market price per share

$15\% = 1.00/p_0$

$p_0$  = $6.67, or $7.67 cum div

100% of the total return is provided in the form of dividend.

**Option 2**

Under the assumptions relating to earnings stated above, the share price will be the same as that calculated for option 1, ie $6.67 per share. However, in this case 50% of the expected return is in the form of dividend and 50% as capital appreciation.

A numerical example will clarify the position.

The rate of growth of dividends g may be expressed as:

$g = rb$

Where 
- $r$ = required rate of return
- $b$ = proportion of profits retained

In this case therefore, with dividends at 50 cents per share:

$g = 0.15 \times 0.5 = 0.075$

$$p_0 = \frac{d_1}{r-g} = \frac{0.5 \times 1.075}{0.15 - 0.075} = \$7.17$$

$7.17 plus 50c dividend at $t_0$ = $7.67 cum div.

**Option 3**

This is the same as for option 2, but 25% of the expected return is in the form of dividend and 75% as capital growth.

$g = 0.15 \times 0.75 = 0.1125$

$$p_0 = \frac{0.25 \times 1.1125}{0.15 - 0.1125} = 7.42$$

$7.42 plus 25c dividend at $t_0$ = $7.67 cum div

**Option 4**

In this case, for a share price of $6.67, investors would need to believe that retained profits will be invested in projects yielding annual growth of 15% and that the share price will grow at this rate. 100% of the expected return is provided in the form of capital appreciation under this option.

(c) **Factors influencing share price**

The figures calculated above assume that the **share price** is wholly dependent on the **rate of return required by shareholders** and that the shareholders are indifferent as to the form which the return takes. In practice, this is but one element in the range of factors which influence share prices. Other significant influences include the following:

(i) The **level of funds available for investment**
(ii) **Investor confidence**
(iii) The **tax situation and income requirements of investors**
(iv) The **availability of alternative investments**

The figures calculated are helpful to the directors only insofar as they direct attention away from the share price: they demonstrate that it is the **level of returns** and the **rate of return required** by investors which drive the share price.

**Investment policy**

It would be more helpful for the directors to look in detail at the options available to them in terms of **investment** and to assess these against the **cost of capital**, taking account of the differing **degrees of risk** entailed. For the share price to be maximised in the long term, it is the effect of **investment policy** on the net worth of the business which is important, ie the **net present value** of operating cash flows. This may mean that in the short term the share price declines, but the directors may decide that this is a worthwhile sacrifice to make for the long-term profitability of the business. They may also need to consider whether the company needs a further injection of capital in addition to an increase in retentions in order to fund its development.

# 3 Remuneration

The choice of an appropriate remuneration policy by a company will depend, among other things, on:

(a)   **Cost**: the extent to which the package provides value for money

(b)   **Motivation**: the extent to which the package motivates employees both to stay with the company and to work to their full potential

(c)   **Fiscal effects**: government tax incentives may promote different types of pay. In times of wage control and high taxation this can act as an incentive to make the 'perks' a more significant part of the package

(d)   **Goal congruence**: the extent to which the package encourages employees to work in such a way as to achieve the objectives of the firm – perhaps to maximise rather than to satisfice

## High basic salary

In this context, option (a) is likely to be **relatively expensive** with no payback to the firm in times of low profitability. It is unlikely to encourage staff to maximise their efforts, although the extent to which it acts as a motivator will depend on the individual psychological make-up of the employees concerned. However, many staff prefer this type of package since they know where they are financially. In the same way, the company is also able to budget accurately for its staff costs.

## Profit bonus

The firm will be able to gain benefits from operating a **profit-related pay scheme** (option (b)), as **costs** will be **lower**, though not proportionately so, during a time of low profits. The effect on motivation will vary with the individual concerned, and will also depend on whether it is an individual or a group performance calculation. There is a further risk that figures and performance may be **manipulated** by managers in such a way as to maximise their bonus to the detriment of the overall longer-term company benefit.

## Share option scheme

A share option scheme (option (c)) carries **fiscal benefits**. It also minimises the cost to the firm since this is effectively borne by the existing shareholders through the dilution of their holdings. Depending on how pricing is determined, it may assist in **achieving goal congruence**. However, since the share price depends on many factors which are external to the firm, it is possible for the scheme to operate in a way which is unrelated to the individual's performance. Thus such a scheme is unlikely to motivate directly through links with performance. Staff will continue to obtain the vast majority of their income from salary and perks and are thus likely to be more concerned with maximising these elements of their income than with working to raise the share price.

# 4 Stakeholders

(a)   **A company seeking a stock market listing**

When an unlisted company converts into a listed company, some of the existing shareholder/managers will sell their shares to outside investors. In addition, new shares will probably be issued. The dilution of ownership might cause loss of control by the existing management.

The stakeholders involved in potential conflicts are as follows:

(i)   **Existing shareholder/managers**

They will want to sell some of their shareholding at as high a price as possible. This may motivate them to overstate their company's prospects. Those shareholder/managers who wish to retire from the business may be in conflict with those who wish to stay in control – the latter may oppose the conversion into a listed company.

(ii)   **New outside shareholders**

Most of these will hold minority stakes in the company and will receive their rewards as dividends only. This may put them in conflict with the existing shareholder/managers who receive rewards as salaries as well as dividends. On conversion to a listed company there should be clear policies on dividends and directors' remuneration.

(iii)   **Employees, including managers who are not shareholders**

Part of the reason for the success of the company will be the efforts made by employees. They may feel that they should benefit when the company seeks a listing. One way of organising this is to create employee share options or other bonus schemes.

(b)   **Directly attributable costs**

The way in which **environmental costs and benefits** are included in the appraisal process will depend on the nature of the environmental implications, and the way in which the company intends to approach them. One method is to include in the appraisal only those elements of environmental cost that are **directly attributable** to undertaking the project, and to evaluate any further actions that the company may wish to undertake as a separate issue. In some cases, this may be relatively simple, particularly if legislation exists that defines the environmental standards to be applied.

**Technological options**

The company will then be faced with a variety of **technological options** that it could use to reduce the contamination to the required levels; for example, if volumes are large enough, it may be appropriate to build a treatment plant to decontaminate the effluent – alternatively it could enter into an agreement with a waste treatment company to tanker away the waste and dispose of it off site. Each of these options will have a **definable cost** which can be evaluated and incorporated into the overall project appraisal. In this situation, there are **no quantifiable benefits** as such, since the environmental issues take the form of a constraint on the project. The costs arise as a direct result of undertaking the project, and as such must be incorporated into the appraisal.

### Further expenditure

The problems arise where the company sees the opportunity to go beyond its statutory duties and to act in such a way as to **maximise** the **environmental benefits**. In the example cited above, it may be that the most cost-effective method from the point of view of the company is to **tanker the waste** to a remote treatment plant. However, it may view this as unacceptable on the grounds that it wishes to **minimise** the **disturbance** to the area around the site, and thus not to generate high volumes of tanker traffic in the local area. In this situation, the **higher cost option** of **on-site treatment** may become more attractive, although this is not a direct requirement of the project being undertaken. The benefits that arise are difficult to quantify and will not accrue directly to the company undertaking the investment.

In this situation, two approaches are possible:

(i) The company could decide that its own environmental standards form a financial constraint on the project, and thus that the project should be **evaluated at its full environmental cost**.

(ii) Alternatively, it could decide that the additional costs of on-site treatment over and above the cost of meeting the statutory requirements represent a **separate environmental investment**. If the company sets aside a budget for environmental and social issues, these excess costs could then be taken away from the project and allocated against this environmental budget.

Both approaches are valid and will depend on the objectives and policies of the company with regard to environmental issues.

# 5 Ethical dimension

(a) The main responsibilities faced by companies when developing an ethical framework are:

(i) Economic
(ii) Legal
(iii) Ethical
(iv) Philanthropic

The ways in which these responsibilities can be addressed are:

### Economic

(i) Management should always be acting in the best interests of the company's shareholders, and should therefore always be actively making decisions that will increase shareholders' wealth.

(ii) Projects that have positive NPVs should be pursued as far as funds will allow, as such projects will increase the value of the company and thus shareholders' wealth.

(iii) While management may have a different attitude towards risk than do the shareholders, they should always manage risk according to shareholders' requirements.

(iv) Financing – the optimal financing mix between debt and equity should be chosen as far as possible.

(v) Dividends – there is no legal obligation to pay dividends to ordinary shareholders, but the reasons for withholding dividends must be in the interests of the company as a whole (for example, maintaining funds within the company in order to finance future investment projects).

### Legal

(i) Companies must ensure that they are abiding by the rules and regulations that govern how they operate. Company law, health and safety, accounting standards and environmental standards are examples of these boundaries.

(ii) Failure to abide by the rules can cost companies dearly. One only has to look at the fate of WorldCom and Enron bosses, as well as Nick Leeson of Barings Bank, for examples of how

failure to operate within the legal framework can cause companies to collapse, taking with them the jobs (and often pension funds) of thousands of employees.

### Ethical

(i)    Ethical responsibilities arise from a moral requirement for companies to act in an ethical manner.

(ii)   Pursuit of ethical behaviour can be governed by such elements as:

- Mission statements
- Ethics managers
- Reporting channels to allow employees to expose unethical behaviour
- Ethics training and education (including ethics manuals)

### Philanthropic

(i)    Anything that improves the welfare of employees, the local community or the wider environment.

(ii)   Examples include Tesco's 'Computers for Schools' campaign (UK); provision of an employees' gym; sponsorship of sporting events; charitable donations.

(b)    Main functional areas of a firm include:

(i)    Human resources
(ii)   Marketing
(iii)  Market behaviour
(iv)   Product development

### Human resources

(i)    Provision of minimum wage. In recent years, much has been made of 'cheap labour' and 'sweat shops'. The introduction of the minimum wage is designed to show that companies have an ethical approach to how they treat their employees and are prepared to pay them an acceptable amount for the work they do.

(ii)   Discrimination – whether by age, gender, race or religion. It is no longer acceptable for employers to discriminate against employees for any reason – all employees are deemed to be equal and should not be prevented from progressing within the company for any discriminatory reason.

### Marketing

(i)    Marketing campaigns should be truthful and should not claim that products or services do something that they in fact cannot. This is why such campaigns have to be very carefully worded to avoid repercussions under Trade Descriptions Acts etc.

(ii)   Campaigns should avoid creating artificial wants. This is particularly true with children's toys, as children are very receptive to aggressive advertising.

(iii)  Do not target vulnerable groups (linked with above) or create a feeling of inferiority. Again, this is particularly true with children and teenagers, who are very easily led by what their peer groups have. The elderly are also vulnerable, particularly when it comes to such things as electricity and gas charges – making false promises regarding cheaper heating for example may cause the elderly to change companies when such action is not necessary and may in fact be detrimental.

### Market behaviour

(i)    Companies should not exploit their dominant market position by charging vastly inflated prices (this was particularly true when utilities were first privatised in the UK; also transport companies such as railway operators which have monopolies on certain routes).

(ii)   Large companies should also avoid exploiting suppliers if these suppliers rely on large company business for survival. Unethical behaviour could include refusing to pay a fair price for the goods and forcing suppliers to provide goods and services at uneconomical prices. In the past this has been a particular problem for suppliers in developing countries providing goods and services for large companies in developed countries.

### Product development

(i) Companies should strive to use ethical means to develop new products – for example, more and more cosmetics companies are not testing on animals, an idea pioneered by such companies as The Body Shop.

(ii) Companies should be sympathetic to the potential beliefs of shareholders – for example, there may be large blocks of shareholders who are strongly opposed to animal testing. Managers could of course argue that if potential investors were aware that the company tested their products on animals then they should not have purchased shares.

(iii) When developing products, be sympathetic to the public mood on certain issues – the use of real fur is now frowned upon in many countries; dolphin-friendly tuna is now commonplace.

(iv) Use of Fairtrade products and services – for example, Green and Blacks Fairtrade chocolate; Marks & Spencer using Fairtrade cotton in clothing and selling Fairtrade coffee.

# 6 Developments

Adverse effects of increased globalisation on multinational companies:

### Government regulation

(a) Increased regulation due to greater number of industries being characterised by oligopoly.

(b) Anti-trust scrutiny – for example, British Airways and American Airlines alliance to prevent cross-border oligopolies.

(c) Such regulation creates obstacles to trade, as companies must comply with regulations that may prevent efficient and effective operations.

### Pressure groups

Pressure is being put on governments to take measures against multinational companies – in the UK for example there is increasing resistance to supermarket chains setting up in opposition to small shops in city suburbs. The pressure groups are becoming more and more successful at curbing multinationals' activities.

### Political risks

(a) Multinational companies are becoming more vulnerable to political developments in home and host countries. Global conflicts have led to trade embargoes, restrictions on operating in certain countries and sanctions.

(b) Tariffs and capital restrictions; import quotas; export subsidies; exchange controls are all barriers that can affect multinational activity, as host countries try to protect domestic industries.

# 7 Transfer prices

> **Top tips.** You can go wrong quite easily in part (a) if you don't think carefully about the layout of your computation. For each of the options you need to split the calculation between what happens in the countries where the subsidiaries are located, and what happens in the country where the holding company is located. Remember also to assess the effect of the withholding tax separately from the other local taxes.
>
> (b) demonstrates how strategic issues can be brought into the discussion part of an answer. It is not sufficient just to discuss government action. Local issues are important, as well as trying to ensure goal congruence throughout the group.

(a)    The current position is as follows.

| | UK company B$'000 | Ceeland company B$'000 | Total B$'000 |
|---|---|---|---|
| *Revenue and taxes in the local country* | | | |
| Sales | 84,000 | 210,000 | 294,000 |
| Production expenses | (68,000) | (164,000) | (232,000) |
| Taxable profit | 16,000 | 46,000 | 62,000 |
| Tax (1) | (4,000) | (18,400) | (22,400) |
| Dividends to Beeland | 12,000 | 27,600 | 39,600 |
| Withholding tax (2) | 0 | 2,760 | 2,760 |
| | | | |
| *Revenue and taxes in Beeland* | | | |
| Dividend | 12,000 | 27,600 | 39,600 |
| Add back foreign tax paid | 4,000 | 18,400 | 22,400 |
| Taxable income | 16,000 | 46,000 | 62,000 |
| Beeland tax due | 5,600 | 16,100 | 21,700 |
| Foreign tax credit | (4,000) | (16,100) | (20,100) |
| Tax paid in Beeland (3) | 1,600 | – | 1,600 |
| | | | |
| Total tax (1) + (2) + (3) | 5,600 | 21,160 | 26,760 |

An increase of 25% in the transfer price would have the following effect.

| | UK company B$'000 | Ceeland company B$'000 | Total B$'000 |
|---|---|---|---|
| *Revenues and taxes in the local country* | | | |
| Sales | 105,000 | 210,000 | 315,000 |
| Production expenses | (68,000) | (185,000) | (253,000) |
| Taxable profit | 37,000 | 25,000 | 62,000 |
| Tax (1) | (9,250) | (10,000) | (19,250) |
| Dividends to Beeland | 27,750 | 15,000 | 42,750 |
| Withholding tax (2) | 0 | 1,500 | 1,500 |
| | | | |
| *Revenues and taxes in Beeland* | | | |
| Dividend | 27,750 | 15,000 | 42,750 |
| Add back foreign tax paid | 9,250 | 10,000 | 19,250 |
| Taxable income | 37,000 | 25,000 | 62,000 |
| Beeland tax due | 12,950 | 8,750 | 21,700 |
| Foreign tax credit | (9,250) | (8,750) | (18,000) |
| Tax paid in Beeland (3) | 3,700 | – | 3,700 |
| | | | |
| Total tax (1) + (2) + (3) | 12,950 | 11,500 | 24,450 |

The total tax payable by the company is therefore reduced by B$2,310,000 to B$24,450,000.

(b)    **Government action**

In practice, governments usually seek to prevent multinationals' reducing their tax liability through the manipulation of transfer prices. For tax purposes governments will normally demand that an **'arm's length' price** is used in the computation of the taxable profit and not an artificial transfer price. If no such 'arm's length' price is available then there may be some scope for tax minimisation through the choice of transfer price.

**Other factors**

If it is possible to manipulate the transfer price in this way, there are further factors that the company must take into consideration before making a final decision.

(i)    The level of transfer prices will affect the **movement of funds** within the group. If inter-company sales involve the use of different currencies the level of the transfer price will also affect the group's **foreign exchange exposure**. These factors must be taken into account as well as the tax situation.

(ii)   The level of profit reported by the subsidiary could affect its **local credit rating** and this could be important if the company wishes to raise funds locally. It could also affect the ease with which credit can be obtained from suppliers.

(iii)  The reported profit is likely to have an **effect** on the **motivation** of managers and staff in the subsidiary. If reported profits are high then they may become complacent and cost control may become weak. If, on the other hand, profits are continually low they may become demotivated.

(iv)   Transfer prices that **do not reflect market levels** may lead to subsidiaries making 'make or buy' decisions that do not optimise the performance of the group as a whole.

# 8 Solden

**Top tips.** Exam questions would not be purely numerical as this one is, but this question does provide an excellent demonstration of the level of detail you will have to cope with in a foreign investment appraisal. Planning is very important, working out what format you will need and what workings will be required.

You can assume that the rates of return are money rates of return, which means that the sales and costs have to be adjusted for price increases.

Possible pitfalls in this question are getting the timing of the exchange rate movements wrong, forgetting that the working capital figure in the cash flow analysis is the **change** in working capital (not the total amount) and including the full cost of materials in (b) rather than just the contribution (remember the UK company is going to have to pay cost price to obtain new materials).

## (a) Investors in Ober

| Year | | 0 | 1 | 2 | 3 | 4 | 5 | 6 |
|---|---|---|---|---|---|---|---|---|
| | | G'000 | G'000 | G'000 | G'000 | G'000 | G'000 | G'000 |
| Contribution | 1 | | 320.0 | 369.6 | 426.9 | 493.0 | 569.5 | |
| Materials – UK | 2 | | (40.0) | (43.7) | (47.7) | (52.1) | (56.9) | |
| Selling costs | | | (40.0) | (44.0) | (48.4) | (53.2) | (58.6) | |
| Licence fee (10% sales) | | | (64.0) | (73.9) | (85.6) | (98.6) | (113.9) | |
| Tax-allowable depreciation (800 × 25%) | | | (200.0) | (200.0) | (200.0) | (200.0) | | |
| Taxable profit/(loss) | | | (24.0) | 8.0 | 45.2 | 89.1 | 340.1 | |
| Tax at 20% | | | | 4.8 | (1.6) | (9.0) | (17.8) | (68.0) |
| Plant | | (600.0) | | | | | | |
| Equipment | | (200.0) | | | | | | |
| Tax-allowable depreciation | | | 200.0 | 200.0 | 200.0 | 200.0 | | |
| Working capital | | (64.0) | (9.9) | (11.7) | (13.0) | (15.3) | 113.9 | |
| Terminal value (3 × 436.3*) | | | | | | | 1,308.9 | |
| Tax on terminal value at 30% | | | | | | | | (392.6) |
| Net cash flow in year | | (864.0) | 166.1 | 201.1 | 230.6 | 264.8 | 1,745.1 | (460.6) |
| Discount factor at 15% | | 1,000 | 0.870 | 0.756 | 0.658 | 0.572 | 0.497 | 0.432 |
| PV | | (864.0) | 144.5 | 152.0 | 151.7 | 151.4 | 867.3 | (199.0) |
| NPV | | 403.9 | | | | | | |

*436.3 = Year 5 cash flows to this point.
The project is acceptable to investors in Ober.

*Workings*

| Year | | 0 | 1 | 2 | 3 | 4 | 5 | 6 |
|---|---|---|---|---|---|---|---|---|
| Exchange rate | | 16.00 | 16.00 | 16.64 | 17.31 | 18.00 | 18.72 | 19.47 |
| 1 | Sales – units | | 4,000 | 4,200 | 4,410 | 4,630 | 4,862 | |
| | Ober contribution per unit (160 – 80, increasing by 10%) | | 80.0 | 88.0 | 96.8 | 106.5 | 117.1 | |
| | Ober contribution (G'000) | | 320.0 | 369.6 | 426.9 | 493.0 | 569.5 | |
| 2 | Materials (UK) – assuming fixed cost increasing with inflation | | | | | | | |
| | Cost in pounds | | 2,500 | 2,625 | 2,756 | 2,894 | 3,039 | |
| | Cost in gurgles (G'000) | | 40.0 | 43.7 | 47.7 | 52.1 | 56.9 | |
| 3 | Working capital | | | | | | | |
| | Balance – 10% sales | | 64.0 | 73.9 | 85.6 | 98.6 | 113.9 | |
| | Increase/(decrease) | | 64.0 | 9.9 | 11.7 | 13.0 | 15.3 (113.9) | |

## (b) Investors in UK

| Year | 0 | 1 | 2 | 3 | 4 | 5 | 6 |
|---|---|---|---|---|---|---|---|
| | £ | £ | £ | £ | £ | £ | £ |
| From Ober subsidiary (W1) | (54,000) | 10,381 | 12,085 | 13,325 | 14,711 | 93,221 | (23,662) |
| Adjustments in UK | | | | | | | |
| Licence fee (W2) | | 4,000 | 4,441 | 4,946 | 5,478 | 6,080 | |
| Contribution on materials | | 500 | 525 | 551 | 579 | 608 | |
| Lost exports | | (5,000) | (5,250) | (5,513) | (5,788) | (6,078) | |
| Total adjustments | | (500) | (284) | (16) | 269 | 610 | |
| Tax thereon, lagged one year | | | 165 | 94 | 5 | (89) | (201) |
| Net | (54,000) | 9,881 | 11,966 | 13,403 | 14,985 | 93,742 | (23,863) |
| DF at 10% | 1.000 | 0.909 | 0.826 | 0.751 | 0.683 | 0.621 | 0.564 |
| PV | (54,000) | 8,982 | 9,884 | 10,066 | 10,235 | 58,214 | (13,459) |

The NPV is positive, at £29,922.

*Workings*

| | | 0 | 1 | 2 | 3 | 4 | 5 | 6 |
|---|---|---|---|---|---|---|---|---|
| 1 | From Ober subsidiary: | | | | | | | |
| | Cash flow in G'000 | (864.0) | 166.1 | 201.1 | 230.6 | 264.8 | 1,745.1 | (460.6) |
| | Pound equivalent | (54,000) | 10,381 | 12,085 | 13,325 | 14,711 | 93,221 | (23,662) |
| 2 | Licence fee in G'000 | | 64 | 73.9 | 85.6 | 98.6 | 113.8 | |
| | Licence fee in pounds | | 4,000 | 4,441 | 4,946 | 5,478 | 6,080 | |

# 9 Mover

**Top tips**. Do not assume that because a tunnel is a very high-risk project its discount rate must be extremely high. For a diversified investor, the relevant risk in the discount rate is systematic risk. However, construction as an industry does have fairly high systematic risk.

**Examining team's comment.** In (a) candidates needed to use a realistic (not too low) discount rate, justify the discount rate used, and treat estimates beyond year 10 in a sensible fashion. However, many discount rates used were too low, and in some cases the inflation rate was used. Some candidates also failed to appreciate the difference between real and nominal rates. Most candidates also failed to discuss wider issues, such as the reliability of the cash flows, the risks, and Mover's activities other than the tunnel project.

(a) **Use of real rate**

The expected cash flows of the tunnel should be discounted at a suitable cost of capital, taking into account the **risk** of the project. Since the cash flow projections exclude inflation, the cost of capital should also be a **real rate**.

**Estimate of the real rate**

(i) The current domestic **risk-free rate** is approximately 6% while inflation is approximately 2%, giving an approximate real risk-free rate of 4%.

(ii) The market premium is 7%.

(iii) The tunnel project is assumed to have a **high level** of **systematic risk**, say a beta of 1.3.

(iv) The pension fund is well diversified and therefore only subject to **systematic risk**.

This implies a real discount rate of approximately 4% + (7% × 1.3) = approx. 13%

Assuming the tunnel has an indefinite life, post-20Y0 cash flows are discounted in perpetuity:

| Year | $m | 13% df | PV $m |
|---|---|---|---|
| 20X0 | (450) | 0.885 | (398) |
| 20X1 | (500) | 0.783 | (392) |
| 20X2 | (550) | 0.693 | (381) |
| 20X3 | (650) | 0.613 | (398) |
| 20X4 | (200) | 0.543 | (109) |
| 20X5 | 200 | 0.480 | 96 |
| 20X6 | 300 | 0.425 | 128 |
| 20X7 | 320 | 0.376 | 120 |
| 20X8 | 340 | 0.333 | 113 |
| 20X9 | 360 | 0.295 | 106 |
| 20Y0 | 400 | 0.261 | 104 |
| 20Y1 onwards* | 400 | 0.261/0.13 | 803 |
| | | | (208) |

*These are PVs of perpetuity cash flows.

At this estimated discount rate the NPV is **negative**, and therefore the project should be rejected. For a more comprehensive assessment, **sensitivity analysis** should be used.

### Other considerations

(i) The use of NPV ignores the value of any **embedded or real options**. Such options might include the option to develop land either side of the tunnel.

(ii) **Economic factors** may be critical to the accuracy of the forecast cash flows.

(iii) **Assumptions** concerning costs and competitive issues (the costs of alternative transport links) should be reviewed. In particular there may be a high probability that costs will be greater than forecast, and also that the project will be delayed, leading to further costs and delays in revenues. In addition, the costs of **upkeep** of the tunnel have not been included in the calculations.

(iv) The **contractual role** of the construction company should be reviewed – is the project government supported?

(v) While the tunnel project is presumably the most important project that Mover will be undertaking over the next few years, the company's continued existence may not depend on it. The trustees should therefore consider the likely results of the **other contracts** that Mover will be undertaking over the next few years.

On a project of this size, and dependent on the level of the pension fund investment, such factors should be modelled in more detail, perhaps using **sensitivity analysis** or **simulation**.

(b) **Effect of inflation**

**Inflation erodes** the **purchasing power** of money. It therefore has an **effect** on the **returns** an investor will require, and consequently on the appraisal of capital investment decisions by companies. As the **inflation rate increases so will the minimum return required** by an investor.

### Example

A return of 5% on a sum invested of $100 will provide $105 back in one year's time. If inflation is running at 15% then at the end of one year $105 will only buy 105/1.15 = $91.30 worth of goods at today's prices. In order to be able to purchase $105 worth of goods at today's prices the investor will need a nominal return of 1.05 × 1.15 = 1.2075, ie 20.75%. Thus with inflation at 15%, a nominal rate of interest of 20.75% is required to give the investor a real return of 5%. This effect can be expressed as:

**(1 + money (or nominal) rate) = (1 + real rate) × (1 + inflation rate)**

### Choice of approaches

Companies therefore have a **choice** of approaches when accounting for inflation in the appraisal of capital projects. They can either **inflate all the elements** of the cash flow at the appropriate rates and then **discount at the nominal (or money) rate of return**. Alternatively they can **exclude inflation** from the cash flows and **discount at the real rate**.

# 10 PS Ltd

> **Top tips.** Part (a) gives you practice in using the Black-Scholes formula. Go back to Chapter 6 and work through the example again if you got stuck. We have used interpolation to find N ($d_1$) and N ($d_2$). However, understanding the principles behind the Black-Scholes formula is more important than being able to plug numbers into the formula. Expect therefore to see discussion parts similar to parts (b)(i) and (ii) featuring in questions on Black-Scholes.

(a) Using the Black-Scholes formula

$$d_1 = \frac{\ln(P_a \div P_e) + (r + 0.5s^2)t}{s\sqrt{t}}$$

$$d_1 = \frac{\ln(3/2.50) + (0.05 + 0.5 \times 0.2^2) \times 0.25}{(0.2 \times \sqrt{0.25})}$$

$d_1 = (0.1823 + 0.0175)/0.1$

$d_1 = 2.00$

$d_2 = d_1 - s\sqrt{t}$

$\quad = 2.00 - 0.2\sqrt{0.25}$

$\quad = 2.00 - 0.1$

$\quad = 1.90$

$N(d_1) = 0.5 + 0.4772$
$\quad\quad = 0.9772$

$N(d_2) = 0.5 + 0.4713$
$\quad\quad = 0.9713$

$c = P_s N(d_1) - P_e N(d_2) e^{-rT}$

$\quad = (3 \times 0.9772) - (2.50 e^{-0.05 \times 0.25} \times 0.9713)$

$\quad = 2.9316 - (2.50 \times 0.9876 \times 0.9713)$

$\quad = 53.35p$

(b) (i) The **Black-Scholes pricing model** was developed to value traded call options on quoted shares and can be adapted to value any options. The input variables are:

(1) **The market price of the underlying share**

If the **share price rises**, the **value** of the **call option** will **increase**.

(2) **The exercise price (or strike price)**

A **call option** gives the holder the **right to buy** the share at a fixed price, known as the **exercise price**. The **higher the price** of the **underlying share** compared with the exercise price (above), the **more valuable** the **option**.

(3) **The time to expiry**

The longer an option has to run before it expires, the more chance there is that the **value of the underlying share will increase**. Time to expiry therefore **adds value** to an option.

(4) **The volatility of the underlying share (standard deviation of share price variations)**

Options provide **unlimited opportunities for gains** but **losses** are **limited to the purchase price**. This asymmetrical probability distribution of gains/losses means that volatility of the underlying share **adds value** to the option.

(5) **The interest rate**

This is the **risk-free rate of interest**, which gives the **time value of money** and is relevant because the option is valued today but is exercisable on a future date.

The difference between 1 and 2 is known as the '**intrinsic value**' of the option, but it has a minimum value of zero. The combination of 3, 4 and 5 gives its '**time value**'. The total value of the option is the sum of intrinsic and time values.

(ii) **Real options**

Real options are **choices** which **arise** in **real capital investments**, for example the opportunity to renew a lease at a fixed price or to renew a licence agreement after an introductory period. The party able to make the choice effectively holds an option, the value of which should be considered when appraising the investment.

**Example**

Suppose a capital project involves paying a franchise fee to a company which has patented a key process. Our agreement gives us the **right** (but not the obligation) to **renew this franchise** after 3 years for a further 5-year period at a fixed cost of $5 million. The value of this option can be estimated by adapting the 5 input variables:

(1) The **current market cost** of a 5-year franchise (say $4 million). This would need to take into account potential competitors who may wish to take over our business.

(2) The **$5m cost of the 5-year renewal licence** agreed in our contract (ie the **exercise price**). This option currently has an intrinsic value of zero.

(3) The **3-year period** until we have to choose.

(4) The **volatility of the franchise price**, which depends on its susceptibility to general market factors and specific factors, including our success at using it.

(5) The **risk-free interest rate**, as in the original model.

# 11 Nile plc

(a) The net dividend has increased 1.5 times from the end of 20X4 to the end of 20X8, a period of 4 years. This represents an approximate annualised growth rate of 10.67% (being $\sqrt[4]{1.5}$ ).

Cost of ordinary share capital in after-tax terms = $\dfrac{30(1.1067)}{476} + 0.1067 = 0.176$ or 17.6%

Cost of debentures = $77 (with interest) is the current market price per cent. The cost of debentures (%) is the internal rate of return of the following cash flows.

| Year | MV $ | Interest $ | Tax saving $ | Cash flow $ |
|---|---|---|---|---|
| 0 | (77) | 8 | (2.8) | (71.8) |
| 1–15 | | 8 | (2.8) | 5.2 |
| 15 | | 100 | | 100.0 |

At a discount rate of 7% the NPV is +$11.8, and at a discount rate of 9% the NPV is –$2.4. The IRR is (by interpolation)

$7 + [11.8 / (11.8 + 2.4)] \times 2 = 8.7\%$

It is assumed that the new issue of shares and debentures will be weighted in accordance with the existing gearing ratio as measured by market values.

The market price of debentures is $77 but an interest payment is about to be made so this needs to be adjusted to an ex-interest price of $77-8 = $69. The total market value of the debentures is calculated as the book value of $800,000 x the price of $69 per $100 nominal = $552,000.

The weighted average cost of capital is:

| | Cost (%) | Market value | | Hash total |
|---|---|---|---|---|
| Ordinary share capital | 17.6% × | 4,760,000 | = | 837,760 |
| Debentures | 8.7% × | 552,000 | = | 48,024 |
| | | 5,312,000 | | 885,784 |

Weighted average cost of capital = $\dfrac{\$885,784}{5,312,000} \times 100\% = 16.7\%$

(b) **Difficulties and uncertainties that should be mentioned are:**

(i) Will the growth rate in dividend remain the same as in previous years?

(ii) Should a premium for risk be added to the weighted average cost of capital; eg should the test discount rate for projects be, say, 20% or more rather than 16.7% (or 17%)?

# 12 Crystal Inc

> **Top tips.** (a) demonstrates the complications that may occur in weighted average cost of capital calculations. When you calculate the cost of equity, you will need to do more than just plug the figures into the formula. Don't forget to check whether shares are quoted cum or ex div. Here you also need to use Gordon's growth model to calculate g.
>
> With debentures, the most serious mistake you can make is to treat redeemable debentures as irredeemable. Because the debentures are redeemable, you need to carry out an IRR analysis. Remember that this calculation is done from the viewpoint of the **investor**. The investor pays the market price for the debentures at time 0, and then receives the interest and the conversion value in subsequent years. You must bring tax into your calculation, although you could have assumed that tax was paid with a one-year time delay.
>
> Lastly don't forget that the weightings in the WACC calculation are based on **market** values, **not book** values.
>
> (b) demonstrates that the calculation of the weighted average cost of capital is not a purely mechanical process. It makes assumptions about the shareholders, the proposed investment and the company's capital structure and future dividend prospects. Given all the assumptions involved, the result of the calculations may need to be taken with a large pinch of salt!

(a) The post-tax weighted average cost of capital should first be calculated.

(i) **Ordinary shares**

| | $ |
|---|---|
| Market value of shares cum div | 3.27 |
| Less dividend per share (810 ÷ 3,000) | 0.27 |
| Market value of shares ex div | 3.00 |

The formula for calculating the cost of equity when there is dividend growth is:

$$k_e = \frac{D_0(1+g)}{P_0} + g$$

where $k_e$ = cost of equity
$D_0$ = current dividend
$g$ = rate of growth
$P_0$ = current ex-div market value

In this case we shall estimate the future rate of growth (g) from the average growth in dividends over the past four years.

$$810 = 620 (1 + g)^4$$

$$(1 + g)^4 = \frac{810}{620} = 1.3065$$

$$(1 + g) = 1.069$$

$$g = 0.069 = 6.9\%$$

$$k_e = \frac{0.27 \times 1.069}{3} + 0.069 = 16.5\%$$

(ii)     **7% debentures**

In order to find the post-tax cost of the debentures, which are redeemable in ten years' time, it is necessary to find the discount rate (IRR) which will give the future post-tax cash flows a present value of $77.10.

The relevant cash flows are:

(1)     Annual interest payments, net of tax, which are $1,300 × 7% × 70% = $63.70 (for 10 years)

(2)     A capital repayment of $1,300 (in 10 years' time)

It is assumed that tax relief on the debenture interest arises at the same time as the interest payment. In practice the cash flow effect is unlikely to be felt for about a year, but this will have no significant effect on the calculations.

|  | Present value $'000 |
|---|---|
| Try 8% |  |
| Current market value of debentures (1,300 at £77.10 per cent) | (1,002.3) |
| Annual interest payments net of tax £63.70 × 6.710 (8% for 10 years) | 427.4 |
| Capital repayment £1,300 × 0.463 (8% in 10 years' time) | 601.9 |
| NPV | 27.0 |

|  | $'000 |
|---|---|
| Try 9% |  |
| Current market value of debentures | (1,002.3) |
| Annual interest payments net of tax 63.70 × 6.418 | 408.8 |
| Capital repayment 1,300 × 0.422 | 548.6 |
| NPV | (44.9) |

$$IRR = 8\% + \left[ \frac{27.0}{27.0 - -44.9} \times (9-8) \right]\%$$

$$= 8.38\%$$

(iii)    **The weighted average cost of capital**

|  | Market value $'000 | Cost % | Product |
|---|---|---|---|
| Equity | 9,000 | 16.50 | 1,485 |
| 7% debentures | 1,002 | 8.38 | 84 |
|  | 10,002 |  | 1,569 |

$$\frac{1,569}{10,002} \times 100 = 15.7\%$$

The above calculations suggest that a discount rate in the region of 16% might be appropriate for the appraisal of new investment opportunities.

(b)     Difficulties and uncertainties in the above estimates arise in a number of areas.

(i)     **The cost of equity**. The above calculation assumes that all shareholders have the **same** marginal cost of capital and the same **dividend expectations**, which is unrealistic. In addition, it is assumed that dividend growth has been and will be at a **constant rate** of 6.9%. In fact, actual growth in the years 20X5/6 and 20X8/9 was in excess of 9%, while in the year 20X7/8 there was no dividend growth. 6.9% is merely the average rate of growth for the past 4 years. The rate of future growth will depend more on the return from future projects undertaken than on the past dividend record.

(ii)    **The use of the weighted average cost of capital (WACC)**. Use of the WACC as a discount rate is only justified where the company in question has achieved what it believes to be the optimal capital structure (the mix of debt and equity) and where it intends to maintain this structure in the long term.

(iii)    **The projects themselves**. The WACC makes no allowance for the business risk of individual projects. In practice some companies, having calculated the WACC, then add a premium for risk. In this case, for example, if one used a risk premium of 5% the final discount rate would be 21%. Ideally the risk premium should vary from project to project, since not all projects are equally risky. In general, the riskier the project the higher the discount rate which should be used.

# 13 Espondera Inc

In order to calculate the cost of debt we first need to assign a credit rating to the company. The values of the equation variables are as follows.

Size = Total assets = $120m

$$\text{Profitability} = \frac{\text{Net income}}{\text{Total assets}} = \frac{\$6m}{\$120m} = 0.05$$

Debt = Subordinated = 1

$$\text{Leverage} = \frac{\text{Long -term debt}}{\text{Total assets}} = \frac{\$14m}{\$120m} = 0.117$$

$$\text{Interest} = \frac{\text{Income before interest and taxes}}{\text{Interest payments}} = \frac{\$8m}{\$1m} = 8$$

$$\text{Cov} = \frac{\text{Standard deviation of earnings}}{\text{Average value of earnings}} = (0.937/3.68) = 0.255$$

*Workings*

(1)    The average value of earnings is: $\dfrac{(5 + 4.2 + 3.2 + 3.8 + 2.2)}{5}$ = $3.68m

(2)    The variance of earnings is:

$$\frac{(5 - 3.68)^2 + (4.2 - 3.68)^2 + (3.2 - 3.68)^2 + (3.8 - 3.68)^2 + (2.2 - 3.68)^2}{5} = 0.878$$

(3)    The standard deviation of earnings is the square root of the variance and is: $\sqrt{0.878} = 0.937$

(4)    Inserting the values of the variables in the Kaplan-Urwitz model we have:

Y = 4.41 + 0.001 × 120 + 6.40 × 0.05 − 2.56 × 1 − 2.72 × 0.1178 + 0.006 × 8 − 0.53 × 0.225 = 1.88

(5)    The value of the model assigns a credit rating of BBB and on the basis of observed market rates for bonds of this rating the cost of debt is 8.4%.

# 14 Canada

**Top tips.** Method (1) involves a year by year conversion of the receipts, making sure that you adjust the exchange rate by the correct amount each year. In Method (2) the adjusted discount rate is computed in the same way as a nominal discount rate is computed from a real discount rate and an inflation rate.

Your answer to (b) needs to bring out the costs that will be incurred, and how the risks of loss (and chance of gain) will be limited or enhanced by borrowing abroad.

(a)    **Method (1)**

| Years | 0 | 1 | 2 | 3 | 4 |
|---|---|---|---|---|---|
| Investment C$'000 | (150) | | | | 50 |
| After tax cash flows C$'000 | | 60 | 60 | 60 | 45 |
| Net cash C$'000 | (150) | 60 | 60 | 60 | 95 |
| Exchange rate | 1.7000 | 1.7850 | 1.8743 | 1.9680 | 2.0664 |
| Net cash £'000 | (88.24) | 33.61 | 32.01 | 30.49 | 45.97 |
| 14% discount factors | 1.000 | 0.877 | 0.769 | 0.675 | 0.592 |
| PV in £'000 | (88.24) | 29.48 | 24.62 | 20.58 | 27.21 |
| NPV in £'000 | **13.65** | | | | |

**Method (2)**

**Adjusted discount rate**: equivalent discount rate in C$, allowing for 5% appreciation of the pound, is given by 1 + r = 1.14 × 1.05 = 1.197. Discount rate = 19.7%.

| Years | 0 | 1 | 2 | 3 | 4 |
|---|---|---|---|---|---|
| Net cash C$'000 | (150) | 60 | 60 | 60 | 95 |
| 19.7% discount factors | 1.000 | 0.835 | 0.698 | 0.583 | 0.487 |
| PV C$'000 | (150) | 50.10 | 41.88 | 34.98 | 46.27 |
| NPV C$'000 | 23.23 | | | | |
| Exchange rate | 1.7000 | | | | |
| NPV £'000 | **13.66** | | | | |

To provide a 14% rate of return in UK and to cope with a 5% annual strengthening of the pound, a dollar invested in Canada would have to grow by 14% to $1.14 and by a further 5% to $1.14 × 1.05 = $1.197. In other words, it would have to show a rate of return of 19.7%. The company's cost of capital, translated into Canadian dollars, is therefore 19.7%.

In a system of **free floating exchange rates**, if the Canadian dollar depreciates by 5% per year against sterling, the cost of borrowing in Canadian dollars is likely to be about 5% more expensive than borrowing in sterling.

(b)    **Finance by borrowing**

The decision to **finance** a **foreign investment** by **borrowing** in the foreign country's currency is influenced by a number of factors.

**Loan in the same currency**

For any income-generating foreign investment there is a risk that the foreign currency **depreciates**, resulting in a reduced value of income when converted to the home currency. If, however, borrowings are taken out in the **same currency** as that in which the **income** is generated, then the **reduced income** is at least partially offset by reduced **loan interest costs**. However, it should be noted that this hedging effect also **reduces** the chances of **currency gains**: if the foreign currency appreciates, then the increased value of income is offset by an increased loan interest cost when converted to the home currency.

**Unexpected losses**

**In the example**, the Canadian dollar steadily devalues against the pound. Borrowing in Canadian dollars would therefore enable currency risk to be managed better than if borrowing is arranged in sterling. However, in a system of free floating exchange rates, if the Canadian dollar depreciates by 5% per year against sterling, the cost of borrowing in Canadian dollars is likely to be about 5% **more expensive than borrowing** in sterling. This **increased interest cost** will take away the advantage of the devaluation of the Canadian dollar loan. If currencies always moved in predictable ways, there would be little advantage in financing the Canadian investment with a Canadian loan. However, currency **devaluations** can sometimes be **unexpected** and much larger than predicted. It is to prevent these **unexpected losses** that hedging using a foreign loan is recommended.

### Cost of foreign loans

The **cost of foreign loans** may be higher than the theoretical equivalent cost of a domestic loan because the company does not have such a **good credit standing** in the foreign country. Better rates may be obtained from the **euromarkets** or by arranging a **currency loan swap**. Care should be taken to match the duration of the loan with the **expected duration** of the project (four years in this question), unless further foreign investments are anticipated. A further consideration is the availability of **tax savings** on the loan interest. The effect on the company's **overall tax charge needs** to be included in the decision process.

### Impact of political risk

For countries with high political risk, which may impose exchange controls, or even expropriate assets, **borrowing** in the **local currency** is recommended to **offset** investment losses which might result from political action.

# 15 Organic growth

(a)  **Advantages of organic growth**

(i)  The company will be developing a new vehicle that has the group's existing culture rather than acquiring a **subsidiary** with a **different culture**.

(ii)  Growing organically may be cheaper in the long run, as it is more likely to **be financed** by **retained earnings** rather than new sources with issue costs, and it will not involve paying a premium for a desirable subsidiary.

(iii)  Planned development of a subsidiary should mean that there is **no duplication of resources** with existing operations.

(iv)  Organic growth offers **more opportunities** for **current employees**.

(v)  Organic growth is more likely to be in areas where a company **currently has expertise**, limiting the risk of failure.

(b)  **Advantages of acquisition**

(i)  Acquisition can offer **speedier entry** into an overseas market than organic growth.

(ii)  Merging with **established firms abroad** can be a means of **purchasing market information**, **market share**, **distribution channels** and **reputation**.

(iii)  **Other synergies** include **acquisition of management skills** and **knowledge**, **intangibles** such as brands and trademarks, and **additional cash** and **debt capacity**.

(iv)  Acquiring a subsidiary may be a means of **removing trade barriers**.

(v)  Acquisition can be a means of **removing a competitor**.

(vi)  **Start-up costs** will not be incurred.

Ultimately the risk of acquiring an established operation may well be less than starting up a subsidiary in an area where the company has **not previously operated**.

# 16 Canon Burger

(a)  There are a number of synergies that the acquisition of Templar can create.

Financial synergies arising from the diversification into other areas reducing the volatility of earnings. The acquisition will also increase the debt capacity of Canon, as Templar has no debt.

Revenue synergies are also expected to arise, as Templar will be able to use the marketing and advertising services of Canon.

The management of Canon may also improve the performance of Templar and may exploit its brand value and clientele.

(b) Present value of additional cash flow in perpetuity = $\dfrac{\$25,000}{0.12}$ = $208,333

The net present value of the acquisition is given by value from the acquisition minus the cost of the acquisition:

NPV = $208,333 – $200,000 = $8,333

The acquisition should proceed.

(c) Unchanged level of gearing of the combined entity means that the cost of capital remains the same at 16%.

NPV = $\dfrac{\$25,000}{0.16}$ – $200,000 = $156,950 – $200,000

$\qquad\qquad\qquad\qquad = -\$43,750$

The acquisition should not proceed if there is no reduction in the cost of capital.

# 17 Takeovers

> **Top tips.** This question discusses the issues surrounding mergers and takeovers. (b) illustrates why companies are acquired and (c) what can go wrong. Together they constitute a checklist of the sorts of issues to look out for in a takeover question.

(a) **Shareholder wealth** in a company can be expressed as the **present value of the future cash flows** of the business. Therefore if a takeover of another company is to increase shareholder wealth then the present value of the combined entity must exceed the sum of the present values of the two individual businesses.

PV combined business > PV bidding company + PV target company

(b) In order for a takeover to lead to an increase in wealth for the bidding company's shareholders there must be gains that would not have arisen if the two companies had not combined.

### Economies of scale

When two businesses combine this creates a **larger business** which can **lead to economies of scale**. For example, there could be direct cost savings by eliminating duplication of costs, or market power could be exerted by the larger entity in order for example to gain lower purchase prices for buying larger quantities.

### Complementary resources

One company may decide to buy another company as a method of directly acquiring resources the other company may have. For example, a manufacturing company may acquire a company with a strong research and development division which will eventually improve the bidding company's products.

### Competition

The motivation for a bidding company to acquire a competitor may be in order to eliminate that market competition and improve market share. This in turn might mean that the combined entity is in more of a position to influence prices and increase profits. However, as this will not always benefit the final consumer, such an acquisition may not be allowed by government.

### Undervalued shares

In some circumstances, due to market imperfections, the shares in the target company may be undervalued and therefore the bidding company is effectively buying a bargain.

### Underutilisation of resources

The target company may have been chosen due to a perception by the bidding company management that the resources of the target are being underutilised and by introducing a new management team additional profits can be earned.

(c) In other cases, although the bidding company management might have expectations of an increase in wealth for its shareholders, this may not always transpire.

### Paying too high a price

In a takeover bid, particularly a contested one, it is entirely possible that the bidding company may pay a **higher price for the target company shares** than they are worth. This is often the case, as it is common for a **premium** to be offered to the target company shareholders in order to persuade them to sell their shares. If the premium is greater than the benefits from the takeover then this will be a direct transfer of wealth from the bidding company shareholders to the target company shareholders.

### Integration of the businesses

After a takeover it is often **hard to integrate the two businesses** to such an extent that any anticipated benefits can be realised. This may be due to **differences in culture, management style or operational or organisational matters**. The problem is particularly highlighted where the bidding company tries to impose its own systems, culture and management on the target company.

### Unforeseen problems

Despite thorough investigation and due diligence procedures being carried out during a takeover bid it is entirely possible after the combination to **discover problems** in the target company which were not evident before the bid and which will eliminate any anticipated increases in wealth.

### Management problems

In some cases the management of the bidding company **lose motivation** after a takeover and assume that the benefits foreseen will just happen without additional effort on their behalf. This is rarely the case and continued management effort and motivation will be required in order to achieve the desired results.

# 18 Univo Inc

**Top tips.** Hopefully you remembered that the fundamental theory of share values is based on linking share values with **future** dividend patterns, whatever these patterns are assumed to be. (Chartism assumes that past dividend patterns will be repeated in the future.)

This question gives you the beta of equity, so you can just insert it into the formula. In the exam you are more likely to have to calculate it using the principles of gearing and ungearing betas. The main complication in (a) is knowing how to cope with the different dividend growth rates. The calculation of the intrinsic value of share has two elements.

(a) The present value of dividends in 20X2 and 20X3

(b) The market value of the shares in 20X3, using the formula but remembering to discount its result

In (b) you have to carry out the same calculation making the assumption that as the return on fixed interest securities has increased, the return required from shares must also have increased. Don't get confused into making adjustments to the actual dividends received (the question tells you that they are unaffected by the change in interest rates); it is the discount factor that needs to change.

(a) The **dividend growth model** may be formulated as follows.

$$P_0 = \frac{D_0(1 + g)}{(r - g)}$$

where: $P_0$ = market price of the share (ex div)
$D_0$ = current net dividend
$r$ = cost of equity capital
$g$ = expected annual rate of dividend growth

In this example, the first step is to calculate the cost of equity capital. This may be done using the CAPM:

$$E(r_j) = r_f + [E(r_m) - r_f]\beta_j$$

where: $E(r_j)$ = cost of capital
$\beta_j$ = beta factor relating to the type of capital in question
$E(r_m)$ = expected market rate of return
$F_r$ = risk-free rate of return
$E(r_j)$ = 4% + (9% − 4%) × 1.02 = 9.1%

Dividend growth between 20W9 and 20X1 has been 5.5% per year. It is estimated that growth in 20X2 and 20X3 will be 15%, thereafter reverting to 5.5%. Dividends for the next 3 years can be estimated as follows.

| | Total dividend | Dividend per share |
|---|---|---|
| | $ | Cents |
| 20X1 | 2,800,000 | 7.00 |
| 20X2 | 3,220,000 | 8.05 |
| 20X3 | 3,703,000 | 9.26 |
| 20X4 | 3,906,665 | 9.77 |

Then we can estimate the intrinsic share value as follows.

| | $\rho$ | Discount factor @ 9% | PV Cents |
|---|---|---|---|
| 20X1 dividend | 7.00 | − | − |
| 20X2 dividend | 8.05 | 0.917 | 7.38 |
| 20X3 dividend | 9.26 | 0.842 | 7.80 |
| 20X3 value of shares in 20X3 per dividend model | 271.37* | 0.842 | 228.49 |
| | | | 243.67 |

$$* \frac{d_{20X3}(1 + g)}{K_e - g} = \frac{9.26(1 + 0.055)}{0.091 - 0.055} = 271.37c$$

Estimated intrinsic value = 243.67c

The actual market price of the shares (ex div) is 260 cents per share. A fundamental analyst would therefore regard the shares as being overpriced and would recommend their sale.

(b) If the interest rate increased by 2%, the return required on equity is likely to increase by a similar amount to approximately 11%. The PV of dividends to be used in calculations will therefore fall.

| | Total dividend | Dividend per share | Discount factor @ 11% | PV |
|---|---|---|---|---|
| | $ | Cents | | Cents |
| 20X1 | 2,800,000 | 7.00 | | |
| 20X2 | 3,220,000 | 8.05 | 0.901 | 7.25 |
| 20X3 | 3,703,000 | 9.26 | 0.812 | 7.52 |
| 20X4 | 3,906,665 | 9.77 | | |
| | | | | 14.77 |

The PV of the expected dividend can be calculated as follows.

$$P_0 = \frac{D_1}{(ke - g)} \times 0.812$$

where: $P_0$ = market price of the share (ex div)

$D_1$ = net dividend in the following year (9.77c)

$k_e$ = cost of equity capital (11%)

$g$ = expected annual rate of dividend growth (5.5%)

$$P_0 = \frac{9.77}{(0.11 - 0.055)} \times 0.812 = 144.24c$$

To this must be added the PV of the dividend for 20X2 and 20X3:

Estimated intrinsic value = 144.24 + 14.77 = 159.01c

# 19 Black Raven Co

> **Top tips.** This question provides comprehensive practice of valuation techniques. In the exam you would most likely be expected to use three or four of these techniques to carry out calculations that would form the basis of discussions. Even in this question, you do need to make clear the basis of your calculations and the assumptions you are making (in (a) the assumptions are that the purchaser will accept the valuation, that the last five years are an appropriate indicator and so on).
>
> Other important issues which this question raises include:
>
> - Valuation (if any) of intangible assets
> - Lack of likelihood that asset valuation basis would be used
> - Adjustment to P/E ratios used in calculations because company is unquoted
>
> Don't take all of the figures used in this answer as the only possibilities. You could for example have made adjustments to estimated earnings in (c) to allow for uncertainty, or used a different figure to 17%.

(a) **Earnings basis valuations**

If the purchaser believes that earnings over the last five years are an appropriate measure for valuation, we could take average earnings in these years, which were:

$$\frac{\$465,000}{5} = \$93,000$$

An appropriate P/E ratio for an earnings basis valuation might be the average of the three publicly quoted companies for the recent year. (A trend towards an increase in the P/E ratio over three years is assumed and, even though average earnings have been taken, the most recent year's P/E ratios are considered to be the only figures which are appropriate.)

|  | P/E ratio |  |
|---|---|---|
| Albatross Inc | 8.5 | |
| Bullfinch Inc | 9.0 | |
| Crow Inc | 10.0 | |
| Average | 9.167 | (i) |
| Reduce by about 40% to allow for unquoted status | 5.5 | (ii) |

Share valuations on a past earnings basis are as follows.

|  | P/E ratio | Earnings $'000 | Valuation $'000 | Number of shares | Value per share |
|---|---|---|---|---|---|
| (i) | 9.167 | 93 | 852.5 | 300,000 | $2.84 |
| (ii) | 5.5 | 93 | 511.5 | 300,000 | $1.71 |

Because of the unquoted status of Black Raven Co, purchasers would probably apply a lower P/E ratio, and an offer of about $1.71 per share would be more likely than one of $2.84.

Future earnings might be used. Forecast earnings based on the company's five-year plan will be used.

|  |  | $ |
|---|---|---|
| Expected earnings: | Year 1 | 100,000 |
|  | Year 2 | 104,000 |
|  | Year 3 | 108,160 |
|  | Year 4 | 112,486 |
|  | Year 5 | 116,986 |
|  | Average | 108,326.4 (say $108,000) |

A share valuation on an expected earnings basis would be as follows.

| P/E ratio | Average future earnings | Valuation | Value per share |
|---|---|---|---|
| 5.5 | $108,000 | $594,000 | $1.98 |

It is not clear whether the purchasing company would accept Black Raven's own estimates of earnings.

(b) **A dividend yield basis of valuation with no growth**

There seems to have been a general pattern of increase in dividend yields to shareholders in quoted companies, and it is reasonable to suppose that investors in Black Raven would require at least the same yield.

An average yield for the recent year for the three quoted companies will be used. This is 12%. The only reliable dividend figure for Black Raven Co is $45,000 a year gross, in spite of the expected increase in future earnings. A yield basis valuation would therefore be:

$$\frac{\$45,000}{12\%} = \$375,000 \text{ or } \$1.25 \text{ per share}$$

However, a purchasing company would be more concerned with earnings than with dividends if it intended to buy the entire company, and an offer price of $1.25 should be considered too low. On the other hand, since Black Raven is an unquoted company, a higher yield than 12% might be expected.

(c) **A dividend yield basis of valuation with growth**

Since earnings are expected to increase by 4% a year, it could be argued that a similar growth rate in dividends would be expected. We shall assume that the required yield is 17%, rather more than the 12% for quoted companies because Black Raven Co is unquoted. However, in the absence of information about the expected growth of dividends in the quoted companies, the choice of 12%, 17% or whatever is not much better than a guess.

$$P_0 = \frac{D_0(1 + g)}{(r - g)} = \frac{45,000(1.04)}{(0.17 - 0.04)} = \$360,000 \text{ or } \$1.20 \text{ per share}$$

(d) **The discounted value of future cash flows**

The present value of cash inflows from an investment by a purchaser of Black Raven Co's shares would be discounted at either 18% or 14%, depending on the view taken of Black Raven Co's assets. Although the loan of $400,000 is secured on some of the company's property, there are enough assets against which there is no charge to assume that a purchaser would consider the investment to be backed by tangible assets.

The present value of the benefits from the investment would be as follows.

| Year | Cash flow $'000 | Discount factor 14% | PV of cash flow $'000 |
|---|---|---|---|
| 1 | 120 | 0.877 | 105.24 |
| 2 | 120 | 0.769 | 92.28 |
| 3 | 140 | 0.675 | 94.50 |
| 4 | 70 | 0.592 | 41.44 |
| 5 | 120 | 0.519 | 62.28 |
|  |  |  | 395.74 |

A valuation per share of $1.32 might therefore be made. This basis of valuation is one which a purchasing company ought to consider. It might be argued that cash flows beyond year 5 should be considered and a higher valuation could be appropriate, but a figure of less than $2 per share would be offered on a DCF valuation basis.

(e)    **Summary**

Any of the preceding valuations might be made but, since share valuation is a largely subjective matter, many other prices might be offered. In view of the high asset values of the company an asset stripping purchaser might come forward.

# 20 Margate

> **Top tips.** In this case study there are **many** alternative answers for all parts of the question, but the main requirement throughout the question is to demonstrate your knowledge of the principles involved by writing explanatory notes and comments.
>
> In part (a), try to choose three ratios with different purposes (eg profitability, liquidity, gearing) – but the P/E ratios are already given – so presumably no marks for calculating them, even though it is a relevant ratio!
>
> In part (b), there is a huge range of justifiable values for the company, even without estimating possible merger gains, on which no information is given. Again, the key is to justify the assumptions you make. Giving a range of possible answers means the expectations of different commentators are taken into account, and an indication of the risk involved is given.
>
> For the report in part (c), the most sensible figure to choose for a bid price would be something with a premium over current market value. The 'offer terms' means suggesting how many shares of Margate would be exchanged for a given number of Hastings' shares (eg 7 for 8). The bulk of the discussion marks can be earned by considering principles of takeover defences and reasons for merger synergy and needs to range quite widely. Your calculation for the value of the combined company should show how much would be owned by the original shareholders of Margate and how much by former Hastings shareholders.

(a)    **Three key ratios**

**Profitability: return on shareholders' funds**

|  | Margate Group plc £m | Hastings plc £m |
|---|---|---|
| Earnings £m | 503 | 300 |
| Shareholders' funds £m | 2,020 | 1,450 |
| Return on shareholders' funds | 25% | 21% |

This ratio shows the **rate of return of equity earnings** compared with the book value of shareholders' funds. Margate Group plc has a **higher return** at present, a fact that is consistent with its lower P/E ratio, but inconsistent with its lower equity beta. The measure is **limited** by the fact that **book values** are used.

**Gearing: debt ratio**

|  | Margate Group plc £m | Hastings plc £m |
|---|---|---|
| Long-term debt | 1,450 | 950 |
| Shareholders' funds | 2,020 | 1,450 |
| Total long-term funds | 3,470 | 2,400 |
| Debt ratio | 42% | 40% |

Both companies have **higher debt ratios** than the industry average (30%), indicating that use of **debt finance** for the merger would probably be **inadvisable**. The figure for Hastings could be understated if its substantial overdraft is effectively used as long-term debt. Including the overdraft of £420 million, the debt ratio becomes 1,370/2,820 = 49%.

### Liquidity: current ratio

|  | Margate Group plc £m | Hastings plc £m |
|---|---|---|
| Current assets £m | 1,125 | 645 |
| Current liabilities £m | 755 | 785 |
| Current ratio | 1.490 | 0.822 |

At less than 1, the current ratio of Hastings looks low. This is despite the fact that it carries **higher inventory levels** than Margate. The high overdraft probably needs restructuring into long-term funds, otherwise a period of rapid growth may cause severe liquidity difficulties.

(b) **Range of possible values for Hastings plc**

### P/E ratios

Hastings' **current P/E ratio** is 16, giving its equity shares a current market value of 16 × equity earnings £300 million = £4,800 million. It is highly unlikely that any offer below this figure would be attractive to shareholders, who would have no incentive to sell. Measured by the industry average P/E of 13, Hastings would be worth 13 × £300 million = £3,900 million. The higher value that Hastings enjoys at present is because of its **above-average growth expectations** and, probably, expectations of gains from a merger with another company.

### The dividend valuation model

> **Top tips.** Many different calculation assumptions may be offered here. Two or three valuations would be sufficient.

The current dividend is £135 million. The cost of equity for Hastings can be estimated from the **Capital Asset Pricing Model**, $k_e = 6\% + (12\% - 6\%)\ 1.2 = 13.2\%$.

### Possible valuation method

Using this cost of equity in the dividend valuation model, we obtain the following possible valuation figures.

(i) If, as some experts believe, the **supermarket contract results in zero growth**, the company's equity value would be 135/0.132 = £1,023 million, well below current market value.

(ii) On the optimistic side, if there was **dividend growth of 10% per year to perpetuity**, the equity value would be 135 × 1.1/(0.132 – 0.10) = £4,640 million. This is more in line with current market value.

(iii) Dividend growth of 10% per annum for 5 years followed by a period of lower growth would result in a **valuation figure between these two values**.

### Adjusted present value method

Hastings is relatively highly geared, which has the effect of increasing its equity beta. Since the acquisition would be financed by equity shares, the adjusted present value method would use a discount rate based on the **cost of ungeared equity** to value Hastings, and there would be no gearing side effect. The cost of ungeared equity for Hastings would be lower than 13.7%, let us say 1.0, giving a cost of equity of 12%. The computations above would then lead to higher figures.

(i) **No dividend growth**: 135/0.12 = £1,125 million
(ii) **Growth of 10% p.a. to perpetuity**: 135 × 1.1/(0.12 – 0.10) = £7,425 million
(iii) **Growth of 10% for 5 years**, followed by slower growth: a figure between these two values

### Summary

Based on existing information, the value of Hastings' equity can be calculated as somewhere between £1,023 and £7,425 million, with its **current market value** at £4,800 million.

(c)  To:        Board of Directors, Margate Group plc
     From:      Financial Manager
     Date:      13 December 20X1
     Subject:   Report on the proposed acquisition of Hastings plc

## Introduction

This report provides a financial evaluation of the proposed acquisition, recommends offer terms and discusses strategic issues.

### (i)  Recommended bid price and offer terms

Our calculations show that the intrinsic value of Hastings as a standalone company is somewhere in the **range** £1,000 million to £7,400 million. On the basis of the efficient market hypothesis, the **current market value** of £4,800 million is probably as good a guide to the company's value as any, but it should be remembered that the market will undoubtedly have factored some expected merger gains (see below) into the share price as a result of the recent bid by the US company.

#### Premium

However, if we are to make a bid, we will not be successful unless we offer a **premium over current market value**, giving the Hastings shareholders an incentive to sell. An offer price of approximately £5,000 million is suggested.

#### Synergy

It should be noted that if the possibility of merger gains is already factored into Hastings' share price, this offer price can only be justified if we have clear **plans** for **creating synergy** from the combination. Before going ahead, I suggest that we thoroughly investigate the possibilities, as indicated below.

#### Consideration

A share for share exchange should be offered as the terms for this merger, because:

(1)  We have **insufficient cash**.

(2)  As the **debt ratios** of both companies are above the industry average, I do **not recommend** any further **increase in borrowings** to finance this deal.

(3)  Our company's shares have an **above average P/E ratio that**, though not as high as Hastings', indicates that they are a relatively good 'currency' at the moment.

I recommend that we offer **7 of our own shares for every 8 in Hastings**. At our current share price this would value Hastings' shares at $7 \times 671p/8 = 587.125$ pence, giving a total market value for Hastings' equity of £4,991 million, a premium of 3.9% over the current market value.

*Workings*

1    Our share price is currently 671 pence.

2    Hastings' total number of shares in issue is 850 million. At a total value of £5,000 million, Hastings' share price would be 588 pence.

3    The terms of the offer should be 588 of our shares for 671 of Hastings', which are approximately 7 of ours for 8 of theirs.

#### Revised bid

When we make our initial bid, the market will assess it. The effect on the share price will depend on whether the market anticipated the sort of bid that we shall be making, but it is possible that we may have to make a revised offer.

(ii) **Strategy for making the offer**

To minimise the **risk of outright rejection** by the Hastings plc board, our strategy needs to take the following factors into account.

(1) We must follow the **City Code** on Takeovers and Mergers, stock exchange regulations and the law, especially that on **insider dealing**. We are allowed to approach the board of directors of Hastings for informal talks, but must maintain **absolute secrecy** until we make a formal offer.

(2) We will need to ensure that Hastings' directors are given **key roles** on the board of the combined company. This bid is most likely to succeed if management arrangements are those of a genuine merger rather than a takeover by ourselves.

(3) We need to **emphasise the similarities** between the management styles of our companies, and the advantages of joining forces to compete effectively in Europe against world competition.

**Risks in making the bid**

(1) The US company may decide to make a **counter offer**, resulting in an auction for Hastings' business, bidding up the price to an unrealistic level.

(2) Hastings may appeal for an **investigation** by the Competition and Markets Authority, on the grounds that our bid is against the public interest.

(3) Hastings' board may decide to **counter our offer** by making an offer to acquire us.

(4) Hastings' staff may decide to **mobilise public opinion** against us. Some key members may leave (see below).

(5) Hastings' directors may have strengthened their **contract termination terms**: this needs to be investigated.

**Risks of post-merger failure**

(1) There may be a **conflict of cultures** between the management of the two companies. Disagreements at board level may lead to widespread loss of morale. Key staff of Hastings may leave and set up on their own or join another competing company. For example, the US company may decide to poach staff rather than making an increased offer for Hastings' business.

(2) Our objective of achieving synergy may not be realised because of **poor planning**, lack of resolve to tackle the key issues, or shortage of funds for necessary capital investment.

(3) **Incompatibility of information systems** between the companies is a common merger problem.

(iii) **Strategic and financial issues**

The rationale for the bid depends on the advantages that a combination of our companies would have over the existing 'standalone' businesses. Such combinations can create synergetic merger gains (the whole is worth more than the sum of the parts) by a number of mechanisms.

**Increased market power**

Elimination of Hastings as a major competitor might allow us to charge **more realistic prices** to customers on some of our less profitable operations. We are also likely to be able to negotiate **more favourable deals** with suppliers in terms of costs and payment terms. However, in this respect we must be careful to avoid the accusation that we have become a monopoly. Our combination will have more than a 25% share of the UK market and the Competition and Markets Authority may decide to mount an investigation.

### Access to new market

The merger would enable us to **grow more rapidly** in Europe, where Hastings already has a strong base.

### Combining complementary resources

Hastings' **superior knowledge of markets in Europe** fits well with our dominant position in the UK.

### Achieving critical mass to enable effective competition

As trade barriers fall, our competition is worldwide rather than just the UK. Our defence to the potential monopoly accusation is that our **market share** in the **European Union** is still relatively small and we need this merger in order to be able to compete effectively in international markets.

### Elimination of duplicated resources

Our research shows that recent restructuring of both our companies does **not** leave **much scope** for **staff reductions** except at the head offices, but there will be possibilities for rationalising our warehouse and depot locations, for example.

### Elimination of management inefficiencies

For example, Hastings' **financial management** could be **improved** with savings in financing costs.

### Post-acquisition value of combined group

Our company has 1,050 million shares in issue and Hastings has 850 million.

At offer terms of 7 for 8, we will issue 7/8 × 850m new shares in Margate = 743.8m.

Total Margate shares in issue would then be 1,050 + 743.8 = 1,793.8m shares.

To maintain our existing share price, the value of the combined company would need to be 1,793.8 × 671p = £12,036m, shared as follows.

|  | No. of shares | Share price p | Value £m |
|---|---|---|---|
| Original Margate shareholders | 1,050.0 | 671 | 7,045 |
| New shareholders from Hastings | 743.8 | 671 | 4,991 |
|  | 1,793.8 |  | 12,036 |

The existing market capitalisation of the two companies is as follows.

|  |  | £m |
|---|---|---|
| Margate | as above | 7,045 |
| Hastings | £300m × P/E16 | 4,800 |
|  |  | 11,845 |

### Size of synergistic gains

To maintain our existing share price, we would need to generate synergetic gains of £191 million (above those gains which have already been factored into the current share prices), which would accrue to the new shareholders from Hastings (£4,991m – £4,800m).

(1) On the downside, if we assume that a more realistic value for Hastings as a standalone company is in the region of £4,000 million, the synergy needed is closer to £1,000 million. Clearly we need to start work immediately on evaluating whether this is a **realistic proposition** and, if so, developing plans for implementing our ideas as swiftly as possible.

(2) On the optimistic side, if the market value of Hastings is realistic and our offer is accepted and we can generate an **additional synergy** of **£500 million**, say, the value of the company would be £12,345 million, split as follows.

| | No. of shares | Value £m | Original value £m | Gain £m | % gain |
|---|---|---|---|---|---|
| *Original* | | | | | |
| Margate shareholders | 1,050.0 | 7,226 | 7,045 | 181 | 2.6 |
| New shareholders | | | | | |
| from Hastings | 743.8 | 5,119 | 4,800 | 319 | 6.6 |
| | 1,793.8 | 12,345 | | 500 | |

The gains made by Hastings shareholders would be higher in percentage terms.

### Financial advantages

Given that the preferred bid strategy is a share for share exchange, if the bid goes through, the combined group's debt/equity ratio will be lower than either of the current companies. We can either accept that this reduction in financial risk would be beneficial (as the gearing of both companies currently is high for the industry), or we can take the opportunity to issue further debt. Perceived business risk is unlikely to fall because the merger does not involve diversification, and because of the uncertainties surrounding the supermarket project.

### Conclusion

While a merger would have some significant benefits, we would need to convince our shareholders that Hastings is not overvalued, before they approve the issue of the consideration shares. Other issues, in particular the reaction of Hastings and the Competition and Markets Authority, also need to be considered carefully.

# 21 Canadian Inc

MEMORANDUM

To: The Finance Director
From: Accountant
Date: 12 December 20X5
Subject: Proposed investment in local coal mine

(a) **Overall summary and conclusion**

I have performed an analysis of the available figures using the adjusted present value (APV) technique. This method is appropriate because the project:

(i) Represents an activity **fundamentally different** from that of the company
(ii) Has a **different risk profile**, as evidenced by the differing betas, from Canadian
(iii) Is to be financed using a **gearing ratio different** from the company
(iv) Is a **significant investment** for the company (ie is not a marginal investment)

An alternative to this method might be the **adjusted discount rate method**, in which an estimate is made of the appropriate discount rate to use and the project cash flows discounted at this rate. However, insufficient data is available to perform this sort of analysis.

APV demonstrates that while the project appears to be marginally attractive under the stated assumptions (a positive NPV of $86,000), the total project allowing for the financing effects has a positive net present value of $2,010,000. These positive financing effects result from the interest savings on the Regional Development Board loan, plus the tax effects of the additional debt capacity of the firm.

However, I should stress that these figures assume a great deal about the future, as regards both the values of the factors that have been taken into account and the factors that have been ignored. I would refer you to the later sections of this memo, but broadly:

(i)   There would be **substantial implications** for power station X if this pit were to close. These costs should also be considered in coming to our conclusion.

(ii)  Even if the power station is judged viable in the absence of the pit, **buying coal from overseas** will expose us to **currency fluctuations** which would need to be managed.

(iii) **No sensitivity analysis** has been carried out. It would appear likely that the project is highly sensitive to the price of coal, and to the level of redundancy and environmental cleanup costs. This implies a high degree of political risk, which will be outstanding for five years.

(b)   **Workings**

The APV represents the NPV of the project based on an all equity financed situation, adjusted for any finance costs/benefits.

The appropriate discount rate is found from the formula:

$$\beta_a = \beta_e \frac{E}{E + D(1-t)} + \beta_d \frac{D(1-t)}{E + D(1-t)}$$

This should be based on the betas for the coal mining industry, which obviously has a different risk profile from that of the power generation industry.

$$\beta_a = 0.7 \times \frac{1}{1 + 1(1-0.3)} + 0.2 \times \frac{(1-0.3)}{1 + 1(1-0.3)} = 0.494$$

Therefore the appropriate discount rate is:

$$K_e = 8\% + (16\% - 8\%) \times 0.494$$
$$= 12\%$$

The cash flows generated by the project are therefore discounted at 12% to find the base NPV.

*Cash flow forecast, $'000*

| Year | 0 | 1 | 2 | 3 | 4 | 5 | 6 |
|---|---|---|---|---|---|---|---|
| Inflows | | | | | | | |
| Value of coal production | | 10,000 | 10,000 | 10,000 | 10,000 | 10,000 | |
| Outflows | | | | | | | |
| Operating costs (3,000 × 3% inflation factor) | | (3,090) | (3,183) | (3,278) | (3,377) | (3,478) | |
| Initial investment | (12,000) | | | | | | |
| Final payment (17,000 × 1.03⁵) | | | | | | (19,708) | |
| Tax | | | (1,173) | | (1,313) | (1,347) | 4,525 |
| | | | | | | | |
| Tax from year 3 | | | | | (1,258) | | |
| Net cash flow | (12,000) | 6,910 | 5,644 | 6,722 | 4,052 | (14,533) | 4,525 |
| PV factor (12%) | 1.000 | 0.893 | 0.797 | 0.712 | 0.636 | 0.567 | 0.507 |
| | | | | | | | |
| PV | (12,000) | 6,171 | 4,498 | 4,786 | 2,577 | (8,240) | 2,294 |
| NPV | 86 | | | | | | |

*Working*

| Year | 1 | 2 | 3 | 4 | 5 |
|---|---|---|---|---|---|
| Tax calculations | | | | | |
| Operating cash flows | | | | | |
| Inflows | 10,000 | 10,000 | 10,000 | 10,000 | 10,000 |
| Outflows | (3,090) | (3,183) | (3,278) | (3,377) | (3,478) |
| Capital allowances | | | | | |
| On equipment | (1,500) | (1,125) | (844) | (633) | (1,898) |
| On mine | (1,500) | (1,500) | (1,500) | (1,500) | |
| Termination costs | | | | | (19,708) |
| Net taxable flow | 3,910 | 4,192 | 4,378 | 4,490 | (15,084) |
| Tax on taxable flow | 1,173 | 1,258 | 1,313 | 1,347 | (4,525) |

Financing effects are as follows.

**Borrowing effect**

The company can borrow a total of $6 million (the regional development loan) plus the $3 million increase in the borrowing capacity as a result of this project. This means that debt benefits flow on a total of $9 million of additional debt. This is worth:

Debt benefit = Total debt × Canadian's borrowing rate × tax rate

Canadian's borrowing rate can be found using CAPM as:

$K_d = 8\% + (16\% - 8\%) \times 0.25 = 10\%$

Therefore the increase in debt capacity is worth:

$9 million × 10% × 30% = $270,000 p.a.

This tax benefit will be received between years 2 and 6, and should be discounted at the cost of debt (10%).

$$\$270,000 \times 3.791 \times \frac{1}{1.10} = \$931,000$$

**Regional development loan**

The value of the subsidy can be related directly to the cost of debt that Canadian Inc would otherwise have paid (10%).

Therefore the saving in interest charges is:

$6 million × (10% − 4%) = $360,000 p.a.

Again, this is discounted at the cost of debt. However, there are two things to notice.

(i)     The benefit of the interest rate reduction is received in years 1–5.

(ii)    There is an associated reduction in the tax benefit, detrimental in years 2–6, of the interest cost × tax charge.

Present value of interest saved in years 1-5:

$360,000 × 3.791 = $1,365,000

Present value of tax benefit forgone in years 2–6:

$$\$6 \text{ miilion} \times 6\% \times 30\% \times 3.791 \times \frac{1}{1.10} = \$372,000$$

The expected APV of the project, including financing effects, will therefore be:

|  | $'000 |
|---|---|
| NPV of project | 86 |
| NPV of tax shelter on interest | 931 |
| NPV of interest saved | 1,365 |
| NPV of tax benefit forgone on interest saved | (372) |
|  | 2,010 |

(c) **Assumptions behind this report**

As regards the data used in the report, it assumes the following:

(i) The various output and costing **figures** are reasonably **accurate**.

(ii) The **cleanup** and **redundancy costs** are **correctly estimated** – this assumes a stable political environment over the next five years.

(iii) The **price of coal** will **stay at the current level** for the foreseeable future.

(iv) The **RPI** can be **accurately used** as a measure of the cost inflation factors that will affect the pit.

(v) The Regional Development Board **loan is obtained**.

(vi) **Retained earnings** are **available** to finance the equity component of the project. If additional equity finance were required then issue costs could make this project unviable.

(vii) That the **debt capacity** added to the firm is **accurate**. It is not known how this figure is arrived at, but the project might well affect the total perceived risk of the firm for both equity and debt, and therefore change borrowing capacities for the rest of the firm.

(viii) The **tax regime** is at least as **favourable** as regards capital allowances as at present over the next five years.

As regards the APV model, it assumes the following:

(i) The value of the **tax shield** is the **full corporate tax rate**. This is questionable when shareholders obtain the benefit of a dividend imputation system and annual capital gains tax allowances.

(ii) The **project** will **contribute** a **full $9 million** to the borrowing capacity of the group for the whole of its useful life. In reality it is likely that the asset base, and therefore the borrowing capacity, will diminish over time.

(iii) The **CAPM** can be used to arrive at an **ungeared cost of capital**, which can then be used to discount the cash flows over five years. The CAPM is an annual model, so the assumption must be questioned.

(d) **Areas for further research**

(i) This memo is incomplete without a **detailed sensitivity analysis** being carried out. Such an analysis would seek to determine which of the above assumptions was likely to change, and by how much.

(ii) It is also not possible to assess whether this project is advisable in isolation from other **capital opportunities** and needs of the firm. It is unclear whether capital is in short supply.

(iii) The scenario presumes that there is **no alternative bidder for** the mine. However, it is possible that supplies to Station X might be secured by offering a fixed price contract to an alternative bidder for the supply of coal. In this case, we ourselves can avoid the risks inherent in this industry, about which we know so little, and concentrate on our strengths.

# 22 Peden and Tulen

> **Top tips.** (a) illustrates how shareholders gain from creditors in a bankruptcy scenario because of their limited liability. The key is that when Peden is a standalone company, the minimum value of its equity is zero, causing a drop in the value of debt, but when combined with a low-geared company the debt recovers its value at the expense of equity.
>
> **Examining team's comment.** Many candidates aggregated equity and debt without considering their individual values, and produced implausible solutions. Candidates also ignored the narrative in the question that stated that operational synergy did not occur.

(a) **Value of Peden's shares**

To find the **value of Peden's equity shares**, subtract debt of $45m from the total value.

| Peden | Recession | Slow growth | Rapid growth |
|---|---|---|---|
|  | $m | $m | $m |
| Equity | (3) | 10 | 30 |
| Debt | 45 | 45 | 45 |
| Total | 42 | 55 | 75 |

This gives a **negative value to equity** in the recession scenario, which cannot happen because the shares have limited liability. Assume the shares are zero value and the debt has declined to $42m because of bankruptcy risk. The expected value of equity of debt can then be computed.

| Peden | Recession | Slow growth | Rapid growth | Expected value |
|---|---|---|---|---|
| Equity | 0 | 10 | 30 | 12.50 |
| Debt | 42 | 45 | 45 | 44.55 |
| Total | 42 | 55 | 75 | 57.05 |

**Value of Tulen's shares**

To find the value of Tulen's equity shares, subtract debt of $10m from the total value.

| Tulen | Recession | Slow growth | Rapid growth | Expected value |
|---|---|---|---|---|
| Equity | 53 | 70 | 110 | 75.45 |
| Debt | 10 | 10 | 10 | 10.00 |
| Total | 63 | 80 | 120 | 85.45 |

**Effect of merger**

When the companies merge, **add** the **economic values** of **equity** and **debt** together. This means using the negative $3 million value for Peden's equity in the recession scenario. Its debt will be restored to $45 million because the bankruptcy risk will have disappeared by combination with a low-geared company. This is known as the **coinsurance** effect.

| Combined | Recession | Slow growth | Rapid growth | Expected value |
|---|---|---|---|---|
| Equity | 50 | 80 | 140 | 87.50 |
| Debt | 55 | 55 | 55 | 55.00 |
| Total | 105 | 135 | 195 | 142.50 |

**Summary**

Expected equity values

|  | $m |
|---|---|
| Peden | 12.50 |
| Tulen | 75.45 |
| Total | 87.95 |
| Combined company | 87.50 |
| Loss in equity value after combination | 0.45 |

Expected debt values

|  | $m |
|---|---|
| Peden | 44.55 |
| Tulen | 10.00 |
| Total | 54.55 |
| Combined company | 55.00 |
| Gain in debt value after combination | 0.45 |

After the combination, in the absence of synergy, the total economic value of the businesses remains at $142.5 million, but the total expected value of debt has increased by $0.45m at the expense of equity. This is because, under the recession scenario, there is **no longer a bankruptcy risk** for the debtholders of Peden. The previous advantage conferred on Peden equity by limited liability has now disappeared.

Furthermore, the cash flows of the combined company may **reduce in volatility** because of the portfolio effect and this may further reduce the cost of debt, increasing its value.

(b) **Significance of financial post-audits**

(i) **Incentive for strategic planning**

The knowledge that a post-audit will take place will **discourage growth** by acquisition **without** proper strategic **analysis** and **planning**.

(ii) **Problem identification**

They **identify problems** which have occurred since the merger or acquisition, identify whether these were unexpected or whether contingency plans had been made, and ensure that management confront the problems.

(iii) **Forecasting methods assessment**

By **analysing results** against **forecasts** made before the merger or takeover, they provide valuable feedback on the **reliability** of the **forecasting** and **planning** methods used.

(iv) **Future plans**

They identify **factors** which may have been **overlooked** and which need to be incorporated into future merger and takeover proposals.

# 23 Gasco

**Top tips.** This case study is a welcome change to most 'general questions' on mergers and takeovers, as it provides a lot of detail for use as illustrations of synergy, stakeholder expectations and post-merger problems. You should state the general principles involved and illustrate them with examples drawn from the question.

(a) There is frequently a mix of good and bad reasons behind a takeover bid. Among the good reasons, the most significant is the possibility of creating **synergy**, which means that the value of cash flows from the combined business is higher than the value of cash flows from the two individual businesses. Although CarCare and Gasco are in different market sectors, there are a number of areas which may generate synergy.

(i) **Elimination of duplicated resources**. The most obvious areas are the marketing systems, the call centre systems and local offices and training facilities for mobile repair/emergency staff. Head office overheads may also be reduced.

(ii) **Cross-selling**. Opportunities exist to cross-sell products to customers on the other company's database.

(iii) **Building a critical mass** for non-core business. This might apply to the financial services areas of both businesses. The credit card and insurance businesses may gain from a combined brand name.

(iv) **Reduction in the risk of the company's cash flow profile**. CarCare receives membership subscriptions in advance, whereas Gasco's customers will pay mainly in arrears. The combined cash flows will be perceived as less risky by shareholders and lenders.

(v) The takeover of CarCare will **abolish its mutual status** and will allow equity funds for expansion to be raised more easily, by share issues made by the parent company, reducing the cost of capital.

Among the many possible bad reasons for takeover are:

(i) The directors of Gasco **seeking the prestige** of a larger company

(ii) Diversification with **no real strategic objective**

(iii) Gasco using up surplus cash, **again with no strategic objective**

(b) **Stakeholders**

The major stakeholders of CarCare are its members, who are both owners and customers, its directors and employees, and its creditors. Competitors will also be highly interested in the takeover.

**Members**

The members will have **mixed reactions**. The replacement of mutual status with marketable equity shares or cash will give them an immediate **'windfall' gain**, which many will welcome. However, the cost of this is **lost influence** on the future direction of CarCare. As customers, many may fear a reduction in the quality of service, particularly in the light of increased competition in the market and the fact that Gasco has to demonstrate that it is making a **return on its investment**. Others may disagree, on the basis that Gasco will be able to raise money for expansion, modernisation and improvements more easily than CarCare could as a mutual organisation.

CarCare's directors have a duty to ensure that they act in the **best interest** of **members**. However, they will also be concerned about their own positions after the takeover and will wish to seek suitable positions in the new company's management structure. Some may fear loss of their jobs.

**Employees**

Employees will have **mixed reactions** depending on whether they are likely to be presented with additional opportunities or loss of status or redundancy. There is likely to be some **rationalisation** of the workforce except for those with highly specific skills, and for those who remain there may also be the threat of relocation. Employees will be seeking answers to these questions before the takeover happens, but are unlikely to receive comprehensive answers.

**Payables**

Payables, including bankers, will probably be happy with the merger provided that Gasco has no financial problems.

**Competitors**

Some competitors will fear that they will **lose market share** if the takeover enables new finance for expansion, improvement and marketing of CarCare. Others will be more optimistic, believing that CarCare will become less sensitive to the needs of customers.

(c) Gasco may face a number of problems after the takeover has been achieved.

(i) Former members of Gasco who did not agree with the takeover, and who may have been actively resisting it, may decide to **change their service provider** to another organisation. The parent company will have to be proactive in giving confidence to all its CarCare customers.

(ii) The two organisations probably had **different management styles**, Gasco being a stock exchange quoted company with a clear need for financial results and CarCare being more orientated to serving its customers and acting as a pressure group to represent their needs. Conflicts may arise between directors, managers and employees of CarCare after the takeover as a result of an enforced change in management style from Gasco.

(iii) Actual and feared redundancies, relocations, changes in work practice, training methods and other problems may **demotivate CarCare employees**, causing resistance and a drop in productivity. In this respect, delays in information provision and decision making can make the situation worse.

(iv) **Competitors may take advantage** of reorganisation problems at CarCare in order to gain market share.

# 24 Olivine

**Top tips.** Our answer to part (a)(ii) assumes that the administrative savings have been achieved. Otherwise the answer to (a)(ii) is $(25 + 9.6)m/60m = 57.7$ cents per share, and subsequent answers also change.

**Examining team's comments.** The calculations in the first two parts of the question were generally well answered but the final part which required discussion of the calculations was not particularly well done. The terms of the proposed takeover favoured the target company's shareholders and candidates should have identified the need to achieve a more equitable outcome between the two shareholder groups by changing the offer price.

(a)  (i)  **The total value of the share offer**

Earnings per share = $25m/40m = $0.625
P/E ratio = 20
Share price = 20 × $0.625 = $12.50 per share
Share offer = 5 shares × (16m shares/4) = 20m shares issued
Value of share offer = $12.50 × 20m = $250m

(ii)  **Olivine earnings per share**

Earnings = $25m + $9.6m + $2.4m = $37.0m
Number of shares = 40m + 20m = 60m
Earnings per share = $37.0m/60m = 61.7c per share

(iii)  **Share price of Olivine**

Earnings per share (part ii) = 61.7c per share
Price/earnings ratio = 20 × (100 − 5)% = 19
Share price = 19 × $0.617 = $11.72 per share

(b)  **Effect on wealth of shareholders**

**Olivine shareholders**

Original holding = 40m shares @ $12.50 per share = $500m
New share price = $11.72
New share value = 40m shares @ $11.72 = $468.8m
Loss in shareholder wealth = $500m − $468.8m = $31.2m or 6.24%

**Halite shareholders**

Original earnings per share = $9.6m/16m shares = $0.60
Price/earnings ratio = 15
Share price = 15 × $0.60 = $9.00 per share
Original holding = 16m shares @ $9.00 = $144m
New holding = 20m shares @ $11.72 = $234.4m
Gain in shareholder wealth = $234.4m − $144m = $90.4m or 62.78%

(c)  The market capitalisation of the separate businesses is (40m × $12.50) + (16m × $9.00) = $644m. When combined, the market capitalisation will be 60m × $11.72 = $703.2m so there are benefits to be gained in overall terms.

BPP
LEARNING MEDIA

### Effect on share price

The **total share value** of Halite prior to the acquisition is $144 million. However, the intended share issue by Olivine of 20 million shares has a value at Olivine's current share price of $250 million. The issue of so many shares to achieve this premium means that there is a small reduction in the size of the earnings per share of Olivine even when the earnings of Halite and the benefits of the acquisition are taken into account. This reduction in earnings per share together with a 5% reduction in the price/earnings ratio of Olivine after the acquisition would lead to a reduction in Olivine's share price from $12.50 per share before the acquisition to $11.72 per share after the acquisition. The estimate of the revised P/E ratio is possibly too high and needs further scrutiny.

This reduction in share value for Olivine shareholders would **result in a loss in shareholder value** from the acquisition of $31.2 million (6.24%). In contrast, the generous premium being considered for the shares of Halite would lead to an increase in the value of the shares held by former Halite shareholders of $90.4 million (62.78%).

### Beneficiaries of offer

If the proposed offer is made, all the benefit of the acquisition will accrue to the Halite plc shareholders and the Olivine shareholders will suffer a loss in share value. However, the dividend per share for Halite shareholders is likely to be lower in the future than it is at present.

The directors of Olivine might wish to consider a less generous offer than the current premium of $106 million ($250m – $144m) on the purchase of Halite. For example, a share for share exchange would value the offer at $200 million (16 million shares @ $12.50 per share) thereby still providing a substantial premium for the Halite shareholders but with no loss to the Olivine shareholders.

# 25 Takeover regulation

(a) Takeover regulation in the UK, centred around the City Code, is based on what is often referred to as a **'market-based model'** designed to protect a wide and **dispersed shareholder base**. This system which also prevails in the Commonwealth countries and the US is based on **case law** and the legal rules resulting from it. These seek to a great extent the protection of shareholder rights.

The second system, prevalent in continental Europe, is referred to as the **'block-holder'** or **stakeholder system** and relies on codified or civil law seeking to protect a broader group of stakeholders, such as creditors, employees and the wider national interest.

The two systems differ not only in terms of their **regulatory framework** (**civil** versus **common law**) but also in terms of the underlying structure of ownership and control that they seek to address.

In the UK and the US the system is characterised by **wider share ownership** than in continental Europe where companies tend to be owned by **majority** or **near-majority stakes** held by a small number of investors.

In the Anglo-American model, the emphasis is on the **agency problem** and the protection of the **widely distributed shareholder base**.

The civil law countries rely via **legislation** on the monitoring by large shareholders, **creditors** and **employees**.

The **Takeovers Directive** lays down for the first time minimum EU rules concerning the regulation of takeovers of companies whose shares are traded on regulated markets. It is one of the measures adopted under the EU Financial Services Action Plan and aims to strengthen the single market in financial services.

The **Takeovers Directive** requires that certain activities of the **Takeover Panel** are placed within a legal framework bringing an end to the non-statutory approach to regulation in the UK. In terms of approach, the new regulatory model leads to the **convergence** of the **European system** to the **UK-US** one by adopting many of the elements of the **City Code**. The City Code is divided into general principles and detailed rules which must be observed by persons involved in a merger or takeover transaction.

(b) Some mergers, referred to as friendly, take place when the management of the respective firms negotiate an agreement that is beneficial to both sides.

However, not all takeovers are negotiated in this way and those that are perceived as hostile are likely to be resisted by the directors.

The defensive measures that can be taken to resist a hostile bid have developed over the years, mainly in the US during the wave of takeover bids of the 1980s.

The more aggressive tactics, designed to make the target less attractive to the bidder, often risk shareholders' interests in favour of those of management.

Examples of such aggressive tactics include the following.

### Golden parachute

This is where large compensation payments are agreed with top management in the case of a takeover.

### Poison pill

Poison pills have many variants but the basic objective behind them is to give rights to existing shareholders to buy shares at a very low price or special preferential terms.

### Crown jewels

This tactics is where the directors decide to sell the firm's most valuable assets, making the firm less attractive as a result.

### Restricted voting rights

Multiple voting rights can often be used as a means of allocation to certain shareholders' disproportionate voting rights, enabling them to frustrate a bid.

In the US these takeover defences are allowed to a greater extent, as they are subject to a very sophisticated and ever-developing set of rulings based on case law established during a period of over 25 years of court judgements.

In the UK, one of the principles of the Takeover Code is the requirement that the directors of the target company are not permitted to take any steps to frustrate a bid without the prior approval of the shareholders. This principle seeks to minimise the danger of the directors adopting measures that would risk the shareholders' interests in favour of their own.

In Europe an attempt was made by the Takeover Directive to introduce the break-through rule whereby a bidder with a specified proportion of shares would be able to break through the company's multiple voting rights and exercise control as if one share-one vote existed. However, this was considered unpopular and was introduced as an optional measure in continental Europe.

# 26 Atlas International

(a) We need to find the value of Global under the assumption that it will grow at 7%. We do not know the cost of equity for Global so we find it implicitly for the share price.

$$P = \frac{D1}{k - g}$$

Or $22 = \dfrac{\$0.90}{k - 0.05}$ or $k = \dfrac{\$0.90}{\$22} + 0.05 = 0.0909$

The value of the target company is:

$$\frac{\$0.90}{0.0909 - 0.07} = \$43.04 \text{ per share}$$

The value of Global's equity will therefore be:

43.04 × 500,000 = $21,521,739

The value will increase by:

21,521,739 – 11,000,000 = $10,521,739

(b) The acquisition premium is:

$30 – $22 = $8 per share

or $4,000,000

The NPV of acquisition is:

NPV = Additional revenues – Costs of acquisition
    = 10,521,739 – 4,000,000
    = $6,521,739

The acquisition should proceed.

(c) Atlas needs to issue another 250,000 shares. The value of the combined company will be 70,000,000 + 21,521,739 = $91,521,739

The value of each share will be:

$$\frac{91,521,739}{1,250,000} = \$73.22$$

Cost of acquisition = 250,000 × 73.22 – 11,000,000 = $7,304,348

NPV of acquisition = 10,521,739 – 7,304,348 = $3,217,391

The acquisition should proceed.

# 27 Brive Inc

**Top tips.** In this question you are given details of the proposed reconstruction whereas in the exam you may have some input into its design.

There are no real traps in answer to (a), and if you adopted a methodical layout you should have scored full marks. The principal advantage of the layout we've used is that it highlights the adjustments.

In (b) with each of the parties you first assess what the position would be if liquidation did occur, and then the consequences (certain and uncertain) of reconstruction. Knowledge of the order of priority in a liquidation is vital. You need to show that the shareholders' and debentureholders' position is not clear-cut. If liquidation proceeds, they will certainly lose money; however, if the reconstruction proceeds, they will have to pay out more money in return for uncertain future returns **and** other possibly undesirable consequences (change in control, lack of security).

Don't forget when considering the debentureholders' and bank's position in the event of reconstruction to include the opportunity cost of the cash forgone from liquidation.

The conclusion sums up the benefits to everyone but also emphasises the uncertainties.

(a) and (b)

REPORT

To:        Board of Directors
From:      M Accountant
Date:      17 September 20X1
Subject:   Proposed capital reconstruction

**Introduction**

The purpose of this report is to evaluate the implications of the proposed capital reconstruction of Brive Inc for the various affected parties, including the shareholders, debentureholders, unsecured payables and

the bank. Calculations showing the effect of the reconstruction on the statement of financial position are included as an appendix to this report.

**Ordinary shareholders**

In the event of Brive going into liquidation, the ordinary shareholders would be most unlikely to receive anything for their shares, since the net proceeds of the liquidation would be as follows.

| | $ |
|---|---|
| Property | 2,000,000 |
| Plant | 1,000,000 |
| Inventory | 1,700,000 |
| Receivables | 1,700,000 |
| Liquidation costs | (770,000) |
| | 5,630,000 |

The total amount due to the payables, bank and debentureholders is $8,600,000, leaving nothing available for the shareholders.

If the reconstruction is undertaken, the existing shareholders will have to provide an additional $1m of capital in subscribing to the rights issue. However, if the projections are correct the effect of this should be to bring Brive back into profit, with earnings after interest amounting to $1.4m ($1.75m – $0.35m) per annum. This amounts to earnings per share of 28c which should permit Brive to start paying a dividend and providing some return to the shareholders again. The fact that the company is returning to profit should also make it possible to sell the shares if required which is presumably difficult at the present time. However, there would be a substantial shift in the balance of control, with the existing shareholders being left with only 40% of the equity, the balance being in the hands of the present debentureholders.

**Secured debentureholders**

Under the existing arrangements, the amount owing to the debentureholders is $3 million. Although the debentures are secured on the property which has a book value of $3 million, in the event of a forced sale this would only be likely to realise $2 million, giving a shortfall of $1 million. The debentureholders would rank alongside the bank and the other payables for repayment of this balance. As has been calculated above, the amount that would be realised on liquidation and available to the unsecured payables would be $3.63 million (net of property proceeds). The total amount owed is:

| | $m |
|---|---|
| Debentureholders | 1.0 |
| Bank (overdraft) | 1.6 |
| Payables | 4.0 |
| | 6.6 |

The debentureholders would therefore only receive 55 cents in the dollar on the balance owing, giving a total payout of 85 cents in the dollar (($2m + $0.55m)/$3.0m).

Under the proposed scheme, the debentureholders would receive $2.8 million of new capital in return for the old debentures ie 93.33 cents in the dollar in the form of capital rather than cash. Of this, $1.3 million would be in the form of 14% unsecured loan stock, and the remainder in the form of equity. They would also have to subscribe an additional $1.5 million to take up the rights issue. Their total investment in the reconstruction would therefore be:

| | $m |
|---|---|
| Cash forgone from liquidation | 2.55 |
| Additional cash investment | 1.50 |
| | 4.05 |

Returns would be:

| | $ |
|---|---|
| Interest ($1.3m × 14%) | 182,000 |
| Return on equity ($3m × 0.28) | 840,000 |
| | 1,022,000 |

This represents a return of 25.23% which is likely to be above that which could be earned elsewhere thus making the scheme attractive to the debentureholders. However, in addition they would have to forgo their

security on the property and rank partly with the unsecured payables and partly with the equity. They should therefore be confident of the ability of the management to deliver the projected returns before consenting to the scheme.

### The bank

Since the overdraft is unsecured, the bank would rank for repayment alongside the unsecured payables. As calculated above, the amount to be repaid would be 55 cents in the dollar, and the bank would thus recover $880,000 in the event of a liquidation. In the reconstruction, the bank would have to write off $400,000 ($1,600,000 debt – $1,200,000 loan stock), but would receive interest of 14% per annum leading to repayment of the balance in 5 years' time.

The investment that the bank would be making would therefore be the cash forgone from the liquidation of $880,000. The annual returns would be $168,000 (14% × $1.2 million) which represents a return on the incremental investment of 19.1%. Provided that the bank is confident of the financial projections of the management, it stands to receive $1.2 million in 5 years' time. The effective return of 19.1% in the meantime should be in **excess of current overdraft rates**, and the level of security is improved since there would no longer be secured debentureholders ranking ahead of the bank for repayment. The scheme is therefore likely to be attractive to the bank.

### Unsecured payables

If Brive goes into liquidation the unsecured payables will receive 55 cents in the dollar ie $2.2 million. Under the proposed scheme they would stand to receive 75 cents (25% written down) in the dollar with apparently no significant delay in payment. If Brive continues to operate they will be able to continue to trade with the company and generate further profits from the business. The proposed scheme therefore seems **attractive** from their point of view.

### Conclusions

The proposed scheme appears to hold benefits for all the parties involved. It is also in the interests of Brive's customers and workforce for the company to continue to trade. However, these benefits will only be realised if the directors are correct in their forecast of trading conditions and if the new investment can achieve the projected returns. All parties should satisfy themselves as to these points before considering proceeding further with the reconstruction.

| | Before | a | b | c | d | e–g | After |
|---|---|---|---|---|---|---|---|
| | $'000 | | | | | | $'000 |
| Non-current assets | 5,700 | (2,100) | | | | 2,500 | 6,100 |
| Current assets | | | | | | | |
| Inventory | 3,500 | (800) | | | | | 2,700 |
| Receivables | 1,800 | (100) | | | | | 1,700 |
| | 5,300 | | | | | | 4,400 |
| Payables | (4,000) | | | | | 1,000 | (3,000) |
| Overdraft | (1,600) | | | | 1,600 | | 0 |
| Working capital | (300) | | | | | | 1,400 |
| Total assets less current liabilities | 5,400 | | | | | | 7,500 |
| 10% debentures | (3,000) | | | 3,000 | | | 0 |
| 14% stock | | | | (1,300) | (1,200) | | (2,500) |
| Net assets | 2,400 | | | | | | 5,000 |
| | | | | | | | |
| Capital and reserves | | | | | | | |
| Share capital | 4,000 | (3,000) | | 1,500 | | 2,500 | 5,000 |
| Reserves | (1,600) | | 1,600 | | | | 0 |
| | 2,400 | | | | | | 5,000 |

# 28 Reorganisation

(a) Potential problems with management buyouts:

(i) Deciding on a fair price – management will obviously want to pay the lowest price possible, while the vendor will want to secure the highest possible price.

(ii) Any geographical relocation may result in the loss of key workers.

(iii) Maintaining a good relationship with suppliers and customers, particularly if key contacts that suppliers and customers were used to dealing with decide to leave as a result of the buyout.

(iv) Availability of sufficient cash flow to maintain and replace non-current assets. This is one of the main problems with buyouts – cash is often very tight at the beginning of the venture.

(v) Changes in work practices may not suit all employees.

(vi) Maintaining financial arrangements with previous employees may be difficult – for example, pension rights.

(vii) Many suppliers of funds will insist on representation at board level in order to maintain some control over how the funds are being used.

(b) In order to estimate the change in the value of equity, we can use forecast retained earnings figures, assuming dividends to be at the maximum 12% level.

(All figures are in $'000)

|  | 0 | 1 | 2 | 3 | 4 | 5 |
|---|---|---|---|---|---|---|
| EBIT | – | 2,200 | 3,100 | 3,900 | 4,200 | 4,500 |
| 9.5% interest | – | 713 | 713 | 713 | 713 | 713 |
| Earnings before tax | – | 1,487 | 2,387 | 3,187 | 3,487 | 3,787 |
| Tax | – | 446 | 716 | 956 | 1,046 | 1,136 |
| Earnings after tax | – | 1,041 | 1,671 | 2,231 | 2,441 | 2,651 |
| Dividend (12%) | – | 125 | 201 | 268 | 293 | 318 |
| Retained earnings | – | 916 | 1,470 | 1,963 | 2,148 | 2,333 |
| Equity | 17,500 | 18,416 | 19,886 | 21,849 | 23,997 | 26,330 |

$$\text{Compound growth interest rate} = \left[ \sqrt[5]{\frac{26,330}{17,500}} \right] - 1 = 8.5\%$$

The 8.5% growth rate is considerably less than the 15% rise predicted by management, therefore it can be concluded that the management's estimate does not appear to be viable.

# 29 Treasury management

> **Top tips.** A few easy marks may be available for discussing the role of the treasury function. (b) looks at the role from another angle.

(a) **Management of cash**

A central treasury department will normally have the responsibility for the **management of the group's cash flows** and borrowings. Subsidiaries with surplus cash will be required to submit the cash to the treasury department, and subsidiaries needing cash will borrow it from the treasury department, not from an external bank.

**Borrowing**

A central treasury will also be given the **responsibility for borrowing** on behalf of the group. If a subsidiary needs capital to invest, the treasury department will borrow the money required, and lend it on to the subsidiary. The subsidiary will be responsible for **paying interest** and **repaying the**

**capital** to the treasury department, which will in turn be responsible for the interest and capital payments to the original lenders.

### Risk management

Another function of the treasury department will be to **manage the financial risk** of the group, such as currency risk and interest rate risk. Within broad guidelines, the treasurer might have authority to decide on the balance between fixed rate and floating rate borrowing, and to use swaps to adjust the balance. The department would also be responsible for arranging forward exchange contracts and other hedging transactions.

### Taxation

The central treasury department could also be responsible for the **tax affairs** of the group, and an objective would be to minimise the overall tax bill. To accomplish this effectively, the treasury must have **authority to manage transfer prices** between subsidiaries in the group, as a means of transferring profits from high-tax countries to lower-tax countries.

(b)     The treasury function needs information from within and outside the organisation to carry out its tasks.

    (i)     From each subsidiary within the group, it will need **figures for future cash receipts and payments**, making a distinction between definite amounts and estimates of future amounts. This information about cash flows will be used to **forecast the cash flows of the group**, and identify any future borrowing needs, particularly short-term and medium-term requirements. Figures should be provided regularly, possibly on a daily basis.

    (ii)     Information will also be required about **capital expenditure requirements**, so that long-term capital can be made available to fund it.

    (iii)     Subsidiary finance managers should be encouraged to **submit information** to the **treasury department** about local market and business conditions, such as prospects for a change in the value of the local currency and a change in interest rates.

    (iv)     From outside the group, the treasury will need a **range of information** about current market prices, such as exchange rates and interest rates, and about which banks are offering those prices. Large treasury departments will have a link to one or more information systems such as Reuters and Bloomberg.

    (v)     The treasury department should be alert to any **favourable market opportunities** for raising new debt capital. The treasurer should maintain regular contact with several banks, and expect to be kept informed of opportunities as they arise.

    (vi)     Where the treasury is responsible for the group's tax affairs, information will also be needed about **tax regulations** in each country where the group operates, and changes in those regulations.

# 30 Expo Inc

> **Top tips.** The numerical part of this question is a good example of how you might be tested on forward and money market alternatives to hedging. However, the rest of the question demonstrates that you need to be able to discuss why and how risk can be dealt with. Remember that hedging everything will be expensive, but only hedging certain transactions may be more expensive still. (b) shows the importance of matching; remember that the company may be able to use a hard currency if the local currency cannot be used. However, there are other possibilities and your answer should briefly mention these.

(a)　To:　　　　The Treasurer
　　　From:　　 Assistant
　　　Date:　　　12 November 20X7

　　(i)　Comparison of two methods of hedging exchange risk

### Method 1

Expo borrows SFr750,000.

3 months' interest is SFr750,000 × 3% × 3/12 = SFr5,625.

The customer pays SFr750,000, which repays the loan principal but not the interest. The interest must be paid by converting dollars. Since the interest is known in advance, this can be covered on the forward market at a cost of 5,625/2.3688 = $2,375.

Meanwhile, the SFr750,000 is converted to dollars at the original spot rate 2.3834 to give $314,677. Assume that this is used to repay the company's short-term borrowings. Interest saved will be $314,677 × 6% × 3/12 = $4,720.

So, at the end of 3 months, the net dollar cash from the transaction is:

$314,677 + $4,720 − $2,375 = $317,022.

### Method 2

The exchange rate is agreed in advance. Cash received in three months is converted to produce 750,000/2.3688 = $316,616.

### Conclusion

On the basis of the above calculations, Method 1 gives a slightly better receipt. Banker's commission has been omitted from the figures.

　　(ii)　**Factors to consider before deciding whether to hedge foreign exchange risk using the foreign currency markets**

### Risk-averse strategy

The company should have a clear strategy concerning how much foreign exchange risk it is prepared to bear. A highly risk-averse or 'defensive' strategy of hedging all transactions is expensive in terms of commission costs but recognises that floating exchange rates are very unpredictable and can cause losses high enough to bankrupt the company.

### Predictive strategy

An alternative 'predictive' strategy recognises that if all transactions are hedged, then the chance of currency gains is lost. The company could therefore attempt to forecast foreign exchange movements and only hedge those transactions where currency losses are predicted. The fact is that some currencies are relatively predictable (for example, if inflation is high the currency will devalue and there is little to be gained by hedging payments in that currency).

This is, of course, a much more risky strategy but in the long run, if predictions are made sensibly, the strategy should lead to a higher expected value than that of hedging everything and will incur lower commission costs as well. The risk remains, though, that a single large uncovered transaction could cause severe problems if the currency moves in the opposite direction to that predicted.

### Best strategy

A sensible strategy for our company could be to set a cash size for a foreign currency exposure above which all amounts must be hedged, but below this limit a predictive approach is taken or even, possibly, all amounts are left unhedged.

### Matching

Before using any technique to hedge foreign currency transactions, receipts and payments in the same currency at the same date should be offset. This technique is known as 'matching'. For example, if the company is expecting to receive SFr750,000 on 31 March and to pay SFr600,000 on the same day, only the net amount of SFr150,000 needs to be considered.

Matching can be extended to receipts and payments which do not take place on exactly the same day by simply hedging the period and amount of the difference between the receipt and payment. A company like ours which has many receipts and payments in European currencies should consider matching assets with liabilities in the same currency. For example, if we have total Swiss debtors of SFr2 million, we should borrow SFr2 million on overdraft to match the debtor.

(b)   **Matching**

If the foreign subsidiary is selling predominantly **matching** in its own country, the principle of matching assets and liabilities says that the subsidiary should be **financed as far as possible** in the **currency of that country**. Ideally the subsidiary will be highly geared with loans and overdrafts in the developing country's currency. If local finance has not been used and the sales invoice which is about to be sent is large, then an overdraft in the same currency should be taken out and the receipt converted to sterling immediately.

### Positively correlated currency

If it is impossible to borrow in the local currency, Expo Inc should attempt to find a **hard currency** which is **highly positively correlated** with the local currency. For example, some countries have a policy of pegging their currency to the US dollar. The receipt can then be hedged by selling the US dollar forward.

However, this technique is open to the risk that the local currency suddenly devalues against the dollar, as happened in 1997 with a number of Asian currencies. The likelihood of this happening is high if there is high inflation in the country and it has low reserves.

If Expo Inc is fairly certain that the local currency is going to devalue and that it cannot borrow in that currency, the remaining alternatives are:

(i)    To **increase the sales price** by the amount of the expected devaluation and bear the risk

(ii)   To **invoice in a hard currency**, for example US dollars, which can then be sold forward

(iii)  To **arrange a 'counter-trade' agreement** (ie barter) in which the sale of Expo's textiles is paid for by the purchase of local raw materials or other products

# 31 Fidden plc

(a)   Techniques for protecting against the risk of adverse foreign exchange movements include the following:

   (i)    A company could trade only in its own currency, thus transferring all risks to suppliers and customers.

   (ii)   A company could ensure that its assets and liabilities in any one currency are as nearly equal as possible, so that losses on assets (or liabilities) are matched by gains on liabilities (or assets).

   (iii)  A company could enter into forward contracts, under which an agreed amount of a currency will be bought or sold at an agreed rate at some fixed future date or, under a forward option contract, at some date in a fixed future period.

   (iv)   A company could buy foreign currency options, under which the buyer acquires the right to buy (call options) or sell (put options) a certain amount of a currency at a fixed rate at some future date. If rates move in such a way that the option rate is unfavourable, the option is simply allowed to lapse.

   (v)    A company could buy foreign currency futures on a financial futures exchange. Futures are effectively forward contracts, in standard sizes and with fixed maturity dates. Their prices move in response to exchange rate movements, and they are usually sold before maturity, the profit or loss on sale corresponding approximately to the exchange loss or profit on the currency transaction they were intended to hedge.

   (vi)   A company could enter into a money market hedge. One currency is borrowed and converted into another, which is then invested until the funds are required or funds are received to repay the original loan. The early conversion protects against adverse exchange rate movements, but at a cost equal to the difference between the cost of borrowing in one currency and the return available on investment in the other currency.

(b)   (i)   (1)   Forward exchange market

The rates are:

|                   | $/£             |
|-------------------|-----------------|
| Spot              | 1.7106–1.7140   |
| 3 months forward  | 1.7024–1.7063   |
| 6 months forward  | 1.6967–1.7006   |

The net payment three months hence is $£116{,}000 - \dfrac{\$197{,}000}{1.7063} = £546.$

The net payment six months hence is $\dfrac{\$(447{,}000 - 154{,}000)}{1.6967} = £172{,}688.$

Note that the dollar receipts can be used in part settlement of the dollar payments, so only the net payment is hedged.

   (2)   Money market

$197,000 will be received three months hence, so:

$$\frac{\$197{,}000}{(1 + 0.09 \times \frac{3}{12})} = \$192{,}665$$

may be borrowed now and converted into sterling, the dollar loan to be repaid from the receipts.

The net sterling payment three months hence is:

$$£116{,}000 - \frac{\$197{,}000}{1 + (0.09 \times \frac{3}{12})} \times \frac{1}{1.7140} \times (1 + (0.095 \times \frac{3}{12})) = £924$$

The equation for the $197,000 receipt in three months is to calculate the amount of dollars to borrow now (divide by the dollar borrowing rate) and then to find out how much that will give now in sterling (divide by the exchange rate). The final amount of sterling after three months is given by multiplying by the sterling lending rate.

$293,000 (net) must be paid six months hence. We can borrow sterling now and convert it into dollars, such that the fund in six months will equal $293,000. The sterling payment in six months' time will be the principal and the interest thereon. A similar logic applies as for the equation above except that the situation is one of making a final payment rather than a receipt.

The sterling payment six months hence is therefore

$$\frac{293,000}{1+0.06\times^6\!/_{12}}\times\frac{1}{1.7106}\times(1+0.125\times^6\!/_{12}) = £176,690$$

(ii) Available put options (put, because sterling is to be sold) are at $1.70 (cost 3.45 cents per £) and at $1.80 (cost 9.32 cents per £).

Using options at $1.70 gives the following results.

$$\frac{\$293,000}{1.70\$/£} = £172,353$$

Contracts required $= \dfrac{£172,353}{£12,500} = 14$ (to the next whole number)

Cost of options $= 14 \times 12,500 \times 3.45c = \$6,038$

(translated at today's spot rate = £3,530)

14 contracts will provide, for £12,500 × 14 = £175,000, $(175,000 × 1.70) = $297,500.

The overall cost is £175,000 $+ \dfrac{\$293,000+\$6,038-\$297,500}{1.6967} = £175,906$

As this figure exceeds the cost of hedging through the forward exchange market (£172,688), use of $1.70 options would have been disadvantageous.

Using options at $1.80:

$$\frac{\$293,000}{1.80\$/£} = £162,778$$

Contracts required $= \dfrac{£162,778}{£12,500} = 14$ (to next whole number)

Cost of options $= 14 \times 12,500 \times 9.32c = \$16,310 \ (\div 1.7106 = £9,535)$

14 contracts will provide, for £12,500 × 14 = £175,000, 175,000 × 1.80 = $315,000.

The overall cost is £175,000 $+ \dfrac{\$293,000+\$16,310-\$315,000}{1.7006} = £171,654$

This figure is less than the cost of hedging through the forward exchange market, so use of $1.80 options would have been preferable.

(iii) Foreign currency options have the advantage that, while offering protection against adverse currency movements, they need not be exercised if movements are favourable. Thus the maximum cost is the option price, while there is no comparable limit on the potential gains.

# 32 Exchange rate forecasts

> **Top tips.** In (a)(i) and (b) there are two alternative versions of the International Fisher effect and purchasing power parity formulae. Either one will give the correct result. In (a)(ii) you must distinguish between the terms 'unbiased' and 'accurate', and state some of the assumptions behind the IFE formula. In (b) the best type of hedge where it is uncertain whether cash is needed is a currency option.
>
> In (a) marks were split 50% IFE calculations, 50% comment. Five out of eight marks were available in (b) for calculations of the tender price and conclusion, with three marks being available for the alternative hedges.

(a) (i) To: Managing Director
From: Financial Analyst

### Predictions of $/euro exchange rate

If exchange rates are freely floating and interest rates are also freely determined by market forces then, according to the International Fisher effect, interest rate differentials between two countries can be applied to the current exchange rate to give an unbiased predictor of the future exchange rate.

Predicted future exchange rate = spot rate $\times (1 + i_{us})/(1 + i_{\epsilon})$

This gives year 1 exchange rate as $1.667 \times 1.035/1.06 = 1.6277$, and year 2 as $1.6277 \times 1.035/1.06 = 1.589$ $/euro.

The non-executive director is wrong, having applied the formula wrongly as $1.667 \times (1 + 0.02358)^2$ = $/euro.

(ii) ### Errors in prediction

The fact that a predicted exchange rate is **unbiased** does not make it accurate. Unbiased simply means that the rate is as likely to be above the prediction as below it. The margin of error on the prediction over two years will be very large, even if other factors remain the same, which is unlikely. Over the next two years interest rates are almost certain to change with changing economic conditions.

### Assumptions

The **assumptions** behind the IFE model are also **unlikely to hold**. The model assumes that the currencies are freely traded on the market with, for example, no government intervention, and that the current exchange rate represents an equilibrium position. The forecast exchange rate is therefore very unlikely to be accurate.

(b) ### Currency options

The best form of protection against foreign exchange risk, in a situation where it is uncertain whether there will be a need for the currency to be exchanged, is a **currency option**. A forward contract cannot be avoided if the contract is lost and could create a currency loss, whereas a currency option can be allowed to lapse if it is not advantageous. The disadvantage of a currency option is the 'up-front' premium, which is non-refundable and can be expensive.

### Period of option

The option is needed **from the date** the **tender is made** to **the date the results are announced**. Beyond that point, if the contract is won, currency protection could be achieved by a money market hedge (borrowing dinars on the strength of the future sales proceeds) or by another option, but forward contracts do not appear to be available.

Since the date of award of the contract is unknown, an alternative hedge would be to take out an **option** for the **whole 18-month period**. The company would purchase an option to sell (put) dinars for euros in 18 months' time.

### Prediction of exchange rate

If no hedge is used, a prediction of the exchange rate in 18 months is needed to estimate the tender price.

The spot rate is 0.256 – 0.260 euros per dinar. The rate for selling dinars is 0.256 (when you sell dinars you will get the lower number of dinars).

The formula is: $\dfrac{(i_E - i_D)}{(1 + i_D)}$

The euro is predicted to strengthen against the dinar: $\dfrac{(3\% - 9\%)}{1.09} = -5.505\%$ per year.

In 18 months (1.5 years) the exchange rate is predicted to be:

$0.256 \times (1 - 0.0505)^{1.5} = 0.235$ euros per dinar.

Purchasing power parity has been used instead of the International Fisher effect, as it is regarded as more reliable.

The euro cost in 18 months' time is predicted to be €340,000. A 25% margin gives a price of €425,000.

If no hedge is used, the recommended tender price is: $\dfrac{425,000}{0.235} = 1,808,511$ dinars.

If an option hedge using today's exchange rate is used, the price should be 425,000/0.256 = 1,660,156 dinars **plus** the cost of the option.

# 33 US options

**Top tips**. To compare the participating option with the traded option, it is best to look at the same exercise price for both ($1.65 = £1). Since you need to look at the outcomes for a range of possible exchange rate movements, it is convenient to use the range from $1.55 to $1.70 given in the traded option table. The company is selling its dollar (term currency) receipt, therefore the bank is buying the dollars high. Collars are often worth mentioning in questions on options.

(b) provides useful revision of other hedging methods. Matching can be an important technique. Watch out also for references to currencies being pegged to another currency (generally the $).

**Examining team's comment**. Poorer candidates confused futures and options, showed a lack of understanding of option premia or the possibility of options lapsing.

(a) **Current spot rate**

At the current exchange rate of $1.6100 = £1, the receipt of $1,800,000 will produce £1,118,012.

**Participating option**

Using the **participating option**, there is no premium. An examination of possible receipts under four possible exchange rates in six months' time shows the following.

|  | $1.55 £ | $1.60 £ | $1.65 £ | $1.70 £ |
|---|---|---|---|---|
| *Spot market* |  |  |  |  |
| At opening spot rate $1.8m/$1.61 | 1,118,012 | 1,118,012 | 1,118,012 | 1,118,012 |
| At closing spot rate $1.8m/closing rate | 1,161,290 | 1,125,000 | 1,090,909 | 1,058,824 |
| Gain/(loss) | 43,278 | 6,988 | (27,103) | (59,188) |
| *Options market* |  |  |  |  |
| Buy at | 1.65 | 1.65 | 1.65 | 1.65 |
| Sell at | 1.55 | 1.60 | 1.65 | 1.70 |
| Exercise? | No | No | Yes/No | Yes |

**Outcome of option position**

| Net outcome | £ | £ | As for $1.65 on spot market £ | As for $1.65 on spot market £ |
|---|---|---|---|---|
| Gain/(loss) | 43,278 | 6,988 | (27,103) | (27,103) |
| Half gain to bank | (21,639) | (3,494) | | |
| Net gain/(loss) | 21,639 | 3,494 | | |

## Traded option

### Set up option

(i)  Contract date June

(ii)  Option type call

(iii)  Strike price $1.65 and $1.70 have premium costs less than £10,000. Choose $1.65 for comparison

(iv)  Number of contracts

$$\frac{1,800,000 \div 1.65}{31,250} \approx 34.9 \text{ contracts, say } 35$$

(v)  Tick size = 31,250 × 0.0001
= $3.125

(vi)  Premium = $\dfrac{1.1}{100}$ × 31,250 × 35

= $12,031 @ 1.605

= £7,494

### Closing prices

As for participating option.

### Outcome

| | | $1.55 | $1.60 | $1.65 | | $1.70 |
|---|---|---|---|---|---|---|
| (i) | Options market | | | | | |
| | Strike price call | $1.65 | $1.65 | $1.65 | | $1.65 |
| | Closing price | $1.55 | $1.60 | $1.65 | | $1.65 |
| | Exercise? | No | No | Yes/no | | Yes |
| | Tick movement | | | | 500 | |
| | Options outcome | | | | 500 × 35 × 3.125 = $54,688 | |
| | | | | | | |
| (ii) | Net outcome | £ | £ | £ | | £ |
| | Spot market gain/(loss) as for participating option | 43,278 | 6,988 | (27,103) | | (59,188) |
| | Options market gain ÷ spot rate | | | | | 32,169 |
| | Options premium | (7,494) | (7,494) | (7,494) | | (7,494) |
| | | 35,784 | (506) | (34,597) | | (34,513) |

Comparison of the two pay-off schedules shows that using the participating option is probably preferable, as the resulting cash receipt is less sensitive to exchange rate fluctuations and, in particular, shows a lower maximum loss.

### Creation of straddle option

As a more advanced use of traded options, the company could consider creating a straddle option. In order to hedge the purchase of pounds with dollars, the company should buy call options and sell put options at the same exercise price.

For example, the cost of purchasing $1.60 call options (5.3 cents) can be offset by selling $1.60 put options (4.0 cents). The net premium cost per £ is 1.3 cents.

Receipt   = 1,800,000/1.60
            = £1,125,000

Premium   = $1.3/100 × 1,125,000

             = $14,625,   which at today's spot rate of $1.6055 would be £9,109, which is within the £10,000 limit.

### Effect of straddle

The combination of two options on the same exercise price **fixes** the exchange rate to £1 = $1.60. When the net premium cost is added, the effective exchange rate for buying pounds with dollars is £1 = $1.613. This is an alternative to using forward or futures contracts.

### Collars

Use of collars with calls and puts on different exercise prices gives a **pay off schedule** with a **risk profile intermediate** between a fixed return and the call option pay off shown above.

(b) ### Matching assets and liabilities

If the foreign subsidiary is selling predominantly in its own country, the principle of **matching assets and liabilities** says that the subsidiary should be financed as far as possible in the currency of that country. Ideally the subsidiary will be highly geared with loans and overdrafts in the developing country's currency. If local finance has not been used and the sales invoice which is about to be sent is large, then an overdraft in the same currency should be taken out and the receipt converted to sterling immediately.

### Use of hard currency

If it is impossible to borrow in the local currency, the company should attempt to find a hard currency which is highly positively correlated with the local currency. For example, some countries have a policy of pegging their currency to the US dollar. The receipt can then be hedged by selling the US dollar forward.

However, this technique is open to the risk that the local currency suddenly devalues against the dollar, as happened in 1997 with a number of Asian currencies. The likelihood of this happening is high if there is high inflation in the country and it has low reserves.

### Other options

If the company is fairly certain that the local currency is going to devalue and that it cannot borrow in that currency, the **remaining alternatives** are:

(i)   **Increase the sales price** by the amount of the expected devaluation and bear the risk

(ii)   **Invoice in a hard currency**, for example US dollars, which can then be sold forward

(iii)   **Arrange a 'countertrade' agreement** (ie barter) in which the sale of the company's textiles is paid for by the purchase of local raw materials or other products

# 34 Curropt plc

(a) The department's view that the US dollar will strengthen is in **agreement** with the **indications** of the forward market and the futures market. Forward and futures rates show a **stronger dollar** than the spot rate. The forward rate is often taken as an **unbiased** predictor of what the spot rate will be in future. However, future events could cause large currency movements in **either direction**.

(b) The **company needs to buy dollars in June**.

### Forward contract

A forward currency contract will fix the exchange rate for the date required near the end of June. If the exact date is not known, a range of dates can be specified, using an **option forward contract**. This will remove currency risk **provided that the franchise is won**. If the **franchise is not won** and the group has no use for US dollars, it will still have to buy the dollars at the forward rate. It will then have to sell them back for pounds at the spot rate which might result in an exchange loss.

### Futures contract

A currency hedge using futures contracts will attempt to create a **compensating gain** on the futures market which will **offset** the **increase** in the **sterling cost** if the dollar strengthens. The hedge works by **selling sterling futures** contracts now and closing out by **buying sterling futures** in **June** at a lower dollar price if the dollar has strengthened. Like a forward contract, the exchange rate in June is effectively fixed because, if the dollar weakens, the futures hedge will produce a loss which counterbalances the cheaper sterling cost. However, because of inefficiencies in future market hedges, the exchange rate is not fixed to the same level of accuracy as a forward hedge.

A futures market hedge has the same weakness as a forward currency contract in the franchise situation. If the franchise is not won, an **exchange loss** may result.

### Currency option

A currency option is an ideal hedge in the franchise situation. It gives the company the **right but not the obligation** to sell pounds for dollars in June. It is only exercised if it is to the company's advantage; that is, if the dollar has strengthened. If the **dollar strengthens** and the franchise is won, the exchange rate has been **protected**. If the dollar strengthens and the **franchise is not won**, a **windfall gain** will result by **selling pounds** at the exercise price and buying them more cheaply at spot with a stronger dollar.

(c) **Results of using currency hedges if the franchise is won**

### Forward market

Using the forward market, the rate for **buying dollars** at the end of June is 1.4310 US$/£. The cost in sterling is 15m/1.4310 = £10,482,180.

### Futures

**Date of contract**

June future

**Type of contract**

Sell sterling futures

**Number of contracts**

$$\frac{15,000,000}{1.4302 \times 62,500} = 167.8 \approx 168 \text{ contracts}$$

**Tick size**

$0.0001 \times 62,500 = \$6.25$

### Closing futures price

This can be estimated by assuming that the difference between the futures rate and the spot rate (ie basis) decreases constantly over time. On 30 June there will be 0 months left of this June contract so the basis should have fallen to zero.

|  | 1 March | 30 June |
|---|---|---|
| Futures price | 1.4302 | |
| Spot rate now | 1.4461 | |
| Basis (future – spot) | –0.0159 | 0 |

Three possible spot price scenarios

1.3500
1.4500
1.5500

Assuming basis = 0 then the futures price will be the same as the spot price.

### Hedge outcome

|  | 1.3500 | 1.4500 | 1.5500 |
|---|---|---|---|
|  | $ | $ | $ |
| Opening futures price | 1.4302 | 1.4302 | 1.4302 |
| Closing futures price | 1.3500 | 1.4500 | 1.5500 |
| Movement in ticks | 802 | (198) | (1,198) |
| Futures profits/(losses) | 842,100 | (207,900) | (1,257,900) |
| 168 × tick movement × 6.25 | 842,100 | (207,900) | (1,257,900) |

### Net outcome

|  | $ | $ | $ |
|---|---|---|---|
| Spot market payment | (15,000,000) | (15,000,000) | (15,000,000) |
| Futures market (profits)/losses | 842,100 | (207,900) | (1,257,900) |
|  | (14,157,900) | (15,207,900) | (16,257,900) |
| Translated at closing rate | £10,487,333 | £10,488,207 | £10,488,698 |

This gives an effective rate of $15m / £10.488m (approx.) = 1.4303

A **shortcut** that will deliver **approximately** the same answer is:

---

**Opening futures price – closing basis = effective futures rate**

Here this gives:
1.4302 – 0 = 1.4302

Applying this rate gives an outcome in £s of $15m / 1.4302 = £10,488,044

This is the answer for all 3 scenarios, and is the preferred approach for tackling futures questions because it is so much quicker.

---

The slight difference arises because this shortcut does not account for the fact that the futures hedge is for 168 contracts, not 167.8.

### Options

### Date of contract

June

### Option type

Buy put

**Exercise price**

| Exercise price | Premium | Net |
|---|---|---|
| 1.4000 | 0.0038 | 1.3962 |
| 1.4250 | 0.0068 | 1.4182 |
| 1.4500 | 0.0238 | 1.4262 |

Choose 1.4500

**Number of contracts**

$$\frac{15,000,000 \div 1.4500}{31,250} = 331.03 \approx 331 \text{ contracts}$$

**Tick size**

$31,250 \times 0.0001 = \$3.125$

**Premium**

$0.0238 \times 31,250 \times 331$ = \$246,181 at 1.4461
= £170,238

**Outcome**

| | 1.3500 | 1.4500 | 1.5500 |
|---|---|---|---|
| | $ | $ | $ |
| **Option market** | | | |
| Strike price | 1.4500 | 1.4500 | 1.4500 |
| Closing price | 1.3500 | 1.4500 | 1.5500 |
| Exercise? | Yes | No | No |
| Outcome of option 331 × £31,250 × 1.45 = | $14,998,438 | – | – |
| Shortfall in $s vs $15m needed | $1,563 | | |
| At spot rate of 1.35 (alternatively forward rate could be used) | £1,157 | | |

**Net outcome**

| | 1.3500 | 1.4500 | 1.5500 |
|---|---|---|---|
| | $ | $ | $ |
| Spot market payment | | (15,000,000) | (15,000,000) |
| Options | | | |
| | | (15,000,000) | (15,000,000) |
| | £ | £ | £ |
| Translated at closing spot rate | | (10,344,828) | (9,677,419) |
| Option exercised (331 × £31,250) | (10,343,750) | | |
| Shortfall | (1,157) | | |
| Premium | (170,238) | (170,238) | (170,238) |
| | 10,515,145 | 10,515,066 | 9,847,657 |

**Note.** There are a number of possible approaches to evaluating options.

**Summary**

The company will either choose to purchase a **forward** or an **option**. Although forwards are slightly more advantageous at lower exchange rates, the net benefits of using an option are significant if the exchange rate moves in Curropt's favour eg to $1.55. Also, given that the transaction is not certain to be required an option will be more suitable because it can be sold on if it is not needed. On this basis an option is recommended.

# 35 Carrick plc

(a)    **Interest rate exposure**

**Interest rate exposure** arises when a company's borrowing is such that a change in interest rates might expose it to interest charges that are unacceptably high. For example, if a company has a large tranche of debt at a fixed rate of interest that is due for repayment in the near future, and the loan is to be replaced or renegotiated, the company would be vulnerable to a sudden increase in market interest rates.

**Risk management**

Risk management in this context involves using **hedging techniques** to reduce or 'cover' an exposure. However, hedging has a cost, which will either take the form of a **fee** to a financial institution or a **reduction in profit**, and this must be weighed against the reduction in financial risks that the hedge achieves. The extent to which the exposure is covered is known as the **'hedge efficiency'**. A perfect hedge has an efficiency of 100%.

Methods of managing interest rate risk include the following.

**Forward interest rate agreements (FRAs)**

An FRA is an agreement, usually between a company and a bank, about the **interest rate** on a future loan or deposit. The agreement will **fix the rate of interest** for borrowing for a certain time in the future. If the actual rate of interest at that time is above that agreed, the bank pays the company the difference, and *vice versa*. Thus the company benefits from effectively fixing the rate of interest on a loan for a given period, but it may miss the opportunity to benefit from any favourable movements in rates during that time. An FRA is simply an agreement about rates – it does not involve the movement of the principal sum – the actual borrowing must be arranged separately.

**Futures**

A financial future is an agreement on the **future price** of a **financial variable**. Interest rate futures are similar in all respects to FRAs, except that the terms, sums involved and periods are **standardised**. They are traded on the London International Futures and Options Exchange (LIFFE).

Their standardised nature makes them less attractive to corporate borrowers because it is not always possible to match them exactly to specific rate exposures. Each contract will require the payment of a small initial deposit.

### Interest rate options

An interest rate guarantee (or option) provides the **right to borrow** a **specified amount** at a guaranteed rate of interest. The option guarantees that the **interest rate will not rise** above a specified level during a specified period. On the date of expiry of the option the buyer must decide whether or not to exercise their right to borrow. They will only exercise the option if actual **interest rates** have **risen above the option rate**. The advantage of options is that the buyer cannot lose on the interest rate and can take advantage of any favourable rate movements. However, a **premium** must be paid regardless of whether or not the option is exercised. Options can be negotiated directly with the bank or traded in a standardised form on the LIFFE.

### Caps and collars

These can be used to set a **floor** and a **ceiling** to the range of interest rates that might be incurred. A **premium** must be paid for this service. These agreements do not provide a perfect hedge, but they do limit the range of possibilities and thus reduce the level of exposure.

(b) Collars make use of **interest rate options** to limit exposure to the risk of movement in rates. The company would arrange both a ceiling (an upper limit) and a floor (a lower limit) on its interest yield. The use of the ceiling means that the cost is lower than for a floor alone.

### Choice of options

Since Carrick requires protection for the next 7 months, it can use **September options** in order to cover the full period. It is assumed that the floor will be fixed at the current yield of 6%. This implies that it will buy call options at 9400. At the same time, Carrick will limit its ability to benefit from rises in rates by selling a put option at a higher rate, for example 7% (or 9300).

The level of **premiums payable** will **depend** on the different **sizes of collar**. The number of three-month contracts required for seven months' cover will be:

$$\frac{£6m}{£0.5m} \times \frac{7}{3} = 28 \text{ contracts (£14m)}$$

The premiums payable at different sizes of collar (in annual percentage terms) will be:

| Call | Premium | Put | Premium | Net premium | £ cost* |
|------|---------|------|---------|-------------|---------|
| 9400 | 0.40 | 9350 | 0.35 | 0.05 | 1,750 |
| 9400 | 0.40 | 9300 | 0.14 | 0.26 | 9,100 |
| 9400 | 0.40 | 9250 | 0.06 | 0.34 | 11,900 |

(* eg £14m × 0.05% × ¼ = £1,750)

If Carrick does take out the options as described above, the effect will be as follows.

(i)    If interest rates fall below 6%, Carrick will **exercise the call option** and effectively fix its interest rate at 6%. The loss on the interest rate will be borne by the seller of the call option.

(ii)   If interest rates remain between the 6% floor and the 7% ceiling, Carrick will **do nothing** but will benefit from the effect of any increase in rates above 6% within this band.

(iii)  If interest rates rise above 7% the buyer of the put option will **exercise** their **option**, provided that the futures price falls below 9300. Carrick will effectively achieve an interest rate of 7%, but the benefit of any premium on rates above 7% will accrue to the buyer of the put option.

In practice, costs will be higher due to the transaction costs that will be incurred.

The potential gross interest rate gain, and the net gain taking premiums into account if rates do rise to the various exercise prices, are as follows. The interest rate gain is calculated on £6 million for seven months.

| | Interest rate % rise | Interest gain £ | Premium £ cost (above) | Net gain £ |
|---|---|---|---|---|
| 9350 | 0.50 | 17,500 | 1,750 | 15,750 |
| 9300 | 1.00 | 35,000 | 9,100 | 25,900 |
| 9250 | 1.50 | 52,500 | 11,900 | 40,600 |

This suggests that Carrick could make the greatest potential gain by **selling put options** at 9250. However, this gain will only be realised if actual rates rise to 7.5%. If they stay at around 6% then Carrick will still incur costs without realising benefits. The actual put price chosen will depend on the view of the directors on the likely movements in rates over the period in question but, if it seems likely that rates will increase by up to 1%, then a put price of 9300 would be the most appropriate.

# 36 Burger Queen

(a) Burger Queen could enter into December futures contracts to sell for 92.70. Since each contract has a notional value of $500,000 it should sell:

$$\frac{\$10,000,000}{\$500,000} = 20 \text{ contracts}$$

(b) Since interest rates have risen to 9% the price of the futures contract will fall to 91 (= 100 – 9).

The gain on the futures contract is as follows:

92.70 – 91 = 170 ticks

Each tick is worth $12.50 and the profit on the futures contract is:

170 × $12.50 × 20 = $42,500

Although there is gain in the futures position, the company has to pay a higher rate for the loan. The extra amount of interest paid on the loan is: 9 – 7.3 = 1.70% or:

$10m × 0.017 × $^3/_{12}$ = $42,500

This extra cost is offset by the profit on the futures position so the effective rate is 7.3% even though interest rates have risen.

(c) The effective rate is still 7.3%.

This time there will be loss on the futures contract since the price of the futures contract has risen. The price of the futures contract is now 94 (= 100 – 6). The loss is 94 – 92.70 = 130 ticks or:

130 × $12.50 × 20 = $32,500

The lower interest rate on the loan means that there is a saving on interest payments equal to:

$10m × (0.073 – 0.06) × $^3/_{12}$ = $32,500

The gain on the interest is again offset by the loss on the futures position, so that the cost of borrowing remains the same at 7.3%.

# 37 Theta Inc

(a) Theta borrows $10 million with interest at six-month LIBOR plus 1%. In the swap, it receives six-month LIBOR and pays fixed interest at 8.5%. The net effect is to acquire a fixed rate obligation at 9.5% for the full term of the swap.

| | % |
|---|---|
| Borrow at LIBOR plus 1% | –(LIBOR + 1%) |
| Swap: receive (floating rate) | +LIBOR |
| pay (fixed rate) | –8.5% |
| | |
| Net payment (fixed rate) | –9.5% |

Theta will therefore fix its payments at $475,000 (10 million × 9.5% × 6/12) every six months for the five-year term of the swap.

At each six-monthly fixing date for the swap, the payment due from Theta to the swaps bank or from the bank to Theta will depend on the market rate for six-month LIBOR at that date.

(b)   (i)   **LIBOR 10%**

Suppose that on the first fixing date for the swap, at the end of month six in the first year, six-month LIBOR is 10%. The payments due by each party to the swap will be as follows.

| | $ |
|---|---|
| Theta pays fixed rate of 8.5% | |
| ($10m × 8.5% × 6/12) | 425,000 |
| Swaps bank pays LIBOR rate of 10% | |
| ($10m × 10% × 6/12) | 500,000 |
| Net payment from bank to Theta | 75,000 |

This payment will be made six months later at the end of the notional interest rate period. Theta will pay interest on its loan at LIBOR + 1% which for this six-month period is 11% (10% + 1%). Taken with the payment received under the swap agreement, the net cost to Theta is equivalent to interest payable at 9.5%.

| | $ |
|---|---|
| Loan payment at 11% | |
| ($10m × 11% × 6/12) | 550,000 |
| Payment received from the swap bank | (75,000) |
| Net payment (equivalent to 9.5% interest) | 475,000 |

(ii)   **LIBOR 7.5%**

Suppose that at the next six-monthly fixing date, six-month LIBOR is 7.5%. The swap payments will be as follows.

| | $ |
|---|---|
| Theta to swap bank (fixed at 8.5%) | 425,000 |
| Swap bank to Theta (at 7.5%) | 375,000 |
| Net payment by Theta to swaps bank | 50,000 |

Under its loan arrangement, Theta will pay 8.5% (LIBOR + 1%) for the six-month period. Adding the net swap payment gives a total cost for the six-month period of $475,000, equivalent to an interest rate of 9.5% for the period.

| | $ |
|---|---|
| Loan payment at 8.5% | |
| ($10m × 8.5% × 6/12) | 425,000 |
| Swap payment | 50,000 |
| Total payment (equivalent to 9.5% interest) | 475,000 |

# 38 Kilber Inc

(a)   The management of risk is one of the most important aspects of the treasury function. Excessive volatility in the cash flows of the company, caused by changing business conditions, changes in exchange rates or interest rates, will adversely affect the value of the firm. Hedging is in general considered to enhance the value of the company.

The most serious risk that Kilber faces is the falling kilbe prices. Since Kilbe prices are highly correlated with copper prices, it is reasonable to use copper futures contracts to lock into certain future value. Suppose that Kilber has sold a sufficient number of copper futures contracts maturing in three months. Suppose further that during this period, the price of both Kilbe and copper have fallen. On expiration of the contract, the company will have a loss due to the fall in the price of the Kilbe but a gain on the copper futures contract.

Whether the gain in the futures contract will offset the loss due to the fall in the price of the Kilbe it will depend on whether the price of copper has fallen by the same percentage as the price of Kilbe. If it has fallen by the same percentage then the price of copper will be behaving exactly like the price of Kilbe, the copper futures contract will be the exact equivalent of a Kilbe futures contract.

However, when the price of Kilbe and copper is not perfectly correlated, then the copper futures contract is an imperfect hedge.

The remaining risk is called basis risk and arises from the imperfect correlation between the hedging instrument and the hedged asset.

(b)     The main benefit of OTC derivatives is that they can be tailored to the needs of the two parties; their major drawback is that they pose a higher risk of default than do exchange-traded derivatives. Some very specialised agreements may also be illiquid.

(c)     Kilber could use a variety of instruments to hedge interest rate risk depending on its time horizon. For short-term protection the company could use forward rate agreements, short-term interest rate futures and interest rate options. For long-term protection, it could use interest rate swaps to convert the variable interest rate debt to fixed rate.

Note that forward rate agreements, futures and swaps lock into a particular borrowing rate and the company does not benefit from a fall in interest rate. Interest rate options, on the other hand, set a ceiling on the interest rate to be paid but allow the company to benefit from a fall in interest rates.

# Bibliography

BBC. (11 February 2014) Myanma Air signs nearly $1bn leasing deal. *BBC* [Online] Available from: http://www.bbc.co.uk/news/business-26131019 [Accessed 25 September 2016].

BBC. (25 March 2015) Kraft shares soar on Heinz merger. *BBC* [Online] Available from: http://www.bbc.co.uk/news/business-32050266 [Accessed 27 September 2016].

BBC. (12 October 2015) Dell agrees $67bn EMC takeover. *BBC* [Online] Available from: http://www.bbc.co.uk/news/business-34505553 [Accessed 27 September 2016].

BBC. (14 July 2016) Nintendo shares up more than 50% since Pokemon Go release. *BBC* [Online] Available from: http://bbc.co.uk/news/ business-36791275 [Accessed 23 September 2016].

Bondsonline. (15 Decem 2015) Reuters Corporate Bond Spread Tables. Available from: http://www.bondsonline.com [Accessed 26 September 2016].

Davies, R. (15 December 2015) Starbucks pays UK corporation tax of £8.1m. *Guardian* [Online] Available from: https://www.theguardian.com/business/2015/dec/15/starbucks-pays-uk-corporation-tax-8-million-pounds [Accessed 25 September 2016].

Economist. (21 July 2016) The Big Mac Index. *Economist* [Online] Available from: http://www.economist.com/content/big-mac-index [Accessed 27 September 2016].

Financial Times. (September 4 2014) Goldman Sachs issues its first Islamic bond. *Financial Times* [Online] Available from: https://www.ft.com/content/1af110fe-3448-11e4-b81c-00144feabdc0 [Accessed 23 September 2016].

Goergen, Martynova and Renneboog (2005) Corporate governance convergence: evidence from takeover regulation reforms in Europe, *Oxford Review of Economic Policy*

ICAEW. (May 2012) The impact of the Eurozone crisis on UK business Available from: https://www.icaew.com/-/media/corporate/files/about-icaew/what-we-do/business-confidence-monitor/special-reports/business-opinion-report-may-2012-impact-of-the-eurozone-crisis.ashx [Accessed 24 September 2016].

IMF. (19 July 2016) IMF Cuts Global Growth Forecasts on Brexit, Warns of Risks to Outlook. *IMF* [Online] Available from: https://www.imf.org/en/News/Articles/2016/07/18/18/11/NA07192016-IMF-Cuts-Global-Growth-Forecasts-on-Brexit-Warns-of-Risks-to-Outlook [Accessed 24 September 2016].

Jetuah, D. (16 April, 2008) Prudential takes £459m fair value hit. *Accountancy Age* [Online] Available from: https://www.accountancyage.com/aa/news/1756051/prudential-takes-gbp459m-fair-value-hit [Accessed 24 September 2016].

Johnson, G, Scholes, K and Whittington, R (2008) *Exploring Corporate Strategy: Text and Cases*. 8th edition. Harlow: Pearson.

New York University Stern School of Business. (January 2016)  Price and Value to Book Ratio by Sector (US)  Stern NYU [Online] Available from: http://pages.stern.nyu.edu/~adamodar/New_Home_Page/datafile/pbvdata.html [Accessed 27 September 2016].

Reuters. (22 March 2015) U.S. multinationals set to face much more pain from strong dollar  *Reuters* [Online] Available from: http://www.reuters.com/article/us-usa-earnings-dollar-analysis-idUSKBN0MI0DC20150322 [Accessed 27 September 2016].

Reuters. (16 November 2015) As stock buybacks reach historic levels, signs that corporate America is undermining itself  *Reuters* [Online] Available from: http://www.reuters.com/investigates/special-report/usa-buybacks-cannibalized/ [Accessed 20 September 2017].

Reuters. (29 December 2016) DEALS-Corporate makeovers drive corporate takeovers in 2016 M&A bonanza  *Reuters* [Online] Available from: http://www.reuters.com/article/global-ma-deals/deals-corporate-makeovers-drive-corporate-takeovers-in-2016-ma-bonanza-idUSL1N1EE12J [Accessed 20 September 2017].

Reuters. (24 January 2017) S&P downgrades Rolls-Royce credit rating after bribery settlement *Reuters* [Online] Available from: http://uk.reuters.com/article/us-rolls-royce-hldg-ratings/sp-downgrades-rolls-royce-credit-rating-after-bribery-settlement-idUKKBN1581IX. [Accessed 21 September 2017].

Ryan, B. (2007) **Corporate Finance and Valuation**. 1st edn. Thomson.

SEC. (8 November 2015) Shedding light on dark pools. *SEC* [Online] Available from: https://www.sec.gov/news/statement/shedding-light-on-dark-pools.html [Accessed 25 September 2016].

Standard & Poor's. (30 April 2015) Default, Transition, and Recovery: 2014 Annual Global Corporate Default Study And Rating Transitions Available from http://aeri.es/irconference/docs/agenda/1710%20Carlos%20Garrido%20Rating.pdf [Accessed 26 September 2016].

Tovey, A. (17 April 2015) Former factory floor worker helps lead £26m management buyout of Jablite. *Telegraph* [Online] Available from: http://www.telegraph.co.uk/finance/newsbysector/industry/engineering/11566039/Former-factory-floor-worker-helps-lead-26m-management-buyout-of-Jablite.html [Accessed 27 September 2016].

Tovey, A. (6 August 2016) Concerns G4S could cut dividend as debt levels weigh. *Telegraph* [Online] Available from: http://www.telegraph.co.uk/business/2016/08/06/concerns-g4s-could-cut-dividend-as-debt-levels-weigh/ [Accessed 27 September 2016].

Watson, D. and Head, A. (2013) **Corporate Finance principles and practice**. 6th edn. Pearson Education Limited.

# Index

## Review Form – Advanced Financial Management (AFM) (01/18)

Please help us to ensure that the ACCA learning materials we produce remain as accurate and user-friendly as possible. We cannot promise to answer every submission we receive, but we do promise that it will be read and taken into account when we update this Study Text.

Name: _____

Address: _____

_____

_____

**How have you used this Study Text?**
*(Tick one box only)*

☐ On its own (book only)

☐ On a BPP in-centre course _____

☐ On a BPP online course

☐ On a course with another college

☐ Other _____

**Why did you decide to purchase this Study Text?** *(Tick one box only)*

☐ Have used BPP Texts in the past

☐ Recommendation by friend/colleague

☐ Recommendation by a lecturer at college

☐ Saw information on BPP website

☐ Saw advertising

☐ Other _____

**During the past six months do you recall seeing/receiving any of the following?**
*(Tick as many boxes as are relevant)*

☐ Our advertisement in *ACCA Student Accountant*

☐ Our advertisement in *Pass*

☐ Our advertisement in *PQ*

☐ Our brochure with a letter through the post

☐ Our website www.bpp.com

**Which (if any) aspects of our advertising do you find useful?**
*(Tick as many boxes as are relevant)*

☐ Prices and publication dates of new editions

☐ Information on Text content

☐ Facility to order books off-the-page

☐ None of the above

*Which BPP products have you used?*

| | | | | | |
|---|---|---|---|---|---|
| Study Text | ☑ | Passcards | ☐ | Other | ☐ |
| Kit | ☐ | i-Pass | ☐ | | |

*Your ratings, comments and suggestions would be appreciated on the following areas.*

| | Very useful | Useful | Not useful |
|---|---|---|---|
| *Introductory section* | ☐ | ☐ | ☐ |
| *Chapter introductions* | ☐ | ☐ | ☐ |
| *Key terms* | ☐ | ☐ | ☐ |
| *Quality of explanations* | ☐ | ☐ | ☐ |
| *Case studies and other examples* | ☐ | ☐ | ☐ |
| *Exam focus points* | ☐ | ☐ | ☐ |
| *Questions and answers in each chapter* | ☐ | ☐ | ☐ |
| *Fast forwards and chapter roundups* | ☐ | ☐ | ☐ |
| *Quick quizzes* | ☐ | ☐ | ☐ |
| *Question Bank* | ☐ | ☐ | ☐ |
| *Answer Bank* | ☐ | ☐ | ☐ |
| *Index* | ☐ | ☐ | ☐ |

| *Overall opinion of this Study Text* | Excellent ☐ | Good ☐ | Adeqate ☐ | Poor ☐ |
|---|---|---|---|---|

**Do you intend to continue using BPP products?**     Yes ☐     No ☐

**On the reverse of this page is space for you to write your comments about our Study Text We welcome your feedback.**

**The BPP Learning Media author of this edition can be emailed at: accaqueries@bpp.com**

## TELL US WHAT YOU THINK

Please note any further comments and suggestions/errors below. For example, was the text accurate, readable, concise, user-friendly and comprehensive?